The Welsh Cistercians

The Chapter house of Margam Abbey before its collapse in 1799.
(From an engraving by F. Chesham (after S.H. Grimm) 1780;
From the collections of the National Museums and Galleries of Wales: 2849 Top).

THE WELSH CISTERCIANS

Written to Commemorate the Centenary of the Death of

STEPHEN WILLIAM WILLIAMS
(1837–1899)

(The Father of Cistercian Archaeology in Wales)

David H. Williams

First published in 2001

Gracewing
2 Southern Avenue, Leominster
Herefordshire HR6 0QF

ISBN 0 85244 354 4

Typesetting by
Action Publishing Technology Ltd, Gloucester GL1 5SR

Printed in England by
MPG Books Ltd, Bodmin PL31 1EG

CONTENTS

List of Figures

Acknowledgements

The author is very grateful to those persons and bodies who have given permission to include in this book their work, or material they hold and/or to which they have the copyright. In these respects, he is indebted for the under-mentioned illustrations to:

Dr Lawrence Butler (Figs. 30, 54; plate VI-B), Dr Paul Courtney (Fig. 58), Dr Jeremy Davis (Fig. 128), Professor Michael Fulford (Fig. 119), Dr Cyril Hart (Plate XIII-B), Mr Roscoe Howells (Plate XVI-A), Mr Christopher Jones-Jenkins (Fig. 46, Plate VI-C), Mr Neil Ludlow (Figs. 47, 126), Mr Geoffrey Mein (Fig. 127), Dr Paul

Remfry (Fig. 76), Dr Stephen Rippon (Fig. 108), Mr Graham Thomas (Fig. 75), Mr Howard Thomas (Fig. 105), Mr John Wait (Pl. XI-B), Dr Peter Webster (Fig. 95).

The late Mr Richard Kay (Figs. 61, 64, 79, 90, 91, 94). All Mr Kay's thirty-nine field-notebooks, a mine of information, plans and sketches, meticulously collected over the period of 1936 to 1993, were deposited by him with the Ancient Monuments Record, Royal Commission on Ancient and Historical Monuments of Wales, Crown Building, Aberystwyth.

Archaeoleg Cambria (Figs. 47, 126).
The British Library. Crown copyright (Figs. 49, 129; Plates IX–1, IX-8, X-B).
Cadw: Welsh Historic Monuments. Crown copyright (Figs. 31, 33, 34, 37, 45, 46, 48, 52, 53, 56, 58; Plate IV-B).
Cambridge University Collection of Air Photographs. Copyright reserved (Plates XI-A, XII-A. XII-B).
Cardiff County Council Library Service (Fig. 67; Plates VIII-B, IX-4).
The Carmarthenshire Archives, Carmarthen (Pl. IX-6).
The Clwyd-Powys Archaeological Trust (Fig. 35).
The Ministry of Defence, Crown copyright (Plates I, XII-C).
The National Library of Wales (Figs. 29, 44, 55, 63, 65, 66, 75, 80, 83, 85, 86, 92, 104, 109b, 113; Plates IX-3, X-A, XV-A).
The National Museums and Galleries of Wales (Frontispiece; Plates II, V-C, VIII-A, IX-2, IX-7, XIII-A).
The Ordnance Survey (Crown Copyright: Licence NC/01/001; Figs. 84, Maps II-XIII).
The Trustees of the Powis Estate (Fig. 28).
The Pembrokeshire Record Office (Plate XVI-A).
The Powys Archives, Llandrindod Wells (Fig. 106).
The Public Record Office. Crown copyright (Fig. 71, Plate IX-4).
The Royal Commission on Ancient and Historical Monuments of Wales. Crown copyright. (Figs. 93, 112); Ordnance Survey Record Card (Fig. 120).
The Council of the Royal Society of Antiquaries of Ireland (Fig. 38).
The West Glamorgan Archive Service, Swansea, for items it holds (Figs. 68, 72, 109a) .

The Editor of *Archaeologia Cambrensis* (Figs. 30, 32, 59, 60, 62, 95, 125).
The Editor of the *Transactions of the Bristol and Gloucestershire Archaeological Society* (Fig. 119).
The Editor of the *Transactions of the Caernarfonshire Historical Society* (Fig. 54).
The Editor of the *Transactions of the Cardiff Naturalists' Society* (Fig. 50).
The Editor of the *Transactions of the Cardiganshire Antiquarian Society* (Plate XV-B).
The Editor of *Medieval Archaeology* (Fig. 58).
The Editor of *The Monmouthshire Antiquary* (Figs. 16, 96, 108).
The Editor of *The Montgomeryshire Collections* (Fig. 14).

PREFACE

In the last fifteen years since my two volume work entitled *The Welsh Cistercians* appeared, there has been a considerable flowering of Welsh Cistercian studies. It seemed to me that the time was ripe for a new book, very much updated, revised and recast. Three years ago, Gracewing published in fine format my life's work *(The Cistercians in the Early Middle Ages)*, and so I am very pleased that Tom Longford, Managing Director, and Jo Ashworth, Publishing Manager, are ensuring the appearance of this new volume which also reflects a lifelong interest.

I am especially grateful to Dr David Robinson, of English Heritage, for constructively criticising points made regarding the monastic buildings, to Dr Madeline Gray for suggesting amendments to my list of the lands of Llantarnam, and to Mr Julian Harrison for correcting the first proofs. Other collaborators find mention in the captions and notes. Years ago, various scholars who accompanied me on field trips included Dr Cyril Hart, Mr Jeremy Knight and the late Mr Richard Kay. More lately, my companions have included: Mr John Burton (at Rogerstone Grange), Mr Geoff Mein (at Porthcaseg Manor), Mr Graham Thomas (at 'black dyke' near Hafod Owain) and Mr Leslie Toft (at Walterstone Grange). Three years ago, a successful conference was held in Cardiff to mark the 900th anniversary of the Cistercian Order; several of its papers, when published, will complement the relevant sections in my volume.

Those maps and plans in this book which were first published in my *Atlas of Cistercian Lands in Wales* (University of Wales Press, Cardiff, 1990) derive their fine appearance from the expert cartography of Miss M.H. Bigwood, formerly of the Department of Geography, University College of Wales, Aberystywth. Those illustrations which have appeared in other of my recent writings reflect the skilled draughtsmanship of Mr Colin Williams, formerly Senior Assistant in the Department of Archaeology and Numismatics at the National Museum of Wales. For this present volume, I have added a number of hitherto unpublished original figures. To those who have assisted me in the past, as also to the staffs of the public bodies of Wales: the Archaeological Trusts, Cadw, the County Record Offices, the National Library, the National Museum and the Royal Commission, I express my grateful thanks. I have listed separately those who have kindly given me permission to reproduce illustrations.

The publication of this book at an economic price has only been made possible by grants from the Gwendoline and Margaret Davies Charity, the James Pantyfedwen Foundation, the Marc Fitch Fund, the West Glamorgan Archives Committee, and the Welsh Church Acts Funds of Flintshire County Council and Wrexham Borough Council. I hope that on seeing this new volume they will feel their support has been fully justified.

David H. Williams
Borth, Ceredigion.
Epiphany, 2001.

FISCAL NOTE

In the reading of any work relating to the Middle Ages, it is important to take into account the current equivalent of medieval monetary values. Even within the medieval period, there could be considerable fluctuations from decade to decade. Thus, one pound sterling in 1280 and 1300 was the equivalent of £410 in 1999, but in 1290 approximated to £547 in today's values. £1 in 1320 and 1360 would have been worth £328 today, but the pound sterling in 1340 again equalled around £547 in modern terms. From 1380 to 1520, the pound was generally the equivalent of £410 today. To sum up, from the mid-13th century until almost the time of the Suppression of the monasteries, if the reader mentally multiplies any monetary value given in ths book by 400, a fairly accurate idea of that amount in modern real terms will be gained.

The equivalent value of the pound to that of our times fell sharply over the Reformation years, and a multiplier of 300 should be applied to figures of that period, like the pensions awarded to ousted abbots and monks.

(These notes are based upon the Bank of England information sheet entitled, *Equivalent Contemporary Values of the Pound. A Historical Series from 1270 to 1999*. The author is indebted to the Royal Mint, Llantrisant, for supplying him with a copy.)

1 mark = 13s 4d, $^2/_3$ of the pound sterling.

CHAPTER 1

THE AGE OF SETTLEMENT (1130–1226)

Introduction[1]

Towards the close of the 11th century, certain monks of the French Benedictine abbey of Molesme felt a need for spiritual renewal. Led by their abbot, Robert, they transferred in 1098 to Cîteaux, in a marshy and forested area of Burgundy, and it is from that place's Latin name *(Cistercium)* that the word 'Cistercian' is derived. The monks' custom of wearing habits of undyed wool led to their nick-names: the 'grey monks' or, more often, 'the white monks'. The stability of Cîteaux owed much to Alberic, its second abbot; the constitutions of the fledgling Order to the third, Stephen Harding.

These founders of the 'New Monastery' at Cîteaux can have had no idea that they were sowing the seeds of a religious Order which would come (aided by the driving force of Abbot Bernard of Clairvaux – a household name in the 12th century) to comprehend well over six hundred male abbeys throughout Europe, and stretching into the Near East. Many of these were new foundations, but some were existing religious communities which became Cistercian by incorporation, or else had their sites taken over by the Cistercians. Added to which, from the late 12th century on, there was a considerable influx of nunneries into the new Order.

At the heart of the charism of the Order lay withdrawal from the world, hence where possible – it wasn't always – remote sites were sought for its abbeys. Mostly these were low-lying riverine locations which afforded means of water-power, transport, fishing, drainage and sanitation. Many abbeys experienced one or more changes of site, and for a variety of reasons, which included growing awareness of the limitations of the original position and physical attacks by human agencies. Solitude necessitated self-sufficiency and manual labour in the fields, preceded in virgin territory by the clearance of woodland (assarting) and, perhaps, drainage or irrigation.

Such work took place, on the scale it did, only because of a large body of helpers – the unpaid *conversi* (lay-brothers, who in the late 12th century might outnumber the monks by two to one) aided by wage earning labourers *('mercenaries')*. The preparatory tasks completed, there came the establishment of monastic farms – the granges, sometimes mini-monasteries in themselves. Based on a network of such granges, within the limitations of the local geography and to an extent retarded by the troubled nature of the times, the White Monks endeavoured to use agricultural potential to the full. No less than in the marginal areas of the continent, the Cistercians were frontiers-men, and a civilising influence, in a real sense.

Archdeacon Walter Map (who died in 1210) drew a sharp (and critical) contrast between the White Monks and the Welshry of his day: 'The Cistercians have numbers of coats, the Welsh none; the one class has boots and shoes, the other goes barefoot and barelegged .... The monks eat no meat, the Welsh no bread'.[2] The

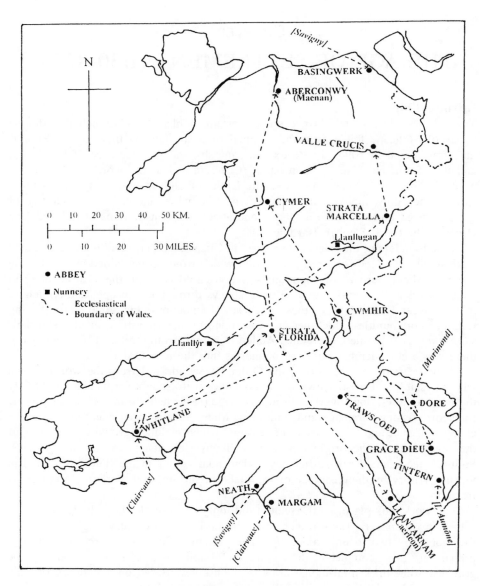

Fig. 1: Cistercian Expansion in Wales.
(Simplified; for intermediate sites, see: Fig. 9).

documentary evidence is so fragmentary, that it is difficult to assess the influence of the Cistercians in those formative years for the Order in Wales. Doubtless, though, their abbeys were places of relative security, of learning and literature, of charity and hospitality, and of spiritual and temporal prestige.

The Political Background

The Norman Conquest of England was followed, in the late 11th century, by a series of incursions into Wales from castles built at strategic points in the March. Welsh princes were held in captivity, Norman knights were rewarded with grants of confiscated land, small towns were established and alien Benedictine monks settled in urban priories. In the 12th century, especially after the death of Henry I (1135), and under leaders like Owain Gwynedd (*d.* 1170) and the Lord Rhys in Ceredigion (*d.* 1197), much of north and west Wales returned to Welsh rule, although the south and south-east remained primarily a Norman sphere. This division was to hold good more or less until the Edwardian Conquest (1277–82), and it was to lead to differences of political allegiance within the Cistercian family in Wales.

The resurgence of Welsh power assisted the growth of the Order in north and west Wales.[3] Even where the initial founder may have been a Norman baron or knight – as at Whitland (1140) and Strata Florida (1164), it was the patronage of the Lord Rhys which made those two abbeys the significant establishments they became. He also settled Premonstratensian Canons at Talley and Cistercian nuns at Llanllŷr. The growth of native power may be a major factor in explaining the series of Cistercian houses founded in the 1170s: Strata Marcella (1170, by Owain Cyfeiliog, Prince of Powys); Cwmhir (1176, by Cadwallon ap Madog, Prince of Ceri and Maelienydd – though, the foundation charter early lost or destroyed, his name does not appear in extant confirmations of the abbey's charters),[4] and Llantarnam (about 1179, by Hywel ab Iorwerth, Lord of Caerleon). The transient abbeys of Pendâr and Trawscoed were probably also foundations of this period. At the close of the century, Prince Llywelyn ab Iorwerth afforded his patronage to the new abbeys of Aberconwy and Cymer – the latter founded by his cousins, Maredudd and Gruffydd ap Cynan,[5] whilst Madog ap Gruffydd, Lord of Iâl, founded Valle Crucis.

Most of the abbeys in North and Central Wales shared two things in common: (i) descent from Clairvaux *via* the premier Welsh house of Whitland, and (ii) identification with the national aspirations of the Welsh princes and people. The White Monks of Wales, however, did not seek to imitate or be influenced by the ancient Celtic *clas* system of monasticism. Much of south and south-east Wales lay under the over-lordship of the earls of Gloucester – members first of the Consul family and later of the de Clares. They also espoused the Cistercian cause: Robert Consul founded Margam (1147); earlier his Constable, Richard de Granville, had established Neath (1130), whilst a de Clare, Walter (as Lord of Chepstow) founded Tintern (1131). Tintern ranks thus as the first Cistercian abbey in Wales, Neath being Savigniac until its incorporation in 1147 (an *annus mirabilis* for the Order).

The composition of the south Walian Cistercian communities, and their political leanings, reflected the very different post-Norman Conquest pattern of settlement in this region. The odd man out was the monastery of Llantarnam: an agreement (of about 1203) allowed Margam to acquire what it could 'from the French and the English', Llantarnam 'from the Welsh'.[6] The cultural environment was very different from that obtaining in the lands of the Welsh princes. With the settling of the last foundation, Grace Dieu near Monmouth, there were thirteen Cistercian abbeys in Wales which endured until the Suppression. With Dore (also founded in 1147 and straddling the boundary between the dioceses of Hereford and St. David's) they came to be regarded as a rudimentary Welsh 'province' within the Order.[7]

Not all mooted abbeys came into being, nor did all new foundations survive. No more is heard of a request to the General Chapter (1203) from the 'king of Wales' (presumably Prince Llywelyn ab Iorwerth) for leave to found an abbey.[8] Another would-be patron was William de Braose (1204), an important baron of the March.[9] The Coggeshall chronicler records him as having constructed a Cistercian abbey in Wales.[10] It is may be that he had meant to found a monastery at Llanfair hermitage, in north Gwent, which he gave to Dore abbey and which became one of its granges.[11]

Two transitory Cistercian abbeys were Pendâr and Trawscoed. Gruffydd ab Ifor, lord of Senghenydd, granted land to Margam abbey (*c.* 1175) through an intermediary – the noted hermit, Meiler.[12] (Gruffydd, a son-in-law of the Lord Rhys, desired to be buried at Margam but died at Llantarnam).[13] The land given (to make: 'A hermitage or abbey upon the Taff') lay in the northern part of his lordship, and was, presumably, Pendâr. A little later, Caradog Merbeis gave 'the brethren of Pendâr' land in Llanwynno in Miscin,[14] and the fledgling community may have moved there. Wherever Pendâr was located, it was certainly for a short while a Cistercian establishment, independent of, though perhaps subordinate to, the mother-house of Margam: witness the preamble to an early charter: 'We grant to St Mary and the Cistercian Order and the house of Margam ... We grant *also* to St Mary and the

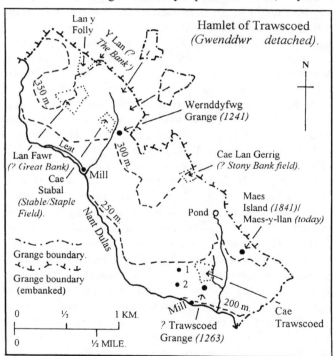

Fig. 2: Trawscoed, Breconshire. *(The site of the abbey was perhaps at Lower Trawscoed).*

Cistercian Order and the house of Pendâr'.[15] (Later, after a protracted dispute, the Llanwynno lands passed to Llantarnam abbey).[16]

The monastery of Trawscoed in Breconshire *(Fig. 2)* owed its origins to the grant to Dore (*c.* 1173) by Walter de Clifford, lord of Bronllys, of land in Cantref-selyf for an abbey: 'For the increase of the Cistercian Order', together with timber for the construction of the building. He hoped that 'the abbey shall remain in Cantref-selyf for ever'.[17] It didn't: Giraldus Cambrensis mentioned a visit to the new abbey by Abbot Canawg of Cwmhir,[18] but, in a later writing, grumbled that Dore had degraded Trawscoed from the status of a conventual abbey into merely a grange.[19] This was perhaps in accord with the enabling statutes of the General Chapter in 1189 and 1204;[20] the statutes may also explain the loss of independence by Pendâr.

Various other sites have been suggested as the location of Cistercian monasteries, but all appear to have been no more than outlying cells or major granges of parent abbeys. Such were: 'Cridia', close to Montgomery and adduced by Matthew Paris as being burnt by Henry III in 1228,[21] the 'monks of Mochraiadr', referred to about 1284,[22] and the 'abbey' traditionally located at Cyffin.[23] They were granges, respectively, of Cwmhir, Basingwerk, and Strata Marcella. None of these transient, or reputed, foundations find mention in the great ecclesiastical valuation of 1291.

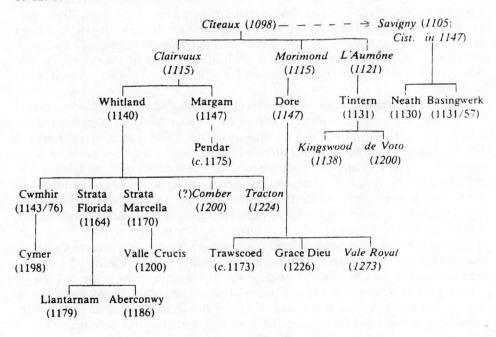

Fig. 3: Cistercian Expansion in Wales: Genealogical Table.

The Permanent Foundations

The premier Welsh abbey of Whitland was founded (directly from Clairvaux) around 1140–44 by Bishop Bernard of St David's at Trefgarn in Deugleddyf, according to the

Annales Cambriae.[24] When the monks moved to Whitland – to a site provided by John of Torrington – they do not appear to have retained this early property, but it is hardly likely that the chronicler was mistaken, and that their first site was at Trefgarn, 4^1/$_2$ miles [7km.] south-west of Whitland and adjacent to its Blaengwyddno Grange.[25] Further, a situation on land owned by the church of St David's makes sense.

Whitland, directly or indirectly, gave rise to seven further foundations, thus enabling an abbot of Fountains (in 1517) to remark that: 'Nearly all the monasteries of Wales are of the filiation and generation of Clairvaux'.[26] This 'priority of Whitland' endured until the dissolution, and was indicated when a former monk of Cwmhir (in 1549) referred to Whitland's last abbot as: 'Head of that religion and Visitor of their house'.[27] Yet Whitland's south-western position, away from the power bases of the Welsh princes, made Aberconwy and Strata Florida the more notable houses in 13th century politics.

In 1164 Whitland sent monks into Ceredigion, under the leadership of Abbot David, to found an abbey by the Fflur brook, the latter lending it the name of Strata Florida *(Ystrad Fflur)*.[28] The original patron was perhaps the Norman baron, Robert fitzStephen, as lord of Pennardd, credited by Giraldus Cambrensis with founding a Cistercian house.[29] Robert lost this district the next year to the Lord Rhys, who erected permanent buildings for the new monastery which, he said: 'He loved and cherished'.[30] Strata Florida, in turn, established the daughter-houses of Llantarnam (*c.* 1179) – in conjunction with Hywel ab Iorwerth, Lord of Caerleon,[31] and of Aberconwy (1186) – perhaps with the backing of Rhodri ab Owain Gwynedd, Lord of Arfon.[32]

Monks from Whitland settled at Cwmhir (1176) with Cadwallon ap Madog, Prince of Ceri and Maelienydd, as patron,[33] but an earlier foundation there (perhaps abandoned after the Anglo-Conquest of Maelienydd in 1144) has been suggested.[34] Whitland had by now also founded Strata Marcella, and, at the close of the century, these two abbeys established their own daughter-houses, thus completing the 'Whitland family' in Wales. Monks from Cwmhir settling at Cymer in Meirionydd in 1198 – under the patronage of Gruffydd and Maredudd ap Cynan, and religious from Strata Marcella – assisted by Madog ap Gruffydd, Lord of Dinas Brân, Bromfeld and Iâl, founded Valle Crucis (1200).[35] [Gruffydd ap Cynan died in 1200, clothed in Cistercian habit, at Aberconwy.] One author sees the removal of monks to Cymer as that of refugees fleeing from the current troubles in Maelienydd. Cymer's foundation led to difficulties for Cwmhir with Aberconwy – perhaps regarding grants in Llŷn.[36]

In anglicised Wales, Tintern took pride of place, and Churchyard wrote that it was 'as old a sell, as within the land'.[37] It was the second Cistercian abbey to be founded in England and Wales – but it did not rank with the great Benedictine establishments, and John Russell, in the 15th century, was quick to point out that 'Tintern with Westmystere shalle nowher sitte ne stande'.[38] Colonised from the French abbey of L'Aumône, the founder was Walter de Clare, lord of Chepstow,[39] but it was Earl Roger Bigod of Norfolk (1270–1306) who enabled the present abbey church to be completed, and who also substantially enhanced the possessions of the house. He was retrospectively even seen as the founder, and his arms were glazed on the east window of its church.[40] Within eight years Tintern had sufficient monks to settle the monastery of Kingswood across the Bristol Channel (1138)[41] and, later, founded an Irish house – Tintern Secunda or 'the abbey of the Vow' (1200).[42] Also in Gwent were Llantarnam and Grace Dieu – a daughter-house of Dore, founded by John, Lord of Monmouth.[43]

In Glamorgan, Margam was, like Whitland, an offshoot of Clairvaux. Both were settled during St Bernard's rule of that house, and it was to St Bernard's brother, Nivard, that the site of Margam was granted at a ceremony in Bristol.[44] Its first abbot was William, a monk from Clairvaux.[45] In the same county, Neath – being a daughter-house of Savigny – was dedicated not to the Blessed Virgin Mary, as normal for Cistercian abbeys – but to the Holy Trinity.[46] Also Savigniac was Basingwerk in the far north-east of Wales; its date of foundation and the identity of its founder are both uncertain. Its initial patron (1131–32) may have been a baron, William Peverell,[47] but its major benefactions came from Earl Ranulf II of Chester (to whom Peverell's lands passed in 1153).[48] The *Brut y Tywysogyon* ('the Chronicle of the Princes') implied that the abbey was founded by Owain Gwynedd.[49] Whatever the truth, Basingwerk, whilst technically 'in Wales', was not 'of it' in nationalist feeling. Its presence in the four Cantrefs – to which he lay claim – may have been welcomed by Earl Ranulf for political purposes. As a filiation of Savigny, Basingwerk became Cistercian in 1147. Ten years later the abbot of Savigny placed it under the oversight of Buildwas abbey, an unpopular move which Basingwerk resisted (unsuccessfully) for decades.[50]

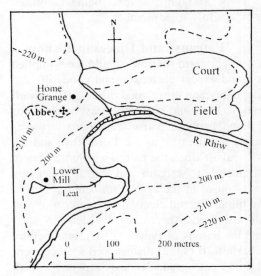

Fig. 4: Llanllugan Abbey.

The Cistercian Nunneries

There were two lasting Cistercian nunneries in Wales – surprisingly few.[51] Llanllugan in Cydewain (*Fig. 4;* initially sited at Hydan, perhaps about 1170 to 1190)[52] was endowed with substantial lands in Llanllugan by Maredudd ap Rhotpert, the local lord, possibly as late as 1217.[53] One tradition has it that the convent sprang from an ancient Celtic community.[54] Llanllŷr (*Fig. 5*) in Ceredigion was founded by the Lord Rhys – probably well before his death in 1197.[55] Giraldus Cambrensis called it 'a small and poor house', and (reflecting the only semi-official status within the Order of nunneries at that time) he told how its nuns followed from the outset, as far as was permissible, the outward habit and inner life of the Cistercians.[56] (An inscribed stone, of perhaps the 8th century, found at Llanllŷr and bearing the name of a Celtic saint, Modomnoc, might reflect an earlier religious foundation there).[57]

Medieval poets saw the nunneries as 'proud Llanllugan' and 'holy Llanllŷr', and, alluding to the nuns' habits, wrote of 'the chalk-white ones' of Llanllugan[58] and the 'white maidens' of Llanllŷr.[59] Llanllugan – overlooking the southern Rhiw, lay under the oversight of Strata Marcella,[60] Llanllŷr – on the Aeron floodplain, under that of Strata Florida[61] whom Giraldus Cambrensis accused of despoiling it.[62] The location of an earlier nunnery – located by Giraldus at Llansanffraid in Elfael – was at best a transient foundation.[63]

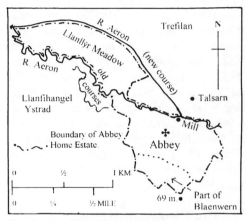

Fig. 5: Llanllŷr Abbey. *(Based upon an estate plan of 1768, and the parochial tithe-map of 1841).*

Dates of Foundation

Certain general points concerning the monasteries are worthy of note: the date of their establishment, the privileges of their 'patron' and their relationship to the diocesan bishop. Not surprisingly, the dates ascribed to the actual settlement of monks practically all fall within the warmer weather of the summer. They range from 24 April (in the case of Grace Dieu) to 23 November (in the instance of Margam); several being colonised in July to September.[64]

'Patrons' and Diocesan Bishops

The term 'patron' should have implied a local magnate from whom the monks could expect protection and goodwill, and for whom they would render prayers, hospitality and other good offices. (Cromwell was promised that, if he spared Aberconwy, he would be 'daily prayed for as for a founder of the house'; 1537).[65] The bond between patron and monastery was strongest where the patron lived in relative proximity – as the Lord Rhys and his descendants in the case of Strata Florida, weakest when the patron was more remote – as the earls of Gloucester in the instances of Margam and Neath – perhaps accounting for the sufferings of those two houses in the early 13th century.[66]

A patron should have played no part in the unfettered election by monks of a new abbot – Prince Llywelyn ab Iorwerth promised Aberconwy freedom in such matters,[67] but after the Charltons acquired the barony of Powys (1309), and thereby the patronage of Strata Marcella, John Charlton III (1332) disregarded such convention.[68] Official relations with the local episcopate gradually acquired in the 12th century a similar independence, so far as Cistercian monasteries were concerned.[69] The bishop's rights became restricted to blessing newly-elected abbots and the visitation, not of an abbey, but of its impropriated churches. Bishop John de Trillek of Hereford (1360) noted the exempt, extra-diocesan status of Strata Marcella.[70]

Abbey Sites

Cistercian abbeys were generally built in lowland areas, mostly in a riverine situation which provided running water for drainage purposes and as the motive force of the abbey mill. Fishing and transport potential were also realised. Valley sites were common – hence the official Latin names for Cwmhir, *'Longa Vallis'* ('the abbey of the long valley'),[71] and for Valle Crucis ('the vale of the cross' – deriving from the nearby Eliseg's Pillar. Valle Crucis actually lay in the bed of an abandoned meander of the deeply incised river Dee.[72] Important as the main river may be, a situation near the junction of a tributary was equally significant, for it was often the waters of the latter which were led off to flush an abbey's drainage channels and to service its mill leat. 'Cymer',

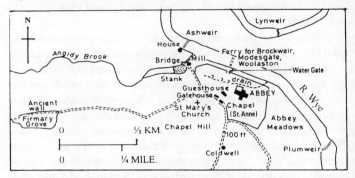

Fig. 6: Tintern Abbey, at the confluence of the river Wye and the Angidy brook.

indeed, took its name from the adjacent 'confluence' of the Wnion with the Mawddach. Tintern's 'park' lay between: 'The torrent called Angetty and the stream of Wye' (*Fig. 6;* 1527).[73]

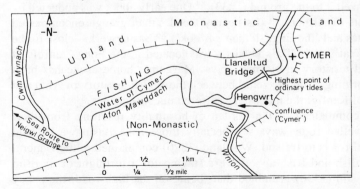

Fig. 7: Cymer Abbey, at the confluence of the rivers Mawddach and Wnion.

Such lowland situations, close to running water, meant that good drainage was essential. Maenan (Aberconwy III) was, therefore, sited on rising ground surfaced with alluvial deposits.[74] Though they might have been in lowland situations, the Welsh monasteries could never be far from the uplands – those 'desolate mountains' as an abbot of Strata Florida once described them.[75] Cwmhir, over 250 metres high, was (in 1232) seen as being set 'in a remote, mountainous district'.[76]

Several Welsh houses chose estuarine positions; indeed a few abbeys may have been first colonised by sea. Tintern lay on the right bank of the river Wye, an artery of traffic throughout the Middle Ages. Its boats plied to Bristol, and the tidal waters yielded salmon. Proximity to the estuary of the river Mawddach, close to its lowest bridging point, allowed the monks of Cymer *(Fig. 7)* easy access to their arable properties in Llŷn; it had fisheries there as well as in the Mawddach itself.[77] Alas, one of its monks was accidentally drowned.[78] Margam's site – close to the Bristol Channel – gave it like advantages, but also inherent difficulties – marine inundation of its coastal lands, encroachments by blown sand, and the 'horrid intemperance' of the wind (1384).[79]

The Cistercians sought situations for their monasteries in sparsely populated areas – to facilitate contemplative life. Such a position also permitted easier estate building. Even in rural Wales, most Cistercian sites were not entirely un-peopled,[80] and local folk might need to be displaced: when Valle Crucis was founded (1200) inhabitants of Llanegwestl were removed to Northcroft and Stansty, townships of Wrexham within the founder's lordship of Bromfeld and Iâl.[81] Several Welsh foundations stood relatively close to military fortifications, which gave them a measure of security. This was true of Aberconwy's second site (in clear view of Prince Llywelyn's citadel at Deganwy),[82] of Neath (across the river from a pre-existing Norman castle), and of Tintern (but eight kilometres from the de Clare fortress of Striguil). In the 13th century, Basingwerk was to find a near neighbour in the Edwardian castle of Flint, whilst Valle Crucis saw the Welsh hill-top Dinas Brân re-established. Their close proximity was later remarked upon by the travelling antiquary, John Leland: 'Dinas Brane Castel on a rokky hille stondith almost as neere as Valle Crucis to Dee ripe'.[83]

The 'border' situation of some abbeys aggravated their troubles in difficult political times. Grace Dieu was built – so the Welsh alleged – on land wrested from them by the English; they razed it to the ground (1233).[84] One early abbot was abducted by the Welsh 'descendants of Arthen'.[85] (Its nearby Coed Ythan grange encompassed both Welsh place-names and 'the English men's brook').[86] Basingwerk – close to the Saxon boundaries of Wat's and Offa's Dykes – was located in the Four Cantrefs of Perfeddwlad, disputed territory in Norman days. Margam's home estate has been seen as deliberately forming a 'buffer zone' between the Welsh territory of Afan and the Norman lordship of Kenfig; the monastery suffered in consequence.[87]

Not a few abbeys complained of the burden of hospitality resulting from their proximity to well-travelled route-ways – especially those (like Basingwerk[88] and Neath[89]) by the coastal roads to Ireland. Whitland (1220) complained to the General Chapter that both English and Irish abbots were staying for a fortnight or more in the monastery.[90] Margam (1336) grumbled that 'being on the high road, the abbey is continually over-run with rich and poor strangers'.[91]

There is little evidence that the location of the Cistercian abbeys of Wales bore any relationship to previous ecclesiastical sites. The concentration of Celtic stone crosses near Margam, and upon certain of its granges, has led to the suggestion that there may previously have been an important *clas* church at Margam.[92] Earlier religious foundations have also been suggested for Neath (of St Catwg),[93] Valle Crucis[94] and Strata Marcella,[95] as well as for the Cistercian nunneries.

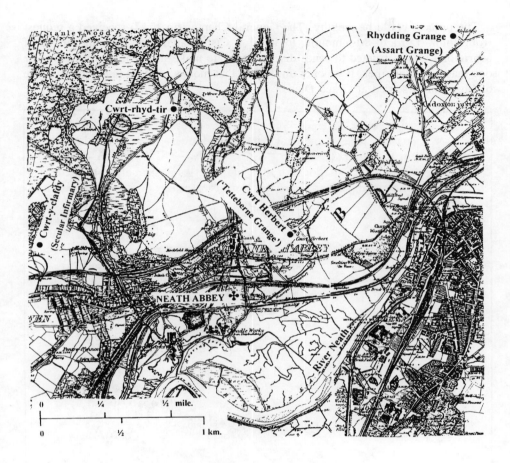

Fig. 8: Neath Abbey in its Setting.
(Reduced from the 1ˢᵗ edn. of the 6" O.S. Map).

Site Changes ('Cloister Translation')

Cistercian abbey sites were chosen with care. It was 'a rather complicated operation, involving a number of interested parties: first, there had to be an invitation to
settle, with the approval of the local diocesan, and then, if the General Chapter of
the Order agreed, the ground had to be inspected and the actual site selected'.[96] In
addition the two abbots sent to negotiate with the would-be founder had to ensure
that the initial benefactions promised would ensure the material stability of the new
monastery.

The process could be lengthy. The General Chapter (in 1217) received a request from John, Lord of Monmouth, to build a Cistercian house, and the abbot of Morimond was instructed to send 'discreet men' to make 'diligent enquiries'.[97] For one reason and another, it was not until 1226 that monks of Dore (a daughter-house of Morimond) settled at Grace Dieu.[98]

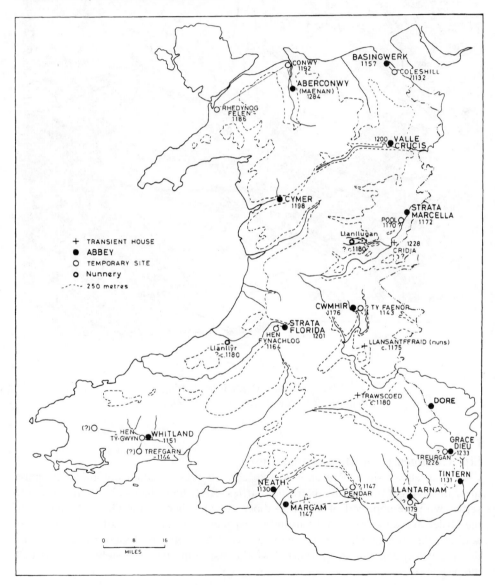

Fig. 9: Cistercian sites in Wales.

About one-third of the Cistercian abbeys of Europe found it necessary to change their location.[99] This may have been simply a transfer from a location temporarily occupied whilst permanent buildings were erected. In many instances, though, it was for reasons beyond the control of the monks – like an inadequate site or oppression by enemies. In only two cases in Wales (Aberconwy and Grace Dieu) are the motives known, and in only two instances (Aberconwy and Strata Florida) can foundations of an earlier site be detected. Occasionally, such moves can only be ascertained from the term 'old abbey' used in later documentation.

White Monks settled in Gwynedd at Rhedynog-felen in 1186, but, not later than 1192, they transferred to a site at the mouth of the Conwy river – though lands at Rhedynog remained in monastic ownership.[100] A century later, after the Edwardian Conquest, Edward I, whilst staying at Aberconwy abbey (from 13 March to 9 May 1283) and realising the strategic value of its position, determined to build Conwy Castle there.[101] This enterprise clearly necessitated the removal of the monks, the sovereign (in mid-September 1283) taking possession of the township of Maenan, seven miles (11 km.) up the Conwy valley, as the site for their new abbey (Aberconwy III).[102] He also compensated financially both the community (for the loss of their monastery and lands at Conwy), and also the five landowners dispossessed in Maenan.[103] The extra-parochial monastic territory thus created at Maenan accounts for the deviation of the county boundary of Caernarfonshire eastwards, away from the Conwy river.[104]

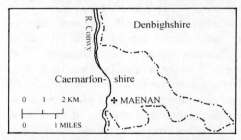

Fig. 10: Location of Aberconwy III (Maenan).

Work on the new abbey was inaugurated on 26 March 1284, the king visiting the site. Present also on 8 October that year, when the first buildings were dedicated, Edward I gave 580 marks for the construction of the new edifice, and a grant of £60 for further works – including the bake-house and brew-house,[105] as well as lands in Anglesey – compensating for the concomitant loss of Creuddyn Grange.[106] On 23 October, at Caernarfon, Edward I formally gave the community possession of the site in a detailed charter. Pope Honorius IV saw Maenan as a new (and royal) foundation to which the former abbey – endowed by the Welsh princes – was united,[107] and to which the monks took the body of Llywelyn ab Iorwerth for reburial.[108]

Only seven years after its foundation, the humble abbey of Grace Dieu was burnt during the joint rebellion of Prince Llywelyn ab Iorwerth and Earl Richard Marshal of Pembroke against King Henry III (1233). The Welsh alleged that its site stood on land 'wrested from them' by John of Monmouth, the monastery's founder.[109] The *Annals of Waverley* suggest that the house was 'completely overthrown'.[110] The General Chapter delegated the abbots of Bruern and Kingswood to 'induce the founder either to make peace with his enemies or give the monks a more suitable place where they can live without damage'.[111] The latter course was adopted, and

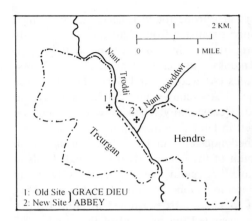

Fig. 11: The Location of Grace Dieu Abbey.

in 1236 the monks moved to a new site,[112] Henry III granting timber from the Forest of Dean to help in the new abbey's construction.[113] (Later – in 1276 – Grace Dieu experienced fresh difficulties, and a further site change was mooted – but there is no record of it taking place).[114] The first site of Grace Dieu probably stood in the former small medieval township of Treurgan ('Parc Grace Dieu' today) – which remained extra-parochial well into modern times.[115] The final site seemingly lay to the east, immediately across the Troddi stream.[116] Exploratory excavation[117] and geophysical survey[118] here have revealed substantial foundations deeply buried under later alluvial deposits – the product of repeated flooding once monastic drainage channels failed to be maintained.[119] A late-medieval field-name of 'old abbey close',[120] whilst its precise location is lost, shows that the final site was at no great distance from the initial position *(Fig. 11)*.

In north-east Wales, the monks of Savigny settled originally at a place known as 'the chapel of Basingwerk', situated somewhere other than the site at Greenfield ultimately occupied by the abbey in 1157.[121] This was later made clear when Edward III confirmed to its monks 'the chapel of Basingwerk in which they first dwelt'.[122] This earlier site may have been three miles distant – at a place in Coleshill called Hên Blas.[123] The reasons for the move are unknown. In south-west Wales, the monks of Whitland transferred from Trefgarn (*f.* 1140–44) to their final site in 1151, but there is a possibility of an intermediate stop-over at Hen Dy Gwyn, a mile south of Whitland proper.[124]

The initial site of the monks of Strata Florida, at what is today known as 'Hen Fynachlog' *(Fig. 12)*,[125] may have been intentionally temporary, for the Lord Rhys noted in his charter of 1184 that he had 'begun to build the abbey'.[126] The thesis of a fire at the old abbey being the cause of transfer has little to commend it.[127] At the first site the foundations of the church (over 35 m./120 ft. long) were once traceable.[128] Not far distant survives the name of Ty'n-llidiart ('gate-house').[129] The monks took to the new abbey the original name of Strata Florida *(Ystrad Fflur)*, despite the move away from the Fflur brook by which the first house had stood.[130]

Strata Florida's daughter-house of Llantarnam also knew a site change. This is indicated by the property listed as 'old abbey' in the *Taxatio Ecclesiastica* in 1291,[131] and by the description of Abbot John (1476) as: 'Abbot of Llantarnam, lord of the old abbey'.[132] The first site may have been at Pentre-bach (formerly called Cefn-mynach Grange);[133] this was in the parish of Dewma – an alternative early name for the abbey.[134] There is no cast-iron evidence to support alleged site changes by the monks of Cwmhir (in 1176 from nearby Ty Faenor),[135] nor of Strata

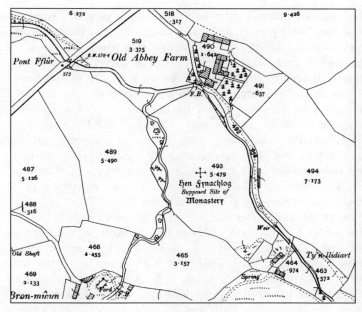

Fig. 12: The Location of Strata Florida I.
(Reduced from the 1ˢᵗ Edn. O.S. 6″ Map).

Marcella (in 1172 from a site nearer Welshpool).[136] It is important to note, however, that John Leland referred to the 'first' foundation of Cwmhir,[137] and that its daughter-house at Cymer was occasionally called 'Y Vaner'.[138] At Tintern, architectural evidence shows the building of the 13th century church on the site of the Norman one; one can discount the suggestion of a site change made by 'The Troubled Spirit of Tintern Abbey' in *Lord Halifax's Ghost Book*.[139] More assuredly, the nuns of Llanllugan first lived on the property which became their Hydan Grange,[140] and by that name (corrupted as 'Hudham') the nunnery was first known.[141]

Dual Nomenclature

Closely bound up with changes of site, but not always deriving from them, was the relative frequency with which some abbeys bore alternative names. Every Cistercian monastery had an official Latin name recorded in the 'table of the Order', kept by the precentor of Cîteaux, but many were also known by more collo-quial names.[142] The abbey of Valle Crucis – so named from its proximity to Eliseg's Pillar – was often called Llanegwestl (perhaps more correctly Llynegwestl) from the original Welsh name for its site.[143] Whitland was generally described by its Latin form 'Albalanda', or as 'Blanchland', but within the pages of one work – the *Taxatio Ecclesiastica* of 1291 – it finds description as both 'Wytelond' and as 'Alba Domus'.[144] Far less frequently was it termed 'Ty Gwyn ar Tav'.[145] Strata Marcella had (throughout the Middle Ages) the sometimes less formal name of 'Pool' – deriving from the nearby castle-town (now Welshpool). Leopold Janauschek thought there were two separate monasteries, and referred to 'Pola, filia Stratae-Marcelli',[146] but, so interchangeable were the two names, that it was possi-ble for one charter in its list of witnesses to place in juxtaposition – as if they were two separate entities- 'T. and I. monks of Strata Marcella, D. and K. *conversi* of

Pool'.[147] There is other internal charter evidence[148] – as well as official Cistercian records[149] -to show that they were part of the same community, but the confusion may reflect a temporary dwelling whilst the abbey proper was being completed.

The matter of Llantarnam is even more complex, and may derive from a known site change.[150] The late-12th century *Brenhinedd y Saeson* points to the problem; of the year 1179 it says that: 'A community was established at Nant-teyrnon, others call it the monastery of Dewma, others the monastery of Caerleon-on-Usk'.[151] ('Dewma' was the parish of its first site, 'Caerleon' the lordship of its foundation).[152] Until 1239 the monastery was almost exclusively termed 'Caerleon',[153] but from 1266 the use of 'Llantarnam' (a corruption of Glan-teyrnon) creeps in. Some later records (down to 1513) refer to the abbey of 'Caerleon *alias* Llantarnam'.[154] The more colloquial 'Dewma' occurs in the *Brut y Tywysogyon*, in the *Red Book of Hergest*,[155] in the verse of Welsh Tudor poets,[156] and – as 'Duma' – even in the register of the Bishop of Hereford (1449).[157] The General Chapter of the Order had tried (in 1272) to rectify matters: 'Concerning the name of the abbey of Llantarnam, which is also called by another name, Vallium *(perhaps a mis-transcription for Carliun)*,[158] it is always to be allotted that name by which it is designated in the table of Cîteaux'.[159] The searcher of indices in older published works (as of the Rolls Series) must take care to look for these variants, as also 'Morgan' for 'Margam', 'Neth' for 'Neath', 'Kymer' for 'Cymer', and so on.

The Troubled Background

The resistance offered by the native population to the advent of the Normans to

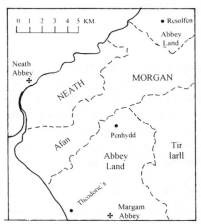

Fig. 13: Margam Abbey, and the granges attacked in 1227.

south Wales affected the monasteries severely – especially where they were seen as objects of Norman patronage.[160] A monk of Neath recorded (in the late 12th century) that whenever a lord of Gower died, his territory was devastated by the Welsh and the abbey's holdings there declined appreciably in value.[161] The period was also a time of considerable difficulty for Margam, Henry II taking the abbey under his protection, notifying the Lord Rhys of his action, ordering the powerful baron William de Braose and the 'faithful Welshry' to capture its enemies.[162] Despite the Earl of Gloucester's 'Welsh Hundred of Morgan' (by 1183) agreeing not to molest the monastery,[163] and a papal bull (1203) forbidding 'theft, arson, bloodshed' at the abbey as well as further royal charters (1204, 1228, 1236) of protection,[164] severe difficulties continued – including attacks by 'men of Brecknock and Senghenydd' (about 1205).[165] The 1220s were especially troubled years, and saw 'perverse men' burning over a thousand of the abbey's sheep in 1223, two of its 'familiars' and a shepherd-boy killed by the Lord of Afan (Morgan ab Owain) in 1224, and further attacks on its stock at several granges in 1227 *(Fig. 13)*. A temporary interlude of peace seems to have been marked, or occasioned by, the abbey receiving the body of Morgan Gam for burial (1241).[166]

The possibility of trouble was foreseen also in north Wales. The confirmatory charter given to Cymer by Prince Llywelyn the Great (1209) ten years after its foundation, was so lest its monks be 'unjustly molested by breach of the peace'. The forms such 'breach of the peace' might take are so detailed as to suggest that the community may have experienced some of them already: at least they feared the worst 'by burning of houses, by shedding of blood within the precincts of the monastery, or also of the granges . . . by committing theft . . . irreverence'.[167] Such difficulties inhibited the full and free spiritual and economic development of the several abbeys in their formative decades. So, too, did financial constraints: as the levy imposed on all Cistercian houses to pay for the ransom imposed of Richard I;[168] in addition to which came the heavy fine imposed by King John: not least on Strata Florida – £800, a debt and a millstone around its neck for years. Margam, which twice gave the monarch and his army hospitality, was exempted.[169]

Difficulties came, too, from within the Order: from unruly lay-brethren, and from a number of contentions between its Welsh monasteries as to pasture rights and other matters. By the close of the 12th century, the Welsh lay-brethren *(conversi)* were sometimes difficult to handle[170] and drink appears to have been the root of the problem. Beer drinking was forbidden on the granges, but (in 1190) on Margam's lands this rule was 'held in contempt',[171] difficulties ensued[172] and the General Chapter (1195) demanded that on the Welsh granges 'neither beer nor other drink except simple water' was to be had.[173]

Conversi of Cwmhir (1195) stole their abbot's horses, 'because he had refused them beer',[174] and erring lay-brethren were at the centre of 'brawls and excesses' at Strata Florida (1196).[175] Ten years later, the *conversi* of Margam (1206) rose in rebellion, chased the abbot away, threw the cellarer off his horse, refused to give the monks food, and barricaded themselves in their dorter. The General Chapter ordered the dispersal of the ring-leaders, and a temporary halt to the recruitment of *conversi* at Margam.[176]

As the monasteries expanded their estates and spheres of influence, a number of disputes almost inevitably arose between neighbouring abbeys. In all such cases recourse was had to arbitration and judgement by representative abbots appointed by the General Chapter.[177] These contentions were most frequent in the first half of the 13th century; by 1250 matters appear to have become more stabilised and rights and ownership more clearly defined and accepted.

Disagreements between the almost proximate abbeys of Margam and Neath – largely concerning territorial and pasture rights – lasted on and off for years (1173–1238), and sometimes found expression in raids by one party or the other.[178] Margam also had long-standing difficulties (1203–56) with Llantarnam, concerning lands and pastures in the Rhondda.[179] Basingwerk (1201) objected to Poulton (the later Dieulacres) building a grange close to its lands.[180] Strata Florida (1209), after arbitration by several Welsh abbots, agreed not to infringe any more the liberties and properties of Dore in Cantref-selyf.[181] Tintern was involved in disputes with Llantarnam (1221),[182] Dore (1239)[183] and Grace Dieu (about 1248).[184]

An analysis has been made of the principles upon which investigating abbots were appointed.[185] In a dispute between Margam and Neath (1208) seven abbots drawn widely from England and Wales met at the former's Orchard Grange, three as arbitrators, four as assessors; no apparent reason appears for their selection, save that the abbot of Combermere (like Neath a Savigniac house) was brought in to safeguard its interests.[186] A dispute between Cwmhir and Strata Marcella (1227) (regarding pasture rights granted in 1201 by Prince Gwenwynwyn[187]) saw three abbots (of Dore, Whitland and Llantarnam) appointed.[188] Whitland was the mother-house of both monasteries, the others were impartial. No less than fifty senior monks of the Order, including two further abbots, met as 'associates' at Radnor.[189] The judgement given was that: 'All things were to be restored to their former status'. Of the disputed territory (between the brooks Chorw and Einion) Cwmhir was to have that part belonging to Ceredigion; that part pertaining to Cyfeiliog, Strata Marcella was to enjoy. Land between the Llwyd and Biga streams was divided, so that the part towards the Llwyd went to Strata Marcella, the southern section to Cwmhir *(Fig. 14).*[190]

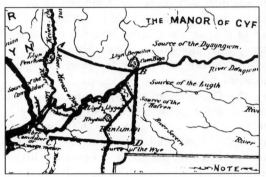

Fig. 14: The 1227 Settlement. *(M.C. Jones, 1872; by Courtesy of the Editors of the Montgomeryshire Collections).* ABC = pasture for Strata Marcella; BCD = pasture for Cwmhir.

Conventual Life

What little is on record regarding the interior life of the monasteries in this period, mostly concerns various short-comings – just as bad news to-day often alone hits the headlines. The stable and spiritual – even holy – lives, lived by many monks and *conversi* pass unrecorded. The student of medieval Cistercian history can truly say: 'Behold, the half was not told me' (1 Kings 10:7). The multiplication of houses – particularly in the 1170s and around 1200 – suggests that not a few Welsh folk took the habit in the late 12th century. Thereafter, enthusiasm may have waned: Gerald of Wales – a critical witness – alleged that Bishop Geoffrey of St David's (1203–14) allowed 'a great many regulars and lay-brothers in Maelienydd and Elfael, who had taken the habit of religion and worn it for some time, to return to wearing secular clothes'.[191] Cwmhir lay in Maelienydd. Gerald also – in three of his works – related the story of Abbot Enoch of Strata Marcella who, having founded a nunnery in Elfael, eloped with one of its nuns, but later 'humbled and amended' returned to monastic life at the mother-house of Whitland where he submitted to a severe flogging.[192] 'Enoch' may have been a fictitious name, a play on his character. Gerald told a not dissimilar tale regarding Abbot Cynan of Whitland.[193]. Both stories emanated in part from the hermit, Meilyr of Caerleon, perhaps the same personage who played a role in the foundation of Pendâr, and possibly even of Llantarnam.[194]

The statutes of the General Chapter reveal occasional departures from Cistercian rule and custom. Abbot William of Tintern was deposed (1188)[195] – but might this have been due to advanced age? The Abbots of Aberconwy, Llantarnam and Valle Crucis (founded only a year or so before) were said (in 1202) to 'most rarely celebrate' Mass[196] – could this have reflected the growing number of priest-monks? The monks of Tintern (1217) were rebuked for singing the office in harmony ('in the manner of seculars'), and its abbot was criticised for breaking the night silence, and for allowing women to live near, and even work on, a grange.[197]

In a sequence of events which paralleled those of Giraldus *(infra)*, Rotoland, the sub-prior of Aberconwy, was twice elected to the see of Bangor (*c.* 1190, 1197) but the Archbishop of Canterbury refused to consecrate him.[198] Rotoland was a Welshman, 'a fellow countryman' Giraldus called him.[199] He took his case three times, unsuccessfully, to Rome,[200] and his lengthy absences from his monastery incurred him the displeasure of the General Chapter (1202).[201] The same was true for another monk of Aberconwy, Philip (1200), who claimed to have been created a bishop.[202] Two other Cistercians *were* consecrated to the episcopate: Cadwgan, Abbot of Whitland, as Bishop of Bangor (1215),[203] and Abraham, monk of Aberconwy, for the see of St Asaph (1225).[204] These appointments, and the unsuccessful endeavours of Rotoland, may have had the backing of Prince Llewelyn.[205]

As Archbishop Baldwin of Canterbury made a peregrination in Wales in 1188, preaching the Crusade, he and his company were received at several Cistercian houses. One of his number was Giraldus Cambrensis, who told of the 'faithful attendance' upon them of Abbots John of Whitland and Seisil of Strata Florida – both of whom preached at Llanbedr-pont-Steffan (Lampeter),[206] and Seisil – a second sermon – in Anglesey.[207] During the primate's stay at Whitland, twelve archers (from the St Clear's garrison) who had committed a murder were signed with the Cross, as a punishment for their crime.[208] Other notable events of the period included: the burial of Owain Cyfeiliog at Strata Marcella (1197),[209] and the opening of the new church at Strata Florida (1201)[210] – the next year a delirious monk had a vision of three angels censing its altar during Lauds on Whit-Sunday.[211]

Notable abbots of the times included Gilbert, formerly a monk of Louth Park who founded an Irish house, and later became Abbot of Basingwerk – dying there in 1155. He related a vision of Owain, his Irish interpreter, to Henry of Saltrey, who included it in his 'Purgatory of Saint Patrick'.[212] As a young man, Abbot Henry of Tintern (1148–57) had been a brigand. Converted by the anchorite, Wulfric of Haselbury, he took the Cistercian habit and after his time at Tintern was translated to the abbacy of Waverley – where he died in 1182. Said to have met both the Pope and St Bernard, John of Ford told how Abbot Henry had the charism of the 'gift of tears', especially when celebrating the Eucharist.[213] Another worthy, long-serving superior was John of Goldcliff at Margam (1213–37), who soon made his mark, being named (1218) as one of five 'father-abbots' in England and Wales whose advice could be sought if problems arose which needed resolution before the next ensuing General Chapter.[214]

As for Cadwgan of Bangor – a brother of whom was a monk of Llantarnam[215] – Giraldus Cambrensis had little good to say about him,[216] accusing him – whilst a monk of Strata Florida – of forcing Gerald to sell his books to the monastery instead of accepting them on pledge (*c.* 1201), of engineering his own election to the abbacy of Whitland (1203), of disowning his father (a Welsh-speaking Irish priest), and of gaining the bishopric of Bangor (1215) through the influence of Prince Llywelyn.[217] (Gerald's evidence is suspect, not least because he himself had no good word to say about Peter, the deposed Abbot of Whitland).[218]

In 1236, Cadwgan retired to be 'honourably received' at the abbey of Dore; there he was professed as a monk of the house – seemingly with special privileges.[219] It may be the latter that led the General Chapter (1239) to observe that Cadwgan failed to observe the observances of the Order – by breaking silence, by his mode of living, and by fostering dissension and scandal. He died two years later, and was buried at Dore.[220] A very different picture of Cadwgan is portrayed in the *Cronica de Wallia*: 'An extraordinarily eloquent and wise man',[221] and from his noted religious writings which have been described as 'thoroughly Celtic in spirit and expression'.[222] Written perhaps during his time at Bangor, they included commentaries on the Creation, the Eucharist and St Bernard, as well as tracts concerning Our Lady.

Giraldus also painted a black picture of Abbot Gilbert of Margam (1203–13), portraying him as an abbot of acquisitive nature, hated by his subjects – the rebellion of its *conversi* took place during his rule (1206). He told, with some delight, of how the abbot became an epileptic and was eventually deposed (1213).[223] Gilbert was a north countryman and retired to Kirkstead Abbey, dying there the following year. Was this a false portrait, or did the chronicler of Margam have his tongue in his cheek when he wrote of Gilbert as being: 'Of honoured memory'?[224]

Giraldus Cambrensis and the Welsh Cistercians

Towards the close of the age of Cistercian settlement in Wales, the forceful ecclesiastic – Archdeacon of Brecon – and prolific writer, Giraldus Cambrensis ('Gerald of Wales'), had a love-hate relationship with the Order in Wales and beyond. His earlier writings often praise the Cistercians, but his later works frequently show an embittered criticism. His views on the Order were mixed and prejudiced because of the unfriendly way in which, he alleged, some White Monks had treated him.[224a] Some of his statements – as those concerning the Herefordshire abbey of Dore – were based on hearsay,[225] but he had a first-hand knowledge of several of the Welsh houses. He frequently visited Strata Florida and, perhaps, Cwmhir. Accompanying Archbishop Baldwin preaching the Crusade he stayed at several others. At the close of 1201 he preached at Aberconwy and Strata Marcella and, a little later, at Valle Crucis.[226] He certainly had a predilection for the Order; describing his relief and political map of Wales, he told how he plotted on it: 'Many monasteries, above all of the Cistercian Order'.[227] How one wishes that map had survived!

Gerald had some pleasant words for the Welsh Cistercians: he praised the charity Margam exercised towards the poor (1188),[228] he saw Abbot Cynan of Whitland (*d.* 1176) as a 'good and saintly' man,[229] and he lauded the stance taken towards Bishop Geoffrey of St David's by Abbot Ririd of Cwmhir (*c.* 1213).[230] More often than not, his comments were critical. In particular, he castigated the Cistercians for their alleged avarice, quoting an apparently contemporaneous proverb: 'They are bad neighbours, just like the white monks'.[231] He accused Strata Florida of robbing Llanllŷr nunnery of its Hafodwen Grange,[232] Whitland of wanting to absorb the Premonstratensian monastery at Talley,[233] and Aberconwy for oppressing: 'A community of Culdees at the foot of Snowdon' – probably the *clâs* of Beddgelert.[234] (The former accusation may have resulted from the inability of the nuns, strictly enclosed from 1213, to work their own lands;[235] the latter may have reflected – not to be borne out in these instances – the substantial movement of other religious houses into the Cistercian Order).[236]

Giraldus criticised both Black and White Monks in Wales for practising as physicians – sometimes with disastrous results.[237] He was upset when Abbot Canawg of Cwmhir, formerly a friend, neglected to visit him at his home at nearby Llanddew when staying at Trawscoed Abbey.[238] The archdeacon also told how, 'in the hour of violent persecution', he had often betaken himself to Strata Florida, but relations became soured when that abbey – on the instructions of its father-abbot of Whitland and the Earl of Essex – placed him 'in the public hall among the common guests and the noise of the people', and declined to give him a guide to conduct him over the mountains.[239]

Gerald's severest strictures were reserved for Abbot Peter of Whitland. He was disconcerted because Peter – who was, before he became a Cistercian, a clerk in his own household[240] – competed against him for the bishopric of St David's.[241] He accused Peter of bastardy, incontinence and ambition,[242] claiming that almost all the canons of St David's (responsible for the election) were of the abbot's kith and kin – a surprising assertion given the fact that Gerald had been the chapter's first preference in 1198 and that Peter was also unsuccessful.[243] He had no good word to say about Peter, relating instead a story of a boy in a dream seeing Giraldus attacked by three wolves – of which the Abbot of Whitland was one.[244]

Despite his personal and hurt feelings – and it has been suggested that 'Gerald was writing not for a public but for himself'[245] – it is his evidence, biased and exaggerated as it is, that has much to tell us of the Welsh Cistercians at the turn of the 12th century. (Two recent articles deal at length with his descriptions of the Order in southern Britain[246] and in Wales[247]). What he wrote about the Order in general can be taken, as little other corroboratory or contradictory evidence is available at this period, as reflecting the achievements of the White Monks in Wales. On an economic level Gerald knew the accomplishments of the early Cistercians: 'Give them a wilderness or a forest, and in a few years you will find a dignified abbey in the midst of smiling plenty'.[248] A decade after his unhappy experiences concerning the see of St David's and the loss of his books, he could still write of the Order as being: 'Such a favourite throughout the world, and such a strong pillar of the Church'.[249]

NOTES

1. This section is based upon the Introduction to the author's *Atlas of Cistercian Lands in Wales* (Cardiff, 1990).
2. *Walter Map* 53; *Opera G.C.* IV, 139, 219–220.
3. Lloyd, J.E. 1939, I, 598–600, 603–04.
4. *Cwmhir Charter* 70; Remfry P.M. 1995.
5. Beverley Smith J. 1999, 104; *Cf. Statuta* I, 230 (1198/41), 236 (1199/21); *Cf. Brut* (1952) 79.
6. Cowley F.G. 1977, 27, *Cf.* 53–54.
7. *Letters to Cîteaux* 262 (No. 134).
8. *Statuta* I, 294 (1203/48).
9. *Ibid.* I, 305 (1204/43).
10. Cowley F.G. 1977, 39.
11. Williams D.H. 1976, 35–36.
12. *Penrice* I, 10 (Charter 23).
13. *Cronica de Wallia* 34.
14. *Penrice* I, 19–20 (Charter 54).
15. *Cartae Glam.* I, 127 (CXXX); *Episc. Acts* II, 646; *Cf.* NLW, Penrice and Margam Ch. 10; BL, Harleian Ch. B.29 (Grant to: 'The Cistercian Order, Brother Meiler, and the brethren of Pendâr').
16. NGR: SO 049951.
17. *Episc. Acts* I, 276; *Mon. Angl.* V, 555b; *Cf.* PRO, E 315/50/74.
18. *Opera G.C.* I, 241.
19. *Ibid.* IV. 206.
20. *Statuta* I, 111 (1198/3), 295 (1204/2): If a monastery had less than twelve monks, apart from the abbot, it should be closed or reduced to grange status.
21. Salmon M. 1927, 137; *Cf.* Morris E.R. 1889, 353–55, 369; RCAHMW, 1 (*County of Montgomery*; 1911) 60 (No. 314).
22. *Mont. Collns.* VI (1873) 384–85.
23. *Arch. Camb.* 1856, 330.
24. *Ann. Camb.* 43.
25. Ludlow N. *et aliis*, MS Report 2000, 3 (Archaeoleg Cambria).
26. *Letters to Cîteaux* 245 (No. 126).
27. PRO, C 1/304/36.
28. Williams G. 1962, 19; Williams S.W. 1889, 100, Appx. i.
29. Radford C.A.R. 1974, 1.
30. Williams S.W. 1889, Appx. x.
31. Williams D.H. 1967, 1.
32. Hays R.W. 1963, 4, 6, 9.
33. Lloyd J.E. 1939, I. 600; Williams D.H. 1976a, 73–74.
34. Lloyd J.E. 1939, I. 594.
35. Price G.V. 1952, 3, 13, 15.
36. Beverley Smith J. 1999, 104–05; *Cf. Statuta* I, 237–38 (1199/22).
37. Knight J.K. 1972, 39.
38. Brakspear H. 1910, 51.
39. Williams D.H. 1976, 94–95.
40. *Itin. Wm. Worcestre* 61.
41. Williams D.H. 1976, 102.
42. *Ibid.* 103–04.
43. *Ibid.* 59.
44. Cowley F.G. 1977, 22–23.
45. *Ann. Mon.* I, 14.
46. Birch W. de Gray. 1902, 35, 37; *Cf. Cartae Glam.* V, 1679 (MCCXX); Guilloreau L. 1909, 321.
47. Auvry D.C. 1896. II, 190; Taylor A.J. 1971, 2.
48. Jones A.J. 1933, 171; *Cf. Arch. Camb.* 1921, 401; *Cal. Charter R.* II, 289–91.
49. Salmon M. 1972, 78.
50. *Statuta* I, 149 (1192/18), 192 (1195/70), *Cf.* II, 34 (1253/24); *Eccl. Charters* 51–54; *Thesaurus* I, 433–34; VCH. *County of Chester* III (1980) 151–52; *Gervase* I, 569 (for Basingwerk's English leanings).
51. Cartwright J. 1997, 21, 24, 37.
52. Jones M.C. 1869, 301–02; Williams D.H. 1975, 157, 163.
53. Morgan R. 1985, 116–19.
54. Thomas D.R. 1913. I, 484.
55. *Opera G.C.* IV, 152.
56. *Ibid.* IV, 152–53.
57. *Arch. Camb.* 1859, 338; Rhys J. 1896, 119–25; Westwood J.O. 1863, 258–59.
58. Parry T. 1952, 298.
59. Harris L. 1953, 70; Williams G. 1962, 190.

60. Williams D.H. 1975, 159; *Cf.* PRO, E 315/104, f. 177d (2nd nos).
61. Williams D.H. 1975, 164; *Cf.* Itin. J. Leland III, 51.
62. *Opera G.C.* IV, 152–53.
63. *Ibid.* II, 248; IV, 168; Cartwright J. 1997, 21–23.
64. *Orig. Cist.* passim; Williams D.H. 1984. I, 11.
65. Hays R.W. 1963, 178.
66. Cowley F.G. 1977, 197.
67. Hays R.W. 1963, 20.
68. Cal. Close R. 1333, 93–94; PRO, SC 8/239/11937; *Anc. Pet.* 400–01; Williams D.H. 1976b, 168.
69. Williams D.H. 1998, 31–33.
70. *Reg. J. Trillek* 632.
71. *Orig. Cist.* 74–75; *Cf. Gervase* II, 443
72. Bond J. (at Cardiff Cistercian Conference, 1999).
73. NLW, Badminton Manorial 1663, m. 2d.
74. Butler L.A.S. 1963, 28; 1980, 1.
75. *Cal. Patent R.* 1442, 95.
76. *Cal. Papal Reg. (Letters)* I, 131.
77. *Augm. Rec.* 122–23, 443; PRO, LR 1/212, f. 214.
78. *Llywelyn's Charter* 49.
79. Birch W. de Gray. 1897, 321; *Cf.* Williams D.H. 1969, 28.
80. Williams D.H. 1984. I, 14.
81. Price G.V. 1952, 260; Ellis T.P. (?) 1924, 109.
82. Butler L.A.S. 1982, 36.
83. *Itin. J. Leland* III, 70.
84. Williams D. H. 1976, 59–60.
85. Harrison J. 1998, 25–29.
86. PRO, E 40/A.14,282.
87. *Pers. comm.*: the late Mr Leslie Evans.
88. *Anc. Corr.* 185.
89. *Cartae Glam.* V, 1685 (MCCCXLIV).
90. *Statuta* I, 521 (1220/22); Cowley F.G. 1977, 205.
91. Birch W. de Gray. 1897, 100 (but date is not 1326, as Dr Cowley has kindly pointed out).
92. Cowley F.G. 1977, 71; *Cf.* Birch W. de Gray. 1897, 27.
93. Butler L.A.S. 1982, 35; Birch W.
94. de Gray. 1902, 32.
Butler L.A.S. 1982, 35; Price G.V. 1952, 118.
95. *Arch. Camb.* 1889, 7*n*; Jones M.C. 1871, 8–9.
96. Donkin R.A. 1963, 182.
97. *Statuta* I, 48 (1217/67).
98. Williams D.H. 1964, 85–86.
99. Williams D.H. 1998, 181–84.
100. Hays R.W. 1963, 4–6.
101. *Ibid.* 61–62 (pp. 61–77, for a detailed account of the transfer); *Cf. Lanercost Chr.* 33.
102. Hays R.W. 1963, 57–58; Taylor A.J. 1974, 338; Bryan A. 1999, 125–49.
103. Hays R.W. 1963, 70; Butler L.A.S. 1981, 28.
104. Fig. 10; *Cf.* Butler L.A.S. 1981, 32–33 (inset map).
105. Taylor A.J. 1974, 339–40.
106. *Anc. Pet.* 112 (76); Hays R.W. 1963, 70–71.
107. *Anc. Corr.* 225; Taylor A.J. 1974, 339*n*.
108. Fenton R. 1917, 163.
109. *Ann. Camb.* 79; *Ann. Mon.* II, 312.
110. *Ann. Mon.* II, 312.
111. *Statuta* II, 137 (1234/49), 147 (1235/36).
112. *Ibid.* II, 155 (1236/13).
113. *Cal. Close R.* 1235, 44; 1240, 185; 1253, 11.
114. *Statuta* III, 161 (1276/62), 200 (1280/29); Williams D.H. 1976, 60–61.
115. *Cf.* PRO, E 318/569.
116. Williams D.H. 1976, 67–68.
117. Williams D.H. 1970, 55–58.
118. Phillips N. and Hamilton M. 2000, 51–54.
119. *Cf.* PRO, C 1/596/42.
120. *Grace Dieu Docs.* 196.
121. Taylor A.J. 1971, 2; Williams C.R. 1961, 70, 76*n*.
122. *Arch. Camb.* 1846, 103; *Cal. Charter* R. 1328, 225.
123. Leach G.B. 1960, 36–60; *Cal. Patent R.* 1391, 510; *Cf. Cal. Inq. Misc.* I, 43 No. 123).
124. Williams D.H. 1984. I, 20.
125. NGR: SN 717645.

126. Jones Pierce T. 1950, 25; Williams S.W. 1889, Appx. x.
127. Williams S.W. 1889, 22, 88–89.
128. *Ibid*. 19–20.
129. NGR: SN 719644.
130. Taylor A.J. 1947, 146; [Not to be confused with *Vallis florida =* Cleeve Abbey].
131. *Taxatio Eccl*. 281b.
132. Pugh T.B. 1953, 28.
133. NGR: ST 285921; Coxe W. 1801, 118; Evans C.J.O. 1953, 301.
134. Williams D.H. 1976, 77.
135. Williams D.H. 1976a, 74.
136. Donkin R.A. 1957, 257; *Mon. Angl*. V, 636n.
137. Williams J. 1905, 306–08.
138. *Llywelyn's Charter* 62. Nearby was 'Dol*vaner*' : *Augm. Rec*. 443.
139. Fontana 1961, 197–200.
140. NGR: SJ 147070.
141. BL, Cotton MS Cleopatra A. XII, f. 58; *Gervase* I, xxix; II, 443; Jones M. C. 1869, 302.
142. Williams D.H. 1998, 14.
143. As in the *Brut* (1952) 81; PRO, C 1/356, m. 84 (where: 'Fflanegwest otherwys called Valle Crucis'; *Cf*. Williams D.H. 1984. I, 21 and *n*.
144. *Taxatio Eccl*. 203, 276b–277.
145. *Itin. J. Leland* III, 58.
146. *Orig. Cist*. 159.
147. *Strata Marcella Ch*. 210–11 (No. 69).
148. *Cf*. Williams D.H. 1984. I, 21–22; 1997, 129.
149. *Tax Book* 74 (where: *'Stramagir sive Pola'*, *c*. 1354); *Letters to Citeaux* 191 (No. 94: 'Strata Marcella *alias* Pola').
150. Williams D.H. 1984. I, 22.
151. NLW, MS 7006; BL, Cleopatra B. v. 152. Prof. Ceri Lewis of U.C. Cardiff, kindly advised me regarding Dewma, some years ago.
153. Sometimes mis-transcribed: e.g. 'Parlion' (1223), 'Querelon' (1257), 'Tallion' (1291): Alphonse T. 1979, 77.
154. *Cal. Papal Reg. (Letters)* V,
507–08; *Reg. R. Mayew* 263; *Arch. Camb*. 1852, 70.
155. *Brut* (1941) 129, (1952) 72, (1955) 168.
156. Harries L. 1953, 112.
157. *Reg. R. Beauchamp* 13.
158. *Statuta* II, 287 (1244/61); III, 111 (1272/34).
159. *Ibid*. III, 115 (1273/3).
160. Cowley F.G. 1977, 197.
161. *Ibid*. 10.
162. *Cartae Glam*. VI, 2271 (MDL); VCH, *Glamorgan* III (1971) 34.
163. *Cartae Glam*. VI, 2277–78 (MDLVI); *Cf*. Birch W. de Gray. 1893. I, 118.
164. *Cartae Glam*. II, 278–79, 292–93, 455, 507.
165. *Ibid*. II, 301–02 (CCXCVII).
166. *Ann. Mon*. I, 34–36, 116.
167. *Llywelyn's Charter* 59.
168. Lekai L.J. 1977, 215.
169. Hays R.W. 1963, 43–44.
170. Cowley F.G. 1977, 119–20.
171. *Statuta* I, 123 (1190/21).
172. *Ibid*. 138 (1191/23).
173. *Ibid*. I, 193 (1195/76).
174. *Ibid*. I, 191 (1195/66).
175. *Ibid*. I, 199 (1196/8).
176. *Ibid*. I, 324 (1206/23).
177. Sayers J. 1964, *passim*.
178. Cowley F.G. 1977, 124, 125n.
179. Williams D.H. 1976, 82.
180. *Statuta* I, 268 (1201/26).
181. *Catal. Ancient Deeds* I, 282 (B. 727).
182. *Statuta* II, 10 (1221/47).
183. *Ibid*. II, 209 (1239/34).
184. *Ibid*. II, 382 (1252/31).
185. Sayers J. 1964, *passim*.
186. Birch W. de Gray. 1902, 62.
187. *Strata Marcella Ch*. 24, 173–75 (No. 34).
188. *Statuta* II, 41 (1225/31).
189. *Strata Marcella Ch*. 23, 213; Banks R.W. 1888, 206–12.
190. *Strata Marcella Ch*. 211–14 (No. 70); Jones M.C. 1871, 318–22.
191. *Spec. Duorum* 264–65.
192. *Opera* G.C. II, 248; IV, 168–69; VI, 59; Golding B. 1995, 12; *Hist. Works* 375–76; *Journey through Wales* 118–19.

193. Golding B. 1996, 12.
194. *Ibid.* 112; Williams D.H. 1984. II, 232.
195. *Ann. Mon.* II, 242, 245.
196. *Statuta* I, 281 (1202/35).
197. *Ibid.* I, 472 (1217/30–31).
198. Hays R.W. 1963, 25–29; *De Invect.* 94–96, 116, 118–20, 153–54, 217.
199. *Opera G.C.* III, 240.
200. *Cal. Papal Reg.* I, 14; *Letters Inn.* III. *79 (No. 481); Cf. 55–56 (Nos. 336, 338).*
201. *Statuta* I, 281 (1202/34).
202. *Ibid.* I, 262–63 (1200/70); Hays R.W. 1963, 31.
203. Williams D.H. 1976, 10.
204. Hays R.W. 1963, 37–38.
205. *Ibid.* 26–27, 37–38.
206. *Journey through Wales* 178, 186, 196; *Hist Works* 433.
207. Cowley F.G. 1977, 190.
208. Salmon M. 1927, 103–04.
209. *Reg. Aberconway* 7.
210. *Ann. Mon.* IV, 100.
211. Cowley F.G. 1977, 97–98 (quoting Ralph of Coggeshall).
212. *D.N.B.* XXI, 314.
213. Bell M. 1933, xxxiv *et seq.*, *John of Salisbury I, 263.*
214. Cowley F.G. 1977, 115, 123–35.
215. Alphonse T. 1979, 187.
216. Harrison J. 1994, 253–54.
217. Cowley F.G. 1977, 122–23.
218. Williams D.H. 1984. I, 28.
219. PRO, E 135/24/3; *Cf.* BL, Add. MS 1823/5845, 11b; *Cal. Papal Reg.* I, 151.
220. *Statuta* II, 206 (1239/20).
221. *Cronica de Wallia* 35.
222. Talbot C.H. 1959, 19; *Cf.* Williams D.H. 1976, 10.
223. Cowley F.G. 1977, 115, 123–25.
224. *Ann. Mon.* I, 32; Birch W. de Gray. 1897, 197.
224a. As an abbot of Biddlesden, whose deposition he helped to procure: *Gir. Camb.*I, 203-04, 216–18.
225. Williams D.H. 1976, 8–9.
226. *Opera G.C.* I, 10; *Hist. Works* 457; Conway Davies J. 1947, 265.
227. *Opera G.C.* I, 44–45; the map perished in a fire at Westminster Abbey in 1694 [Conway Davies J. 1949, 50].
228. Cowley F.G. 1977, 207-08; Golding B.J. 1996, 11.
229. Golding B.J. 1996, 9; Williams D.H. 1984. I, 29 (*n.* 223).
230. *Journey through Wales* 119; *Spec. Duorum* 279–80.
231. Owen H. 1904, 183.
232. *Opera G.C.* IV, 152–53.
233. Cowley F.G. 1977, 73–74.
234. Owen H. 1904, 181–82.
235. Williams D.H. 1998, 404-05.
236. *Ibid.* 21.
237. Owen H. 1904, 184.
238. *Opera G.C.* I, 241.
239. *Autobiog. G.C.* 266; *Episc. Acts* II, 318.
240. Golding B.J. 1996, 20.
241. Williams D.H. 1984. I, 30.
242. Cowley F.G. 1977, 122.
243. *Autobiog. G.C.* 197, 223.
244. *De Invect.* 220; Owen H. 1904, 110, 181.
245. Golding B.J. 1996, 22.
246. Castora J.C. 1997, 73–97.
247. Golding B.J. 1996, 1–26.
248. King A.A. 1954, 3.
249. *Spec. Duorum* 279.

CHAPTER 2

INVOLVEMENT IN WALES
(1200–1277)

The 13th century in Wales has been called: 'The age of the two Llywelyns',[1] for its political history was dominated by Llywelyn ab Iorwerth ('the Great'; Prince of Gwynedd, 1194–1240) and his grandson, Prince Llywelyn ap Gruffydd ('the Last'; 1246–82). The latter took advantage of the troubled times to extend his authority far beyond the confines of Gwynedd. The first Llywelyn, despite having married Joan, the daughter of King John (1205), spent much of his time fighting her father's army, and later (1231) invading south Wales. Conflict was continued through the reign of Henry III by Princes David (1240–46) and Llywelyn the Last, save for interludes of peace (as in 1234–40 and 1267–72). It was a century of difficulty from which the Cistercians could not escape uninvolved or unscathed.[2]

By and large, the eight abbeys of the family of Whitland served the Welsh princes well, but also looked to them for support – as in the confirmatory charters which Llywelyn the Great accorded Aberconwy and Cymer. In their loyalty to the native princes the white monks had little option; had they sided with the English Crown local retribution might have been speedy and disastrous. Not for nothing did English royal officers note of the abbot of Strata Florida (1220) that he was: 'In the power of Llywelyn'.[3]

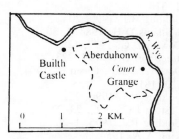

Fig. 15: Aberduhonw Grange.

The Welsh monasteries indeed irked the Crown. Whilst (in 1207) Strata Florida had no option but to give lodging at its Aberduhonw Grange (Fig. 15) to an earl of Gloucester – unsuccessfully attempting to storm Builth Castle,[4] more usually the monasteries afforded a measure of protection for those fleeing from the English army. King John (1212) noted that Strata Florida: 'harbours our enemies' – and ordered its destruction, amplifying his command to his officers with the realistic words: 'so far as you are able'.[5] In the impost he placed on all Cistercian abbeys (1209–10) Strata Florida was fined £800 (compared with £100 expected of Basingwerk).[6] It was a debt with which the monastery was saddled beyond 1248,[7] when Abbot Gruffydd 'made peace with the king with respect to the debt for a long time owed'.[8] Under the terms of the agreement, instalments were still being repaid as late as 1253.[9]

No sooner was King John dead than an earlier Abbot of Strata Florida – in the name of several Welsh superiors – protested at the interdict laid on Wales (November 1216) because of the support given by the nation to a projected invasion by Louis VIII of France.[10] The abbot went unchecked by his father-abbot of

Whitland, and the upshot was that both abbots (and five priors) were removed from office by the General Chapter (1217).[11] Strata Florida remained in the forefront of Welsh affairs, and was chosen by Llywelyn ab Iorwerth to be the venue (1238) where 'all the princes of Wales swore fidelity to the lord David', his son – thus securing the succession to, and the stability of, the principality after Llywelyn's demise (1240).[12]

The Troubled Background

Abbey Cwmhir suffered during the uprisings led (in 1228 and 1231) by Prince Llywelyn against the king's forces, and with the new Lord of Montgomery (Hubert de Burgh) as a particular adversary.[13] Matthew Paris describes how (in 1228) Cridia: 'An abbey of white monks, five miles from Montgomery', was burnt by the royal troops because 'it was a refuge for Welshmen to fly unto'.[14] In fact, this may have been Cwmhir's Gwern-y-go Grange. Another grange (of a mid-Wales monastery) was burnt (in 1231) because a Cistercian monk, allegedly at the behest of Llywelyn, had directed English troops into an ambush near Hay or Montgomery.[15] That year Llywelyn swept into south Wales and exacted a tribute of sixty marks from Margam.[16]

Grace Dieu (1233) was razed to the ground in the joint rebellion of Llywelyn and Earl Richard Marshal, and the next year local men of Gwent stole its corn.[17] It may have been at this time that its abbot was abducted by 'the descendants of Arthen', and led across mountains and valleys to Faenor *(Fig. 16)*.[18] As for Earl Richard, in December 1233 he received at Margam Henry III's negotiator, Bl. Agnellus of

Fig. 16: The location of Grace Dieu Abbey, in relation to Faenor *(Monm. Antiq. XIV: 1998)*.

Pisa, first provincial of the Franciscans in England.[19] In times such as these, royal grants to Welsh Cistercian houses were conditional upon them 'not assisting the king's enemies'. In particular, they were not to trade with them, nor supply them with food.[20]

Llywelyn the Great died in 1240 and was buried at Aberconwy. Already (in 1230) its monks had set up in his honour the Levelinus Stone on their lands in Hiraethog.[21] Renewed warfare during the short reign of his son, David, brought difficulties for Cymer. In 1241, Henry III reached the Mawddach valley, tried to extract information from one of its monks, and caused part of the abbey buildings to be burnt.[22] Its current difficulties led to the dispersal of its monks (an official safety-valve used by the Order to help troubled communities)[23] being enjoined, but – the General Chapter noted – not executed because of the abbot's non-compliance.[24]

The significant role which Welsh Cistercian abbots continued to play in national politics was highlighted by Prince David's action (in 1244) in persuading Innocent IV to order King Henry III to appear before the Abbots of Aberconwy and Cymer, acting as the pope's delegates.[25] Shortly thereafter (8 April 1245) a papal bull invalidated whatever 'may have been done by the abbots in pursuance of papal letters commanding them to absolve prince David from an oath which he took to obey the king of England'.[26]

Aberconwy, clearly not in the King's good books, suffered that August, The royal forces looted the monastery and damaged the church.[27] Henry III may have suffered qualms of conscience – granting damages of seventy marks to the abbey,[28] and taking it under his protection.[29] Prince David (who restored Holywell church to Basingwerk)[30] died in February 1246, and was also laid to rest at Aberconwy.[31] In the first campaigns of Llywelyn ap Gruffydd (the 'great war' in Wales) forces loyal to the Crown attacked Whitland by night (4 February 1258), plundering the abbey, assaulting the community and killing servants.[32] The troubled conditions of that year meant the dispersal of the monks of Strata Florida was mooted.[33] Then, in 1263, when English troops, sheltering by the Severn in the barn of the abbey's Abermîwl Grange, were slain by Welsh forces, the bailiff of Montgomery burnt the barn in revenge.[34]

In the spill-over from the principal conflicts during the reign of Henry III, and undoubtedly encouraged by the patriotic fervour aroused by Llywelyn ap Gruffydd, were the troubles endured by Anglo-Norman abbeys. The Abbot of Neath (1247) referred to the 'profusion of wars', and to 'his persecutors'.[35]

The neighbouring house of Margam suffered from the Welshry for years – damage to its stock and crops to the tune of £477 in 1246[36] and, the next year, losses to the value of £60 at one grange (Eglwys-geinor) alone.[37] The principal offender in 1246 (Morgan ab Owain) compensated the monks by reducing (to one-tenth) the rent they paid for Hafod-heulog Grange.[38] The settlement with Cnaytho ab Iago (leader of the band of thirty-seven vandals in 1247) saw an armed guard of twenty-four Welshmen formed to protect the abbey's properties.[39] It was not the end of monastery's problems;[40] as late as 1268 the community was excused (for five years) from receiving guests[41] – another device adopted by the Order for houses in grave difficulty.[42]

The Border monasteries walked a tightrope – favour to one side meant offence to the other. The Herefordshire abbey of Dore experienced constant interference on its lands in Cantref-selyf in Brecknock.[43] Its adversaries included Walter Clifford III, Lord of Bronllys, and his bailiff (1240–41)[44] – Prince David[45] and the Bishop of St David's[46] taking the Dore's lands under their protection. The Abbot of Cwmhir arbitrated in another dispute with Clifford (1252),[47] whilst the Prior of Chepstow, as 'keeper' of Dore's privileges (1263), admonished the Archdeacon and Rural Dean of Brecon on its behalf.[48] By 1264, the monks of Dore felt more secure: 'having established their rights in the cantref'.[49]

Cwmhir (1252) saw 'men of Montgomery' damage its woods in Ceri,[50] but enjoyed a fruitful relationship with the Mortimer dynasty – whose members it allowed to hunt on its lands.[51] Strata Marcella profited from the patronage of

Gruffydd ap Gwenwynwyn, Lord of Powys, (1241–86/7).[52] He had a Cistercian monk as chaplain (1277),[53] and when seriously ill was a patient in a Cistercian abbey (*c.* 1257)[54] – probably Strata Marcella. When Gruffydd allied himself with Edward I (1274), Prince Llywelyn confiscated far-flung lands of the abbey at Pennant-tigi and in Penllyn.[55]

Further Diplomatic Activity

Throughout the difficult century prior to the Edwardian Conquest both English monarch and Welsh prince made much use of the White Monks as emissaries and mediators. In 1198, 'monks and *conversi*' (very probably of Strata Florida) kept the peace between the sons of the lately deceased Rhys ap Gruffydd,[56] whilst in 1202 'learned men' (perhaps monks of Strata Marcella) intervened to prevent warfare between Llywelyn ab Iorwerth and Prince Gwenwynwyn of Powys.[57] In 1203, the Abbot of Aberconwy was the leading recipient of the papal missive allowing Llywelyn to marry the daughter of King Reginald of Man – though he wed Joan, a daughter of King John.[58] This identification of the Cistercians with the nation was emphasised when Welshmen of princely stock were buried in a Cistercian house, and when their abbeys set down a permanent record of Welsh affairs in their annals and chronicles.

The ecclesiastical status of the Cistercians and their membership of an international Order helped them to enter 'no-go' areas safely, even to penetrate behind enemy lines.[59] Henry III in this way sent a letter to Llywelyn ab Iorwerth (then at Denbigh) by the hands of the Cistercian abbot of Vaudey (Lincolnshire; 1230),[60] and he

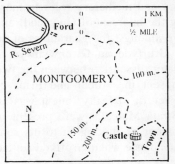

Fig. 17: The Ford of Montgomery.

appointed the Abbot of Grace Dieu as one of the go-betweens to meet at Montgomery to receive compensation from Llywelyn for his incursions (1236).[61] Other Cistercian abbots to attend on the king's behalf at the Ford of Montgomery *(Fig. 17)* were the superiors of Tintern (1268)[62] and of Dore (1273).[63] The Abbots of Tintern (very much of the Englishry) had frequent duties outside Wales,[64] amongst them acting as assessor of tallage in the port of Bristol (1271),[65] and as auditor of the collectors and receivers of a fine levied on the burgesses of that city (1277).[66]

The dominant note of Cistercian political life in Wales lay more generally in monastic activity for the native princes. It would be a mistake to over-estimate their contribution – superiors of other religious houses also played a part and, sometimes, Welsh Cistercian abbots had only a supporting role in missions led by members of the episcopate – but equally the Cistercian involvement should not be undervalued. Llywelyn ab Iorwerth had indicated how such ecclesiastics ranked in his mind when, early in 1216, he sent to Prince Gwenwynwyn of Powys: 'bishops and abbots, and other *men of great authority*'.[67]

Successive Abbots of Aberconwy were to the fore in diplomatic missions: pleading with Henry III for, and escorting – with the Abbot of Strata Florida –

the body of Prince Gruffydd ap Llywelyn from the Tower of London to Aberconwy for burial (1248);[68] as one of a pair attending the Mad Parliament at Oxford to arrange a truce as representatives of Llywelyn (1258);[69] in the company of the Bishop of Bangor, negotiating at the Ford of Montgomery a prolongation of the truce (1260);[70] travelling – for the same purpose – to Westminster as Llywelyn's sole representative (1262);[71] and, again with the Abbot of Strata Florida, bearing a letter from Llywelyn – to the convocation of bishops assembled in London – falsely promising to do homage to Edward I (1275).[72]

The close relationship between the Welsh Cistercians and Llywelyn ap Gruffydd was exemplified in the wake of severe criticisms of the prince voiced by Bishop Anian II of St Asaph, when he had censured Llywelyn and his followers for continually demanding hospitality from the monasteries, and making unjust exactions and extortions from them. The seven Cistercian abbots of Welsh Wales (Whitland, Aberconwy, Cwmhir, Cymer, Strata Florida, Strata Marcella and Valle Crucis) jointly defended the prince in a letter written at Strata Florida (7 March 1275) to Pope Gregory X. In it they suggested that the bishop had 'spoken falsely', and that: 'the Prince has shown himself protector, not only of our Order but of each and every Order in Wales'.[73]

The evidence is that the abbots may have been under some duress, because there was perhaps more than a grain of truth in the bishop's assertions. (The affair is another pointer to Whitland – though the senior house – being off the beaten track, and yielding to Strata Florida in practical importance, it being more central in Wales and nearer to the stirring events of those days).

The Welsh abbots also had significant conciliatory and mediatory roles in more local affairs.[74] The Abbot of Aberconwy (reflecting the interests of Gwynedd) and the Abbot of Strata Marcella (those of Powys) were amongst the guarantors of an agreement reached between Prince Llywelyn and Gruffydd ap Gwenwynwyn at Ystumanner (1263),[75] and were also involved in a later dissension between the two magnates (1274).[76] In December 1274, Llywelyn sent the Abbot and Prior of Cymer to Welshpool to try to induce Gruffydd to return to fealty, but it was an unsuccessful mission.[77] The Abbot and Prior of Strata Marcella were present in Welshpool Castle when Gruffydd made over the manor of Buttington to his son, Llywelyn (1271),[78] whilst its abbot James was in attendance when Gruffydd settled his estates on his eldest son, Owain (c. 1277).[79]

Cistercian ecclesiastics often witnessed deeds executed by Welsh princes and nobility, and – as when the Abbots of Aberconwy and Basingwerk were witnesses (at Caernarfon in 1272) to a territorial settlement between Llywelyn and his brother, Rhodri – their seals and those of other onlookers might be appended to the relevant deeds 'for greater security'.[80] Part, at least, of the monies due to Rhodri were paid out at Aberconwy.[81]

The involvement of the Abbot of the anglicised house of Basingwerk is a reminder that it, a Border house, was useful to political adversaries.[82] Henry III (1246) chose its abbot to 'escort personally' Isabella, the widow of Prince David, from Dyserth Castle to 'live honourably' at Godstow nunnery close to Oxford.[83] Llywelyn ap Gruffydd, for his part, used an Abbot of Basingwerk (1256) to convey a letter to Henry III.[84]

Princely Usage of the Granges

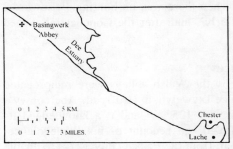

Fig. 18: Basingwerk's Lache Grange.

Basingwerk's grange of 'La Lith' (probably Lache, near Chester; *Fig. 18*) was used by Henry III (1241) for a conference between his council and the Bishop of Bangor and Prince David's clerk.[85] The grange was a suitable point – as war was imminent in Perfeddwlad; and a fitting choice – the monks were English, yet recently favoured by David. It was an appropriate neutral meeting ground.

The Welsh princes found the monasteries, and their granges more particularly, suitable halting-points or places of refuge.[86] The isolated instances on record of such usage of monastic lands suggest many more visits of which we are unaware. Llywelyn ap Gruffydd stayed 'with a large army' – one night early in Advent 1256 – at Strata Florida's Morfa Mawr Grange, and there Maredudd ab Owain came to swear fealty to the prince.[87] He is also known to have made use of remote mountain properties of Aberconwy (Llanfair Rhyd Castell in 1273, 1274 and 1276; Hafod-y-llan in 1281),[88] and of

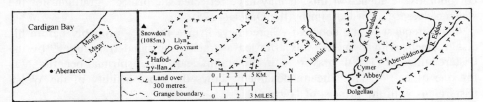

Fig. 19: left: Strata Florida's Morfa Mawr Grange; *centre:* Aberconwy's properties in and near Snowdonia; *right:* Cymer Abbey and its Abereiddon grange.

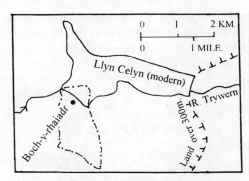

Fig. 20: Boch-y-rhaiadr Grange.

Cymer (notably Abereiddon, his headquarters at least twice – in 1275 and 1279).[89] After Llywelyn's death (1282) some of his belongings found at Abereiddon and at Cymer itself were removed by Roger Le Strange, the royal commander.[90]

Such hospitality was seen by the English monks of Basingwerk as a heavy imposition. Llywelyn ab Iorwerth and his son, Prince David, had expected its Boch-y-rhaiadr Grange *(Fig. 20)* to provide bread, butter, fish and cheese, for a hunting party of three hundred of their men once a year; Llywelyn ab Gruffydd increased this requirement to food for five hundred persons, with money *in lieu* when there was no hunting.[91] Edward I (1278) told Llywelyn 'to treat the abbey fairly', and after the Conquest abolished these demands.[92]

Other Relations with the Welsh Princes

The hospitality and good offices afforded by the Welsh abbeys were reciprocated in favours – particularly financial – by Prince Llywelyn ab Gruffydd. Aberconwy's allegiance gained it the tithes of Llanbadrig (*c.* 1255),[93] and it acknowledged its indebtedness to the prince in the sum of £40, on account of his 'benevolence' (1281).[94] An Abbot of Cymer received a loan from the Prince (July 1274) to enable him to travel to the General Chapter at Cîteaux,[95] and in return for a further loan (£12 in 1281) the abbey pledged its 'grange of Cyfeiliog' to Llywelyn.[96] (His brother, David (1282) exacted a rental (39/-) from Cymer for its Neigwl Grange in Llŷn).[97]

To expedite and sustain Abbot Madog of Valle Crucis on business of his abbey at the Roman curia (1275–76), Prince Llywelyn loaned the house a total of £40.[98] In 1280 he had only been repaid £6. It has been suggested that these loans may have compensated for heavy taxation of the monasteries by Llywelyn,[99] but there is little corroborative evidence of this. It may have reflected the prince's gratitude for the staunch defence afforded him by the Order (1275).

At the request of the abbot of Aberconwy, Prince David – probably before his disagreement with Cymer – was afforded a grant of spiritual fraternity[100] by the Cistercian Order (1280): prayers – 'in life and in death', and spiritual benefits – 'as for one of us'.[101] The Cîteaux document shows the close affinity of the Welsh Cistercians with the princes of Gwynedd.

As for David's brother and Wales' born leader, Llywelyn ap Gruffydd, he met his death on 11 December 1282. It has been suggested that he spent his last days hiding at a monastic grange called 'Thaulweyr'.[102] What is certain is that he was killed (without being immediately recognised) whilst reconnoitring English positions near Builth. His head was sent to King Edward I, the rest of his body: 'headless and mutilated',[103] found burial at the nearest Cistercian house, Cwmhir abbey[104] – the size of whose church may have owed much to his largesse. Their prince was indeed with the White Monks: 'in life and in death'.

NOTES

1. Jones Pierce T. 1959, 113.
2. Williams D.H. (Lecture given at the Machynlleth Tabernacle Festival, 1995).
3. PRO, LTR III, m. 11d.
4. *Cronica de Wallia* 33.
5. *Rot. Litt. Claus.* I, 122.
6. Hays R.W. 1963, 43–44.
7. *Cal. Close R.* 1227, 1; 1248, 8.
8. Williams S.W. 1889, Appx. ii.
9. PRO, LTR III/1(2), 11d; V (*Memo. R.* 7 Hen. III) mm. 8, 13 (2nd); XIV, m. 8; XX, mm. 2d, 4d, 8, 10; XXI, 21/1; KR 19d; *Cf. Cal. Close R.* 1248, 8; 1250, 338–39; 1253, 398; *Brut (1955)* 235.
10. Cowley F.G. 1977, 211–12.

11. *Statuta* I, 484 (1217/83).
12. *Cronica de Wallia* 38; *Ann. Camb.* 82; *Cal. Papal Letters* I, 87 – for Llywelyn's concern for this succession much earlier.
13. Lloyd J.E. 1939. II, 667–69.
14. Williams R. 1882, 88; *Cf.* Morris E.R. 1889, 354–56, 361–64, 369; Williams D.H. 1976a, 77.
15. Dunn E. 1967, 31; Stedman Davies D. 1934; Williams S.W. 1890, 405–07; Williams D.H. 1976a, 80.
16. *Ann. Mon.* I, 39.
17. *Cal. Close R.* 1234, 445.
18. Harrison J. 1998, 25–29.
19. Gillespie K. 1964, 28–29.
20. *Cf. Cal. Close R.* 1231, 547; 1232, 53; 1246, 430; *Cal. Charter R.* 1232, 155.
21. Hays R.W. 1963, 15.
22. Ellis T.P. 1928, 62–63.
23. Williams D.H. 1998, 152–53.
24. *Statuta* II, 238 (1241/45).
25. Hays R.W. 1963, 46–47.
26. PRO, SC 7/20/19.
27. Hays R.W. 1963, 47.
28. *Cal. Liberate R.* II, 66, 352.
29. *Cal. Patent R.* 1247, 504.
30. Jones A. 1933, 171–72; Jones H.L. 1846, 107.
31. Lloyd J.E. 1939, II. 705–06.
32. *Ann. Camb.* 92; *Cf. Cronica de Wallia* 40.
33. *Statuta* II, 444 (1258/27).
34. Williams S.W. 1889, 143.
35. Cowley F.G. 1977, 246; *Statuta* II, 318 (1247/17).
36. Cowley F.G. 1977, 213.
37. Birch W. de Gray. 1897, 263.
38. *Cartae Glam.* II, 532 (DXXVI).
39. *Ibid.* II, 544–45 (DXXXIV).
40. Williams D.H. 1984. I, 37.
41. Cowley F.G. 1977, 205.
42. Williams D.H. 1998, 152.
43. Williams D.H. 1976, 38–39.
44. PRO, E 326/11586; *Episc. Acts* I, 369–70 (D. 520); *MSS in BM* III, 538–42 (No. 803); IV, 904–05 (Nos. 1775, 1778).
45. *MSS in BM* IV, 909 (No. 1792a).
46. PRO, E 326/9817; *MSS in BM* IV, 904 (No. 1776b).
47. PRO, E 326/8398; *Cf. MSS in BM* III, 625 (No. 1085).
48. *Episc. Acts* I, 404 (D. 659).
49. *MSS in BM* IV, 902 (No. 1766).
50. *Cal. Close R.* 1252, 143; 1254, 20.
51. Williams D.H. 1976a, 94–95.
52. Williams D.H. 1976b, 182; *Cf.* 163.
53. *Cal. Chancery R. var.* 174.
54. *Anc. Corr.* 19–20.
55. Williams D.H. 1976b, 163; Jones M.C. 1872, 127–38.
56. *Cronica de Wallia* 32.
57. O'Sullivan J.F. 1947, 15.
58. *Letters Inn. III* 77 (No. 469); Hays R.W. 1963, 27.
59. Williams D.H. 1984. I, 32, 38–39, 40–41.
60. *Anc. Corr.* 37 (No. VI, 155).
61. *Cal. Close R.* 1236, 343.
62. *Cal. Patent R.* 1268, 254.
63. *Ibid.* 1272, 1; *Cal. Close R.* 1272, 2.
64. Williams D.H. 1976, 105–06.
65. *Cal. Patent R.* 1271, 592.
66. *Cal. Close R.* 1277, 392.
67. *Brut* (1955) 295; Hays R.W. 1963, 44.
68. *Brut* (1955) 241; they used: 'pressing solicitation' [Williams S.W. 1889. Appx. lii.]
69. *Litt. Wallie* 13–14, 27–29; Hays R.W. 1963, 50.
70. Hays R.W. 1963, 50.
71. *Litt. Wallie* 17–18.
72. Hays R.W. 1963, 53–54.
73. *Councils* I, 498–99; O'Sullivan J.F. 1947, 67–68.
74. Williams D.H. 1984. I, 40–42.
75. *Litt. Wallie* 77–79, 111–13; Bridgeman G.T.O. 1868, 117–19.
76. *Litt. Wallie* 108–10.
77. *Ibid.* lv.
78. *Ibid.* 132.
79. *Welsh Assize R.* 40n.
80. *Ibid.* 49; *Cal. Close R.* 1278, 506.
81. *Litt. Wallie* 42; *Cf.* 85.
82. Williams D.H. 1984. I, 41.
83. *Cal. Close R.* 1246, 415.
84. *Ibid.* 1257, 115.
85. *Cal. Patent R.* 1241, 257; [NGR: SJ 399649].

86. Williams D.H. 1984. I, 39.
87. *Ann. Camb.* 91 [NGR: SN
     504656].
88. *Anc. Corr.* 127, 162; *Litt. Wallie*
     175; Hays R.W. 1963, 53 [NGR:
     SH 827528, 629513].
89. *Anc. Corr.* 27, 75, 85, 87; *Litt.
     Wallie* 32; *Llywelyn's Ch.* 63
     [NGR: SH 800219; Hen-gwrt-
     uchaf, today].
90. *Cal. Inq. Misc.* I, 392 (No.
     1357); Jones A. 1933, 173.
91. *Ibid.* [NGR: SH 847397].
92. *Cal. Chancery R. var.* 174–75,
     301, 304; *Welsh Assize R.* 48.
93. Hays R.W. 1963, 116–17.
94. *Litt. Wallie* 25 (No. 30).

95. *Ibid.* 33 (No. 45).
96. *Ibid.* 45–46; PRO, E 36/274.
97. *Cal. Patent R.* 1316, 394.
98. *Litt. Wallie* 33 (No. 46), 36 (No.
     53), 40 (No. 58).
99. Hays R.W. 1963, 56; Waters
     W.H. 1935, 26–29.
100. Williams D.H. 1998, 65–66.
101. *Litt. Wallie* 153 (No. 270); it is
     not recorded in *Statuta*.
102. Morris R.H. 1911, 28.
103. *Chr. Bury St Edmunds* 75; *Bart.
     Cott.* 163; *Reg. J. Peckham* III,
     1073.
104. Salmon M. 1927, 179; Willis-
     Bund J. 1900, 74; Williams D.H.
     1976a, 80–81.

CHAPTER 3

THE ENGLISH YOKE (1277–1348)

The refusal (in 1277) of Prince Llywelyn to do homage to Edward I, and the Passion Week (1282) attack by his brother, David, on Hawarden Castle, led to the Edwardian Conquest of Wales: a war in each of those years being separated by an interlude of comparative peace, but accompanied by military activity in west and central Wales organised by royal officials and Marcher barons. Even after Edward's triumph there were further revolts, albeit on a more limited scale: that of Rhys ap Maredudd (1287) during the King's absence abroad, and a series of risings (1294–95) led by Madog ap Llywelyn in north Wales, Maelgwyn Fychan in west Wales, and Morgan ap Maredudd in south Wales. Yet another rebellion occurred in Glamorgan (1314–16), inspired by Llywelyn Bren.

In all these encounters the property of the Cistercians suffered, sometimes severely. More than that, the Conquest accomplished, there followed for the White Monks in Wales a time of readjustment to the new political order; a period which ended roughly in 1348 – not so much because of the Black Death, but from the establishment of their privileges in the *Quo Warranto* proceedings of that year.

As Edward I progressed into north Wales in the summer of 1277, the monks of Basingwerk found the sovereign encamped on their doorstep for several days (21–25 August) and sold him a property[1] (perhaps its 'Sovereign Grange' which came back into its hands)[2] for the not insubstantial sum of 55 marks. The war ended on 9 November with the Treaty of Conwy; on that occasion the Abbot of Aberconwy seems likely to have been present. A few days later (15 November) an Italian merchant carrying Aberconwy's wool to Chester did so with royal safe conduct; a probable sign of favour.[3] In west Wales, Whitland – quite possibly against its inclination – was the projected scene of a meeting (Easter Monday, 29 March 1277) held by Payn de Chaworth (Lord of Cedweli and royal Keeper of Armaments in the south-west) with 'the more discreet men of the district', to plan their campaign against local rebels – notably Rhys ap Maredudd, ensconced in his new castle in Emlyn.[4]

Strata Florida was also affected in these years: the construction of a royal castle at Llanbadarn Fawr (1277) saw the abbey compensated for the loss of some land involved.[5] Towards the close of 1278, one of its monks, Clement, was deputed to negotiate with the King regarding what they considered unjustified exactions.[6] On the construction of Flint Castle (1280) a monk of Basingwerk was engaged as chaplain to the royal garrison.[7] The troubled conditions saw letters of protection afforded to the abbots (and communities) of Basingwerk (1276, 1278), Aberconwy (1277) and Neath (1280).[8] Safe conduct was also granted to a monk of Strata Marcella, John of Cydewain, travelling to his abbey (1277),[9] and to the Abbot of Cistercian Hailes (Gloucs.) *en route* to visit the Premonstratensian canons at Talley (1278).[10]

Edward I's experiences in the campaign of 1277 led him to order three abbeys to clear woodland, lying near frequented route-ways and strategic points, so as to lessen the chances of ambush and surprise attack.[11] Basingwerk was required (in 1278) to clear Gelli Wood, but, despite a reminder (1280), it was seven years (1285) before this was fully accomplished.[12] The monks of Strata Florida were also tardy to obey a command (1278) to enlarge the passes in their woods.[13] They, the monks of Whitland, and other Welsh notables (1280) were urged to proceed with the task; it was 'expedient for the keeping of the peace, and for the security of those passing through'.[14]

Similar injunctions were issued (in 1284) to Madog, a *conversus* of Strata Florida and Geoffrey, Lord of Pennardd.[15] Restoration of Strata Florida abbey after the troubles of 1294 was subject to the condition that 'the woods and ways around it, which may become a source of danger in the future, be cut down *(i.e: the woods)* and repaired *(i.e: the roads)*.'[16] To stop secondary vegetation springing up, all three abbeys were ordered to bring the cleared land into cultivation.

During the second campaign of Edward I (1282–83) all the Cistercian houses of north, central and west Wales suffered war damages for which they were later partially compensated. At the height of the trouble (October 1282) Basingwerk was granted royal letters of protection, but this safeguard was conditional upon the monks not giving any aid or comfort to the Welsh rebels.[17] (Other abbeys received letters of protection[18] – perhaps to avoid military reprisals – in the aftermath of the war [April–August 1283], as Cymer[19] and Valle Crucis).[20]

The King ineffectually forbade his troops to take Basingwerk's corn, for the monastery suffered from his motley army. Basque soldiers rustled stock and stole corn from its granges on Deeside, Gascon sailors plundered its lands in Englefield, whilst houses and corn were burnt on its more distant Gwernhefin Grange in Penllyn *(Fig. 21)*.[21] Holywell, too, was burnt and the abbey's villeins abducted – perhaps for forced labour with the King's pioneers in the forests.[22] Some of the Welshry took advantage of the difficult times, and stole lead and cash from the monastery[23] which, all in all, suffered damages to the extent of over £200 during the reign of Edward I.[24]

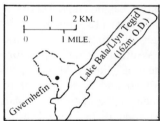

Fig. 21: Gwernhefin Grange.

The subsequent war damage compensation awarded to Basingwerk was £100; this was second only to the £160 accorded to Valle Crucis. The properties of both abbeys had been in the thick of the fighting, as had those of Aberconwy – which also received £100. Other abbeys – somewhat removed from the main battle-front – received less, ranging from £80 in the case of Cymer to £26 13s 4d for Llanllŷr nunnery.[25] A few houses also received very small sums in respect of damage to impropriated churches: Basingwerk (13s 4d) for Holywell, and Valle Crucis (£4) for Bryneglwys and (30s) for Llangollen.[26] Much of the war damage was perhaps to stock and crops, both sides taking their pick in order to sustain their armies, or burning farms to spite their opponents. The Justice of Chester rode into Edeyrnion and found: 'Great abundance of corn in granges not burned in all this war, the enemy has a great lair there, and much assistance in supplies'.[27]

Following Edward I's decision (15 June 1284) to make restitution to those ecclesiastical bodies which had suffered, a small commission of three – led by the prior of Rhuddlan – enquired into the damages sustained in the dioceses of Bangor, St Asaph and St David's,[28] and later (2 to 6 November 1284) sat at Chester Abbey to disburse the agreed payments. Representatives of the Cistercian abbeys attended, armed with letters of authority from their communities.[29] As the prior of Cymer, and the monk of Strata Florida representing the abbess of Llanllŷr, did not have the seals of those houses with them, they appended to their receipts the seals of the Abbots of Strata Marcella and Valle Crucis.[30] The restitution made to the White Monks was only fair, as the Order in England and Wales had contributed £661 to Edward's campaign in Wales.[31]

Did the Conquest have any direct effect upon the personnel of the monastic communities? At Cymer, Abbot Llywelyn, who still ruled the house on 7 November 1281, had, by 1284, been succeeded by Cadwgan – probably previously master of the *conversi*.[32] At Aberconwy, Abbot Maredudd (1278–81) gave way to an Abbot David (1284).[33] Did they die naturally, or lose their life in the troubles, or – the Conquest over – were they forcibly removed from office? There is no sure evidence. At Strata Florida, Abbot Philip Goch appears to have died naturally (1281).[34] Growing tension in Wales may have accounted for the absence of four Abbots (Strata Florida, Strata Marcella, Llantarnam and Tintern) due at the General Chapter at Cîteaux in the autumn of 1281.[35] In the summers of 1283 and 1284 respectively, the Abbots of Cymer and Basingwerk did journey to France;[36] a welcome respite from the troubles back home!

In the uprisings of 1294–95 properties of Aberconwy were 'ruined and destroyed'[37] – including perhaps its mill at Cornwy Llys[38], described as 'broken and valueless' (1294).[39] Whitland's lands suffered damages ('in the last war in Wales') assessed at £260.[40] The failure of the Abbot of Strata Florida to fulfil his promise (May 1295) to bring the Welsh rebels of Ceredigion into submission, caused an irate Edward I to order the countryside to be burnt. The abbey buildings and its crops were badly affected – though the King later claimed the monastery had been burnt 'contrary to our wishes'.[41]

Llantarnam (although very much a Welsh house) was (in 1315) forced to cede lands to Llywelyn Bren during his revolt in Glamorgan. Its monks described him as being of 'great mastery in that country'. They 'dared not withstand him'.[42] After Llywelyn was executed (1316), Llantarnam petitioned Edward II for the return of their lost properties.[43] During the rebellion, Neath was 'plundered of its goods,[44] whilst to this period may also be ascribed the damage done to the stock and crops of Whitland by Scottish mercenaries.[45] The monks of Aberconwy spoke (also in 1315) of how 'lean years and debt' had caused them to mortgage many of their lands.[46]

In addition to the consequences of the Edwardian campaigns and the later Welsh uprisings, practically all the Cistercian abbeys experienced other and substantial thorns in the flesh during, and perhaps partly originating in, the disturbed condition of these times. Infringements of their lands and liberties were frequent, and led some houses into costly and time-consuming litigation. Powerful men, like the de Clares and the Mortimers[47] oppressed certain of the monasteries, but they were by no means the only offenders. Amongst the complaints that Cistercian houses made were those by Strata Florida (1291) that Edmund Mortimer, Lord of Cydewain with a base at

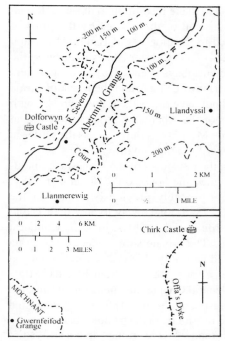

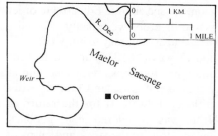

Fig. 22: top: Abermiwl Grange;
base: Gwernfeifod Grange.

Fig. 23: Overton Weir.

Dolforwyn, expected it (at Abermiwl Grange; *Fig. 22*)[48] to 'find for him and his household all necessary victuals every Friday of the year';[49] and by Valle Crucis (1305) that Roger Mortimer, Lord of Chirk, had deprived it of land in Mochnant (perhaps its Gwernfeifod Grange; *Fig. 22*)[50] and built houses upon it, and, further, had forced its men to make 'divers works at his castle'.[51] Its previous good relations passed, Cwmhir suffered at the hands of his nephew, Roger Mortimer III. After the latter's imprisonment, the abbey gained from Edward II (1322) the restoration of its rights.[52]

Lesser magnates of the March also found themselves in litigation with the White Monks, chiefly concerning land disputes and pleas of trespass.[53] Amongst them were: Peter Corbet (lord of Caus) with whom Cwmhir had differences regarding land in Hopton (1279–81),[54] and Robert le Crevecoeur (Lord of Maelor Saesneg, until 1283) who deprived Valle Crucis of fishing rights at Overton Weir.[55] Strata Marcella was involved in protracted litigation before several sessions of the Welsh Assize (1279–81) with Robert Pigot, a free tenant in Caus.[56]

The monks may have been in part to blame for such lengthy proceedings by their 'favourite device of non-appearance'.[57] It might be that 'changes to English law and court procedure that had no parallel under Welsh law had bewildered the monks'.[58] Not all the difficulties stemmed from the Marcher lords. Cynan ap Maredudd ab Owain disputed the boundaries of Strata Florida's Mefenydd Grange (1280). Agreement came after arbitration by the Abbots of Whitland (its mother-house) and Llantarnam (its daughter-house) protecting its interests, and Gruffydd ap Maredudd reflecting his brother's concerns.[59]

In south Wales, Earl Gilbert of Gloucester (and Lord of Glamorgan) took over (between 1289 and 1295) large tracts of monastic land at the Heads of the Valleys. Neath lost some of its mountain granges, and was forced into a one-sided deal.[60] Margam (two of whose granges had been seized by the sheriff of Glamorgan in 1285) and Llantarnam were still seeking redress long after the break-up of the de Clare estates in 1314.[61] Grace Dieu (perhaps from Border violence in 1276) lay (by 1280) in a state of ruin.[62] Margam suffered further – in the Despenser troubles of the 1320s.[63] Natural disasters also had to be faced – murrain killed off much of Aberconwy's stock (1315–16),[64] whilst a severe fire at Strata Florida – sparked off by lightning – devoured its belfry and roofs.[65] Only the presbytery was spared, and this mercy was attributed to the presence there of the Reserved Sacrament: 'The body of Our Lord on the great altar under lock'.[66] Excavation has revealed molten lead in the interstices of the walls.

The Cistercians in Wales had thus much else to contend with, apart from the Edwardian campaigns. By 1281, their monasteries were considered as being a depressed group: for that year the Herefordshire abbey of Dore successfully petitioned the General Chapter that for taxation purposes it might be (because of its poverty) grouped amongst the Welsh houses.[67] Depressing though these years were, there came occasions of joy. At Strata Florida, two happy events found worthy of note in its chronicles were the raising of 'the great bell' in 1254, and its consecration by the bishop of Bangor, and later (in 1282) the singing of his first Mass in his diocese by Thomas Bek, the new Bishop of St David's.[68] His episcopate was roughly co-terminus with the abbacy of Anian Sais – himself to be elevated (1294) to the see of Bangor.

After the Conquest

As the wars of Edward I drew to their close, the White Monks – reluctantly or otherwise – had to give the same facilities and render the same good offices to their new English masters which hitherto the native princes had enjoyed. For his part, the King 'relied on the Cistercians for help in the pacification of Wales and the introduction of English institutions';[69] the monks in their turn were 'realists and came to terms with the new political situation'.[70] In 1301, Abbot David of Aberconwy was amongst those swearing allegiance to the newly created Prince of Wales at Conwy.[71] In 1343, the Abbot of Cymer did fealty to the Black Prince's commissioners at Harlech, as did the Abbot of Strata Florida at Llanbadarn Fawr and, with the Abbot of Whitland, at Carmarthen. (At Harlech, the absence of the Abbots of Basingwerk and Strata Marcella was noted).[72] The Conquest brought the Cistercians certain privileges and favours, but it also entailed duties of one kind or another – sometimes burdensome.

In the last months of his final campaign, Edward I was resident for some weeks (13 March to 9 May 1283) at Aberconwy,[73] the abbey bringing corn from Ireland for the royal army,[74] and presenting the King with a relic of the True Cross (*Croes Naid:* 'the Cross Neith').[75] Appreciating the strategic nature of its site, Edward moved the monks eleven kilometres (7 miles) upstream to Maenan, building a notable castle at Conwy instead *(Chapter 1)*. Cymer, which too had given hospitality to Prince Llewelyn, saw the monarch and the royal treasury installed (by 14 to 20 May 1283).[76] From the Crown money now held in the abbey, two panniers – each containing £100 – were sent under guard to Harlech towards the expenses of building the king's new castle there.[77]

The Conquest over, King Edward made a royal progress through Wales, taking in a pilgrimage to St David's, visiting several Cistercian houses. Journeying from Shrewsbury to Corwen (18 December 1283) he undoubtedly saw the war-damaged buildings of Valle Crucis, and that Christmas-tide gave the abbey a present of £26 13s 4d.[78] In March 1284, the King gave Basingwerk no less than £42[79] for building its grange at Gelli[80] – the once wooded area he had caused its monks to cut down. In the autumn (30 October) he revisited Cymer, made an offering of 14d for Masses for the soul of Sir Payn de Gamach, and gave £5 towards building work in the monastery.[81] All this was additional to the war damages received a few days later at Chester. Then, on 12 December, he presented Neath with a fine baldachin.[82]

Revisiting Wales in connexion with the revolts of 1295, the monarch came again to Cymer (11 May), Valle Crucis (15–16 July) and Whitland (5 June).[83] His call at Valle Crucis resulted in 'oblations of the King at the great altar' of two 'cloths'.[84] Shortly before his capture and death, Edward II visited Tintern, Margam and Neath, but briefly and as a fugitive *(Chapter 9)*.

In the interlude of peace between the campaigns of 1277 and 1282, Edward I appointed a three-man commission of enquiry into Welsh law and custom (1280–81).[85] The Abbots of Strata Florida and Whitland gave evidence in this respect at Llanbadarn Fawr, and two monks of Basingwerk at Rhuddlan. One of the latter said he had no knowledge in the matter, and the other that he had no documents which would throw any light on the subject. They were uninterested English monks.[86] The Welsh superiors were far more knowledgeable and influential, and Edward I clearly felt their advice and presence invaluable and politic as Wales settled down to a new order.

The stature of Abbot David of Aberconwy was such that (together with the Abbot of Vale Royal and another monk) he was attached to the king's court for nearly four months in 1284.[87] In the troubled decade of the 1290s, the monarch requested the abbot's exemption from attendance at the General Chapter in France (1293), and likewise, in 1298, when (together with the Abbot of Valle Crucis) he was 'staying in Wales for the king's business and the quiet of the land'.[88] Abbot David was also one of four people (including the English sheriff of Anglesey) who visited the monarch at Waldingfield in Suffolk (1296), to gain his assurance that he regarded the people of north Wales as his 'faithful and devoted subjects'.[89]

Other abbots to be assigned significant duties on behalf of the Crown included: Cadwgan of Cwmhir (1287; to admit to the king's peace the followers in Ystrad Tywi of the rebel leader, Rhys ap Maredudd);[90] Llywelyn of Whitland (1290; member of a commission examining the costs and progress in rebuilding Llanbadarn Fawr [Aberystwyth] Castle);[91] the same with John of Strata Florida (1299; to enquire into complaints of financial exactions by royal officials in west Wales);[92] and the Abbot of Valle Crucis (1294; in whose fidelity the monarch mentioned his: 'especial confidence') was to care for the lands of Roger of Mold absent in Gascony on the king's service.[93]

Another, and honourable, duty incumbent upon certain abbots – in the wake of the Conquest – lay in attendance at Parliament during the latter part of the reign of Edward I (1295–1307). The basis upon which they were summoned may have lain in the potential expertise and individual stature they were known to possess. During this period, the Abbot of Strata Florida was summoned to attend Parliament on no less than seven occasions, the Abbot of Basingwerk six times, of Tintern five, and of Whitland twice.[94] The regard felt for Abbot Ralph of Tintern had also been demonstrated (1294) when he was summoned to a Council meeting called to consider retaking Gascony from the French.[95] The absence of extant writs summoning the Abbots of Margam and Neath suggests that the presence of abbots representing Welsh interests was not always paramount. The failure to summon the trusted Abbot of Aberconwy was perhaps a reflection of his age: in 1298, he was said not to be 'in a fit bodily state to travel'.[96] The Abbot of Basingwerk was the only Welsh Cistercian abbot summoned during the reign of Edward II, and none were so in the time of Edward III.

Taxation

As the English yoke settled upon the former principality of Llywelyn, various burdens, as well as privileges,[97] came to trouble the Welsh Cistercians. Not only were they increasingly expected to pay various tenths and subsidies, calculated basically upon the value of their spiritualities (ecclesiastical possessions), but also their abbots were frequently nominated as collectors, or deputed as sub-collectors, of the same. Margam, Strata Florida, Tintern and Whitland were amongst many houses excused payment of a tenth in 1297,[98] but, meanwhile, several abbeys had been taxed in the subsidy of 1292, as Cymer and Strata Marcella.[99] Care was taken by royal officials in recording payments made, but errors might occur, and so (in respect of this latter subsidy) the monks of Whitland claimed 'to have made fine for their fifteenth about which it is not written in the great roll'.[100]

Other occasional demands included royal requests for help towards the marriage costs of Edward III's sister (Basingwerk, £5 in 1333),[101] and loans on account of 'the great burdens of the realm and the dangers threatening the English Church' (1346/47). Basingwerk sought exemption from the £20 expected of it in this latter connexion, pointing out that it had just 'contributed towards the thousand marks granted to their lord, the Prince of Wales, in the county of Chester'.[102]

Monastic Privileges Challenged

In the aftermath of the Conquest, liberties which the White Monks had previously taken for granted were frequently challenged – especially by Crown officials. Many were the consequent petitions they submitted to the king, requesting redress and relief. Early on (*c.* 1284–95), the monks of Valle Crucis drew attention to 'the hardship in being obliged always to go to seek remedy where the king may be'.[103] Aberconwy's complaints (1313) centred on the sheriffs of Anglesey and Caernarfon and other royal officers who 'frequently harrass them against the tenor of their charters'.[104] The response to its petitions is unknown, but there is no further record of amercements imposed on the house.[105] The abbey's voice was perhaps justly heard.

Cymer (*c.* 1305) protested at being expected to pay suit at the county courts of Caernarfon and Meirionydd, at a levy imposed on its manor of Neigwl in Llŷn, at interference by the woodwards of the new (English) Prince of Wales in its forests, and at a summons to appear before the Justice of north Wales to answer for burying a monk, accidentally drowned, without the coroner's licence.[106] The monks were fairly, if tardily, dealt with. In 1310, the Prince – now King – sent a schedule of petitions from Cymer to his Chancellor (the Bishop of Worcester) requiring him to remedy matters 'according to the law and usage of those parts'.[107] An enquiry (delegated to the Justice himself, Roger Mortimer: 1308–15) revealed honestly how unjust situations had arisen in the adjustment to English rule,[108] and the Justice and the Chamberlain of Caernarfon were told to supersede their demands. Royal letters (1315/16) excused Cymer from the Neigwl rental[109] and from suit at the two county courts,[110] and it was also absolved from a demand (of the Justice's lieutenant) that it build a bridge over the Mawddach river.[111]

Few monasteries, if any, escaped the effects of the Conquest. Basingwerk (1317) found itself required to pay the Earl of Chester over £14 for his 'recognizance' of the abbey;[112] the same year, the monks of Llantarnam complained of the royal foresters of Machen 'selling by force' their Ebbw valley woodland.[113] There was a concerted effort by Whitland and Strata Florida to be exempt from paying suit of court at Cardigan, in respect of their properties in Ceredigion. The former monastery asserted that the lands concerned had been granted *in frankalmoign* ('pure and perpetual alms'), and that therefore no suit should be required;[114] the latter abbey alleged 'grievous distraint' by the constable of Cardigan, to force it to do suit of court.[115]

Their abbots were instructed to exhibit their charters in Chancery and gain the necessary writs (1336); Edward III took note, and Strata Florida was to be impleaded only at Llanbadarn Fawr.[116] But, in 1344, it was still said before the justices of the Black Prince that not only Whitland and Strata Florida, but also Cwmhir and the nunnery of Llanllŷr, had not paid their 'customary' suit at Cardigan for forty years.[117] Tintern (in 1330) gained discharge from rent it paid for lands in Hewelsfield (Gloucs.), it being shown that royal officials fifty years before (1280) had forged letters patent of the monastery committing it to this exaction.[118]

So far as Aberconwy and Cymer were concerned, a conclusive opportunity to assert their rights came (in 1348) when justices of the Black Prince held Proceedings *quo warranto* at Caernarfon.[119] Both abbots were amongst those summoned to prove their title, to show 'by what warrant' they held their respective liberties. This they successfully did by presenting the charters granted to their abbeys by Llywelyn ab Iorwerth, and by reference to inspections of their charters by Edward I and to confirmations of them by Edward III.[120] Their rights were upheld and sustained, though the question of whether Aberconwy had made improper use of its liberties was remitted for further consideration – of which there is no record.[121] The fascinating submission by the abbot of Cymer spelt out in some detail the usage by the house of the rights granted it, in respect of fishing, forestry, mining and metallurgy.[122]

Further Difficulties

Well before the Black Death wrought havoc in Wales, the tribulations of the White Monks formed a veritable catalogue of woes. A variety of factors, including 'sterility' of their lands (Basingwerk, 1346),[123] accounted for the straitened circumstances in which most Cistercian monasteries found themselves in the 1330s and 1340s. Some were heavily in debt, having borrowed from Italian merchants of Lucca (Tintern, £74 in 1340) and the Bardi (Cymer, £80 in 1343; Aberconwy, £200 in 1344).[124] These amounts may represent wool bought in advance, but Aberconwy also owed 'a great sum' to the Black Prince (1346).[125]

In difficult circumstances, too, were: Grace Dieu (1335)[126] and Strata Florida (1338)[127] – both unable to pay a tenth due to the Crown, and Margam (1337) – forfeiting Llangeinor manor on failure to pay the rent due to the lord of Ogmore.[128] Strata Florida (1339) was said to be 'manifestly oppressed with the burden of poverty'.[129] Those abbeys which could sought additional income and food in kind by appropriating parish churches and their tithes. Neath received three churches (Llandeilo Talybont, 1334; Aberafan and Castell Nedd, 1343–44) within a decade.[130] Whitland and Strata Florida came to a tithe composition with the bishop of St David's (1339–40; *Chapter 19*).

The Abbot of Margam (who in 1324 had claimed inability to pay his taxes because of the Despenser wars,[131] and in 1329 had blamed the long past de Clare depredations for having had to reduce the number of monks by ten)[132] gave a gloomy picture of his monastery's difficulties in a report (of 1336) to the General Chapter.[133] He asserted that flooding of coastal land frequently destroyed abbey crops; that a 'terrible mortality' had struck his stock – this was especially grievous as the monastic economy was primarily a pastoral one; that enemy attacks had caused immense losses; that 'being on the high road' there was a heavy burden of hospitality; and that the house had thus become unable to pay its pressing debts, let alone its contributions to the Order and taxes to king and pope.

Another source of difficulty lay when local lords sought to impress their will on a community. A classic example lay in the relations of Strata Marcella with John de Charlton , who acquired the barony of Powys in 1309 by marrying the grand-daughter of Prince Gwenwynwyn – with whom (and whose family) the abbey had enjoyed a long and close relationship.[134] Now matters changed, and for the worse.[135] About 1328, Charlton (terming himself 'patron of the monastery')[136] complained to Edward III that the community at Strata Marcella was depleted in numbers, did not properly maintain Cistercian life, and lacked visitation by the father-abbot of Whitland.[137] More damagingly, he asserted that at the abbey: 'Unlawful assemblies to excite contentions and hatred between the English and the Welsh have been entered into'[138] – it was very much a Border monastery. Edward III, at first, accepted his accusations and requested the Abbot of Cîteaux[139] and (repeatedly) the Abbot of Clairvaux that the Abbot of Buildwas (Savigniac, but of Clairvaux's family) should be appointed as Visitor, and that the Welsh monks of the abbey should be dispersed.[140]

What action was in fact taken is uncertain. Neither request seems to have been acted upon on a permanent basis.[141] Local antipathy to Buildwas was shown when (in 1350) 'evildoers in no small number' from Powys plundered Buildwas abbey.[142] A group of English monks at Strata Marcella were ordained by the Bishop of Hereford (in 1346)[143] – but this could simply have reflected a need to fill depleted ranks, and been unconnected with Charlton's petition some fifteen years before. Charlton (who sent his own monk-emissary to Cîteaux in 1328)[144] was by no means an innocent party.

A counter-petition tells how, after the death of Abbot Gruffydd (January 1333), the monks of Strata Marcella went to its daughter-house at Valle Crucis to elect a new abbot (Matthew) freely – away from Charlton's opposition. During their absence, Charlton – they alleged – took control of their property and refused them entry on their return; for a fortnight no services could be held.[145] Edward III ordered the re-admittance of the monks and instructed Charlton to appear in Chancery.[146] A supporting petition, on behalf of Strata Marcella, by the monk-commissary of the Abbot of Clairvaux, informed the king of Charlton's words: 'I am pope, I am king, I am bishop and abbot in my land'.[147]

External forces and pressure groups came increasingly to influence the affairs of the steadily declining communities. A typical example came at Strata Florida from 1344–47, with a dispute as to whom was the rightful abbot.[148] A monk of the house, Clement Richard, claimed that he had been canonically elected on a vacancy in the abbacy,[149] but that another monk, Llywelyn Fychan,[150] ('with no pretence of election') and his accomplices had violently ousted him. The General Chapter deputed the Abbots of Beaulieu and Thame to investigate alleged irregularity by the Abbot of Whitland in installing Llywelyn as abbot – but apparently found in his favour, and the Chapter (September 1344) confirmed him as superior.[151] Clement appealed to Rome, and Pope Clement III (March 1345) ordered an investigation by the Bishop of Hereford. The case dragged on (under different deputies acting for the Bishop) for two years before seemingly finding in Clement's favour.[152]

The Black Prince (to whom Llywelyn appealed) took the latter's side, ordering the Justice of south Wales (July 1346) not to allow Clement's party sustenance at the monastery until they had done obedience to Llywelyn as abbot and had returned goods (including chalices) they had allegedly removed from the abbey.[153] Llywelyn then (27 April 1347) appealed to the Court of Arches (where Clement was represented by counsel),[154] but (in October 1347) had to have further recourse to the Black Prince who again enjoined the Justice to maintain Llywelyn in the abbacy.[155] Indeed, he remained (a notable) abbot there for another thirty-three years. The Black Prince let slip that the whole matter arose 'because of some persons who are interfering to maintain the party in the wrong'.[156] This was the root of the matter; external – probably secular – forces, to whom the choice of abbot mattered, perhaps for family or economic reasons.

Laxity of discipline at Tintern during the abbacy of Roger de Camme (1330–31) may have accounted for the ease with which one of its monks, William Martel, assumed the office of prior at the Benedictine priory of Goldcliff (Monmouthshire) – whose monks as members of the Norman abbey of Bec wore white, not black, habits.[157] He forged a papal bull,[158] claiming to be the pope's nominee, and was admitted as prior by Edward III (Goldcliff being an alien priory) in February 1332. The monarch noted that: 'Although he has not brought the apostolic letters of presentation nor letters from the abbot of Bec nor the Pope, as is customary, yet the King at the request of certain magnates has taken his fealty'.[159] The gentleman of Somerset behind the affair was Sir John Inge, who stood surety for Martel's entry fine of forty marks, and was to do very well out of the deal.[160] Within a few months, Martel wasted the prior's possessions, but he was soon found out.[161] In April 1332 John XXIII ordered his seizure;[162] in June he was formally suspended from his ill-gained position at Goldcliff.[163]

Relatively small numbers, increasing economic problems and other external pressures thus combined to make the period of adjustment to English rule a trying one for the White Monks in Wales. They do not, however, appear to have lost their national consciousness: Strata Marcella (*c.* 1328) being allegedly, and quite probably, a base for Welsh political rallies; Whitland (*c.* 1330) being said to be 'ruled by the levity of the Welsh',[164] whilst Abbot Cynfrig of Aberconwy (1345) was one of several Welshmen attainted of conspiracy and held for a time in Denbigh Castle.[165] With a few exceptions, there was to be a growing lack of contact between the Order in Wales and the English Crown, and this may have assisted a further resurgence of Welsh national feeling in several abbeys which came to the surface in the earlier part of the fifteenth century *(Chapter 4)*.

The Abbots as Tax Gatherers

In 1267, the Abbot of Tintern was appointed to collect a tenth of church revenues in the diocese of Llandaff which had (as throughout the realm) been granted by the pope to the king.[166] In 1274, the Abbot of Margam was enjoined to collect a subsidy in aid of the Holy Land.[167] For the most part, however, the participation of Welsh abbots in such onerous tasks awaited, and was indeed a lasting consequence of, the Edwardian Conquest.[168] Thereon, such duties were imposed from time to time on the abbots of all the Cistercian houses, and included a moiety again in aid of the Holy Land (1294–95),[169] a tenth to provide revenue for the Scotch War (1309),[170] several 'crusading tenths' – as that demanded by Clement V (1318–20),[171] a triennial tenth on account of the war with France (1344–45),[172] a subsidy 'for the defence of the realm' (1487),[173] and a loan for a further war with France (1522).[174]

The imposition of a tenth was usually organised on a diocesan basis, whilst the bishop concerned (technically the collector) or the Crown directly, deputed major religious superiors in his diocese to do the work, and take the responsibility for any failure. There were many instances, as in 1360 – when the Abbot of Cymer was made collector for the whole diocese of Bangor, and the Abbot of Neath for Llandaff.[175] In large dioceses (like St David's) the load might be shared: like in 1401, when the Abbot of Vale Royal was collector for the archdeaconry of Cardigan, and the Abbot of Whitland in that of Carmarthen. In 1513 the Abbot of Strata Florida was responsible for the archdeaconry of Cardigan; in 1517 for that of Brecon.[176] It was a thankless task, and so Edward I (1294) had commanded the Abbots of Aberconwy and Margam to carry out their duty 'laying aside all delay and without tendering any excuse'.[177]

The 'qualification' for appointment as a collector lay in the possession of substantial spiritual income (chiefly the revenue of appropriated churches) in the diocese concerned. The Abbot of Vale Royal (Cheshire), who was the Rector of Llanbadarn Fawr, was, therefore, a collector for the archdeaconry of Cardigan (1401,[178] 1489[179]). If an abbot felt that the amount of his spiritualities did not justify his appointment, there could be contention: an Abbot of Aberconwy (1390) took his case (as did the Bishop of Bangor) to Richard II.[180] Henry IV took Bishop Mascall of Hereford (1406) to task for apppointing the Abbot of Tintern a collector in his diocese, when the bulk of the abbey's possessions lay in the see of Llandaff.[181] Undeterred, Bishop Spofford (1435) did the same.[182] An Abbot of Aberconwy successfully appealed against being made a collector in *both* the dioceses of Bangor and St Asaph.[183]

The episcopal brief appointing four North Walian abbots (Aberconwy, Basingwerk, Strata Marcella and Valle Crucis) as deputy collectors in the diocese of St Asaph (1479) survives, together with a note of their apportioned churches.[184] The value of each church was pretty well established by this time, but (in 1267, prior to the 1291 *Taxatio Ecclesiastica*) the abbot of Tintern (with the Archdeacon of Hereford) had not only to collect in the see of Llandaff a triennial tenth granted to Henry III, but also had to make the preliminary valuation.[185]

Those abbots appointed as collectors or (more often) sub-collectors, presumably delegated monastic or secular messengers to gather in the money. Certainly, some legal or representative assistance became necessary. In 1324, the Abbot of Tintern appointed a merchant of the Bardi as his 'attorney to account', and, in 1330, one of his monks. In 1337, the Abbot of Aberconwy likewise put a lay-man 'in his place, to render account'.[186] Doubtless he received a fee, for the sums raised were considerable. Margam (1318–20)[187] and Aberconwy (1339–41)[188] each levied £130 in one taxation alone. Such a sum represents thousands of pounds today. No wonder collectors were told to send their monies 'under safe and sure conduct', to the Exchequer.[189]

The task of collection had attendant and considerable difficulties, especially in times of Welsh unrest. In 1294, with the devastation resulting from Madog's uprising, the abbot of Aberconwy found the clergy of north Wales unable to pay their tenth, even if willing.[190] During the Glyn Dŵr Revolt (1401–02), Abbot John Wysebech of Tintern found 'great rebelliousness' and 'violent refusal'. He 'did not dare deliver for fear of death', royal letters to the lords of Glamorgan concerning the current tenth.[191]

Abbot Henry Wirral of Basingwerk (1441) could only partly gather in a tenth because of 'insurrections and riots'.[192] Some religious houses might refuse to pay, by virtue of being exempt from the jurisdiction of the local bishop, as (in 1380) the Abbots of Llantarnam, Margam and Neath, even though a fellow abbot (Tintern) was collector.[193] The Bishop of Bangor and Abbot Geoffrey of Aberconwy (*c.* 1533) were 'indited for extortion' by the suspended vicar of Llanfair, who claimed he had been over-taxed.[194]

The burden of this unpopular role as a tax-collector led abbots to seek to be excused it. Abbot Cynfrig of Aberconwy (1347) failed in this, despite having been a collector for a long time to the detriment of his house.[195] Abbot Wysebech of Tintern (1391), granted a seven year respite, did not enjoy the break for the full term.[196] More often, an abbot received a royal missive (or a visit from a Crown official) urging him on in his task and requiring speedy production of the cash levied.

This was especially true where the Black Prince was concerned, as Aberconwy (1347: 'to deliver quickly' £93)[197] and Cymer (1360: 'to apply all possible diligence')[198] found. Payment in instalments might be permitted, either because this was the best way for the Crown to make use of the money and to ensure its safe-keeping until needed (Tintern, 1320),[199] or else because the abbey concerned was in arrears, and this was the most likely way to ensure that the cash eventually reached the royal coffers (Aberconwy, 1337).[200]

Failure to produce a tenth or subsidy could mean both spiritual and temporal sanctions (excommunication and distraint). Collectors were frequently in arrears, like the Abbot of Basingwerk (1346) 'bound in a great sum to the Black Prince'.[201]

Significations of excommunication – perhaps stemming from non-production of a tax, included those directed to Abbots of Tintern (*c.* 1250, 1390). Five writs of distraint against Valle Crucis were issued between 1316 and 1334. The last (and perhaps the others) referred to a collection ordered in the time of the abbot's predecessor.[203]

Inability to collect was the downfall of Abbot Rhys of Strata Florida (*c.* 1440) who, committed to Carmarthen Prison, died there. Distraint meant that his abbey had 'no cloth remaining on any table or bed'.[204] Tintern (*c.* 1402) was 'distrained from day to day ... whereby it is greatly impoverished'.[205] Another means of recovering a debt was for the Crown to assign it to money-lenders, as in the case of Tintern (1337) and the Society of Peruzzi.[206] The 'manifest burden' and 'great damage' to a monastery of tax-collection (Aberconwy; 1347, 1390)[207] was both a serious financial liability and a spiritual hazard.

NOTES

For this period, see especially: Rhŷs W. Hays (1971).

1. *Cal. Close R.* 1277, 401–02; *Cal. Patent R.* 1277, 242.
2. *Cal. Inq. Misc.* I, 379 (No. 1302).
3. Hays R.W. 1963, 55.
4. *Anc. Corr.* 71.
5. Taylor A.J. 1974, 301.
6. PRO, SC 1/120/189.
7. *Welsh Memo R.* 5 (No. 40); Jones A. 1933, 2.
8. *Cal. Patent R.* 1276, 129; 1277, 234; 1280, 405; *Cal. Chancery R. var.* 166.
9. *Cal. Patent R.* 1277, 211.
10. *Ibid.* 1278, 275.
11. Williams D.H. 1984. I, 44.
12. *Cal. Patent R.* 1278, 256; *Cal. Chancery R. var.* 186–87, 301–02.
13. *Cal. Chancery R. var.* 171.
14. *Ibid.* 184–87; Williams S.W. 1889, Appx. xlviii.
15. *Cal. Chancery R. var.* 293.
16. *Cal. Patent R.* 1300, 499.
17. *Cal. Chancery R. var.* 244.
18. *E.g. Ibid.* 269; *Cal. Patent R.* 1283, 73.
19. *Cal. Patent R.* 1283, 68.
20. *Ibid.* 1283, 73.
21. *Cal. Inq. Misc.* I, 379 (No. 1302).
22. Jones A. 1933, 174.
23. *Flint Pleas* 2.
24. Jones A. 1933, 174–75.
25. Hays R.W. 1963, 76.
26. *Litt. Wallie* 62 (No. 94), 64 (102), 73 (135), 81 (150), 88 (172).
27. *Anc. Corr.* 72.
28. *Litt. Wallie* 71 (No. 127), 107–08 (202), 123–26 (214), 162–63 (286), 170 (297).
29. *Ibid.* 80–81 (No. 149), 95–97 (187–90).
30. *Ibid.* 96–97 (No. 190), 132–33 (234).
31. *Ibid.* 147–49 (260, 263), 202 (353).
32. *Ibid.* 45–46 (No. 69), 96 (No. 189).
33. *Fasti Cist. (1)* 1971, 188.
34. Williams S.W. 1889, Appx. ii.
35. *Statuta* III, 214 (1281/49).
36. *Cal. Patent R.* 1283, 68; 1284, 124.
37. *Anc. Pet.* 311 (No. 9298).
38. NGR: SH 316926.
39. Hays R.W. 1963, 109.
40. *Anc. Pet.* 42 (No. 1681); Cowley F.G. 1977, 214–15; *Ann. Mon.* IV, 520.
41. Williams S.W. 1889, 154–55; *Cal. Patent R.* 1300, 499 (licence to rebuild).
42. *Anc. Pet.* 200–01 (No. 5948).
43. Bradney J.A. III: Pt. 2, 225.
44. *Cal. Patent R.* 1315, 263.
45. *Anc. Pet.* 42 (No. 1682); *Cf. Cal. Patent R.* 1315, 388.
46. Hays R.W. 1963, 91.
47. Williams D.H. 1984. I, 48–49.
48. NGR: SO 158944.
49. *Cal. Patent R.* 1291, 459; *Cf.* Williams S.W. 1889, Appx.

xxxiii–xxxv.
50. NGR: SJ 094290.
51. *Rec. Caern.* 219.
52. *Anc. Pet.* 54–55 (No. 1972); Williams D.H. 1976a, 94–95.
53. Williams D.H. 1984. I, 48–49.
54. *Welsh Assize R.* 183, 281, 288, 292, 302, 304, 306; Williams D.H. 1976a, 93–94.
55. *Anc. Pet.* 455 (No. 13385); Cf. *Welsh* Assize R. 284–85. [NGR: SJ 355522].
56. *Welsh Assize R.* 296–97, 323, 326, 330–31, 334, 336; Williams D.H. 1976b, 164–65.
57. *Welsh Assize R.* 183.
58. Hays R.W. 1971, 128.
59. *Welsh Assize R.* 197–98, 300-01.
60. Birch W. de Gray. 1902, 80–81.
61. Cowley F.G. 1977, 216, 224–25.
62. *Statuta* III, 161 (1276/62); 200–01 (1280/29).
63. Cowley F.G. 1977, 213–14.
64. Hays R.W. 1963, 92.
65. Williams S.W. 1889, 153.
66. *Cf. Journey through Wales* 79.
67. *Statuta* III, 210 (1281/21).
68. Williams S.W. 1889, Appx. ii.
69. Hays R.W. 1963, 79.
70. Williams G. 1962, 40.
71. Hays R.W. 1963, 86.
72. Banks R.W. 1873, 164, 173, 175.
73. Hays R.W. 1963, 58.
74. *Anc. Corr.* 42 (IX, 62); *Cal. Chancery R. var.* 269.
75. *Rec. Ward.* xix, xxxv; Taylor A.J. 1976, 119.
76. Taylor A.J. 1977, 255; *Cf.* 256–57, 260; *Litt. Wallie* 180 (311), 192–93 (330).
77. Taylor A.J. 1974, 357.
78. Taylor A.J. 1976, 117.
79. *Ibid.* 117.
80. NGR: SJ 128782.
81. Taylor A.J. 1976, 116–17.
82. Birch W. de Gray. 1902, 79–80.
83. *Book of Prests* 13, 123, 172, 200, 224; Archbishop Peckham stayed at Margam in July 1284: *Reg. J. Peckham* I, 778.
84. *'panni'*.
85. Lloyd J.E. 1915, 1–20; Stephenson D. 1980, 4.
86. *Cal. Chancery R. var.* 198, 207.
87. Taylor A.J. 1976, 121 (he was allowed a total of £7 7s. 6d. for 118 days).
88. Hays R.W. 1963, 81–82.
89. *Ibid.* 83–84.
90. *Cal. Chancery R. var.* 307.
91. *Ibid.* 324; Taylor A.J. 1974, 306.
92. *Anc. Pet.* 367–68 (No. 10959).
93. Taylor A.J. 1974a, 79.
94. Cowley F.G. 1977, 223; *MSS in BM* II, 210 (No. 386).
95. Williams D.H. 1976, 106.
96. Hays R.W. 1963, 82.
97. Williams D.H. 1984. I, 51–55.
98. *Cal. Chancery R. var.* 26, 29, 33–35.
99. *Merioneth Sub.* Passim.
100. Jones F. 1950, 230.
101. *Cal. Patent R.* 1333, 422.
102. *Anc. Corr.* 185 (XXXVII, 183).
103. *Anc. Pet.* 455 (No. 13385).
104. *Ibid.* 40 (No. 1464).
105. Hays R.W. 1963, 87–91.
106. *Rec. Caern.* 217–18; *Llywelyn's* Charter 49.
107. *Cal. Chancery Warrants* 322.
108. Williams D.H. 1984. I, 54.
109. *Cal. Close R.* 1315, 179, 256.
110. *Cal. Patent R.* 1316, 394; *Cf.* 1347, 359; *Welsh Memo R.* 67 (564, of 1325).
111. *Anc. Pet.* 76 (No. 2698).
112. *Chester Recog. R.* (36) 24.
113. *Anc. Pet.* 286 (No. 8368).
114. *Ibid.* 117–18 (4057).
115. *Ibid.* 129 (4335).
116. Williams S.W. 1889, Appx. lxvii–viii.
117. Griffiths R.A. 1972, 14.
118. *Tintern MSS* 2426–2432.
119. Usher G.A. 1974, 1–12.
120. Hays R.W. 1963, 95–97.
121. *Rec. Caern.* 144–50.
122. Banks R.W. 1873, 170; *Rec. Caern.* 199–200.
123. *Anc. Corr.* 185 (XXXVII, 183).
124. *Cal. Close R.* 1340, 492; 1343, 244; 1344, 338.
125. Hays R.W. 1963, 122.
126. Cowley F.G. 1977, 231.
127. *Reg. T. Charlton* 57.
128. Williams G. 1962, 141.

129. Cowley F.G. 1977, 231.
130. *Ibid*. 242–43; Birch W. de Gray. 1902, 128, 132–33.
131. *Welsh Memo. R*. 58 (No. 484).
132. NLW, Penrice and Margam Ch. 203.
133. Birch W. de Gray. 1897, 305 (where wrongly dated).
134. Jones M.C. 1872, 47.
135. O'Sullivan J.F. 1947, 89–91; Williams D.H. 1976b, 166–68.
136. Jones M.C. 1872, 140; Williams D.H. 1998, 11–12 (for 'patrons').
137. *Anc. Pet*. 489–90 (No. 15389); PRO, SC 8/308 (No. 15389); C 81/164 (No. 2804); Jones M.C. 1872, 138–41.
138. *Cal. Close R*. 1330, 150.
139. *Ibid*. 1328, 410.
140. *Ibid*. 1329, 566–67; 1330, 150; 1333, 130.
141. Williams D.H. 1976b, 167.
142. *Cal. Patent R*. 1350, 532.
143. *Reg. J. Trillek* 437, 440.
144. *Anc. Pet*. 490 (No. 15389).
145. *Ibid*. 400–01 (11937); PRO, SC 8/239/11937.
146. *Cal. Close R*. 1333, 93–94.
147. *Anc. Pet*. 411–12 (No. 12354).
148. Williams D.H. 1984, I. 58–59.
149. *Reg. J. Trillek* 52; *Cf*. 37, 62.
150. *Cf. Cal. Papal Reg. (Petitions)* I, 39; *(Letters)* III, 139.
151. *Statuta* III, 494 (1344/65).
152. *Reg. J. Trillek* 112.
153. *Black Prince's Reg*. I, 2.
154. *Reg. J. Trillek* 112–13.
155. *Black Prince's Reg*. I, 132.
156. *Ibid*. I, 44.
157. Williams D.H. 1970a, 45.
158. *Cal. Patent R*. 1332, 406.
159. *Ibid*. 1332, 244; *Cal. Close R*. 1332, 433.
160. *Cal. Close R*. 1337, 175; PRO, E 40/A.3215; 42/342.
161. *Cal. Fine R*. 1332, 316; 1337, 449.
162. *Cal. Papal Reg. (Letters)* II, *350*.
163. *Cal. Fine R*. 1332, 316.
164. *Cal. Close R*. 1330, 150.
165. *Anc. Corr*. 227 (LIV, 37); Hays R.W. 1963, 94–95.
166. Williams D.H. 1976, 97; *Episc. Acts*. II, 751–52 (No. 542).
167. *Cal. Fine R*. 1320, 45.
168. Williams D.H. 1984. I, 59–63.
169. *Cal. Patent R*. 1294, 89; 1295, 173.
170. *Cal. Close R*. 1309, 227.
171. *Cal. Patent R*. 1320, 502.
172. Hays R.W. 1963, 98.
173. *Hist. Hen. VII* II, 181.
174. *LP (Hen. VIII), Addenda* I: Pt. 1,111 (No. 358): the abbot of Neath netted £211 in the diocese of Llandaff (1522).
175. *Cal. Close R*. 1360, 40..
176. *Episc. Acts* I, 211; II, 791, 818.
177. *Cal. Close R*. 1294, 396–97.
178. *Episc. Acts* I, 211.
179. *Hist. Hen. VII* II, 428.
180. *Anc. Corr*. 254–56 (LVI, 111).
181. *Reg. R. Mascall* 588.
182. *Reg. Th. Spofford* 195.
183. Hays R.W. 1963, 98.
184. *Anc. Corr*. 188 (XXXVIII, 92); *Arch. Camb*. 1882, 156–59.
185. *Episc. Acts* II, 751–52 (L. 542).
186. *Welsh Memo. R*. 57 (No. 475), 77 (660; Gilbert of Stowe), 101 (893).
187. *Cal. Patent R*. 1318, 136; 1320, 502, 509–10.
188. Hays R.W. 1963, 93.
189. *Cal. Close R*. 1294, 396–97.
190. Hays R.W. 1963, 84.
191. *Anc. Pet*. 239–40 (No. 7126); 364–65 (10839); *Cf*. Jack R.I. 1972, 153–55.
192. *Cal. Patent R*. 1441, 2.
193. *Cal. Close R*. 1380, 297–98; *Cf*. 1386, 149–50.
194. PRO, STAC 2/2, ff. 76–78.
195. Williams G. 1962, 141.
196. Williams D.H. 1976, 98; Jack I. 1972, 154.
197. *Black Prince's Reg*. I, 121; Hays R.W. 1963, 97–98.
198. *Cal. Close R*. 1360, 40.
199. *Cal. Fine R*. 1329, 45.
200. *Welsh Memo. R*. 103 (No. 910).
201. *Black Prince's Reg*. I, 3.
202. PRO, C 85/159/33; 85/167/32.
203. *Welsh Memo. R*. 42 (345), 54 (449), 74 (635), 82 (702), 92 (799).
204. *Cal. Patent R*. 1442, 95.
205. *Anc. Pet*. 240–41 (No. 7136).
206. *Welsh Memo. R*. 101 (No. 896).
207. *Anc. Corr*. 237–38, 254–56.

CHAPTER 4

PAST THE BLACK DEATH
(1348–1485)

The great bubonic plague took a firm hold on Wales in the spring and summer of 1349, but its direct effects upon the personnel of the Cistercian communities are unknown. It may have contributed to the small numbers in some abbeys later in the 14th century, and it may have caused the deaths of the Abbots of Basingwerk,[1] Tintern[2] and Whitland,[3] but the Abbots of Aberconwy,[4] Margam[5] and Strata Florida[6] survived the pestilence. Tintern's court rolls suggest an unusually high number of deaths on its Porthcaseg manor in mid-summer 1349.[7] At its most valuable manor (Acle in Norfolk) contemporary record related how (at an unspecified date): 'The brute beast plague' raged 'hour by hour'.[8] At Woolaston, Tintern had to appoint a new vicar (3 April 1349) because the incumbent had died.[9]

The indirect effects of the Black Death upon the labour market, and the stimulus it gave to economic and social change, did not pass the White Monks by. Labour scarcity was perhaps reflected when Margam demised eight acres of land at Theodoric's Grange (1349),[10] Neath sought and obtained the greater tithes of Exford (1349),[11] and Dore (1351) formed a company in association with seculars to farm its granges in Cantref-selyf (Brecknock).[12] Grace Dieu's 'depressed state', in 1361, has been attributed to the recurrence of the plague that year.[13] Animal pestilence affected the flocks of Margam (1383),[14] whilst 'pestilences' helped the value of Aberconwy's spiritualities to decline between the survey for the *Taxatio Ecclesiastica* (1291) and that given in the abbey's *Register* (c. 1356).[15]

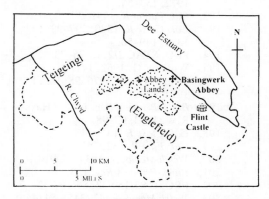

Fig. 24: Basingwerk Abbey's Political Location. *(After Melville Richards).*

The Black Death was not the only tribulation that some Cistercian houses suffered at this time: human agencies also played their part. Basingwerk had difficulties with officials of the Black Prince (1351–58) and the Welshry, so much so, its monks said, that it was 'ruined and destroyed for ever'.[16] The commonalty of Teigeingl tried to have the monastery pay part of a fine in return for privileges granted it by the Prince (1359).[17] The escheator of Flint (1362) allegedly seized 400 acres (160 ha.) of the monastery's land.[18] All in all, for Basingwerk, it was an unhappy period.

Aberconwy (1390) had difficulties at the hands of the Welshry, including two individuals who later were to support Owain Glyn Dŵr.[19] Margam (1394), where 'sons of iniquity' plundered the church and withheld rents,[20] was taken under protection by Thomas le Despenser, Lord of Morgannwg (1396).[21] Margam also had problems, yet again, from natural causes: flooding and encroachment by wind-blown sand on its coastal lands (1384);[22] old age and severe estuarine winds causing its buildings to be on the point of collapse (1385).[23]

Prior to 1398, Llantarnam suffered from a severe fire; its restoration was organised by Abbot John ap Gruffydd, whom Adam of Usk called: 'That man of grace'.[24] He sent two secular priests (the vicars of Basaleg and Woolaston) as emissaries to Rome,[25] where they obtained an indulgence for pilgrims to the monastery who gave alms for its restoration.[26] In 1399, Llantarnam may have obtained extra revenue when given the keeping (for one year) of the alien priory of St Clear's.[27] Additional income was also gained by Grace Dieu (a chantry chapel in Monmouth Castle, from 1357 to at least 1462),[28] and Dore (St Noye's Chapel (*al. Llan-noys*) at Blackbrook,[29] Gwent, for the period of 1360–69, if not longer).[30]

The Schism in the Papacy (1378–1417) was a time of disruption for the White Monks, some of whom (from faithful houses) were accorded the dignity of papal chaplain – including one monk apiece of Basingwerk, Cymer and Whitland, and three of Tintern.[31] The need to hold provincial abbatial councils in Britain led to serious disputes where appointments to vacant abbacies was concerned.[32] At Dore (1396–98) one of the parties backing a rival claimant stole charters, money and stock from the abbey and its daughter-house at Grace Dieu. During the dispute, a Welsh band carried two of Dore's monks to its Welsh Gwenddwr Grange and abused them, hanging them upside down. John Oldcastle, the Lollard, was associated with these brigands.[33]

There were lapses from established order. The Abbot of Strata Florida (1352) translated the Abbot of Cwmhir to the abbacy of Strata Marcella, without leave of the General Chapter. Both abbots were ordered to be deposed, but the sentence was ineffectual for Abbot Llywelyn continued to rule Strata Florida for many more years.[34] An apostate monk of his house was reconciled (1359) but made to live at Cwmhir.[35] The need for legal advice perhaps explains the grant of an annuity by Neath to Robert de Coventry D.C.L. (1349–69).[36] Twenty-one monks of Cwmhir (in the see of St David's) were ordained priest by the Bishop of Hereford (1349–93), geographical convenience in troubled times may have dictated this.[37]

Abbots given papal or royal tasks included: an abbot of Tintern (1355) dealing with the case of an apostate canon of St Kynemark's Priory, Chepstow;[38] the Abbots of Strata Marcella and Valle Crucis (1395) serving on a commission attending to the neglect into which the temporalities of the see of Llandaff had fallen;[39] and an Abbot of Margam (1398) testing the fitness of a priest for the office of notary.[40]

If this period was a troubled one for some abbeys, it was a happier time for two others. Strata Marcella found better relations with the Charlton family. The Abbot in 1361 was godfather to the infant John Charlton,[41] great-grandson of John Charlton who had plagued the monastery in the early 1330s.[42] The child's father, John Charlton III (1367), granted the abbey an important confirmatory charter,[43] whilst two years later Bishop Lewis Charlton of Hereford bequeathed twenty marks towards the fabric of its church.[44]

The long abbacy of Llywelyn Fychan at Strata Florida, despite its troubled start, gave that house a period of relative peace and prosperity. A poet sang Llywelyn's praises, and the English king commended him. Llywelyn ap Meurig of Nannau told of: 'The mild abbot, the praiseworthy Llywelyn Fychan, the noble offspring of another Llywelyn, the lion-like protector of an enraptured people' – possibly an allusion to descent from the house of Gwynedd.'[45] Such poetic licence needs to be viewed with caution, but in Llywelyn's case it receives royal confirmation. Richard II (1377), allowing Strata Florida to appropriate Pencarreg church as this had been the Black Prince's intention, spoke of: 'The high place the abbot held with him, and now holds with us'.[46] Abbot Llywelyn was clearly an esteemed person of stature, and it was perhaps his influence for good in mid-Wales that earned him royal favour.

The Glyn Dŵr Revolt[47]

By the year 1400 a variety of factors, not least heavy taxation and difficult economic circumstances, caused for many Welsh people a smouldering resentment against the English establishment. A local quarrel of Owain Glyn Dŵr – an able forty-five year old lawyer with military experience – and Lord of Glyn Dyfrdwy and Cynllaith Owain – with the English Lord of Ruthin, Reginald Grey, was the spark which set ablaze a nationalist uprising. On 16 September a group of relatives and friends proclaimed Owain as 'Prince of Wales'. Ruthin and other English-settler boroughs were attacked, and there was a parallel rising in Anglesey. Henry IV brought an army and quelled the Revolt, but it broke out again 1401.

In 1402, Owain captured both Lord Grey and the powerful Earl of March. In 1403, the Revolt spread to south Wales: Cardiff was burnt. In 1404, the rebels took Aberystwyth and Harlech Castles, and Owain held a Parliament at Machynlleth. In 1405, 2,500 French troops landed at Milford Haven to augment Owain's 10,000 men, and to make a temporary foray into England. This was the peak of the Revolt: from 1406 there were more reverses than successes, though until 1412 Owain was still chalking up successes. Thereafter he died in obscurity. His rebellion had re-awakened national self-consciousness, but the revolt left in its wake a country devastated in its buildings and agricultural assets – the work of both sides.

It had been, for a few years, a nation-wide uprising – one in which the Cistercians could hardly fail to take sides, one from which they could not escape very damaging consequences. Within weeks of the outbreak of open rebellion in the autumn of 1400, the communities of Aberconwy and Cymer – perhaps fearing reprisals from the English – hastened to obtain letters of protection from Henry IV during the monarch's brief visit to north Wales.[48] The Abbot of Cymer, however, was to be (in 1402) in close touch with Glyn Dŵr – now in control of Meirionydd.[49] The Abbot of Valle Crucis, tradition relates, met and conversed with Owain in the Berwyn Hills, foreseeing in him the later Henry Tudor.[50]

The traditionally Welsh-orientated abbeys of the family of Whitland appear to have supported Glyn Dŵr when they could, especially when he was in the ascendancy and

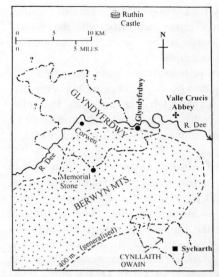

Fig. 25: Owain Glyn Dŵr's homeland. *(After Melville Richards, and advice from Mr Derrick Pratt).*

of local mastery. At other times, some at least served the interests of the Crown: it was a matter of practical politics. About 1404, the Abbot of Aberconwy was giving tactical support to the Crown by sending word to the lieutenant of Conwy Castle of six trading ships from France (with whom Owain was in alliance) approaching Llŷn.[51] Two years later Abbot Hywel ap Gwilym[52] was held as a 'rebel', though pardoned in 1409.[53]

Strata Florida had no choice but three times to become a barracks for English troops. In October 1402, Henry IV and his army occupied the abbey for a time, driving out those monks who favoured Glyn Dŵr. Divine worship was suspended for six months.[54] In 1407, 120 men-at-arms and 360 archers, and in 1415, forty men-at-arms and eighty archers, were stationed there. This was in order to have a base from which : 'To ride after and make war with the rebels, as well in south as in north Wales'. Strata Florida's mid-way position was advantageous in this respect.[55] In south Wales, the Abbot of Whitland was a Glyn Dŵr sympathiser, described as a 'rebel' and penalised accordingly.[56]

Two years later (1405) the Abbot of Llantarnam (John ab Hywel) actively participated at the battle of Bryn Buga, when the Welsh forces launched an onslaught on Usk Castle.[57] He was concerned spiritually for the rebels, personally hearing confessions and giving absolution before the attack. He was also a nationalist. John of Fordun told how 'zealous for the liberty of his country and people', he urged the troops on in their endeavour as they prepared for battle.[58] He then made the supreme sacrifice, for Adam of Usk (who called him 'a man of the highest prudence) recorded how the English soldiers 'slew many, and above all the abbot of Llantarnam'.[59]

The Cistercian houses of Wales were severely affected by the Revolt, not so much because they took one side or the other, but since they were, so to speak, caught in the cross-fire between the opposing armies. In the years that followed, most of the abbeys had a tale of woe to tell. Moreover, there was no carefully assessed royal compensation as that which had ensued upon the Edwardian Conquest, and the monasteries took decades to recover. Some never fully did.

As for Strata Florida, Adam of Usk suggested that despite the king being a 'guest' in the abbey, the English troops (in 1401) pillaged the house and used the church as a stable.[60] It was because of the damage done by the devastation of its lands and by the large royal army that, early in 1402, 'the dispersion of the monks' was feared. Henry IV committed the monastery for two years to the care of the Earl of Worcester and John Belyng. They were to administer its affairs, with the proviso that the first claim on the abbey's resources was to be the maintenance of its community.[61] It was a typical grant of 'secular custody'.[62]

The Crown usage of the abbey as a military post did not please the rebels; the community later (1442) recalled that it was 'spoiled by Glyn Dŵr and his company, the walls of the church excepted'.[63] This may explain why the refectory and infirmary were in ruins before the Dissolution.[64] A relic of these difficult times may be seen in three spurs, of early 15th century pattern, unearthed during excavations at Strata Florida.[65]

Destruction of conventual buildings occurred at other monasteries. John Leland visiting Cwmhir (*c.* 1538) told how 'all the house was spoiled and defaced by Owain Glyn Dŵr'.[66] Might the partition wall at the east end of its nave date from this period?[67] Edward Charlton (1420) noted at Strata Marcella: 'The destruction made by the Welsh rebels to the church and the monastery and its holdings, by plunder and by fire'.[68] Part of this abbey, too, lay in ruins by the Dissolution.[69] At Aberconwy, a charcoal layer detected during relatively recent excavation may also be a legacy of the known burning of that abbey in Glyn Dŵr's time.[70] At Basingwerk (1403), a licence granted it to buy beer in Chester may suggest a breakdown in the normal economy of the abbey at this time.[71]

An indirect result of the Rebellion was the promotion of the abbot of Valle Crucis, Robert of Lancaster, to the bishopric of St Asaph (1410–33) when Bishop John Trevor was banished to St Andrew's.[72] Becoming abbot only in 1409, he may have been a deliberate replacement for his predecessor who talked with, and praised, Glyn Dŵr. [73]

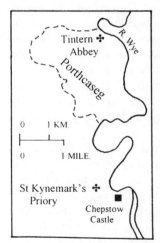

Fig. 26: Tintern *vis-à-vis* St Kynemark's.

The abbeys of south Wales did not escape suffering. On the Border, Dore (1405) had to parley with the rebels 'for the safety of the abbey, which is in great peril of destruction and burning'.[74] At the start of the Revolt (1400-01) the manorial records of Tintern's home estate (Porthcaseg) – with their lengthy lists of presentments for alleged faults and trespasses – may indicate a restlessness on the part of the rustic population.[75] In the autumn of 1401, Eynon, the Welsh Augustinian prior of nearby St Kynemark's,[76] instigated disaffection towards the monks of Tintern.[77] The uprising meant that the abbot could not fulfil his duties as a tax collector, and, by 1406, Tintern (1406) was in debt because much of its lands had been razed by the rebels.[78] The cloister roof may have been damaged.[79] To sustain themselves the monks had to demise land (1411) at their Acle manor in Norfolk.[80]

Margam (1412), so 'utterly destroyed' that its monks 'went about like vagabonds',[81] received a fraternal visit from two monks of Tintern.[82] Much later, Henry VI (1440) referred to its losses 'in the time of the Rebellion'.[83] Neath, too, was reduced to poverty.[84] Following the collapse of the Revolt, Thomas Franklin, abbot of Neath (1424–41) and then of Margam (1441–60), did much to rectify matters for both abbeys in terms of their fabric, numbers, worship and possessions.[85]

Bishop Robert of St Asaph's term as abbot (he lived at the monastery)[86] at Valle Crucis was extended (in 1419) because he had both 'repaired the monastery on its destruction by fire', as well as largely restoring his cathedral.[87] His monks, however, appear to have been drawing away from him, and had to be reminded to obey him.[88] In 1448, although its Abbot was 'eighty and blind', Aberconwy and its properties which had been 'burnt in time of war' were mostly put to right.[89]

Abbot Rhys at Strata Florida (1430–41) was another notable restorer,[90] whilst later in the century Morgan ap Rhys at Strata Florida, Sîon ap Rhisiart at Valle Crucis and Dafydd ab Owain at Aberconwy, continued the labours of others.[91] Restoration, whether of fabric or fortune, cost money, and the devastation wrought during the Rebellion very probably accounts for the encouragement given to pilgrims to visit Holywell (Basingwerk), Pen-rhys (Llantarnam) and Tintern (the Galilee chapel) from the early 15th century on *(Chapter 9)*.

External Pressures and Internal Feuds

In the aftermath of the Revolt, Wales was 'sorely afflicted by the hatreds and rivalries of a divided people, and by the increase in banditry'. Then came the Wars of the Roses (1455–71) and the troubled times which preceded them. 'From the outset Wales was deeply involved, both as a recruiting ground and an important battle field'.[92] It is no wonder that, for several Cistercian houses, there was a continuance of protracted tribulation, and a veritable catalogue of troubles which must have greatly retarded the efforts of those abbeys to rise from the low-water mark caused by the Rebellion.

Neath (*c.* 1423) was pillaged by 'sons of iniquity',[93] and then ransacked (*c.* 1450) during: 'The great war between men of Carmarthenshire and the lordship of Glamorgan'.[94] Tithes and rents were withheld, deeds and documents stolen. To gain extra income it successfully sought the appropriation of the church of Llandeilo Talybont.[95] Officers of the lords of Glamorgan wrongly sought taxes from Margam and interfered with its monopoly on the sale of alcohol.[96] Bailiffs of the Earl of Warwick once threateningly visited the abbey 'with a great multitude of men and horses'.[97] Once again, lords of Glamorgan (the Earl of Warwick: 1422–30, and the Duke of Clarence: 1450, 1471) took the abbey under their 'special protection'.[98]

Some of the difficulties of Abbot Rhys of Strata Florida (1436–41) may have been of his own making, particularly when (in 1435) he was bound over in the sum of £500 not to disturb Vale Royal's property in Llanbadarn Fawr.[99] He clearly had enemies, as Guto'r Glyn indicated: 'No matter what the claims brought against thee by abbots or laymen; no one ever opposed thee, Rhys, but thou didst get the better of him'.[100] The poet spoke too soon: the abbot's nomination as collector of a clerical subsidy (1430), of a moiety (1434), and then of tenths (1437, 1440), but subsequent failure to deliver, saw his (or his successor's) committal to Carmarthen Prison where he died.[101]

As for Whitland, by 1440 it had been so 'diminished by ravages of sword and fire', that the community only numbered eight monks.[102] The abbey, at this time, was fully involved with the Welshry. Abbot David (1434) stood bail for Hywel 'Whymys' of Powys imprisoned in the Tower.[103] About 1443, he was suspected of being implicated in the designs of Duke Humphrey of Gloucester, who was allegedly stirring up revolt in Wales.[104] The abbot was summoned (with other Welshmen) before the Privy Council,[105] whilst a monk (probably a Cistercian) was travelling around Wales 'telling chronicles at *commorthaus* and other gaderynges to the motion of the people'.[106] The flame of nationalism was still alive at Whitland.

Other monasteries affected included Basingwerk (1441) whose Abbot could not complete collection of a tenth because of 'insurrections and riots'.[107] In 1442, a year which was 'a blaze of riot',[108] the Abbot of Vale Royal complained that, trying to journey to Llanbadarn Fawr, he risked being repeatedly assaulted.[109] Dissension between Marcher lords helped to bring to the surface various problems at Cymer (1453), and caused the abbey to be committed to royal custody – the four nominal 'keepers' appointed included prominent Lancastrians.[110] A monk of Grace Dieu (1460) was presented to the Somerset living of Puriton – dying there in 1475 – a move which may reflect the economic difficulties of the Welsh houses.[111] Tintern (whose abbot, Colston had, in 1462, offended against the Statute of Praemunire)[112] received for burial (in 1469) the body of the Yorkist, Sir William Herbert,[113] who was executed after the Battle of Banbury, and who had been the abbey's steward since 1454.[114] In the 1440s its local rustics had been restive yet again.[115]

The mid-15th century was also marked by allegations of misrule within monasteries and by further contentions between rivals for abbatial office. Grace Dieu (1427) suffered from an interloper, Richard Moyne of Margam,[116] whilst two of its abbots felt forced to resign: Roger of Chepstow (1451) because 'of the pressure put on him by neighbours',[117] and John Mitulton (1484) due to harrassment 'by his enemies'.[118] Cajoling by self-interested secular parties hoping to gain economically from a subservient abbot, perhaps by putting one of their own kin into an abbacy, lay behind at least some of these internecine disputes.

Cymer's troubles (1453) came partly from 'dissensions between certain lords of the Marches',[119] whilst Willam Morris resigned the abbacy of Strata Florida (1444) 'having incurred the enmity of powerful men of those parts'.[120] Such external forces might claim that their intervention was necessitated by poor administration of a monastery and its property. David ap Rhys (1433), taking over the abbacy of Whitland, said it had been 'wasted by misrule'.[121] Ill-governance by its abbots allegedly helped to bring Cymer (1453) to its knees.[122] In judging the religious life of these years, it must be remembered that the various communities were not always their own masters.

There is rarely any precise evidence as to the background causes of difficulties such as these: civil war, local feuds, or simply a magnate with a vested interest, may all have been concerned. Even disputes which on the surface appear to have been but quarrels between contending abbots or monks, frequently saw lay involvement with force of arms, and havoc wreaked; divine service might be suspended. When the common seal of an abbey fell into the wrong hands, monastic land could be unjustly leased wholesale to the long-term detriment of the house. The common Crown device of placing a troubled house under 'secular custody' might be reinforced by the Order's own partial and temporary solutions, which included: 1. Dispersing the monks to other monasteries until matters improved; 2. Dispensing a community from the obligation to receive guests; 3. Suspending the admission of novices.

A stormy petrel was John ap Rhys, Abbot (probably) of Aberconwy, Cymer and Strata Florida, successively. Whilst superior of Aberconwy he was alleged to have come to Strata Florida (his mother-house) in mid-Lent 1428 'with a great troop of armed people and archers', to have held the abbey by force for forty days, to have plundered its books, silver and stock to the tune of 2,000 marks, and to have used the common seal to obtain loans 'of great sums of money'. As a result, the community found themselves 'grievously impleaded'.[123]

After an interim period as Abbot of Cymer, John ap Rhys himself succeeded (about 1442) to the abbacy of Strata Florida, but, returning to Cymer with 'divers, riotous misdoers', he evicted his successor Abbot Cobbe, and used its common seal to make irregular leases and grants 'bearing date a long time before his resignation' from that abbacy.[124] Cymer's next abbot, Richard Kirkby (much later to become Abbot of Basingwerk) had to seek protection for the house, as 'divers persons in north Wales propose daily to disturb both his person and his goods temporal and spiritual'.[125] Against such a background, it is a wonder that some monasteries survived!

John ap Rhys became Abbot of Strata Florida by force and deception, but his time there was short-lived. After Abbot Rhys had died in prison, one William Morris had been elected in his stead and installed by the father-abbot of Whitland (David ap Rhys) and the Abbot of Cymer (now John ap Rhys himself). The election was confirmed by the Abbots of Buildwas and Margam, Visitors of the Order, but, after not many months, John ap Rhys pretended to the Crown that Morris had been deposed and that he, ap Rhys, was now abbot. On the basis of letters of protection then issued to the abbey, ap Rhys, 'with many evildoers', expelled Morris and other monks, imprisoning them in Aberystwyth Castle.

Released by Sir William ap Thomas, the deputy Justiciar for south Wales, Abbot Morris (18 Febr. 1443) petitioned the king for redress.[126] Henry VI (3 March) decided that neither party should govern the abbey, but appointed the Abbots of Margam and Whitland as its keepers, ordering the Crown officers in Ceredigion to assist them.[127] In June 1444, Morris was granted a benefice. No more is heard of John ap Rhys, but clearly he had his backers, for the papal register tells that William Morris 'fearing that the monastery might suffer, surrendered it to the father abbot'.[128] Another ap Rhys, Morgan, succeeded him, a great blessing for the abbey, but was there a family connexion with David (of Whitland) or the unworthy John, or, indeed, the troubled Abbot Rhys whom the poets had praised?

The story of Basingwerk in the first half of the 15th century revolves around one abbot, Henry Wirral – whose surname indicated his Cheshire origins. Despite apostasy as a young monk (1399),[129] by 1430 he was *de facto* abbot of the house,[130] though very much a doubtful character. Failing in 1432 'to answer trespasses charged to him',[131] in 1436 he, and others, were bound over (in the sum of £200) to keep the peace towards Thomas de Wevere.[132] In the early 1450s, his monastery was financially embarrassed by 'reason of writs' executed against it by the Justiciar of Chester.[133] Wirral, in fact, was yet another monk who assumed an abbacy without legitimate authority.

Both Abbot Gnossal of Buildwas (now Basingwerk's father-immediate), and an inquiry held during a meeting of Cistercian abbots at Northampton (1432), supported another monk (Richard Lee) as the rightful abbot.[134] Wirral had for a time imprisoned Lee, whose release was ordered (1 December 1431) by Duke Humphrey of Gloucester ('guardian of England'), when he bound both parties over (in the sum of 500 marks each) pending the inquiry.[135] Though the latter awarded Lee the abbacy, Wirral refused to give way. Lee petitioned the Chancellor of England, telling him divine service at Basingwerk was suspended and that its monks (out of fear of Wirral) were residing at Buildwas.[136] The Chancellor's intervention, if any, was ineffective, Wirral continuing as abbot until his arrest in 1454 for participation in felonies in the county of Flint.[137]

Basingwerk's problems were not over, for twelve years later a similar dispute occurred. Richard Kirkby (formerly monk of Aberconwy and Abbot of Cymer) claimed the abbacy in 1465 and sought to oust Edmund Thornebar (previously a monk of Dore). Kirkby was supported in his claim by Gnossal's successor at Buildwas (Henry of Derby), but a high-powered commission of five abbots ordered by the General Chapter, and headed by no less a personage than the Abbot of Cîteaux, thought differently. Meeting at Dijon (16 September 1466) it reported unanimously in favour of Thornebar, accounted him the rightful abbot and deprecated the ill-practices of Kirkby and the Abbot of Buildwas in trying to oust him.[138] It was perhaps a reflection of the diminishing influence of central control in the Order that Kirkby remained *de facto* abbot down to at least 1476.[139] During his rule, a new common seal was engraved for the monastery, replacing that which had Abbot Wirral's initials inscribed upon it.[140]

Notable Abbots

Whilst several houses knew protracted tribulations in the 15th century, not all was unrelieved gloom. Much clearly depended upon the ruling abbots, and several abbeys were fortunate in this respect. It must also be remembered that (just as in a modern newspaper) only bad news hit the headlines; the great mass of good, the spiritual daily round, went unmentioned. Neath (1424–41) and Margam (1441–60) both profited from having the restoring Abbot Thomas Franklin at the helm. A proven superior, he was one of the Visitors to whom the keeping of Strata Florida (1443) was committed, and 'having regard to his labours' he received papal permission to hold *in commendam* for life any other monastery of the Order or a benefice.[141] Whether he so availed himself is unknown.

Another abbot-restorer was John ap Richard of Valle Crucis (*c.* 1455 to at least

1461, perhaps even 1480),[142] whose rule followed a period of alleged neglect by an English superior, John Mason (1438–48).[143] A local man, John ap Richard hailed from Ruabon and the important Trefor family;[144] perhaps Yorkist in sympathy, his duties for the monarch included receiving 'attornments' from the Crown tenants of Chirkland (1461).[145] As for his building work, the bard, Gutun Owain, praised his construction in Iâl of 'a palace of diadem'.[146]

After its bitter troubles, Strata Florida enjoyed a lengthy period of quietude under the governance of Morgan ap Rhys (1444–86). At perhaps a young age, his path to the abbacy was cleared (in February 1444) by receiving the dispensation his irregular birth demanded.[147] Abbot Morgan was yet another church restorer, and his work was itemised in the verse of Dafydd Nanmor, who told how he made an oak roof covered with 'heavy lead', and repaired the damaged choir, 'he cut ten complete windows, half the cost of this went in glass'.[148]

Morgan was, moreover, a scholar who took pride both in his monastery and in his nation, giving his house academic and genealogical distinction. In a (Panton MS) pedigree of Welsh nobility the scribe cites the authority of 'the great roll written by Morgan, abbot of Ystrad Fflur, a skilful and venerable teacher'. Another (Panton MS) pedigree refers to 'Bookys of Remembrans founde in the ancient abbey of Strata Florida ... and the rowls of Morgan Abbot'.[149] Historical works have also been attributed to Abbot William Corntown of Margam (1468–87).[150]

Somewhat surprisingly, a Scottish Cistercian, Thomas Pyle of Dundrennan, was involved in an unsuccessful effort to conserve the community of Bonshommes at Ruthin (1478–79).[151] As for some of the Welsh houses of the Order, little is known of their state as the Tudor age approached. At Grace Dieu (1484), however, the harassed Abbot Mitulton felt obliged to resign, unable there to 'safely and peacefully serve God'. His father-immediate, the Abbot of Dore, described him as being: 'A good man, of honest conversation and wholesome belief', and allowed him a year's sojourn in another monastery, where he could pursue what the Cistercian way of life was all about, a place where he could freely 'render to God his vow'.[152]

NOTES

1. Richard occurs in 1345, Ralph in 1351.
2. Gilbert in 1342, John in 1349.
3. Richard in 1345, Hywel Seys in 1352.
4. Cynfrig, 1345–56.
5. Henry, 1338–59.
6. Llywelyn, 1344–80.
7. NLW, Badm. Manorial 1646.
8. Bryant A. 1970, 385–86.
9. *Reg. J. Trillek* 375.
10. Cowley F.G. 1977, 251.
11. Glam. Archives CL/Deed I/8.
12. PRO, DL 25/1285; Williams D.H. 1984. II, 349.
13. Williams G. 1962, 153.
14. O'Sullivan J.F. 1947, 53.
15. Hays R.W. 1963, 117–19.
16. *Black Prince's Reg.* III, 22, 217–18, 309; *Cf.* 359.
17. *Ibid.* III, 330.
18. *Ibid.* III, 448.
19. Hays R.W. 1963, 129.
20. Birch W. de Gray. 1902, 135.
21. *Cartae Glam.* IV, 1383–84 (MLXX).
22. *Cal. Patent R.* 1384, 483–84 ['the sea sand'.]
23. *Cartae Glam.* IV, 361 (MLVI).
24. *Chron. Adae de Usk* 45, 205.

25.   *Cal. Papal Reg. (Letters)* V, 21, 24 (two Cistercian parishes).
26.   *Ibid.* V, 507–08; *Cf. 154.*
27.   *Cal. Fine R.* 1399, 7; 1400, 51.
28.   Williams D.H. 1976, 62, 73 (*n.*16).
29.   NGR: SO 430210.
30.   M.N.J. 1926, 8, 59–60, 162; *Cf.* NLW, Milborne Deed 78; *Monm. Antiq.* XVI (2000) 112.
31.   *Cal. Papal Reg. (Letters)* IV, 269, 304, 308, 312; V, 117, 213; VI, 174–75.
32.   Jacob E.F. 1961, 294.
33.   Williams D.H. 1976, 19–20.
34.   *Statuta* III, 525 (1352/14).
35.   *Reg. W. Courtenay* 38–39; *Cal. Papal Reg. (Letters)* III, 605.
36.   *Cal. Papal Reg. (Petitions)* I, 290, 339.
37.   *Fasti Cist. (1)* passim.
38.   *Cal. Papal Reg. (Letters)* III, 575.
39.   *Ibid.* IV, 291, 511.
40.   *Ibid.* V, 114.
41.   *Anc. Pet.* 373 (No. 11105).
42.   *Cal. Inq. Misc.* XV, 268–70.
43.   *Mont. Collns.* I (1868) 279, 324–25; *Strata Marcella Ch.* 230–33 (No. 89).
44.   *Mont. Collns.* V (1872) 138; LI (1949–50) 13.
45.   Williams S.W. 1889, 92–93.
46.   *Cal. Patent R.* 1377, 14.
47.   Jacob E.F. 1961, 37–65 (for a general review).
48.   *Cal. Patent R.* 1400, 555 ('during good behaviour').
49.   *Arch. Camb.* 1846, 455.
50.   Williams G. 1966, 60; Wrenn D.P.H. 1975, 27.
51.   *Orig. Lett.* II: Pt. 1, 30–31.
52.   A monk of Aberconwy by 1378: *Fasti Cist. (1)* 200.
53.   Hays R.W. 1963, 131.
54.   O'Sullivan, J.F. 1947, 109.
55.   Williams S.W. 1889, Appx. lvi.
56.   *Cal. Patent R.* 1403, 298.
57.   Williams D.H. 1976, 84; Williams G. 1962, 235.
58.   *Scoti-Chron.* II, 457.
59.   *Chron. Adae de Usk* 103, 282.
60.   *Ibid.* 237; Williams S.W. 1889, 165.

61.   Williams S.W. 1889, Appx. lv; Cf. *Anc. Pet.* 363–64 (No. 10789).
62.   Williams D.H. 1998, 153.
63.   *Cal. Patent R.* 1442, 95.
64.   Williams S.W. 1889, Appx. iii.
65.   *Ibid.* 165.
66.   *Itin. J. Leland* III, 52; Dunn E. 1967, 29.
67.   Rees S.E. 1999, pers. comm.
68.   *Mont. Collns.* VI (1873) 354–55.
69.   Owen E. 1919, 7.
70.   Butler L.A.S. 1980, 14.
71.   *Chester Recog. R.* (36) 25.
72.   Williams G. 1962, 225.
73.   *Cal. Papal Reg. (L)* VII, 528.
74.   *Cal. Patent R.* 1405, 65.
75.   NLW, Badm. Manorial 1654.
76.   Housing now occupies the site.
77.   NLW, Badm. Manorial 1654, mm. 1r, 3r; (he lost his office).
78.   *Reg. R. Mascall* 104.
79.   NLW, Badm. Manorial 1575.
80.   *Cal. Patent R.* 1411, 284.
81.   *Cal. Papal Reg. (L)* VI, 282.
82.   NLW, Badm. Manorial 1575.
83.   Birch W. de Gray. 1897, 342.
84.   *Chron. Adae de Usk* 305.
85.   *Cal. Papal Reg. (L)* IX, 527–28.
86.   Sealing episcopal deeds there: UCNW, Gwysaney Deed B. 424 (1416); *Reg. J. Catterick* 19 (145; 1419).
87.   Price G.V.P. 1952, 45–46; *Cal. Papal* Reg. (L) VII, 117, 177.
88.   *Cal. Papal Reg. (L)* VII, 177.
89.   *Cal. Patent R.* 1448, 227; *Cf.* 296.
90.   Williams G. 1962, 260.
91.   *Ibid.* 384–85.
92.   Rees W. 1972, 48–49.
93.   Birch W. de Gray. 1897, 341; 1902, 136–37.
94.   PRO, C 1/213/106.
95.   *Cal. Patent R.* 1447, 34.
96.   Birch W. de Gray. 1897, 346, 348–49.
97.   Evans H.T. 1915, 112.
98.   Birch W. de Gray. 1897, 346, 348–49.
99.   *Cal. Close R.* 1435, 364.
100. Williams G. 1962, 260; *D. Nanmor* 73–75.
101. *Cal. Patent R.* 1453, 65.
102. *Ibid.* 1440, 380; *Cf.* 486.

103. *Cal. Close R.* 1434, 271–72.
104. *Anc. Pet.* 220 (No. 6464*n*).
105. *Ibid.*
106. Evans H.T. 1915, 33.
107. *Cal. Patent R.* 1441, 42.
108. Evans H.T. 1915, 32.
109. *Ibid.* 32; *Rot. Parl.* 1442, 42–43; Cf. *Anc. Pet.* 39 (No. 1349*n*).
110. *Cal. Patent R.* 1453, 65.
111. *Fasti Cist.* (1) 212, (2) 157.
112. *Cal. Patent R.* 1462, 229.
113. Evans C.J.O. 1953, 492.
114. NLW, Badm. Manorial 1657.
115. See Chapter 13.
116. *Monm. Rec.* II, paras. 81–82.
117. BL, Royal MS 12E. xiv, f. 23r.
118. PRO, E 315/36/228.
119. *Cal. Patent R.* 1453, 65..
120. *Cal. Papal Reg. (L)* IX, 424.
121. *Cal. Patent R.* 1433, 295.
122. *Ibid.* 1453, 65.
123. *Anc. Pet.* 235 (No. 6928).
124. *Ibid.* 503 (No. 15874).
125. *Cal. Patent R.* 1443, 164.
126. *Ibid.* 1443, 151–52.
127. Williams S.W. 1889, Appx. xliv–xlvii (for a full account). Cf. *MSS in BM* III, 551 (No. 832).
128. *Cal. Papal Reg. (L)* IX, 424.
129. *Cal. Patent R.* 1399, 511. Burgesses with like patronym are on record at Flint [1362] and Rhuddlan [1535]: Williams D.H. 1984, I. 77*n*.
130. *Chester Recog. R.* (37: 2) 33–34.
131. *Ibid.* 33.
132. *Ibid.* 33.
133. *Cal. Patent R.* 1452, 547; 1453, 73.
134. PRO, C 1/44/236 [transcribed in Williams D.H. 1981, 331–32]. *Cf.* Knowles M.D. 1979, 128. The year of 1432 is uncertain, as regular meetings at Northampton date only from 1433.
135. *Cal. Close R.* 1431, 167.
136. PRO, C 1/44/236.
137. *Chester Recog. R.* (37: 2) 34; *Cf.* 19.
138. *Statuta* V, 185, 189 (1466, 33, 108); .Cf. BL, Add. Ch. 8527 (for Kirkby in 1465).
139. BL, Harleian MS 2038, f. 119.
140. *Arch. Camb.* CXXXVI (1987) 147 (Nos 238–39).
141. *Cal. Papal Reg. (L)* IX, 527–28.
142. *Arch. Camb.* 1875, 332.
143. Bachellery E. 1950, I. 118, 142; *Arch. Camb.* 1882, 155.
144. Williams G. 1962, 260; Price G.V. 1952, 279.
145. *Cal. Patent R.* 1461, 37.
146. Price G.V. 1952, 279; *Cf.* *Penguin Book of Welsh Verse* (1967) 188.
147. *Cal. Papal Reg. (L)* IX, 413. NLW, Alcwyn Evans MS 12,362D, suggests he was of Caio stock.
148. *D. Nanmor* 73–74 (transl. Mrs. E. Beecham).
149. Knight L.S. 1920, 269.
150. Williams G. 1962, 391.
151. *Cal. Papal Reg. (L)* XIII, 625–26, 698.
152. PRO, E 315/36/228.

CHAPTER 5

CONVENTUAL LIFE IN TUDOR TIMES
(1485–1535)

For the last half-century of Cistercian life in Wales, the state of monastic affairs varied greatly from one house to another. Much depended upon the personality of the ruling abbot.[1] Not all was unrelieved gloom, but there was scope for regular and thorough visitations, and, in particular, for the reforming zeal of Abbot Marmaduke Huby of Fountains. There were, moreover, difficulties created by the cleavage between the great mother-houses of Cîteaux and Clairvaux. As early as 1480, 'excesses' in Wales had 'come to the ears' of that year's General Chapter.[2] As Reformator of the Order, Abbot Huby (1497) told how many monks had 'digressed from the path of holy religion, as well in habit and tonsure as in other usages', although the previous year he had claimed that they were 'beginning to amend their ways'.[3]

The 'other usages' probably included the marital status of certain abbots who lived openly with a spouse and sired children. Amongst them were Thomas Pennant of Basingwerk (1481–1522) and David of Margam (1500–17). One of Huby's emissaries (Abbot David of Strata Marcella; 1496) remarked that: 'By the reception of secular priests and noble sons from the Welsh nation, the Sacred Order of Cîteaux is very much denigrated'.[4] The smallness of numbers in some communities perhaps necessitated the employment of secular chaplains, but in what way the Order was defamed by having personnel of native stock is not clear. The difficulties were both spiritual and economic. A variety of factors *(Chapter 6)* created the situation which led Huby (1517) to refer to 'the very poor' monasteries of Wales.

The inroads on their resources, he said, were 'as if the skins have been stripped off their backs'.[5] Abbot Lleision of Neath (1521) told how: 'Famine and the high price of corn' – such as had not been known for fifty years, meant that the Welsh abbeys could not pay in full the taxes expected of them by the Order.[6] The substantial aid demanded by the Crown (1522) towards the expenses of the French war must have been crippling,[7] varying between £40 and £67. Three smaller houses (Cwmhir, Cymer and Grace Dieu) were exempted, as also was Whitland.[8]

A series of visitations resulted in a considerable shake-up, and a change-over of abbots. A submission from the influential Abbot of Woburn, or a report from a monk of Cîteaux, John Coke – active in Wales in 1479,[9] perhaps led to the appointment (in 1480 by the General Chapter) of the Abbots of Woburn himself, and of Hailes and Louth Park, to make a visitation of the Welsh abbeys.[10] One consequence may have been the promotion of David ab Ieuan ab Iorwerth, monk of Aberconwy, to the abbacy of Valle Crucis (1480).[11] Clearly marked out for advancement, five years later he became a deputy Reformator of the Order in England and Wales,[12] ending his days concurrently as Bishop of St Asaph (1500–03).[13] His appointment may have been an endeavour to renew the Order in Wales from within.

It was a time, too, when high-level visitations from overseas were vetoed for political reasons, as a proposed visit by the abbot of Cîteaux (1490).[14] In the case of a planned visitation by the Abbot of Chaâlis (1532, at the direction of Cîteaux), the Crown spelt out the reasons plainly: 'It was not thought convenient to admit him, being an inhabitant of France'.[15] The international character of the Cistercian Order meant that it could not always escape the constraints which political boundaries and racial differences placed upon it.

Becoming a Reformator of the Order in England and Wales in 1495,[16] Marmaduke Huby had (as bursar of Fountains) already for some years assisted his predecessor as abbot in that capacity, and had more than once, with zeal and despite 'many dangers to his body',[17] taken a close interest in Welsh affairs. He now compelled reluctant Welsh houses to contribute towards a tenth granted to the Holy See. Only one abbot refused, John of Strata Florida,[18] and he was seemingly deposed.[19] Visiting Wales again in 1496, Huby deposed the 'pretended' Abbot of Strata Marcella (Maurice ab Ieuan) and installed his (Huby's) assistant (David Wynchcombe) in his place.[20] Maurice was perhaps the same monk who, in 1491, had been deposed from the abbacy of Whitland for moral laxity and illicit contracts,[21] and who, prior to becoming abbot (1469), may have been expelled from Oxford.[22] Huby also imprisoned a monk of Neath for the premeditated murder of a secular priest in the cloister of Whitland.[23]

It was undoubtedly in the light of Huby's visit to Wales in 1496, that the General Chapter that autumn appointed the Abbots of Aberconwy and Valle Crucis as its commissaries in the Principality.[24] It was indubitably acting on the request of David Wynchcombe, newly installed at Strata Marcella, that Huby forbade the father-abbot of Whitland (Thomas ap Rhys) from holding a visitation there.[25] He likewise enjoined the Abbot of Dore not to visit Grace Dieu until a meeting 'for the reform of our Order' had taken place early in 1497.[26]

Huby's work for Wales lasted from about 1490 until roughly 1514. He sought, in 1517, the continuance of his (and the Abbot of Rievaulx's) commission in this respect. He referred then to 'the monasteries of Wales which we formerly always had – for twenty years, except three years now elapsed – under our reformation'.[27] He wanted the 'very poor' abbeys there to have a respite from financial levy in order to recuperate, so that they could say of him, 'in the same way as he ceased the tribute, he is gathering the tax'.[28] Huby, however, was growing old and infirm, with malcontents back home at Fountains. In Wales, his work as Reformator passed to Abbot Lleision of Neath, whose activity was not always to the liking of the older man he had replaced.

Huby criticised Lleision for the irregular deposition – only one other investigating abbot instead of two being present – of Abbot David of Margam (1517). David, he said, had been forced to resign 'in fear of death and terror of armed force', and an unlearned monk (John Gruffydd) had been substituted in his place.[29] The potential use of secular force in depositions at this time was also exemplified (the same year) when the abbot of Ford (commissary for part of England), aided by the father-abbot of Tintern, ousted Abbot Robert of Kingswood. It was only accomplished at the apparent behest of, and certainly with the aid of help sent by, the Duke of Buckingham (resident nearby at Thornbury).[30] Abbot Robert, deposed (but with a

£12 annual pension) left the chapter-house of Kingswood 'sore weeping and lamenting', and complained of maltreatment both at Kingswood and Tintern.[31] Abbot Huby reported the Kingswood incident to Cîteaux.[32] He also had further occasion to criticise Abbot Lleision, accusing him of effecting 'the triple translation within the space of two years' of David Floyd, abbot of Conwy, first to Cymer and then to Strata Marcella.[33]

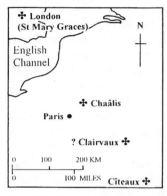

Fig. 27: Distant Abbeys visited by Abbot Lleision of Neath.

Abbot Lleision, like Huby, was also concerned with plans for the reform of the Order, summoning a meeting for this purpose at St Mary Graces in London (1520).[34] He was concerned at the inability of the Welsh abbeys to pay in full their pecuniary dues to the Order; what they did raise he took with him on a visit to Paris and Chaâlis abbey in 1521.[35] *(Fig. 27).* His work as a Reformator was long continued. When the Abbot of Chaâlis was refused entry to Britain, Lleision was one of the five abbots appointed by the Crown (1532) to visit the Cistercian houses of the realm,[36] and (in 1534) he was involved in sorting out troubles at Valle Crucis (1534).

Natural factors, but perhaps also Lleision's guiding hand, may be seen in the several changes in abbacies in 1527 and 1528: the translation of members of the family of Robert ap Rhys (John to Strata Marcella and Hugh to Aberconwy); the accession of William Vayn at Whitland; and the deposition of John Gruffydd at Margam. It was a period of change, as reflected in a list of arrears of fees due to Cardinal Wolsey (1529) for dispensations granted – on account of irregular birth or being under-age – for those aspiring to high office: James ab Ieuan of Valle Crucis and Robert Salisbury, abbot of Valle Crucis, as well as John of Strata Marcella and William of Whitland.[37]

Difficulties at a high level within the Cistercian Order, and especially the increasing gulf between the abbeys of Cîteaux and Clairvaux, were to be reflected even in Wales.[38] Sharp and relentless polemic was prolonged between the two houses – especially from 1484 to 1486 – and there was a real fear of the abbeys of the filiation of Clairvaux seceding from the Order, but Innocent VIII gave his backing to Cîteaux.[39] Two abbots tried to maintain the superiority of Clairvaux in Welsh Wales; not surprisingly, they were the heads of Aberconwy and Strata Florida.

The Abbot of Stratford Langthorne, writing to the Abbot of Cîteaux (12 March 1487) told him that: 'Some Welsh fathers are leaning away from your rule', and that he had imprisoned William Marlow – accounted by Henry VII as the 'rightful abbot' of Strata Florida. Marlow, he said, had acted as a guide to a monk sent from Clairvaux to the king's court at Winchester, had evaded capture at first by monks loyal to Cîteaux and had himself 'vented his poisonous mind' to the King.[40] A few months later (6 June) Marlow, now free, was entrusted by Henry VII with a royal missive to the Abbot of Cîteaux which referred to 'perverse abbots of your Order', and to false evidence regarding Marlow who had been placed 'for no small time in a house of correction'.[41]

By 1490, the question had been raised for some time of the Abbot of Cîteaux personally conducting a visitation in England and Wales. Huby, then bursar at Fountains, had worked hard to bring this about, but, he said, the Abbot of Aberconwy who had great influence at Court had denigrated the idea. Huby, in a letter to Cîteaux, not without satisfaction, told how the Abbot returning from the royal court to Aberconwy was thrown from his horse, broke his neck and died immediately. The (un-named) father-abbot of Strata Florida (for whom Huby was full of praise) who set out for Aberconwy to instal a new superior was taken ill and returned home to die. The truth of the affair was vouched for by three Welsh monks who bore the tidings to Fountains.[42]

The relative weakness of the Order in parts of Wales towards the close of the 15th century probably accounted not only for several monasteries being held *in commendam* by a Cistercian bishop, and secular clergy being assimilated as chaplains, but also for the ease with which at least three English monks were intruded into Welsh abbacies. They were monks with duties for the good of the Order to perform, and an abbacy gave them both status and pecuniary resources.

One such was William Marlow. Another was John Stratford, a monk of Hailes who became Abbot of Cymer (1482);[43] non-resident there by 1487, he was employed on carrying financial contributions from the English monasteries to the General Chapter, and bearing letters from the Abbot of Cîteaux to Henry VII.[44] A later abbot of Cymer, (also formerly a monk of Hailes – by 1461),[45] was David Wynchcombe, who, in April 1495, bore letters from Huby to the Abbot of Cîteaux (then on visitation in Flanders).[46] He, too, cannot have seen much of Cymer; in August that year Huby sent him again to France, bearing letters 'under a simple covering of cloth'.[47] Huby's high regard for Wynchcombe gained him the abbacy of Strata Marcella; the General Chapter twice appointed him as a definitor *(Chapter 10)*.

Individual Houses

In the opening decades of the 16th century, the lengthy abbacies of the superiors of seven Welsh houses brought them a considerable degree of quietude and stability, largely free from internal wrangling or major scandal. The abbots concerned were: Thomas ap Rhys of Whitland (1490–*c*. 1527), Morgan Blethin at Llantarnam (*c*. 1507–33), Lleision Thomas, the Reformator, at Neath (*c*. 1510–39), Richard Talley at Strata Florida (*c*. 1516–39), Lewis ap Thomas at Cymer (*c*. 1517–37), and Richard Wyche at Tintern (1521–36). All these abbeys (save for Tintern) had Welshmen at the helm, and all (Cymer excepted) ended their days with a reasonably sized community. Other abbeys had a more chequered history during these years.

The monastery of Aberconwy, especially, had its ups-and-downs. In the vacancy following the death of Abbot Reginald, with the prior, Gruffydd Goch, in interim control, and despite 'the poverty of the abbey', sizeable annual pensions were awarded for life to two of the monks: 8 florins to Lewis 'Ox. Ianykim', and 40 crowns to a son of Abbot Reginald, David ap 'Pigam'. The General Chapter (1482) ordered the abbots of Hailes and Sawley to investigate, and to 'extinguish' the pensions if found unreasonable or undue. The prior had granted David's mother a house, but the visitors were to make arrangements for her which did not burden the abbey. Finally, they were to compel both monks to lead a regular and stable life. David, who perhaps was quite young, was 'to learn the observance of holy religion in a cloister of the Order'.[48] This might imply he was to be transferred, but how far – at this time – the strictures of the Chapter were effective in a house of the lineage of Clairvaux is debatable.

That same year, 1482, the General Chapter confirmed the 'election' of David Wynchcombe as Abbot of Aberconwy,[49] in time to attend a meeting of Cistercian abbots in Shrewsbury later that year.[50] His appointment (doubtless designed to extend the influence of Cîteaux in Clairvaux dominated Wales) was quickly challenged by a Welsh monk; and once more Gruffydd Goch took temporary charge. The Crown (31 May 1484) ordered the abbey's tenants to pay their rents to the prior 'during the variance and controversy betwixt Dom David Wynchcombe and Dom David Lloyd'.[51] David Lloyd won the day; he was Abbot of Aberconwy on 20 November 1489,[52] and it was probably he who, the next autumn – perhaps not without personal feeling – resisted the projected visitation by the Abbot of Cîteaux. Prior Gruffydd – possibly during one of Abbot David's absences at court – was again in charge for a time in 1490;[53] by 1494 he appears to have become (though not for long) Abbot of Cymer.[54] Later superiors of Aberconwy included the notable David ab Owain; Geoffrey Kyffin (1514–26) – his abbacy was a relatively peaceful period; the young Cambridge student-abbot, Hugh ap Rhys, buried at Saffron Walden in 1528;[55] and Geoffrey Johns (1529–35) – when the house knew financial difficulties.

The tension between Cîteaux and Clairvaux may have been reflected yet again in the appointment of John Stratford from Hailes (of Cîteaux lineage) as Abbot of Cymer (1482), and in the challenge made (in 1486) to his control – perhaps during one of his frequent absences – by a monk, William,[56] who reigned at Cymer by 1491.[57] The rule of its last abbot, Lewis ap Thomas (1517–37), was interrupted on and off for four years (1521–25) by the intrusion of an abbot John[58] – probably John Glyn who later was deposed from the abbacy of Dore but managed to become the last Abbot of Cwmhir. Glyn was seemingly expelled in 1525, and Lewis ap Thomas – regarded as the 'good husband' (i.e: wise guardian) of the abbey[59] – reinstated. Abbot Lewis later took part in the very necessary reformation of Valle Crucis abbey *(infra)* – but perhaps not without a certain measure of self-interest – for he offered large sums of money to its steward (Sir William Brereton; £40) and to Cromwell (£20) in an unsuccessful bid to become abbot there himself.[60] A person of stature, after the Suppression he became bishop of Shrewsbury (1537–61).

Valle Crucis spent much of the Tudor period under the leadership of abbots of note: David ab Ieuan ab Iorwerth (1480–1503) and John Lloyd (Siôn Llwyd; 1503 –*c.* 1527). The latter, described (in 1518) as 'the king's chaplain and doctor of both laws',[61] was one of the Overseers nominated to compile the Welsh pedigree of King Henry VII.[62] Henry VIII suggested to Cardinal Wolsey Lloyd's appointment to the bishopric of St Asaph, but a Franciscan, Henry Standish, obtained the see.[63] Lloyd came of local stock – he was uncle and guardian to a namesake who was later High

Sheriff of Denbigh. After the Suppression, his tombstone was removed from Valle Crucis, and placed outside Llanarmon Church.[64]

Unfortunately for Valle Crucis, the violent reputation of the next abbot – a member of the local and powerful Salusbury family – went before him. Robert Salusbury[65] became abbot by March 1528, with dispensation from Cardinal Wolsey[66] – probably on account of his being under-age.[65] It is probable that Salusbury was intruded by external pressures into the abbacy, and that he had never served a proper novitiate nor been properly professed or elected. His 'coming thither' was not to the liking of the seven professed monks then at Valle Crucis, and five promptly left for other monasteries. In evidence he later gave (1542), Salusbury told that 'he was forced to get seven other strange monks, and give them wages to serve with him'.[67]

This statement reveals that nine monks were felt necessary to maintain divine service, and points to the now prevalent custom of giving even Cistercian monks pocket-money ('wages'). In his deposition he also let slip that he kept the common seal of the abbey in his custody. This, perhaps, enabled him (in one of his first acts as abbot) to grant a generous annuity to one Thomas Arundel (also an annuitant of Tintern) who might have helped him gain the abbacy, and/or with legal advice.[68]

This apparent initial concern for the maintenance of standards, is the only good known of Salusbury. Matters at Valle Crucis degenerated considerably, with great tension appearing in the community. At the instance of the Duke of Richmond (as Lord of Bromfield and Iâl), the Abbot of Neath (Reformator of the Order in Wales) accompanied by the Abbots of Aberconwy, Cwmhir and Cymer, held a visitation (mid-February 1534) at Valle Crucis. The community and Robert Salusbury laid claims and counter-claims against each other. As the abbot and his 'learned counsel' appealed to the Archbishop of Canterbury any action was stayed.[69] [The visitation is of note in revealing the use made by monastic superiors of legal advisers, an employment which gained the lawyers fees and annuities *(Chapter 6)*]

At Valle Crucis, the problems remained, and a concerned William Brereton (Chamberlain of Chester and Steward of Holt Castle) and an anxious Lewis ap Thomas, Abbot of Cymer, tried to right affairs – but both had a certain measure of self-interest: Lewis ap Thomas had already (May 1534) sought the abbacy for himself; Brereton wanted and obtained (in return for a loan of £1000 to Salusbury and his kinsman, Fuke, Dean of St Asaph) the stewardship of the abbey with the tithes of Ruabon as his fee.[70] The loan was to help the abbey, and perhaps the Salusburys personally, out of financial difficulties.

On 22 June 1534 Lewis ap Thomas and Brereton sent for the Reformator (Abbot Lleision of Neath) who was then staying at the White Hind-without-Cripplegate in London.[71] The result was a considerable shake-up at Valle Crucis. On 4 August (the day after Brereton was appointed the abbey's steward), the youthful Abbot Salusbury had to relinquish his authority to the prior (Richard Bromley) and a lawyer (John Brereton) and two others, and was sent to Oxford 'there to continue at his school and learning', but with a generous maintenance grant of £20 p.a. This mode of governance of the abbey, and the abbot's stay at Oxford, were to continue as long as Sir William Brereton saw fit. He had become not simply the monastery's steward, but its effectual master.[72]

Alas! Whilst at Oxford Robert Salusbury became the leader of a band of robbers, keeping half the booty (£140) for himself.[73] In May 1535, he was informed upon by one of his accomplices who had been caught, and fled.[74] Back at Valle Crucis (late August 1535), he was imprisoned by Sir William Brereton – first at Holt Castle and then in Chester Castle.[75] At an uncertain date he was incarcerated in the White Tower at the Tower of London[76] and may have languished there into 1537.[77] Meanwhile (4 or 5 Sept. 1535) he was deprived of his abbacy.[78]

Salusbury's abbacy ended in ignominy. How far better it might have been if the prior, Richard Bromley, had been appointed in his stead. Bromley had been a monk of Valle Crucis since at least 1504, when (staying at the English College) he went on pilgrimage to Rome.[79] Perhaps to ease his disappointment at being passed over for the abbacy in 1528, Cardinal Wolsey granted him (18 August) several privileges – which, in former days, would have been within the prerogative only of the General Chapter or a father-abbot at the very least. He was now absolved from ecclesiastical censure due (if any) for not wearing the habit; he was permitted (because of infirmity) to wear linen next his skin, long leggings of a decent colour (the monks were normally bare legged beneath their habit), and a 'head warmer' under his hood; he was allowed to talk quietly in the dorter (clearly still in use, though perhaps partitioned), and to eat and drink in his own (prior's) chamber.[80]

Moreover, his young wayward abbot (26 June 1528) gave him by way of annuity (which continued after the Suppression) the tithes of Bodellan township, Wrexham.[81] Cardinal Wolsey's deed also allowed Bromley to be promoted to an abbacy – despite being the bastard son of a monk. When this opportunity came a second time, with Salusbury's imprisonment, he declined it, well aware of the abbey's deep financial problems – despite being thought of by the Crown Commissioners surveying the abbey (22–26 August 1535) as 'a virtuous and well-disposed man', and of the six remaining monks the only one fit to be abbot.[82] After the Suppression, he lived in Wrexham where (in 1542) he was 'yet in full life'.[83]

At Strata Marcella, the abbacy of David Wynchcombe (1496–1513), was followed by the brief rule of Lewis ap Thomas and then the little-known period under David Ffloyd (1517–25). He was succeeded by John ap Rhys (*alias* Goyddvarche;[83a] 1527–36), one of the twelve illegitimate sons of Wolsey's friend, Robert ap Rhys, Vicar General of St Asaph, and brother of Abbots Hugh and Richard ap Rhys (*al*. Price) of Aberconwy.[84] Here was favouritism and nepotism indeed! John ap Rhys, however, may have been a worthy choice. He took over at Strata Marcella (aged about thirty-five)[85] towards the close of ten years study in philosophy, civil law and theology, for the B.Th. at Oxford.[86] When he came, he found but a small community (maybe only three in number in 1529),[87] and a monastery already 'to a large extent in ruin'.[88]

Early in his abbacy (about 1528) John ap Rhys tried to rectify matters by issuing an indulgence listing privileges granted by Pope Clement VII and Cardinal Wolsey to those who visited the monastery on certain feasts and/or 'extended helping hands towards it'.[89] Such pilgrims and almsgivers were assured, *inter-alia*, of ten years of pardon, substantial mitigation from the laws of fasting, and a promise of spiritual fraternity. One of the feasts specified was Holy Cross Day – 14 September – Strata Marcella had a relic/shrine of the Cross.[90] A space was left blank on each copy for the name of the individual benefactor to be inserted. This Indulgence is the earliest known printed document relating to Wales, and was the work of Richard Pynson, partner of the celebrated printer, Wynkyn de Worde.[91] Two copies survive.[92]

The Salusbury and Ap Rhys families were not the only ones to dominate Cistercian life in Tudor-age north Wales. For the last half-century of its existence, Basingwerk was governed by two members of the influential Pennant family: father (Thomas) and his third son (Nicholas).[93] This was another instance of a monk begetting a child, and a blatant departure from Church teaching. Yet Thomas Pennant, abbot for over forty years (1480–*c.? * 1522)[94] did much to bolster the fortunes of his house after the internal wrangling it had endured. The evidence (to be treated with caution) of the poet Tudor Aled, is that Pennant was 'dark-complexioned and godly, with a fine taste for minstrelsy, and a lion in battle who has overcome the foreigner'.[95] This may reflect his local origins unlike those of earlier English abbots at Basingwerk.

It is possible that he was the Thomas Pennant who wrote a wide selection of Latin grammatical texts.[96] In his time, the economic interests of the house were streamlined,[97] new guest accommodation was erected at the abbey,[98] new mills built on its lands,[99] and the present fine buildings raised at Holywell shrine.

In Nicholas Pennant's time as abbot the community may have numbered no more than three monks, and under his administration the monastery became even more of a family concern, with several grants of land and tithes to his relatives.[100] A notable incident in his time was the dispute as to who was the rightful vicar of nearby Holywell.[101] Maurice ap David claimed that he had become such on 11 July 1532 'by the presentation of Nicholas, Abbot of Basingwerk, and by the induction of Harry, Bishop of St Asaph'. The other contender, Roger Pigot (who also claimed presentation by the Bishop), was testified as having been inducted on 10 July by Robert Salusbury, parson of Llanrwst, and as having formally taken possession of the living by presenting himself to the Abbot and saying Mass in Holywell church[102].

Pigot alleged that a month later, whilst conveying his tithes of oats to the vicarage, he was assaulted by a band of twenty-one men led by the prior (Robert) and a monk (Thomas) – both armed 'with great quarter-staffs'. He was kept from his living, and asserted that this was at the instigation of Abbot Nicholas who openly said that he would keep the vicarage ready for his bastard son.[103] In the inquiry ordered by the Court of Star Chamber – at Holywell (13 March 1533) with Henry Conwey and Robert ap Rhys ap David as commissioners – the Abbot countered that he had no such son and that Pigot had never been lawfully presented to the living.[104] So great was the local feeling aroused by this affair that the two commissioners did not dare to pronounce judgement, but sent 'the bokes with the depositions' to the Court.[105]

Abbot of Strata Florida in the early 16th century was Richard Dorston (*c.* 1505–13), formerly a monk of Dore (by 1466) who had risen to be abbot first at Grace Dieu (1486–88) and then of Dore itself (1496–1500).[106] His appearance at

Strata Florida is somewhat surprising as he had been effectively deposed at Dore for 'inordinate rule and governance',[107] but it was not without its later parallel when another deposed abbot of Dore, John Glyn, became Abbot of Cwmhir (*c.* 1534).[108] Both these appointments must reflect the weakness of the houses concerned, but also external pressures of which we know nothing. At Cwmhir, Glyn's predecessor but one had been Richard Vaughan (1516–30), later accused of irregularities in his custody and usage of the common seal.[109] In a like case to that of Richard Bromley at Valle Crucis, Glyn's appointment to Cwmhir saw William Leicester, a long-standing monk of the abbey, passed over.[110]

At Strata Florida, Dorston was succeeded by Richard Talley (1516–39), whose ordination to the priesthood had taken place but three years before his accession.[111] His lengthy abbacy was only marred towards its close when one monk tried to oust him, and another (possibly the same one) was imprisoned for coining. The evidence then taken gives a certain insight into monastic life at that time. An inquiry held at Shrewsbury by the Commissioners in the Marches (1 and 2 October 1534) heard two contrary depositions.[112] The first (by Ieuan ab Hywel) admitted that he had brought the monk (Richard Smith) moulds for coining groats, and alleged that on the morning of Saturday, 20 June, Smith came bare-legged to his lodging 'requiring him to come to hear Mass, saying that he had fire ready to make the said coin'. The first results were unsatisfactory so Smith threw them out of his chamber window. Unfortunately for him, another monk passing by picked them up and took them to Abbot Talley, who arrested both Smith and Ieuan and clapped them in irons, setting two other monks to watch over them.

Richard Smith (now about forty years old) gave a different version, alleging that after drinking ale with him in a house 'in the precinct of the monastery', Ieuan tried to induce him to commit forgery, showing Smith two new groats and the moulds. It was a matter of each defendant trying to blame the other! The upshot was that Richard Smith was imprisoned for nearly four months (first at Carmarthen Prison and then in Aberystwyth Castle) before being brought before the Commissioners at Shrewsbury. More than coining may have lain at the heart of this incident. It may be that Talley seized the opportunity to be rid of a rebellious monk; Smith may have been the monk who was 'sworn to obedience' to the abbot by the Council of the Marches.[113] He seems to have returned to his abbey, and was pensioned off a few years later.

Margam, alone of the houses in south Wales, experienced major set-backs in these years. Abbot from 1500 until 1517 was David ap Thomas ab Hywel, possibly of Stradling lineage.[114] It may have been of him that Thomas ab Ieuan ap Rhys sang: 'Never did a white habit adorn a fairer owner'.[115] However, he openly kept concubines by whom he had at least one son and four daughters,[116] and despite Marmaduke Huby's criticism of the tactics used, it is little wonder that the Reformator (Lleision of Neath) insisted upon his resignation. Huby implied that Abbot David was deposed because of his loyalty to Clairvaux.[117] Early in the abbacy of his successor (John Gruffydd; 1517–28), said by Huby to be an 'unlearned' monk, the state of the monastery caused the General Chapter (1520) to order a special visitation there.[118]

In course of time, John Gruffydd was also removed from office, seemingly on the orders of Cardinal Wolsey, to whom representations were made (4 August 1528) with the backing of the king, that Abbot Gruffydd might 'resort home to his place, and enjoy his room there, as he did before'.[119] This was not to be; he was succeeded at Margam by Lewis Thomas, a monk of Neath who had been a Visitor at Mellifont (1517)[120] and both a definitor and a confessor at General Chapter (1530).[121] John Gruffydd may be the monk of that name who went on to occupy the abbacy of Grace Dieu (1534–36), and, after its suppression, to live at Hailes. If this is so, it is yet another instance of an abbot, found unworthy in one house, occupying a like position elsewhere. (The monk of Hailes went on to hold minor ecclesiastical appointments, dying only in 1564).[122]

At Llantarnam a long period of quietude seems to have marked the lengthy abbacy of Morgan Blethyn (1507–33), son of William Blethyn of nearby Malpas. He, too, earned poetic praise, and, alluding to the monastery by its *alias* of Deuma, Ieuan ap Huw Cae Llwyd wrote:

> Fair Deuma, the branch of Morgan is her defence,
> Mary's abbot from the family of Bleddyn.[123]

In the will of Morgan Jones (1532), Blethyn was appointed to act as guardian to Jones' son,[124] John, but the Abbot did not outlive Jones for long; dying in the spring of 1533. It was either he or his successor (Jasper ap Roger)[125] who (on 28 February 1533), with the mayor and other gentry, negotiated a peaceful settlement to armed conflict in Newport between the Morgans of Pencoed and the Herberts of St Julian's.[126] Even at this time, close to the Suppression, at least one Welsh abbot was fulfilling the mediatory role which had been commonplace in the early Middle Ages.

Individual Abbots

A striking feature of Tudor Cistercian life was the number of abbots who received a university education; frequently completing their studies after their installation. This was a deliberate policy for the good of the Order, and the monasteries with graduate-abbots were usually the most stable as the Dissolution approached. In the period of 1501–40 at least seven Welsh abbots studied at Oxford.[127] They included: (presumably) Abbot John Lloyd of Valle Crucis ('doctor of both laws' by 1518);[128] David ab Owain, Abbot of Strata Marcella and Aberconwy (D.C.L.); Lleision ap Thomas of Neath (Abbot by 1510, B.Can.L. in 1511, B.D. in 1512); Richard Talley of Strata Florida (abbot perhaps by 1516, B.D. in 1526); Richard Wyche, monk of Whalley (Abbot of Tintern, and B.Th. 1521);[129] and John ap Rhys of Strata Marcella (Abbot from 1527, B.Th. 1529).[130] The erring Robert Salusbury of Valle Crucis was also sent to Oxford (1534), whilst the youthful Hugh ap Rhys of Aberconwy died whilst a Cambridge undergraduate (1528).[131]

One of the most notable abbots was David ab Owain, who had legal training and who, after giving advice to the Earl of Gloucester as justice of north Wales (1461–67) and favouring thus the House of York, went on to espouse the cause of Henry Tudor and benefited in consequence.[132] The Welsh poets were full of his praise – no fewer than eleven addressed David in their verse – and as one of them said: 'The much-prospered Harry, was glad to recompense thee'.[133] He appears to have become successively Abbot of Strata Marcella (1485 on), perhaps provisor of St Bernard's College, Oxford (about 1495)[134], Abbot of Strata Florida (*c.* 1496–1500), and then Abbot of Aberconwy (*c.* 1501–13), holding this last abbacy in *commendam* whilst concurrently Bishop of St Asaph (1504–13).[135] At Strata Florida he added to Morgan ap Rhys' architectural work, and whilst Bishop of St Asaph oversaw a much-needed restoration of Aberconwy's buildings.[136]

The known abbatial chronology of 1490–1500 is uncertain, and there may have been partial truth (of a temporary nature) in the assertion of a Peniarth manuscript that Abbot David was 'advanced from Ystrad Fflur to Ystrad Marchell and Aberconwy and held the three together',[137] and in the claim of Lewis Môn that 'to the one choir go nine hundred as tenants from our two Gwynedds'.[138] On a personal note, the poets saw Abbot David as 'a bountiful man', an 'accomplished speaker', a huntsman, and as an abbot whose 'white habit was language and law to Powys'.

Abbot David's time at St Asaph was preceded by the three-year episcopate of David ab Ieuan ab Iorwerth (Abbot of Valle Crucis). Something of his career has been traced above. Like has predecessor, John ap Richard, he was a member of the Trefor family,[139] and he continued his work of restoration. Gutun Owain remarked on his care for the monastery, 'how good is the lord who loves to store his wealth, and spend it on Egwestl's noble church', and he praised him for building such 'a noble fabric for God, His cruciform House'.[140]

Two other north Walian abbots of note (David Wynchcombe and Lewis ap Thomas) have also found frequent mention before. For the un-named Abbot of Strata Florida (maybe William Marlow) who died in 1490, Marmaduke Huby was full of praise, mentioning his daily recitation of the rosary, and his rapid advancement (in three days!) from being a secular priest to abbot of the house.[141]

At Whitland, a little while after Abbot Thomas ap Rhys retired, his future was assured (in an arrangement like that for Prior Bromley at Valle Crucis) by the demise of Blaengwyddno Grange (1531) – gaining him a yearly pension.[142] His successor was William Vayn *alias* Thomas. This *alias*, together with the dispensation granted him on entering the abbacy by Cardinal Wolsey,[143] makes it possible that (like the Pennants at Basingwerk) a father was passing on the rule of the abbey to a bastard son.

In south Wales, Lleision ap Thomas of Neath (1509–39) was the foremost Tudor abbot, completing his Oxford studies in the early years of his abbacy.[144] At the General Chapter he was named as a definitor for the family of Clairvaux (1517) and for the lineage of Cîteaux (1518).[145] By this time he was Reformator of the Order for Wales, and his zealous activity in this respect has been noted. In 1521 his work for the Order took him on a visit to Paris.[146] In 1532 he was one of five abbots appointed (by the Crown) to replace the Abbot of Chaâlis on a visitation in England and Wales.[147] That same year, he played an important role in dealing with the affrays between the western and eastern portions of Gower,[148] and in February 1536 he was named (as once before – in 1513)[149] in a Commission of the Peace.[150] His last years were spent trying to ensure the survival of his house *(Chapter 6)*, and when its end eventually came (1539) one of the Crown Visitors said of Abbot Lleision that: 'He had ever lived worshipfully and well'.[151]

The small abbey of Grace Dieu finds little mention in this period, save for one Richard Rotter (1518), 'apostate monk of Grasduw', who now served as a chantry priest at St Briavel's[152] – in the Forest of Dean, not far from the abbey's Stowe Grange. One must not be unkind, but perhaps his surname indicated his character! Tintern finished its days in quite a sound condition *(Chapter 6)*, but not without first suffering difficulties with its steward (the Earl of Worcester).[153] 'Stewards' – as in the instance of Brereton at Valle Crucis – were becoming the masters of their monasteries rather than what they were supposed to be, their 'servants'. The spiritual tone of Tintern in its last years was indicated by the substantial size of its community, and in the personality of its abbot, Richard Wyche, who put first the keeping of 'a high feast of Our Blessed Lady' (her Nativity, 8 September 1534), before obeying a summons from Cromwell.[154]

As the Suppression approached, the condition of the Cistercian houses in Wales clearly varied considerably – in numbers, in leadership, and in spiritual and economic fortune. There were cases of severe neglect and instances of scandal, but in several abbeys, if not in most, there was yet a degree of scholarship and a concern for prayer and the recitation of the divine office. The Cistercian vocation still stood for something, as was evidenced when (in 1530) the Bishop of Hereford, noting the wish to lead 'a holier life' of an Augustinian nun of Limebrook (Herefordshire), Katharine Dodd, granted her permission to transfer to Cistercian Llanllugan where 'the rule is stricter' and the way 'greater and straiter'.[155] (This despite John Leland's description of it as 'a very little poor nunnery').[156]

It is true that numbers in the communities were small, far smaller than had been envisaged in the 12th century. For this reason, as well as the changed social scene, the Welsh Cistercians in Tudor times – with notable exceptions like John Lloyd and Lleision ap Thomas – were not involved in affairs of State and of the Welsh nation to the same degree that their predecessors had been three centuries before. Of greater concern to the Order must have been its impotence to arrange its affairs freely in the face of, first, the domineering activity of Cardinal Wolsey, and then the unscrupulousness of Thomas Cromwell.

NOTES

1. Williams G. 1962, 375.
2. *Statuta* V, 401 (1480/30).
3. *Letters to Cîteaux* 188 (93), 208 (101).
4. *Ibid*. 191 (94).
5. *Ibid*. 247 (127).
6. *Ibid*. 260–61 (133).
7. Williams G. 1962, 370.
8. *LP (Hen. VIII)* III: Pt. 2, 1047 (2483).
9. *Letters to Cîteaux* 64 (No. 15).
10. *Statuta* V, 401 (1480/30); *Cf. Letters to Cîteaux* 81–83 (Nos. 29–30).
11. *Letters to Cîteaux* 83 (30); *Cf. Cal. Papal Reg. (L)* XIII: Pt. 1, 278.
12. Williams G. 1962, 397; BL, Harleian MS 433, f. 209.
13. *Fasti Cist. (1)* 194.
14. *Letters to Cîteaux* 127–30 (Nos. 63–64).
15. *LP (Hen. VIII)* V, 456 (978–6).

16.   *Letters to Cîteaux* 174 (No. 87).
17.   *Ibid.* 132 (66); *Cf.* 180 (88).
18.   *Ibid.* 175 (87).
19.   *Ibid.* 181 (88).
20.   *Ibid.* 191 (94).
21.   *Statuta* VI, 21–22 (1491/47–48, 50); *Cf. Letters to Cîteaux* 131–32 (No. 66).
22.   Emden A.B. 1955. II, 1245; *Reg. Cancell. Oxon.* 310.
23.   *Letters to Cîteaux* 191 (No. 94).
24.   *Statuta* VI, 151–52 (1496/55).
25.   *Letters to Cîteaux* 191 (No. 94).
26.   PRO, E 135/18/6.
27.   *Letters to Cîteaux* 245 (No. 126).
28.   *Ibid.* 247 (127).
29.   *Ibid.* 251 (129); but note: Williams G. 1962, 398–99m regarding this case.
30.   *LP (Hen. VIII)* II: Pt. 2, 1021–22 (No. 3173); III: Pt. 1, 512 (1288).
31.   *Gloucestershire Notes and Queries* IV (1890) 436–39.
32.   *Letters to Cîteaux* 252 (19): For more details, see: Williams D.H. 1976, 109–10.
33.   *Letters to Cîteaux* 251–52 (No. 129).
34.   PRO, E 326/12613.
35.   *Letters to Cîteaux* 260–62 (133–34). (The letter Lleision addressed to Cîteaux on 25 March 1521, arrived five weeks later on 2 May).
36.   *LP (Hen. VIII)* V, 456 (978–6).
37.   *Ibid.* IV, 3048 (6748–4).
38.   Igliozi S. 1976, 1–14.
39.   Lekai L.J. 1977, 111.
40.   *Letters to Cîteaux* 97–98 (No. 40); Williams G. 1962, 397.
41.   *Letters to Cîteaux* 98–100 (41–42).
42.   *Ibid.* 127–30 (64).
43.   *Statuta* V, 432 (1482/13).
44.   *Letters to Cîteaux* 97 (39), 99 (41).
45.   *Bull. Inst. Hist. Research* LIII (127; 1980) 112.
46.   *Letters to Cîteaux* 176 (88).
47.   *Ibid.* 177 (88), 181 (89); *Cf.* 191–92 (95).
48.   *Statuta* V, 438–39 (1482/37).
49.   *Ibid.* V, 432 (1482/14).
50.   Hays R.W. 1963, 135.
51.   *Arch. Camb.* 1882, 71; Price G.V.

52.   1952, 40.
52.   Hays R.W. 1963, 136.
53.   UCNW, Penrhyn Castle Deed 257.
54.   PRO, LR 1/213, f. 270d.
55.   Hays R.W. 1963, 139–40.
56.   *Statuta* V, 536 (1486/18).
57.   *Augm. Rec.* 288.
58.   For more detail: Williams D.H. 1984. I, 87 and *n.*
59.   Williams D.H. 1981a, 45–46.
60.   *LP (Hen. VIII)* IX, 83 (244).
61.   *Ibid.* II: Pt. 2, 1262 (4070).
62.   Lloyd J.Y.W. (1885) V, 150; *MSS in BM* I, 105 (263): The work was later updated down to Edward VI.
63.   *LP (Hen. VIII)* II: Pt. 2, 1262 (4070).
64.   *Arch. Camb.* 1876, 227.
65.   For further detail: Pratt D. 1997, 28–33.
66.   *LP (Hen. VIII)* IV, 3048 (6748–4).
67.   Owen E. 1931 (I); PRO, E 315/117, f. 42.
68.   PRO, E 326/5421.
69.   Price G.V. 1952, 262–63.
70.   PRO, E 326/10140–41.
71.   *MSS in BM* IV, 819 (1670-c).
72.   PRO, E 326/10136; Owen E. 1931 (I). For Brereton and Vale Royal Abbey, see: VCH, *Chester* III (1980) 162.
73.   Pratt D. 1997, 32 (a full account).
74.   *Ibid.* 33; *LP (Hen. VIII)* VIII, 295 (789).
75.   *LP (Hen. VIII)* IX, 83 (244).
76.   *Ibid.* VIII, 397 (1000–3).
77.   *Ibid.* XII: Pt. 2, 59 (181).
78.   *Ibid.* IX, 83 (244).
79.   Pratt D. 1997, 29.
80.   Owen E. 1931 (II) 6.
81.   Pratt D. 1997, 29–30, 63 (*n.*7).
82.   *LP (Hen. VIII)* IX, 83 (244): Pratt D. 1997, 63 [*n.*4] raises the *possibility* of Bromley having been briefly arrested for treason (1534).
83.   PRO, REQ 2/5 (No. 273).
83a. *Strata Marcella Ch.* 238 (No. 100).
84.   Williams G. 1962, 324.
85.   PRO, E 210/D.6238; *Cf.* E 321/37/51.
86.   *Biog. Reg. Oxford* 10.
87.   *Cf.* the signatures on BL, Addit. Ch. 10654.

88. BL, Egertom MS 2410, f. 4.
89. *Ibid.* For a summary, see: *Jnl. National Library of Wales* XIV (1965) 246–47, and Plate XIV.15; for a transcription, see: *Y Cymmrodor* XXIX (1919) 4–13.
90. PRO, SC 6 (Hen. VIII) 5259.
91. For more detail: Williams D.H. 1976b, 175.
92. BL, Egerton MS 2410, f. 4; NLW (Dept. of Printed Books) Ws 1528.
93. Jones A. 1933, 168. For these abbacies: Williams D.H. 1981b, 100–02.
94. *Cf.* Williams D.H. 1984. I, 92 (*n.* 74).
95. Jones A. 1933, 176.
96. Huws D. 1980, 13; *Cf.* Gieben S. 1967.
97. Williams D.H. 1981b, 100.
98. Jones A. 1933, 176.
99. Jones H.L. 1846, 111.
100. Williams D.H. 1981b, 101.
101. Owen E. 1920, 66–69.
102. PRO, STAC 2/34/24/
103. Owen E. 1920, 67.
104. PRO, STAC 5/32/157.
105. *Ibid.* 2/34/24.
106. *Fasti Cist.* (1) 210.
107. Blashill T. 1883, 9; PRO, E 315/238, ff. 72, 75d.
108. Williams D.H. 1976a, 83–84.
109. PRO, C 24/29 (Pt. 2); *Cf.* LR 1/229, f. 153d.
110. See Chapter 6.
111. *Reg. R. Mayew* 261–63.
112. Williams S.W. 1889, Appx. lxxvii–lxxx; *LP (Hen. VIII)* VII, 477.
113. *LP (Hen. VIII)* VII, 87 (1264).
114. Birch W. de Gray. 1897, 352.
115. Thomas L. 1930, 31. Other verse praising Abbot David for repairing 'The broken church', might refer to the David of 1413, abbot in the wake of the Glyn Dŵr Revolt [*MSS in BM* I, 34 (90b)].
116. Williams G. 1962, 399.
117. *Letters to Cîteaux* 251 (No. 129).
118. *Statuta* VI, 558 (1520/29).
119. *State Papers* I (Hen. VIII: I–II) 323 (CXLV); *Cf. LP (Hen. VIII)* IV: Pt. 2, 2005 (4604, 4606).
120. Williams D.H. 1980, 22.
121. *Statuta* VI, 674 (A).
122. *Trans. Bristol and Gloucs. Arch. Soc.* XLIX (1927) 89.
123. Harries L. 1953, 112.
124. PRO, PROB 11/14, f. 21; Williams D.H. 1976, 85–86.
125. Williams D.H. 1976, 86.
126. Alphonse T. 1979, 136–37.
127. *Fasti Cist.* (1) 185–86
128. *LP (Hen. VIII)* II: Pt. 2, 1262 (4070).
129. *Biog. Reg. Oxford* 642.
130. *Ibid.* 10.
131. Hays R.W. 1963, 139–40.
132. *Dict. Welsh Biog.* 107.
133. Williams G. 1962, 402–03.
134. *Letters to Cîteaux* 196 (No. 97).
135. *Fasti Cist.* (1) 194.
136. Williams G. 1962, 384–85. Abbot Geoffrey (1513–26) continued the work at Maenan: Butler L.A.S. 1980, 2.
137. Williams G. 1962, 384 (*n.*7).
138. *Ibid.* 358 (*n.*1).
139. Pratt D. 1997, 10.
140. Price G.V. 1952, 278, 280.
141. *Letters to Cîteaux* 129 (No. 64).
142. PRO, SC 6 (Hen. VIII) 4903, mm. 26d–27r.
143. *LP (Hen. VIII)* IV: Pt. 3, 3048 (6748–4).
144. *Fasti Cist.* (1) 205.
145. *Statuta* VI, 509 (1517/A), 525–26 (1518/A).
146. *Letters to Cîteaux* 262–63 (No. 134a).
147. *LP (Hen. VIII)* V, 456 (978–6).
148. *Dict. Welsh Biog.* 567–68.
149. *LP (Hen. VIII)* II, 1836 (18).
150. *Ibid.* X, 159 (392–48).
151. Williams G. 1967, 96.
152. *Hockaday Abst.* 328.
153. Williams D.H. 1976, 110.
154. PRO, SP 1/85/1133.
155. *Reg. C. Bothe* 241–43; Dodd's name appears on the pension list of Limebrook at its suppression [*LP Hen. VIII* XIV: Pt. 2, 283 (752); did she go to Limebrook, or return to it when Llanllugan was dissolved?
156. *Itin. J. Leland* III, 55.

CHAPTER 6

THE SUPPRESSION
(1536–1539)

It is sad to reflect that the monasteries of the White Monks in Wales have already been suppressed for longer than they were in existence. Only three – Basingwerk, Neath and Tintern, had a life-span barely in excess of 400 years, yet now they have lain inactive for just over 460. By the late spring of 1539, medieval religious life in Wales had been extinguished, the monastic buildings soon fell into decay and ruin, their former inmates were dispersed abroad.

Significant questions remain: How far ahead of the event were the monks aware of their likely fate? To what degree should the dissolution of the monasteries have been accomplished? That some radical action was necessary is shown by the small numbers in some communities – with even English monks and abbots imported into certain once die-hard Welsh houses, by financial indebtedness in several instances, and by the partial state of ruin of the buildings in a few monasteries. The prevailing state of affairs in Tudor times indicates the need there was for renewal and 'reformation', but not wholesale dissolution.

The closure of religious houses was not without precedent.[1] Most alien priories had ceased to exist a century before. Minor spates of suppression – to realise funds and buildings for educational purposes – had been the work more recently not only of Cardinal Wolsey, but also of the saintly Bishop John Fisher of Rochester. Closures were also rampant in the 1520s in Germany and Sweden. By the mid-1530s, the religious of Wales, as elsewhere, must have experienced growing foreboding and a deep insecurity. This manifested itself in monks jockeying for abbatial position and a hoped-for pension – whilst the lay-folk backing one or another aspiring candidate perhaps hoped for a share in the pickings. Monastic estates were broken up, and leases of lands and grants of office given in return for 'favours' – sometimes financial. In March 1536, the first Act of Suppression alleged that the superiors of many houses had been 'dreading the suppression thereof'.[2] The compilation of the Crown survey, the *Valor Ecclesiasticus*, the previous year, left them in little doubt as to what to expect.

Appointment to Abbacies

There were, indeed, several instances of 'bargaining for position and office',[3] but too little is known of their background to accurately deduce the motives behind them. After Robert Salusbury was deposed at Valle Crucis and Lewis ap Thomas was unsuccessful in his bid to succeed him,[4] the monk who did, John Durham of St Mary Graces, had to borrow heavily (£200) to meet the expenses of his 'induction and installation'.[5] This obligation stemmed from money owed to Lord Rochford (Queen Anne Boleyn's brother) who recommended his appointment to

Cromwell. On the eve of his execution (17 May 1536) Lord Rochford was troubled in conscience, because he thought that the abbey was already suppressed and 'the abbot undone', the king now holding the deeds of obligation.[6]

At Cwmhir, John Glyn *(Chapter 5)* became abbot about 1535, despite his having been deposed at two other houses for 'misguiding and decaying them',[7] and despite the preference of the father-abbot of Whitland, and the Earl of Shrewsbury, for William Leicester, who had been a monk there for over forty years, and had administered the abbey briefly after the cession of Abbot Geoffrey Davies, and in doing so had tried to keep John Glyn at bay.[8] His feelings can only be imagined!

The hunger for an abbatial pension – honoured by the Court of Augmentations after the Suppression – was blatantly shown at Grace Dieu. After the cession of John Rowthwell (himself an import from English Buildwas)[9] in 1533, there was a rapid succession of abbots – William Ipsley (from Flaxley – a very transient superior),[10] Thomas Perpin and John Gruffydd (its last abbot, and perhaps the abbot of that name deposed at Margam). Perpin held the abbacy only for a year or so, but received an annuity of 13s 4d (8 December 1534) upgraded nine days later to £4, during an official visit by the father-abbot of Dore.[11] The *Valor* in 1535 noted the pensions paid to Perpin and also to 'two religious persons'.[12] One of them was certainly Rowthwell.[13]

Family influence probably gained Richard ap Rhys the abbacy of Aberconwy, at the age of only twenty-four. (Apart from his abbatial brothers – John and Hugh – an elder brother, Ellis, was appointed as one of the three commissioners to inspect the religious houses of Wales (1535), but his nomination was cancelled after protests by his colleagues – Adam Becanshaw and John Vaughan – concerning his life and reputation).[14] The young Richard, however, had the favour of Bishop Lee, President of the Council of the Marches, a friend of his deceased father, who wrote to Cromwell (1 July 1535) on his behalf.[15] The upshot was that on 30 August the two commissioners received the unwilling resignation of Abbot Geoffrey Johns.[16]

Although Richard ap Rhys was purportedly unanimously elected by the community, and presented his dispensation from Cardinal Wolsey to the commissioners, the latter postponed his installation until they received further instructions. Whilst Bishop Lee saw the young man as 'much loved by his brethren',[17] the outgoing abbot thought very differently. He described Richard as 'a wilful and misruled person who would utterly destroy the abbey'.[18] He proposed, supported by Richard Bulkeley, Vice-Chamberlain of North Wales, a monk, David Owain, who was 'meet to be ruler' (5 May 1536). However, despite making substantial financial offers to Cromwell, Owain was passed over, and (by 3 June 1536) Richard ap Rhys was *de facto* abbot.[19] He had occasion later to remind Cromwell of the 'costs and charges, to his brethren and friends' of his 'promotion'.[20] As elsewhere, bribery and family connections rather than free election and spiritual concerns had become the machinery by which abbots might be appointed.

Late Leases

The first Act of Suppression made explicit mention of the current monastic practice of granting leases of conventual possessions in anticipation of the Dissolution. The

Act, therefore, provided that all such transactions made within the twelve months previous to the promulgation of the Act were 'utterly void and of none effect'.[21] Were such leases allowed to stand, the post-monastic owners of property granted them by the Crown could find their freedom of action concerning them, and indeed the income accruing from them, severely restricted. In the aftermath of the Suppression claims to title to former monastic lands led to no little litigation.

So far as Wales was concerned, the abundant evidence suggests two motives by Cistercian abbots demising properties: first, 'to provide generously for friends and family',[22] and, second, the need to raise money to endeavour to have the monastery spared the evil day of closure. A long catalogue of such late leases can be made.[23] As regards Strata Marcella, it was stated in 1547 that several parties possessed 'parcels of the demesne grounds of the late abbey', by virtue of leases granted them 'within one year before the Dissolution, contrary to the Statute'.[24] A lease made by Dore 'within the period disallowed by statute', was conditional; if the monastery was not after all suppressed ('should stand still'), then the lease was to be surrendered.[25] There were instances of leases being made after the promulgation of the Act (Aberconwy),[26] and even (allegedly) after the Dissolution itself (Basingwerk[27] and Strata Florida).[28]

Amongst late leases made by Abbot Nicholas Pennant of Basingwerk was the grant of the tithes of Brynford to his brother John.[29] He bequeathed the tithes back to (now former) Abbot Nicholas who, in turn, redemised them to a younger generation of Pennants, ensuring that they stayed in family hands for no small time.[30] Of thirty-nine dated leases granted by Strata Marcella, twenty-nine were from the last abbacy, that of John ap Rhys. One was of Berriw Church (1531) to Nicholas Purcell, burgess and draper of Shrewsbury, in return for a £300 loan.[31] The abbot completed the formalities of a later lease whilst in Ludlow, en route to London in connection with the surrender of the monastery.[32]

Cwmhir mortgaged Gwernygo Grange (1534) to the constable of Clun in recompense of a loan of £112 'in ready money and other necessaries'.[33] When Llantarnam demised Pwlpan Grange (1533) it did so to Lewis Blethin, a relative of the penultimate abbot (Morgan Blethin) who had just died.[34] Against this general pattern, must be set rare instances of continuing monastic control, as at Tintern (1535) where two valuable granges had lately been brought back under direct control.[35]

Three abbeys (Neath, Strata Florida and Whitland) escaped suppression until 1539, but only by the payment of substantial sums of money – £150, £66 and £400 respectively, raised by splitting up their estates, re-negotiating existing leases, and demanding heavy entry fines of new tenants. In all this, the appointment of Receivers-General seems to have played a decisive part. At Neath, where fifty-one of seventy-one recorded leases were post-1535, a succession of valuable properties disposed of included Sker[36] and Cwrt-y-carnau[37] Granges, 'all its land in Clydach',[38] and the rectory of Llandeilo Talybont.[39] Nash Grange was split into sixteen demised holdings within a few months; its dismemberment being accomplished in three stages between 12 September 1535 and 3 January 1536.[40] One lessee of property of Neath in Bristol, William Shepman a merchant, had to give the abbey before the sealing of his lease 'a ton of iron and two hogsheads of good Gascon wine'.[41] A Crown official to do well out of Neath was Richard Duke, Clerk of the Court of Augmentations, who gained the lease of its Exford manor in Somerset (1538).[42]

All, save one, of the recorded demises of Whitland date from between 10 May 1537 and 10 February 1539. The last lease was granted only two days before the abbey's suppression. Twenty-four of the leases are dated 10 May 1537, while forty others occur in the short period of 6–20 October 1538.[43] Some of the planning was undoubtedly the work of its adviser, David Nash, appointed its Receiver-General on 9 October that year.[44] That the leases were a conscious effort to raise money to prolong the abbey's life (spared in 1536) was reflected in the substantial entry fine for Ystlwyf Grange (£40) and three years' rent for another holding (£15) paid by Richard Devereux, son of the abbey's Steward (Lord Ferrers), 'towards the 1,000 marks sterling (due) to the king for the redemption of the house'.[45] The effect of this wholesale, and late, demising, was that, in 1576, the Earl of Essex complained that he could make no profit out of lands formerly belonging to Whitland, because the abbot before the dissolution had leased them out for ninety-nine years, for some reason using the seal of the friars of Carmarthen.[46]

Strata Florida, too, made major demises in its last years for 'the redemption of the monastery'.[47] Its Receiver-General (the same Richard Devereux, appointed – 'with plenary powers' – on 12 May 1538) had a hand in the later stages.[48] The properties demised included Morfa Bychan[49] and Nant Bau[50] Granges, and the rectorial tithes of Llangurig[51] and Pencarreg.[52] In each case a substantial sum had been 'beforehand paid'. These grants, part of a succession traceable from 11 December 1536 to 25 November 1538, raised nearly £400 in entry fines.[53] Why, when so much money had been raised, had Strata Florida by Michaelmas 1538, only paid over to the Crown £66 (compared to Whitland's £400) of the 1,000 marks expected?[54] Could some have been salted away? Could the grant of Aberduhonw Grange, said to have been made under counterfeit seal after the Dissolution be any indication? The lessee claimed to have been granted it 'because of a sum of money [100 marks] he paid to the late abbot'.[55] The lease of Nant Bau Grange was eventually held, probably because of its late date, to be 'void in law'.[56]

Efforts to Prolong Monastic Life

The Crown inspection of the Welsh religious houses, stretching from the late summer of 1535 to the spring of 1536, left the monasteries in no doubt at all as to their potential fate. A few may have acquiesced quietly, and made little or no effort to be spared. Strata Marcella, for example, was later said to have been sold to Lord Powis by its community 'before the making of the Act'.[57] The abbot's reward was presentation by the peer (as early as 13 March 1536) to a portion in Pontesbury Church. Indeed he had left the house before its dissolution.[58]

His brother, Richard ap Rhys of Aberconwy, did his utmost to save his abbey – and thus the welfare of 'his brethren and family' – both through the advocacy of his brother, Ellis, and his own two letters to Cromwell. In the first epistle (of 1536) he offered Cromwell an annuity if the house was spared 'by a provision of this Parliament or a special licence from the King'.[59] With his second letter (24 January

1537) he sent Cromwell £40, and promised him daily prayers 'as for a founder of the house'.[60] His pleas fell on deaf ears; within two months Aberconwy was no more.[61]

It is not clear why three abbeys (Neath, Strata Florida and Whitland) were allowed to briefly prolong their lives. Trying to be spared was a risky business, financially, as one of Neath's advocates pointed out when the evil day finally arrived: 'My lord abbot hath of late dangered himself and his friends very far with the redemption'.[62] Apart from its fifty-odd leases, Neath curried favour with Cromwell by the grant of an annuity of £12 (1536),[63] and rewarded with smaller pensions (£2 each; 1538) the Clerk and Solicitor of the Court of Augmentations 'for good advice and favours'.[64] Financial help probably formed part of the 'aids and services' and 'great liberalities shewn', which moved Strata Florida to grant several annuities in 1537.[65] It also received a substantial loan (£100) from its Receiver, Richard Devereux (20 August 1538).[66] Whitland gave an annuity to John Dorman (1537) 'for a pecuniary service',[67] and promised a yearly obit to Gruffydd ap David Ddu (*d.*1538) for the sum of £40.[68]

These efforts meant that Neath was to remain '*in pristino statu*' (30 January 1537).[69] Strata Florida was technically dissolved but, because of its exercise of piety and hospitality, Henry VIII consented 'to erect and renew the abbey ... *for ever*' (30 January 1537).[70] Whitland was formally re-founded 'by virtue of the king's restitution' (25 April 1537).[71] The three abbots kept their positions.[72] In each case a heavy payment was exacted. Whether the communities took on this burden from spiritual motives, and whether the final surrender of Strata Florida (21 February 1539) was the 'spontaneous' act alleged,[73] are debatable questions. Whitland had already been dissolved on 12 February,[74] and Neath was no more by 12 March.[75] The hopes of continuance raised early in 1537, coupled with the large sums of money raised, meant that when the axe fell, so soon, it was a cruel blow. The broken promises were a fraudulent endeavour by the Crown.

State of the Monasteries on the Eve of their Dissolution

Financial Indebtedness

Hardly an abbey in Wales was free from financial embarrassment when the Suppression came – the result of substantial debts, out-goings in the form of annuities and pensions, economic mismanagement, subsidies levied – as for the war with France (1522), and the need (in a few cases) to pay heavy fines imposed in return for the prolongation of monastic life, as well as economic and social circumstances beyond monastic control. The large sums demanded of all but four abbeys for the French war (ranging from £40 to over £66)[76] must have hastened and intensified a general malaise.

The commissioners visiting Valle Crucis (1535) wrote to Cromwell that it was: 'Indebted to the king and others, 300 marks'.[77] This was slightly more than its gross income as recorded in the *Valor* that year.[78] Its principal creditor was William Brereton (4 August 1534; £100)[79] newly appointed its Steward, who was granted the tithes of Ruabon 'for which he paid nothing'.[80] A further £300 (16 December 1535) was borrowed from Sir William Penizon, a royal courtier,[81] and Giles

Brugge,[82] a London clothier. Penizon was rewarded with the lease of Wrexham Abbot manor, and it was he who financed John Durham's appointment to the abbacy.[83] Durham's failure to meet his commitments saw not only Lord Rochford troubled in conscience,[84] but also one of the abbot's sureties 'in irons and strait keeping', in the prison of the King's Bench.[85] In June 1536, Valle Crucis was still owing £100, if not much more indirectly, to the Crown,[86] and it could be that it finished its days in debt to the tune of almost £500.

Llantarnam raised (from William Jones and Lewis Blethin – local gentry) no less than £360 in December 1533–January 1534. At its dissolution some £200 was still owing to twenty-two people.[87] At Aberconwy, the £200 Richard ap Rhys had borrowed from 'his poor brethren', in order to obtain the abbacy,[88] probably stemmed from the £240 lodged at the abbey by his elder brother, Ellis Price, in the autumn of 1534 in return for the mortgage of Hiraethog Grange.[89] Tintern was in debt to Richard Southwell (£40)[90] and Richard Herbert (£49).[91]

The survey of Margam (23 August 1536) noted debts of £32,[92] but was probably ignorant of a far greater obligation (£70) due to the neighbouring abbey of Neath, and granted (12 September 1532) for 'the reparation of our house as in other necessaries'.[93] Of all the abbeys, Neath, perhaps, ended its days in the strongest financial position,[94] yet – as noted before – its last abbot 'dangered himself and his friends very far' with its redemption.[95]

The great bulk of money owed by the abbeys was never repaid by them. It was left to the Court of Augmentations in the immediate post-Suppression years: (i). to determine the validity of the claims presented – they were mostly upheld but sometimes found to have 'no vigour in law'; and (ii) to determine compensation. This might be accorded in full, more often it was partial. Letice Harper received in so-called 'full recompense' but £40 of the £60 lent by her late husband, a merchant tailor of London, to Valle Crucis.[96] Edmund Turner was awarded £10 of the £14 6s 8d. he claimed from arrears of his annuity from Tintern.[97] Abbot Lleision of the still functioning Neath received but £30 of the £40 outstanding from Margam.[98] In these instances, it could be that abbeys had refunded part of their loans but, if so, the Court did not record this. Llantarnam did manage to reimburse half its debt of £360 to Lewis Blethin and William Jones.[99]

Annuities

Many monasteries raised a relatively small amount of ready cash in the last years of monastic life by making grants of corrody (residential entitlement) to lay-folk *(Chapter 9)*, but practicable considerations limited the amount of money obtainable in this way. Another means was by the grant of non-residentiary annuities. Many of these related to pensioned officers and servants – and brought in no down-payment, but others were given in return for unspecified favours, favours which, in part at least, may have been financial. Some annuities went, as the future became uncertain, to powerful potential patrons – as those granted to Thomas Cromwell and officers of the Court of Augmentations. Strata Marcella made an unusually large grant of £13 13s 4d to Lord Powis.[100] Legal personalities receiving monastic annuities included: Maurice ap David, attorney (£1; 1533),[101] and Gruffydd Leyson, 'doctor of laws' (£1 6s 8d; 1538),[102] from Strata Florida, as well as John Price, the London-based 'principal registrar of ecclesiastical causes' (£2; 1535) from Margam.[103]

The motive for a grant of an annuity was frequently masked behind a generalisation: Basingwerk (1534) awarded Sir John Donne of Utkinton £4 p.a. for 'favours and friendship shown';[104] Tintern (1535) gave Edmund Turner £2 p.a. for 'good turns in time of need';[105] Whitland (1537) granted John Prescott £4 p.a. for 'various causes and considerations'.[106] Strata Florida (15 August 1533) allowed a clerk, Philip ap John, £4 p.a. 'out of the coffers of the abbey' for 'good counsel, help and advice'. The next day, his future assured, Philip resigned the parish of Cefn-Llys in favour of one Brother Hugh Jones – maybe a religious the abbey wished to place.[107] The 'favour', 'friendship', 'service', shown was in some cases certainly a fiscal one – as probably the 'great liberalities' which gained John Dorman and Richard Greenway an annuity from Strata Florida (10 May 1537).[108] Whitland's grant six months later, also to Dorman, was explicitly made in return 'for a certain pecuniary service'.[109]

In this way, Strata Florida burdened itself with the promised payment of nearly £20 per year, and three-quarters of this was arranged in its last two full years of life (1537, 1538). Annuities of these kinds totalled some £12 at Neath and £13 at Whitland. In addition, most monasteries had a heavy outgoing in stipends and pensions to officers and servants. Annuities were payable at given dates and, sometimes, the place of payment is specified. John Thomas was to receive his £2 13s 4d from Strata Florida within a month of the feasts of St James (25 July) and St Luke (18 October) 'at the altar of blessed Mary within the monastery'.[110] A pension awarded to a former Abbot of Grace Dieu was to be paid, at stated feasts 'between 8 a.m. and 11 a.m. at the baptismal font in the parish church of Monmouth'.[111] The medieval church, and its baptistry in particular, was a convenient business centre. To make distant payments, monasteries engaged agents and lawyers.

As with alleged loans, the Court of Augmentations scrutinised carefully all monastic grants of annuities, though mostly they were upheld. They were certainly valued by their recipients, as was exemplified at Tintern. On 20 January, 1522, its new abbot (Richard Wyche) granted £5 yearly to one of his monks, John Gethin, because of his 'manifold labours, charges and expenses'. Payment ceased after nine or so years, when the monk, acting through two lay sponsors, sued the abbot 'at the common law'. Arbitration halted these proceedings, but after the Suppression, Gethin, now claiming to be 'in great necessity', sought to have the ex-abbot subpoenaed to appear before the Court of Chancery. Wyche, in turn, complained to the Court of Augmentations that Gethin, and also Edmund Turner, 'do daily vex and sue him in the Court of Chancery'.[112] Turner, an official of the Earl of Worcester, Tintern's former steward, was dead by November 1539.[113]

Conventual Buildings

The state of ruin into which abbey buildings fell after their closure is, by and large, to be attributed to the stripping of lead from their roofs, the plunder of masonry, and so on, but in some instances the process of decay started well before the

Suppression. As early as about 1490, Tintern was 'threatened in ruin in its walls, roofs, houses and granges (by) the passage of years and (by) negligence and incompetence'.[114] By about 1528, the 'greater part' of Strata Marcella was 'broken down',[115] and when, shortly after its dissolution, Lord Powis came to view his property, he found the abbey only 'a mass of walls in decay'.[116]

Margam needed substantial repairs by 1532,[117] whilst in 1535 at Valle Crucis both 'monastery and church' were 'in great decay'.[118] By 1538, at Strata Florida, the refectory and infirmary were 'mere ruins'.[119] Very small communities no longer required the buildings that once occupied far greater numbers, and perhaps could not afford to maintain them properly. A brighter note obtained at Llantarnam (1532) where there were plans to build 'an arch in the body of the church', and a new processional entrance off its cloister.[120]

Numerical Strength

When conventual life ceased between 1536 and 1539, there were still some seventy-five White Monks in Wales,[121] and this must pose the question: Was the total dissolution justified? Would not reformation (in the true sense of renewal) and redeployment have been the fairer ways to proceed? In certain monasteries there were perhaps only two or three monks left,[122] but Tintern and Strata Florida had thirteen and twelve respectively, Neath and Whitland about eight apiece. Ought not the surviving monks to have been regrouped in three revived foundations – perhaps at Neath, Strata Florida and Tintern, giving each house a community twenty-five monks strong? It was not to be, and for at least four old-stagers eviction from their home of many years must have been a bitter and difficult wrench. Apart from Richard Bromley of Valle Crucis and William Leicester of Cwmhir *(Chapter 5)*, they were: Henry Norton, a monk of Strata Marcella for forty-five years or more,[123] and David Vaughan of Aberconwy, about seventy years old when his abbey closed.[124]

In the last years of monastic life few new vocations can be traced in the Welsh houses, but this is, in part, due to the lack of extant ordination lists for three of the Welsh dioceses. Even some traditionally Welsh abbeys had an infilling (for whatever reason) of English monks, as John Porter at Aberconwy[125] and Richard Smith at Strata Florida.[126] There were a few desertions from the ranks. The Oath of Supremacy was signed (in the Usk Deanery in 1534) by a Cistercian, William Burford, 'dismissed from his monastery',[127] but (given his name) he could have been from England. An apostate monk of Valle Crucis (1535) was imprisoned in Holt Castle.[128] Henry Huskin of Neath was given permission to change his habit (for that of a secular cleric) and hold a benefice three years before its suppression.[129]

So far as *spiritual strength* was concerned, enough has been said *(Chapter 5)* to show that matters varied from monastery to monastery. At Valle Crucis no monk was found 'fit for abbot except the prior',[130] but at Tintern Richard Wyche, its last abbot, preferred to keep 'this high feast of our Blessed Lady' with his community, rather than hasten to the beck and call of Cromwell.[131] A former monk of Cwmhir later had affectionate remembrance of his father-immediate (of Whitland) 'our father, William',[132] but at Strata Marcella the Abbot purported to sell the abbey even before the Crown could lay hands on it.[133] Fortunately not all was lost, in several abbeys there were definite signs of life, and these should have been encouraged rather than extinguished.

Evidence of John Leland

Valuable insights are gained from the eye-witness accounts of this traveller and antiquary who visited Wales after the first wave of suppressions (1536/37) and before the total extinction of Cistercian life (1539). He was able to describe Llantarnam as 'lately suppressed',[134] but also to note that 'Ty Gwyn ar Tav *[Whitland]*, Barnardines, still stondeth'.[135] He conversed with surviving monks. The Abbot of Whitland spoke to him in Welsh, and told him 'a meri tale'. A monk of Strata Florida told him 'for a certainty that Newport in Kemeysland is called Tredraith in Welsh'.[136] Neath, it seemed to Leland, was 'the fairest abbey of all Wales', but he saw 'no church of such length' as that at Cwmhir.[137]

Leland drew attention to the Savigniac element within the Cistercian family: the *'fratres grisei'* he noted at Basingwerk and Neath.[138] He commented on the abundant woodland on Cistercian lands, but noted the wastage of it around Strata Florida. He told of the partial state of ruin of that abbey, but also mentioned its 'meanly walled cemetery', the extent of its estates, its lead mine and its inland fishing potential.[139] Another visitor to Strata Florida in its last days was Edward Waters, the Particular Receiver for the monasteries already dissolved, who thanked its abbot for the 'good cheer' afforded him there.[140]

Mechanics of Dissolution

The Suppression of the monasteries was foreshadowed by the Act of Supremacy (1534) and the compilation of the *Valor Ecclesiasticus* (1535).[141] It is perhaps significant that no Cistercian signatures affirming the former are known for Wales, whilst the latter survey had little part, if any, in determining priorities so far as the dissolution of the Welsh abbeys was concerned. Later in 1535, three Commissioners, expert in law, were appointed to visit the religious houses of Wales and to report back to Cromwell. They were Adam Becanshaw (a priest) and John Vaughan of Narberth (Pembs.), as well as Ellis ap Robert whose commission was cancelled.[142] The two remaining toured north Wales in the late summer and autumn of 1535, and visited south Wales between 11 November 1535 and 28 April 1536,[143] spending perhaps part of that winter in London. It may be that Dr Vaughan carried out the concluding stages of the visitation alone.[144]

The findings of the Commissioners are only known from their letters to Cromwell, as the *Registry of Visitation* they kept is now lost.[145] At Aberconwy they effectively deposed the Abbot and planned to do the same at Valle Crucis, but 'the deposition of abbots and traffic in the vacated posts robbed the examination of all integrity and respect'.[146] Dr Vaughan writing to Cromwell (1 March 1536) said: 'I hear *by the common people* that the houses of monks in Wales, also Tintern . . . are greatly abused and have transgressed the king's injunctions'.[147] In another letter (28 April) he penned to his master, he wrote: 'Help me to get one of the abbies . . . so that I may be able to do you more service'.[148] He got Grace Dieu, but later found a more substantial reward in Whitland. Hearsay evidence, and a self-seeking nature, coloured his reports to London.

In the summer of 1536 came the 'survey' of the monasteries. On this occasion they were taken into the King's hands, but then were left in a state of suspended animation[149] for weeks or even months. Precise dates are largely lacking for north Wales, but in south Wales the 'survey' came largely in June 1536: Grace Dieu on the 6th, Llantarnam on the 10th, Tintern about the same time and Margam on the 20th. Cwmhir's 'survey' took place on about 25 August, that of Llanllŷr nunnery not until around 1 October.[150]

The subsequent interval before the actual day of 'suppression' lasted from a little over ten weeks in the case of Margam to roughly six months at Cwmhir. During this period the monasteries could no longer legally transact any business as corporate bodies, and they had to keep careful accounts of their expenditure. Margam kept a book of accounts for this purpose which told of payments totalling £33 made to twenty-seven people, including a launderer and the keeper of Briton Ferry; a further £27 was expended on other essentials – including food, beer, and the hospice.[151] The like accounts for Cwmhir noted the 'twenty-four weeks and five days' of its suspension.[152] Its small community received four bushels of wheat and five of malt; the monks of Llantarnam two cows and six sheep.[153]

It was an interlude of considerable uncertainty for the monks, no doubt hoping their house would be spared. For the most part, it was not to be so. A new set of Commissioners – local gentry – Thomas Johns, Walter Herbert and John Phillips, together with Edward Waters (as Receiver) and Edward Gostwyke (as Auditor) – were appointed in south Wales to attend to the formalities of the actual day of suppression at each doomed abbey.[154] The late summer of 1536 saw the end of Margam (23 August), Llantarnam (27 August), and Grace Dieu and Tintern (3 September).[155] At Margam there is note of the common seal being broken on the day of dissolution,[156] and of various payments being made. The Commissioners recorded these in a 'Book of particulars' now lost, but incorporated into the first Receivers' Accounts.[157]

These accounts note the numbers of monks and monastic servants, and the payments they received, as for: Margam (nine monks, £9 6s 8d, between them; fifteen 'yeoman' servants, sharing £10 8s 4d; thirteen 'hinds' [youths or labourers] £9 17s 0d). Tintern (twelve monks, £8 8s 0d; thirty-five servants, £16 5s 1d); Grace Dieu (one monk – apart from the abbot – 13s 4d); Llantarnam (four monks, 35s; seventeen servants, £5 11s 0d[158] – there had been six monks there on its day of 'survey'; possibly two left before its closure).

The average payment to each monk (taking these abbeys as a whole) works out at 15s 6d, and to each servant, at 9s 7d. It ranged from just over £1 per monk to under 9s at Llantarnam. Did these hand-outs represent arrears of pocket money ('wages') commonly received by the Cistercians at this time,[159] or were they meant as a very necessary aid to religious thrown out into the world, and, if so, was length of service taken into account? Certain monastic officials were secure for the time being (as the bailiffs of Llantarnam and Whitland), performing after the Suppression their accustomed duties but now on behalf of the Crown.

Wintry conditions, difficulties in communications, and political unrest,[160] may have played a part in delaying the suppression of Llanllŷr nunnery until 26 February 1537 and Cwmhir until 2 March.[161] Its Abbot rode to London on 2 February (returning home on 15 February) probably on business to do with its dissolution. The last Abbot of Strata Marcella also rode to London to surrender his monastery, perhaps in the spring of 1536.[162]

The detailed evidence available for the abbeys of south-east Wales is mostly lacking for those of north Wales. Their dates of closure can only be judged approximately. Basingwerk[163] and Valle Crucis[164] probably saw monastic life end during the autumn of 1536 – the monks of the latter received over £10 in 'wages'.[165] Aberconwy[166] and Cymer[167] survived until sometime in the spring of 1537. The commissioners for north Wales were led by William Stumpe, a JP and clothier of Malmesbury, as Receiver.[168] He, too, benefited from the Suppression, receiving not only a lease of Aberconwy's Quirt Grange,[169] but also Malmesbury Abbey itself – part of which he converted into a textile mill.[170]

The delayed suppression (until the early spring of 1539), or, more correctly, the re-foundation, of Neath, Strata Florida and Whitland, may have seen a technical but real break in their corporate existence. When the latter two houses were 'surveyed' in 1536, their superiors were described as 'lately abbot',[171] though both were re-appointed.[172] Strata Florida, whose seal may already have been confiscated, had a new one engraved: 'After the restitution by the king . . . impressed with the arms of the king'.[173]

The extension of conventual life at these abbeys allowed them to be a temporary refuge for a few of the monks cast out of their homes in the closures of 1536–37. Henry Norton, an elderly monk of Strata Marcella, moved to its mother-house of Whitland.[174] William Jones, a former abbot of Cwmhir still living there about 1530, may be the monk of that name residing at Strata Florida in 1539.[175] To Neath came, from the now suppressed abbey of Furness, one John Estgate. Henry VIII was suspicious (perhaps because Furness had been involved in the Pilgrimage of Grace), wondering why 'he prefers that place'.[176] Estgate's choice was perhaps prompted by Neath being, like his own abbey, a Savigniac foundation.

All these were short-lived opportunities, as also for John Gethin and Nicholas Acton, both monks of Tintern, who, on its earlier dissolution, transferred to its daughter-house at Kingswood (Gloucs.) becoming respectively parish priest and cellarer.[177] Contrariwise, a monk of Fountains, Robert Morreby, who had been living at one of the now suppressed abbeys of Wales, returned home to his abbey. On 3 May 1538, at the abbot's table there, he spoke allegedly seditious words. Overheard by influential layfolk, he was executed three months later for treason.[178]

The Fate of the Monks

The monks of the houses dissolved in 1536–37 received, so far as we can tell, no assistance from the State – save for their arrears of pocket-money. Their abbots fared better, receiving annual pensions ranging from £4 p.a. in the case of John Gruffydd of humble Grace Dieu to £24 for Richard Wyche of prestigious Tintern. The status and wealth of a dissolved monastery, rather than length of service, perhaps determined the amount of abbatial pension awarded. The last abbots of Aberconwy and Valle Crucis – who occupied their office for barely a year – received no less than £20 and £23 respectively.[179] (In addition, Richard ap Rhys of the former house also gained the parishes of Eglwys-fach and Llanbadrig).[180] The much longer serving Abbot of Cymer, Lewis ap Thomas (24 November 1538) now Bishop of Shrewsbury, assigned his pension (of only £6 13s 4d)[181] to the Crown Receiver, William Stumpe.[182]

The religious of Neath, Strata Florida and Whitland, which survived until 1539, were the most fortunate. Their abbots received the princely sum of £40 p.a. each;[183] ten times the pittance granted the Abbot of Grace Dieu (1536)[184] and the Abbess of Llanllŷr (1537). (Her £4 was exactly one-tenth of the nunnery's value as credited in the *Valor Ecclesiasticus* – in the compilation of which she at first refused to co-operate).[185] The Abbot of Neath also held the rectory of Cadoxton, worth a further £8 per year.[186] The monks of those three abbeys were also awarded annual pensions, averaging a little over £3.[187] In these cases, length of service may have been taken into account.

A necessary concomitant of the Suppression was the granting of ecclesiastical dispensations to religious, permitting them to wear henceforth secular garb instead of monastic habit. Such licences, recorded in the Faculty Office Registers, are valuable in revealing the names and numerical strength of the Welsh Cistercians at the Dissolution.[188] That there are no records of dispensations for the monks of Basingwerk or Strata Marcella might reflect the extreme paucity then of their communities. The record of only two dispensations for Llantarnam is more surprising: could it be, as has been suggested, that they continued their monastic life remotely in the hills? A similar suggestion for the monks of Cwmhir appears to have little foundation in fact.[189] Llantarnam was a different case. There is good reason to believe that its monks continued their community life at Pen-rhys, protected by the 'sixteen Stradling bastards', and where (as late as 1550) there was 'a full choir of monks'.[190]

Some dispossessed Cistercians found clerical positions after their eviction. Of the abbots, Lewis ap Thomas of Cymer became Bishop of Shrewsbury; Richard Talley of Strata Florida *may* have been Archdeacon of Cardigan;[191] and John ap Rhys of Strata Marcella was to be dean of Pontesbury.[192] His brother, Richard of Aberconwy, became Rector of Eglwys-fach and Llanbadrig, whilst Lleision ap Thomas of Neath, was Rector of Llangatwg-iuxta-Nedd – on his monastery's doorstep. Thomas Perpin (*alias* Pierpoint), sometime abbot of Grace Dieu, was chantry priest of Holy Trinity, Bristol, and, later, perpetual curate of Cirencester.[193]

Of the ordinary monks: David Owain of Aberconwy became vicar of Eglwys-bach;[194] John Gethin and Nicholas Acton of Tintern, after their sojourn at Kingswood, became the parish priests, respectively, of Newnham and Hewelsfield (Gloucs.)[195] – the latter a church formerly of the patronage of the abbey. William Thomas, a monk of Cwmhir in 1527, *may* have been the stipendiary priest of like name (William ap Thomas) at its former grange chapel at Gwernygo in 1547.[196] William Machyn of Tintern served as a chantry priest at Henbury (Gloucs.),[197] whilst John York, the monk-bailiff of two of Strata Florida's granges, now ministered to its former parishioners.[198] Richard Bromley, former prior of Valle Crucis, lived in Wrexham,[199] and

William Leicester, former pretender at Cwmhir, in Llanfihangel-in-Ceri;[200] could it be he also resided at Gwernygo, forming a mini-community there?

The pension lists for 1553 show that at least twenty-one former Welsh Cistercians were then still alive,[201] including six former abbots.[202] William Jones, sometime Abbot of Cwmhir, died shortly after the suppression of his eventide home at Strata Florida.[203] Nicholas Pennant, former Abbot of Basingwerk, died in 1548/9, requesting burial in Holywell churchyard.[204] Bishop Lewis ap Thomas died in 1561,[205] and when Richard ap Rhys, last Abbot of Aberconwy died in or after 1589,[206] there can have been few, if any, Welsh Cistercians still alive.

Provision for Parishioners

Especially in the cases of the remoter monasteries, which had permission to give the Sacraments to their servants and tenants, the closure of the monasteries meant the loss of spiritual services to which the local populace had become accustomed. Within six weeks of the suppression of Cwmhir (2 March 1537) Edward Beawpe and others, planned to 'build a chapel in Maelienydd in the honour of Jesus . . . to have the sacraments and sacramentals administered'. With this in mind, they sought the return from the still-functioning Strata Florida of a famed 'picture of Jesus', formerly the property of Cwmhir which Abbot Talley of Strata Florida had purchased from the Crown Receiver and Auditor.[207] The chapel stood perhaps where the present parish church stands, within or adjacent to the former monastic precinct.

At Strata Florida, the local populace – numbering some three hundred houseling people – and dwelling up to seven or more miles from their parish church, had a chapel built for them within the monastery well before the Dissolution. The two chaplains appointed to serve them were paid out of the revenue of the third part of tithes granted the abbey in 1340. After the Suppression, the Receiver discharged the priests because he had no warrant for them, but local pressure culminated in a stipend of £5 6s 8d for the continuance of worship in 'the chapel of Stratflur', now served by the former monk, John York.[208]

At Margam, repairs were made 'to the chancel', about 1537 to 1539 and again perhaps around 1552.[209] By 1612 its belfry had been 're-edified', and part of the church covered[210] – perhaps the nave, now the parish church.[211] As noted elsewhere, spiritual provision was also maintained in certain former grange chapels: as Gwern-y-go (of Cwmhir), Llanfair (of Dore) and Lân Tav (of Whitland).

Disposal of Effects

The first post-Suppression accounts rendered by the Receivers, included detailed lists of the chattels of the several abbeys;[212] the more valuable items were sent to London,[213] others were sold locally.[214] Precise note was made, by weight, of monastic plate. Richest in this respect was probably Tintern with a total of 496 oz;[215] Margam could boast over 130 oz.[216] Poor Cwmhir had only 9½ oz of silver plate.[217] The scanty nature at some houses of the ornaments listed suggest that (as a cope at Tintern)[218] some had been hidden from the Commissioners. At Tintern were found only one crozier, four chalices and patens, two jewelled silver gilt crosses, and two censers with an incense boat. At Margam comes mention of a reliquary, and at Llantarnam of a red velvet cope with matching Eucharistic vestments.[219] Other goods accounted for by the Receivers included £53 worth of corn at Margam and £14 worth of uncut corn at Tintern[220] – both suppressed perhaps before harvesting had been completed

Not the least of the effects of the Dissolution upon the local populace was that the abbey bells fell silent, and no longer punctuated each day. Valuable objects, they were cut down and later removed, often sold. The six bells of Margam[221] and the three, possibly four, bells of Neath[222] were eventually bought by a London grocer, John Coore, and removed on his behalf to Bristol.[223] He also bought the three bells of Grace Dieu which found their way to Bristol *via* Monmouth, and the solitary bell of Cwmhir – which was transported to Caerleon en route for London.[224] Water transport played a role, but it was not until 1555, or later, that Coore received some of these bells.[225]

Tintern's four bells were bought by the Earl of Worcester;[226] the three bells of Whitland – still hanging in the autumn of 1539 – were sold to 'the town of Whitland',[227] and the three bells of Strata Florida to the parish of Caron.[228] The four bells of Llantarnam were later bought by William Jones (a local bigwig with court connections) and William Morgan.[229]

The two bells of Llanllŷr nunnery were sold to Sir William Thomas, who also bought the four bells of Carmarthen Priory.[230] A solitary bell was noted at Llanllugan,[231] three at Basingwerk,[232] two at Valle Crucis – which eventually found their way to the churches of Baschurch and Great Ness (Shropshire),[233] and three at Strata Marcella – sold, allegedly unlawfully, to the parish of Chirk.[234] The number of bells at Aberconwy is not on record, but, all told, at least forty Cistercian bells fell silent by 1539.

More serious than the cutting down of bells was the removal of lead from the roofs of the monastery churches and conventual buildings, because this initiated and hastened their decay and depredation. The poet of Basingwerk's closing years told how it was 'roofed with lead, and ornamented with glass windows'.[235] This happy state of affairs soon came to an end. As early as 1538, six 'fothers' (5.85 tons) of lead from Basingwerk may have been used for reparations at Holt Castle,[236] and, in 1546, nearly sixty tons were transported to Dublin to cover Dublin Castle and other Crown buildings in Ireland.[237] There yet remained forty-five tons at the former monastery.[238] Lead, being an extremely heavy commodity, had to stay on site until required elsewhere.

This was also true at Tintern, where its lead (valued at £124) was still on site in 1541, when William Wilson and Christopher Dray, 'the king's plumbers', were paid £8 to melt it down.[239] The lead of Strata Florida was eventually moved to Aberystwyth where, as late as 1555, there remained 'eleven score sows' of it, each 'sow'[240] weighing 100 lb.[241] The largest recorded haul of lead available to the Crown came from Margam: some ninety tons, melted down by 1539 into 415 'sows'.[242] Valued at £372, it was later sold (indirectly) to three Glamorgan merchants.[243].

At Llantarnam, the sum of £15 was paid to the 'plumbers, carpenters, tilers and labourers' for cutting down the bells, removing and melting the lead (into eight 'sows'), and weighing both. A further 18s was paid for the carriage of wood for charcoal. The work was completed within one year of its suppression. The comparative paucity of lead at Grace Dieu is implied by the lower wages paid there; they amounted to only 10s 10½d.[244] The lead of Valle Crucis was melted down by workers from Minera.[245] Allegedly unlawful stripping of lead was carried out at Strata Marcella and Whitland. Figures for Cwmhir, Cymer and Neath are not on record.

Further Depredations and Plunder

Much stone from Aberconwy (Maenan), as well as over a hundred oaks from abbey land, were used to repair the Shire or Justice Hall and town walls of Caernarfon. Transport of timber and stone to Caernarfon was by water both from Maenan (using three or four 'pickards' of three, five and seven ton weight) and (several boat-loads of timber) from its grange at Rhedynog-felen.[246] Local gentry bought useful items from the abbey fabric, and Pennant (1773–76) described Gwydir mansion as 'built out of the abbey materials'.[247]

The plunder of Strata Marcella was less legitimate. At fault, seemingly, was Nicholas Purcell, Crown tenant of the abbey and later sheriff of Montgomeryshire (1553).[248] His alleged role in the destruction of the abbey, included the sale of its three bells to the parish of Chirk, of the organ to St Mary's, Shrewsbury, of lead guttering to repair Oswestry Castle, and of large amounts of stone to local inhabitants – some such stone has lately come to light during the demolition of houses in Welshpool. All the glass in the eight or nine windows of the church was removed, and church plate and vestments disappeared.[249] Destruction was long continued: as late as 1634, a new lessee of 'Streetmarshall Farme' (on the site of the cloister) was allowed for repair work 'stone out of the Abbye there'.[250]

In similar activity at Whitland, the chief culprits were Sir John Vaughan, the former commissioner to whom the site had been leased, together with Sir John Perrot – and Richard Vaughan, elder and younger. The commission now appointed to investigate was obstructed at first, but its report told of the wholesale removal of iron and lead, glass and timber. Perrot took much freestone to Laugharne to erect a house for himself, whilst Richard Vaughan exchanged cart-loads of freestone in return for livestock. Only one great chamber and two smaller rooms escaped their attention, as they were under lock and key.[251] Little wonder that remains at Maenan, Strata Marcella and Whitland are today diminutive or nil. No wonder that in the course of their 1911 meeting, the Cambrians, passing by the site of Maenan 'did not consider it worthwhile to pay it even the empty homage of an afternoon call'.[252]

At the dissolution of Valle Crucis, Edward Almer, deputy keeper of Holt Castle, set up legitimately twenty-five 'fote' of its glass in the castle 'for his commodity', but later, together with lead originating from Combermere Abbey, removed it to his own house at Gresford.[253] About 1584, several local inhabitants were accused of making severe depredations to the 'mansion house' of Valle Crucis and pulling down the 'great and high stone walls'. The accused countered that the mansion house had been 'in continual decay since the dissolution', and that many of the stones taken for building their houses were lying scattered around.[254] Two years later, Camden could speak of Valle Crucis as 'wholly decaied'.[255]

Less is on record concerning other monasteries. There is a plausible tradition that some of the coloured glass now in Llanasa church, and the ornate oak roof of the south aisle of Cilcain church, derived from Basingwerk,[256] as may also the wooden sedilia in Nerquis church.[257] Certainly, the choir-stalls of Basingwerk were, soon after the Suppression, set up in the church of St Mary-on-the-Hill, Chester.[258] Architectural evidence (including masons' marks) demonstrates five bays of the north nave arcade of Cwmhir as being erected (in 1542) in Llanidloes church.[259] A late-Norman arch from Margam (much later) found its way to the church of St Bride's-super-Ely.[260] It is very unlikely, though, that (as local legend would have it) the rood screens of Conwy and Llanrwst, Llanegryn, Llananno and (formerly at) Newtown, ever came from Maenan, Cymer, Cwmhir and Strata Florida, respectively.[261]

Monasteries where in later centuries stone was robbed for building purposes probably included Cwmhir (for Abbey Cwmhir and Ty Faenor mansions),[262] Grace Dieu (for the Herbert residence of Parc Grace Dieu, erected by 1588),[263] and Llantarnam (the Elizabethan home of the Morgan family). The latter was rebuilt again (*c.* 1837) by Blewitt, who also demolished its Great Gate.[264] Stone from Cwmhir was used in the reconstruction of Llananno and Llanbister churches, whilst several hundred tons helped to improve the roads of the neighbourhood.[265] Dressed stone from Strata Marcella can yet be seen at the former Pool Quay vicarage (1872),[266] whilst the like was used to ornament the fire place at Penybont Uchaf farm, Llanwrtyd Wells (1770s).[267] At all these monastic sites medieval remains are vestigial. Much more survives at Cymer, even though it was in Elizabethan times 'a quarry for stones'.[268]

Deliberate destruction, let alone lack of maintenance, enhanced natural decay. Cwmhir was stormed by cannon fire during the Civil War (1644).[268a] The chapter house roof at Margam (1799) caved in after severe frosts – for years its only protection from the elements had been 'a thick oiled paper'.[269] The collapse of much of the south transept at Basingwerk (1901) damaged in turn the dormitory and chapter house.[270] Tintern has seen on-going works to ensure safety and stability.

Secular uses to which former conventual buildings were put greatly increased wear and tear. In the early days of the Industrial Revolution, metal smelting took place in the former kitchen at Neath.[271] Sir Thomas Mansel (1612) kept his coach 'in an out Isle of Margam church where lyme and Rubish used to be kept'. Its chapter house was used for coal storage (1736) and its vestibule, out of the cloister, as a brew house.[272] The dormitory of Valle Crucis was used as a hayloft (from at least 1830 to 1878),[273] its refectory was employed as a barn and threshing floor, and the two top steps of its pulpitum stairs were used as sharpening stones.[274] Cymer saw its aisle converted into a cattle shed, and the site of its high altar become a pigsty.[275]

The actual abbey sites were valued at very little at first,[276] and indeed some (Cymer, Llanllŷr, Maenan and Whitland) continued to be held by the former superiors for a few months.[277] Within a few years of the Dissolution, however, the sites were leased, or sold, largely to local people. These included John Vaughan of Narberth (Whitland),[278] Henry ap Harry of Llanasa (Basingwerk),[279] Richard Cromwell *alias* Williams (Neath)[280] and William Pickering (Valle Crucis).[281] Basingwerk later descended, by marriage, to the Mostyns of Talacre.[282] Maenan changed hands a number of times

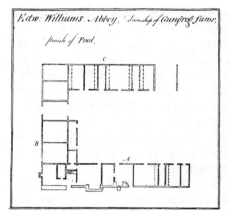

Fig. 28: Abbey Farm, Strata Marcella. *(NLW, Powis Castle Survey, 1780; By courtesy of the Trustees of the Powis Estate).*

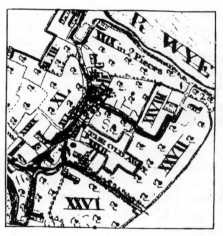

Fig. 29: Tintern: The Eastern Precinct. *(NLW, Badminton Plan, Vol. 2 (6), 1764).*

before 1580, but finally passed to the Wynnes of Melai.[283] Strata Florida, granted first to the Devereuxs, passed to the Stedmans and, by marriage in the 18th century, to the Powells of Nanteos.[284] In some instances, parts of the monastic buildings (modified) were preserved since they became domestic residences, like the cloister (now vanished) at Strata Marcella *(Fig. 28)*[285] and the dorter range at Valle Crucis.[286] Sir Rice Mansel turned part of Margam into his principal residence,[287] whilst Neath, similarly converted, formed a mansion for the Herberts.[288]

The lease of Tintern to the powerful earl of Worcester (1537)[289] undoubtedly safeguarded it from undue and hasty demolition, and left much to be admired. The earl sometimes resided there,[290] but many of its buildings were sub-let by him. These included (in 1568): 'the laundry-house', a room 'above the gate of the abbey parlour', 'the pantry-house', a 'sewery-house' or 'bark-loft', three stables, one being 'otherwise an oste and kyllynhouse', as well as the gate-house chapel of St Anne, now converted into a dwelling-house. Also let out were the graveyard, and an orchard 'towards low water mark'.[291] By 1579 'le library and le cloyster', were also demised.[292] A century on 'the ground called 'Ye Cloyster', was taken by Capt. Herbert for 10/- p.a.'.[293] Later still, squatters occupied portions of the conventual buildings *(Fig. 29)*.[294]

Post-Dissolution Disputes

The Suppression left in its wake a trail of contention and litigation regarding the rightful ownership or tenancy of former monastic lands, and there were not a few instances where the new landlords were unable to obtain the rents, or tithes, they claimed as their due. Contending parties might appeal to alleged leases of different date, but, more commonly, conflict arose where a conventual lease was said to conflict with a later Crown demise. In the former instance one party laid claim to the Court in Wrexham by virtue of a lease granted by Abbot Salusbury of Valle Crucis (1528–35), the other on the strength of a demise by Abbot Durham (1535–36).[295] An example of the latter cause came when (in 1554) one party claimed Gwern-y-go Grange (formerly of Cwmhir) on the 'colour' of a Crown lease (of 1546), the other claimant asserting a pre-Suppression conventual lease.[296] The Earl of Worcester accused Abbot Wyche of Tintern of demising Modesgate Grange 'within a month or so' before the Suppression, but he denied the charge.[296a] The Abbots of Basingwerk (the tithes of Holywell[297]) and Strata Florida (Aberduhonw Grange[298]) allegedly made pretended leases, *after* their abbeys had been suppressed.

In late Elizabethan days such contentions were reflected by numerous instances of assault and battery. An affray on former lands of Strata Marcella (in Talerddig in the early 1590s) saw Thomas ap Oliver, and sixty other persons, heavily armed with 'swords, staves, forest bills, javelins' and other weapons.[299] (Oliver had been responsible for a non-monastic related dispute, on former land of Cwmhir at Gwern-y-go, when the rioters disguised as women evicted a land-owner and beat his wife 'black and blue').[300] The use of women's clothing – a precursor of the Rebecca riots – had been employed in an armed assault on Strata Marcella land (in Llanerfyl) in 1577.[301] When Hugh Gruffydd and others intruded forcibly on to Cymer's former grange at Abereiddon (1584), its tenant (Hywel ap Gwilym) and his fellows said that they 'dare not venture forth by day lest they should be attacked and assaulted'.[302]

Damage to property occurred when landlords tried to make improvements which limited common rights[303] – as at Neath's Cwrt-y-carnau (the breaking down of enclosures in 1577)[304] and Coed-ffranc (the burning of a hedge in 1581).[305] Disgruntled by the entrenching of Strata Marcella's former 400-acre pasture in Gwern Valley, fifty disguised men met in an ale house to plan action. Perhaps fortified by drink, they then broke down the enclosures and hewed down great oaks.[306] Such disputes had repercussions upon the common people. When late leases made by Aberconwy (1531/32) in Penmynydd (Anglesey) had run their term, the new owner, Owain Williams (1581), forcibly ousted the five tenants who were forced to 'lie in the streets'.[307] A dispute regarding Strata Florida's former land at Bryn Merllwyd meant that the expelled plaintiffs had to 'beg their bread upon the highway'.[308]

The Crown Receivers, and the purchasers of monastic property, experienced severe difficulties in the post-Suppression years. At Cwmhir, of sixty-nine tenants claiming a holding by indenture, only five could prove their title; of some sixty-four leaseholders on former lands of Aberconwy none could, or would, do likewise.[309] Tenants on several former properties of Strata Florida[310] and Valle Crucis[311] declined to pay rents and services. At Rhedynog (of Aberconwy)[312] and Mynyddislwyn (of Llantarnam)[313] obstructive tenants tried to get others to adopt the same attitude. Richard Herbert of Montgomery (1593) was to accuse several persons of confederacy to defeat his claim to the tithes of Llanfair Caereinion (formerly of Llanllugan).[314] The Crown bailiff of Whitland, David Nash, was unable to hold customary courts because of life-threatening riotous assemblies; he said the tenants were 'very desperate persons, far out of all good rule and order'.[315] Dislike of the courts held by the Crown lessees was also shown by tenants on lands formerly of Llanllŷr[316] and Strata Marcella.[317]

Some tenants produced forged documents. A lease purported to have been granted by Strata Florida in 1509 was queried much later (*c.* 1580) because the seal appended was the new seal made after the restoration of the abbey (1537).[318] Another demise allegedly made by Strata Florida was noted as having been: 'forged, that is to say 20th *[year]* is made 30th'.[319] Yet another lease ascribed to the same abbey – of Ffynnon O'er Mill to the monastery's notary [John Gwyn] in 1538 – was allegedly made by 'Richard Dorston, abbot'.[320] He had been abbot (*c.* 1505–13),[321] but was long dead. The Brilley Remembrance (of 1590) remarked, of a lease purportedly granted by Cwmhir in 1502, that: 'This lease seemeth to be forged for the seal is of white wax set on the label[322] with the head downwards, and fastened to the label with green wax on the backside'.[323]

Dissolution or Reformation?

Many factors (internal and external feuds, debt and financial impositions, litigation and distraint, and not least the decline in vocations and the placement of unsuitable abbots) brought the Welsh Cistercian houses to a low ebb by Tudor days. This was, though, no excuse for the wholesale butchery meted to them by Henry VIII and his cronies. There were sufficient numbers left to have formed three sizeable re-grouped communities – in itself an opportunity to shed unsatisfactory superiors. There were abbots of stature, as well as signs of spiritual tone and of care bestowed on monastic buildings. Had three abbeys been retained as power-houses of prayer and worship, much of their land could have been sold off to enable the monks to continue accustomed acts of charity, but with sufficient retained to allow them – in the early spirit of the Order – to return to direct farming. Those monasteries surplus to requirements could have become charitable or educational establishments – perhaps under the aegis of the Order – rather than fall wastefully into decay. Renewal and redeployment, rather than dissolution and eviction, would have breathed new life into the monasteries of Wales.

NOTES

1. Woodward C.W.O. 1966, 48–49.
2. Owen E. 1919, 27.
3. O'Sullivan J.F. 1947, 118.
4. See Chapter 5.
5. PRO, C 1/870, m. 4; E 315/91, f. 24.
6. *LP (Hen. VIII)* X, 374 (902).
7. The others were Dore and, probably, Cymer.
8. *LP (Hen. VIII)* VII, 310(818); PRO, E 315/91, SP 1/84.
9. His appointment may reflect the influence of Stephen Green, the last abbot of Buildwas, who himself had been abbot of Grace Dieu [1515–17].
10. *Fasti Cist. (1)* 219.
11. PRO, LR 1/229, ff. 129–31.
12. *Valor Eccl.* IV, 361.
13. PRO, E 315/43/150; *Cf. Reg. C. Bothe* 305, 309, 318.
14. *LP (Hen. VIII)* IX, 205–06 (607–8); Thomas L. 1930, 32–33.
15. *LP (Hen. VIII)* VIII, 448 (150).
16. *Ibid.* IX, 83 (244).
17. *Ibid.* VIII, 448 (150).
18. O'Sullivan J.F. 1947, 120.
19. Hays R.W. 1963, 161.
20. *LP (Hen. VIII)* XII: Pt. 1, 108 (215).
21. Owen E. 1919, 27.
22. Jones A. 1933, 177; *Cf.* 272–73.
23. Williams D.H. 1984. I, 103–05.
24. Owen E. 1919, 27.
25. PRO, E 321/32, m. 84.
26. *Augm. Rec.* 53.
27. Jones A. 1933, 178.
28. PRO, E 321/10, m. 45.

29. *Augm. Rec.* 96–97; Owen E. 1920, 64, 77,
30. Hawarden R.O. D/NA/73, 74, 78.
31. Glamorgan Archives CL/Deeds II/Montg. Box 3.
32. Owen E. 1919, 30.
33. Williams D.H. 1976a, 91.
34. PRO, C 1/870, m. 21.
35. *Valor Eccl.* IV, 370.
36. Birch W. de Gray. 1902, 143–44.
37. PRO, SC 6 (Hen. VIII) 5156, m. 9r.
38. *Ibid*. m. 4r.
39. *Ibid*. m. 11d.
40. *Ibid*. mm. 6r–7d.
41. *Ibid*. m. 10r.
42. *Ibid*. m. 11r.
43. PRO, SC 6 (Hen. VIII) 6/4903 *passim*; LR 1/228, ff. 129d, 182d–183r, 231–235; 1/229, ff. 79–88.
44. PRO, SC 6 (Hen. VIII) 4903, f. 32.
45. *Ibid*. f. 27.
46. *Salisbury MSS* II, 134–35.
47. PRO, SC 6/4868, m. 4d.
48. PRO, E 315/93, f. 106.
49. PRO, E 315/103, ff. 110–111; LR 1/228, F. 135.
50. PRO, SC 6 (Hen. VIII) 4868, mm. 4d–5r.
51. *Ibid*. m. 12r.
52. *Ibid*. m. 10r; LR 1/228, f. 64; E 315/97, ff. 25–26.
53. *Cf.* PRO, SC 6 (Hen. VIII) 4868, *passim*; LR 1/228, ff. 89, 228; E 315/103, f. 118; *Augm. Rec.* 243.
54. *LP (Hen. VIII)* XIII: Pt. 2, 177 (452–3).
55. PRO, E 318/186, f. 22; E 321/10, m. 45.
56. *Augm. Rec.* 243.
57. Owen E. 1919, 21
58. *Reg. E. Foxe* 377.
59. *LP (Hen. VIII)* X, 434 (1046).
60. *Ibid*. XII: Pt. 1, 108 (215).
61. *Ibid*. XIII: Pt. 1, 577.
62. Williams G. 1967, 96.
63. *LP (Hen. VIII)* XIV: Pt. 2, 321 (782); *Cf.* PRO, E 315/93, ff. 107d–108r; 315/96, f. 120d.
64. PRO, E 315/95, f. 122d; 315/100, f. 353d.
65. See later in this chapter.
66. PRO, E 315/104, f. 189 (2nd nos.).
67. PRO, E 315/99, f. 31d.
68. *West Wales Wills* 155.
69. PRO, LR 6/152/1, m. 2r.
70. Williams S.W. 1889, Appx. lxxxiv–v.
71. PRO, LR 6/152/1, m. 3r; SC 6 (Hen. VIII) 4903, m. 16r.
72. Williams D.H. 1984. I, 107.
73. NLW, Cwrtmawr MS 873D, f. 68.
74. PRO, SC 6 (Hen. VIII) 4903, f. 1; NLW, Cilgwyn Deed 92.
75. *LP (Hen. VIII)* XIV, 602 (1355).
76. *Ibid*. III: Pt. 2, 1047 (2483).
77. *Ibid*. IV, 83 (244); Williams D.H. 1984. I, 108 (*n*.83, for greater detail).
78. Williams G. 1962, 347.
79. PRO, E 326/B. 10140.
80. PRO, E 326/B. 10141. (*n*. 101).
81. PRO, E 315/91, f. 24.
82. PRO, E 315/91, f. 27d.
83. PRO, E 315/91, f. 24d; C 1/870, m. m. 21.
84. *LP (Hen. VIII)* X, 216 (374–902).
85. PRO, C 1/870, m. 21.
86. PRO, SP 1/104, f. 258.
87. Williams D.H. 1976, 86–87.
88. PRO, E 315/131, f. 145; E 178/5086.
89. Hays R.W. 1963, 176.
90. Williams D.H. 1976, 112–13 (for Tintern's debts).
91. PRO, E 315/92, f. 23d; LR 6/152/4, m. 7d.
92. *Cf.* Williams D.H. 1984. I,109.
93. PRO, E 315/100, f. 91.
94. Williams D.H. 1984. I, 109–10.
95. Williams G. 1967, 176.
96. PRO, E 315/92, f. 23d.
97. PRO, LR 6/152/4, m. 7r.
98. PRO, E 315/100, f. 91.
99. Williams D.H. 1976, 86.
100. PRO, E 315/105, f. 71d; E 321/44/116; LR 1/212/34.
101. PRO, LR 1/228, f. 59d.
102. PRO, E 315/102, f. 19d.
103. PRO, E 315/96, f. 237.
104. PRO, E 315/91, f. 88; 315/100, f. 19d.
105. Williams D.H. 1976, 112–13.
106. PRO, E 315/104, f. 126d.
107. PRO, C 1/721, m. 11; E 315/95, f. 67.

108. PRO, E 315/94, f. 247.
109. PRO, E 315/99, f. 31d.
110. PRO, E 315/99, ff. 7d–8r; *Cf.* E 315/94, f. 24d; LR 1/228, f. 57d.
111. Williams D.H. 1976, 64; *Cf.* 113; PRO, STAC 2/29/61.
112. PRO, C 1/799/12; E 321/3/73; Williams D.H. 1976, 112–13.
113. *Worcester Lands* I, 192–93, 212.
114. *Cal. Papal Reg. (L)* XVI, 3–4 (No. 5).
115. Owen E. 1919, 7.
116. *Mont. Collns.* X *(1877) 401–02.*
117. PRO, E 315/100, f. 91; *Cf.* LR6/152/4, m. 6r.
118. *LP (Hen. VIII)* IX, 83 (244).
119. Williams S.W. 1889, Appx. iii.
120. PRO, PROB 11/14, f. 21.
121. *Fasti Cist. (1)* 186–87.
122. Basingwerk, Cymer, Grace Dieu, Strata Marcella.
123. *Reg. T. Myllyng* 181.
124. PRO, E 315/31, f. 45.
125. *Faculty Off.* 91.
126. *LP (Hen. VIII)* VII, 477; PRO, E 315/233, f. 219.
127. Thomas L. 1930, 16.
128. *LP (Hen. VIII)* IX, 83 (244).
129. *Faculty Off.* 38.
130. *LP (Hen. VIII)* IX, 83 (244).
131. PRO, SP 1/85, f. 1133; the feast of the Nativity of the BVM: 8 Sept.].
132. PRO, C 24/29 (Pt. 2).
133. *LP (Hen. VIII)* IX, 308, 349–50; *Augm. Rec.* 463; Owen E. 1919, 20–22.
134. *Itin. J. Leland* III, 45.
135. *Ibid.* III, 58.
136. *Ibid.* III, 123.
137. *Ibid.* III, 51–52.
138. *Ibid.* V, 159–60.
139. *Ibid.* III, 118–23; Williams S.W. 1889, Appx. iii–vii.
140. *LP (Hen. VIII)* XII: Pt. 1, 424 (932).
141. Thomas L. 1930, 19–24.
142. *Ibid.* 32–33; *LP (Hen. VIII)* IX, 205–06 (607-08); NLW, Cernioge Coll. 71.
143. Williams G. 1967, 94.
144. Thomas L. 1930, 36.
145. *Ibid.* 35; Williams G. 1967, 94.
146. Thomas L. 1930, 33.
147. *LP (Hen. VIII)* X, 160 (393).
148. *Ibid.* XIII: Pt. 1, 576.
149. Williams G. 1967, 95.
150. PRO, LR 6/151/1–2.
151. PRO, LR 6/152/1, m. 8d.
152. PRO, LR 6/152/1, m. 3d.
153. Williams D.H. 1976, 87.
154. PRO, LR 6/152/1, m. 7d.
155. PRO, LR 6/152/1.
156. Williams G. 1967, 95.
157. PRO, LR 6/152/1, f. 9d.
158. PRO, LR 6/152/1, *passim.*
159. *Cf.* Chapter 5, and: Williams G. 1967, 367*n.*
160. *Cal. State Papers* I: Pt. 2 (Hen. VIII) 455.
161. PRO, LR 6/152/2.
162. *Mont. Collns.* X (1877) 401–02.
163. *Cf.* Owen E. 1920, 60; *LP (Hen. VIII)* XIII: Pt. 1, 577 (152).
164. *Cf.* Pratt D. 1997, 38; *Augm. Rec.* 71.
165. Pratt D. 1997, 38.
166. *Cf. LP (Hen. VIII)* XII: Pt. 1, 108 (215); XIII: Pt. 1, 577.
167. *Cf. LP (Hen. VIII)* X, 515; PRO, SC 6 (Hen. VIII) 5222.
168. Richardson W.C. 1961, 50; Williams D.H. 1984. I, 118 (*n.* 191).
169. *LP (Hen. VIII)* XIII: Pt. 1, 584.
170. Pratt D. 1997, 34–35.
171. PRO, LR 6/152/1, m. 3r.
172. *LP (Hen. VIII)* XII: Pt. 1, 144, 515.
173. NLW, Cwrtmawr MS 873D, f. 25.
174. *Faculty Off.* 206; Williams D.H. 1976b, 174.
175. Williams D.H. 1976a, 82.
176. *LP (Hen. VIII)* XII: Pt. 1, 315, 395, 399.
177. Williams D.H. 1976, 111.
178. *LP (Hen. VIII)* XIII: Pt. 1, 346 (941–2); Pt. 2, 51–52 (142).
179. *Ibid.* XIII: Pt. 1, 575–77.
180. *Ibid.* XII: Pt. 2, 470 (1311/22–6); PRO, LR 1/212, ff. 177d–178.
181. *LP (Hen. VIII)* XIII: Pt. 1, 576.
182. PRO, LR 1/212/ ff. 181d–182r.
183. *LP (Hen. VIII)* XIV, 362 (747), 602–03 (1355); PRO, LR 1/228, ff. 55d, 63d.
184. *LP (Hen. VIII)* XIII: Pt. 1, 576.
185. Williams D.H. 1975, 165, 167.

186. Birch W. de Gray. 1902, 150.
187. *LP (Hen. VIII)* XIV, 362 (747–48); PRO, E 315/223; LR 6/152/1–4; *MSS in BM* IV, 931–32.
188. *Faculty Off.* passim., where Llantarnam is mistaken for Llanthony [*pers. comm.* Dr M. Gray].
189. Williams J. 1905, 307–08.
190. Matthew D. and A. 1929, 70; Thomas L. 1930, 146–47.
191. *Fasti Cist. (1)* 211.
192. PRO, E 321/37/51; V.C.H. *Shropshire* VIII (1968) 283.
193. Baskerville G. 1927, 108.
194. Hays R.W. 1963, 173.
195. Baskerville G. 1927, 88.
196. *Mont. Collns.* XXVII, 112.
197. PRO, LR 6/149/1–5 (*pers. comm.* Dr M Gray).
198. PRO, LR 1/228, f. 65d; *Augm. Rec.* 27–28.
199. PRO, REG 2/5 (No. 273).
200. PRO, C 24/29 (Pt. 2).
201. Williams D.H. 1984. I, 121 (*n.* 233).
202. Aberconwy, Basingwerk, Cymer, Grace Dieu, Strata Marcella, Valle Crucis [Pratt D. 1997, 39].
203. *LP (Hen. VIII)* XIV: Pt. 1, 362.
204. Hawarden R.O. D/NA/723–24: born *c.* 1495.
205. Pryce A.I. 1923, 8, 17.
206. *Augm. Rec.* 190.
207. Williams D.H.1976a, 86–87.
208. *Augm. Rec.* 27–28; PRO, LR 1/228, f. 65d.
209. PRO, LR 6/152/ 2, 4.
210. *Exch. Proc. (2)* 213.
211. Williams G. 1967, 99.
212. PRO, LR 6/152/1–4 (for S. Wales; missing for N. Wales).
213. Youings J. 1971, 214.
214. *Cf.* PRO, C 115/D.21/1937.
215. PRO, LR 6/152/1 [249 oz. silver gilt; 180, parcel gilt; 40, white silver].
216. PRO, LR 6/152/1, m. 3r.
217. PRO, LR 6/152/2.
218. Williams D.H. 1976, 112; *Cf.* 29.
219. PRO, LR 6/152/1, m. 14d; ['shepe = 'incense boat'].
220. PRO, LR 6/152/1.
221. Weight: 5 mils, 2 cwt, 3 qt, 21 lb; Val. £8: PRO, E 117/13/70, m. 9r; LR 6/152/4, m. 11r.
222. PRO, LR 6/152/4, m. 11d.
223. Owen E. 1896, 265.
224. *Ibid.* 264.
225. PRO, E 117/13/70, m. 9r.
226. Thomas L. 1930, 48, 54. [Weight = 21 cwt. Val.= £10].
227. Owen E. 1896, 625 (for £13 6s. 8d.).
228. PRO, E 117/13/70, m. 9r (for £10 13s. 4d).
229. Thomas L. 1930, 56 (for £39); Williams D.H. 1976, 88.
230. PRO, LR 6/152/1–4.
231. PRO, E 117/13/70, f. 22. [It weighed 1 qtr. 14 lb.).
232. PRO, E 117/13/70, f. 2.
233. *Ibid.*, Pratt D. 1997, 40.
234. *Augm. Rec.* 152.
235. Jones A. 1933, 176.
236. *LP (Hen. VIII)* XIII: 1: 231 (624/3).
237. PRO, E 117/13/71, m. 18; Taylor A.J. 1971, 3; Owen E. 1897, 286.
238. PRO, E 117/13/71, m. 18.
239. Williams D.H. 1976, 112.
240. Such an ingot, stamped with Tudor rose and crown, has lately been excavated at Haverfordwest Priory, (*pers. comm.* Dr S Rees, Cadw).
241. PRO, E 117/10, m. 57; *Cf.* E 117/13/71, m. 22; LR 6/152/4, m. 12d.
242. PRO, LR 6/152/1, m. 3r; 152/4, m. 11r.
243. Thomas L. 1940, 53; PRO, E 117/14, No. 130.
244. PRO, LR 6/152/1–2.
245. Pratt D. 1997, 40.
246. Owen E. 1917, 74–77; for the coffin of Llywelyn ab Iorwerth, see: Hays R.W. 1963, 180.
247. Butler L.A.S. 1963, 30; 1980, 2.
248. *Cf. Mont. Collns.* II, 421–32.
249. Owen E. 1919, 27–28; Williams D.H. 1976b, 176–77; PRO, E 315/516/25–27; *Augm. Rec.* 152–53.
250. Antony House, Cornwall: MS BD 13/103 [*pers. comm.* Mr Graham Thomas, NLW].
251. Owen G.D. 1935, 360–63.

252. Owen E. 1917, 71–72.
253. PRO, C 1/1108, mm. 25–27;
      Pratt D. 1997, 42, 66 (*n.* 16).
254. PRO, E 112/60 (Denbigh) 70;
      Exchq. Proc. (1) 166.
255. *Arch. Camb.* I (1846) 31.
256. Glynne S.R. 1897, 286–87;
      Williams G. 1962, 437.
257. *The Antiquary* IX, 188.
258. RCAHMW 2 *(County of Flint;*
      1912) 41.
259. Radford C.A.R. 1982, 70.
260. Evans A.L. 1958, 34, Pl. (opp. 28).
261. Williams G. 1962, 438.
262. Williams D.H. 1976a, 77.
263. Bradney J.A. II: Pt. 1 (1914) 122 *et*
      seq.; Williams D.H. 1976, 50–58.
264. Williams D.H. 1976, 78. [Lord
      Mansel, by 1744, demolished
      Margam's Great Gate: Evans
      A.L. 1958, 35].
265. Williams D.H. 1976a, 77.
266. *Arch. Camb.* 1890, 248, 250;
      Mont. Collns. XXV (1891) 162.
267. *Country Quest*, Dec. 1977, 41
      [Letter from Mr D Jones,
      Abergwesyn].
268. Ellis T.P. 1936, 46.
268a. Davies J.H. 1999.
269. Randolph J.A. 1905, 24; Donovan
      E. 1805. II, 14.
270. Randolph J.A. 1905, 11; *Cf.*
      Pennant T. 1796, 195.
271. Sutton T.S. 1887, 82.
272. Randolph J.A. 1905, 22; Jones
      D.R.L. 1981, 6.
273. Price G.V. 1952, 129.
274. Butler L.A.S. 1976, 96.
275. Ellis T.P. 1936, 46.
276. PRO, LR 1/228/95d–96r.
277. Jones A. 1937, 270–71.
278. PRO, LR 1/228, f. 53. He also
      leased Pill Priory.
279. *Arch. Camb.* 1878, 70.
280. Williams G. 1967, 101.
281. *LP (Hen. VIII)* XIII: Pt. 1, 586.
282. Jones A. 1933, 3; *Cf.* Hawarden
      R.O. Mostyn of Talacre (Add.)
      MS 678 *et Seq.,* UCNW,
      Bodrhyddan Deed 1255.
283. Butler L.A.S. 1963, 30.
284. Jones Pierce T. 1950, 33.
285. Williams D.H. 1992, 82–83.

286. Evans D.H. 1995, 42.
287. Williams G. 1967, 102.
288. Lewis J.M. 1976a, 30.
289. PRO, LR 6/152/4, m. 9r.
290. *Worcester Lands* (1) 212.
291. NLW, Badm. Manorial 1524, m.
      44.
292. Courtney P. and Gray M. 1991,
      155–56.
293. NLW, Badm. Manorial 2445, f.
      15.
294. Courtney P. and Gray M. 1991,
      153.
295. *Augm. Rec.* 71.
296. *Early Chanc. Proc.* 185.
296a. PRO, C 1/1265/39–40.
297. Jones A. 1933, 178.
298. PRO, E 321/10/45; SP 1 (Hen.
      VIII) XVII/380, f. 195.
299. PRO, STAC 5/J.1/27 (17). For
      south Wales, see: Owen G.D.
      1935, 551–78.
300. PRO, STAC 5/J.27 (17).
301. *Ibid.* 5/V.2/5, V.7/8 (4), V. 8/8
      (26); *Cf.* NLW, Powis Castle
      Deed 10250.
302. *Exchq. Proc. (1)* 225.
303. Owen G.D. 1935, 589–610.
304. PRO, STAC 5/P.54/4 (19).
305. *Ibid.* 5/C.24/15 (24).
306. *Ibid.* 5/H 76/17 (17). *Cf.* Owen
      G.D. 1972, 89–90.
307. *Exchq. Proc. (1)* 17.
308. Owen G.D. 1935, 554.
309. Jones A. 1937, 273.
310. *Augm. Rec.* 32–33.
311. PRO, E 321/18/65.
312. *Augm. Rec.* 54.
313. *Ibid.* 135.
314. Williams D.H. 1975, 163.
315. *Augm. Rec.* 28–29.
316. Williams D.H. 1975, 170–71.
317. Owen E. 1919, 27.
318. PRO, E 321/14/6; *Augm. Rec.*
      29–31.
319. NLW, Cwrtmawr MS 873D, ff.
      25, 31.
320. *Ibid.* f. 45.
321. Carmarthen R.O., Lort Deed
      11/554.
322. 'Label' = the seal-tag.
323. Powell A.D. 1964, 24, 27.

CHAPTER 7

THE CONVENTUAL BUILDINGS

Building Programmes

In their own day, more so perhaps even than now, the Cistercian abbeys of Wales were viewed with admiration. The undoubtedly biased author of the *Brut y Tywysogyon* referred to the church of 'fine workmanship' at Strata Florida,[1] Roger of Wendover (1231) mentioned the 'sumptuous buildings' constructed at Cwmhir,[2] and Thomas of Afan (1349), 'having had a diligent view' of Margam, remarked upon 'the noble and magnificent structure *continually* made in the monastery'[3] – indicating the many decades that such building took. Many monks of those years spent their whole religious life on a building site!

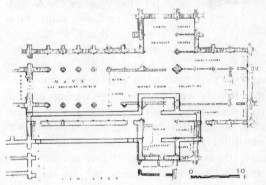

Fig. 30: Neath: the 12th and 13th century churches. *(L.A.S. Butler; Arch. Camb. 1984).*

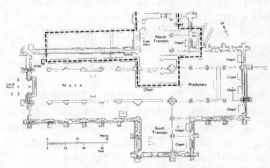

Fig. 31: Tintern: the 12th and 13th century churches. *(Cadw: Welsh Historic Monuments. Crown Copyright).*

These extended building programmes were overseen by officials named as 'master of the works' (Margam, 1307)[4] or 'keeper of the work' (Tintern), 1340–52).[5] Whether, at those late dates, such officers were monks or *conversi*, or secular master-masons, is difficult to say. For labour force, the *conversi* undoubtedly played a major role before the mid-13th century, but, as their numbers declined, lay help became increasingly important. Masons' marks can be identified at several houses – as Margam (over thirty have been recorded),[6] and Strata Florida (twenty-seven).[7]

The note of lands formerly pertaining to 'The office of the master of the works of the *new* church' at Margam (prior to 1307), implies that major structural work was carried out there in the later 13th century, a time when in at least two instances – Neath *(Fig. 30)*[8] and Tintern *(Fig. 31)*[9] – the relatively modest 12th century churches (Late Romanesque in style) were being entirely rebuilt, but in such a way that worship could continue more or less uninterrupted in the old church until the grander edifice was ready. The reasons lay (perhaps) in the munificence of wealthy patrons, and the need for extra altars for increased numbers of priest-monks offering private Masses daily. At both abbeys, the first stone churches became partly or wholly encased within the rising shell of the new buildings.

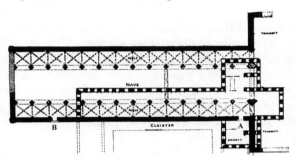

A similar rebuilding programme has been postulated for Cwmhir – based upon the failure of the entrances into the 13th century church for the monks and *conversi (Fig 32: A and B respectively)*, to correspond to the lanes of its cloister.[10] A late 12th century vault boss excavated at Cwmhir is of the same form as those found in the transepts of

Fig. 32: Cwmhir: The postulated 12th and 13th C. churches. *(C.A. Radford, Arch. Camb. 1982).*

Strata Florida, indicating that their east ends may have been similar in form.[10a] At Cymer, of late foundation [1198], the church was completed – except for the western tower – within about twenty-five years,[11] and, save for the eastward extension of its presbytery, the final church at Strata Florida (being on a different site from the first) was also raised relatively quickly.[12]

Documentary evidence of the precise dates of building of any section of a monastery is largely lacking, though architectural detail helps to remedy this deficiency. In the case of Tintern, however, a lost chronicle does record that the church was begun in 1269, and that in 1301: 'The new church of Tintern Abbey, thirty-two years in building was *finished* by Roger Bigod',[13] implying that the Earl of Norfolk's role became crucial in the later stages of the work. Generations of monks were to remember his generosity with gratitude.[14] Half-way through the work of construction the monks were able to celebrate the Eucharist in the new church (15 April 1282), always an event of great moment, and (on 3 October 1288) were able to use the new choir and high altar, but all was not ready for the consecration until (28 July) 1301.[15]

In like vein, the charter granted by the Lord Rhys to Strata Florida tells of how he 'had begun to build' that abbey by 1184,[16] whilst the chronicler of *Brut y Tywysogyon* notes its community as taking possession of their new church on the eve of Pentecost (Whit-Sunday) in 1201.[17] The Lord Rhys' comments perhaps marked the completion of a significant stage in its building – which commenced with the south transept and gradually extended to the crossing, north transept and the initial presbytery before tackling the nave and west front *(Fig. 33)*.[18]

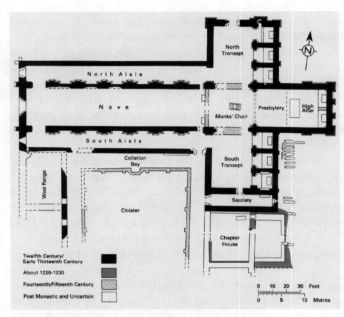

Fig. 33: Strata Florida: Ground Plan.
(Cadw: Welsh Historic Monuments. Crown Copyright).

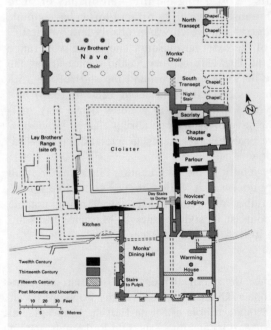

Fig. 34: Basingwerk. *(Cadw: Crown Copyright).*

More often than not, building history has to be determined from visual evidence. This suggests at Valle Crucis (*fd.* 1200) that by 1225 the eastern half of the church was well advanced with a stone roof being raised, whilst by 1240 work had started on the walls and piers of the western section. By the middle of the century it is likely that the western and southern stone ranges of the cloister had been completed.[19]

At Basingwerk (*Fig. 34; fd.* 1131/1157), a reconstruction, which commenced early in the 13th century, saw the church and the east range of its claustral buildings completed first, whilst – about the middle of the century – the refectory was re-oriented on a north-south axis. In the later 14th century, a handsome new arcade adorned the cloister.[20]

Reconstruction at Tintern was also not confined to the church, and included (in the early 13th century) a refashioning of the chapter house, the reorientation of the refectory, the building of a completely new west range (the domain of the *conversi*), and a new cloister arcade. Later in the century, a sizeable infirmary complex was added.[21] All this work of building and rebuilding meant that, for decades, if not centuries, dust and noise, accidents and bustle, must have disturbed monastic peace and calm, nor (in working hours) could a substantial lay presence within the heart of the monastery be avoided.

Reconstruction might be necessitated by damage caused by fire. An extreme example was Grace Dieu, completely burnt in 1233, but next to nothing is known of its architectural development. Strata Florida, badly damaged after lightning struck about 1284, and from military action a decade later, saw more than remedial action. The church was reroofed in stone rather than lead, and the once brightly coloured walls were whitewashed, but also – on the floor of the choir and the transepts – handsome tiles replaced slate paving.[22]

Valle Crucis suffered from several severe fires, the first necessitating rebuilding from the mid-13th century onwards.[23] Damage during the Welsh wars of Edward I may have led to the reconstruction (perhaps in the abbacy of Adam, 1330–44) of the upper west front – which bears the consequent inscription: + ADAM ABBAS FECIT HOC OPUS Ī PACE / QVIESCAT AMĒ.[24] A later abbot (Robert of Lancaster) told (in 1419) in the wake of the Glyn Dŵr Revolt, how he, too, had repaired the monastery after damage by fire.[25] His work *may* have involved the remodelling of the eastern cloister range.[26]

The long years of building and rebuilding the monasteries are evident from clear variations in design. Such changing patterns may be vertical or horizontal. The uppermost lancet windows at the east end of Valle Crucis are narrower and more pointed than those of earlier construction below. The lower church walls incorporate large boulders, but the upper parts – post-dating the fire – are mainly of small flat stones.[27] The exterior of the north transept chapels at Strata Florida have simple chamfered plinths, lacking in the south transept which was probably laid out first.[28]

A distinct change in the character of the external masonry shows the west range at Tintern to have been extended in the late 13th century,[29] and demonstrates the refashioning of part of the east range of Valle Crucis around the start of the 15th century.[30] The final church of Neath was erected (from about 1280 to 1330) in a continuous building operation but stylistic differences in window detail may indicate one break in construction.[31] In the nave of Tintern an abrupt change in window style towards the west end of the nave probably represents an interruption in building work – perhaps when funds ran low.[32]

In those monasteries almost entirely rebuilt in the 13th century, little may remain of the earlier foundation – the sacristy doorway at Valle Crucis[33] and a like round-headed doorway at the north end of the 'day-room' at Tintern[34] being notable exceptions. Perhaps the most vivid contrast in style occurs at Margam: the solid Norman west front as opposed to the graceful Gothic chapter house.

Building Materials

Locally quarried stone inevitably formed the major element in Cistercian construction of their monasteries: a grey gritstone at Cwmhir (*?* from nearby Fowler's Cave; *Fig. 35*),[35] Silurian shale at Maenan,[36] slate rubble at Strata Florida,[37] and glacial boulders and dolerite at Cymer.[38] The use of local strata – as 'Old Red Sandstone' at Tintern (from the Barbadoes Wood quarries close by)[38a] – helped abbeys to blend with their environment. Stone for finer work might also be found at not too great a distance: a pale fine-grained Cambrian sandstone at Cymer; red and white sandstone from Bodysgallen at Maenan;[39] Sutton stone from Southerndown at Margam and Neath;[40] freestone from local Rhuddnant Gritstone at Strata Florida.[41]

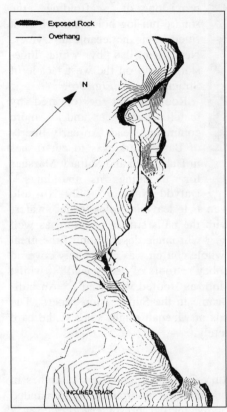

Exposed Rock
Overhang

N

INCLINED TRACK

Scale: 1:750.
Contours at 0.25m. intervals.

Fig. 35: Fowler's Cave, Cwmhir.
(Clwyd-Powys Archaeological Trust)

Abbeys might look further afield, as Cwmhir[42] and, closer to hand Strata Marcella,[43] obtaining freestone from the Grinshill quarries near Shrewsbury. A variety of sources provided dressed stone for Strata Florida, including: oolitic limestone of Cotswold or Bath origin, Caerbwdy sandstone from the south side of St Davids peninsula, and Millstone Grit – from either the Bristol area or the South Wales coalfield.[44] Stone is a bulky commodity, and these distant sources give credence to the tradition that Strata Florida's better quality stone was imported via Cardigan Bay to its property at Llanddewi Aberarth, and then hauled by oxen (but by hand-barrow across Tregaron Marsh) to the abbey.[45]

Timber played no small part in monastic construction: the abbeys were works of 'stone and timber' (Gutain Owain; 1460–1503);[46] this helped make them susceptible to fire. Apart from roofing, wood played an especial part in the fashioning of the choir stalls. Henry III made grants totalling twenty-six trees, including six oaks, to Grace Dieu (1235–53) to help in rebuilding that abbey after its destruction by fire.[47] During Neath's reconstruction even the oppressive Earl Gilbert de Clare (in 1289) gave it 'all the timber necessary'.[48] Lewis Morgannwg (1520–65), in Tudor times, reflected on 'the fine workmanship in wood', to be found at Neath'.[49] At Valle Crucis, parts (like the south range) were originally timber constructions, later rebuilt in stone; some of the vertical timbers being left *in situ* encased in the later wall. All the major construction timbers at Valle Crucis were of oak, and halved trunks were used in the refectory and kitchen as a strengthening raft.[50]

At Cymer, the apparent absence of a west range might suggest (pending excavation) that its *conversi* quarters were wooden structures, never replaced by stone. Walter Clifford's grant of 'all materials in his forest', suggests that the transient

Fig. 36: Strata Florida: the West Front.
(S.W. Williams, 1889).

Trawscoed Abbey was largely a timber edifice.[51] Another important, though only initial, role played by timber was in the provision of scaffolding: the square put-log holes into which it fitted being noticeable at Cymer, Neath (infilled by white limestone), and on the west facade of Strata Florida *(Fig. 36).*[52]

Roofs might be covered by thatch, tiles, and, more commonly, lead. An early liberty of Basingwerk was to cut rushes in Hawarden and Saltney Marshes for thatching its buildings.[53] Dafydd Nanmor (1420–90) told how, at Strata Florida, the roofs were 'so woven as to leave no holes for ice, water, snow or rain'.[54] Blue roofing slates, some with the nails still in position, as well as clay roof tiles, have been found at Maenan.[55] Chronicle description of the great fire at Strata Florida (1284) records that its 'whole church was completely covered with lead'.[56] Dafydd Nanmor spoke of that abbey's 'roofs of heavy lead',[57] whilst Tudur Aled (1480–1526) noted Basingwerk, too, as 'roofed with lead'.[58] An indication of the amount of lead on abbey roofs came in the Suppression papers. The absence of roof lead from archaeological finds at Maenan might suggest the care taken by the Crown to strip the abbey completely.[59]

The Abbey Churches

Some of the earliest, and transient, 12th century Cistercian monastery churches in Wales may have exhibited, like Tintern, the 'simplicity' in architecture demanded by the Order – with an aisleless nave and a rectangular presbytery *(Fig. 37).*[60] Margam and Whitland, which did have aisles, were perhaps the first true 'Bernardine' churches in Wales *(Fig. 47).*[60a] Elsewhere, adaptations and reconstructions in the 13th century saw an increase in size and the addition of aisles, but the retention of a square-ended termination to the east end. What made Cistercian churches, as most other conventual churches, stand out from surrounding parochial architecture was the addition of transepts. The plan of the abbey church was (for practical reasons) that of the sign of the Saviour, the cross. This was noted by Gutain Owain, who spoke of Valle Crucis as 'a noble fabric for God, His cruciform House',[61] and by John Leland (*c.* 1538) who remarked of Strata Florida that its church was 'side ilid and crosse ilid'.[62]

The traditions of the Cistercian Order initially insisted upon uniformity as well as simplicity, but the size of its churches varied greatly (from the 13th century) in relation to the resources of the individual abbeys. There was no constant length or

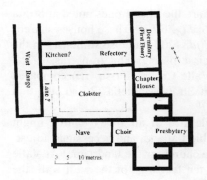

Fig. 37: Tintern in the 12th century. *(Cadw: Welsh Historic Monuments. Crown Copyright).*

width: Cwmhir had a nave of 256ft. (78m.), the total length of Cymer was but 105ft. (32m.).[63] Both abbeys were never finished, their east walls were but clay bonded to the remainder of the structure, and raised when further ambitious building became impossible.[64] Indeed, Leland remarked of Cwmhir that 'no church in Wales is seen of such length as the foundation of walls there begin doth show, but the third part of the work was never finished'.[65]

If there were considerable differences in scale, there were also some close similarities in plan and architecture, both within the monasteries of Wales and to others outside it, as well as to non-Cistercian ecclesiastical structures. So far as the latter are concerned, specific debts can be discerned at Strata Florida from the pier design of St David's Cathedral,[66] whilst the early 14th century west gable of Valle Crucis has a remarkable similarity to that (of the same period) at the non-Cistercian St Etienne, Moudon (Fribourg).[67] Within the Order, there is a close resemblance between the Norman west fronts of Fontenay (consecrated in 1147) and Margam (founded that same year).[68] The plan of the church of Maenan (built from 1284 onwards) may have owed much to that of Hampshire Netley (constructed about 1244–70).[69] The plan of Strata Florida (largely completed by 1201) *may* have been the inspiration for that of Irish Duiske (Graiguenamanagh; founded in 1207), but this is by no means certain *(Fig. 38)*.[70]

Within Wales itself, there were a number of likenesses which seem to have sprung mostly from simultaneous building periods (as for Margam, Neath and Tintern abbeys), and from the close affinity existing within the family of Whitland (like Strata Florida, Strata Marcella and Valle Crucis). The almost exact similarity of dimensions of the churches of Neath and Tintern *(Figs. 30, 31)* once led to a plan of the one being mistaken for the other in the former Ancient Monuments branch of the Department of the Environment.[71] The 'family likeness' noted between Basingwerk and Valle Crucis,[72] may stem from masons at the former going on to work at the latter house.[73] Four of the masons' marks found at Strata

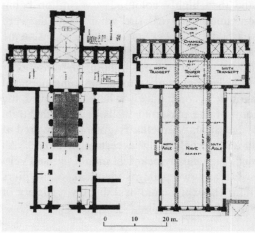

Fig. 38: Strata Florida Church. *(S.W.Williams, 1889).*

Duiske Church. *(R. Cochrane, 1892).*

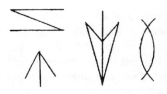

Fig. 39: Masons' Marks, common to Strata Florida and Strata Marcella. *(S.W. Williams, 1889–91).*

Florida *(fd.* 1164) are the like of ones noted at Strata Marcella *(fd.* 1176; *Fig. 39).*[74] These houses shared, with Valle Crucis *(fd.* 1200), a close similarity in the dimensions of their crossings and transepts.[75] The cloister garth at Valle Crucis (79 sq. ft.) compared closely to those at Strata Marcella (76 sq. ft.) and Cymer (74 sq. ft).[76]

The considerable size of an abbey church might outstrip the available flatland, and necessitate adjustments either to the church or the landscape. At Valle Crucis, at a point ten feet west of the west wall, the medieval builders had to cut back into the slope of the hillside and into the natural rock.[77] At Maenan, the ground rose sharply twenty feet to the east of the church limiting any extension in that direction.[78] At most monastic sites a certain amount of building up or of excavation would have been necessary, as suggested by the steps leading downwards to the cloister at Tintern, and upwards to the church of Cymer. At Neath, the church stood on a natural rock shelf, somewhat higher than the cloister ranges.[79]

Internal Simplicity

Fig. 40: Capital: Strata Florida. *(S.W. Williams, 1889).*

Fig. 41: Capital: Strata Marcella. *(S.W. Williams, 1891).*

The architectural restraint which marked Cistercian churches was relieved in several ways, not least in window patterns and, later, tiled floors, but also by painted walls and sculptured pier capitals. Imagery was, at first, frowned on by the Order, but it is clear that the internal walls of Strata Florida were plastered and then highly coloured – vermilion being common, until the great fire when its walls were white-washed.[80] Traces of the original scheme survive in the south transept chapels. At Neath, painted wall plaster remains in both the transepts.[81] At Tintern, false masonry – imitation joints depicted by red lines – common elsewhere – relieved the monotony of the plastered walls.[82] At both Strata Florida and Strata Marcella, fragments recovered of capitals and corbels show a certain affinity.[83] As was usual, they mostly bear leaf moulding, and very rarely were any two patterns identical.[84] The piers of Cwmhir (now at Llanidloes) display a variety of leaf form within one capital.[85]

Ceilings

The interior height of the abbey churches can now only be approximated by estimation, though William Worcestre (1478) fortunately recorded the elevation of the vaulted roof at Tintern as 'eleven vethyms'.[86] Lewis Morgannwg (*c.* 1520) spoke of 'the vast, high roof', at Neath.[87] The church roofs of Neath[88] and Tintern[89] were vaulted in stone throughout. At both abbeys a few bosses – which once marked the rib intersections – remain, including (at Neath) a depiction of Christ in Majesty. At Margam only the east end was vaulted;[89a] at some abbeys the nature of the ceiling is uncertain.

At Strata Florida, the presbytery and transept chapels were stone vaulted, the nave roof probably remaining in timber. It was perhaps the stone vault which spared its presbytery the worse effects of its great fire. The vault ribs were ornamented with a 'domino' or pellet motif, picked out in red and black paint. The transept chapel bore bosses, each with an iron pin which probably held a lamp *(Fig. 42)*.[90] At Valle Crucis, stone vaulting was intended but seemingly never completed.[91] At all the foregoing houses, one or more spiral staircases – encased in the fabric – gave access to the large roof space between the vaulting and the exterior leaded roof covering.

Fig. 42: Chapel Boss, Strata Florida. *(S.W. Williams, 1889).*

Floors

From the mid-13th century, it became commonplace for part at least of the floors in Cistercian churches to be beautified with decorated tiles. Hence it was, that after the great fire at Strata Florida, the flooring of local slate slabs was replaced in the presbytery and transepts by patterned tile pavements. A more modest arrangement in the eastern half of the nave picked out a large cross. As time progressed one floor level might be laid over another. At Margam, the lowest of three such successive pavements comprised plain tiles glazed in white, yellow and green.[92] Much of the church

floor of Tintern was tiled,[93] whilst Lewis Morgannwg (*c.* 1520) spoke of 'the floor of variegated stone' at Neath.[94] No decorative tiles have been recovered from Cwmhir, Cymer or Maenan. A common source (perhaps a Wessex or west Midland tilery) explains the discovery of tiles of like design at Tintern and Cleeve (Somerset), Basingwerk and (its mother-house) Buildwas, as well as Strata Florida and Strata Marcella.[95] Late-medieval imported tiles (from Flanders and Normandy) have been excavated at Llantarnam.[95a] Heraldic tile devices found at

Fig. 43: Neath Abbey Tile Pavement. *(H.H. Knight, 1850).*

Margam, Neath[96] and Strata Florida[97] include the Despenser arms.

Most pavement tiles were decorated – being impressed (Strata Marcella), impressed and infilled with white clay (Tintern), or embossed (Whitland).[98] The designs illustrated include: Saladin in combat with Henry II (Neath),[99] Ezekiel's winged creature (Basingwerk), an *Agnus Dei* (Whitland),[100] and a man eyeing a looking-glass (Strata Florida).[101] At Basingwerk inscribed tiles made up the word: *DEUS*.[102].

No crypts are known in Welsh Cistercian abbeys, though a deep vault has been postulated within the west end of the nave at Tintern.[103]

Window Glass

Early Cistercian churches were confined to employing uncoloured (*grissaille*) glass relieved by pattern-forming lead-work. No remains of this are known in Wales where, by the time the Cistercian churches were being renewed, glazing schemes were more adventurous. Dafydd Nanmor told how Abbot Rhys at Strata Florida (*c.* 1440) 'cut ten complete windows, half the cost of this went in glass'.[104] William Worcestre (1478) described the east window of Tintern as being glazed with the arms (a red lion rampant on a background of gold and green) of Roger Bigod, its great benefactor.[105] Lewis Morgannwg (*c.* 1520) told of the coats of arms on the glass of Neath.[106] Llantarnam and Neath (1504) received bequests towards glazing their west windows.[107]

After the Suppression the 'eight or nine great windows' of Strata Marcella were unlawfully removed,[108] whilst twenty-five *'fote'* of glass was taken from Valle Crucis to ornament Holt Castle.[109] Fragments of stained glass have been excavated at Llantarnam,[110] Strata Florida,[111] Strata Marcella[112] and Valle Crucis.[113] A stone mould for casting window ventilators has been found at Neath,[114] and window lead at Cwmhir.[115] The east window of the former nunnery at Llanllugan contains medieval glass, incorporating an abbess at prayer.[116] Medieval glass, reassembled in the west window of Buttington church (Powys), may have come from Strata Marcella.[117]

Bells and Belfries

Cistercian belfries were (by statute) timber constructions of moderate height, generally resting upon the solid foundations of the crossing, but stone towers were not unknown. Each monastery had at least a 'great' and a 'lesser' bell, whilst a minor bell might adorn the refectory. Forty or more Cistercian bells adorned the Welsh houses, but little is known of their belfries. At Strata Florida, Dafydd Nanmor described: 'A great belfry, lime dressed, big and white', with a cock on top of it.[118] Does 'lime-dressed' imply a stone tower? Was the first tower – which held the 'great bell' raised in 1255 – destroyed in the fire of 1284? At Valle Crucis, where the bell-tower was supported by the four great crossing piers,[119] Guto'r Glyn, aged and deaf, slept through the ringing of its bells.[120] At Neath, the central tower was supported by massive multi-clustered piers.[121] At Tintern, where a mid-15th century bell-pit has been excavated[121a], William Worcestre (1478) noted 'the principal belfry in the middle of the quire'; this was perhaps but a small timber flèche.[122] At Cymer, a stone tower was added at the west end subsequent to the main building phase.

The Altars and the Liturgy

In the church as a whole, the principal feature was the high altar, sometimes free-standing as at Strata Florida. This 'great altar' was the scene of the daily conventual Eucharist, and the place where the Blessed Sacrament was reserved – 'The body of

Our Lord kept under lock' (Strata Florida, 1284).[123] It was upon the high altar at Margam that early benefactors to Margam laid their charters as a sign of their good faith, and of the dedication of their gift to Almighty God. In the south wall of the presbytery at Basingwerk and Cymer remain substantial vestiges of the *sedilia*, where the sacred ministers were seated during High Mass. A stone set in the floor at the entrance to the presbytery at Basingwerk, may have supported a lectern for readings.[124] It was to enhance the liturgy centered upon the high altar, that presbyteries might be stone vaulted whereas naves might only have timber ceilings.

By the late 13th century, each priest-monk offered Mass daily, necessitating several subsidiary altars located in the ambulatory (as at Neath and Tintern), in the transept chapels (in all abbeys), against the west-facing wall of the *pulpitum* (the bases still visible at Strata Florida), or (where there was one, as at Neath and Tintern) in the Galilee vestibule. Further chapels might be sited adjacent to the gate-house, within the guest-house and infirmary complexes, or (as at Tintern) in the abbot's quarters. Eleven altar sites can be identified within the church at Strata Florida *(Fig. 33)*, where oak screens decorated the entrances to the transept chapels.[125] Side-chapels frequently had an aumbry (for holding cruets) and a piscina (to drain away unused water).[126] Double-piscinas survive at Cymer (in the presbytery) and Valle Crucis (in a side-chapel).

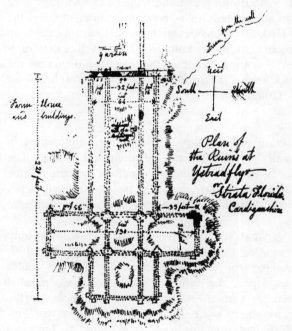

Fig. 44: Strata Florida Abbey Church *(By the Revd. John Parker, c. 1850; National Library of Wales, P 556, 64d).*

Each subsidiary altar had its own especial dedication, including the Holy Trinity (consecrated at Margam in 1187),[127] the Holy Cross (the nave altar, like the 'cross auter' at Neath in 1430),[128] the Blessed Virgin Mary (the usual dedication – under God – of the high altar, but also of 'Our Lady Chapel' at Llantarnam (1532)[129] and of a subsidiary altar at Strata Florida),[130] St Anne (the gate-house chapel of Tintern), St John Baptist (Tintern: 'On the north side of the church', 1531),[131] and St Mary Magdalene (Margam, 1360, and Tintern – 'On the south side of the monastery' – 1531).[132] Such secondary chapels might became meeting places for the transaction of business between the community and secular folk – as at Neath's Holy Cross altar (1430) and Strata Florida's Lady altar (1537).

The monastic choir had wooden stalls ranged lengthwise on either side. Those from Basingwerk were (after its suppression) moved to the church of St Mary-on-the-Hill, Chester.[133] Within the choir at Strata Florida is a stepped stone depression – possibly used in the Saturday evening maundy ceremony, or, more likely it is thought, no more than a drainage inspection pit.[134] Could it be the 'baptismal well' recorded by Parker (*c.* 1850; *Fig. 44*) but perhaps later misplaced by him into the nave?[135]

In latter days the singing of the monks was enhanced by organ music. Cwmhir (1524) received a bequest in order 'to bye a paire of Organs to honour God within the Abbey.'[136] The steps ascending the *pulpitum* at Valle Crucis may have led to an organ loft,[137] and the poets spoke of organ music there.[138] Little else is known of Cistercian music, save for the (officially frowned on) chanting in harmony of parts at Tintern (1217),[139] and for the singing of the *Salve* at Neath. Ieuan Du'r y Bilwg (*fl.* 1470) told how: 'After Vespers, manifold will be the uttering of praise to Mary'.[140]

Other glimpses of Cistercian worship come in references to: the chanting of Matins in the choir at Neath (*c.* 1470),[141] the censing of the altar during Lauds at Strata Florida (Pentecost, 1202),[142] the keeping of Candlemas at Margam (*c.* 1220),[143] and the Office of the Dead (dirge and requiem) performed at Llantarnam (1532).[144] The bequests to Tintern of vestments (1355, 1380),[145] as well as its annual expenditure (£8 in 1535) on bread and wine, wax and oil,[146] are reminders that what mattered in an abbey church was not fine architecture, but the sacramental worship of Almighty God. Religious devotion was also aided (albeit on a very restrained scale in a Cistercian church) by sculptured imagery like the crucifix retrieved from Strata Florida,[147] a (now weathered) tympanum depicting the Ascension (or the Assumption) at Cwmhir *(Plate V-A)*,[148] and the (now headless) image of the Virgin and Child at Tintern.[149]

The Nave

Much of the nave was given over to the worship of the *conversi* (numerous in earlier decades); their wooden stalls would have ranged along either side. The monastic choir (in early arrangements at least) frequently occupied the easternmost bay (or bays) of the nave, extending into the crossing. The two choirs were separated by a structure known as the *pulpitum*, remnants of which are visible at Neath[150] and Strata Florida.[151]

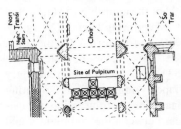

Fig. 45: Tintern Abbey: Site of the Pulpitum.
(Cadw. Crown Copyright).

That at Valle Crucis – perhaps as the community dwindled – was moved eastwards (around 1400) making for a shorter monastic choir.[152] Fully developed, the *pulpitum* would have two parallel screens with a loft above; between them lay the retro-choir, where infirm monks might worship. Sufficient remains have been found of Tintern's *pulpitum (Figs. 45, 46)* to permit a reconstruction,[153] and the surmise that it was the design (about 1325–30) of the west country master, William Joy.[154]

Fig. 46: Tintern Abbey: Reconstruction of the Pulpitum *(C. Jones-Jenkins, 1995, for Cadw: Welsh Historic Monuments. Crown Copyright).*

The architectural simplicity of the nave was relieved by the character of the great piers separating the choir of the *conversi* from the side aisles. There was a marked contrast as between, say, the aesthetic beauty of the clustered columns of Tintern and the feeling of solidity given by the cuneiform Norman piers of Margam. The nave piers at Strata Florida are of at least three different designs, and show an affinity to those of St David's Cathedral.[155] An engraving of 1742 suggests that sculptured monastic heads adorned the north arcade piers at Cymer *(Plate V-B)*.[156]

The entrance door at the west end of the nave might be imposing, like that of Valle Crucis, inserted in the mid-13th century after the great fire, and decorated with dog-tooth ornament.[157] That at Strata Florida, of the late 12th century *(Fig. 36)*, with its six orders of continuous roll mouldings, is unique.[158] The west doorway of Aberconwy II (now St Mary's church, Conwy) is of the monastic period but of a later confection, the arch may derive from the former chapter house entrance.[159] The three lancets above the doorway are windows characteristic of those monasteries not subject to later aggrandisement – there were two layers of lancets in the east wall of Cymer.[160] The rose window, whilst seen at Tintern and Valle Crucis,[161] did not achieve the importance in Wales that it did in some Cistercian churches elsewhere.[162]

In the early centuries the west doorways were more decorative than functional, the monks and *conversi* usually processing into their separate choirs through doorways sited towards the east and west ends of the nave, respectively. The arrangement is best seen at Tintern, where the early 14th century entrance provided for the monks is richly carved. Another entrance into the church (for the sick monks) or departure point (for the bodies of the dead going to burial) was a doorway piercing the presbytery wall close to one or other of the transepts. Without the west door might stand (as at Margam,[163] Neath[164] and Tintern) a stone vaulted 'galilee' porch or 'paradise', which usually contained one or more subsidiary altars. That at Tintern may have been free-standing, and housed an allegedly miraculous image of the Blessed Virgin Mary.[165]

The Claustral Complex

The quadrangle cloister attached to the abbey church was the 'home' of the monk, giving him direct access to the various chambers of his monastery. The cloister was sited to the south of the church – so gaining extra sunlight and protection from cold northerly winds, but local topography sometimes dictated (as at Tintern) that cloisters were placed north of the church – to solve problems of drainage and water supply.

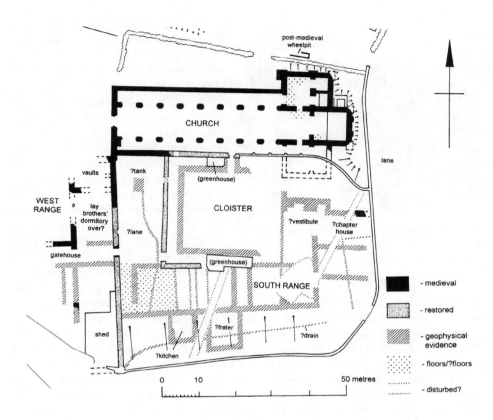

Fig. 47: Plan of Whitland Abbey, the result of superficial excavation of the church and geophysical survey of the conventual buildings undertaken in 1994–99. The church, of simple 'Bernardine' plan without a tower, belonged mainly to a single, mid-12th century building phase, with early 13th century screen walls in the chancel and transept arches. The layout of the conventual complex, suspected from aerial photographs, was confirmed, but survey of the west range was limited to magnetometry. *(By courtesy of Mr Neil Ludlow, Archaeoleg Cambria).*

Certain monasteries – like Strata Florida[166] and Valle Crucis[167] – refashioned their cloisters in the 15th century; perhaps necessitated by damage incurred during the Glyn Dŵr Revolt. William Herbert (1469) bequeathed Tintern a hundred tons of stone for the restoration of its cloister.[168] For one reason or another, the shape of cloisters varied somewhat: almost square (Tintern), practically rectangular (Neath), or definitely trapeziform (Basingwerk and Valle Crucis).[169]

The north walk of the cloister (or the south walk – if the cloister position was reversed) saw the nightly gathering of the community for the collation reading. This necessitated a projection into the cloister garth – to accommodate the reader's *pulpitum* (evident at Strata Florida[170] and Tintern),[171] opposite a 'collation seat' for the abbot recessed into the wall (visible at Tintern). This was the wall pierced close to either end for the entry into their separate choirs of the monks and the *conversi*. This 'making of an arch at the entry of the church out of the cloister', envisaged at Llantarnam as late as 1532,[172] referred perhaps to the proposed aggrandisement of an already existing processional doorway. The unfinished building programme of Cymer means that its monastic entrance to the quire is out of alignment with the cloister.

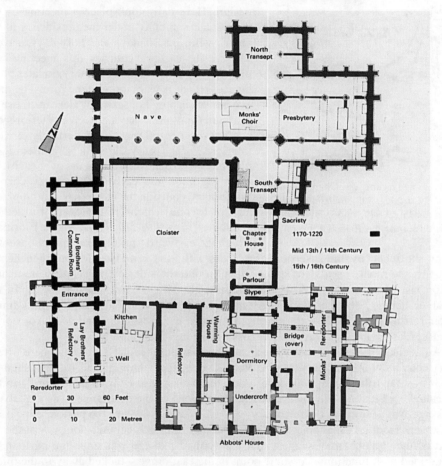

Fig. 48: Neath Abbey: the Cloister Complex.
(Cadw: Welsh Historic Monuments: Crown Copyright).

Next along from this doorway in the eastern walk of the cloister, comes first a relatively narrow and partitioned vaulted chamber, the inner part of which served as the sacristy with a doorway leading (as at Strata Florida)[173] into the presbytery, and the portion nearest the cloister as the book-room (as at Tintern – where the book-room supplemented the still visible 12th century book-cupboards).[174] At Basingwerk, the

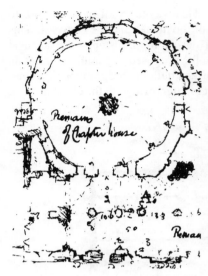

Fig. 49: Margam: the Chapter-House
*(John Carter; 1803: British Library
Addit. MS 29,940, f. 68;* By
permission of the British Library

sacristy contained an altar;[175] at Valle Crucis, the book-room is fronted by a fine stone screen bearing the rough outline of a human face.[176]

In central position in the east range was the chapter house; generally a rib-vaulted structure, its importance was reflected in the beauty of its design. Here daily took place a meeting of the monastic community under the presidency of the abbot, who, on Sundays and holy-days, gave a sermon. In earlier centuries this meeting was primarily spiritual and disciplinary, in later times business matters were more to the fore. The most evocative chapter houses in Wales are those of Margam (unusual in having twelve exterior sides and but one central pier in the perfectly circular interior),[177] and of Valle Crucis (consisting of nine bays with quadripartite vaults over each).[178]

At Margam, the early 13th century chapter house stands outside the east range, and replaces an earlier one which (refashioned) formed its vestibule *(Figs. 49, 50).*[179] At Strata Florida – where the eastward prolonged chapter house was later shortened by the insertion of a cross-wall, the remains of stone benches to support the monks' seats are still evident around the sides.[180] At Tintern, remnants also exist of the seating, as well as of the eight piers and the tiled floor.[181] In the chapter house, abbots and some lay notabilities were interred. Other monks found their resting place in the exterior angle between the presbytery and south (or north) transept, as the ancient graves with cross-headstones at Strata Florida.

Adjacent to the chapter house was the inner parlour (seen at Tintern), where necessary conversation was permitted. At Valle Crucis, the counting of £240, deposited (in 1534) by Dr Ellis Price, was done 'upon the table board ('the higher board') in the parlour'.[182] Sited next to the parlour, at the far end of the east range, was the 'slype' passage-way leading to the infirmary. At Valle Crucis – where the parlour appears to be absent from its usual position – the relocated fine 13th century doorway at the far end of the slype[183] may suggest that the vaulted passage was once the parlour, or combined both functions. At some point in the east range – tucked away in the thickness of the wall at Valle Crucis – the day-stairs led up to the monks' dorter.[184]

Beyond the slype, the east range was extended away from the cloister to provide a lengthy dormitory undercroft (or sub-dorter; some 24m. × 9m. at Neath, 27m. × 9m. at Tintern) which *may* have been partitioned to serve as a scriptorium, 'day-room', or novitiate, and, in some abbeys (like Basingwerk) as the warming-house.[185] The undercroft at Neath – a rib-vaulted chamber of five bays – is a fine example of Cistercian architecture.[186] The far end of this building at Tintern contained sluice-gates allowing the waters of the main drain to flush the monks' rere-dorter.[187]

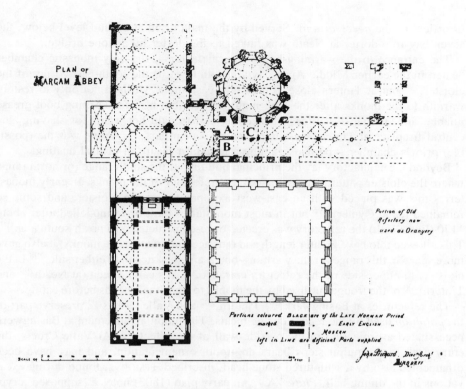

Fig. 50: Margam Abbey: Ground Plan. *(Trans. Cardiff Naturalists' Society, 1881).*
A: Sacristry.   **B:** Book Room.   **C:** Vestibule.

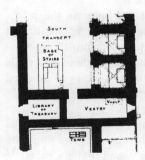

Fig. 51: Strata Florida: Site of the Night Stairs *(S.W. Williams, 1889).*

The dorter of the monks lay over the under-croft, parlour, chapter house and book-room. At its end was a flight of steps (the 'night-stairs') leading the monks directly down to their choir for the night office. The night-stairs have been reconstructed at Tintern on the lines of the original flight;[188] at Neath, the carved hand-rail by which the monks might support themselves is still visible.[189] The chamber under the night-stairs would have found practical uses, as a store or office (if window lit), or perhaps as a prison cell for refractory monks.

The relatively short dorter at Valle Crucis (indicating a comparatively small community) is still intact. At dorter level at Tintern was the treasury (over the sacristy), and a separate chamber – maybe for the prior.[190] At the far end of most dorters, (like Valle Crucis),[191] or to its side (as at Tintern),[192] or even parallel to it (the case at Neath) was the rere-dorter (variously called also the 'house of office' or the *necessarium)*. Served by the main drain at ground-level below, the seven-bay rere-dorter at Neath was linked to the dorter by a stone bridge.[193]

The entrance to the warming-house (or calefactory), the only monastic chamber heated in the earlier Middle Ages, lay at Neath towards the south-east corner of the cloister,[194] but at Tintern close to the north-east angle. Utilised not only to restore warmth to the monks after the long night service, but also for keeping boot grease pliable, and, perhaps, at times of bleeding and to gain hot water for shaving, the central fireplace at Tintern was supported on four pillars.[195] Above was the (possible) prior's chamber – perhaps gaining a certain measure of central heating!

Beyond the calefactory lay the principal building of the south range (or north range where the cloister pattern was reversed): the refectory of the monks. In early monasteries this was placed with an east-west axis parallel to the cloister, and some so remained (as at Cymer),[196] but in most monasteries built or re-modelled after about 1170 (like Neath) the refectory was erected or re-constructed on a north-south axis.[197] This allowed it to have greater length and thus accommodate more monks; it also gave more space in this range for the warming-house and the kitchen to either side.[198] In the cloister, to either side of the refectory entrance, traces can be seen (at Neath[199] and Tintern)[200] of the troughs utilised by the monks to wash their hands before eating.

The refectories at Basingwerk,[201] Tintern,[202] and Valle Crucis[203] preserve part of the *pulpitum* used by the reader during meals. The pulpit arrangement at Basingwerk necessitated a projection in the outside wall of the refectory. At Valle Crucis, the entry arch to the pulpit steps bears dog-tooth ornamentation, and may have been ornamented also by a sculptured stone head, inscribed + MORVS, found during excavations in the dining hall *(Plate V-C)*. An early plan (1803) notes a 'supposed' crypt under the 'refectory' at Margam,[204] but the foundations concerned were perhaps of the infirmary. The Orangery now occupies the site of Margam's dining hall.[205] At Tintern (1438), supervision of the refectory and the meals provided was the domain of a monk 'refectorer', and to his office various rents pertained.[205a]

The kitchen at the end of this range was functionally placed between the refectories of the monks and *conversi*, so as to serve both. At Basingwerk,[206] Neath and Tintern,[207] hatch-ways survive through which cooked food passed into the monastic refectory. The main drain passed under the rear of Tintern's kitchen, and finds of imported pottery show that broken vessels and rubbish must have been dumped into it.[208] Fire caused Valle Crucis' kitchen to be twice rebuilt.[209]

The west range, the abode of the *conversi*, was frequently a lengthy and imposing edifice, measuring no less than 180ft. (55m.) at Tintern.[210] Its ground level was pierced by a passage way which formed the entrance into the cloister, and might be fronted by a porch – added in the 14th century at Neath[211] and Valle Crucis.[212] Between the porch at Tintern and the cloister lay its outer parlour, where business with lay-folk might be done – a practical stone bench being provided.[213] Above the parlour at Tintern was a room which found mention in 1568.[214] Might this have been the 'candle house' mentioned (in 1521) as being a chamber 'above the great door of the abbey, next to the church'?[215] The absence of a substantial west range at Cymer suggests that perhaps it was never completed there in stone.[216]

Plate I: **Tintern Abbey from the air**.
Note: *At base, left:* the Water Gate complex, by the river Wye.
 At base, right: the complex of domestic buildings in the Outer Court.

Crown Copyright/MOD. Reproduced with the permission of the Controller of Her Majesty's Stationery Office. [UR 90].

Plate II: **Valle Crucis Abbey.** Note the ruined castle of Dinas Brân, protectively situated on the hill-top behind the monastery.

Photograph: Kevin Thomas and Denis Donovan.
Plate: National Museums and Galleries of Wales.

Plate III-A: **Margam Abbey**. The West Front, of the late 12th century.

Plate III-B. **Strata Florida Abbey**. The West Front, of the early 13th century.

Plate IV-A: **Valle Crucis Abbey**. The Chapter House, of perhaps the mid-14th century.

Plate IV-B: **Neath Abbey**. The Dorter Undercroft, of the second quarter of the 13th century.　　　　*(Cadw: Welsh Historic Monuments, Crown Copyright).*

Plate V-A: **Cwmhir Abbey**. Tympanum, depicting perhaps the Ascension, possibly the Assumption. (Now built into a garden wall).

Plate V-B: **Cymer Abbey**.
Human faces (*?* monastic), formerly seen on the consoles of the north arcade piers.

Buck S. and N. 'Antiquities' III (1742) No. 49. Cf. National Library of Wales PB 755 (63/2).

Plate V-C: **Valle Crucis Abbey**.
13th C. sculpted head, excavated in the refectory. Inscribed: +
MORVS.
(National Museums & Galleries of Wales).

Plate VI-A: **Grace Dieu Abbey**. Possible foundation wall excavated in 1970.

Plate VI-B: **Maenan Abbey**. Base of stair turret in north transept, looking east. Excavated 1925–26. *(Courtesy of Dr Lawrence Butler).*

Plate VI-C: **Woolaston Grange** (of Tintern Abbey). Cobbled surface, uncovered in 1998.   *Plate: C.O. Jones-Jenkins.*

Plate VII-A: **Strata Marcella Abbey**. Lesser Drainage Channel.

Plate VII-B: **Strata Florida Abbey**. A stepped depression in the Quire.
(? A drainage inspection pit, or the site of the weekly Washing of the Feet ritual).

Plate VIII-A: **Neath Abbey**. 14th century Tiles. *top left:* a shield, the *three clarions* of Robert Consul, Earl of Gloucester; *top right:* a shield, the *three chevrons* of the De Clares, Earls of Gloucester and Lords of Glamorgan; *centre:* a mounted knight, Saladin; *base:* a hunting scene. *Photograph: Eric Broadbent; Plate: National Museums & Galleries of Wales.*

Plate VIII-B. **Whitland Abbey**.

Heraldic panelling. *Left: top and base*, A double rose, and a portcullis (Tudor badges). *Right: top:* A shield of the Tudor royal arms, with the sinister supporter, a greyhound. *Right, base:* A dragon, the dexter supporter of the Tudor arms (the shield and sinister supporter missing). Perhaps datable to the early part of the reign of Henry VIII.

Description: Dr Michael Siddons, F.S.A., Wales Herald Extraordinary. *Drawing:* Charles Norris, 1838. *(By courtesy of Cardiff County Council Library Service)*.

Plate IX: **Selected Welsh Cistercian Seals** (illustrative of the several seal types).
1. Llantarnam *alias* **Caerleon Abbey**. Early Abbot's Seal (hand grasping staff), as used in
1203 *(By permission of the British Library, Harleian Charter 75 A. 32).* **2. Tintern Abbey**.
Early Abbot's Seal (hand grasping staff), as used in 1245–53 *(By permission of the National
Museums & Galleries of Wales:* copy of that attached to Canterbury Cathedral, *Carta Antiqua*
I, 234). **3. Margam Abbey**. Early Abbot's Seal (abbot three-quarters length, with staff), as
used about 1170–1249 *(National Library of Wales, Penrice and Margam Charter 26).* **4.
Llantarnam** *alias* **Caerleon Abbey**. Abbot's Seal (abbot standing, with staff), as used in
1237 *(Cardiff County Council Library Service, MS 4.335. Drawn by Bartholomew Howlett,
d. 1827).* **5. Aberconwy Abbey**. First Common Seal (abbot kneeling before the Blessed
Virgin and her Child), as used in 1350 *(Public Record Office, E 42/321].* **6. Strata Florida**.
Signet Seal of Abbot Richard Dorston, 1509–13 (a two-headed eagle). *(Carmarthenshire
Archives, Lord Deed 11/554).* **7. Neath Abbey**. Seal of Abbot William (depicting the Blessed
Virgin). Date unproven, but between 1345 and 1425. Found (1999) on Baglan Bay beach,
Port Talbot *(By permission of the National Museums & Galleries of Wales).* **8. Whitland
Abbey**. Counter-Seal (hand grasping staff), as used in 1303 *(By permission of the British
Library, Additional Charter 8414).*

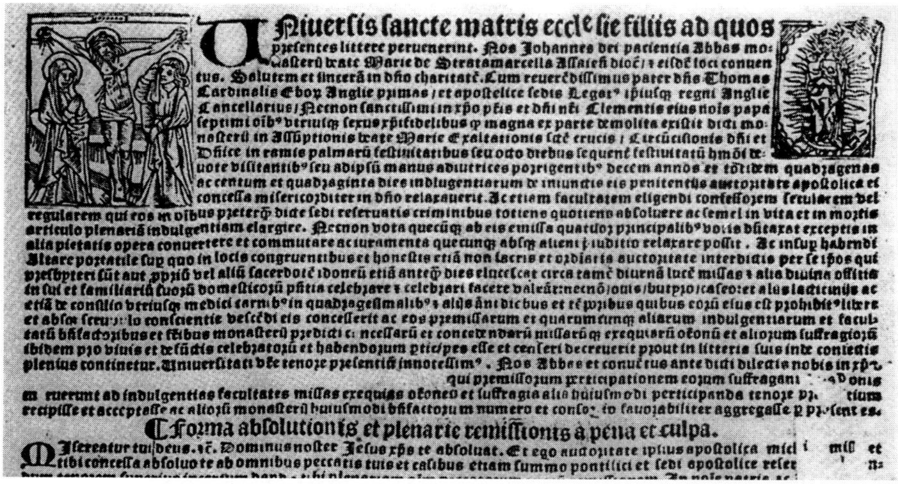

Universis sancte matris eccl[es]ie filiis ad quos

Forma absolutionis et plenarie remissionis a pena et culpa.

Plate X-A: **Strata Marcella Abbey**. The printed Indulgence, issued about 1528. *(National Library of Wales).*

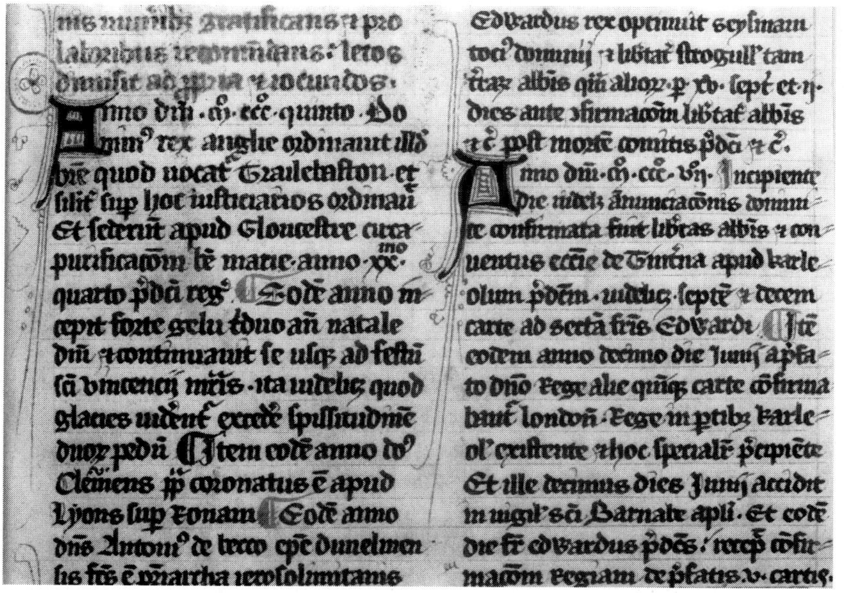

Plate X-B: **Tintern Abbey**. Extract from its additions to a copy of *Flores Historiarum*, telling of the confirmation in 1307 of the abbey's charters by Edward I. *(By permission of the British Library, MS Royal C.vi, fo. 254r).*

Plate XI-A: **Margam Abbey**. S.E. of the abbey church lies its polygonal chapter-house. On the hillside *(foreground)* is sited Capel Mair, Cryke, within (perhaps) a circular enclosure. Below it lies Cryke mill-pond.
(Cambridge University Collection of Air Photographs (BKA 30). Copyright reserved).

Plate XI-B: **Tintern Abbey**. The Gate-house complex, as it stood in 1822.
(Reproduced from a water-colour by J. Nichols, by kind permission of Mr John Wait).

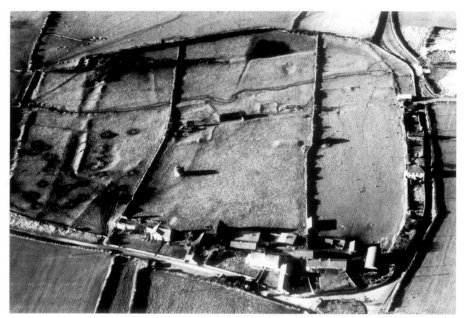

Plate XII-A: **Monknash Grange** (of Neath Abbey; *Cf.* Fig. 93 in text).
(Cambridge University Collection of Air Photographs (BPJ 32). Copyright reserved).

Plate XII-B: **Grangefield, Redwick**,
Double Moated Enclosure, on lands of
Tintern Abbey. *(Cambridge University
Collection of Air Photographs.
Copyright reserved. (CBW 39).*

Plate XII-C: **Mynachdy, Llangynllo**.
Moated Enclosure, with homestead
(top of centre right), on lands of
Cwmhir Abbey.
(Crown Copyright/MOD (EN 80)).

Plate XIII-A: **Gelli Grange** (of Basingwerk Abbey), about 1810.
An article regarding this house, in the *Liverpool Daily Post* at least thirty years ago, records the date of 1325 carved into one of the oak floor-boards of an attic. (Information from Mr Derek Williams, Mold).
(Photograph: Mr Eric Broadbent. Plate: By permission of the National Museums & Galleries of Wales).

Plate XIII-B: **Woolaston Grange Chapel** (of Tintern Abbey), about 1956.
This chapel, which had a cellar/crypt beneath, has since been largely demolished.
(Courtesy of Dr Cyril Hart).

Plate XIV-A: **Rogerstone Grange Mill** (of Tintern Abbey), in the late 1960s. The mill has since been demolished, on safety grounds.

Plate XIV-B: **Nant-y-arian Grange Mill** (of Cwmhir Abbey). Note *(far right)* the outline of the former mill wheel at the base of the gable wall. (The leat is traceable on the ground).

Plate XV-A: **Strata Florida Abbey**. The excavator, Stephen. W. Williams *(top left)* with a visitor, perhaps during a visit by some Cambrians on 20 August 1888 (St Bernard's Day). *(NLW, Photo Album 1206).*

Plate XV-B: **Strata Florida Abbey**: The First County Gathering, 23 June 1909. Seated by the Plan is probably Professor Tyrrell Green of St David's College, Lampeter. Addressing the Gathering is perhaps the Revd. J.F. Lloyd.
(Reproduced, by permission of the Society, from Vol. 1, of the Transactions of the Cardiganshire Antiquarian Society).

Plate XVI-A: **Caldey Abbey**. The Community (late spring, 1984). [The author stands second from left].
(Pembrokeshire Record Office, HDX 933/162). (Courtesy of Mr Roscoe Howells).

Plate XVI-B: **Holy Cross Abbey, Whitland**. The Community (summer, 2000).

To either side of the cloister entrance lay the *conversi* range with their refectory and another chamber which may (sub-divided) have served various purposes, including storage and crafts. Above the entire length of the ground-floor lay the *conversi* dorter; remnants of their night-stairs leading down to their choir exist at Tintern. The foundations of the *conversi* rere-dorter can be seen at Neath[217] and have been excavated at Valle Crucis.[218] In some abbeys (like Basingwerk,[219] Neath[220] and possibly Whitland)[220a] can be traced a narrow alley, the *conversi* 'lane', which lay between the west range and the west cloister wall and led to the processional entrance into their choir.

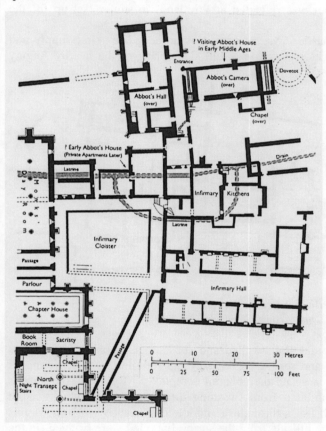

Fig. 52: Tintern: the Abbatial and Infirmary complexes. *(Cadw: Welsh Historic Monuments. Crown Copyright).*

Set somewhat apart from the cloister were the monastic infirmary and the abbot's quarters *(Fig. 52)*. The infirmary at Strata Florida, into which a delirious monk had been carried in 1202,[221] lay in ruins by Suppression (1539),[222] but the infirmaries of Valle Crucis and Margam were still in use in 1528[223] and 1531[224] respectively. The 'infirmary-master' at Margam was a monk or brother of some consequence in its early days.[224a]

At Tintern – where (*c.* 1240) the shoulders of the deer taken in Trelech Park were granted as food for its monks[224b] – the infirmary great hall – of nave and two aisles delineated by round piers – measured 107ft. × 54ft. (33m. × 16m.).[225] In the 15th century, the aisles were separated from the nave by screen walls, and converted into individual chambers. Thus William Worcestre (1478) recorded the nave as being '34 yards long and 8 yards wide.'[226] He called the hall 'the infirmary chapel'. A covered passageway led into the quire of the church.

The medieval Cistercian abbot, needing to entertain and do business, had from the 13th century on his own accommodation. At Tintern, this was at first appended (under the same roof) to the monastic dorter and under-croft. Later that century, a separate abbot's house was erected, with a grand hall and small chapel added in the 14th century. Here was 'the abbot's table' where sat 'the gentlemen of his household'.[227] There was also a dovecot.[228] At Valle Crucis, the northern part of the dorter was converted (in the 15th century) into the 'common hall of the abbot',[229] necessitating an external staircase.[230] At a like date, the abbots of Neath adapted for their use the southern end of its dorter, undercroft and refectory.[231] This enhanced status of the abbot was reflected at Whitland, in stones 'set up for the *picture of the abbot*'.[232]

A vital necessity in monastic days, as now, was an adequate water supply and drainage system. Deriving its water from a hill side spring or the nearby Angidy

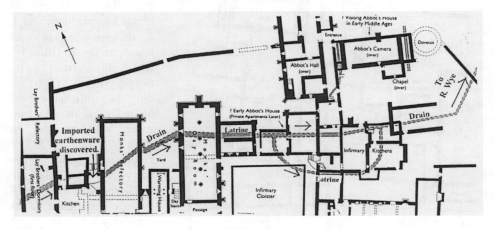

Fig. 53: Tintern Abbey: the Principal Drainage System.
(Cadw, Welsh Historic Monuments. Crown Copyright).

Brook, the partly underground stone-walled and substantial channel at Tintern is still in evidence (*Fig. 53*), and served the kitchen and rere-dorter, and, by means of side-channels, the infirmary and the abbatial complex.[233] By 1528, the tenants of the abbey had to be inhibited from 'washing dirty clothes, or other corrupt matter, in the stream which flows through the middle of the abbey'.[234] The drains at Valle Crucis ran down the hillside from the spring-line, and were bridged (in the west range) by stone or slate slabs.[235] The drainage of Strata Florida was carried to the river Teifi by a sewer constructed in stone;[236] excavation might reveal the character of the channel – deriving its water from the river Severn – which served Strata Marcella.[237] The rere-dorter of Maenan (*Fig. 54*) lay over Nant Llechog.[238] Lead water pipes served the refectories at Tintern and Valle Crucis, and a lead pipe conducted water to Strata Florida from the spring 'Dyffryn Tawel',[239] whilst fragments of lead piping have been found at Cwmhir[240] and Whitland.[241]

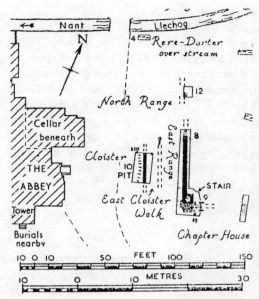

Fig. 54: Maenan Abbey: Excavation of 1963. (*L.A.S. Butler; Trans. Caernarfonshire Historical Society*).

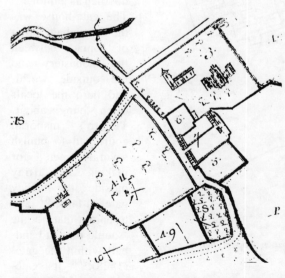

Fig. 55: Strata Florida (1765): Field A 11 = 'Y Green'. (*National Library of Wales, Nanteos Deposit 302*).

Within the precincts of all monasteries were a variety of ancillary domestic-orientated structures, like the brew-house, bake-house, laundry-house and pantry-house, listed for Tintern in a rental of 1568.[242] Aerial photography shows the large acreage devoted to such buildings at Tintern, and in recent years its guest-houses and evidences of early industrial activity have been excavated.[243] A robber (in 1445) stole both ale and dregs from its brew-house,[244] it had its brand of 'better beer',[245] and Margam its 'strong beer'.[246] There is note at Grace Dieu of its 'Bakehouse Meadow',[247] and at Whitland of its buttery.[248] The work and comings-and-goings associated with these, and other trades, made the outer court of every abbey bustle with activity.

The entire monastic complex – church, claustral buildings, and ancillary edifices – was ideally encompassed by a precinct wall; the enclosure thus formed comprehended 11 hectares (27 a.) at Tintern.[249] The open space afforded without the west door at Strata Florida was called 'the Convent Green' [*Cowart Grene*, 1543; *Fig. 55*].[250] Leland (about 1538) said of it that 'the base Court or Camp afore the Abbay is veri fair and large'.[251] Few substantial remains of precinct walls still stand; at Cwmhir only traces may be seen in nearby low banks.[252] At Strata Marcella aerial photography suggests a possible precinct wall. At Valle Crucis, the field-name of *lwyn-y-palys* may indicate that it was no more than an earthen rampart topped by a stake fence.[253]

Lands in Margam (1543) were described as being 'within and without the walls' of the monastery.[254] Gutun Owain wrote that at Basingwerk 'there is a stone wall by Cilgwri, and upon it a gate-house'.[255] The 'great gate', normally the only lawful means of entry, was the first impression of an abbey that visitors gained, and, being a substantial structure, parts of it may remain when much of the rest has disappeared.

Margam (1532),[256] Llantarnam (1534)[257] and Tintern (1536)[258] had their 'Great Gate'. That of Neath still has its porter's room.[259] The gate-house at Whitland, had its 'porter's lodge', and two major chambers, each with 'two windows of free-stones of three lights'.[260] It was at the great gate that the needy assembled for dole: Giraldus Cambrensis noted this of Margam,[261] and Guto'r Glyn noted at Strata Florida: 'The gate-way that has neither lock nor door-keeper'.[262] In course of time, subsidiary gates appeared: like the 'west gate' at Margam,[263] and the 'southern gate'[264] and 'money gate' *(Penny Perth)* at Strata Florida.[265]

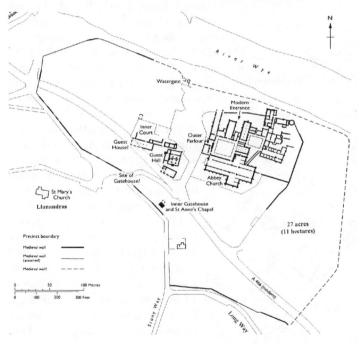

Fig. 56: Tintern Abbey: the Precinct.
(Cadw: Welsh Historic Monuments. Crown Copyright).

At Tintern the Great Gate incorporated the monastic prison, perhaps in the garret. Its last lay porter (whose duties including opening and closing the Great Gate at night) doubled as janitor.[266] The gate-house was the immediate point of contact between the monastery and the outside world, and here the locals often hung about. Tintern's manorial court had to punish several men for making an affray outside the abbey gate (1444),[267] and to enjoin that no-one 'should play at hand-ball within the gate' (1528).[268] Its gate-house had a chapel (St Anne's, with its own church-yard) converted by 1568 into a dwelling house.[269] Land routes – like the Stony Way and the Long Way – focussed on Tintern's Great Gate; the former was then the highway to Chepstow.[270] Its precinct wall was also pierced by its Water Gate,[271] which gave access (by the river Wye) to

Bristol, Chepstow and Monmouth, and (by its own ferry across the river) to its Brockweir Grange and its Manor of Woolaston.

The Monasteries as Repositories

In an age before there were any banks, large sums of money might be held in monasteries, partly because their abbots were frequently deputy collectors of subsidies and tenths, and partly because of the relative security an abbey afforded. When, in 1320, the Abbot of Tintern was appointed collector of a tenth he was enjoined to keep the money 'in a safe place'.[272] There is mention of 'the coffers' of Strata Florida (1533).[273] In a Cistercian house, the treasury – which safe-guarded both cash and valuable deeds – was commonly at dorter level, above the book-room and sacristy. It was a relative security: an abbot of Margam, that same year, told that 'the place of the abbey was too perilous to receive treasure',[274] whilst – like at Neath in the mid-15th century – deeds were not infrequently stolen from Cistercian houses.[275] Lhuyd (1707) noted that, to give added protection, certain records of Valle Crucis were kept (in monastic times) at 'a place, Y Twr, pretty near the Castle *[of Dinas Brân]*';[276] quite possibly a purpose-built abbey dependency.

There is evidence demonstrating the banking services offered by Welsh Cistercian houses, apart from the monies gained from tenths and safe-guarded for the Crown, and pecuniary aid afforded to the native princes. In his will, George Lewis of Netherwent (1508) arranged for Tintern to hold £9 yearly for ten years to provide for the marriage of his daughters.[277] £240 was deposited at Valle Crucis (1534) to provide £20 p.a. for the children of Robert ap Rhys, the abbot's father.[278] Hugh of Hereford (about 1187) borrowed nine silver marks from Margam,[279] which abbey (in 1255) paid £3 to two British Jews on behalf of Simon le Wyk.[280] Abbot Richard Mason of Valle Crucis (1448) acknowledged the repayment of a five mark debt by Sir Geoffrey Warburton.[281]

The private deeds of lay-folk might also be given into the safe-keeping of a Cistercian community. An abbot of Basingwerk (1328) undertook 'to hold, keep safe, and deliver', the indentures of an agreement between William de Hoton and his son, Henry.[282] Tintern (about 1465) had in its custody the evidences of the lands in Trelech of John ap Hopkin.[283] The Council of the Marches (1535) ordered that the deeds relating to the current Turberville-Loughor dispute be kept at Neath, in 'a fair chest'.[284] Other items entrusted to Cistercian abbeys included books (to Strata Florida by Giraldus Cambrensis)[285] and wine (to Tintern by King John).[286]

The personal and financial standing of some abbots led to their occasionally acting as a surety to a bond or to stand bail – although Innocent III, in his bull for Margam, ruled that no monk or *conversus* was to become a surety without the permission of his abbot and community.[287] Clearly, this was to avoid potential embarrassment. An abbot of Cwmhir (1276) was one of several sureties for the release of John ab Hywel from Prince Llywelyn's prison.[288] An abbot of Whitland (1434) helped to secure the release on bail of Hywel 'Whymys' of Powys from the Tower of London.[289] These are perhaps not isolated instances of such aid to fellow-Welshmen.

NOTES

1. *Brut* (1955) 183; Williams S.W. 1889, Appx. i.
2. *Chron. R. Wendover* III, 11–12.
3. *Arch. Camb.* 1867, 37.
4. NLW, Penrice and Margam Ch. 192.
5. NLW, Badm. Manorial 1645, m. 9; 1657, m. 12d.
6. Adams J. 1981, 87–91.
7. Harrison S. A. unpubl. report.
8. Butler L.A.S. 1984, 147–51.
9. Blashill T. 1881, Pl. 3.
10. Radford C.A.R. 1982, 58–76.
10a. Robinson D.M. pers. comm..
11. Taylor A.J. 1949, 314.
12. Robinson D.M. 1998, 28.
13. *Itin. Wm. Worcestre* 61 (and *n*).
14. Harrison S.A. et al. 1998, 182–85.
15. *Itin. Wm. Worcestre* 61; Craster O.E. 1956, 4.
16. Williams S.W. 1889, Appx. x, lvii–lviii.
17. Jones Pierce T. 1950, 25.
18. Robinson D.M. 1998, 28.
19. Evans D.H. 1995, 15.
20. Robinson D.M. 1996, non-paginated.
21. *Ibid.* 1995, 31–32.
22. *Ibid.* 1998, 31–32.
23. Evans D.H. 1995, 16.
24. RCAHMW, *County of Denbigh* (1914) 164.
25. Price G.V. 1952, 45–46.
26. Evans D.H. 1995, 16–17.
27. *Ibid.* 1995, 16, 30.
28. Harrison S.A. and Robinson D.M., forthcoming.
29. Robinson D.M. 1995, 31.
30. Evans D.H. 1995, 35.
31. Robinson D.M. 1998a, 150.
32. *Ibid.* 1990, 24.
33. Evans D.H. 1995, 15.
34. Robinson D.M. 1995, 57.
35. Rees S.A. unpubl. report.
36. Butler L.A.S. 1963, 37.
37. Cowley F.G. 1977, 55.
38. Neaverson E. 1949, 281.
38a. Lott G.K. 1998, 2.
39. Butler L.A.S. 1963, 37.
40. Newman J. 1995, 425.

41. Davies J. and Waters R. unpubl. report.
42. Cowley F.G. 1977, 55.
43. *Arch. Camb.* 1892, 5.
44. Davies J. and Waters R. unpubl. report; Williams S.W. 1889, 197–98, 211, 215.
45. Williams S.W. 1889, 105, 107.
46. Price G.V. 1952, 278.
47. *Cal. Close R.* 1235, 44; 1240, 185; 1253, 11.
48. Birch W. de Gray. 1902, 82.
49. *Op. cit.* 139.
50. Butler L.A.S. 1976, 93–94, 115–16.
51. *Episc. Acts* I, 276; *Mon. Angl.* V, 555b; *Cf.* PRO, E 315/50/74.
52. Butler L.A.S. 1976, 93–94, 115–16; Williams S.W. 1889, 221–22.
53. *Bromfield Extent* 60.
54. *D. Nanmor*, 74–75.
55. Butler L.A.S. 1963, 37; 1980, 5.
56. Williams S.W. 1889, 153.
57. *D. Nanmor*, 74.
58. Jones A. 1933, 176.
59. Butler L.A.S. 1963, 37; 1980, 8.
60. Robinson D.M. 1998a, 40.
60a. Robinson D.M. pers. comm.
61. Price G.V. 1952, 278, 280.
62. Williams S.W. 1889, Appx. iii.
63. Robinson D.M. 1998a, 96–97.
64. Rees S.A. unpubl. report; Robinson D.M. 1998a, 97.
65. *Itin. J. Leland* III, 52.
66. Harrison S.A. and Robinson D.M., forthcoming.
67. Taylor A.J. 1977, 291.
68. Cowley F.G. 1979.
69. Butler L.A.S. 1980, 16.
70. Carville G.C. 1979, 25–27.
71. Info. of Mr J.K. Knight. [Neath's church was 68 m. long, Tintern's 69.2 m; Neath's north-south transept width was 44.2 m., Tintern's 45.7 m.
72. Williams G. 1979, 64.
73. Price G.V. 1952, 95–96.
74. Williams S.W. 1891, 195.
75. Price G.V. 1952, 84.
76. Butler L.A.S. 1976, 95.

77. *Ibid.* 1976, 81.
78. *Ibid.* 1980, 6.
79. *Ibid.* 1976a, 13.
80. Harrison S.A. and Robinson D.M., forthcoming; Robinson D.M. 1998, 31, 49.
81. Butler L.A.S. 1976a, 17.
82. Robinson D.M. 1995, 44.
83. *Ibid.* 1998a, 179.
84. *Cf.* Williams S.W. 1890,
85. Robinson D.M. 1998a, 96.
86. *Itin. Wm. Worcestre* 61 ['vethym' = 'fathom'].
87. Lewis J.M. 1976, 3.
88. Butler L.A.S. 1976a, 13–14.
89. Robinson D.M. 1995, 45.
89a. *Ibid.* pers. comm.
90. Harrison S.A. unpubl. report; Robinson D.M. 1998, 31, 50, 52.
91. Evans D.H. 1995, 15, 24, 30.
92. Evans A.L. 1958, 30.
93. Lewis J.M. 1999, 260–61; Robinson D.M. 1995, 44–45.
94. Lewis J.M. 1999, 241–45; Jones A.L. 1996; some tiles are now on display in the National, Rhayader, Tenby and Welshpool Museums.
95. Lewis J.M. 1976, 3; Williams S.W. 1891, 189–95.
95a. Mein A.G. 1990, 102–03.
96. Evans A.L. 1958, 30–31.
97. Lewis J.M. 1999, 253–259; Robinson D.M. 1998, 32.
98. Lewis J.M. 1976, for much of this section.
99. Robinson D.M. 1993, non-paginated.
100. Lewis J.M. 1976, 37, 39; 1999, 226–28.
101. Robinson D.M. 1998, 32.
102. Lewis J.M. 1976, 3.
103. Heath (1828): 'About six yards, on the right, from the west entrance'.
104. *D. Nanmor*, 73.
105. *Itin. Wm. Worcestre* 61; Robinson D.M. 1990, 37.
106. Birch W. de Gray. 1902, 139; *Cf.* Dineley T. 1684 (1888 edn.) 309.
107. Williams G. 1962, 562.
108. *Augm. Rec.* 153.
109. PRO, C 1/1108, mm. 25–27.
110. Info. of Mr Geoff Mein.
111. Williams S.W. 1889, 227.
112. *Ibid.* 1891, 173, Pl. 14.
113. Butler L.A.S. 1976, 109.
114. Rigold S.E. 1977, 334–36, Pl. LXIb.
115. Now in Rhayader Museum.
116. Lewis M. 1970, 7, 11, 39, 68–69.
117. Jones M.C. 1873a, 29–33; [the glass was then in the east window of the church.]
118. Robinson D.M. 1998, 33.
119. Evans D.H. 1995, 28.
120. Parry T. 1962, 552–53.
121. Butler L.A.S. 1976a, 15.
121a. Courtney P. 1989, 117–21.
122. *Itin. Wm. Worcestre* 61 [his remarks imply that there were other belfries]; Robinson D.M. 1995, 48.
123. Williams S.W. 1889, 153.
124. Robinson D.M. 1996, unpaginated.
125. Robinson D.M. 1998, 48, 51–52.
126. Evans D.H. 1995, 32–33.
127. *Ann. Mon.* I, 20.
128. PRO, C 1/213, m. 106.
129. PRO, PROB 11/14, f. 21.
130. PRO, E 315/99, ff. 7d–8r.
131. *Visit. Wales* 38.
132. NLW, Penrice and Margam Ch. 2067.
133. RCAHMW, *County of Flint* (1912) 41.
134. Suggestion of Mr Stuart Harrison.
135. NLW, Dept. of Maps and Prints, P 556 *(Parker's Drawings* II*)* 64d.
136. PRO, PROB 11/21, f. 35.
137. Evans D.H. 1995, 28.
138. Price G.V. 1952, 164; Parry T. 1962, 553–53.
139. *Statuta* I, 472 (1217/31).
140. Hirsch-Davies J.E. de. 1916, 123.
141. *Op. cit.* 123.
142. Cowley F.G. 1977, 97.
143. *Cartae Glam.* II, 403.
144. PRO, PROB 11/14, f. 21; Williams D.H. 1976, 85.
145. PRO, PROB 11/21, f. 2.
146. *Valor Eccl.* IV, 371.

147. Robinson D.M. 1998, 49.
148. Now in the adjacent private garden.
149. Lewis J.M. 1976a, 37.
150. Butler L.A.S. 1976a, 15.
151. Robinson D.M. 1998, 48.
152. Evans D.H. 1995, 28.
153. Harrison S.A. and others. 1998, 177–268.
154. Robinson D.M. 1995, 48.
155. Harrison S.A. unpubl. report; Robinson D.M. 1998, 47.
156. Buck S. and N. 1742. III, No. 49.
157. Evans D.H. 1995, 23.
158. Robinson D.M. 1998, 44–45.
159. Robinson D.M. 1998a, 64.
160. Randolph J.A. 1905, 18.
161. Evans D.H. 1995, 24.
162. Williams D.H. 1998, 221–22.
163. Suggested by the roof line above the west door.
164. Butler L.A.S. 1976a, 13.
165. Robinson D.M. 1995, 42.
166. *Ibid*. 1998, 52.
167. Evans D.H. 1995, 34.
168. Williams D.H. 1984. I, 141.
169. Further research is needed here.
170. Robinson D.M. 1998, 52.
171. *Ibid*. 1995, 53.
172. PRO, PROB 11/14, f. 21.
173. Robinson D.M. 1998, 53.
174. *Ibid*. 1990, 42.
175. *Ibid*. 1996, unpaginated.
176. Evans D.H. 1995, 36.
177. Robinson D.M. 1998a, 140.
178. Evans D.H. 1995, 36–37.
179. Robinson D.M. 1998a, 140.
180. *Ibid*. 1998, 54–55.
181. *Ibid*. 1990, 42–43.
182. PRO, E 315/131, f. 45r.
183. Evans D.H. 1995, 42–43.
184. *Op. cit*. 37.
185. Robinson D.M. 1996, unpaginated.
186. Butler L.A.S. 1976a, 19.
187. Robinson D.M. 1997, 58
188. *Op. cit*. 39.
189. Butler L.A.S. 1976a, 17.
190. Robinson D.M. 1995, 60.
191. Evans D.H. 1995, 43.
192. Robinson D.M. 1995, 58.
193. Butler L.A.S. 1976a, 20.
194. *Op. cit*. 21.
195. Robinson D.M. 1995, 59.
196. *Ibid*. 1990a, unpaginated.
197. Butler L.A.S. 1976a, 21; Robinson D.M. 1990, 18–19 (for Tintern).
198. Robinson D.M. 1995, 60–62.
199. Butler L.A.S. 1976a, 21.
200. Robinson D.M. 1995, 60.
201. *Ibid*. 1996, unpaginated.
202. *Ibid*. 1990, 47.
203. Evans D.H. 1995, 45.
204. BL, Addit. MS 29,940, f. 68 (J. Carter).
205. Prichard J. 1881, 50–53; Russell A.D. 1979, 42.
205a. NLW, Badm. Manorial 1657, m. 2d.
206. Robinson D.M. 1996, unpaginated.
207. *Ibid*. 1990,m 48.
208. Lewis J.M. 1976a, 32 (Nos. 54–55).
209. Evans D.H. 1995, 45.
210. Robinson D.M. 1995, 62–63.
211. Butler L.A.S. 1976a, 22.
212. Evans D.H. 1995, 47.
213. Robinson D.M. 1995, 63.
214. NLW, Badm. Manorial 1663, m. 4d.
215. PRO, E 315/92, f. 97d.
216. Robinson D.M. 1990a, unpaginated.
217. Butler L.A.S. 1976a, 23.
218. Evans D.H. 1995, 47.
219. Ludlow N.D. and others; unpubl. report.
220. Robinson D.M. 1996 (plan).
221. Butler L.A.S. 1976a, 22.
222. Williams S.W. 1889, Appx. iii.
223. NLW Deed 915.
224. PRO, E 315/92, f. 1d.
224a. Birch W. de Gray. 1897, 23; (N.B: the 'Barber's Land' at Neath's Sker Grange: Birch W. de Gray. 1902, 143).
224b. *Cal. Charter R*. III, 98.
225. Robinson D.M. 1995, 64–66.
226. *Itin. Wm. Worcestre* 59.
227. PRO, E 315/92, f. 97d.
228. Robinson D.M. 1995, 67–68.
229. PRO, E 315/91, f. 61r-d.
230. Evans D.H. 1995, 40–41.

231. Butler L.A.S. 1976a, 23.
232. Owen G.D. 1935, 363.
233. Craster O.E. 1956, 11–12 (plan).
234. NLW, Badminton Manorial 1663, m. 4d.
235. Butler L.A.S. 1976, 82–86.
236. Williams S.W. 1889, 223.
237. Williams D.H. 1992, 83–84.
238. Butler L.A.S. 1963, 25–26.
239. Williams S.W. 1889, 224.
240. Now in Rhayder Museum.
241. Donovan E. 1805. II, 254.
242. NLW, Badm. Manorial 1524, f. 44.
243. Courtney P. 1989, 99–143.
244. NLW, Badminton Manorial 1657, m. 7r.
245. PRO, E 315/92, f. 97d.
246. *Cartae Glam*. III, 1132 (DCCC–CXXIV).
247. Owen E. 1950, 196.
248. Owen G.D. 1935, 360–62.
249. Robinson D.M. 1995, 18.
250. Williams S.W. 1889, Appx. xciii.
251. *Op. cit*. Appx. iii.
252. Clwyd-Powis Arch. Trust., unpubl. report; Williams S.W. 1890, 412–13.
253. Pratt D. 1997, 46.
254. Birch W. de Gray. 1897, 363.
255. *Arch. Camb*. I (1846) 111.
256. NLW, Penrice and Margam Ch. 539.
257. PRO, SC 6 (Hen. VIII) 2497, f. 2d.
258. PRO, LR 1/228, f. 6d.
259. Butler L.A.S. 1976a, 27.
260. Owen G.D. 1935, 360–62.
261. *Journey through Wales* 127.
262. Hartwell Jones G. 1912, 379.
263. Evans A.L. 1958, 35.
264. Hartwell Jones G. 1912, 379.
265. PRO, SC 6 (Hen. VIII) 4868, m. 7.
266. PRO, LR 1/228, f. 6d.
267. NLW, Badm. Manorial 1657, mm. 6r, 9r.
268. *Ibid*. m. 4d.
269. NLW, Badm. Manorial 1524, f. 44; [In 1651, it was mistakenly noted as 'Agnes Chappel':NLW, Badm. Manorial 2445, f. 12].
270. NLW, Badm. Manorial 1021, f. 1 (of 1694).
271. Part of its fabric now incorporated into the Anchor Hotel.
272. *Cal. Fine R*. 1320, 45.
273. PRO, C 1/721, m. 11.
274. *Cal. Chancery Warrants* I, 517.
275. PRO, C 1/213, f. 106.
276. Lhuyd E. 1707. II, 41.
277. PRO, PROB 11/10 (Bennett).
278. PRO, E 315/131/ f. 45r.
279. *Cartae Glam*. I, 196–97 (CXC).
280. NLW, Penrice and Margam Ch. 2060; le Wyk granted the abbey its lands in Saltmarsh, Gloucs., by way of recompense.
281. Price G.V. 1952, 249.
282. *Chester Deeds* 187–88.
283. PRO, SC 8/344, E. 1313.
284. *Arch. Camb*. 1853, 243 (where: 'a fir chest').
285. Cowley F.G. 1977, 122.
286. *Rot. Litt. Claus*. I, 230.
287. Birch W. de Gray. 1897, 173.
288. *Litt. Wallie* I, 230.
289. *Cal. Close R*. 1434, 271–72.

CHAPTER 8

THE MONASTERY PERSONNEL

Despite the: 'almost unheard of rigour of their life',[1] the founding monks in the Cistercian abbeys of Wales attracted considerable numbers of people of native stock to join their ranks as choir monks or *conversi*. Recruitment was assisted, in respect of Strata Florida, by Alexander III (1159–81) who forbade anyone 'to receive or return any brother, cleric or lay, after profession had been made',[2] whilst Llewelyn ab Iorwerth disallowed any claim or action against Aberconwy (1199) 'by reason of its reception of any man, no matter what his status, once he had become a monk'.[3] In both cases there were exceptions, and the protection did not normally cover the first probationary year.

Within or near the monastic precincts was a wider community comprised of permanent secular residents (familiars, servants, corrodians) and temporary visitors (the traveller, the guest, the pilgrim, the poor, the sick and the dying). An abbot of Margam (1384) claimed that he had to provide for 'an hundred people',[4] whilst, on the eve of its Suppression (1537), Aberconwy's resources had to support forty persons 'besides poor people and strangers'.[5] The 'community' proper consisted of those (men only) who had made their religious profession, but they were by no means the only settlers within, or close to, the walls of the monasteries.

The Choir-Monks

The evidence regarding the size of the early Cistercian communities in Wales consists very largely of statements made some considerable time after the age of settlement – yet they have a ring of truth about them. Whitland (1440) claimed to have been able 'at the time of its foundation' to house one hundred monks.[6] This was perhaps an exaggeration, (and may have included its roll-call of resident *conversi*), but within thirty years of its foundation (1140) it was able to found three new abbeys, and later went on to establish two more in Ireland.[7] The minimum complement for a new monastery was an abbot and twelve monks, whilst an early statute of the General Chapter insisted that an abbey was not to found a daughter-house unless it itself had a complement of at least sixty monks.[8]

Three quite independent pieces of evidence for three abbeys of Whitland's lineage stress this same number. A petition from Llantarnam to Edward II (1317) states how it had 'but twenty monks instead of sixty as formerly'.[9] John Charlton, lord of Powys (1328), claimed that 'there used to be sixty monks', at Strata Marcella;[10] whilst the antiquary, John Leland (*c.* 1538), related of Cwmhir that its 'first foundation was made for sixty monks'.[11] A contemporaneous clue to community size comes in the numbers present at arbitration between Cwmhir and Strata Marcella (1226): 'From the seniors and counsellors of their houses about fifty persons'.[12]

The deliberate keeping of a balance between economic resources and the numbers in a community[13] was exemplified at Margam (1329) when, having suffered from the

De Clare depredations, it needed ten more monks to bring its numbers 'up to strength',[14] and when (1383) its appropriation of Afan church gained papal approval only on condition that it increased its complement of monks by three.[15] As noted before, the Abbot of Valle Crucis (1528) made up his numbers by importing 'strange monks';[16] in other words, deriving from other houses of the Order. In these Tudor times a few abbeys may have received reinforcements from English houses.

The Welsh wars of the late 13th century and the growth in popularity of the mendicant Orders – thirty-nine Dominican friars at Haverfordwest in 1285[17] – were probably amongst the factors causing a considerable decline in the size of the Cistercian communities well before the Black Death laid its icy hand on Wales. Only Margam (1336) is known to have possessed a substantial community at this time: thirty-eight monks and forty *conversi*.[18] Llantarnam (1317)[19] and Basingwerk (1347)[20] had only twenty monks each, and Strata Marcella (1328) but eight.[21] By the latter part of the 14th century (1388) several houses were down to single figures (as Aberconwy – six,[22] and Cymer – five[23]). At least two abbeys showed an ongoing consistency in their numbers: Tintern, with fifteen monks in 1395,[24] still had thirteen in 1536;[25] and Whitland, noted as having seven monks in 1388, is credited with eight in 1440[26] and seven again in 1539, but the size of Margam's community (1532–36) seems to have substantially declined.[27]

The total company of medieval White Monks in Wales probably exceeded two thousand, of whom the names of some 750 are known.[28] The leading Christian names borne in religion were John, William, Thomas, Richard and David. Relatively few (forty-three) bore this latter name of Wales' patron saint and two of its notable princes, and, of the nation's other holy men of pre-Norman times, only Deiniol (at Strata Florida) finds solitary mention. It is maybe a reflection of the anglicisation of Tintern that whilst almost every other house had its Davids, Tintern had none. On the other hand, only two Edwards are on record; both were monks of Tintern, a house much favoured by Edward I. Both occur in the period 1307–73, during the reigns of Edward II and III, and not so long after the translation of Edward the Confessor. The name of Llywelyn (borne by six religious of Cymer, Strata Florida and Whitland) is limited to the period 1274–1380, which saw the closing years of Llywelyn ap Gruffydd's life, and when his memory was still vivid in Welsh minds. These facts reflect both the political realities of Wales and the differences in racial mix within its abbeys.

The evidence for the houses of north Wales suggests thoroughly Welsh communities prior to the Edwardian Conquest, and the great bulk of their members thereafter as still being of local origin. At Aberconwy, at least two-thirds (perhaps much more) of the known religious were of undoubted Welsh background, and, with the exception of two imported abbots in the late 15th century, a significant English component only appears at the time of the Suppression.[29] A list of the monks of Valle Crucis (1275) is entirely Welsh: Anian Rufus (prior), Madog, Tudur, Madog Iorwerth, Sigymab, Hywel and David.[30] In the first half of the 15th century this house had English abbots intruded, but thereafter abbots of local stock ruled – as John ap Richard (of Ruabon) and John Lloyd (of Bodidris).[31]

Matters were very different in the Flintshire house of Basingwerk, situated in the disputed Perfeddwlad. By 1281, the eve of the Conquest – if not well before, the county of Cheshire provided most vocations. One abbot (1346) told how his monks lived 'among the Welsh', implying that they themselves were aliens.[32] Only with the abbacy of Thomas Pennant (1481–1522) did the monastery gain anything of a Welsh character. His guest, and bard, Tudur Aled, wrote of him as being 'a lion in battle, who has overthrown the foreigner'.[33] Whether this referred to the previous rule of English abbots (as Henry Wirral and Richard Kirkby), or to freedom from the yoke of Buildwas, is less certain.

In central Wales, the names of but thirty-five monks and eleven *conversi* of Strata Florida have come down to us. They are practically all Welsh down to Tudor times, when the presence of monks such as Henry Howtone (1515), James Whitney (1515) and Thomas Durham (1539), suggests a wider net being cast for vocations. The 13th century community at Strata Marcella was strongly Welsh, and the surnames of some monks reveal their local origin, as Adam of Pole (1246) and John of Cydewain (1277), but, after the troubles with John Charlton *(Chapter 3)* a Border element appears – like Nicholas Worthen (1346) and Thomas de Wrockwardine (1360). A similar picture occurs at Cwmhir, where at least two-thirds of the forty known monastic names are of Welsh provenance. Again, a Border (but still Welsh) presence is evident in the 14th century, exemplified by monks like Gervase of Heyope (1365) and William of Ceri (1362) – a locality where the abbey had substantial lands. Yet again, an English component appears in Tudor times – as Richard of Chester and William Leicester.

In Welsh Wales, the Celtic members remained in the majority, but what language did these monks speak? Their earlier deeds were written in Latin, some of their later ones in English, none seemingly in Welsh. This does not mean that Welsh was not spoken; far from it. In 1228, it was the vernacular employed at Tracton in Ireland by the monks Whitland had sent there four years previously, so clearly Welsh was widely employed at Whitland at that time. Indeed, Stephen Lexington (Abbot of Stanley and later of Savigny and Clairvaux) on visitation there, strongly objected, asserting that 'certain members of Whitland are more concerned that the abbot of Tracton and his community speak the Welsh language, than that they do the will of God and the Order'.[34] The later evidence of John Leland (*c.* 1538) suggests a bilingual nature (Welsh and English) to everyday speech at Strata Florida and Whitland in his time.[35]

In south Wales, the maintenance of a large number of Anglo-Norman monks at Margam and Neath may have been a deliberate policy of the Earls of Gloucester (as lords of Glamorgan).[36] Of the seventy known pre-1270 religious of Margam, about fifteen came from England but the bulk were of local Anglo-Norman stock – like Robert Poynz and Walter Luvel (of notable families) and Walter Baglan and Philip of Kenfig (of lesser breed). Not one bore an unmistakeably Welsh name, though some Welsh monks may have sheltered (as did Prior Clement of Neath) behind an Anglo-Norman name in religion.[37] Further, until the 16th century, perhaps none of the abbots were truly derived from the Welsh nation, though – like William Corntown (1468–87) – they might be natives of Glamorgan. In his day, the presence of Richard Stradling as cellarer, shows that the monastery still attracted local vocations of good family.

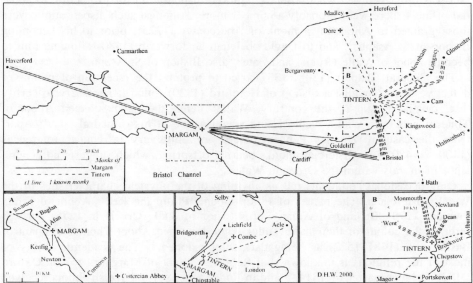

Fig. 57: Places of Origin of Some of the Monks of Margam and Tintern.

In south-east Wales, Welsh names were almost unknown amongst the one hundred known monks of Tintern, but at least five were Bristol men and four came from the Forest of Dean. The Wye valley and Gloucester were other important recruitment areas, and local vocations are also indicated in the names of monks like John Went (1385) and Richard Magor (1395). From its Norfolk manor of Acle came John 'Akyll' (1460). Just as Basingwerk was the odd man out in north Wales, so too was Llantarnam in the south-east. Most of the known twenty-six monastic names appear to be of a Welsh background, and some indicate quite local vocations – as David Newport and Stephen Went (1426).

There was a limited movement from one abbey to another (possibly on expulsion or dispersal or promotion), and from the sphere of influence of one monastery to membership of another. Tintern had in its community Roger of Kingswood (its Gloucestershire daughter-house, 1291), as well as Henry and William of Combe (1331) and John of Dore (1406). On the other hand, we find a Thomas Tintern as Abbot of Stanley (1452), a John Tintern as Abbot of Buildwas (1471), and a Matthew Whitlonde at Dore (1451). A monk of Grace Dieu, Philip Kingstone (1366) bore the name of a grange of Abbey Dore, its mother-house.[38]

Not a few monks were of irregular birth, resulting as they did from clerical concubinage. The notable Cadwgan of Bangor (Abbot of Whitland, 1203–15) was said to be the son of an Irish priest and a Welsh mother.[39] The last Abbot of

Basingwerk, Nicholas Pennant (1529–36) was the third son of his predecessor.[40] At least seven other monks are on record as being of illegitimate birth, but – as the fact was only recorded when a monk required dispensation for promotion to abbatial office – there were probably a number more. Amongst such dispensations were those granted to Abraham, a monk of Aberconwy (1225), prior to his becoming Bishop of St Asaph,[41] and to David ab Ieuan ab Iorwerth (1480) allowing him to become abbot of Valle Crucis, and, later, also Bishop of St Asaph.[42]

The General Chapter (1308, 1337) tried to prohibit the reception of monks of defective birth,[43] whilst a bishop of Hereford (1320) found it necessary to certify that, despite gossip to the contrary, Walter Penk, the newly elected Abbot of Tintern, was born within wedlock and was a native of his cathedral city.[44] Apart from the case of Thomas Pennant, there are only very infrequent references (1400,[45] 1480[46]) to Cistercian monks bearing offspring, which suggests no general lapse of morals within the Order in Wales.

Only occasional comments tell us anything of the physical characteristics of the Welsh Cistercians. The names of Philip Goch ('Philip the Red', Abbot of Strata Florida, 1278–80), and of Anian Rufus (prior of Valle Crucis in 1278) perhaps refer to the colour of their hair. Tudur Aled described Abbot Thomas Pennant of Basingwerk (1481–1522) as being dark-complexioned.[47] The academic ability of most of the religious is unknown, but Robert, a monk of Margam, was an Oxford DD and regent master by 1314,[48] and in Tudor times several Welsh abbots received an university education.[49] One monk of Tintern, Thomas Brockweir (1478), was an alchemist.[50] The medieval pace of life allowed some monks to become jubilarians – like John Cherville (at Tintern by 1388 and until at least 1437), and Henry Norton (already at Strata Marcella when made deacon in 1491, and, after its suppression, living at Whitland until 1539).[51]

The lifelong stability in their monastery undertaken from the time of their profession did not preclude abbots and monks travelling on the necessary business of their house – the cellarer especially, on missions for bishops and secular magnates, to work on the granges, to further their studies, to present themselves to the diocesan bishop for their ordination or abbatial blessing, or to attend the General Chapter. Travel was the exception rather than the norm, and Innocent III ruled (in his second bull for Margam, 1203) that 'no professed brother was to depart without permission of the abbot, and no one was to harbour him without a certificate'.[52] The monks of Llantarnam, finding it inconvenient whilst journeying to observe Cistercian custom fully, received papal dispensation (1398) to eat meat, if necessary, when away on business;[53] as did a monk of Aberconwy (1398).[54] Holidays were never taken, nor were pilgrimages entered upon.[55]

Young monks seeking ordination usually travelled to the local cathedral or the chapel upon an episcopal manor – not a few Welsh religious were ordained in Hereford diocese, but one monk of Strata Florida, John ap Rhys (1370), received holy orders in St Paul's, London.[56] Further afield, Nicholas de Stanton (1351), a monk of Grace Dieu probably on his abbey's affairs, was said to be detained in Rome 'by the difficulties and toil of the journey'.[57] It was not uncommon – perhaps hastened by the strain of travelling on horseback – for monks to die on a journey and not see their house again. Abbot Hugh de Wyke of Tintern died in London 'about the middle of the night', on 10 November 1320, and was buried in the Cistercian abbey nearest at hand – Stratford in Middlesex.[58] More happily, a monk of Basingwerk, Walter de London (1348), who had been staying at Merevale, returned home with letters of commendation. Merevale was sorry to lose him, and its abbot praised 'his religious conversation and probity of conduct'.[59]

Few choir-monks, in the early days of large communities, could aspire to the abbatial dignity. The chances were greater as the communities became smaller, and sometimes contentions and intrigues arose – as noted before of the 15th and early 16th centuries. As early as 1259, in a vacancy at Tintern 'a clandestine election' had been held, though the result was allowed to stand.[60] Proven abbots might find themselves promoted to the governance of other, perhaps more important, monasteries. Ralph, Abbot of Tintern (1232–45), was translated first to Dunkeswell (1245–52) and then to the premier English abbey of Waverley (1252–66). David Wynchcombe, originally a monk of Hailes, was abbot in turn of Aberconwy (1482–88), of Cymer (1495–96) and of Strata Marcella (1496–1513).[61] More often than not, an abbot emerged from those monks already holding a position of responsibility in their monastery or a daughter-house, like Gervase at Neath (1218), formerly its prior; Henry Newland at Tintern (1493), previously its cellarer; and perhaps Cadwgan at Cymer (1284), earlier the master of its *conversi*.[62] Without a doubt and certainly in the later Middle Ages, the post of cellarer was the usual stepping stone into the abbacy of Tintern.

Seven or eight Welsh Cistercians were elevated to the episcopate. Frequently they were already abbots of their respective houses, and – as described before – sometimes continued to hold this office simultaneously with the episcopal dignity. Robert of Lancaster was concurrently Abbot of Valle Crucis and Bishop of St Asaph for twenty-three years (1409–33); this arrangement undoubtedly assisted him financially, and perhaps solved an accommodation problem in the wake of the mayhem caused by the Glyn Dŵr Revolt.[63]

Some Cistercians – as Rotoland and Philip of Aberconwy (c. 1200) – claimed the episcopal office unsuccessfully,[64] whilst one abbot of Valle Crucis (John Lloyd, 1518) was passed over.[65] Three Cistercian bishops with no apparent Welsh background ministered in Wales: Thomas, a monk of Merevale, becoming a Bishop *in partibus*, assisted in Llandaff (1361); Tideman of Winchcombe, a monk of Netley in royal service as the king's physician, became abbot of Beaulieu and then Bishop of Llandaff (1393–95) and later of Worcester (1395–1401); Thomas Skevington, also Abbot of Beaulieu – where he mostly lived – was concurrently Bishop of Bangor (1509–33).[66] Said to be 'the richest monk in England', his patronage allowed Abbot Baddesley of Merevale to appropriate the tithes of Llangynhafal.[67]

The *Conversi*

The multitude of lay-brothers (correctly termed the *conversi*) who at first manned the granges of the White Monks, and who, in their heyday, often outnumbered the choir monks by more than two to one, were not an innovation of the Order but received greater emphasis as a distinctive institution within it. The *Charter of Charity* held them 'to be our brothers, and equally with our monks, sharers of our goods both spiritual and temporal'.[68] They did not wear the cowl, only a cloak; they were not tonsured but did have a distinctive hairstyle and, unlike the monks, they grew beards. Yet they were true religious, for they vowed obedience, lived a common life, and, if they left the Order, might not marry. They were not all of lowly birth, nor perhaps were they all unlettered, though this was the general rule.[69] They were generally local men, and so, even at Anglo-Norman Margam, many in the early 13th century were of the Welshry: like Anian, Cnaithur, Caradog and Rhiryd.[70] Tintern's *conversi* had very different, but still local surnames, as John of Aylburton and William of the Marsh.[71]

In the Order at large, by the close of the 12th century, men of doubtful quality, motivated by self-interest, were amongst those entering the ranks of the *conversi*.[72] This could well help account for the troubles with drink (1190–96), for rebelliousness (1206), and for widespread apostasy (in Elfael, *c.* 1205), described before. So far as Margam was concerned, men seeking admittance as *conversi* were mostly expected to be single and without financial difficulties. Indeed, several were not without private means and were possessed of their own distinctive seals. A classic instance was that of Gille Seis (*c.* 1200) who was 'to take the habit of a *conversus*', unless debarred by marriage or debts. He was able to transfer to the abbey the ownership of twenty-four acres of land, and such admissions appear to have been encouraged by Margam as it built up its estates.[73] The reluctance of Margam to take on any burdens was shown when Madog Vydir (*c.* 1290) became a *conversus*; his three sons were obliged to meet all debts and liabilities due to the Earl of Gloucester by their father.[74]

Madog was perhaps now a widower, whilst the entry of (presumably previously) married men as *conversi* is also reflected in the note of 'Matthew ap David, of the diocese of St David's, son of a Cistercian lay-brother'.[75] Other motives for becoming *conversi* included the wish for security if disabled by physical defect or old age. In these cases, little work could have been expected of them, but an abbey often received with their profession substantial amounts of land: Margam gained the nucleus of its Stormy Grange when Geoffrey Sturmi (by 1173) entered on becoming infirm,[76] and its valuable property at Resolfen (*c.* 1200) accrued from Morgan ap Caradog, Lord of Afan, when it took in one of his tribesmen, Canaythen, blinded whilst a political hostage.[77] Some early *conversi* may not have been entirely illiterate – like Espus, Hugh and Rhiryd, who were witnesses to important charters.[78]

For most of the 13th century, the *conversi* might be assisted not only by hired labour, but also by 'familiars', living in close association with them and doing much the same work, but without the same religious profession and obligations.[79] This institution was all but abolished in 1293, as the presence of 'familiars' in a community was found to be unconducive to the strict keeping of the religious life by its other members.[80] It is possible that the *famuli* of Margam and Neath killed by the local Welshry (1224–27)[81] may have been familiars, rather than ordinary hired hands, such as the *servitores* mentioned in a similar raid on Whitland (1258).[82]

The *conversi* were under the authority – where work and discipline were concerned – of the abbey cellarer, but had, as spiritual mentor and confessor, a monk appointed as 'master of the *conversi*'.[83] Such 'masters of the lay-brethren' find mention in Wales throughout much of the 13th century, suggesting a still considerable presence of *conversi* in the houses of the Principality.[84] Theirs was a post, as that of cellarer, of considerable responsibility, fitting them for advancement, like Philip at Valle Crucis (1234) who became its prior, and Cadwgan of Cymer (1281) who seemingly was elected its abbot.[85] One of the master's duties was to visit the granges regularly: there is note of Dore's 'master' going to its Welsh grange at Trawscoed to give Communion to the brethren there one Easter.[86]

Most of the *conversi* lived and worked on the granges, ideally returning to the abbey for worship on Sundays and great festivals. Those dwelling permanently at the abbey had their own quarters in the west range *(Chapter 7)*. Whilst physically separated from the choir-monks, certain missions and work were shared from time to time. In 1198, 'monks and *conversi*' (probably of Strata Florida) meditated in a territorial dispute between two sons of the recently deceased Prince Rhys ap Gruffydd, indicating that some lay-brethren were of ability and standing.[87] At harvest-time, choir-monks would assist the *conversi* in the fields, as when both 'monks and brothers' of Cwmhir (1231) reaped the corn at its Carnaf and Gabalfa Granges by the river Wye.[88]

A *conversus*, the 'granger' or 'master of the grange', had day-to-day charge of each grange, as Richard, granger at Margam's Llanfeuthin [1199].[89] At Margam, *conversi* assisted in the guest-house: like Richard and Thomas [c. 1230]),[90] and helped as porter, as did an earlier Richard [c. 1200].[91] There is note of *conversi* fulfilling a variety of tasks, like mill-construction [Llantarnam's Maestir Mill, 1204],[92] clearing woodland [of Strata Florida, 1284],[93] guarding the monastic flocks [on Cwmhir's Nant-yr-Arian Grange, 1291],[94] and having overall charge of an abbey's fisheries [like Tintern's John de Walweir, 1322].[95] The surnames of *conversi* may suggest the tasks they performed, as John Faber ('smith') at Margam [1205]),[96] and Richard 'the parmenter' ('furrier') at Tintern [1261],[97] or suggest their physical characteristics, like early on at Margam, William Grosso (? William the Fat) and Walter Rufus (? Walter the Redhead).[98]

The changing social conditions of the early 14th century, accelerated by the Black Death, were to cause a rapid diminution in the numbers of *conversi*, but the decline was already underway as early as 1274, when the General Chapter drew attention to a considerable shortage.[99] *Conversi* were still being recruited at Aberconwy (1311), the monastery being fined for admitting two of the king's villeins, Adam and Rhiryd, into their ranks.[100] None are known at Strata Florida after 1294, whilst the decline in their numbers at Valle Crucis is demonstrated by a 14th century change in use for their refectory.[101] Only at Margam (1356) is there evidence of substantial numbers (forty, as opposed to thirty-eight monks) in the midst of the century.[102] It still had 'monks and *conversi*' in 1396.[103]

In these latter decades of their presence, not all *conversi* were faultless, and it was reported to the General Chapter (1294) that many did not want to do manual work.[104] *Conversi* of Neath (1269) stole some of the visiting Abbot of Savigny's horses, in order to make a getaway.[105] Four *conversi* of Strata Marcella (1277, 1281) found themselves imprisoned in Montgomery Castle.[106] Two of Margam's lay-brothers were acquitted at Glamorgan County Court (1358) on charges of robbery and harbouring a felon.[107] At a later date, a *conversus* of Dore stationed at its Trawscoed Grange was said to be so evil, although young and handsome, that the sacred Host would not enter his mouth.[108]

Cultural Activity

'Barely a dozen books can now be identified with certainty as belonging to a Welsh Cistercian house'.[109] Nevertheless, their monks had a definite partiality for books, and a distinct sense of loss when they were damaged or stolen. Gerald of Wales held it against the community of Strata Florida that they had tricked him out of his books (*c.* 1200), whilst books formed part of the subject matter of a dispute between Aberconwy and Basingwerk (1215). Books of the former house were looted by English soldiers (1245), and also 'stolen in the disturbance in Wales' (1448).[110] At Llantarnam (1398) 'the books of the church' were devastated by fire.[111] The *ex libris* inscription in many a monastic library book called down spiritual sanctions upon any purloiner – witness that of the *Novum Digestum* owned by Neath: 'A book of St Mary of Neath, whoever takes it away without the consent of the abbot and convent, may he be anathema'.[112] One *ex libris*, of a former book of Valle Crucis, is now so faded as to be readable only under ultra-violet light.[113]

Earl Robert of Gloucester, who founded Margam, was a patron of both William of Malmesbury and Geoffrey of Monmouth, so it is not surprising that its library contained a copy of the former's *De Gestis Anglorum* and of the latter's *Historia Regum Brittaniae*, as well as a 12th century abbreviation of the Domesday Book.[114] The few books known to have once belonged to a Welsh house have survived changes of ownership, and are now to be found in the libraries of such institutions as Eton College (Valle Crucis' *Dialogues*)[115] and Hereford Cathedral (Neath's *Digestum Novum*).[116] Many works have simply disappeared, whilst the books of Neath *may* have gone to the now dispersed Stradling library at St Donat's,[117] and those of Tintern to the Worcester stronghold of Raglan Castle – but lost after its surrender (1646) during the Civil War.[118] The *Book of Usages*, held at Strata Florida in 1202, is no more.[119]

One work which does survive – in the British Library – a 12th century edition of the *Homilies of St Gregory*, tells its own history on its flyleaf. The property of Llantarnam, it was given away in 1248 to the newly-established abbey at Hailes, when Earl Richard of Cornwall – Hailes' founder – wrote round to other Cistercian houses for gifts for its library.[120] This was not uncommon.[121] Long before the volume left Llantarnam, a monk scribbled notes on the rear flyleaf telling of the building of the Maestir Mill (1204), near Risca. A flyleaf of one of Margam's books notes a court of the abbey held in 1421.[122] Such miscellaneous monastic jottings often render valuable information of the times.

A reminder of monastic literacy came (in 1262) when a monk of Margam, Philip of Carmarthen 'wrote with his own hand' that abbey's appeal to Rome when engaged in a dispute with Gloucester Abbey.[123] The White Monks were thus equipped to play an invaluable role in Wales by the compiling of annals and chronicles. Pride of place goes to Strata Florida which (about 1175 – only ten years after its foundation) took over from the *clas* at Llanbadarn the *Brut y Tywysogyon* (the Chronicle of the Princes).[124] It seems to have been written up in Welsh by a monk of the abbey not long after 1282, with one version (*Peniarth MS 20*, copied at Valle Crucis) having an extension down to 1332.[125] Once the native princes were no more, the impetus for its compilation – which had culled information from other houses of north and west Wales[126] – had disappeared. At a date when the memory of monastic days was still fresh in older people's minds, Humphrey Lloyd in the *History of Cambria* (1584), published after his death, told how: 'The succession and acts of the Princes of Wales', were recorded at Aberconwy and Strata Florida. He called the *Brut*, 'the Brytish booke of Stratflur', and noted that (under 1213) it 'set down the earnest repentance of King John'.[127] It also gave valuable details of the history of Strata Florida itself.[128]

Whitland, rather than Strata Florida, [129] may have been the place where the *Cronica de Wallia* (1190–1216) was copied, and its extensions made, judging from the interest it shows in the descendants of the Lord Rhys and their families.[130] The abbreviated *Domesday Book* of Strata Florida seems to have been a copy of an edition held at Margam.[131] On it is written an independent Latin version (for 1203–86) of the *Annales Cambriae*, the last entry referring to the conflagration at Strata Florida in 1286.[132]

Other transcriptions credited to Cistercian houses include the *Mabinogion* (to Strata Florida or Strata Marcella)[133] and the *Book of Aneirin* (to Basingwerk).[134] Thomas Pennant, penultimate abbot of the latter house, may have added marginal notes to the *Llyfr Du Basing* (the *Black Book of Basingwerk*) also ascribed to it.[135] A 'lost chronicle' of Tintern may have been the source for additions (covering the period of 1305 to 1323) made to a copy of *Flores Historiarum* (*Plate X-B*) from the Benedictine abbey of Holme St. Benets (Norfolk). The additional material shows a distinct interest in Tintern, telling of the death of Abbot Hugh de Wyke, the election of Walter of Hereford, and of the confirmation of Tintern's charters.[136]

The *Annals of Margam* were 'a primary source of great value for Glamorgan history'.[137] Covering the years from the death of Edward the Confessor down to 1232, they draw upon William of Malmesbury for the pre-Cistercian period prior to 1147. The Margam chronicler was clearly Anglo-Norman in sympathy with little liking for the Welshry.[138] As others of his time, he drew attention to severe weather conditions (in the winters of 1204 and 1222),[139] but he was the only British annalist to give a detailed account of the murder of Arthur of Brittany (in 1203) by his uncle, King John, a monarch who later encamped twice at the monastery.[140] The scribe concerned had other (archival and secretarial) duties, and 'his activities reveal the bureaucratic versatility Margam's scriptorium had developed by the mid-13th century'.[140a]

Not so revealing as its name suggests is the extant *Register and Chronicle of Aberconwy* – a late-medieval copy held at Hailes Abbey – which includes lists of its territorial possessions and those of its mother-house (Strata Florida), an incomplete account of the *Quo Warranto* Proceedings (of 1348), and a 'Chronicle' down to 1283: again, interest seems to have flagged after the Edwardian Conquest.[141] The only extant portions of the so-called 'Chronicle of Tintern' are largely genealogical in nature,[142] but Tintern did have a fuller chronicle – which William of Worcester noted on his visit there (1478).[143] A different, and liturgical work, composed at most abbeys – like Margam – was their 'martyrology', which included the obits of their founders and benefactors.[144]

Other writings emanating from Margam included a concordance to St Bernard's *Song of Songs* – a copy of this work (by an un-named abbot) found its way to the Flanders abbey of the Dunes.[145] It now reposes in Bruges Municipal Library. Leland noted the existence of a book of verse on birds and beasts composed by Walter, a monk of Margam; he was one of only two Welsh Cistercian authors listed by 16th and 17th century bibliographers[146] – the other was Cadwgan of Bangor *(Chapter 2)*. William of Corntown (Abbot of Margam: 1468–87) has been described as a writer of historical works.[147] Another Cistercian poet was Abbot Adam Vras (13th–14th C.) of Valle Crucis, some of whose *brudiau* are extant in manuscript form.[148]

There are only scanty signs that the abbeys of south Wales may have fulfilled something of an educational role in Tudor times. Poetic evidence had it that in those days Neath was 'greatly resorted to by scholars'.[149] At Llantarnam, the penultimate abbot accepted the orphaned John Jones with the intention of bringing him up 'as well in learning and virtue as in necessary clothing'.[150] Dafydd Benwyn, perhaps with poetic licence, told how at Llantarnam there was 'great learning and choice knowedge'.[151] There is inconclusive evidence of Cistercian schools at Basingwerk and Valle Crucis, charging 1d. per week, and of the former having the later Abbot, Thomas Pennant (1481–1522), as its master of pupils.[152]

NOTES

1. Lekai L.J. 1977, 451 *(The Exordium Parvum)*.
2. Davies J.C. 1945, 202.
3. Hays R.W. 1963, 22.
4. Birch W. de Gray. 1897, 321.
5. *LP (Hen. VIII)* X, 434 (1046).
6. *Cal. Patent R.* 1440, 380.
7. Cowley F.G. 1977, 46.
8. *Analecta S.O. Cist.* 6 (1950) 29.
9. *Anc. Pet.* 286 (8368).
10. *Op. cit.* 489–90 (15389).
11. Williams J. 1905, 306-08.
12. *Mont. Collns.* IV (1871) 230–31 Advice might be tendered to an abbot by his 'council' of senior monks. This 'special council' numbered 14 at Margam in 1228 [*Letters from Ireland* 19].
13. Williams D.H. 1998, 52–53.
14. NLW, Penrice and Margam Ch. 203.
15. *Cartae Glam.* IV, 1350–51 (MLXIX).
16. PRO, E 315/117, f. 42.
17. Cowley F.G. 1977, 135.
18. Birch W. de Gray. 1897, 305.
19. *Anc. Pet.* 286 (8368).
20. *Anc. Corr.* 185 (XXXVII. 183).
21. *Anc. Pet.* 489–90 (15389), *Cf.* 492.
22. Hays R.W. 1963, 128.
23. Williams G. 1962, 560.
24. BL, Addit. MS 7488; *MSS in BM* III, 680.
25. *Fasti Cist. (1)* 187.
26. *Cal. Patent R.* 1440, 380.
27. *Fasti Cist. (1)* 187.
28. For much of what follows, see: *Fasti Cist. (1)* 183–84; Williams D.H. 1984. I, 149–51.
29. *Cf.* Williams D.H. 1984. I, 150–52.

30. PRO, C 85/167/12.
31. Price G.V. 1952, 46–47.
32. *Anc. Corr.* 185 (XXXVII. 183).
33. Jones A.J. 1933, 176.
34. *Letters from Ireland* 206.
35. *Itin. J. Leland* III, 123.
36. Cowley F.G. 1977, 49.
37. *Ibid.* 50.
38. Williams D.H. 1984. I, 152–53.
39. Cowley F.G. 1977, 169.
40. Jones A. 1933, 169.
41. *Cal. Papal Reg. (Letters)* I, 102.
42. *Op. cit.* XIII: Pt. 2, 728; *Cf.* Williams D.H. 1984. I, 153.
43. *Statuta* III, 318 (1308/1), 446–47 (1337/7).
44. *Reg. Ade de Orleton* 185.
45. *Cal. Papal Reg. (Letters)* VII, 460.
46. *Statuta* V, 438–39 (1482/37).
47. Jones a. 1933, 176.
48. Cowley F.G. 1977, 142; *Munimenta Acad. Oxon.* I, 100–01.
49. *Fasti Cist.* 185–86.
50. *Itin. Wm. Worcestre* 77–79.
51. *Fasti Cist. (1)* 186, 198, 200.
52. Birch W. de Gray. 1897, 173.
53. *Cal. Papal Reg. (Letters)* V, 154.
54. Hays R.W. 1963, 129.
55. Williams D.H. 1998, 63.
56. *Reg. Simon de Sudbury* 77, 80, 82.
57. *Cal. Papal Reg. (Letters)* III, 385.
58. *Flores Hist.* III, 343.
59. PRO, E 315/45, No. 232.
60. *Statuta II, 453 (1259/25).*
61. *Fasti Cist. (1)* 195.
62. *Litt. Wallie* 46, 96.
63. See Chapter 4.
64. Hays R.W. 1963, 25–29, 31.
65. *LP (Hen. VIII)* II, 1262 (4070).
66. *Fasti Cist. (1)* 214, 216–17.
67. Pryce A.I. 1923, xiv, 215.
68. Lekai L.J. 1977, 450.
69. Williams D.H. 1998, 80.
70. *Fasti Cist. (1)* 225–27.
71. BL, Arundel MS 19, f. 33d.
72. Williams D.H. 1998, 81, 87–88.
73. NLW, Penrice and Margam Ch. 78.
74. *Cartae Glam.* VI, 2356–57 (MDCXXVII).
75. *Cal. Papal Reg. (Petitions)* I, 77.
76. NLW, Penrice and Margam Ch. 1944, 1977.
77. *Cartae Glam.* II, 347–48 (CCCXLVII); Cowley F.G. 1977, 50.
78. *Op. cit.* II, 471 (CCCLXXIII).
79. Williams D.H. 1998, 88–90.
80. *Statuta* III, 261 (1293/3).
81. *Ann. Mon.* I, 34–35.
82. *Ann. Camb.* 92.
83. Williams D.H. 1998, 85.
84. Williams D.H. 1984. I, 158.
85. *Fasti Cist. (1)* 208, 192, respectively.
86. Bannister A.T. 1927, 10.
87. *Cronica de Wallia* 32.
88. *Cal. Close R.* 1231, 547.
89. Birch W. de Gray. 1897, 125.
90. *Cartae Glam.* VI, 2301 (MDLXXX).
91. Birch W. de Gray. 1897, 168.
92. Williams D.H. 1976, 80.
93. *Cal. Chancery R. var.* 293.
94. *Taxatio Eccl.* 276–77.
95. Williams D.H. 1976, 138.
96. Birch W. de Gray. 1897, 137.
97. BL, Arundel MS 19, m. 3d.
98. Birch W. de Gray. 1897, 29, 62.
99. *Statuta* III, 128 (1274/12).
100. Hays R.W. 1963, 90.
101. Butler L.A.S. 1976, 93.
102. Birch W. de Gray. 1897, 305.
103. NLW, Penrice and Margam Ch. 240.
104. Bernard F. 1965, 49.
105. Cowley F.G. 1977, 121.
106. Williams D.H. 1976b, 164.
107. NLW, Penrice and Margam Ch. 229.
108. Bannister A.T. 1927, 210–11.
109. Lewis J.M. 1976a, 14.
110. Hays R.W. 1963, 47, 142.
111. *Cal. Papal Reg. (Letters)* V, 507–08.
112. Lewis J.M. 1976a, 16.
113. *Op. cit.* 18.
114. *Op. cit.* 18–20; Williams G. 1976, 104–05.
115. Lewis J.M. 1976a, 19 (No. 27).
116. *Op. cit.* 16 (23).
117. Williams G. 1976, 104.
118. *Cf.* Evans C.J.O. 1953, 461.

119. Cowley F. G. 1977, 70*n*.
120. BL, Addit. MS 48984; *Cf.* Lewis J.M.1976, 17–18; Williams D.H. 1976, 78, 80.
121. *E.g.: Cal. Patent R.* 1271, 505.
122. Lewis J.M. 1976a, 20.
123. *Episc. Acts* II, 743.
124. Cowley F.G. 1977, 148.
125. Jack R.I. 1972, 30; Williams G. 1962, 24–25.
126. Williams G. 1962, 25.
127. Powel D. 1969, Introd, and 270.
128. *Cf.* Williams S.W. 1889, Appx. i–ii.
129. Beverley Smith J. 1963, 282; for other suggested works of Whitland, see: Jenkins D. 1982, 19–20, 26*n*, 27*nn*.
130. Exeter Cathedral MS 3514; transcribed in *Bull. Board Celtic Studies* XII (1946) 27–44.
131. Jack I. 1972, 86. For other works, see: Williams D.H. 1984. I, 162.
132. O'Sullivan J.F. 1947, 11; *Ann. Camb.* 109.
133. Williams G. 1962, 25–26.
134. Cowley F.G. 1977, 157.
135. *Ibid.* 143; Thomson D. 1982, 76.
136. Harrison J. 2000, 84–98.
137. Cowley F.G. 1977, 150.
138. *Glamorgan County History* III (1971) 537.
139. *Ann. Mon.* I, 28, 33.
140. Cowley F.G. 1977, 150.
140a. Patterson R.B. 1992, 210.
141. Transcribed in *Camden Miscellany* I (1847); *Cf.* Hays R.W. 1963, 144–45; *MSS in BM* II, 404–06 (No. 5091); Insley C. 1999, 238, 249.
142. BL, Harleian MS 6148, f. 16; Lansdowne MS 447, f. 61r–d.
143. Harrison J. 2000, 91–98.
144. *Cartae Glam.* VI, 2381 (MDCXLVI).
145. Williams G. 1976, 105.
146. Cowley F.G. 1977, 153, 155.
147. Williams G. 1962, 391.
148. Price G.V. 1952, 42.
149. Birch W. de Gray. 1902, 140; *Cf.* Knight L.S. 1920.
150. PRO, PROB 11/24, f. 21; Williams G. 1962, 562–63.
151. Bradney J.A. II: Pt. 2 (1914) 202–03.
152. Thomson D. 1982, 76–80.

CHAPTER 9

THE SECULAR COMMUNITY

The early Cistercian communities, with their often large numbers of *conversi*, probably endeavoured to be self-sufficient. As the centuries progressed, however, the typical abbey community came to be more broadly based and, in a sense, less clerically dominated. Not just passing guests and sundry paupers, but a wide array of resident servants and pensioners, of sick folk and almsmen, together with those tenants and labourers living near the abbey gates, came to make for a much more diversified monastic population.

Servants

As the numbers of *conversi* declined, so the need for servants and labourers increased. Cistercian communities had, though, employed 'hired workers' from the early years. As the *Exordium Parvum* (deriving perhaps from about 1135) put it: 'They realised that without the help of these men they would be unable to observe fully the precepts of the *Rule* by day and by night'.[1] In Wales, the presence of servants comes to the fore in the thirteenth and fourteenth centuries – those of Whitland find mention in 1257;[2] hired hands were numerous on the granges of Tintern by 1387.[3] At Margam (1325) a leading 'free servant' or 'sergeant', who gained his appointment by surrendering lands in Kenfig to the abbey, undertook to serve freely within or without the monastery, wheresoever he might be assigned, so long as his health held out. In return he received his 'livery' – a stipend of 6s. 8d. p.a., four pairs of shoes yearly, pasturing for two animals, as well as three loaves and a gallon of 'strong beer' daily.[4] Lucky fellow!, but it was a sign of the increasing importance of lay helpers and officers.

In Tudor times, the larger abbeys had substantial numbers of servants: Tintern no less than thirty-five, Margam fifteen 'yeoman' servants and thirteen 'hinds' (youths or labourers).[5] The *Valor Ecclesiasticus* (1535)[6] lists fully the officers and servants of Tintern: six in the abbot's household, three or so in the kitchen, a similar number of fishermen, and a tailor, a barber, an ostler and a woodcutter. Their annual stipends (perhaps excluding 'perks') varied from £1. 6s. 8d. (in most cases) to £2. Four other servants enjoyed corrodies said (erroneously) to date 'from the original foundation'. They were the porter (whose rights were worth £5 p.a.), the launderer (£4),[7] the clerk of the church (£4. 10s.), and the ferryman (£4). A tailor is also noted at Margam,[8] a butler at Strata Florida,[9] and the presence of a barber is implied at Valle Crucis.[10] At its suppression, poor humble Grace Dieu listed but three servants.[11]

The nature of the 'corrodies', 'liveries', or 'exhibitions' enjoyed in Tudor times by the principal resident servants, both active and retired, is well attested.[12] They consisted basically of 'meat and drink, clothes and chamber' (Margam, 1531).[13] The recipients included such officials as bailiffs (like John Leyshon, Margam's bailiff at Hafod-y porth, his entitlement granted in 1533);[14] and porters (as John Edmund at Tintern, 1536),[15] as well as those being rewarded for assistance as 'adviser and scribe' (like David Nash at Whitland, 1535)[16] or for 'praiseworthy helpfulness and services' (as John and Margaret Dorman at Margam, 1533).[17]

Four main elements comprised the typical corrody: a chamber (within the precincts) with provision for heat and lighting, meals with daily fixed rations of bread and beer, clothing rights, and an annual monetary stipend. Some deeds of agreement are couched in brief, general terms; others spell out the officer's entitlement in some detail. The Dormans were to inhabit 'a suitably appointed chamber in the monastery' and 'food for dinner and supper', as well as two conventual loaves and one gallon of 'the best ale or better drink' each day.

Richard ap John (also at Margam) 'if he be sick or diseased . . . and may not come out of his chamber to take his refection', was to have food brought to his chamber in like measure for any monk in the infirmary.[18] John Edmund (at Tintern) was to receive 'sufficient fuel from the monastery wood'; David Nash (at Whitland) stabling and fodder for a horse. The fiscal element varied with the duties performed, varied (in the known cases) from 13s 4d to 40s. p.a.

One feature of servants' dress that the grants of corrody show is the distinct liveries adopted by the greater abbeys. Strata Florida's bailiff at Nant Bau (1528) was granted annually 'one tunic *like the other servants*'.[19] John Edmund, porter-designate at Tintern, was to receive a *'toga'*, in the abbey's own livery, or else 7s. to buy one. An especial livery *may* also have bedecked John Dorman at Margam: a robe (valued at 16s 8d), and David Nash at Whitland: two tunics a year – perhaps because he had to travel on monastery business. No provision, in respect of clothing, was specified for Mrs Dorman – presumably she had to make her own dress!

Temporary rights were granted to certain officials when on duty. Neath's steward between Neath and Tawe (appointed 1532) received £2 yearly, and, whilst at the abbey, 'food and hospice with fodder for his horse' – the latter could also be pastured in Cadog's Mead.[20] The Vaughans, clerks of court for Hafod-y-porth, likewise received sustenance whilst at Margam for court-days.[21] Such 'benefits' would surely today attract the attention of the Inland Revenue!

After the Suppression, the residential servants generally lost their homes and perquisites, but were compensated by an annual pecuniary pension fixed by the Court of Augmentations, presumably in proportion to the value of their previous entitlement. There was a time-lag whilst so many cases were considered, but arrears (since the Suppression) were made good, and intermediaries (in London) received the pension on behalf of the individuals concerned. David Nash (in 1542) appointed Hugh ab Hywel, clearly a Welshman, and one of the 'yeoman ushers' to the Lord Chancellor, to obtain his money.[22]

Such compensatory pensions, whilst they guarded the former monastic employees from penury, can rarely have made up for loss of home and job. The Dormans received no known stipend from Margam; their corrody was perhaps more of a retirement present, but the court records show that their meals had been worth 3d. per day (£4 11s 3d p.a.), they had a robe valued at 16s 8d, and 13s 4d for firewood, annually:

a total of £6 1s 3d. In addition, they had received a chamber and daily allowances of bread and beer. Their new £4 pension was but partial compensation.[23]

Corrodians

Another class of permanent monastic residents consisted of the corrodians in the strict sense, by virtue of having purchased their livery as a means of assuring security in their old age, or because the monastery appreciated services they had rendered. Yet other persons enjoying an eventide home were those retired abbots who lived in conditions of some dignity either in their own house, or on moving to another monastery of the Order.[24] In earlier times an abbot ceding office *(Chapter 8)* made his profession of obedience anew and perhaps enjoyed little in the way of privilege, like Gilbert of Margam (1213) who, deposed, 'was made a monk' at Kirkstead in Lincolnshire, dying there the next year.[25]

In later centuries formal provision was made, as for Abbot Roger of Grace Dieu who, resigning in 1451, was granted a large annuity of £20, freedom from claustral observances, a chamber, servants, and food 'as much as for two or three monks'.[26] Philip Morgan, retiring as Abbot of Dore in 1495, was professed as a monk of Whitland in theory, but in practice was given a £12 annuity and permitted – 'for his comfort in his age' – to live at the Dominican Priory in Hereford.[27] As the last Abbot of Fountains wrote to Cromwell (1536): 'By a statute in our religion, an abbot who has ruled well for ten years is to have a competent pension'.[28]

Corrodians can be traced well back into the 13th century at several Welsh houses. The earliest case on record, perhaps, is that of Cedifor ap John and his wife, who, in return for loaning money towards the building of Llantarnam's Maestir Mill (1204), were to take their 'necessaries' at the grange there.[29] Actual residence is not implied here, nor, probably, in the instance of Agnes Gramus (1245) to whom Margam agreed to give weekly rations of bread and ale, and annual allowances of gruel, beans and salt, instead of a yearly rent due to her husband.[30] This may have been to provide security should she be widowed. Grants by Margam to Susan de Bonville[31] and Alice Peruath (from 1320)[32] may have followed their husbands' deaths. At Neath (1293) land was given to the abbey by William of Corneli because the monks had treated his father honourably in food and clothing.[33] The granting of corrodies, as well as of *conversi* and fraternity status, was one means by which Margam and Neath expanded their landed property in their formative period.[34]

The monarch might – in return for favours shown previously to an abbey – lay claim to the right to nominate a retiring servant to a vacant corrody. Such a corrodian was an absolute charge on the house concerned and the obligation was occasionally resisted – as when Henry III (1255) wished to settle Jewish 'converts' at Dore and Tintern,[35] and when Edward II (1314) sought a place for David Gough at Maenan. Its monks pointed out that they had fallen on hard times.[36] There was rarely more than one 'royal' corrodian in a monastery at any particular time, and the only certain placements made in Wales were at Tintern, where Edward I (1304) sent Geoffrey de Lastressen. His successor was John de Ispannia (1314), who had 'long served' Edward II.[37]

Edward I perhaps singled out Tintern because of the temporary surrender (in 1302) by its great benefactor, Earl Roger Bigod, of his estates to the Crown. Edward II may have seen Maenan as a royal foundation by virtue of Aberconwy's establishment (1284) on that site by his father. No more attempts appear to have been made to settle 'royal' corrodians at Maenan, the monks claiming that it would be contrary to the terms of Edward I's charter,[38] but they continued to be received at Tintern. In 1319, Edward II sent there William de Bromfield, a monk of Holm Cultram badly affected by the Scots. In 1412, John Wolde, 'sergeant of the king's chamber', went to Tintern 'to such maintenance as Walter Archier, deceased, had in that house'.[39]

Legal security was sought when the monks of Tintern were required to make 'Letters patent under their seal', 'delivering' his rights to Ispannia. Such provisions were to be for life and were to befit a retiring royal officer; it was to be 'suitable to the requirements of his estate'. David Gough – who had 'long served' both Edward I and II – unsuccessfully sought of Maenan 'his warreson of meat, of robes, and other necessities'.[40] In the later 15th century, the only recorded corrody in a Welsh Cistercian house was that granted John Puleston (1455) at Valle Crucis. It assured him of a stipend and two places in the abbey, with 'two servants, three horses, two harehounds, and four bloodhounds to his sole life'.[41] In Tudor times, Henry VIII required several abbeys, including Llantarnam and Tintern, to take in poorer servants from the dissolved household of Princess Mary.[42] Their abbots would hardly have dared to refuse!

John Puleston received his corrody 'for good counsel and aid', which *may* have stemmed from helping John ap Richard become abbot. Most recorded corrodies in the last years were in recompense for financial gifts, like those awarded John Howe (Valle Crucis, 1530) for £20 placed 'at the use of the monastery';[43] Philip Powell (Whitland, 1532) partly for 'service of £5 to us in our need';[44] Hywel ab John and his wife (Grace Dieu, 1534) 'for a certain sum of money beforehand paid';[45] and John Owain and his wife (Grace Dieu, 1535; he was bailiff of its Stowe Grange, Gloucs.) '£10 ready money beforehand paid'.[46] The Owains had also enjoyed a corrody at Tintern since 1521.[47] In later depositions regarding their entitlement, Thomas Kynnyllyn of Monmouth (1538), a person of some consequence,[48] asserted that 'he wrote the grant, and was at Grace Dieu when it was sealed and delivered, by the assent of the abbot and the whole convent'.[49]

The same elements entered into corrodies obtained by purchase as existed in those granted to retiring servants. First, there was a retirement home: at Tintern, the Owains had the chamber called '"the candlehouse" above the great door next to the church', together with a garden nearby. Later, at Grace Dieu, they received 'the whole house called the gatehouse, to inhabit and dwell'. This grant presumably excluded 'the west end of the gatehouse and the underplace, with garden and apple tree', given to the Johns the previous year. At Valle Crucis, Howe's chamber was to contain 'an adequate bed with sheets'. At Whitland, Powell received a meadow – presumably for his horse. Similarly, at Grace Dieu, the Johns had the 'finding of a horse for to do their business'.

For meals Howe was to receive 'food and drink daily at dinner and supper and other customary hours'. The Owains, at Grace Dieu (where they self-catered) were assigned weekly rations of wheat and oat malt. So, too, did the Johns, who were further granted 1 qt. of beef 'against Christmas', and a pig, 'lawful to make bacon of, against St Martintide'.[50] They could also have sustenance for two kine, with 'a house for their kine', as well as keeping hens, pullets and a pig. At Valle Crucis, John Howe was to take his food 'at the trestle table in the common hall of the abbot within the monastery, just as the Receiver and other officers did'. If ill, he had room service to his chamber. At Tintern, John Owain could take his meals at the abbot's table with the other members of his household. Their wives ate at home!, but the Owains had daily 'two conventual loaves of white bread and a gallon of the better beer'.

Rights of fuel were granted to the Owains by Tintern – 'Sufficient fuel at the discretion of the abbey's foresters', but they had to pay for its carriage. Grace Dieu gave its corrodians 'wood for their fire, sufficiently winter and summer, at a reasonable place assigned'. At Valle Crucis, Howe's 'perks' included candles for lighting, barbering and laundering, and – again a sign of an abbey's pride – a tunic each year in the monastery's livery. Howe appears to have been not only a beneficiary of the abbey, but also an officer. After the Suppression, the former corrodians – like the servants – were awarded compensatory pensions by the Court of Augmentations. Generally speaking, they did not make up for all that had been lost[51] – but the Court did allow the Johns to continue to live in the west end of the gate-house at Grace Dieu.

Those who were corrodians by purchase were not numerous – perhaps no more than one or two even at a great house like Tintern, and for several Welsh houses there is no extant record of them. It could be that there were others of whom we do not know, who may have had other resources and felt that the expense and trouble of approaching the Court of Augmentations was not worthwhile. Artheland Owain and John Edwards were listed as corrodians of Strata Marcella at the Dissolution, their cases do not appear in the decrees of the Court, yet they received commuted payments (of 26s 8d and 13s 4d respectively) as late as 1556.[52]

Travellers and Guests

A transient, but often substantial, component in the wider monastic community was comprised of those seeking refuge or hospitality; the *Rule of St Benedict* had dictated that 'all who arrive as guests are to be welcomed like Christ'.[53] In Wales, the charter in favour of Aberconwy attributed to Prince Llywelyn (1201+) noted that 'it belongs to the monks to give food and lodging to travellers and guests'.[54] The critical Gerald of Wales told how 'the monks of this Order, more than any others, exercise acts of charity and beneficence towards the poor and strangers'.[55] Such charity persisted throughout the Middle Ages. The last Abbot of Aberconwy told how he had to support: 'poor people and strangers'.[56] The Crown withdrew temporarily from suppressing Strata Florida (1537), in part so that its monks might 'devoutly extend hospitality'.[57] In rural Wales, where there was little in the way of accommodation for the passing travellers, the monastic guest-house assumed no small importance.

For those houses which lay close to well-frequented routeways, like Basingwerk (in north Wales), Margam and Whitland (in the south), all adjacent to the coastal highways leading to Ireland, the reception of guests could prove to be a considerable economic liability. In 1220, Whitland obtained a decree from the General Chapter limiting the free stay there of English and Irish abbots to fifteen days.[58] In 1210, King John with his army encamped at Margam en route to and from Ireland.[59] The abbey's guests in this period also included at least two Irish abbots – Gregory of Mellifont and Isaiah of Jerpoint.[60] A century later, Margam (1336) complained that 'being on the high road, and far from other places of refuge, the abbey is continually overrun by rich and poor strangers'; sentiments echoed fifty years later.[61] In similar vein, the Abbot of Basingwerk (*c*. 1346) told how it, being 'near the road, has a heavy burden of hospitality'.[62]

In times of financial stringency and bad harvests, a community might approach the General Chapter for a temporary dispensation from the reception of guests – though it is not absolutely clear as to whether this meant all guests, or simply personnel of the Order itself.[63] Strata Florida (1258) and Margam (1268) were so dispensed for three and five years, respectively.[64] Gilbert de Clare, Earl of Gloucester (1218–30), observing – perhaps suspiciously – the frequent coming of the local Welshry to Margam, told the community to observe its ancient customs and not to shelter, or feed in the abbey, persons coming 'to the parliament or the army'.[65]

The reference by the Abbot of Margam to 'rich and poor strangers', is an indication that charity and hospitality were offered to all social classes, and Guto'r Glyn (*d*. 1493) wrote that Strata Florida 'feeds many, rich and poor'.[66] Very probably, there was some distinction made in the treatment of the more important, vis-à-vis the humbler guests.[67] Gerald of Wales (*c*. 1200) more than hinted at this when he complained of being placed – at Strata Florida – 'among the common guests and the noise of the people'.[68] Recent excavation at Tintern suggests differing provision, certainly by the 16th century, for high-status guests.[69]

Monastic guests might range from the highest to the lowest in the land, and most Welsh houses received visits from English kings or Welsh princes at sometime in their history. Monarchs visiting Margam, en route to and from Ireland, included not only King John (1210)[70] but also Richard II (in 1394 and 1399).[71] Henry II visited Whitland (1171).[72] The travels of Edward I have been noted before *(Chapters 2 and 3)*. Edward II stayed briefly at Tintern, Margam and Neath, during his last days of freedom in the autumn of 1326.[73] Henry IV encamped at Strata Florida during the Glyn Dŵr Revolt *(Chapter 4)*. The Lord Rhys probably visited Whitland much more than his one recorded visit in 1171,[74] and Gwenwynwyn of Powys must have called frequently at Strata Marcella on his doorstep, like the occasion when he dated a charter there (1198).[75] The use made by Llywelyn ap Gruffydd of Aberconwy and Cymer and their granges is detailed above *(Chapter 2)*.

Ecclesiastical visitors of note included Agnellus of Pisa (received at Margam in 1233 as an emissary from Henry III by Earl Richard Marshal),[76] and Archbishop Baldwin of Canterbury, himself a Cistercian (who stayed at several houses in 1188 whilst preaching the crusade).[77] The Bishop of Worcester stayed at Tintern (1289) with a large party of thirty horses, but he bore his own expenses.[78] Numerous visiting members of the Order included Abbot Stephen Lexington who, prior to his visitation in Ireland, called at Margam early in 1228, but later that year told how 'the road through Wales has been closed to us by war',[79] and Abbot Robert of Rievaulx (*c.* 1310) who died and was buried at Margam.[80] To Margam also came, in 1353, a monk of Boxley, Stephen Heche, sent away from his own monastery for bad behaviour[81] – a typical Cistercian punishment.[82] Two secular travellers left their impressions in writing. William Worcester, who spent the weekend of 4 to 7 September 1478 at Tintern, coming by water from Aust Cliff via Chepstow, recorded valuable facts on the abbey's history and architecture *(Chapter 7)*, whilst, about 1538, John Leland came to several monasteries with similar enquiring bent *(Chapter 6)*.

More permanent guests, in late-medieval and Tudor times, were the Celtic bards and poets, who in their writings repaid monastic hospitality with extravagant praise of the monasteries and especially of their abbots.[83] If allowance is made for poetic licence, their verse can be important in revealing not a few facets of monastic life and economy. There is little evidence of such poetic work before the mid-14th century, and such as there is suggests that early bards may have hoped for reception into the 'fraternity' at their end with appropriate burial.[84] This is suggested by the contention of Cynddelw Brydydd Mawr (*fl.* 1155–1200), at odds with the monks of Strata Marcella, who, he said, refused him interment.[85]

In later centuries, most of the monasteries had associated bards living in the house or nearby. One of the most notable was Gutun Owain (1460–1503) who wrote at least fifteen poems in praise of Cistercian abbots.[86] He seems to have stayed at Basingwerk and Valle Crucis,[87] but Strata Florida may have been his favourite residence, and there he was buried, as was another great poet, Dafydd ap Gwilym (d. *c.* 1370).[88] The abbot who attracted most attention was David ab Owain, superior of Strata Marcella, Strata Florida and Aberconwy consecutively (1485–1513); no less than thirteen poets addressed him in their verse. Three of them were 'typical begging poems', as was one dedicated to an earlier Abbot of Aberconwy, David Lloyd, by Ieuan Deulwyn (*fl.* 1460–90) asking for oxen for the use of Henry Tudor's supporter, Rhys ap Thomas.[89]

Other resident poets included Guto'r Glyn (1440–93), who knew Strata Marcella well and spent much time at Strata Florida, but – aged, lame, blind and deaf – spent his last years at Valle Crucis where he was buried.[90] He saw its Abbot Dafydd as 'Bernard's lamb', and said 'a foster-father he's been to me'. Valle Crucis was the final haven of another bard, Lewis Môn (1480–1527), whose will was drawn up there and witnessed by some of the monks.[91] Tudur Aled (1480–1526) also stayed there, as well as at Aberconwy and Basingwerk. He praised Abbot David Lloyd of the former monastery for his greatness and generosity,[92] and described Abbot Thomas Pennant of the latter house as 'a generous patron of bards'.[93]

In Tudor south Wales, Dafydd Benwyn saw the poet Sawnder Siôn as 'the lion' of Llantarnam. Although living at Llangovan, Sawnder was buried 'in the choir of St Michael', the proximate monastic church of Llanfihangel Llantarnam.[94] One of the last monks of Margam, John Leyshon, may have been a wandering poet who came there to end his days.[95] Those closing years of monastic life lend us a note of caution in assessing the worth of the poetic evidence. Lewis Morgannwg (1520–65) who once wrote of Neath that 'the peaceful songs of praise proclaim the frequent thanksgivings of the White Monks', changed his tune after its suppression and now sang of 'the false religious of the choir'.[96]

Guests were received in a 'guest-house' or 'hospice' within the precinct but separate from the cloister, and having its own kitchen and refectory. There was a guest-master. At Margam, Roger (1196–1203) was *'hospitatus'* and Henry (1199–1203) was *'hospitalis'*. The latter could have had charge of the lay infirmary. It is possible that both were *conversi*, as also were Richard and Thomas: *'Conversi* of the hospice', in the early 13th century.[97] Earlier (*c.* 1180), there is note of Robin, *'famulus'* ('familiar' or servant) of its hospice).[98] With a wide social range of guests, they will have had their hands full! It was in Margam's 'Guesten Hall' that, about 1180, a young man was killed in a brawl.[99] Class distinction at Strata Florida (*c.* 1200) saw the 'common guests' placed in 'the public hall'.[100]

The penultimate abbot of Basingwerk (Thomas Pennant: 1480–1522) built new houses for guests, who were still so numerous that they had to take their meals in two sittings.[101] At Tintern a recently excavated building *(Fig. 58)* closely parallels the early 13th century aisled guest-hall at Kirkstall Abbey.[102] The reasonably well-to-do guest came on horseback, and tradition has it that Cae Ceffyle ('Horse Field') at nearby Pentre Farm was reserved for the steeds of visitors to Valle Crucis.[103] Some business between visitors and monks was transacted in the parlour room off the cloister *(Chapter 7)*. Tradition has it also that 'Parlour Farm' proximate to Grace Dieu fulfilled a similar function.[104] There is no evidence to support the theory that Strata Florida kept hospices for pilgrims and travellers at Ysbyty Ystwyth and Ystrad Meurig, and Whitland likewise at Tavernspite.[105] Guests certainly stayed on the larger granges – like Prince Llywelyn the Last *(Chapter 2)*, whilst Strata Florida appears to have entertained the lords of Cydewain at its Abermiwl Grange.[106]

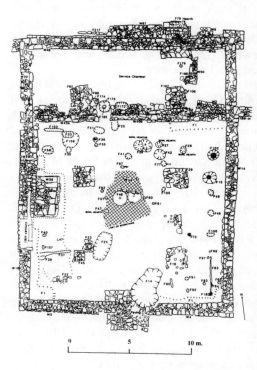

0   5   10 m.

Fig. 58: Tintern Abbey: The Aisled Hall.
(Paul Courtney, 1989; Cadw: Welsh Historic Monuments. Crown Copyright).

Refugees

Monastic shelter was appreciated by those who were fleeing from political foes, who were criminal fugitives from justice, or who simply wanted to get away from the pressures of life in the outer world. King John (1212) noted that Strata Florida 'harbours our enemies';[107] Henry III (1228) had burnt a grange of Cwmhir as it was 'a refuge for Welshmen to flie unto';[108] and in the Border troubles of 1263 many of the defeated Welshry in the Abergavenny area 'fled to the monasteries and the moors'.[109] These were political refugees. So far as the run-of-the-mill criminal was concerned, Prince Llywelyn the Great allegedly absolved Aberconwy of any liability if such were taken on its property,[110] but cases of the harbouring of felons by religious of Tintern (1270)[111] and of Margam (1358)[112] incurred lordly displeasure. As for a change of scene, Gerald of Wales told how he had 'most often betaken himself (to Strata Florida) in the hour of violent persecution'.[113]

The giving of sanctuary – a significant feature at Beaulieu Abbey in Hampshire[114] – was not unknown in Wales, on properties belonging to St Dogmael's Abbey, St Mary's College (St David's), and the Order of St John.[115] As for the Cistercian houses, John Leland (*c.* 1538) wrote of Margam that 'it has the privilege of sanctuary, which the Welsh rarely or never made use of', and of Tintern 'there was a sanctuary granted, but it hath not been used many a day'.[116] Lhuyd (*c.* 1700) told how at Neath there were 'some distance from the Abby, several parcels of a wall that is called 'ye Sanctuary wall', and within it a great stone att ye mouth of an old vault where some say Edward ye Second was taken'.[117] Proof positive comes in the note of 'ye sanctuary wall' in its Suppression accounts (1539).[118]

Pilgrims

Many pilgrims were attracted, especially in the later Middle Ages, to Cistercian abbeys and shrines. To encourage them, Valle Crucis claimed to possess a speaking statue of Christ, Strata Florida a mazer bowl with healing powers (the 'cup of Nanteos'),[119] Cwmhir a famed 'picture of Jesus',[120] and Strata Marcella a relic of the Holy Cross.[121] Alleged pilgrim routes focused on Strata Florida.[122]

Pilgrims were enticed to Llantarnam by a papal indulgence granted (in 1398) to those who, over the feast of St John the Baptist, visited the monastery and gave alms for its repair after a disastrous fire. Another indulgence (in 1414) concerned an alleged miraculous image of the Blessed Virgin at Tintern, 'on account of which a very great multitude resort there'.[123] Stories of such irremovable statues of Our Lady were common, and it is difficult to assess the credibility of such occurrences if they find no mention before the 15th century when – in the wake of the havoc caused by the Black Death and the Glyn Dŵr Revolt – most monasteries needed extra funds.

Of much older origins was the pilgrimage to St Winefride's Well – in Holywell, Flints. Its chapel and well were granted in 1093 to the monks of Chester, but passed – by gift of Prince David – to Basingwerk in 1240, together with the patronage of Holywell church.[124] This new acquisition encouraged the monastery (and Buildwas also) to gain the General Chapter's approval (1253) for the saint's feast-day (3 Nov.) to be a Feast of Twelve Lessons in their abbeys.[125] The popularity of the pilgrimage was enhanced by Henry V (1416) undertaking it on foot from Shrewsbury,[126] and by indulgences granted by Pope Martin V (1427) to those visiting and giving alms to the chapel, 'the buildings of which are now collapsed'.[127] Isabel, Countess of Warwick (1439) left her gown of russet velvet to adorn the saint's statue on festivals.[128] Edward IV (1461–83) visited the shrine, and placed some of the soil there on to his crown.[129] Richard III (1484) gave ten marks yearly towards the chaplain's stipend.[130] Mid-15th century chronicles told how 'at Basingwerk springeth a holy well',[131] unlike Gerald of Wales who (much earlier) had failed to mention it.[132]

The great majority of the pilgrims would have been ordinary folk, and (in 1398) Vicar Benedict of Holywell was planning to erect a hospice for the poor amongst them.[133] A century later, during the abbacy of Thomas Pennant, the present Perpendicular buildings were erected, partly due to the munificence of Margaret, Countess of Richmond (mother of Henry VII).[134] In 1535, the *Valor* recorded the offerings made at the shrine at being then no more than £10.[135] A few years later, deponents told how there was 'an image of St Winefride with a box before it, in which people have long put their oblations, and where they offered their oxen, kine and other things'.[136] A modern royal pilgrim thither was James II (in 1686).[137]

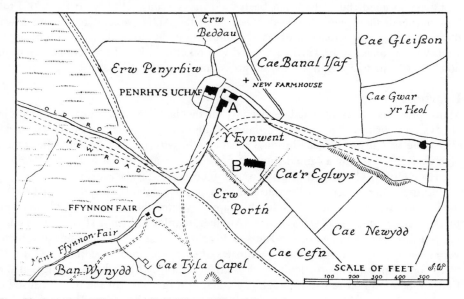

Fig. 59: Pen-rhys Pilgrimage Cell, Ystrad Rhondda.
(Archaeologia Cambrensis, 1914, by permission of the Editor).
A: Probable Site of Hostelry. B: Chapel. C: Well.

In south Wales, the shrine of the Blessed Virgin Mary at Pen-rhys, on lands in the Rhondda belonging to Llantarnam,[138] was of similar significance but not heard of until lauded by the poets in the mid-15th century.[139] Field names indubitably

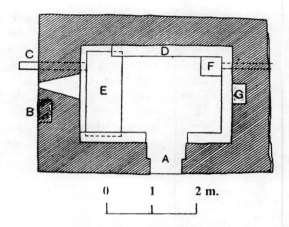

Fig. 60: Pen-rhys Holy Well.
(Archaeologia Cambrensis, 1914; J Ward).
A: Doorway, B: Recess, C: Overflow Pipe, D: Bench,
E: and F. Cistern, G: Aperture for Access of Water.

indicate the former presence here of a church [*Cae'r Eglwys:* 'Church Field'], cemetery [*Erw Beddau:* 'the Acre of Graves'; *Y Fynwent:* 'the Graveyard'], and an enclosure with gate-way [*Erw Porth:* 'the Gate-land'].[140] There is documentary evidence of the pilgrim's hospice here – called 'the Tavern House' in 1536.[141] At a little distance away was *Ffynnon Fair* [St Mary's Well], now happily restored. The pilgrims descended by steps into the well-house to bathe in the spring water.[142]

The poetic evidence, even if embellished, tells of a substantial 15th century – and later – stream of pilgrims to Pen-rhys, especially by the poorer classes and the sick who hoped to find healing. Gwilym Tew (*fl.* 1470–80) wrote: 'I will go to Pen-rhys in my one shirt, for fear of ague, upon my knee a taper a fathom'. He described 'the prayer of the labourers, where at Pen-rhys is ever a host of them'. Rhisiart ap Rhys (1480–1520), addressing Our Lady of Penrhys, told how 'the diseases of the multitude who wait upon thee, after their weeping, are healed the second night.[143] Thomas Cromwell's pamphleteer, Grey, told of the pilgrims 'gaddyng, with few clothes on our backes, but an image of wax, for the lame and for the blynde'.[144]

Gwilym Tew also wrote of 'the image of the Virgin with her colour golden', which was noted by Rhisiart ap Rhys as 'an image at Pen-rhys, that is mentioned afar, of the tall maid'.[145] It was the very popularity of this statue that led to its speedy removal at the time of the Reformation by command of Cromwell (14 September 1538); it was taken to Chelsea for public burning,[146] so that very shortly thereafter John Leland could speak in the past tense of 'Penrise village, where the pilgrimage was'.[147] Offerings of wax continued to be made at Pen-rhys as late as 1550.[148] Another statue now stands at Pen-rhys, and pilgrims continue to walk to the shrine. The initial devotion, and tales of the irremoveable statue, *may* have been engineered in the 15th century to raise funds for the monastery of Llantarnam, and Pen-rhys – like some other pilgrimage sites – has been made a holy place rather by the footsteps of the many who have so sincerely thronged there with genuine devotion.

Neath possessed a holy well at St Margaret's Chapel in Coed-ffranc,[149] sited perhaps upon an earlier hermitage.[150] The Abbot of Neath petitioned the General Chapter (1247) to allow the celebration of the feast of St Margaret in his abbey,

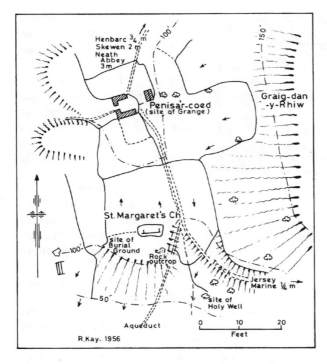

Fig. 61: St Margaret's Chapel, Coed-ffranc, Neath.
(Richard E. Kay, 1956; Ancient Monuments Record,
Royal Commission on Ancient and Historical
Monuments in Wales).

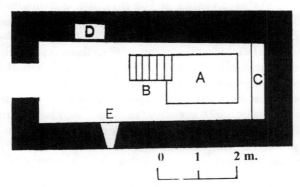

Fig. 62: Holy Well, Margam. (Archaeologia Cambrensis,
1914). A: Cistern. B: Steps down. C: Stone Bench
D: Recess. E: Loop for Light.

in order to 'more easily obtain the favour of his persecutors who hold that virgin in great veneration, and have a chapel dedicated to her'.[151] In 1504, the rector of Newton Nottage bequeathed 2s. for the upkeep of its fabric.[152]

Margam had perhaps a healing well at the so-called 'Monks' Bath' fed by Ffynnon Gyffyr ('Medicine spring'), with a cistern nearly 5ft. deep.[153] 'Ffynnon Mair' ('Mary's Spring' or 'Well') occurs on granges of Margam (at Crug),[154] Neath (at Monknash),[155] and on Whitland's Maenor Forion (at Dancapel).[156]

Fig. 63: St John's Well, Rogerstone
Grange.
(NLW, Badminton Plans, vol. 2, no. 2).

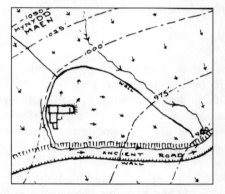

Fig. 64: Llanderfel, Gwent *(Richard E.*
Kay); (Ancient Monuments Record, Royal
Commission on Ancient Monuments,
Aberystwyth).

St John's Well (on Tintern's Rogerstone Grange; *Fig. 63*) was the precursor of the modern Chepstow Water Works.[157]

Apart from Pen-rhys, Llantarnam had a secondary pilgrimage centre at Llanderfel, Gwent, of Celtic origins,[157a] three miles north-west of the abbey, some 300 metres high on the slopes of Mynydd Maen *(Fig. 64)*. The enclosing bank and ditch are clearly visible, and tiles and traces of interments have been found.[158] In offerings, its value was one-third that of Pen-rhys.[159]

Appropriated churches attracting pilgrims, and doubtless offerings, included Margam's Llangynwyd (with its rood),[160] Whitland's chapel of Eglwys Fair Lan Tâf[161] and its church at Llanfihangel Abercywyn – where are 'Pilgrims' Stones', and (formerly) a Pilgrim's Lodge.[162]

The Poor

When the monks of Tintern were allowed to appropriate the church of Woolaston (Gloucs., *c.* 1190), the Bishop of Hereford noted that it was, in part, to allow them to relieve 'the necessities of those who gather there, that they may be able more readily to attend upon the poor in the showing forth of their charity'.[163]

It was a reminder that the poor flocked to monastery gates hoping for dole. At a time of famine (1188) Margam sent a ship to Bristol to obtain corn for 'a very large crowd of beggars', and Giraldus Cambrensis praised the abbey for its great charity.[164] Much later (*c.* 1346), in partial recompense for his confirmation of its possessions, Hugh le Despenser, Earl of Gloucester and lord of Glamorgan, expected Margam to mark annually the anniversary of his birthday by 'feeding, clothing and shoeing' seven paupers.[165] Similarly, its appropriation of Afan church (1383) was partly conditional upon the abbey maintaining three poor people and clothing them three times a year.[166]

Extra alms were often disbursed (as by Tintern)[167] on Maundy Thursday, that great day for showing charity – taking its name from the 'new commandment' of Christ. Morgan ap Caradog (*c.* 1200) gave Margam 6s. 4d. for a *maundy* for the poor on this day.[168] Tintern gave regular alms of corn – presumably at harvest-time – both at the monastery and at its properties as far afield as Acle (Norfolk), Lydd (Kent), and Woolaston (Gloucs.). It also gave out alms at the monastery on six feast-days in memory of its great 13th century benefactor, Earl Roger Bigod.[169] Ten years after the abbey's suppression the distribution of corn at Woolaston ceased, despite litigation by the parishioners.[170] One of the last abbots of Tintern, Henry Newland (in 1501), founded an almshouse at the east end of Woolaston churchyard – a building which survived until 1818.[171]

Neath proffered alms in memory of its founder, Richard de Granville, as well as 'Our Lady's loaf of half a bushel' weekly to the needy.[172] Margam maintained six almsmen by the time of its suppression;[173] the later almshouses are still standing. All told, Margam and Tintern each expended an amount equivalent to about 8 per cent of their annual income on almsgiving.[174] The name of a gate at Strata Florida called, in 1539, 'penny porth' ('money gate') may imply the work of charity there.[175] Valle Crucis seemingly had almshouses in Llangollen, whilst Guto'r Glyn said of Abbot David (1480–1503): 'His strong hand maintains the poor, a whole township at the door of his hall'.[176]

The Sick

Some Cistercian monasteries included monks with medical qualifications which they used to aid ailing laity of the neighbourhood.[177] Gerald of Wales, however, attacked both the Black and the White Monks in the Principality for setting themselves up as physicians – without medical skill and sometimes with disastrous results.[178] The sick and aged fortunate enough did find an home in the 'external' or 'secular' (lay) infirmary of the larger monasteries. These included the 'Firmar House' of Strata Florida (1292),[179] the 'Secular Farmer' of Tintern (1440; *Fig. 65*),[180] and Cwrt-y-clafdy of Neath.[181] Both it and Tintern's lay infirmary lay in hill country, a mile or so away from their respective monasteries, probably to safeguard against any ready spread of infection.

Fig. 65: Firmary Grove, Penteri (1763) *(NLW, Badminton Plans vol. 2, no. 7).*

Margam's lay infirmary stood 'A quoit's cast' (forty paces) from its church. It had its own chapel and infirmary garth;[182] a field-name: 'Infirmary Ground', long survived (*Fig. 68*).[182a] Strata Florida (1294) had 'special charters', concerning the 'acres of the lepers' at nearby Ystrad Meurig, perhaps implying its own leper-house.[183] Gruffydd ap Gwenwynwyn (*c.* 1260) was once 'very ill in a certain monastery',[184] – indubitably Strata Marcella. William Egwad wrote of Abbot David (1485–90) at Strata Marcella, 'to the sick he has ever been a bountiful man'.[185] The note of a monk-alchemist at Tintern, Walter Brockweir (1478), may point to Cistercian medical care.[186]

The Dying

As their last end approached, some layfolk came to reside at the monasteries, not only because of increasing infirmity, but also to make a good death – perhaps technically admitted as novices or even professed as monks and clothed in the habit of the Order. It was like taking out an insurance policy, pecuniary benefits undoubtedly accruing to the abbeys concerned.[187] A common practice down to the mid-13th century, it embraced members of all social classes like Prince Llywelyn ab Iorwerth, dying at Aberconwy (1240)[188] and Geoffrey Sturmi (by 1173) at Margam.[189] Owain Cyfeiliog, founder of Strata Marcella, died there (1197) 'at a great age, having taken upon him the habit of religion'.[190]

Between 1176 and 1249 several of Welsh noble stock so died at Strata Florida.[191] Even women might be admitted: Matilda de Braose (1209–10), widow of Gruffydd ap Rhys – interred at Strata Florida – received the Cistercian habit before her death at Llanbadarn Fawr and was then buried at that abbey.[192] Gerald of Wales told of the monks of Dore taking dying layfolk to their abbey, including the mother of John of Monmouth, founder of Grace Dieu. She, he said, was 'solemnly hooded and made into a monk, with a promise of the gate of heaven opening to her soul'.[193]

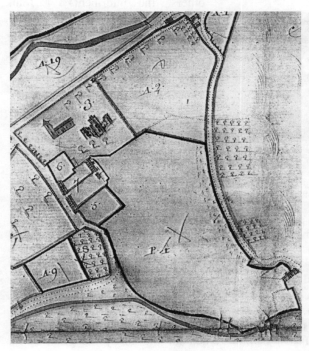

Fig. 66: Strata Florida (1765).   *(NLW, Nanteos 302).*
A.2: Yr hen fynwent ('The old cemetery').
P. 4: Y fynwent fawr ('The great cemetery').

The Dead

The early *Charter of Charity* disallowed burial to an outsider: 'Unless he is a guest or one of our hired workers who dies within our monastery'.[194] This provision was varied, allowing kings and queens, bishops and founders, to be buried in an abbey church. From 1217 the burial of other seculars was permitted if their parish priest agreed. Nobles came to be buried before the high altar or in the chapter-house (normally reserved for dead abbots), lesser folk in an external cemetery.[195] Cymer's cemetery[196] lay between the abbey and the vaccary.[197] There was a graveyard 'outside the gate of Margam'.[198] John Leland (*c.*1538) noted of Strata Florida: 'The cemetery wherein the country about doth bury is very large, and meanly walled with stone' *(Fig. 66)*.[199] Dafydd Nanmor (d. 1490) said of it: 'Between her walls are acres for burying lords'.[200]

Dignitaries buried before a monastic high altar included Maredudd ap Rhys at Whitland (1228)[201] and Llywelyn ab Iorwerth at Aberconwy (1197). His body was later translated to Maenan, which may account for the stone-lined grave excavated there in a central position in the presbytery. Burials have been also found at Maenan in the quire aisles,[202] whilst at Llantarnam modern construction work discovered several interments.[203] At Strata Florida, at least ten lay burials took place in the new chapter-house, ranging from that of Rhys ap Gruffydd ap Rhys in 1222 to that of Owain ap Maredudd in 1275.[204] Earl Gilbert Strongbow (d. 1148) found a final resting place in the chapter house of Tintern.[204a] Tomb recesses are visible at Cwmhir (nave),[204b] Cymer (presbytery),[205] and Strata Florida (side-chapel).[206]

Over twenty sculptured grave slabs record burials at Valle Crucis. Now displayed in its dorter, they include that of Madog ap Gruffydd *(d.* 1306) – grandson of the abbey's founder (also buried here) – which lay formerly before the high altar.[207] Guto'r Glyn, in his 'Lament for Llywelyn ap y Moel' *(d.* 1440) mentions the 'tombs' of Strata Marcella.[208] Surviving gravestones at Tintern record, amongst

Fig. 67: Tintern: Tomb of William Herbert *(d.* 1469).
(Courtesy of Cardiff County Council Library Service: Phillips MS 12134).

others, the interments of John Willifred (perhaps an abbey fisherman – his slab inscribed with salmon and trout), and of William Vilemaydo (a titular abbot, for some time an hermit).[209] Two tombs – originally in the early Norman church – have been opened at Tintern. The remains in one had been sewed up in an oxhide prior to burial; the other had been wrapped in a shroud.[210] The tombs of William Herbert, Earl of Pembroke (d. 1469; *Fig. 67*), and of his namesake *(d.* 1491) had long-lost striking monuments at Tintern.[211] The nature of the first's tomb hardly accords with the note (of 1531) that he was buried 'in the quire before the high altar'.[211a]

Tintern was the burial place of members of the Marshal family, including Isabel, countess of Pembroke (1220), two of her sons (1246) and a daughter, Matilda (1248), who was carried into the quire by her four knight-sons.[212] Provision of a light perpetually burning by Isabel's tomb gained for the abbey the grant of its Rogerstone Grange.[213] Several 13th century land-owners gave Margam land in return for the burial of their bodies.[214] So it was that Lleision ap Morgan (*c.* 1220) confirmed 'grants and agreements', made by his father when requesting interment there.[215] Centuries later, David ap Meurig Vychan left his body for burial at Cymer with an offering of one mark, and a 10s. gift for the abbey fabric.[216] Gruffydd David Ddu (d. 1538), bequeathed to Whitland 40s. for 'a *De Profundis* every Sunday for my soul'. It was also bound in the sum of £40, for a loan he gave, to perform a yearly obit and exequies.[217] Alas for him, the next spring the monastery was no more! A benefactor of Llantarnam (Morgan Jones, 1532), shortly before his death, desired there to be a yearly Dirge and Requiem Mass, and also 'a stone of marble with scripture graven in letters purporting my name with these words: IH'V XTE FILI DEI, MISERERE MEI' ('Jesus Christ, Son of God, have mercy on me').[218]

Adjacent Settlement

The monasteries could not, in later centuries, but attract lay-folk who settled without their walls and even within their precincts. The reasons are not far to seek: monastic buildings now in disuse, the demise of property to tenants, the need for servants. At Strata Florida (1534), John ap Dyo had a house, possibly a tavern, within the precincts.[219] By the 15th century, a sizeable lay community – including shopkeepers – was forming outside the walls of Tintern and in the adjacent Chapel Hill area. The abbey court for the manor of Porthcaseg had to frame rules for their good behaviour, and punish cases of brawling. In 1447, the address of two lay-folk was 'of the Abbey', whilst in 1451 Jenkin Gwyneth built himself a new house on Chapel Hill.[220]

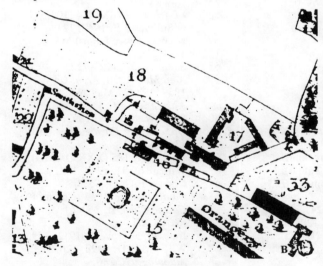

Fig. 68: Margam: the Hamlet *without the walls* (1814). *(From a photograph of the original Margam Estate Plan held by West Glamorgan Archive Service: D/D Ma/E1).* A: Abbey Church. B: Chapter House. 18: Infirmary Ground.

Outside the gate of Margam was a settlement referred to as 'the town without the walls' (1544) or 'the hamlet without the walls' (1562).[221] Excavation suggests a post-medieval date for this (now cleared) village, but its origins clearly preceded the Suppression.[222] (There was also 'a cemetery outside the gate' at Margam in the late 12th century – possibly of Early Christian origin).[223]

The monastic community consisted of the monks and (in earlier centuries) the *conversi*, but, as their numbers declined, so proportionately greater became the roll-call of servants, corrodians, and lay-folk settled nearby, as well as the ever-present 'Poor people and strangers'.[224]

NOTES

1.   Lekai L.J. 1977, 459 (XV).
2.   *Ann. Camb*. 92.
3.   NLW, Badm. Manorial 1571.
4.   *Cartae Glam*. III, 1131–32 (DCCCCXXIV). [Two of the loaves were called "liver-souns", deriving from 'livery'].
5.   PRO, LR 6/152/1.
6.   *Valor Eccl*. IV, 371.
7.   NLW, Badm. Manorial 1663, m. 4d: [Tintern's "Laundry House", 1568].
8.   NLW, Penrice and Margam Ch. 3093.
9.   PRO, E 315/103, f. 159r.
10.   PRO, E 315/91, f. 61r-d.
11.   *Valor Eccl*. IV, 371.
12.   Williams D.H. 1983, *passim*.
13.   PRO, E 315/92, f. 1d.
14.   PRO, SC 6 (Hen. VIII) 5155, mm. 13d–14r.
15.   PRO, LR 1/228, f. 6d.
16.   PRO, E 315/103, f. 82d; SC 6 (Hen. VIII) 4903, f. 33r.
17.   PRO, E 315/101, f. 58r-d.
18.   PRO, E 315/92, f. 1d.
19.   PRO, LR 1/228, f. 98d.
20.   *Ibid*. ff. 82d–83r.
21.   PRO, E 315/91, f. 72d.
22.   PRO, E 210/9448.
23.   PRO, E 315/91, f. 58r-d.
24.   Williams D.H. 1998, 75–76.
25.   Birch W. de Gray. 1897, 375; Cowley F.G. 1977, 117.
26.   BL, Royal MS 12E, f. 24r (kind info. of the late Dr C.H. Talbot).
27.   PRO, C 1/304/36; Williams D.H. 1976, 22.
28.   *LP (Hen. VIII)* X, 170 (424).
29.   BL, Addit. MS 48984, f. 127r.
30.   *Cartae Glam*. II, 526–27 (DXXI).
31.   *Catal. Penrice* I, 23 (Charter 64); *Cartae Glam*. II, 536–37 (DXXVIII).
32.   Llewellyn R.W. 1898, 146.
33.   *Cartae Glam*. III, 895–96 (DCCLXXXVII).
34.   Williams D.H. 1998, 81.
35.   Greatrex J. 1994, 19–20.
36.   Hays R.W. 1963, 91–92.
37.   *Cal. Close R*. 1314, 192.
38.   Hays R.W. 1963, 92.
39.   *Cal. Close R*. 1319, 208; 1412, 363.
40.   *Anc. Pet*. 385 (233).
41.   Price G.V. 1952, 261.
42.   *LP (Hen. VIII)* IV: Pt. 2, 1811 (4096).
43.   PRO, E 315/91, f. 61.
44.   *Ibid*. E 315/95, f. 79.
45.   *Ibid*. E 315/91, ff. 33d–34r.
46.   *Ibid*. E 315/100, ff. 16d–17r.
47.   *Ibid*. E 315/92, ff. 97d–98r.
48.   *Early Chanc. Proc*. 228 (1020/49).
49.   PRO, E 315/23/59; Cf. *Augm. Rec*. 130; Williams D.H. 1976, 65.
50.   Martinmas (11 November).
51.   Williams D.H. 1984. I, 170.
52.   *Mont. Collns*. VI, 362; BL, Addit. MS 8102, f. 76d.
53.   *RSB* 40.
54.   Hays R.W. 1963, 22; *Cf*. Insley C. 1999, *passim*.
55.   Cowley F.G. 1977, 73.
56.   *LP (Hen. VIII)* X, 434 (1046); O'Sullivan J.F. 1947, 121.
57.   NLW (Alcwyn Evans) MS 12,362D.
58.   *Statuta* I, 521 (1220/22
59.   *Ann. Mon*. I, 30; *Arch. Camb*. 1859, 197 (27 May and 28 August).
60.   Birch W. de Gray. 1897, 152.
61.   *Op. cit*. 305; *Cartae Glam*. IV, 1360 (MLVI).
62.   *Anc. Corr*. 185 (XXXVII, 183).
63.   Williams D.H. 1998, 152.
64.   Cowley F.G. 1977, 205.
65.   *Catal. Penrice* II, 13 (Charter 8); *Cartae Glam*. II, 360–61 (CCCLXI)
66.   Jones G. H(artwell). 1912, 379.
67.   Williams D.H. 1998, 126–27.
68.   *Autobiog. GC* 236.
69.   Courtney P. 1989, 99.
70.   *Ann. Mon*. I, 30; *Arch. Camb*. 1859, 197; Birch W. de Gray. 1902, 64.
71.   Cf. *Cal. Patent R*. 1394, 477, 491, 499, 501, 503; 1399, 566, 569.
72.   *Brut* (1952) 67; *Itin. G.C*. I, 184.
73.   *Cal. Close R*. 1326, 619; 1336,

578; *Cartae Glam*. III, 1137 (DCCCXXIX); Ormrod W.M. 1988, 107–12.
74. *Episc. Acts* I, 275.
75. Jones M.C. 1871, 32, 34.
76. Gilliespie K. 1964, 28–29.
77. *Journey through Wales* 35–36, 126, 140, 178, 196.
78. Stevens B.J. 10; Williams D.H. 1976, 99.
79. *Letters from Ireland* 7, 134 (No. 68).
80. Birch W. de Gray. 1897, 119–20.
81. *Statuta* III, 521 (1352/19).
82. Williams D.H. 1998, 60–61.
83. Williams G. 1962, 379.
84. Cowley F.G. 1977, 157; *Cf.* 160.
85. Jones M.C. 1871, 179.
86. Bachellery E. 1951. I, 113–87.
87. Jones A. 1933, 169.
88. Cowley F.G. 1977, 160.
89. Hays R.W. 1963, 155–56.
90. Williams G. 1962, 383; Parry T. 1962, 552–53; Clancy J.P. 1965, 209, 221–24; Pratt D. 1997, 11; *Welsh Verse* 175–76.
91. Williams G. 1962, 383.
92. Hays R.W. 1963, 155; Price G.V. 1952, 170.
93. Jones A. 1933, 169, 176.
94. Bradney J.A. II: Pt. 2 (1913) 202–03.
95. Williams G. 1962, 383; For Margam, see: Evans A.L. 1958, 90–91 *County History of Glamorgan* III (1971) 510–12.
96. Williams G. 1962, 537–38.
97. Birch W. de Gray. 1897, 62, 76, 81.
98. *Op. cit.* 31; NLW, Penrice and Margam Ch. 17.
99. *Hist. Works G.C.* 384.
100. *Autobiog. G.C.* 236.
101. Jones A. 1933, 176.
102. Courtney P. 1989, 104.
103. Ellis T.P. 1927, 4.
104. Info. of the late Mr M.P. Watkins, solicitor, of Monmouth.
105. Cowley F.G. 1977, 206.
106. *Op. cit.* 205–06.
107. *Op. cit.* 212.
108. Morris E.R. 1889, 355.
109. *Anc. Corr.* 53 (XI. 71).
110. Hays R.W. 1963, 22.
111. PRO, E 32/28, 29 (info. of Dr Cyril Hart).
112. NLW, Penrice and Margam Ch. 229.
113. *Autobiog. G.C.* 226.
114. St John Hope W.H. 1906, 175–78.
115. *Cal. Papal Reg. (Letters)* IX, 455, 501–03; Williams G. 1977, 241.
116. *Monasticon* V, 265, 740; Cf. *Mont. Collns*. X, 402.
117. Lhuyd E. 1707. III, 69; *Cf.* Donovan E. 1805. II, 78; Leland J. 1715. I, 104.
118. PRO, SC 6 (Hen. VIII) 5156, m. 3d.
119. Jones Pierce T. 1950, 31.
120. Williams D.H. 1976a, 86–87.
121. PRO, SC 6 (Hen. VIII) 5259.
122. Powell S.M. 1931, 9–24.
123. *Cal. Papal Reg. (Letters)* V, 507–08; VI, 452.
124. Charles Edwards T. 1971, 6.
125. *Statuta* II, 394 (1253/24).
126. David C. 1969, 7.
127. Thomas D. 1964.
128. *Arch. Camb.* 1921, 398–99.
129. David C. 1969, 7.
130. *MSS in BM* II, 141 (35 Ox).
131. *Polychron R. Higden* I, 428–31; *Eulogium Hist.* II, 139.
132. Jones A. 1933, 170.
133. NLW, MS 8942E.
134. *Arch. Camb.* 1921, 400.
135. Owen E. 1920, 60.
136. *Augm. Rec.* 96.
137. Charles Edwards T. 1971, 7.
138. For an excellent account: Slater F. 1972.
139. Williams G. 1962, 490.
140. Ward J. 1914, 258, 362, 371; Cummings R. 1974, 206.
141. PRO, LR 1/229, f. 5; SC 6 (Hen. VIII) 2497, m. 8d.
142. Ward J. 1914, 371–78.
143. *Op. cit.* 395–405.
144. *Pen-rhys* (C.T.S. Cardiff; Anon. n.d).
145. Chidgey P. 1962, 8.
146. Thomas L. 1930, 74.
147. Harris S.M. 1951.
148. Alphonse T. 1979, 147.
149. Howel R. 174.

150. Phillips D.R. 1925, 89.
151. Cowley F.G. 1977, 246.
152. Howel R. 425.
153. Ward J. 1914, 406; Gray T. 1905, 92; NGR: SS 803869.
154. NGR: SS 801865.
155. NGR: SS 906701.
156. NGR: SN 403382.
157. Williams D.H. 1999, 29; NGR: ST 506969.
157a. Edwards D.A.W. 1976, 35–39.
158. Williams D.H. 1976, 81; Wood B.J. 1953; NGR: ST 264953
159. *Valor Eccl.* IV, 365.
160. *County History of Glamorgan* III (1971) 153.
161. PRO, SC 6 (Hen. VIII) 4903, m. 32r.
162. *Arch. Camb.* 1856, 332; 1886, 122–27; 1893, 245; Jones G. H(artwell). 1912, 372–73.
163. Cowley F.G. 1977, 185.
164. *Op. cit.* 208; Birch W. de Gray. 1897, 130–31; *Gir. Camb.* VI, 67–69; *Journey through Wales* 126–27.
165. *Cartae Glam.* IV, 1265 (DCCC–CXCIV).
166. *Ibid.* IV, 1350–51 (MXLIX).
167. *Valor Eccl.* IV, 371.
168. NLW, Penrice and Margam Ch. 87.
169. Gloucester City Library, *Hockaday Abstracts* (Woolaston).
170. VCH, *County of Gloucester* X (1972) 118.
171. Rudder S. 1779, 845.
172. Birch W. de Gray. 1902, 153.
173. Williams G. 1976, 106.
174. Williams G. 1962, 381.
175. PRO, SC 6 (Hen. VIII) 4868, m. 7.
176. Pratt D. 1997, 14.
177. Williams D.H. 1998, 121–22.
178. Owen H. 1904, 184.
179. Williams S.W. 1889, 123. [A field name a little west of the abbey (in 1765) was: 'Cae Main Dol Lazerus': NLW, Nanteos 302].
180. NLW, Badm. Manorial 1657, m. 4r; its location is evidenced by 'Firmary Grove' [NGR: ST 521999].
181. NGR: SS 725977.
182. Jones D.R.L. 1981, 8–9.
182a. West Glamorgan Archive Service, D/D Ma/E1 (Plan of *c.* 1814).
183. Williams S.W. 1889, Appx. lxix.
184. *Anc. Corr.* 19–20 (III. 162).
185. Lloyd H.W. 1872, 33.
186. Williams D.H. 1976, 99.
187. Williams D.H. 1998, 133.
188. Hays R.W. 1963, 47–48.
189. NLW, Penrice and Margam Ch. 1944, 1977.
190. Jones M.C. 1871, 29.
191. *Cronica de Wallia* 32.
192. *Brut (1955)* 191.
193. Williams D.H. 1976, 8.
194. Lekai L.J. 1977, 450 (XXIV).
195. Williams D.H. 1998, 134–36.
196. Ellis T.P. 1927, 4.
197. PRO, LR 1/213, f. 119d.
198. NLW, Penrice and Margam Ch. 18.
199. Williams S.W. 1889, Appx. iii.
200. *D. Nanmor*, 74.
201. *Brut (1952)* 235.
202. Butler L.A.S. 1980, 11.
203. Mein A.G. *pers. comm.*
204. Williams S.W. 1889, 124.
204a. *Visit. Wales* 38, and *n.* k.
204b. *Arch. in Wales* 38 (1998) 140.
205. Robinson D.M. 1990a.
206. Williams S.W. 1889, 124.
207. Evans D.H. 1995, 48–49.
208. Clancy J.P. 1965, 209.
209. Williams D.H. 1976, 102.
210. *Arch. Camb.* 1938, 131.
211. Cardiff Central Libr. Phillips MS 12134 [info. Dr. David Robinson].
211a. *Visit. Wales* 38.
212. Williams D.H. 1976, 101–02.
213. *Cal. Charter R.* III, 104.
214. Chapter 11 *infra*.
215. NLW, Penrice and Margam Ch. 110a.
216. NLW, Dolrhyd Deed 2.
217. *West Wales Wills* 155–56.
218. Alphonse T. 1979, 129.
219. Williams S.W. 1889, lxxvii.
220. Williams D.H. 1969, 21–22.
221. Birch W. de Gray. 1897, 359, 362.
222. RCAHMW, *Glamorgan* III: Pt. 2 (1982) 219–20.
223. NLW, Penrice and Margam Ch. 18.
224. *LP (Hen. VIII)* X, 434 (1046).

CHAPTER 10

EXTERNAL RELATIONS

No Cistercian abbey stood in isolation; rather, each was a member of a large and widely-flung family. The late Professor E.G. Bowen liked to draw comparisons between the Order in medieval Europe and the modern association of independent countries in the Common Market. The spiritual and temporal well-being of the whole body, and of each of its individual monasteries, was achieved by two basic and binding customs: (i). The annual General Chapter of the Order, and (ii). The practice of annual visitation. These were intended to ensure simplicity and uniformity in Cistercian life.[1]

Attendance at the General Chapter

Every Cistercian abbot was, in theory, expected to attend the General Chapter held at Cîteaux in mid-September until 1439, when it was moved backward to May. As the Order expanded to distant places, and as times became troublesome, many mitigations of this rule became necessary. As early as 1209 the Welsh abbots had requested that only some of them need attend annually; the matter was referred to the Abbot of Clairvaux (of whose line most Welsh houses sprang), but the immediate outcome is unknown.[2] By the late 13th century, if not well before, only a representative number presented themselves at Cîteaux. In 1281, the group expected – the Abbots of Llantarnam, Strata Florida, Strata Marcella and Tintern – were excused, because of the current political difficulties in Wales. In 1305, it was reported that the abbots of England and Wales need attend only other year.[3] Individual excuses for absence included infirmity (the abbots of Aberconwy (1216) and Tintern (1277),[4] and the command of the king (Aberconwy and Valle Crucis, 1298).[5]

Records of abbatial attendance only occur when royal permission to travel was required, when foreign exchange was obtained, or when specific abbots are mentioned in the records of the Chapter. The presence of four Welsh abbots is noted in 1309 and of three in 1313.[6] The journey was a lengthy one, planned and undertaken in good time, and one not to be attempted alone nor without money. The Abbot of Cymer (1274) borrowed £12 from Prince Llywelyn to assist his travel to Cîteaux as early as 9 July, two months before the date of the meeting.[7] The Abbot of Whitland (1217), in the far west of Wales, passed through Chepstow about 21 July, pausing at its castle to obtain letters of protection – both for himself and 'those with him', – a reference to a fellow-monk or servants or, indeed, fellow abbots travelling together for mutual protection – a medieval caravan or convoy![8] An abbot of Tintern (1331) had royal leave to cross from Dover 'with his horses and harness and reasonable expenses'.[9] In the 15th century, letters of exchange were obtained from London-based merchants-cum-moneylenders: an abbot of Neath (1424) took twenty marks in this way;[10] an abbot of Aberconwy (1431) £20.[11]

Ability to attend the General Chapter was much affected by the Hundred Years' War (1337–1453) and by the Schism in the Papacy (1378–1417). The consequence was the convoking of provincial assemblies of British abbots. In 1312, six Welsh abbots had attended a meeting in London of superiors of the Order called by Arnald, a cardinal-legate, and himself a Cistercian.[12] In 1342, the Abbot of Tintern was one of a trio who summoned together 'all the abbots of the province of Canterbury, forming their own statutes and imposing punishments on wrongdoers'.[13] The General Chapter realised that 'if this continues the unity of the Order will be lost', but from 1433 it did cause provincial assemblies to be convoked at Northampton for some six years.[14]

The significance of the General Chapter itself was not as great in Wales at that time as it might have been, taking cognisance of some only of the problems and shortcomings of the Welsh Cistercians. In an effort to maintain an effective system, the Abbot of Margam (1439) was appointed Definitor-General for the abbeys of Wales and Ireland.[15] Very much earlier, in 1218, the then Abbot of Margam had been selected as one of five who could advise when serious matters arose in between meetings of the General Chapter.[16]

The majority of the Cistercian abbeys in Wales were in the lineage of Clairvaux, though with two daughters of Savigny (Basingwerk and Neath), one of L'Aumône (Tintern), and two second generation abbeys of the family of Morimond (Grace Dieu and Trawscoed), broadening the representation of the Order. The concept of all the monasteries having a common identity as a Welsh group was implied in 1281 – when Dore petitioned to be classed like the Welsh abbeys for taxation purposes,[17] and in 1479 – when the Welsh houses were omitted from a list of the Cistercian abbeys in the province of Canterbury.[18] In a taxation list of 1521, there is explicit recognition of 'the Welsh province' within the Order.[19]

Welsh links with the supreme legislative body of the Order were maintained almost to the end. Abbot David Wynchcombe of Strata Marcella was appointed a definitor for the family of Pontigny at the General Chapter in 1496, and for the generation of La Ferté in 1510[20] – though his own house was of neither lineage. Abbot Lleision of Neath was a definitor in 1517–18, and Abbot Lewis of Margam, both a confessor and a definitor at the Chapter of 1530.[21]

The System of Visitation

It was intended initially that a father-abbot would inspect his immediate (first-generation) filiations in person each year, but, as the Order expanded, the distances and the numbers of monasteries involved meant that delegation sometimes became inevitable. Despite Wales being so strongly Clairvaux-dominated, there is no evidence that St Bernard (during whose abbacy both Margam and Whitland were founded) ever visited the British Isles, let alone the Principality.[22] In addition, certain especial visitations were ordered by the General Chapter when circumstances rendered them necessary – like that in 1188 which led to the resignation, or deposition, of the then abbot of Tintern.[23]

Close ties existed between daughter- and mother-houses: a monk of one might well be translated to high office in the other, and, apart from the annual routine inspection, official visits by a father-immediate or his delegate could be expected in times of difficulty, and on the occasion of the resignation or election of the abbot of his daughter-house. Foreign Visitors (probably from Clairvaux) were at Margam in 1203 to instal Abbot Gilbert, and, perhaps, also at Whitland to effect the deposition of Abbot Peter.[24] Unknown visitors – acting on the command of the Abbot of Clairvaux – removed Abbot Gilbert from office ten years later.[25] In 1233, Clairvaux's duty of inspection was delegated to the Abbot of Boxley (Kent) who was 'gone to Wales, to make a visitation of the Cistercian houses in those parts'.[26] In 1250, Visitors from Clairvaux were in Wales en route to Ireland.[27] Continuing contacts were shown by the presence of Bernard, a monk of Clairvaux, at Margam in 1336.[28]

Tintern's father-immediate from the French abbey of L'Aumône was probably at Tintern in 1192[29] and 1196; the prior of L'Aumône attended the installation of Abbot Walter in 1321,[30] and in 1330 the Abbot of L'Aumône was in Britain 'to visit divers houses subjected to the Cistercian Order'.[31] Doubtless, Tintern was amongst them. The Abbot of Savigny was present at Neath in 1175,[32] and this monastery – as well as Basingwerk – was probably inspected by Visitors sent by Savigny in 1243.[33] Visitations from overseas became less regular as the centuries progressed – hindered not least by wars, and sometimes even strenuously opposed – like the projected visitations by the abbots of Cîteaux (1490)[34] and Chaâlis (1532),[35] leading to the appointment of Reformators for the Order in Wales *(Chapter 5)*.

Visitations from England or the Continent were partly balanced by a reverse process – as when several Welsh abbots had occasion to make visitations in Ireland. It is possible that the Abbot of Neath undertook duties in respect of two French houses.[36] About 1190, the Abbots of Margam and Neath deposed the cellarer of Biddlesden (Bucks.),[37] whilst, in 1228, the Abbot of Tintern deputised for the Abbot of Buildwas in the visitation of Buckfast and Quarr.[38] In 1279, his successor was one of three abbots investigating the challenged election of the abbot of Boxley.[39]

Within Wales itself, there is enough evidence to suggest that – despite biased criticism at times – the abbots whose duty it was were reasonably assiduous in performing their annual inspections. Occasionally, circumstances dictated that father-abbots were instructed by the General Chapter to especially check when problems arose: like Whitland (1196) in respect of the 'excesses' of the *conversi* at Strata Florida,[40] and as Strata Florida (1253) regarding the keeping of Llantarnam's territorial agreement with Margam.[41] As for a prejudiced attack, John Charlton of Powys (*c.* 1328) alleged that 'for default of good care and visitation by the abbot of Whitland, the house of Strata Marcella is coming to nothing' *(Chapter 3)*.[42]

The continuing relations between Tintern and its Gloucestershire daughter-house at Kingswood are worthy of note. When Abbot William of Tintern was deposed (1188), he was succeeded by Abbot Vido of Kingswood.[43] A few years later (1192–93), the abbot of Waverley claimed Kingswood as his daughter-house, but the General Chapter decided in favour of Tintern's right of visitation there.[44] The dispute arose out of two site changes by the monks of Kingswood much earlier in the century, and the temporary settlement in their place of monks from Waverley.

There are glimpses of the continuing contacts between the two abbeys, as when (in 1240) the Abbot of Tintern visited Hazleton, a former site and now a grange of Kingswood, and when (during 1263) the abbot, prior, and two monks of Kingswood visited their mother-house.[45] In 1262, the solicitude of Tintern for its daughter-house had been reflected in Kingswood's accounts, which included the payment of 3d. to 'a young man of Tintern who brought salmon'.[46] The bond endured to the close of monastic life. In 1517, Abbot Morton of Tintern deposed his daughter-abbot *(Chapter 5)*.[47] After Tintern's suppression (1536) two of its monks, Nicholas Acton and John Gethin, resided and held responsible positions at Kingswood *(Chapter 6)*.[48]

The Herefordshire abbey of Dore maintained links quite effectively with its relatively proximate daughter-abbey at Grace Dieu, west of Monmouth. Occasional references exist to abbots of Dore fulfilling their role as Visitor there – as in 1427 (when Grace Dieu was alleged to be suffering from 'ill-governance'),[49] in 1451 (receiving the resignation of Abbot Roger of Chepstow),[50] in 1484 (when Abbot John Mitulton wished to cede office),[51] and in 1534 (presiding over the grant of a pension to former Abbot Thomas Perpin).[52] Grace Dieu was useful to its mother-house: it provided a brief place of refuge for a persecuted Abbot Holand of Dore (1397),[53] and it was a means of preferment to an abbacy for at least three monks of Dore – John Wysebech, Richard Clifford and Richard Dorston.[54] There was financial benefit, too: Grace Dieu rendered one mark yearly to 'our Visitor'.[55]

Visitation meant travel and had the potential for weariness: one abbot of Strata Florida (1490) en route to instal a new abbot of Aberconwy was taken ill, returned home and died.[56] A good visitor might inspire confidence and be remembered with affection: a former monk of Cwmhir in later years was able to recall the last abbot of Whitland as 'our father William'. Cwmhir was a daughter-abbey of Whitland, so he was able to describe Abbot William as 'head of our religion'.[57] An aggressive Visitor might try to exceed his powers: in 1496, the Abbots of Dore and Whitland had to be restrained from undue interference in the affairs of Grace Dieu[58] and Strata Marcella,[59] respectively.

Irish Affairs[60]

The position of Wales, facing west across the Irish Sea, meant that there were considerable and continuing contacts between the Cistercians of Wales and Ireland, a reflection of the days of Celtic monasticism.[61] The Welsh abbeys most involved were those lying on or near the coastal routes which led to the Irish Sea – like Margam, Tintern and Whitland. The latter two houses founded monasteries in Ireland, other abbeys – especially Margam, were heavily involved in Irish Cistercian life, and – like Basingwerk – the maritime houses received members of the Order travelling to or from Ireland *(Chapter 9)*.

The few Irish houses founded directly from Wales had, not unnaturally, a very definite marine or estuarine situation. Whitland *may* have founded Comber (County Down) on 25 January 1200,[62] and, if so, it will have featured in the itinerary of Abbot Peter of Whitland who, later that year was, Giraldus Cambrensis asserted, 'engaged upon a visitation which had been enjoined upon him *(probably by the*

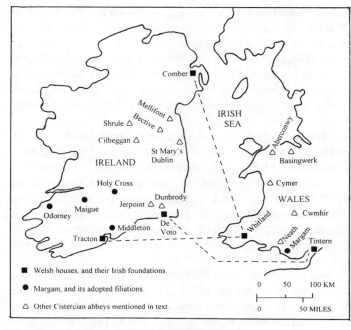

Fig. 69 Welsh-Irish Cistercian Connections.

Abbot of Clairvaux) in the remote parts of Ireland'.[63] More certainly, monks from Whitland settled a monastery at Tracton (County Cork) in 1224, taking there with them the vernacular use of the Welsh language.[64]

Tintern also colonised an Irish house in 1200 – Tintern Minor or Secunda. Colloquially it was known as the abbey *De Voto* ('Of the vow') – referring to William Marshal, Earl of Pembroke and Lord of Chepstow, founding the new abbey in fulfilment of a vow made during a storm at sea.[65] Basingwerk, too, entered the Irish scene at this time, complaining to the General Chapter (1201) that Mellifont had constructed an abbey too close to other Cistercian lands. It may have been representing the interests of its sister-Savigniac abbey, St Mary's, Dublin, with regard to the foundation of Abbeyshrule.[66] Much earlier, Gilbert, a monk of Louth Park (d. 1155), became Abbot of Basingwerk after founding an abbey in Ireland.[67]

The Abbot of Margam played a leading rôle in Ireland (1228) accompanying there Abbot Stephen Lexington of Stanley on his mission in connection with the 'Mellifont conspiracy', when assiduous efforts were made to correct the interior life and often rebellious nature of nationalist-tending monasteries.[68] The then long-ruling Abbot (John of Goldcliff) was clearly highly thought of, and Lexington, travelling en route to Ireland, in the presence of Margam's community insisted on their Abbot accompanying him.[69] He praised him for agreeing even though his abbey was currently 'harassed by enemies'.[70]

The measures taken to break up the Mellifont sub-family resulted in the affiliation to Margam of no less than four Irish houses: Holy Cross, Maigue, Middleton and Odorney,[71] and the Abbot of Margam was still father-immediate of these houses in 1445.[72] Further, the rebellious prior of Maigue, Patrick, was exiled to Margam.[73] The tension in his house may have been heightened by the other monks and *conversi* which Margam sent to assist in the reformation of the Irish abbeys.[74]

Lexington, also in 1228 and fearful of the consequences, dissuaded the Abbot of Whitland from visiting Tracton, by referring to the long and costly journey, and the current need for the Abbot to be in his own house.[75]

A spirit of exclusive nationalism remained in the abbeys housing monks of Irish stock, the consequence being that a later abbot of Margam (John de Cantelo, 1321) was sent by the Crown, with the Abbot of Dore, to see that the Cistercian houses of Ireland received not only Irish religious, but 'all who wished, without exception'.[76]

Even an Anglo-Norman abbey might suffer from the Anglo-Irish troubles of the times. An Abbot of Tintern (1356) who tried to visit in person his Irish daughter-abbey, Tintern Secunda, was obstructed by 'opponents and rebels'.[77] When a later abbot (1413) feared that Tintern Secunda might be 'laid waste and destroyed by rebels', he had a silver gilt cross brought back to Wales for safe-keeping.[78] Quite commonly, the relevant Welsh abbots delegated Irish superiors to act for them. The Abbot of Tracton (1346), on behalf of Tintern, deposed the Abbot of Tintern Secunda;[79] an Abbot of Dunbrody (1363) visited Tracton in the stead of the Abbot of Whitland.[80]

Henry of Lancaut, a monk of Tintern, who became Abbot of Tintern Secunda, later retiring to the mother-house – where his grave-slab still lies – will not have been the only Welsh monk to be translated to the abbacy of an Irish daughter-house. There were occasional difficulties. A monk of the Welsh Tintern (1411) was alleged to have unjustly deposed the Abbot of Tintern Secunda.[81] A bastard monk of Whitland (1441) – John de Barry – tried to usurp the abbacy of Middleton, in an episode reminiscent of the contentions for abbacies not unknown back in Wales. Eventually, he became Abbot of Tracton (1450).[82] A monk of Neath (1533) tried – with some backing within the Order – to supplant the Abbot of Whitland. The aggrieved Abbot referred to a 'pretended visitation' by the Abbots of Jerpoint and Tintern Secunda, acting on commissary letters of doubtful authenticity drawn up at two Welsh abbeys: Neath and 'Nimgavia'.[83]

NOTES

1.   Williams D.H. 1998, 38–40.
2.   *Statuta* I, 367 (1209/50); Cowley F.G. 1977, 127.
3.   Cowley F.G. 1977, 116–16.
4.   *Op. cit.* 115.
5.   Hays R.W. 1963, 82.
6.   Cowley F.G. 1977, 129.
7.   *Litt. Wallie* 33.
8.   *Cal. Patent R.* 1217, 80; *Cal. Close R.* 1332, 586; Cowley F.G. 1977, 130.
9.   *Cal. Close R.* 1331, 331.
10. *Cal. Patent R.* 1424, 487; *Cf.* 1426, 374.
11. Hays R.W. 1963, 123.
12. Desmond L.A. 1971, 153.
13. *Statuta* III, 469–70 (1342/1).
14. Talbot C.H. 1939, 12.
15. *Statuta* IV, 471 (1439/31).
16. Cowley F.G. 1977, 115.
17. *Statuta* III, 210 (1281/21).
18. *Letters to Cîteaux* 59–60.
19. *Op. cit.* 262.
20. *Statuta* VI, 123, 377. [Whilst once visiting Llantarnam, he wrote to Dore requesting a subsidy due to the Order: PRO, E 315/48].
21. *Statuta* VI, 509, 525, 674.
22. Williams D.H. 1998, 42–43.

23. *Ann. Mon.* II, 242, 245.
24. Cowley F.G. 1977, 116–17.
25. *Ann. Mon.* I, 32.
26. *Cal. Patent R.* 1233, 14.
27. *Ibid.* 1250, 61.
28. NLW, Penrice and Margam Ch. 211.
29. *Statuta* I, 153 (1192/97).
30. Brakspear H. 1910, 51, 72.
31. *Cal. Close R.* 1330, 145.
32. Birch W. de Gray. 1897, 48.
33. Cowley F.G. 1977, 117.
34. *Letters to Cîteaux* 127–29 (63–64).
35. *LP (Hen. VIII)* V, 456 (978–6).
36. Letter from the Director of the Archives of Côte d'Or [64A–1568 of 16/10/1964].
37. Cowley F.G. 1977, 117.
38. *Letters from Ireland* 42 (20).
39. *Statuta* III, 185 (1279/11), 199–200 (1280/23, 29).
40. *Statuta* I, 199 (1196/8).
41. Williams S.W. 1889, Appx. xxx–xxxi.
42. PRO, C 81/164 (No. 2804).
43. *Ann. Mon.* II, 242, 245.
44. Williams D.H. 1976, 102.
45. *Kingswood Docs.* 194 (XII), 215–17 (XXV-Col. II).
46. *Op. cit.* 216–17 (XXV).
47. Williams D.H. 1976, 109–10.
48. *Op. cit.* 111.
49. *Monm. Rec.* II, 81, 82 (Info. of Mr Keith Kissack).
50. BL, Royal MS 12E xiv. F. 23r (Info. of the late Dr C.H. Talbot).
51. PRO, E 315/36/228 (where a misleading catalogue entry).
52. PRO, LR 1/229, ff. 129–131.
53. Williams D.H. 1976, 19.
54. *Fasti Cist. (1)* 205, 210.
55. *Valor Eccl.* IV, 361. (It also paid 73s. to the Holy See).
56. *Letters to Cîteaux* 127 (63).
57. PRO, C 24/29 (Pt. 2).
58. PRO, E 135/18/6; Williams D.H. 1976, 23.
59. *Letters to Cîteaux* 191 (94); Williams G. 1962, 397.
60. Williams D.H. 1980, *passim*.
61. Bowen E.G. 1969, *passim*.
62. *Orig. Cist.* 204 (DXXVI); Stalley R.A. 1987, 243.
63. *Autobiog. G.C.* 77–78.
64. O'Dwyer B.W. II (1976) 26, 96–97.
65. Hore P.H. I (1901) 4; *Lit. Cant.* III, 99 (No. 985).
66. *Statuta* I, 268–69 (1201/27).
67. Williams D.H. 1981, 96.
68. Williams D.H. 1998, 58.
69. *Letters from Ireland* 19–20 (3).
70. *Op. cit.* 35 (15).
71. *Op. cit.* 48 (22), 56 (24), 150 (77), 152–53 (78); *MSS in BM* III, 550 (825).
72. *MSS in BM* III, 551 (828); Birch W. de Gray. 1897, 345.
73. *Letters from Ireland* 28 (9).
74. *Ann. Mon.* I, 36; Birch W. de Gray. 1897, 222.
75. *Letters from Ireland* 18 (2), 206–07 (98).
76. *Cal. Close R.* 1321, 404.
77. Hore P.H. I (1901) 54; *Cf.* 50–51, 58–59.
78. PRO, C 1/2 (6).(6).
79. Gwent Record Office, D.902.2, p. 55.
80. Gwynn, A. 1970, 143.
81. *Statuta* IV, 155 (1411/72).
82. *Cal. Papal Reg. (Letters)* X, 300, 510; XII, 559.
83. Conbhuí C.S.Ó. 1958, 162–63.

CHAPTER 11

LANDED PROPERTY

Introduction

The basis of Cistercian economy lay in the acquisition, often by donation but also by purchase or exchange, of large tracts of both arable and pasture land. Their very size and widespread distribution throughout Wales allowed the White Monks to give to the Welsh folk in their localities the example of large-scale management and expertise – as witnessed in the great 13th century flocks of sheep under the care of *conversi*, and as evidenced by the careful administration of their estates – not least in the consolidation of their holdings.

Giraldus Cambrensis praised the Cistercians for their 'good management'.[1] This, in turn, was reflected by the cartularies of houses like Neath and Whitland, the cellarers' and manorial rolls and grange accounts of Tintern,[2] and in the unique survival of a slate talley employed by a reeve of Strata Florida.[3] In addition, the use of enclosures,[4] the breeding of pedigree dairy herds (at least by Llanllŷr nunnery), and the practice of manuring (certainly by Neath and Tintern),[5] must all have contributed to give both peasant farmers and a growing tenantry food for thought. Initiative and impetus was also given by the Cistercians to the milling and early mining industries of Wales, and, not least, to wool production and trade.

A rough idea of the relative prosperity of the various abbeys can be obtained from the several valuations compiled at intervals during their history – but all suffer inherent problems of compilation and interpretation making absolute comparison difficult. The *Norwich Taxation* (1254) gives Neath (£269) the edge over Margam (£251), with Tintern (£108) far behind. It is a survey restricted to the diocese of Llandaff.[6] The *Taxatio Ecclesiastica* (1291) has Margam as leading the way and valued at £256 (gross), Neath coming second (£236) and Tintern third (£145)[7] – later it was to receive additional valuable properties.

The Cistercian *Tax Book* (1354–55) keeps Margam in first place (£34 'medium' tax), closely followed by Strata Marcella (£33) with Tintern (£22) still lagging behind.[8] The list of contributions for the support of Cistercian scholars at Oxford (1400) now shows Tintern (£2 13s 4d) in first place, with Margam and Neath (£2 6s 8d) running second.[9] A subsidy arranged for the expenses of the General Chapter (1521) gives Tintern and Neath the lead,[10] whilst Tintern still holds sway in the *Valor Ecclesiasticus* (1535).[11] The subsidy expected by the Crown towards the expenses of the French war (1522) couples, surprisingly, Llantarnam and Valle Crucis in first place with Tintern (£66 13s 4d).[12] If these figures are multiplied by 300, some idea is gained of their value in modern real terms.[13]

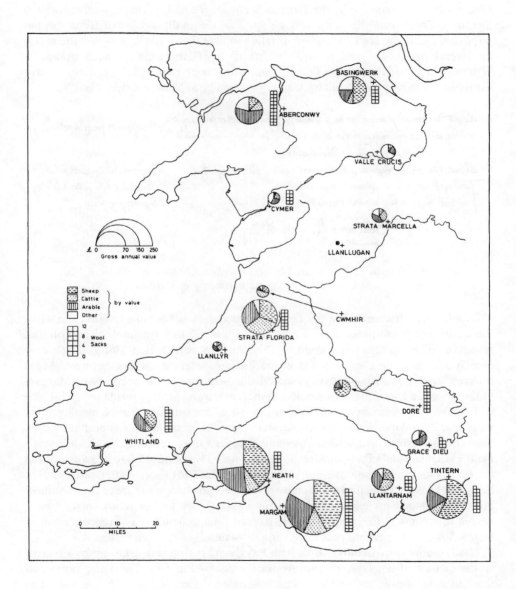

Fig. 70: Economic values, 1291, of the Welsh Cistercian houses.
based chiefly upon the *Taxatio Ecclesiastica* of 1291; Record Commission, 1802).

These great surveys, whilst broad and useful illustrations, lack complete reliabil-
ity. Some important properties were not taken account of – like Tintern's
Gloucestershire manors – by the *Taxatio Ecclesiastica* and, perhaps, by the *Norwich
Taxation*. The *Taxatio* listed the abbey's spiritualities in the diocese of Hereford, but
omitted those in the see of Llandaff. It failed to note that Valle Crucis was the rector
of several parishes,[14] and it made no mention of Aberconwy's huge grange at
Nanhwynan. The *Taxatio* also failed to quote any stock numbers for Cwmhir – save
for those animals upon its solitary Ceredigion grange at Nant-yr-arian *(Fig. 70)*.[15]

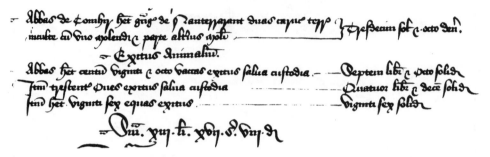

Fig. 71: *Taxatio Ecclesiastica*, 1291 *(Public Record Office E 164/14, f.393).*
Stock of Cwmhir in the Archdeaconry of Cardigan

Despite such discrepancies, the *Taxatio* formed the basis for clerical taxation – like
the tenths payable at times to the Crown – down to the Reformation.[16] The Poll Tax
return of 1379 was also based upon it. This credits Strata Florida with 1,327 sheep –
exactly the same number as listed in the *Taxatio* nearly a century before.[17] More
accurate and updated later surveys included a valuation of the property of Margam
(1336),[18] and a list of the possessions of Aberconwy and Strata Florida (*c.* 1356).[19]

The *Valor Ecclesiasticus* (1535) is also a list where caution must be employed, as
its preparation depended to a considerable extent upon the details submitted by the
heads of the houses themselves.[20] A number of its values appear to be an under-estimate:[21] Llantarnam's Pwl-pan Grange valued at £13 was estimated to be worth £20 in
the first post-Suppression Ministers' Accounts (1535–36) shortly afterwards.[22] Had
the abbeys feared increased taxation it was to their advantage to render lower values,
but if they hoped for exemption from suppression then higher returns would have
served them best.[23] In some instances, the last minute demises and renegotiation of
leases *(Chapter 6)* perhaps account for the substantially increased values.

The last abbess of Llanllŷr, Elizabeth Baynham, at first refused to make a return,
so the income of her convent was arbitrarily assessed at £40. The *Valor* notes that
the nunnery 'afterwards sent a certain schedule', estimating its value at £18. The
compilers then seem to have added both figures together, giving Llanllŷr the
surprisingly high assessment of over £57, as compared to an average of £25 in the
Ministers' Accounts covering the first few post-Suppression years.[24]

Other factors which may detract from these valuations as precise quantitative assessments are: (1). The degree to which land was demised – much of the apparent value of a grange depended upon this; (2). The corollary – where much direct working of land continued there was a substantial 'hidden income' (in the form of grain and stock) to the abbeys concerned.[25]

Benefactors and their Motives

The grantors who settled landed property upon the Cistercian houses of north and west Wales were Welsh practically to a man – like the uncles and cousins of Prince Llywelyn, and the Prince himself, who greatly enriched both Aberconwy[26] and Cymer.[27] Owain Cyfeiliog and his son, Gwenwynwyn, gave Strata Marcella its major acquisitions,[28] and to the Lord Rhys Strata Florida, Whitland and the nunnery of Llanllŷr all owed much.[29] In the far south-east of Wales, by contrast, benefactors were almost exclusively Anglo-Norman – as members of the de Clare and Marshal families in respect of Tintern, and the Lords of Monmouth in the case of Grace Dieu.[30]

Several monasteries had a distinct racial mixture amongst their grantors – like Margam, an Anglo-Norman foundation expanding its territory by obtaining a series of quitclaims from Welsh freeholders.[31] The varying fortunes of Border warfare meant that some houses gained from alternating régimes. Basingwerk received its home manor from Earl Ranulf of Chester, but it obtained its Gelli Grange from Prince Llywelyn ab Iorwerth, and Holywell church from his son, Prince David.[32] Cwmhir had Welsh patrons like Prince Gwenwynwyn (who gave it Cwmbiga), but also enjoyed benefactions – like Brilley and Dolhelfa – from the Mortimers.[33]

There is insufficient evidence to determine what hidden, perhaps sometimes political, motives encouraged benefactors to part with land. If the charters are to be believed, then spiritual considerations played a major role. Prince Gwenwynwyn (1191) made a grant to Strata Marcella 'moved by piety, for the salvation of my soul, and those of my father and mother, and all my ancestors and successors'.[34] This concern for the departed and one's own soul after death was echoed by numerous grantors, like Roger Mortimer who, giving a charter to Cwmhir (1199), was mindful of the salvation of 'those who have died in the conquest of Maelienydd'.[35]

Many benefactors made grants conditional upon being buried in a monastic cemetery, for them hallowed ground – as Llywelyn ap Rhirid promised by Margam burial 'as for one of the familiars',[36] and like Madog ap Seysil (*c.* 1245) who gave land to Dore 'for his soul and the burial of his body'.[37] All these donors were taking out a spiritual insurance policy!

Substantial benefactors might spell out specific chantry obligations.[38] Henry III (1226) granted Stowe Grange to Grace Dieu on condition that two monks maintained divine service there for his soul.[39] When, in the reign of Richard II (1377–99), this obligation went by default, the property passed temporarily out of the monks' hands.[40] Hubert de Burgh, as Lord of the Three Castles (*c.* 1235), gave Llyncoed and Llanfair granges to Dore in return for Masses said daily – in the former case at the abbey, in the latter instance by monks stationed at the grange itself.[41]

Hugh le Despenser (by 1347), in addition to an obit and other spiritual services, expected of Margam a solemn Mass on his birthday.[42] Richard Turberville (1360) sought a daily Mass at the altar of St Mary Magdalene in the monastery, as well as the insertion of his name 'in its martyrology, between its founders'.[43] Close to the Suppression, Morgan Jones (1532) envisaged at Llantarnam a yearly *'dirige and masse of requiem'*.[44] So far as can be ascertained, such obits continued until the Dissolution, as well as the associated alms.

Some of the Welshry gave land to Margam in return for reception into 'full fraternity'. This may have simply meant benefiting from a spiritual association with its monks, as did Richard Norreis received into 'the fraternity of the monastery', together with his wife and sons.[45] Frequently, however, the grantors (by the early 13th century) became numbered amongst the *conversi*, like Geoffrey Sturmi – who gave the nucleus of Margam's Stormy Grange,[46] and Thomas Lageles – who sold the monks (for very little) 100 acres in Laleston – and who was 'received as brother and partaker of all its goods until the end'.[47] This echoed the words of the Order's *Charter of Charity* which said of the *conversi:* 'We hold them to be our brothers and, equally with our monks, sharers of our goods both spiritual and temporal'.[48]

Grants of land might be made by parents whose sons were entering the religious life, like the property on 'Ralph's Down' given to Margam by William ab Algar, and Margery his wife, a reminder that, to secure land against claims by aggrieved heirs, family agreement was essential.[49] An early grant to Margam was made by 'Philip ap Gruffydd, and Morgan my son, and my wife'.[50] The filial consent was very necessary as Philip was seeking admission 'into the fraternity of the house'.

Charitable deeds done by, or expected of, the monks, encouraged recipients to make a gift or sale of land. Hugh of Hereford (*c.* 1187) cancelled a debt owed him by Margam because the abbey had gained his freedom from the prison of the Earl of Gloucester.[51] Robert Russel (1261) 'with the assent of Agnes his wife and Thomas his heir', gave Margam iron and lead mining rights in return for 'no small benefits in his most urgent need'.[52] Hugh le Despenser (*c.* 1347), confirming Margam's ownership of Resolfen, required the abbey to feed, clothe and shoe seven poor men yearly.[53] Far greater obligations were expected by the Welsh princes of the English-orientated Basingwerk. Its lands in Penllyn had to provide for hundreds of their men one night each hunting season *(Chapter 2)*,[54] but Edward I abolished these provisions after the Conquest.[55]

Lands 'granted' to the White Monks were perhaps rarely outright 'gifts', free of any condition or return. Some property was bought for cash or, occasionally, acquired by barter; other land might be held by payment of an annual rent or an 'acknowledgement' of some kind.[56] In its estate formation prior to 1300 Margam spent at least £160 on the purchase of land, and took on the annual burden of £24 for rented property. Family involvement was again to the fore when Geoffrey Sturmi received from Margam not only twelve marks, but also a cloak and four gold pieces for each of his three sons.[57] There were several instances of the abbey buying up land from people who were 'in great necessity' or 'urgent need'.[58] Thomas Grammus (*c.* 1250) sold an acre in Kenfig to Margam 'for 20s. given him by the monks for charity'.[59] Land might be mortgaged; William Franklin (1258) gave an acre by Coalbrook for 1 mark 'with power of redemption on paying the mark and the cost of improvement',[60] a significant note of monastic agrarian practice.

Financial outlay was also the lot of Grace Dieu (1230–32) – £120 to Henry III for the manor of Penyard Regis (Herefs.), paid in three instalments.[61] Of the charters given by Prince Gwenwynwyn to Strata Marcella (1185–1215) several – especially the earlier deeds – make no mention of pecuniary return, a few later ones note his 'sale' of land to the abbey for unspecified sums, but others show an outlay by the abbey of well over £40.[62] Earl Roger Bigod gave Tintern additional lands at Modesgate (Gloucs.) – but for this so-called 'gift' the abbey paid him twenty-five marks.[63]

Payment by an abbey might be partially by barter – according well with Celtic custom. One donor of Margam sought 30s 'in goods and money'.[64] Such trade-ins included cows,[65] sheep, lamb-skins,[66] beans, and shoes.[67] Rentals might also be partly paid in kind: Walter Luvel expected of Margam (1253) 2 qrs. of wheat each July, and a coulter and a ploughshare for his plough each Easter,[68] indicating the dates of seed-time and of harvest.

Where land was leased, an abbey might well try to lessen the annual burden of rent by negotiating quit-claims from the lessors, but sometimes a significant sum had to be laid down.[69] Margam gave forty marks for the quit-claim of lands in Bonvilston (1281), and a further fifteen marks for the return to the abbey of land held of it by the same donor.[70] One of the best reductions in rent Margam achieved was from Morgan Gam, lord of Afan (1240): 20s. p.a. down to 2s. on account of the damages he had inflicted on the monastery.[71] Margam (c. 1225) also benefited from Morgan ap Cadwaladr's promise not to expect any rent from pasture rights he afforded the monks, if they were unable to use them on account of war: a reflection of both current Anglo-Welsh difficulties, and internecine strife amongst the Welshry.[72]

When a quit-claim was obtained, royal dues might still be payable, as also an 'acknowledgement' to the previous owner and his heirs. This was to safeguard against any future demand of 'feudal service, exaction and custom', as when Ralph of Lahee (1234) gave Bachwilim to Strata Marcella in return for 'two pairs of spurs', at each Lammas Day (1 August).[73] Such annual payments included (by Margam): twenty-four lambs' pelts,[74] a pair of gloves,[75] and 1lb. of wax.[76] In Gwent, Madog ap Seysil granted 4½ bovates to Dore, but on condition the monks rendered 6s 9d yearly to the Crown. After his death, his widow remitted her 'widow's third' to the abbey.[77]

Charters and Confirmations

The granting of land to a monastery could be accompanied by due ceremony, as when Hugh of Llancarfan (c.1190) extending Margam's lands at Llafeuthin 'solemnly deposited the charter on the high altar of the abbey, in the presence of many bystanders';[78] an indication – like the burial of Matilda Marshal at Tintern (1248)[79] – that on occasion the laity entered the quire and presbytery. Some grants to Margam were sworn upon the abbey's relics,[80] not least that of the Holy Cross.[81] Certain of its donors swore upon the tomb of St Teilo in Llandaff Cathedral, especially where the bishop or chapter were arbitrators or witnesses to an agreement.[82] Successive abbots of Grace Dieu (from 1361) had to affirm by corporal oath, in the presence of the Constable of St Briavel's, that the chantry services by which it held Stowe Grange were still being performed in the abbey.[83]

The need for charters giving the precise boundaries of monastic properties – streams, ditches and other landmarks – was pointed out by Prince Gwenwynwyn (1191) – who reflected that 'nothing opposes forgetfulness and false-claim more effectively than a written record'. Further, 'to prevent any false claim arising in the future, he has confirmed his gift [to Strata Marcella] by the signatures of witnesses and with the protection of his seal'.[84] The witnesses sometimes constituted a powerful array. Where a grantor was a person of lower status with no seal of his own, or whose seals was not widely recognised, confirmation by a superior secular or ecclesiastical lord was vital. Bishop Alan of Bangor (1195) appended his seal to a gift of Cadwaladr ab Hywel to the same abbey: 'Because the present age is prone and disposed to evil, and attempts to break falsely whatever it seeks to extort gain'.[85] The seals of the Bishop of Llandaff and of the Abbots of Margam and Neath corroborated a grant by Cnaithur ap Herbert and his brothers to Margam (*c.* 1170) as they had no seals.[86]

The drafting of early charters to Welsh monasteries may have owed something, perhaps much, to the monks themselves – being literate and versed in Latin. This did happen, but the phrase in Llywelyn's great charter to Cymer (1209): 'By the hand of Abbot Esau',[87] is more likely a phrase of investiture than a statement that the abbot himself engrossed the text. A very strong case has been made to show that the charter allegedly given by Llywelyn to Aberconwy in 1199, at least as it now survives, may have been produced (by the monks themselves) no earlier than 1284, as a response to post-Conquest assaults on the abbey's privileges. The early nucleus of the charter may have been a confirmation by Llywelyn (about 1201) of grants to the abbey by his uncles and cousins.[88]

Almost as important as the initial grants of land were the subsequent charters of confirmation, and many original deeds, now lost, are known only through such confirmations. Confirmatory charters from an overlord of the grantor might be sought almost immediately, especially at times of political change – like Prince Llywelyn's charter to Cymer (1209), coming only seven years after he achieved suzerainty of Meirionydd. Basingwerk (1285) obtained an important *inspeximus* from Edward I of eleven charters soon after his conquest of Wales.[89] Tintern later (1306), perhaps knowing the sick condition of that king, hastened to obtain the monarch's confirmation of its charters – one of its monks travelling to Carlisle for this purpose.[90]

Monasteries frequently deemed it necessary to obtain confirmation of their charters when their lands and privileges were threatened or infringed. To be effective in such circumstances, a warning of ecclesiastical penalties (excommunication) might be sought: Margam did this by obtaining comprehensive confirmatory bulls from Innocent III (1203) and Alexander III (1261).[91] Damage to, or wear and tear of, the original deeds was another cause. Neath (1336) petitioned Edward III 'to view and confirm the charter of King John, which charter by war in these parts has been ruined and worn'.[92] Likewise, 'for the defence of the monastery', Llantarnam (1398) requested papal confirmation of rights granted in 1257 (to the Cistercian Order as a whole), since 'the said letters are beginning to be consumed with age'.[93] Whitland (1447, 1508), having lost letters patent of Richard II, twice gained their exemplification.[94]

Successive confirmations could be necessary. The Lord Rhys in 1184 'now again' confirmed, with his three sons, the possessions of Strata Florida at a gathering in Rhayader church. He died in 1197, and the abbey hastened to obtain further confirmatory charters from his sons, Maelgwyn and Rhys, at the close of 1198. There followed a series of royal confirmations – in 1200 (John), 1229 (Henry III), 1336 (Edward III),[95] 1369 (Prince Edmund), 1380 (Richard II) and 1423 (Henry VI).[96] In four of those instances it was felt politic to seek a new confirmatory charter fairly soon after the accession of a new sovereign. The charter of Henry VI was inspected nearly a century later by Henry VII (1508)[97] – it listed eleven previous charters and confirmations. Amongst them was that of Cynan ap Maredudd (1294) who called down spiritual rewards upon those who maintained the terms of his charter, but, as for any who infringed it, 'let not his name be written in the book of life'.[98]

A similar series of royal confirmatory charters can be traced for both Cymer and Strata Marcella.[99] Very significant also to the latter house were the charters granted by the Charlton dynasty, who inherited the barony of Powys by marriage (1309),[100] and, especially, the great confirmation of Edward Charlton (1420) – a deed necessitated by the suffering of the abbey in the Glyn Dŵr Revolt.[101] After their ascent to power in Maelienydd (1199), the Mortimers gave substantial grants and confirmed the original charters of Cwmhir;[102] again royal endorsement followed – from John (1214),[103] Henry III (1232) and Edward II (1318).[104]

Fig. 72: Richard de Granville's Foundation Charter for Neath Abbey (*c.* 1129).
(Held by West Glamorgan Archive Service, A/N 1).

Such successive confirmations were not cheap: royal demands varied from 100 marks by Henry III for his charter in favour of Margam, to the light sum of £3 charged Aberconwy by Edward III.[105] Nonetheless, the ultimate advantages must have outweighed the initial costs – as for Cymer when it exhibited its confirmation from Edward III at the *Quo Warranto* Proceedings (1348), and its rights were upheld and sustained.[106]

Later charters may be of interest in expanding upon the bare bones of the originals, perhaps because of monastic concern to spell out precisely what earlier had been taken for granted. Amongst the foundation grants to Tintern (1133) was 'Merthyr-gerain'; Earl Gilbert of Pembroke's confirmation lists: 'Merthyr-gerain, with the church' (*c*.1140); and, a century later, Gilbert Marshal expanded yet further: 'Merthyr-gerain, with the church and the wood'.[107] Prince Llywelyn's charter for Basingwerk (prior to 1230) mentions the 'mill before the gate'. His son, Prince David (1240), was able to speak in the plural, 'the mills near the abbey gate'.[108]

Estate Building

The considerable acquisition of land made in Wales by the Cistercians in their formative period was not without criticism, sometimes biased and severe, because of its human effects: the displacement of people and the occasional destruction of churches, as well as, allegedly, the use of foul means as well as fair to achieve monastic objectives.

Not the least of their critics was the prejudiced Giraldus Cambrensis *(Chapter 1)*. Giraldus – who once quoted an apparently contemporaneous proverb reflecting badly on the Cistercians: 'They are bad neighbours just like the White Monks'[109] – did acknowledge that the monks' avidity for land came 'not from any bad intentions'.[110] Even he realised their need (in his day) to support large communities and to sustain a considerable burden of hospitality and charity *(Chapter 9)*. Coloured though critical evidence may be, it does seem that the Cistercians of the early 13th century had a strong will where land acquisition was concerned, and their heavy burdens may have forced them into means not always ethical. This may, or may not, have been true of Margam's policy of buying up land from people who were 'in great necessity'.[111]

Amongst the accusations levelled by Giraldus were that Strata Florida had robbed Llanllŷr nunnery of land (perhaps its Hafodwen Grange);[112] that Whitland had removed the grange of Rhuddlan Deifi out of the hands of the Premonstratensians of Talley;[113] and that Aberconwy had tried to annex lands of the *clas* of Beddgelert.[114] Giraldus castigated the acquisitiveness of Margam during the abbacy of Gilbert (1203–13), alleging its oppression of the neighbouring abbey of Neath[115] – Cistercian, but of the family of Savigny not of Clairvaux.

The Margam-Neath conflicts persisted for over half a century, with disputes as to the ownership of Sker Grange,[116] as well as problems regarding pasture rights in the lordship of Afan (1205-08)[117] and in Corneli and Newton Downs (*c*. 1237).[118] Margam was not entirely at fault, nor was Neath wholly blameless. Morgan ap Caradog, lord of Afan admitted (in 1205) that 'overcome by lust of money', he granted rights to Neath in the same pastures which he had previously conceded to Margam,[119] whilst Walter Map (d. 1210; both an ecclesiastic and royal officer) accused Neath of altering a charter so that a grant of sixteen acres read one hundred.[120]

The bulk of monastic estates were often acquired within a few decades of an abbey's foundation, but consolidation and expansion might last for well over a century. With the possible exception of lands in Pennal, Cymer had the whole of its property settled upon it within a decade (1198–1209),[121] and the building up of the estates of Strata Florida[122] and Strata Marcella was more or less completed by 1226.[123] The main elements of Margam's domain were achieved by about 1230, but a process of expansion continued until around 1320.[124]

Tintern received most of its major properties within twenty years of its foundation (1131), but had substantial later additions (1223–24, 1302).[125] The houses of north Wales also participated in the search for new lands – like Basingwerk accused (in 1251) of appropriating royal territory in Glossop (Derbys.),[126] and Aberconwy (1306, 1311) allegedly ploughing up land which did not belong to it.[127] All in all, however, a map depicting Cistercian lands in Wales in 1240 would not have been vastly dissimilar from one showing their extent at the Dissolution three hundred years later.

Consolidation of estates meant easier management and greater economic efficiency, and was achieved by two processes: *exchange* – not always a voluntary action, and *extension* – buying up, leasing, or obtaining the outright gift of land within, or contiguous to, that which a monastery already owned. Amongst many examples, Neath (before 1243) exchanged a distant property at Hornblotton (Somerset) for the local Gower fee of Walterstone.[128]

Dore (1285) traded thirteen small parcels of land in the Lordship of the Three Castles (north Gwent) to Prince Edmund for four larger properties.[129] Aberconwy (1350) gave up the somewhat remote Ffriwlwyd Grange in return for the advowson of nearby Eglwys-rhos church.[130] In most instances of exchange the motive was to bring abbey lands closer together and nearer to the monastery. This was not evident when Tintern exchanged lands at Penterry for Woolaston manor (1148+), nor property at Plataland for what became Aluredeston Grange (1302), but in both instances more potentially profitable lands were seemingly being acquired.[131]

Earl Gilbert of Gloucester (*c.* 1290), Lord of Glamorgan, forced exchanges upon three Cistercian houses which were to their detriment. He acquired from Margam Resolven Grange and other lands, in return for the restitution of Theodoric's Grange and New Grange – which he had seized previously, but he also awarded the abbey pasture and milling rights. Forty years later (1329) the exchange was annulled, after Margam pointed out that the net result had been a shortfall in its income, and a consequent reduction in the number of monks it could sustain by ten.[132]

The Abbot of Llantarnam (1317) also complained of being insufficiently compensated when his abbey exchanged lands with the Earl.[133] The Earl gave Neath £100-worth of rents in Cardiff, Caerleon, Cowbridge and Neath, in return for lands in Briton Ferry and Cadoxton. Neath may have acquiesced because of a need to finance building works at the time, but, at the Suppression, the abbey was drawing less than half of the £100 rent so acquired. The lands the Earl had his eye on were undoubtedly already well tilled by the monasteries concerned.[134]

The extension of monastic land is well evidenced in Gwent and the Border. Dore enlarged and consolidated its grange at Llanfair (obtained from Hubert de Burgh in 1201–43), by gaining grants of contiguous land, by exchange, and by buying up privately owned land 'within the lands of the monks'.[135] It also leased secondary waste land in Grosmont Hill (1249–50) lying outside its granges.[136] Walter Marshal (1242–46), Lord of Chepstow, added forty acres of land *(munedam)* rising above the marshy Levels to Tintern's Merthyr-gerain Grange,[137] and Earl Roger Bigod (1302) gave an extra twenty-eight acres at its Modesgate Grange.[138] In 1262, it added sixty-two acres to its Estavarney Grange,[139] whilst Grace Dieu (1338) obtained the leasehold of thirty-six acres of waste adjacent to its grange at Stowe.[140] (Modesgate and Stowe both lay in the west of Dean Forest). In north Wales, Basingwerk was expanding its lands – in the Wirral [141] and in Flintshire – as late as 1351.[142]

The deeds of Margam make frequent mention of land extensions – as twenty-four acres acquired (1190),[143] and then a further seven,[144] next to its St Michael's Grange, and like the grant (as the 13th century opened) of thirty-seven acres at Llanfeuthin 'next to the old cemetery on the western side'.[145] From 1254 to about 1325, additional land was acquired piecemeal in the Kenfig area, sometimes in return for partial or full corrodies granted to the donors.[146] Many of these extensions were only of one or two acres, or of strips of land 'of five rods width'.[147]

One of the most impressive and discerning pieces of estate building was the progressive growth and consolidation from roughly 1150 to 1320 of the continuous strip of land which Margam came to own east of Pyle *(Fig. 73)*: this gave it not only good arable, but also access to iron, lead and lime. It lay on either side of a medieval road, the Portway. This land extension meant the abandonment by the grantors of small castles, like those at Llangewydd and Stormy.[148]

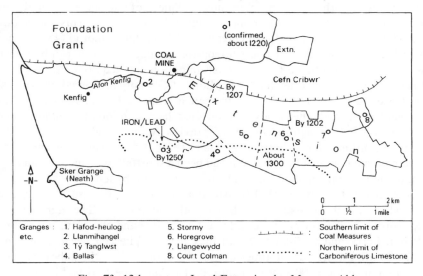

Fig. 73: 13th century Land Extension by Margam Abbey.

There is evidence to show that the Cistercians in their pursuit of consolidated estates did sometimes remove the peasantry already dwelling on land the monks had acquired. Compensation seems to have been paid, or the dispossessed given the opportunity of settling elsewhere.[149] The scores of deeds and quitclaims gained by Margam from the late 12th century on may well be evidence of such depopulation.[150] The process gained critical comment from Archbishop Peckham that where the White Monks 'plant their foot, they destroy towns, take away tithes',[151] and from Giraldus Cambrensis 'all the monasteries of Wales ... are wont to occupy the parishes ... expelling the parishioners ... even razing the churches'.[152]

A well documented example of displacement was at Llangewydd where Margam, after progressively acquiring control of the knight's fee over twenty-five years, converted it into an eight-carucate grange and then (1202) erased the church overnight.[153] King John (1207), confirming land to Neath, safeguarded the existing tenants, saying that the monastery 'might not remove them, but have only their homage and rent'.[154] The evidence is patchy for much of Wales, though the men of Merton (Flints., *c*. 1281) complained that Reginald de Grey, justice of Chester, dispossessed them of sixteen carucates of land – giving it to Basingwerk.[155]

The evolution and continuing possession of the monastic estates was not without disputes as to boundaries and rightful ownership, and the need for prolonged negotiations and adjudications, even more formal litigation. Apart from the depredations of Earl Gilbert de Clare, Margam (*c*. 1196–1200) had, *inter alia*,[156] to obtain a favourable ruling from the Bishop of Llandaff when objections were raised to David Scurlage giving it the fee of Llangewydd, alleging that he was under-age.[157] A young Welshman (*c*. 1200), said to be mentally disturbed, claiming lands which had been given the abbey, set fire to one of its corn-filled barns.[158] Much later (1420), Margam lost certain pasture rights in Afan on the decision of a twelve-man jury.[159]

In Gloucestershire, Tintern had problems with the Augustinian priory of Llanthony Prima, both houses being owners of adjacent manors, and contended that the men of the canons had caused some £112 worth of damage to its Aluredeston Grange. Before a deal was struck (1318), the cellarer of Tintern took forceful counter-measures, the Abbot of Tintern – Hugh de Wyke, noted for his defence of the abbey's properties – was present at one stage 'with a great number of the Welshry'.[160]

Such contentions were not limited to south Wales. Cwmhir had problems with both Peter Corbet, lord of Caus (1280)[161] and with Chirbury Priory (1311).[162] Arbitration involving the abbots of Whitland (its mother-house) and Llantarnam (a daughter-house) closed a contention between Strata Florida and Cynan ap Maredudd ab Owain concerning the boundaries of Mefenydd Grange. Their concord was submitted to the Justices of Assize (1280).[163] All monastic lands suffered at times like the Conquest and the Glyn Dŵr Revolt, and from the many lesser irritants described throughout this volume.

Extent of the Cistercian Estates *(Numbers refer to the Map Section, No. 1)*

All *Aberconwy*'s lands were situated in north-west Wales, both on the mainland and in Anglesey.[164] It had some 16,000 hectares (40,000a.), at least half of which was mountain pasture. The upland granges were of great size – like Nanhwynan *(No. 12 on the Map)*, a 4,900ha. property on the slopes of Snowdon, which being largely rough pasture supported only nine tenants at the Dissolution.[165] Two other major pastoral units were Hiraethog Grange *(No. 17*; about 3,200ha./over 8,000a.)[166] and Ardda-Darllas Grange *(No. 13*; some 1,600ha./close on 4,000a.). The arable granges – much smaller in area – included valuable properties in Anglesey – as the seven-carucate Gelliniog Grange *(No. 7)* which had an important 'Great Field', and Bodgedwydd *(No. 5)* and Cornwy Llys Granges *(No. 1)* – three carucates apiece.

The lands of Basingwerk extended widely away from its home lordship of Fulbrook-Greenfield *(No. 19)*, which encompassed three granges, the lands of Merton Abbot *(No. 21)* and part of Holywell town.[167] Gelli Grange and Tre'r Abbot *(No. 22)* lay near. Other substantial arable properties – as Caldy Grange *(No. 23)* – were in the Wirral, whilst large acreages of pasture – centred on properties like Boch-y-rhaiadr and Gwernhefin *(No. 27)* were held in the mountains of Meirionydd. There the abbey owned an important asset – Llyn Tegid (Lake Bala). Like Tintern, however, its most valuable manor – Glossop (Derbyshire) – lay outside Wales.

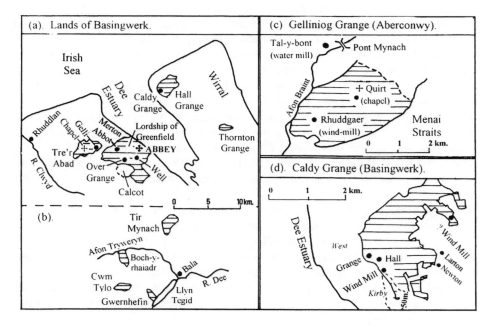

Fig. 74: Lands of Basingwerk, and a Grange of Aberconwy.

Valle Crucis held two urban manors: Llangollen Abbot (with mill and fishery; *186*) and Wrexham Abbot (with its 'court' and mill; *195*).[168] Other important properties included: half the township of Mwstwr (*187*), the township of Stansty Abbot next to Wrexham, and the manor of Halghton (with its 'court' and two mills; *196*). Amongst the abbey's other possessions were a string of properties along the Alun river: the pastures of Hafod-yr-abad *(189)*, the township of Buddugre'r Abad *(190)*, and the granges of Banhadlan and Creigiog *(192a, b)*.

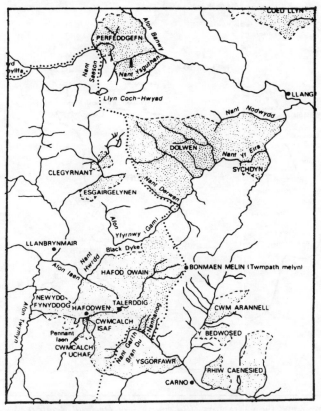

Fig. 75: Upland Properties of Strata Marcella, between the rivers Banwy and Carno.
(Courtesy of Mr Graham Thomas, and of the National Library of Wales).

Much of the early granges of *Strata Marcella*[169] were organised eventually into two manors, both known as Tir-y-Mynach. That in the Severn valley was predominantly arable (11 carucates of ploughland) and included the home estate – also called Strata Marcella Abbot *(152–153)*, with several mills, substantial woodland, a 400-acre great pasture, and a 38-acre 'great mead' adjacent to the abbey site. Neighbouring granges included Moydog and Trefnant *(166)*. In the uplands of west Powys, the second manor – primarily pastoral and centred on Talerddig – contained detached lands in no less than eleven parishes *(160–165)*.

The remote nature of the manor accounted for grange chapels (like Dolwen and Talerddig), and for the tradition of monastic 'cells' (as at Cyffin; *158*). In the more distant mountains was the abbey's Bala-Penllyn Grange *(156)*, whose lands abutted on possessions of Basingwerk and Valle Crucis. Lesser properties, on the Shropshire border, included the township of Rhos-goch *(155)* and an adjacent detached portion of Wollaston parish.

Fig. 76: Lands of Abbey Cwmhir and their Grantors. *(By courtesy of Dr Paul Remfry).*

Much of *Cymer*'s land lay in three blocks in the mountainous region close to the monastery.[170] The first block, in Nannau, lay in the angle between the Mawddach and Mynach streams, included the abbey site and at least three early granges *(41–43)*. (Four or five granges – in the parishes of Brithdir, Llanfachreth and Trawsfynydd – came, in time, to be overseen by one bailiff.) In Trawsfynydd, and forming part of the later 'Forest of Snowdon',[171] was a large block of mountain property between the rivers Mawddach and Gain *(44)*. The isolated settled holdings here were confined to the south of the area – the grange of Cwm Cedryn – a zone where mining and transhumance made their mark. Other upland granges were those of Cwmcadian *(46)* and 'Cyfeiliog'*(45)*, whilst by Cardigan Bay lay Gellisarog Grange *(47)*, a complex of separate holdings – perhaps because the mode of settlement precluded the alienation of a large block of land to the monks.[172] Cymer's most valuable possession, and its leading arable grange, was Neigwl Mynach in Llŷn *(48)*.[173]

The greater part of *Cwmhir*'s immediate lands *(29, 30, 33)* were likewise situated in hilly country, relatively little was below 250 metres, or gently sloping.[174] The abbey leaned heavily on more low-lying, and distant, properties, to be its 'bread-baskets': like the 'mynachtai' of the Lugg and Teme valleys *(36, 37)* and its Galbalfa-Carnaf complex by the river Wye *(39, 40)*. The home manor of Golon *(29)*, accounting for one-third of its annual income, was largely a sheep-rearing and oats-producing property. Yet another significant pastoral possession was Nant-yr-Arian Grange in Ceredigion *(31)*. A leading, and mixed economy, grange on the Shropshire border was Gwern-y-go *(34)* – with which were held the township of Caeliber Isaf and two parts of Hopton. Substantial lands, of uncertain bounds, were held across the Herefordshire boundary, stretching towards Michaelchurch from Brilley *(38)*.

In central Wales also, *Dore* owned substantial parts of Cantref-selyf, with four granges: Gwenddwr *(51)*, Nanteglwys *(52)*, Trawscoed and Wernddyfwg *(53)*.[175] *Vale Royal*, the Cheshire daughter-house of Dore, had property, including the Parson's Mill, in its appropriated parish of Llanbadarn Fawr (near Aberystwyth) *(183)*.[176] Lastly, there were the lands of the two Welsh Cistercian nunneries. *Llanllugan*, in Powys, possessed the township of that name lying between the two Rhiw streams *(63)*, but more valuable was its Hydan Grange (with corn mill and fulling mill; *64*).[177] Amongst its other early properties was a grange 'between Coldmore and the river Severn',[178] which seems to have later passed to Chirbury Priory *(65a)*.[179] In Ceredigion, *Llanllŷr* was ascribed some ten carucates of arable land, split between some seven or eight small granges – not all identifiable today, but including Glanrhiwfallen *(68)*.[180]

Strata Florida had fifteen granges,[181] mostly lying at no very considerable distance away, with a consolidated estate of contiguous possessions centred around it – including Hafodwen (extending into five parishes; *147*) and Blaenaeron (into three; *133*). Mefenydd *(134)* and Pennardd *(132)* Granges were both in excess of 2,000 hectares (5,000 a.). Natural boundaries often delimited properties: the river Teifi, for example, separated Mefenydd from Pennardd. The great extent of granges like Cwmteuddwr *(135)*[182] masks the fact that much of its area was wild open country, whilst the administration of these vast lands was based upon a quasi-manorial Celtic pattern with attendant dues and customs, demesne cultivation being of lesser importance.[183] There were outlying granges – important arable units – in more favoured areas – like Aberdihonw by the Wye *(150)* and Abermiwl by the Severn *(137)*, and along the coast of Cardigan Bay – as Morfa Bychan *(141)*[184] and Morfa Mawr *(143)*[185] – on fertile raised beach boulder clay sites.

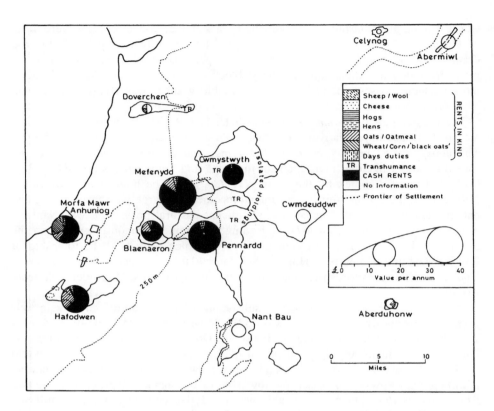

Fig. 77: Economic study of the Granges of Strata Florida Abbey *(based upon values contained in PRO, SC 6 (Henry VIII) 4858, and, especially, NLW, Cwrtmawr MS 873D).*

Whitland had eleven granges, of which two (Rhuddlan Deifi *[209]* and Castell Cosan *[202]*) accounted for nearly half its income from landed property.[186] The former was a grange allegedly stolen from Talley Abbey and never returned; the latter was named after the local Castell Mawr, and came to incorporate earlier grange units like Blaenpedran and Cilgryman. Other major units were: Maenor Forion Grange (*210*; where Tudor abbots had their summer residence), Iscoed Grange (*198*; which included the abbey site and the valuable Cardiff Forest),[187] and Ystlwyf Grange (*199*; with the appropriated church and pilgrimage stopover of Llanfihangel Abercywyn).[188] Amongst the abbey's other properties were the smaller 'grange' or 'lordship' of Llanfihangel Cilfargen (*211*) granted by the Lord Rhys,[189] and the (perhaps earlier lazar house?) St Leonard's Chapel on the banks of the Tywi in St Ishmael's (*212*).[190]

Much of *Neath*'s land was originally a completely undeveloped site consisting of about 2,600ha. (6,400a.) lying between the Neath and Tawe rivers.[191] Its leading granges (Gelligarn *[123]* and Nash *[124]*) lay further afield. Apart from its eleven or so granges (Betws *[109]* and Cwrt Sart *[111]*)[192] it possessed townships of

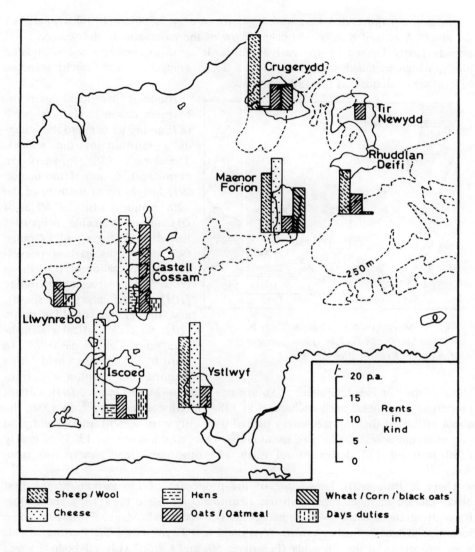

Fig. 78: Economic study of the Granges of Whitland Abbey
(based chiefly upon values contained in PRO, SC 6 [Henry VIII] 4903).

considerable size – as Blaen-honddan *[112]* and Coed-ffranc *[108]*. Some lands, like Walterstone Grange *[129a]*, lay in Gower,[193] and the abbey owned a valuable manor at Exford (Somerset). As noted before, the result of its exchange agreement with Earl Gilbert de Clare was that it lost lands, like Crynant Grange *[119]*, in the upper reaches of the valleys[194] but, theoretically, gained more than one-quarter of its gross income from the rents of urban holdings in Cardiff and elsewhere.

Margam's major endowment took the form of over 7,000ha. (18,000a.) between the rivers Afan and Kenfig, 'from the brow of the mountains to the sea-coast',[195] already partly farmed by the native Welsh. It came to comprise a consolidated block, which included several of its two dozen granges,[196] and which, as noted before, was extended in the 13th century.

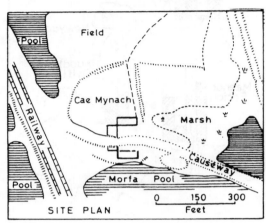

Fig. 79: Margam's New Grange (Cwrt Newydd) in Afan Marsh. *(R.E. Kay, 1948; Ancient Monuments Record, Aberystwyth).*

Amongst its local granges, Margam counted: Hafod-y-porth (*83;* giving its name to the immediate lordship of the abbey), Theodoric's (*88;* formerly an hermitage),[197] and Hafod-heulog (*91;* bought up at the turn of the 12th century). In the Vale of Glamorgan, valuable properties included Llangewydd Grange (*96;* one of its earliest possessions), the manor of Bonvilston (*100;*[198] with Greendown Grange *[101]* immediately to its south), and the grange of Llanfeuthin (*102;* an ecclesiastical establishment in Celtic days).[199] In Cardiff, Margam held two manors, one 'within the franchise' (Cibwr or Heath Grange; *105*), and one without (Moor Grange; *104*). Distant properties were held, until exchanged in 1484, in Gloucestershire.[200] In 1336, the abbot estimated that the monastery owned over fifty carucates of arable land, and one thousand acres (400ha.) of meadow.[201] The gross income (in 1535) of nearly £190 included £70 derived from tithes and tithe-barns, and nearly £80 from rents.[202]

There is little early knowledge of the properties of *Llantarnam*,[203] the first broad picture of them coming in the *Taxatio Ecclesiastica* (1291).[204] The majority of its granges came to be organised as two 'manors': Magna Porta (the home lordship; *70*) and, further north, Wentsland and Bryngwyn *[75]*. Further afield, were properties in the Rhondda (Pen-rhys; *80*) and Cardiff (Llystalybont Grange; *78*).[205] Its upland granges (such as Cil-onydd *[74]*[206] and Dorallt; *NGR: ST 266940*) were balanced by smaller, but more arable, units on the lowlands of Gwent (like Cefn-fynach *[ST 285921]* and Gelli-lâs; *297953*). An outstanding grange was Pwl-pan *[77]* – twelve carucates of arable in 1219, and accounting, in 1535, for nearly one-seventh of the abbey's gross income.[207] It encompassed well-drained soils and also pasture and meadow on the adjacent Caldicot Levels, and must have stood cheek-by-jowl with a manor (of the same name) pertaining to Goldcliff Priory.

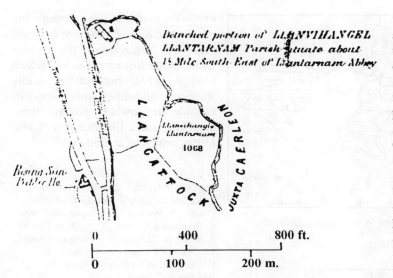

Fig. 80: Extract from the Llanfihangel Llantarnam Tithe Map (1846).
(National Library of Wales).

Like other abbeys, Llantarnam held detached, and sometimes quite isolated, portions of land. The presence of one such plot [No. 1068 on the tithe-map; *Fig. 80*] of the parish of Llanfihangel Llantarnam, surrounded by the parish of Llangatwg-iuxta-Caerleon and situated by a brook flowing into the river Lwyd, suggests that it pertained to the monastery.

Four miles [6.4 km.] west of Monmouth, stood the abbey of *Grace Dieu*;[208] a poor monastery, perhaps because by the time of its foundation (1226) there was little available land for potential donors to bestow upon it.[209] Apart from the home Hendre estate *[59]*, its principal granges included: Coed-ythan *[?62a]* and Penrhos *[60]*, in close proximity; Beaulieu (*62b;* in the parish of Dixton), and Stowe *[62]* in the Forest of Dean – a gift of Henry III. From 1227–67, the abbey also owned (by purchase) the Herefordshire manor of Penyard Regis, partly on account of its iron-extraction potential.

In north-east Gwent, the Herefordshire abbey of *Dore* also had four granges (*Fig. 81*): Llanfair Cilgoed *[56]*, Llyncoed (*alias* Campston; *54*), Cold *[55]* and Morlais *[57]*.[210] The abbey also held (at least from 1360 to 1369) St Noye's Chapel, Blackbrook, Skenfrith, where there was St Noye's bridge and holy well.[211]

The lands of *Tintern* straddled the river Wye (*Fig. 81*), the abbey owning some eight granges in Gwent (as Moor *[179]* and Merthyr Gerain *[178]*) and five in Gloucestershire (like Modesgate *[173]* and Woolaston *[174]*). Three of the former lay in the monastery's manor of Porthcaseg *[167]* whilst the latter all formed part of its manor of Woolaston. [In 1302, Earl Roger Bigod gave Tintern its most valuable possession – the Norfolk manor of Acle. Its acquisition led Tintern to rise from third place in value amongst the Welsh abbeys in the *Taxatio* (1291) to first place in the *Valor* (1535)]. Tintern's economy saw differentiation between primarily arable granges such as Rogerstone *[170]* on a low limestone plateau, and chiefly pastoral units like Moor Grange *[179]* on the estuarine Levels. Study of the geology

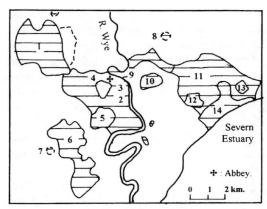

Fig. 81: The Lower Wye Valley Lands of
Tintern.

of Wentwood suggests that the
monks had a discerning eye in clearing for cultivation the better
Brownstone soil areas (as at Trelech
Grange; *171*), but leaving acidic
Tintern Sandstone soils wooded.
Outside the lowland granges were
detached lands, like one plot 'Close
to the cemetery at Redwick'. [212]

[1. Trelech Grange, 2. Porthcaseg Manor,
3. Ruding Grange, 4. Secular Firmary
Grange, 5. Porthcaseg extra-parochial area,
6. Rogerstone Grange, 7. Lands in Howick,
8. Wood in Harthill, 9. Modesgate Grange,
11. Manor of Woolaston,12. Ashwell
Grange, 13. Aluredeston Grange, 14.
Woolaston Grange].

Tintern had isolated holdings widely scattered,
as in Llanishen parish, and as far afield as the
neighbourhood of Usk. One such was a meadow
by the river Olway, later known as 'Tintern's
Lugg'. Monmouth Priory may also have had
property there.

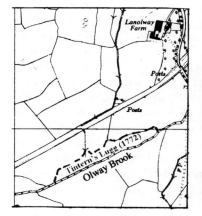

Fig. 82: 'Tintern's Lugg',
Gwehelog, nr. Usk. *[derived
from: NLW, Badminton Plans,
vol. 10, no. 9]*.

Mapping Cistercian Lands[213]

Of primary importance in mapping Cistercian
lands are the broad surveys of monastic properties given in confirmatory charters (like that of
the Lord Rhys in favour of Strata Florida), and in
the summary lists of the *Taxatio Ecclesiastica*
(1291) and the *Valor Ecclesiasticus* (1535). As
noted before, the former has its pitfalls, omitting,
for example, Aberconwy's vast Nanhwynan Grange and Tintern's valuable
Woolaston manor. Further, some of its place-names are now lost or only recognis-
able with difficulty. This is the case in regard of properties of Llantarnam, like
Cil-onydd, Dorallt and Maestir Granges, rendered in the *Taxatio* as Cadlonet,
Torald and Mayster, respectively. More valuable than the later *Valor* are the immediate post-Suppression Minister's Accounts, detailing the holdings of individual
tenants. Place-name evidence also assists as the word 'grange' or its Welsh equiv-
alents: 'cwrt' *(court)* and 'mynachty' *(the monks' house)* frequently survive, even
on small-scale Ordnance Survey maps.

Once a property is known to have been Cistercian-owned, recourse should be had to the parochial tithe-map. The Order's monasteries had, in respect of many of their lands, the privilege of not paying tithe *(Chapter 12)*. They jealously guarded this right, which passed at the Suppression to the later secular owners of former monastic lands. The consequence was that the tithe-maps and schedules compiled subsequent to the Tithe Commutation Act of 1836 reveal with great precision the extent of many Cistercian granges. They also bring to mind long forgotten place-names, and the location of former monastic mills and mines. The tithe map *(Fig. 83)* for Whitland's Blaenpedran Grange shows the medieval names of Cae'r Mynach *(the monks' field)* and Glyn-mynach *(the monks' valley)* rather than the modern Blaen-gilfach.

Fig. 83: Portion of the West Cilrhedyn tithe-map. *(National Library of Wales).*

Early estate plans (like the Badminton Plans held at the National Library of Wales with their detailed surveys of Tintern's Rogerstone and Trelech Granges) depict traces of monastic economy – like wells and fish-ponds. Aerial photo-graphy gives a clear delineation of Cwmhir's moated enclosure at Mynachdy (Radns.; *Pl. XII-C)*, and vividly tells something of the make-up of Monknash Grange *(Pl. XII-A)*.

Individual granges have not, as yet, received much atten-tion by either excavation or geo-physical survey. It would be rewarding if they did!

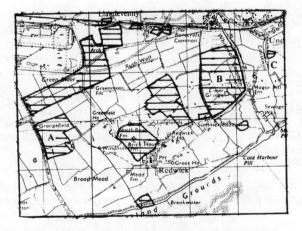

Fig. 84: Tithe-free Lands of Tintern in the Caldicot Levels. *(By kind permission of the Ordnance Survey © NC/01/001).* **A:** Grangefield (moated site); **B:** Moor Grange; **C:** Monks' Mead.

NOTES

1. *Journey through Wales* 103
2. Chapter 14 *infra*.
3. Jones E.D. 1950, 1–6; Lewis J.M. 1976, 25–26 *(illus.)*.
4. Chapter 15 *infra*.
5. Chapter 16 *infra*.
6. *Cartae Glam*. III, 953–54 (DCCCXXXII).
7. *Taxatio Eccl*. 282–84.
8. *Tax Book* passim.
9. Fowler R.C. 1908, 84–85.
10. *Letters to Cîteaux* 262 (No. 134a).
11. *Valor Eccl*. IV, passim.
12. *LP (Hen. VIII)* III: Pt. 2, 1047 (No. 2483).
13. Midmer R. 1979, 216.
14. *Cf*. Cowley F.G. 1977, 92–94.
15. *Taxato Eccl*. 276b–277.
16. Jack R.I. 1972, 152.
17. Williams G. 1962, 174.
18 . Birch W. de Gray. 1897, 304–05.
19. Hays R.W. 1963, 105–112; *Reg*. Aberconway 8 (Abc.), 9 (SF – not named in text).
20. The Abbot of Tintern, for example, made his return on 27 September [*Valor* Eccl. IV, 365].
21. *Cf*. Thomas L. 1930, 23.
22. *Valor Eccl*. IV, 365; PRO, SC6 (Hen. VIII) 2497, mm. 8d–9r.
23. Williams D.H. 1984. I, 199.
24. *Valor Eccl*. IV, 397.
25. Williams D.H. 1984. I, 200.
26. Hays R.W. 1963, 7.
27. *Llywelyn's Charter* 47, 57; *Arch*. Camb. 1888, 207.
28. Williams D.H. 1976b, 182.
29. Williams S.W. 1889, 65, 107; Cowley F.G. 1977, 25, 194; Williams D.H. 1975, 163–64.
30. Williams D.H. 1976, 113.
31. *Glamorgan County History* III (1971) 33.
32. Williams D.H. 1981, 105; Jones A. 1933, 171–72; O'Sullivan J.F. 1947, 25–27.
33. Williams D.H. 1976b, 87–89.
34. *Strata Marcella Ch*. 151–52 (No. 11).
35. *Cwmhir Charter* 68.
36. NLW, Penrice and Margam Ch. 1955.
37. *Kansas* 1/11.
38. Williams D.H. 1984. II, 202–03.
39. *Rot. Litt. Claus*. II, 132; *Cal. Charter R*. 1227, 4.
40. *Cal. Inq. Misc*. IV, 87; *Gloucs. I.P.M*. VI, 208–09; Williams D.H. 1976, 69–70.
41. *Kansas* 1/1; Williams D.H. 1976, 35–36.
42. *Cartae Glam*. IV, 1264 (DCCC–CXCIV).
43. *Ibid*. VI, 2380–81 (MDCXLVII).
44. PRO, PROB. 11.24, f. 21 [*'Dirige'*, from the first antiphon at Matins of the Dead – hence 'dirge'].
45. NLW, Penrice and Margam Ch. 2013; *Cf*. BL, Harleian Ch. 75B. 28.
46. NLW, Penrice and Margam Ch. 1944, 1978.
47. *Ibid*. 2008.
48. Lekai L.J. 1977, 450 (No. XX).
49. Birch W. de Gray. 1897, 151.
50. *Cartae Glam*. I, 127–28 (CXXX).
51. NLW, Penrice and Margam Ch. 34.
52. Birch W. de Gray. 1897, 273.
53. *Ibid*. 311.
54. Jones A. 1933, 173.
55. *Cal. Chancery R. var*. 301–02.
56. Williams D.H. 1998, 261–62.
57. NLW, Penrice and Margam Ch. 1978.
58. *E.g*: NLW, Penrice and Margam Ch. 1992, 1999, 2010, 2062–63 (spanning *c*. 1195–1281).
59. Birch W. de Gray. 1897, 186.
60. *Ibid*. 190; *Cf*. 191 (1261), 195 (1253).
61. Williams D.H. 1976, 69.
62. *Strata Marcella Ch*. passim.
63. *Cal. Charter R*. III, 99–100.
64. NLW, Penrice and Margam Ch. 172 (of 1261).
65. PRO, E 315/53/174 (Dore, in Cantrefselyf).
66. NLW, Penrice and Margam Ch. 11.
67. *Cartae Glam*. I, 191 (CLXXXII).

68. NLW, Penrice and Margam Ch. 47.
69. *E.g: Cartae Glam*. II, 493–98 (CCCXCIII–XCV), 641–42 (DCVII), 697–98 (DCXLII); NLW, Penrice and Margam Ch. 48–50, 57.
70. NLW, Penrice and Margam Ch. 2062–63.
71. Birch W. de Gray, 1897. 198–99.
72. NLW, Penrice and Margam Ch. 1957.
73. *Strata Marcella Ch*. 222–24 (No. 82).
74. *Episc. Acts* I, 360–61 (No. D.491).
75. Birch W. de Gray. 1897, 186, 192.
76. *Cartae Glam*. I, 210; II, 236.
77. *Kansas* 1/13.
78. Birch W. de Gray. 1897, 62.
79. *Arch. Camb*. 1860, 190.
80. *E.g:* Birch W. de Gray. 1897, 198; NLW, Penrice and Margam Ch. 8.
81. Birch W. de Gray. 1897, 227.
82. *Cartae Glam*. II, 513–14 (DVII).
83. *Cal. Patent R*. 1361, 11.
84. *Strata Marcella Ch*. 156 (No. 14).
85. *Strata Marcella Ch*. 158 (No. 16).
86. *Episc. Acts* II, 658 (L. 169).
87. *Llywelyn's Ch*. 59.
88. Insley C. 1999, 235–50.
89. O'Sullivan J.F. 1947, 25, 27.
90. *Flores Hist*. III, 329; *Cal. Charter R*. III, 88–89, 96–100, 106.
91. *Cartae Glam*. II, 282–87 (CCLXXXII), 632–37 (DCII).
92. *Anc. Pet*. 404 (No. 241); Cf. *Rot*. Chart. 174.
93. *Cal. Papal Reg. (Letters)* V, 164.
94. *Cal. Patent R*. 1447, 55; 1508, 568.
95. Williams S.W. 1889, Appx. xi–xviii, lxvii.
96. *Anc. Pet*. 129n.
97. *Cal. Patent R*. 1508, 567.
98. *Rec. Caern*. 199.
99. Williams D.H. 1984. II, 209.
100. *Strata Marcella Ch*. 228–233 (Nos. 88–89).
101. *Ibid*. 230–33 (No. 89).
102. *Cwmhir Charter* 68–70; Tintern [1415] secured confirmation of Roger Bigod's charter at the Sessions for the lordship of Striguil [Glamorgan Archives, CL/Manorial 2].
103. *Rot. Chart*. 205b; *Rot. Litt. Patentium* 125b; Bridgeman G.T.O. 1868, 242.
104. *Cal. Patent R*. 1318, 163.
105. Williams D.H. 1984. II, 210.
106. *Rec. Caern*. 199. For Tintern [1456] exhibiting a charter in Bristol: *Little Red Book* II, 199.
107. *Cal. Charter R*. III, 88, 97–98.
108. *Arch. Camb*. I (1846) 106-07.
109. Owen H.T. 1904, 183; *Giraldus Camb*. IV, 207.
110. *Hist. Works*, 361; *Journey through* Wales 103.
111. See Ref. 58 above, as also: *Episc. Acts* II, 673 (L.218), 676 (L.225); Birch W. de Gray. 1897, 186, 273–74, 290.
112. *Gir. Camb*. IV, 152–53.
113. Cowley F.G. 1977, 73–74.
114. Hays R.W. 1963, 30–31.
115. *Gir. Camb*. IV, 129–43.
116. Birch W. de Gray. 1902, 310: Margam had sold Sker to Neath without warranty.
117. Cowley F.G. 1977, 123–24.
118. Birch W. de Gray. 1897, 250: the Abbots of Rievaulx, Kingswood and Vaudey arbitrated.
119. *Arch. Camb*. 1867, 6.
120. Cowley F.G. 1977, 74.
121. *Llywelyn's Ch*., 54–59.
122. Williams S.W. 1889, Appx. xv–xvii.
123. Williams D.H. 1976b, 182.
124. Cowley F.G. 1977, 75.
125. Williams D.H. 1976, 113–14.
126. Jones A. 1933, 172.
127. Hays R.W. 1963, 89–90.
128. Cowley F.G. 1977, 76.
129. PRO, DL 25/L.326.
130. Hays R.W. 1963, 107–08.
131. *Cal. Charter R*. III, 31, 96–97, 105–06.
132. Cowley F.G. 1977, 248–49; *Cf*. 347, and *Cartae Glam*. III, 1153–56 (DCCCCXXXIX).

133. *Welsh Memo R.* 41 (No. 332).
134. Cowley F.G. 1977, 246–47; *Cf.*
     Anc. Pet. 404 (No.241).
135. *Kansas* 1/7, 11 (3), 12.
136. BL, Addit. Ch. 20414.
137. *Cal. Charter R.* III, 105.
138. *Ibid*. III, 99.
139. Bradney J.A. 1904. II: Pt. 2,
     257–58.
140. *Cal. Fine R.* 1338, 65; *Gloucs*.
     I.P.M. V, 268; *Hockaday Abstr*.
     328.
141. *Chester Recog. R.* 25; *Black*
     Prince's Reg. III, 49–50.
142. *Cal. Patent R.* 1360, 443.
143. *Cartae Glam*. I, 208 (CCII);
     NLW, Penrice and Margam Ch.
     52, 1999.
144. Five of which lay: 'Near the
     stream at the west end of the
     grange' [Birch W. de Gray.
     1897, 72–74].
145. *Episc. Acts* II, 673 (L.218).
146. NLW, Penrice and Margam Ch.
     198–201.
147. *E.g:* Birch W. de Gray. 1897,
     188–91, 194–95; Cowley F.G.
     1977, 90.
148. Spurgeon C.J. 1980, 70, 79–80.
149. Williams D.H. 1998, 278.
150. Cowley F.G. 1977, 80.
151. *Ibid*. 81.
152. *Ibid*. 76–77; *Cf*. 181.
153. *Ibid*. 80–81, 182.
154. Cowley F.G. 1977, 79.
155. *Arch. Camb*. 1846, 108–09; *Reg*.
     J. Peckham II, 461.
156. Williams D.H. 1984. II, 216–17.
157. NLW, Penrice and Margam Ch.
     130.
158. *Arch. Camb*. 1887, 6; *Journey*
     through Wales 127.
159. Birch W. de Gray. 1897, 340;
     Cf. 356.
160. PRO, C 115/K.2/6683, ff. 94r,
     95r. ['Welshry': an indication of
     how Wye valley folk were seen].
161. *Welsh Assize R.* 183, 288 (m.23).
162. PRO, E 326/B.11526.
163. *Welsh Assize R.* 197–98, 300–01
     (m. 26d).
164. *Cf*. Butler L.A.S. 1982, 167–73;
     Gresham C. 1939, 123–62; 1983,

311–47; Hays R.W. 1963,
123–62; Jones Pierce T. 1951,
21.
165. Hays R.W. 1963, 10–16.
166. *Cf*. Hawarden R.O: Map of the
     Enclosure of the Waste Lands of
     Tir Abbot Ucha (1871).
167. *Cf*. Jones A. 1933, 176–78;
     Owen E,. 1920, 48–65; Williams
     D.H. 1981, 105–10; Lloyd
     J.Y.W. 1876, 236–38 (for
     Penllyn).
168. For the abbey's lands, see: Pratt
     D. 1997, 4, 24, 36, 45–49,
     52–54; Price G.V. 1952, 57–82.
     For Wrexham property, see:
     Dodd A.H. 1957, 17–18; Palmer
     A.N. 1903, 183–92.
169. For the monastery's lands, see
     especially: *Strata Marcella*
     Charters 112–28, and the detailed
     maps at the end of that volume;
     Morris E.R.(1982) 135, (1983)
     revised map; Lloyd J.Y.W. 1876,
     235; Williams D.H. 1976b,
     84–88.
170. For the abbey lands, see:
     Gresham C.A. 1984, 142–57;
     Richards R. 1959, 246–49;
     Williams D.H. 1981a, 36–58;
     1984. II, 220–21; *Llywelyn's*
     Charter 45–78; *Merioneth Sub*.
     22, 43, 67, 74; UCNW, Bangor,
     Nannau-Hengwrt Deeds.
171. PRO, E 310/36/219, f. 26;
     Augm. Rec. 438.
172. Gresham C.A. 1984, 153.
173. Gresham C.A. 1976, 11 (map) –
     14, 18–31, 36, 42.
174. For the abbey lands, see:
     Williams D.H. 1976a, 73–101;
     1984. II, 221. For Dolhelfa
     Grange, with map, see: Percival
     D. 1993, 42–45.
175. For these lands, see: Williams
     D.H. 1976, 37–39;1984. II, 222;
     PRO, SC 6/1156/21, 1157/1; *Cf*.
     PRO, E 303/5/88–130, E
     315/238/58–87d; E 326/B.1598.
176. *Exchq. Proc*. (2) 102.
177. Morgan R. 1985, 116–19;
     Williams D.H. 1975, 161–63,
     168–69 (map).

178. PRO, E 210/D.3323.
179. NLW, Powis Castle Deeds: Box 14, Deed 33 (of 1517).
180. Williams D.H. 1975, 166–70.
181. For the abbey lands, see: Bowen E.G. 1950, 34–37; Owen G.D. 1935, 10–27; Williams S.W. 1889, Appx. lxxxvii–viii, xc–xci, xcvii, cvi; NLW (Alcwyn Evans) MS 12,362D.
182. Banks R.W. 1880, 30–50; Williams S.W. 1889, Appx. vii (for Leland's evidence).
183. Jones Pierce T. 1950, 28–29.
184. It included land: 'By the ford of Melin Fach and Morfa yr Ankar, with the water that is called Ystwyth' [PRO, E 315/103, ff. 110d–111r].
185. Its agricultural potential reflected in the research station presently there.
186. For the abbey's lands, see: James T. 1978, 71–78; Owen G.D. 1935, 53–67; NLW, MS 486D [a transcription of PRO, SC 6 [Henry VIII] 4903].
187. PRO, SC 6 (Henry VIII) 4903, m. 1r; E 310/34/208.
188. Jones G. H(artwell). 1912, 372–73.
189. *Cal. Inq. Misc.* II, 11 (No. 45).
190. Evans G. 1915, 130.
191. For the abbey lands, see: Birch W. de Gray. 1902, *passim*; Cowley F.G. 1967, 5–26, 1977, 75–76; Howell R. 1922, *passim*; *Neath Charters*, 86–115; Nicholl L.D. 1936, 117–19; Phillips D.R. 1925, 66–67, 85–90; Williams G. 1974, 76–77; RCAHMW 1982, 251–65; Evans A.L. 1956, 5–10 (Sker Grange).
192. Lhuyd E. 1707, III. 122.
193. Rees D. 1984, 58–60; Toft L.A. 1983, 145–48; 1996, 55.
194. *Cf.* RCAHMW 1982, 248.
195. Cowley F.G. 197, 23.
196. For the abbey lands, see: Cowley F.G. 1967, 5–26; 1977, 79–81; Gray T. 1903, 161–81; 1905, 11–29; Birch W. de Gray. 1897, *passim*; Jones D.R.L. 1981, 7–9;

Evans A.L. 1958, 37–47, 55–62; RCAHMW 1982, 266–97.
197. Hemp W.J., 1963, 188–89.
198. The 'manor' acquired in Bonvilston, in 1230, was extended later that century: *Glamorgan County History* III: 2 (1982) 132.
199. Lewis J.M. and Knight B. 1973, 147–53.
200. *Cartae Glam.* II, 141 (CXLIII, of *c.* 1160; *Cal. Patent R.* 1485, 511; PRO, SC 6 (Hen. VIII) 5155, m. 14d.
201. *Cartae Glam.* IV, 1196–99 (DCCCCLXII); Birch W. de Gray. 1897, 304–06; Cowley F.G. 1977, 272.
202. *Valor Eccl.* IV, 351–52; PRO, SC 6 (Hen. VIII) 5155, mm. 1, 10.
203. For the lands of the abbey, see: Williams D.H. 1967, 131–48; 1976, 88–89. For maps, see: PRO, MPE 175 and MR 1061, and J. Aram's, 1779 *Survey of Llantarnam* (Pontypool Park Estate).
204. *Taxatio Eccl.* 281b, 284b–285; *Cf.* Valor Eccl. IV, 365..
205. *Cf.* Evans A.L. 1958, 27.
206. *Cf. Arch. in Wales* 38 (1998) 126–28.
207. *Taxatio Eccl.* 281b; *Valor Eccl.* IV, 365; *Cf.* PRO, SC 6 (Hen. VIII) 2497, m. 8.
208. For the lands of the abbey, see: *Grace Dieu Deeds*, 188–99; Williams D.H. 1964, 90–94; 1976, 69–73; 1984. II, 225–26.
209. Kelly G.J. 1940, 12.
210. For the lands of Dore in Wales, see: Williams D.H. 1976, 34–39; 1984. II, 222, 225. *Cf.* Gwent R.O. *W and T.* 80, 758; *JCH* 0611.
211. NLW, Milborne Deed 78; NGR: SO 433207.
212. NLW, Badminton Deeds, Group 2, 14482.
213. For a fuller account, see: Williams D.H. 1990, 58–63; 1994, 311–18.

CHAPTER 12

THE GRANGE IN WALES

(For a listing of the Welsh granges, and their enumeration on the maps, see Appendix 3).

Cistercian lands were organised, ideally, into a series of farms called *granges*, which, theoretically, lay no more than a day's journey from the parent monastery – to allow effective control and for the *conversi* to be within reach.[1] They were meant to be sited at some distance (possibly some eleven kilometres or more) apart – perhaps to avoid over-stocking of pastures and friction between shepherds.[2] The relevant statutes have been lost, but the construction of a grange 'within the limits constituted by the General Chapter' was a matter of complaint by Basingwerk (1201) against the Cheshire abbey of Poulton (later Dieulacres).[3]

Some granges were little more than glorified sheep-runs, but others were substantial complexes, important not only for agriculture but also for the transaction of business, and for the hospitality they afforded. At Margam's Orchard Grange (1208) no less than eight abbots gathered to arbitrate in its pasture dispute with neighbouring Neath.[4] Prince Llywelyn ap Gruffydd made much use of the mountain granges of Aberconwy and Cymer; some of his chattels being found (after his demise – 1282) at a grange of the latter.[5] In Tudor times, the Abbots of Whitland used its Maenor Forion Grange as a holiday home, 'a place of diversion for summer'.[6] An abbot of Grace Dieu (1264), on a journey, stopped over at Llantarnam's Llystalybont Grange (near Cardiff) and dated a letter there.[7]

Many granges were the model farms of their day, and their nucleus comprised a refectory and dorter, an oratory, a granary and other necessary farm buildings. There might also be a precinct wall, gateway and hospice. The buildings were a mixture of timber and of stone – as the chapel where there was one. Dore was granted timber from Grosmont Forest 'for making its buildings in Llyncoed Grange' (1233),[8] whilst Tintern's servants at Merthyr Gerain Grange (1387) sought (in Bernardswood and Wentwood) for dyewoods for the new byre being erected there. Later, it was thatched.[9] Tiles, and the service of a tiler, were used in the re-roofing of Tintern's Woolaston Grange (1412).[10] Women were noted (1217) as living 'by the gate of a grange of Tintern',[11] and gate-way structures have been plotted at its Merthyr Gerain Grange.[12]

The granges have left their mark in place-names, like Grangetown (derived from Margam's Moor Grange in Cardiff). Some, like Tintern's Trelech Grange, are plainly marked on the 1" Ordnance Survey maps. In Welsh Wales, the term 'mynachty' often denotes a former Cistercian grange, like Cwmhir's farm in the Lugg valley *(Fig. 107)*.

Another indicative name, occurring sometimes as a prefix or suffix, is (in Welsh) 'cwrt', in English 'court' *(Fig. 86)*. Neath had its Cwrt Sart and Margam its Notteschecourt. In these instances, 'court' was synonymous with 'grange', but 'court' frequently denoted only the central complex of grange buildings, (and, perhaps, in particular that where the abbey's manorial court sat). Of many such, Valle Crucis had its 'court' by the river Alyn in its manor of Budugre'r Abad. There might be permutations of 'cwrt', like Hengwrt (close to Cymer) and Quirt (on Aberconwy's Gelliniog Grange, close to the Menai Straits: *Fig. 74c*).

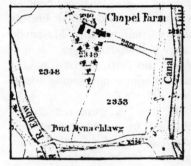

Fig. 85: Chapel Farm, Cwmcarn, before modern development. *(Mynyddislwyn tithe map, 1846).*

There are today but scant relics of medieval grange buildings. Several of Margam's granges disappeared with the expansion of Port Talbot and the construction of its steel works. Its former Heath Grange (in Cardiff) gave way (in 1899) to the Gladstone Road schools.[13] On former lands of Tintern, both a grange chapel (at Woolaston) and a grange mill (at Rogerstone) have been demolished in recent times – partly on safety grounds. Granges have also given way to housing estates – such as the Mynachdy Estate in Cardiff and the Court Farm estate in Cwmbrân, and industrial estates – like the Chapel Farm Industrial Estate, Cwmcarn *(Fig. 85)*, and the Grange Industrial Estate, Cwmbrân.

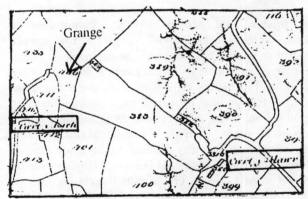

Fig. 86: Whitland's grange in Dyffryn Tawe, Carms. *(NLW, Llanboidy tithe-map).*

Occasionally, a grange nucleus lost to memory is only traceable by field- and place-names shown on tithe-maps, as for Whitland's property in Dyffryn Tawe where occur: 'grange', 'cwrt-y-bach' and 'cwrt y mawr' *(Fig. 86)*.[14] Several granges have been subject to field survey, but none (in Wales) to a thorough excavation. Several would repay the effort, including Dore's Llanfair Cilgoed and Neath's Monknash.

Grange size and situation varied enormously. Granges which were primarily arable concerns lying in favourable low-lying areas, were generally much smaller than upland properties, mostly employed for sheep-rearing – like Strata Florida's Mefenydd and Pennardd Grange, both in excess of 2,000 hectares (5,000 acres).[15] Several of the former, 'bread-baskets' for their monasteries, lay by the sea with the ability to transport grain to the monastery by water. Such included: Aberconwy's Gelliniog Grange in Anglesey, Cymer's Neigwl Grange in Llŷn, and Tintern's Woolaston Grange in Gloucestershire. The last monastic lessee of Whitecross Grange had to allow Margam 'easement for carriage of glebe to the sea'.[16]

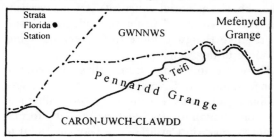

Fig. 87: Part of the Boundary between Strata Florida's Mefenydd and Pennardd Granges.

Rivers and streams frequently delineated grange boundaries,[17] as the Teifi separating Strata Florida's Mefenydd and Pennardd Granges. At Gors-dol-beudiau (south of the old Strata Florida railway station) the Mefenydd grange boundary no longer follows the Teifi, the river having changed course and swung southwards *(Fig. 87)*.

The granges were not always delimited by parish boundaries. Strata Florida's Hafodwen extended into five parishes; Whitland's Castell Cosan included detached lands in no less than nine, partly due to the incorporation of earlier, smaller granges. Occasionally, a grange nucleus might be repositioned – as happened at Margam's Resolfen, about 1185,[18] lending it the later name of the 'New Grange'.[19]

Communications

Overland haulage of monastic produce was perhaps mostly accomplished on unpaved 'greenways', like those which touched upon Margam's Llangewydd Grange[20] and connected Grace Dieu to its Penrhos Grange.[21] Some monastic paths, at least for short stretches, were paved or cobbled – like Tintern's Stony Way (so called by 1451) which climbed some 150 metres (500 feet) from the abbey gatehouse to its vill at Porthcaseg.[22] It was the principal local thoroughfare to Chepstow.[23] Other paths, like 'the Long Way',[24] focussed on the abbey, which showed concern for the upkeep of its roads – paying a man at Merthyr Gerain Grange (in 1388) 'for clearing of rubbish the way leading to St Bride's'.[25] A medieval road-sweeper! The abbey court fined (1440, 1444) several tenants who did not properly maintain their portions of the Lodeway crossing its Rogerstone Grange *(Fig. 96)*,[26] whilst its tenants at Trelech Grange seemingly had the upkeep of 'the way leading from the chapel to Fyshepole' *(Map Section, Fig. 16)*.[27] The paths approaching this grange from Llanishen and Trelech were paved.[28]

Other paved or cobbled monastic paths included: 1. The way leading from Brockweir to Tintern's ferry there[29] – the ferryman was a stipendiary servant of the abbey;[30] 2. A road leading to Neath's Cwrt-y-betws, and 3. The 2.3 km. long causeway, Heol-y-deiliaid, connecting Margam to its New Grange in Afan Marsh *(Fig. 88)*.[31] It utilised stone culverts to pass over ancient dykes. Monastic paths, then and later, might bear names such as Wtra Abbot ('The Abbot's Lane') on property of

Strata Marcella at Plas Newydd in Llanwnog,[32] and the Monks' Lane in Cibwr, Cardiff (1478), where Margam had a grange.[33]

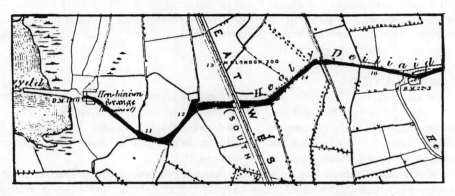

Fig. 88: The western portion of Heol-y-Deiliaid (Margam). *(1ˢᵗ edn., 6" O.S. Map).*

Communication was also assisted by grants of free rights of way (as for Aberconwy – on the 'common road' between Gelliniog Grange and its Talybont Mill),[34] and of free ferry passage (enjoyed by the same abbey, in respect of its Creuddyn property, on the Conwy ferry).[35]

Monasteries had duties as well as privileges. Edward I (1300) expected Strata Florida to make the roads crossing its lands safer from rebels for travellers by cutting down the woodland on either side. The abbey had also to *mend* the roads 'to avoid dangers and hazards'.[36] Pot-holes and ruts presumably had to be filled in, perhaps a hard core laid down in places.[37]

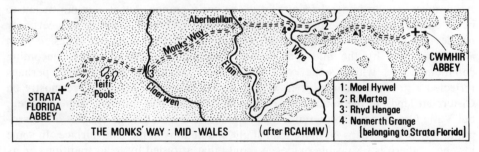

Fig. 89: The Monks' Way *or* Monks' Trod, Mid-Wales.

A routeway which, tradition has it, linked the abbeys of Cwmhir and Strata Florida was the Monks' Way or Monks' Trod (*Fig. 89*), passing up hill and down dale. It was, it appears, a green-way, slightly raised above the surrounding level, with an average width of up to three metres (8–10 ft.).[38] This must have been the route followed (in 1199) by Giraldus Cambrensis who, en route to Rome, 'travelled from Strata Florida, hurrying through the mountains of Maelienydd towards Cwmhir'.[39]

Land communications necessitated bridge building: 'pont-y-fynach', 'pont-mynach', and like terms, still describe bridges by Aberconwy's former Talybont Mill[40] and Llantarnam's Chapel Farm (Abercarn).[41] As Margam extended its marshland holdings in the 13th century, it received licence to build a bridge over the river Afan.[42] Tintern's manorial court (1400) ordered a tenant to repair the bridge at its nearby Angidy Mill.[43]

Eremitical Origins

In several instances, Welsh monastic cells and granges absorbed Celtic eremitical sites, and, possibly, their personnel. This reflected the general trend in western Europe from the mid-12th century onwards whereby the solitary life was greatly modified, either by being institutionalised – as in the Charterhouse, or by absorption into the new Orders – like the Cistercians.[44]

Welsh granges which were previously hermitages before being granted to the Cistercians included: Dore's Llanfair Cilgoed *[56]*,[45] Grace Dieu's Stowe Grange *[62]*,[46] and Margam's Theodoric's Grange *[88]*.[47] The churches of the first two named doubled up thereafter as grange and chantry chapels. Neath's St Margaret's Chapel[48] may have been on the site given it of the hermitage of Ralph, overlooking Crymlyn Bay.[49] Margam also received a meadow belonging to a hermit, Coh (1205),[50] whilst an influential hermit, Meiler, seems to have brought his cell of Pendâr into the Cistercian Order and the fold of Margam.[51] The latter's Llanfeuthin Grange *[102]* inherited a Celtic ecclesiastical site with cemetery.[52] Previous eremitical connections may also be seen in the prefix *'cil'* on monastic lands, like Cil-onydd Grange (of Llantarnam; *74*) and Cil-gryman Grange (of Whitland; *[202]*).

Grange Chapels

An oratory was an integral feature of every early grange, but it was not meant to be a 'chapel' in the sense that the Eucharist was celebrated there; it was certainly not devised for the general public, nor was any priest-monk intended to reside upon a grange. But, by the mid-13th century, such grange chapels were becoming commonplace,[53] whilst some, of 15th century origins or elaboration, perhaps reflected a growing tenantry.[54] In Wales, *recorded* grange chapels were mostly on Cistercian lands in the south and south-east. Margam had thirteen, Tintern seven, but Valle Crucis none for certain. The remains of Welsh grange chapels are disappointingly few, perhaps no more than slight undulations in the land surface. In some instances, there is no visible evidence – only that afforded by local tradition, or by place- and field-names.[55]

Such field-names (mostly afforded by the mid-19th century tithe map schedules)[56] include: *Chapel Field* (Llantarnam's Pwl-pan Grange), *Chapel Mead* (Tintern's Modesgate Grange), *Little Chapel Meadow* (Grace Dieu's Treurgan extra-parochial area), *Cae Capel* (Strata Marcella's Dolwen Grange),[57] *Cae Eglwys* (Llantarnam's Cil-onydd Grange), *Buarth-yn-y-Caple* (Aberconwy's Nant Call Grange),[58] *Llwyn-y-capel* (Strata Florida's Cwm-deuddwr Grange), *Waun-y-capel* (Margam's Hafod-y-porth Grange), and *Dancapel* Farm (close to the site of Capel Mair on

Whitland's Maenor Forion Grange). Neath's Cwrt-y-*betws* ('chapel court'), speaks for itself. Writers, such as Lhuyd (1707) and Pennant (1790), told of Basingwerk's *'hen gapel'* at Tre'r Abbot, its location evidenced by the Whitford tithe-map.[59]

Early maps can be of assistance: Mercator (1594) plotted as 'Talgarth' Strata Marcella's former Capel Talerddig;[60] Speed (1610) and an Admiralty chart (1859) mapped Margam's chapel at Hafod-y-porth.[61] Neither building remains today. Further evidence of chapel sites comes in enduring traditions and finds of burials – as for Quirt in Gelliniog (Aberconwy), at Aluredeston and High Woolaston (Tintern), and Cwrt-uchaf[62] and Hafod-y-porth (Margam). A few of these interments (as at Dore's Llanfair Cilgoed and Neath's Sker) may be of later recusant date, but reflect a pre-existing practice continuing into modern times. Indicative field-names include, at Llantarnam's Pen-rhys, *Y Fynwent* ('the grave-yard') and *Cae Beddau* ('the field of graves').[63] Skeletons were once unearthed close to Llantarnam's Chapel Farm (Abercarn), whilst Chapel Farm Terrace was popularly called Skeleton Row.[64] Tradition asserts that, in early modern times, the estuarine grave-yard at Neath's former St Michael's Chapel, Cwrt-y-carnau, was used to inter unbaptised infants and murderers.[65]

Chapels of Margam included Capel Mair *alias* Cryke Chapel, built, its architectural style would suggest, in the 15th century – its circular enclosure suggests a possible Celtic origin to the site. It was in ruins by 1617.[66] Chapels were noted at Hafod-heulog and Penhydd-neer in 1234, the former was a tithe barn in 1617.[67] St Meuthin's Chapel, Llanfeuthin,[68] and the 'new chapel' at Resolfen *[106]*,[69] were built about 1190–1200. The Bishop of Llandaff (*c.* 1225) allowed Mass to be said in the latter, but not for the general public, and Mass also in the old chapel of the grange on the anniversary of its dedication.[70] In the 1230s, the bishop dedicated a chapel 'within the court' of Llangewydd Grange *[96]*,[71] and, from 1239, Mass was permitted in St Thomas's Chapel, Melis Grange *[85]*.[72] The later lay tenants of Theodoric's Grange (1470; *88*) were bound to allow access to it on the feast of St Theodoric the Priest.[73] Other Margam chapels were at Stormy Grange (*94;* its font is preserved at Margam today), Llanmihangel Grange (St Michael's; *92*) and at Eglwys Newydd *[84]*.[74]

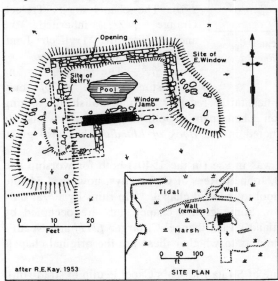

Fig. 90: St Michael's Chapel, Cwrt-y-carnau, Gorseinon.
(R.E. Kay, 1953; Ancient Monuments Record, Royal Commission, *Aberystwyth).*

The foundations of Neath's chapel at Cwrt-y-carnau *[127; Fig. 90]* are now submerged at high tides – clear indication of a rising sea-level. At Neath's Monknash Grange *[124]*, the chaplain (in 1539) received a 13s 4d stipend.[75] Lhuyd (1707) noted four chapels in the parish of Llangatwg-iuxta-Nedd, but only one – at Crinant *[119]* – may have originated as a grange chapel.[76]

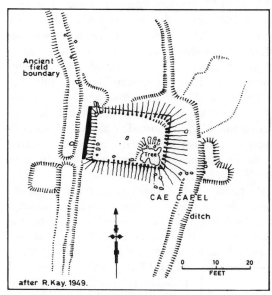

Fig. 91: Estavarney Grange Chapel, near Usk. (*R.E. Kay, 1949; Ancient Monuments Record, Aberystwyth*).

As at Dore's Llanfair Cilgoed *[56]* and Whitland's Lan Taf,[77] the post-Suppression lessee of Cwmhir's Gwern-y-go Grange *[34]* was bound to provide a priest to serve the chapel.[78] In monastic days (1397) one John Gwyn had been ordained to its title;[79] in 1548, one William Thomas, perhaps a former monk of that name of Cwmhir, was in office there. Gwern-y-go Chapel was a school in the 17th century.[80]

Tintern's grange chapels included those at Estavarney (Monkswood; *182; Fig. 91*) and Rogerstone Grange (St John; *170*). The chapel at its Trelech Grange *[171]* inherited the ancient site of 'Tryllech Lann Mainuon', noted in the *Book* of *Llandaff*.[81] The chapel at its Woolaston Grange *[176]* may have found use as a school, but has fairly recently been demolished. Nothing remains of St Bridget's Chapel on Llantarnam's Gelli-lâs Grange,[82] whilst its chapel at Pont Tref-y-carn (also noted in the *Book of Llandaff*) has also given way to modern development.[83]

Strata Marcella's Capel Dolwen was in use (in the 1540s) both for worship and as a school. Looking back, in 1590, John ap Rees of Cefn-y-llys, now aged 54, did 'well remember that he went to school to the said chapel'.[84] In ruins by 1792, only its approximate site is now known. Some grange chapel sites are occupied by parochial churches today (like Whitland's Llanfihangel Cilfargen *[211]* and Neath's Monknash *[124]*), but it is not certain as to whether these are the original chapels restored.

A modern church stands on the site of Strata Florida's Capel Peulin (Ystrad-ffin), Fenton (1811) talked of it in the past tense.[85] The site of the abbey's Capel Madog was preserved by the monastic historian and railway engineer, Stephen Williams (1837–99).[86] George Eyre Evans (in 1911; *Fig. 92*) drew its holy water stoup – then at Noyadd.[87]

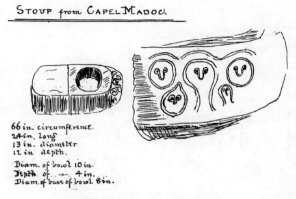

Stoup from Capel Madoc

66 in. circumference.
24 in. long
13 in. diameter
12 in. depth.

Diam. of bowl 10 in.
Depth of --- 4 in.
Diam. of base of bowl 8 in.

Fig. 92: Drawn by George Eyre Evans (1911). (NLW, MS 13452A, p. 120).

The issue of the spiritual oversight of lay servants and of tenants could cause tension between the Cistercians and the secular clergy, as when a 13th century rural dean of Brecon objected to Dore's ministrations to its servants in Cantrefselyf – where it had at least one chapel (Gwenddwr).[88] Monasteries might cover themselves, when administering the Sacraments to lay-folk, by gaining papal approval, as did Cwmhir (1232) being 'in a mountainous area, remote from parish churches'.[89] Llantarnam (1257, confirmed 1398, 1423) celebrated the Sacraments in its grange chapels.[90] Strata Florida (1339) made an agreement with the bishop of St David's, whereby its tenants made oblations at Capels Madog and Peulin, but received the Sacraments at the hands of their parish priests.[91] By the Suppression (1539) a chapel specially built within the abbey, and served by two stipendiary chaplains, served the needs of some 300 houseling people of the neighbourhood.[92] Whitland (1499) remitted to the bishop of St David's ecclesiastical jurisdiction over its tenants, but gained the probate of their wills and the administration of the property of the intestate.[93]

At Grace Dieu's chapel in Trivel Forest,[94] and at Dore's Llanfair Cilgoed chapel (served by monks as late as 1529), the Sacraments were not, in theory, ministered to outsiders – yet Trivel church had a 'font-stone', reputedly moved to Kilpeck church after the Dissolution. After the Suppression, a priest was engaged to say at Llanfair, 'mattyns, masse and evensong', on Sundays, Wednesdays and Fridays, 'as the inhabitants dwelt far from the parish church'.[95] In all such instances, the bone of contention concerned the offerings and surplice fees the parochial clergy would forfeit, if the faithful received the Sacraments at the hands of their monastic landlords. The chaplain at Llanfair Cilgoed, as late as 1570, was a former monk of Dore (John Didbroke, now aged about seventy-three), and there was still 'the cloister's chamber' at the grange.[96]

Notable Individual Granges

In Wales, a rough grouping can be made of: 1. Granges with a central and almost solitary nucleus – like Cwmhir's Gwern-y-go and Dore's Llanfair; 2. Granges with two nuclei – as Neath's Cwrt-y-carnau and Strata Florida's Nant Bau, and 3. Diffuse granges – with less obvious nucleation, as Aberconwy's Gelliniog and Whitland's Castell Cosan. Of the first group, Neath's Gelli-garn *[123]* is a good example.[97] A farm of over 300ha. (800a.), the nucleus was marked by a banked and ditched 11ha. (28a.) enclosure, within which, in a smaller 2.2ha. (5.4a.) enclo-

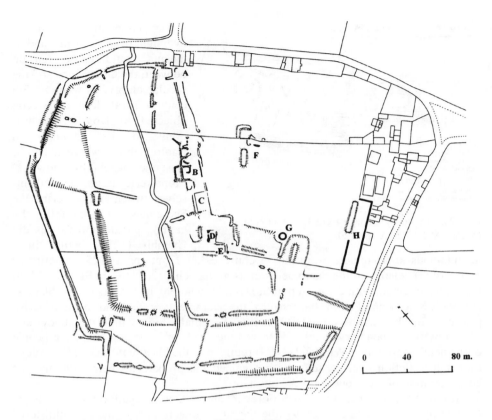

Fig. 93: Monknash Grange (of Neath; *Cf. Plate XII-A*).
(Crown copyright: Royal Commission on the Ancient and Historical Monuments in Wales, 1982).
A: Entrance, **B to E:** Building Sites, **F:** Rectangular Platform, **G:** Dovecot, **H:** Granary.

sure, its central complex included a dovecot and fish-ponds. Close by was the grange chapel – dating from pre-monastic days, but the location of its three mills[98] (one was for fulling) is uncertain. A wayside cross may have marked its northern boundary.[99]

The grange *par excellence* in Wales was Neath's Monknash *[124; Fig. 93]*, comprehending some 340ha. (840a.), of which 8ha. (20a.) are delineated by a pentagonal banked enclosure.[100] The now diminutive Clawdd-y-Mynach bordered the grange on the north, and Heol Lâs did the same to the east. There were a large granary (64m. long) and a dovecot. The grange chapel was possibly dedicated to St Osmund, and it was very probably the present church (licensed for the sacraments in 1607).[101] There were three mills, including perhaps one windmill. One unit with Monknash, at the time of the Suppression (1539), was Marcross Grange *[124a]*, much of which fell within a rectilinear enclosure and had a barn and a pond.[102]

Lands probably administered from Monknash included Cwrt-y-Mynach in Wick parish *[NGR: SS 914716]*, where also was an ancient barn *[NGR: SS 026711]*.

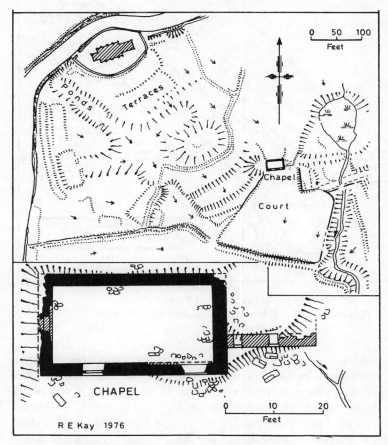

Fig. 94: Llanfair Cilgoed Grange, Monmouthshire.
(Specially surveyed for the author by the late Mr Richard Kay).

In north-east Gwent, Dore's grange at Llanfair Cilgoed *(Fig. 94)* included a chantry chapel[103] *(see above)*, a connected series of ponds (which could have been for fish), and a sequence of shallow terraces with a southerly aspect (possibly for viticulture). The grange nucleus was enclosed by a precinct wall, and records tell that (in Tudor times) there was a heron-aviary here.[104] There are obvious foundations of other buildings within its precincts. The precinct wall may date back to 1268, when Dore had leave 'to obstruct the road through the court of the grange'.[105]

At Tintern's Merthyr Gerain Grange *(Fig. 95)*, which had a byre, vaccary, sheep-cot, stable and granary,[106] excavation and survey[107] have located several stone enclosures. The metre thick perimeter walls were broken in the north by a gate-house entrance. The mill lay on the north-west bounds of the grange. Merthyrgeryn church, given to Tintern by Gilbert Marshal the elder, stood perhaps close by at Salisbury (which lay in the parish of Merthyr Gerain).[108] By 1560, it was in a state of ruin.[109]

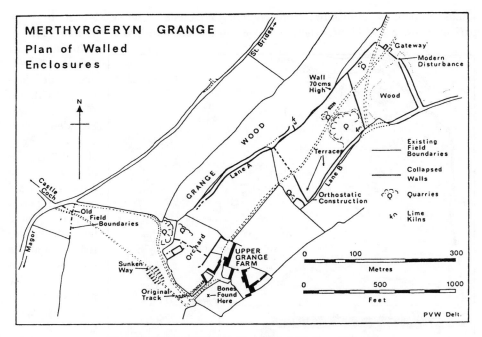

Fig. 95: Merthyr Gerain Grange (of Tintern Abbey).
(L.N. Parkes and P.V. Webster; Arch. Camb. CXXIII: 1974).

At Rogerstone, adjacent to the parish of St Arvan's (SE Gwent), Tintern inherited an existing settlement – perhaps named after one of the 12th century Clare family.[110] An important arable grange (4 carucates in 1291; *Fig. 96*), it was developed on gently sloping relief, the underlying geology being mostly limestone. Boundary stones, and the Long Wall, marked the grange limits. At its heart stood the grange buildings, with the water-mill and St John's Chapel. A series of watercourses and small dams fed the mill-pond, whilst immediately west lay a fish-pond. The former St John's Well[111] has given way to Chepstow Waterworks. With the grange went the large Bernard's Wood[112] to its south, whilst its oxen might pasture in Mynydd-y-Gaer to the north. With associated lands in the adjacent Howick and St Arvan's parishes, the grange comprised nearly 300 hectares (700 acres).

Granges with two focal centres included Cwrt-y-carnau (of Neath), Maenor Forion (of Whitland) and Nant Bau (of Strata Florida). *Nant Bau* probably had its original grange centre at Ystrad-ffin (granted to Strata Florida by 1202; *Fig. 97*), here the abbey had tithe-free lands, and here, too, was its Capel Peulin. The grange mill and 'bron-y-*cwrt*' occur towards the south, at Nant Bau itself. The whole property was coterminous with the later township of Rhandir Abad.[113]

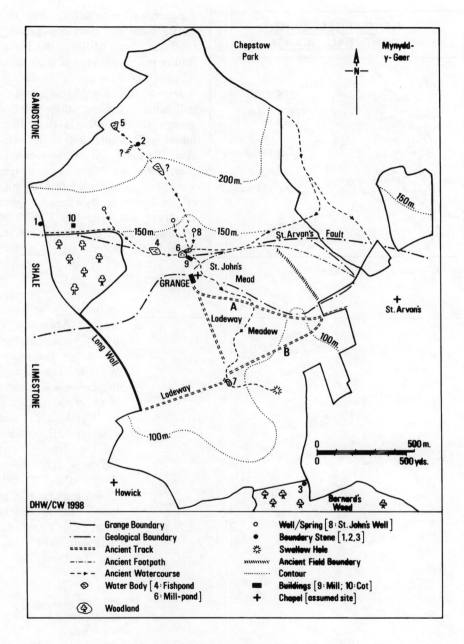

Fig. 96: Rogerstone Grange (of Tintern Abbey).
(Monmouthshire Antiquary XV, 1999).

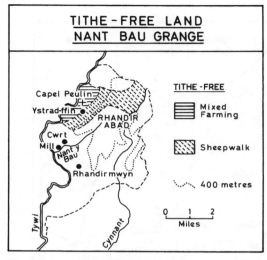

TITHE - FREE LAND
NANT BAU GRANGE

Capel Peulin
Ystrad-ffin
RHANDIR
ABAD
Cwrt
Mill
Nant y
Bau
Rhandirmwyn

TITHE - FREE

Mixed
Farming

Sheepwalk

400 metres

0   1   2
Miles

Tywi
Cynnant

Fig. 97: Based on tithe-map evidence.

Maenor Forion's *(Fig. 98)* two nuclei were the *cwrt* and granary (with the Court Mill and the Pandy fulling mill nearby), but the chapel (Capel Mair) was at Dancapel, nearly a kilometre south-east – indicating perhaps the original grange site.[114] Burials have been found at Dancapel, and in the adjacent field.[115] At *Cwrt-y-carnau (Fig. 99)*, the 'cwrt' and chapel were sited on the western extremity of the grange by the Loughor estuary, but the mill (Melin Mynach) and coal mine were towards its eastern edges, within the confines of modern Gorseinon.[116]

Diffuse granges included Gelliniog (of Aberconwy), which incorporated an early grange at 'Cyfydd' (now lost), the court and chapel at Quirt, a wind-mill at Rhuddgaer, and a water-mill (outside the perimeter) at Talybont *(Fig. 69c)*. Whitland's Castell Cosan grew out of at least three early granges – Cilgryman, Nantweirglodd and Dyffryn Tawe.

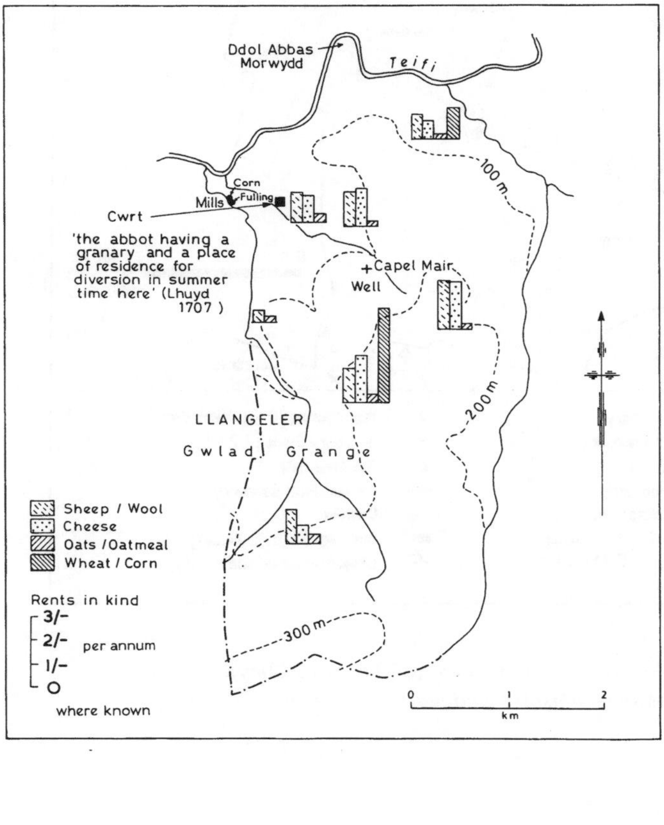

Ddol Abbas
Morwydd
Teifi

Corn
Mills   Fulling
Cwrt
'the abbot having a
granary and a place
of residence for
diversion in summer
time here' (Lhuyd
1707)

100 m

+Capel Mair
Well

200 m

LLANGELER
Gwlad   Grange

Sheep / Wool
Cheese
Oats /Oatmeal
Wheat / Corn

Rents in kind
3/-
2/-   per annum
1/-
0
where known

300 m

0   1   2
km

Fig. 98: Maenor Forion Grange (of Whitland). *(Based upon PRO, SC 6 (Hen. VIII) 4903, and Lhuyd E. 1707).*

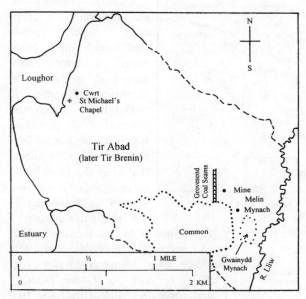

Fig. 99: Cwrt-y-carnau Grange (of Neath Abbey).

Tithe-free Lands

The Cistercians had a 'hidden benefit' in that they were, in large measure, immune from the payment of tithes. They were, indeed, mostly exempt from such dues from 1132 to the Fourth Lateran Council (1215) with regard to all lands cultivated by the monks directly. The hostility aroused by such a blanket privilege, especially from the parochial clergy who might well see their income considerably reduced, led that Council to decree that tithe-exemption was to be maintained in respect of land acquired before the Council – and still cultivated by the monks, but henceforth only on lands they *newly* brought into cultivation.[117] Previously, Innocent III had defended abbeys such as Margam (1203)[118] and Llantarnam (1208)[119] whose tithe-exemption had been challenged.[120] Boniface VIII (1302) extended the privilege to monastic lands demised to tenants – a situation becoming increasingly common – providing no one had been collecting tithes from them up to that time. By virtue of this bull, the Bishop of Llandaff (1339) confirmed Margam's exemption from the payment of tithes in respect of its lands in Hafod-y-porth, Penhydd and Resolfen.[121]

Tithe-exemption was long enduring, and enjoyed by the monks' successors in ownership of the relevant lands even until the final abolition of the payments in 1936. The many instances of such tithe-free properties[122] included: 140 hectares (350a.) in Tir-y-mynach township (formerly of Strata Marcella),[123] about 240ha. (600a.) at Cornwy Lys (formerly of Aberconwy),[124] and about 60ha. (150a.) at each of Llantarnam's Cil-onydd and Gelli-lâs granges.[125] Tithe payments were sometimes modified:[126] the grange lands of Cwmhir at Gwern-y-go (190ha./472a.; *Fig. 100.*) were tithe-free, but its non-demesne lands adjacent in Caeliber Isaf paid a one-thirteenth tithe.[127] Strata Florida's Aberduhonw Grange (240ha./590a.) rendered, instead of tithes, thirty-six bushels of oatmeal, which were to be gauged by 'Winchester measure'.[128] Later tenants at Basingwerk's Tre'r Abbot rendered a *modus* in lieu of tithes.[129]

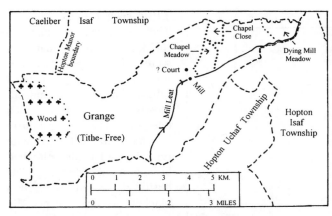

Fig. 100: Gwern-y-go Grange (of Abbey Cwmhir).

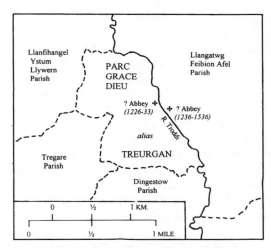

Fig. 101: Parc Grace Dieu, Monmouthshire.

Closely associated, and generally co-terminous with, certain tithe-free lands were areas of later *extra-parochial* status. The centuries of monastic possession – with no external parochial involvement nor collection of tithes – meant that after the Dissolution these lands were not viewed as belonging to any particular parish.[130] Examples in Wales included: Sker (formerly of Neath)[131] and Parc Grace Dieu (*alias* Treurgan; *Fig. 101*), formerly of Grace Dieu,[132] and probably indicating its first site). Tintern possessed a substantial extra-parochial rectangular portion of Greenmoor sandwiched between the parishes of Bishton and Redwick, Monmouthshire (*Fig. 79*).

Cymer's lands in Cyfeiliog, being extra-parochial, caused a reorientation (after the Dissolution) of the boundary between the dioceses of Bangor and St Asaph.[133] Some extra-parochial lands, frequently with existing chapels, gave rise to new parishes after the Suppression, amongst them: Dore's Gwenddwr,[134] Margam's Llangeinor,[135] Tintern's Trelech Grange,[136] and, probably, Whitland's Llanfihangel Cilfargen.

NOTES

1.　Lekai L.J. 1977, 295. (Resident *conversi*, with hired labourers, formed the grange staff, supervised by a senior *conversus*: the 'master of the grange' or 'granger'.)
2.　Dimier A. 1964, 182.
3.　*Statuta* I, 268 (1201/26).
4.　Birch W. de Gray. 1902, 62.
5.　Jones M.C. 1873, 185.
6.　Lhuyd E. 1707. III, 77.
7.　PRO, E 135/21/5, No. 9.
8.　Kansas 1/1.
9.　NLW, Badm. Manorial 1571, m.1.
10.　*Ibid.* 1575.
11.　*Statuta* I, 472 (1217/30).
12.　Parkes L.N. and Webster P.V.

1974, 147–49.

13. Jones T. 1950, 47, 51.
14. NLW, tithe-map, Llanboidy pa., Carms.
15. Owen G.D. 1935, 25.
16. Gray T. 1905, 90.
17. Owen G.D. 1935, 13–14.
18. *Episc. Acts* II, 671.
19. *Cartae Glam.* III, 902 (DCCXCII).
20. Cowley F.G. 1977, 90.
21. Oral communication of Mr N.T. Fryer.
22. Williams D.H. 1976, 133; NLW, Badm. Manorial 1657, m. 11r.
23. NLW, Badm. Manorial 1021, m. 1.
24. *Ibid.* 1657, m. 2d.
25. *Ibid.* 1651.
26. NLW, Badm. Manorial 1657, 3d, 6r.
27. *Ibid.* m. 6r.
28. As *c.* NGR: SO 484025.
29. VCH, *County of Gloucester* X (1972) 105. N.B: Abbey *Passage* Farm nearby.
30. Its 'keeper of the passage' (*Valor Eccl.* IV, 371). In 1282, he was Henry *le Passur*, (VCH, *Gloucester* X (1972) 105).
31. RCAHMW, *Glamorgan* III: Pt.2 (1982) 256, 274.
32. Jones M.C. (1869) 114–15.
33. NLW, Tredegar Park Deeds, Box 46, No. 20.
34. Hays R.W. 1963, 18.
35. Davies H.R. 1942, 3.
36. *Cal. Patent R.* 1300, 499.
37. Williams D.H. 1998b, 244.
38. RCAHMW III (*Radnor*, 1913) 104 (No. 412A); NLW, MS 13452A (Day-Book of George Eyre Evans) 20–21 (partial map)..
39. *Gir. Camb.* I (1869) 117.
40. NGR: SH 455668.
41. NGR: ST 216937.
42. *Cartae Glam.* VI, 2291 (MDLXXI).
43. NLW, Badm. Manorial 1654, m. 3d.
44. *Cîteaux* XXIX (1978: 1–2) 130–31.
45. Williams D.H. 1976, 35; PRO, SC 6 (Hen. VIII) 7319, m.10r; E

46. *Rot. Litt. Claus.* II, 132; *Cal. Charter R.* 1227, 4; Wakeman Papers (Society of Antiquaries) 790 (26) 183.
47. Gray T. 1903a, 133.
48. NGR: SS 705940.
49. Howel R. 174..
50. Gray T. 1903a, 149.
51. Cowley F.G. 1977, 23–24.
52. Lewis J.M. and Knight B. 1973, 147–53.
53. Williams D.H. 1998, 286–87.
54. Williams G. 1962, 174.
55. Williams D.H. 1984. II, 234–36.
56. Appendix 3 for grid references.
57. *Mont. Collns.* V, 121; *Exchq. Proc. (1)* 278; RCAHMW, I (*County of Montgomery*; 1911) 81–82.
58. UCNW, Plas Coch Deed 377.
59. Lhuyd E. 1707. I, 72–73; Pennant T. 1796, 714; Wade-Evans A.W. 1910, 101 (based on a list of 1733).
60. RCAHMW, I (*Montgomery*) 1911) 66 (No. 314); Owen G. 1892. IV, 671.
61. Gray T. 1903, 176.
62. *Arch. Camb.* 1857, 55.
63. Cummings R. 1974, 206; Ward J. 1914, 358, 370.
64. Pugh R.H. 1934, 19–20.
65. Morgan W. Ll. 1899, 9–11; Spurgeon C.J. and Thomas H.J. 1975, 58–59.
66. Appendix 3 for grid references.
67. Gray T. 1903, 176; Lhuyd E. 1707. III, 125; Jones D.R.L. 1981, 9; Evans A.L. 1958, 40; *Cartae Glam.* II, 255, 492; PRO, LR 6/152/4, f. 4d.
68. NLW, Penrice and Margam Ch. 38.
69. Evans A. 1979, 53, 57.
70. Cowley F.G. 1977, 183.
71. *Cartae Glam.* II, 473 (CCCCLXXV).
72. Cowley F.G. 1977, 183.
73. RCAHMW, III: Pt. 2 (*County of Glamorgan*, 1982) 271.
74. Evans A.L. 1958, 37–43, 116.
75. PRO, SC 6 (Hen. VIII) 5156, m.13r.

318/875.

76. Lhuyd E. 1707. III, 69, 123.
77. *NGR:* SN 201162.
78. PRO, E 318/875; SC 6 (Hen. VIII) 4907, m.8r.
79. *Reg. J. Trefnant* 221.
80. Morris E.R. 1893, 113–14, 131–32.
81. *Liber Land.* 452.
82. NGR: ST 297953.
83. *Liber Land.* 480–81. [*NGR*: ST 216938].
84. PRO, E 134/Eliz. Hilary 16. [*NGR: c.* SH 977075].
85. Fenton R. 1917, 68. [*NGR:* SN 788471].
86. RCAHMW III (*County of Radnor*; 1913) 104. [*NGR:* SN 939658].
87. NLW, MS 13452A, p. 120.
88. *Episc. Acts* I, 404; PRO, E 315/52/88.
89. *Cal. Papal Reg. (Letters)* I, 131.
90. *Ibid.* V, 164; VI, 74; VII, 290.
91. Williams S.W. 1889, Appx. lii–liv.
92. *Augm. Proc.* 27.
93. BL, Harl. Ch. 1249, ff. 141b–142; *MSS* in BM II, 248 (428g5, h5).
94. PRO, E 134/8 Jac. I (Hilary 9; Heref. and Monm.); E 112/107/60 (8 Jac. I); Williams D.H. 1984. II, 233–34. Trivel church stood where Park Hall was later located. Grace Dieu had tithes from Trivel [*Valor Eccl.* IV, 361].
95. PRO, E 318/875; SC 6 (Hen. VIII) 7319, m.10r.
96. Jones J. 1997, 89 (No. 28).
97. Spurgeon C.J. and Thomas H.J. 1982, 260–62 (MG 16).
98. *Taxatio Eccl.* 282; PRO, SC 6 (Hen. VIII) 5156; Birch W. de Gray. 1902, 30.
99. Spurgeon C.J. and Thomas H.J. 1982, 262 (at *NGR:* SS 9596 7852).
100. *Ibid.* 262–65 (MG 17).
101. Hopkins T.J. 1967, 88–89, 94; *Glamorgan County History* III (Cardiff, 1971) 414.
102. Spurgeon C.J. and Thomas H.J. 1982, 258–60 (MG 15).
103. Williams D.H. 1976, 35–36.
104. PRO, SC 6 (Hen. VIII) 7319, m.10r (*'herenshawys'*).
105. K I/9.
106. Williams D.H. 1976, 128–34.
107. Parkes L.N. and Webster P.V. 1974,
108. PRO, E 134/44Eliz/East12.
109. PRO, E 134/44–45 Eliz. (Mich. 31); Williams D.H. 1999, 54–55.
110. Williams D.H. 1999a, 22–32.
111. NGR: ST 506969.
112. Its western portion, Prior's Grove, is nowadays mis-spelt as 'Briers Grove'.
113. Williams S.W. 1889, Appx. lxiv–lxv.
114. *Cf.* Lhuyd E. 1707. III, 77.
115. Information of the local farmer.
116. *Cf.* NLW, Badm. Deeds (Group 2) 2021; PRO, E 315/103, f.132.
117. Williams D.H. 1998, 268–69.
118. *Cartae Glam.* II, 280–81 (CCLXXXI).
119. *MSS in BM* III, 710–11.
120. 'Much litigation' preceded the quitclaim to Margam (1271) of tithes claimed by Gloucester Abbey [Gloucester Cathedral MS I, 5].
121. *Cartae de Glam.* IV, 1234–35.).
122. *Cf.* Williams D.H. 1984. II, 241.
123. Simpson Jones T. 1899, 143.
124. Evans A.O. 1928, 194.
125. Llanfihangel Llantarnam tithe-map.
126. Williams D.H. 1984. II, 241 and *n.*
127. *Ibid.* 1976a, 91.
128. Llanddewi'r-cwm, Brecs., tithe-map.
129. Pennant T. 1796, 115.
130. Williams D.H. 1998, 269.
131. Birch W. de Gray 1902, 46.
132. Bradney J.A. II: Pt. 1, 122; Ordnance Survey, *Book of Reference* to Plan of Parc Grace Dieu (1882).
133. Gresham C.A. 1984, 153.
134. A chapelry, with an incumbent subject to the abbot of Dore: 'as his ordinary' [PRO, E 303/5/96, *Cf.* E 326/B.4660].
135. *Glamorgan County History* III (1971) 118.
136. In 1533, described as: 'A parish' [NLW, Badm. Deed Group I, 331].

CHAPTER 13

CISTERCIAN MANORS

The early spirit of the Order, spelt out in the Charter of Charity, forbade the owner-ship of 'manors, serfs, land-rents, ... and all other incomes of this kind, as contrary to the purity of the monastic vocation'.[1] Such possessions could not, in time, be avoided, and the Welsh Cistercians came to own manors, with the atten-dant courts, dues and services, by grant, by purchase, or more often (as demise proceeded apace) by the gradual modification and ultimate transformation of a grange. Long before the Suppression, the lands of several monasteries were effec-tively organised into a series of manors, often including more than one of the initial granges within their borders.

Much of the property of Llantarnam came to be grouped into the manors of Magna Porta and of Wentsland-Bryngwyn. Strata Marcella's Tir-y-Mynach (Talerddig) manor contained lands in nine parishes. Grace Dieu's home manor (Treurgan) administered properties 'up to four miles distant'.[2] Valle Crucis' urban manor of Wrexham Abbot included the nearby township of Stansty Abbatis (*alias* Issa). Serfs (and their offspring) on lands early granted to the monks, if not displaced, became their villeins, accounting for those present (in 1291) on the estates of Margam at Bonvilston and Tanglwst.[3]

A survey, ten years after Aberconwy (1284) received lands in Anglesey at Cornwy Lys and Penmynydd, shows that the abbey had inherited villeins, rents, and associated customs and services.[4] A Celtic equivalent of the manor, the *trefi*, may have prevailed upon the Ceredigion lands of Strata Florida before the abbey acquired them. The typical grange economy never perhaps came to dominate here, but worked side by side with Welshry rendering for their holdings in cash, kind and service. It did have early grange *nuclei* there, like 'the grange which is called Castell Flemish', noted by the Lord Rhys (1184).[5]

The transition of a grange economy to a manorial structure was evidenced when Neath demised its former Somerset grange at Exford (1322). It had become a manor 'with services both of free tenants and of villeins'.[6] When Aberconwy ceded Ffriwlwyd (in 1350) it was no longer described as a grange, but as a manor and vill.[7] Another 14th century transition was at Tintern's Merthyr Gerain Grange where, by 1388, three or four manorial courts were held each year.[8] The terms 'grange' and 'manor' came to be interchangeable, or used very loosely, a sign of the piecemeal modification of the primitive grange economy. Strata Marcella's lands at Bronrotpol (Alberbury, Shropshire) were called both a 'manor' (1342) and a 'grange' (1344) within the space of a few years.[9]

Three manors of Tintern are worth a fuller description. *Woolaston* (Gloucestershire) granted, in part, at the abbey's foundation (1131), came to stretch from the Severn estuary to the river Wye, and to include five granges. The

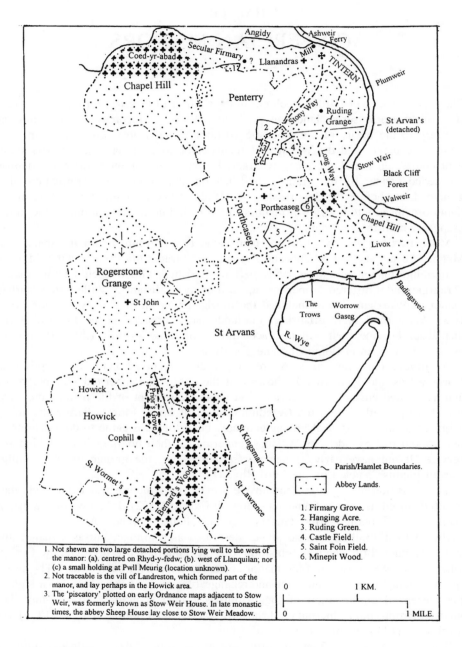

Fig. 102: Tintern Abbey's Porthcaseg Manor (Monmouthshire).

monastery distributed annual gifts of corn in the manor by way of charity,[10] whilst Abbot Newland (1501) gave a site and building by Woolaston church as an almshouse.[11] *Porthcaseg* (lower Wye valley; *Fig. 102*) included the abbey site, the Angidy valley (with mills, honey, fishing and tanning activities), a Sheep House (near Stow Weir) and two granges. In 1302, Earl Bigod confirmed the vill of Porthcaseg also;[12] this probably hastened the demise as a parochial edifice of Porthcaseg church – previously owned by St Kynemark's Priory (1291).[13] The manor saw, in time, a substantial tenantry develop, and its bailiff administered demised holdings in several local hamlets – like Howick and St Wormet's.[14]

Earl Bigod, in the same year, also gave Tintern its most valuable manor, one of several in the Norfolk lordship of Acle.[15] Its tenants resented the firm hand of Abbot Wyke,[16] alleging that he demanded services of them other than those customary since the Conquest, but they failed in litigation against him. In addition to the accustomed suit of court, heriot on the death of ancestors, a penny rent per acre, and mowing services, Abbot Wyke, they said, expected the carriage of hay, the payment of 'merchet' tax for the marriage, took heriot at will, and taxed them 'in high and low'.[17] The same difficulties with the Acle tenantry resurfaced forty years later.[18] It may be that the need to finance an ongoing building programme lay behind such monastic resolve,[19] but changing social conditions in general – as a growing independence of the rustic population – also probably played their part. What the abbey demanded at Acle, it undoubtedly also expected of its Border tenants.

Jurisdiction

The Cistercians enjoyed possession of their lands free from many secular exactions, though the extent of their liberties varied from house to house, and from age to age, and so it is difficult to generalise. Llywelyn ab Iorwerth's charter in favour of Aberconwy (1199) ensured that wayward monks were 'corrected in their chapters' – not in any lay court.[20] Tintern was exempt from 'blodwyte, flithwyte, hengwite and flemenswite' – fines, respectively, for the shedding of blood, harbouring fugitives, public violence, and the wrongful hanging of a thief.[21] Edward I (1284), amongst similar provisions afforded to Aberconwy, provided that if a man under the abbot's jurisdiction was fined in the king's courts, the money should be payable to the abbey. In 1350–52 alone, it received in this way some £7 from the sheriff of Caernarfon.[22]

Exemption from judicial process was not absolute. The monks of Margam might be impleaded before the Earl of Gloucester or the sheriff of Glamorgan.[23] Two brothers of Margam were indeed tried, and acquitted, at Cardiff County Court (1358); one on a charge of robbery, the other for habouring a felon.[24] The Abbot of Whitland (*c.* 1320), obviously a target of litigation, said that he had 'suffered much from Welsh law, which does not permit a respondent in a suit to have a sergeant'.[25] Once English law took hold, Whitland could only be summoned before the king's Justice.[26]

The right to hold inquest varied. The *famulus* of the County of Cardiff performed the duty of coroner for Margam's lands there (1299).[27] Tintern had its own stipendiary coroner 'by custom, from the original foundation', but his salary was disallowed by the *Valor* Commissioners (1535).[28] Cymer was brought to account by the Justice of north Wales for burying a monk, accidentally drowned, without the local coroner's licence.[29]

The juridical rights of the monasteries themselves could be wide-ranging. Tintern was granted 'soc and sac, tol and them, and infangenethef'; respectively – the juris-diction of a manorial lord; the right to buy and sell, hold a market, and determine the ownership of goods within one's estates; and the right to judge a thief taken on one's lands.[30] Aberconwy (but not Tintern) could also claim 'utfangenethef' – the right to judge a thief taken outside one's own land.[31] Indeed, the Justice of north Wales (1397–98) handed over three men to the abbey's Steward for trial.[32] One Steward of Aberconwy (Sir Richard Pole, 1503) investigated, at Nantgwynant, charges laid against two alleged horse thieves and cattle rustlers.[33]

The growth of tenantry obliged monasteries to hold their own manorial courts leet with cognisance of petty offences, of land disputes and pleas of debt. Earl William of Gloucester (*c.* 1150) afforded Neath the right 'to freely hold its courts anywhere over its men'.[34] Earl Richard de Clare (1230–62) allowed Margam 'to have a court of all pleas and forfeits in its lands, but not of felony'.[35] The men of Valle Crucis' Stansty township (1254) were to 'stand to judicial trial for all their excesses to the abbot and his court – except for judgement of homicide and robbery'.[36]

Regular court leets on monastic land may account, in some instances, for the later occurrence of *'cwrt'* in place-names, as the Court Farm (Strata Florida) and Court Field (Llanllugan). In south Wales especially, 'suit of court' – generally twice a year, was written into the obligations of new tenants by monasteries like Margam[37] and Tintern.[38] Court perquisites included – by way of fines – a never very substan-tial income. Tintern, in this way, received at its Porthcaseg Manor (1448) 22s 3d at one court, 12s 7d at another.[39]

The degrees of potential and realised legal jurisdiction varied from monastery to monastery. Llywelyn's great charter (1209) did not ascribe any juridical rights to Cymer, but its abbot (of 1396) claimed the power to impose amercements on 'all his tenants residing eight leagues from Harlech and Bala'.[40] Strata Florida held courts concerned with tenurial rights, but never seems to have been granted 'the slightest exemption from the secular courts of the princes of south Wales, and later of the English Crown'.[41] One abbot (*post*-1327) said that his predecessors and *tenants* had always answered 'all manner of pleas and suits in the king's court at Llanbadarn'.[42]

Certain abbeys came to exercise capital punishment. Tintern was granted (in 1302) by Earl Bigod: ' Gallows, and judgement of life and limb'[43] – but it had been accused (by Walter Map) a century before, of hanging a man at Woolaston Manor (by the Severn estuary) for stealing apples, and then hiding his body in the sand.[44] Later maps show a 'Hangman's Field' at Woolaston Grange[45] and a 'Hanging Acre' at Penterry[46] – adjacent to, if not on, abbey land. Aberconwy had a gallows at Maenan (1348),[47] whilst a tradition endures of gallows formerly sited on the hill above the 'cwrt' of Strata Florida's Dywarchen Grange.[48]

Llantarnam (1398) and Margam (1423) obtained papal confirmation of rights common to the Cistercians, making their tenantry free of ecclesiastical courts, but

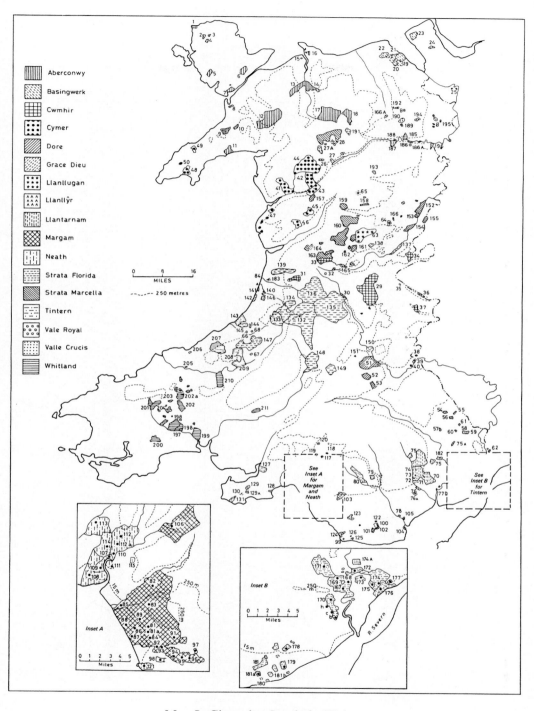

Map I: Cistercian Lands in Wales.
(Maps II–XII following are revisions of those in: Atlas of Cistercian Lands in Wales, Cardiff, 1990).

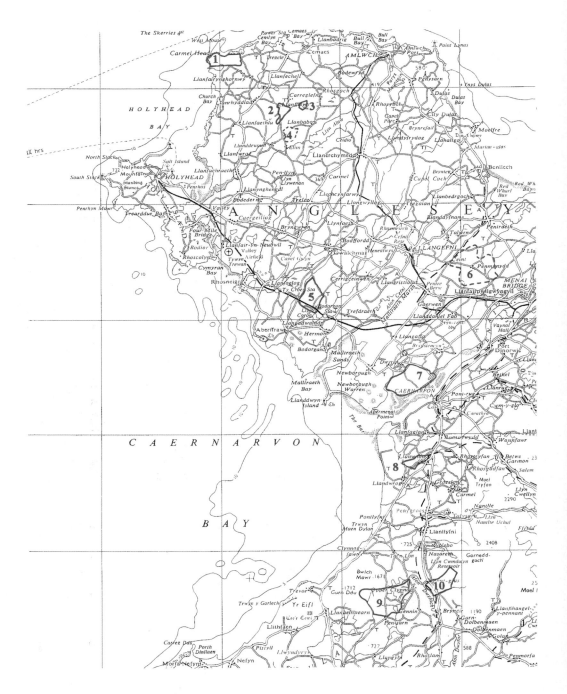

Map II: Cistercian Lands in North-West Wales.
(Reproduced by kind permission of the Ordnance Survey © Crown Copyright NC/01/001).

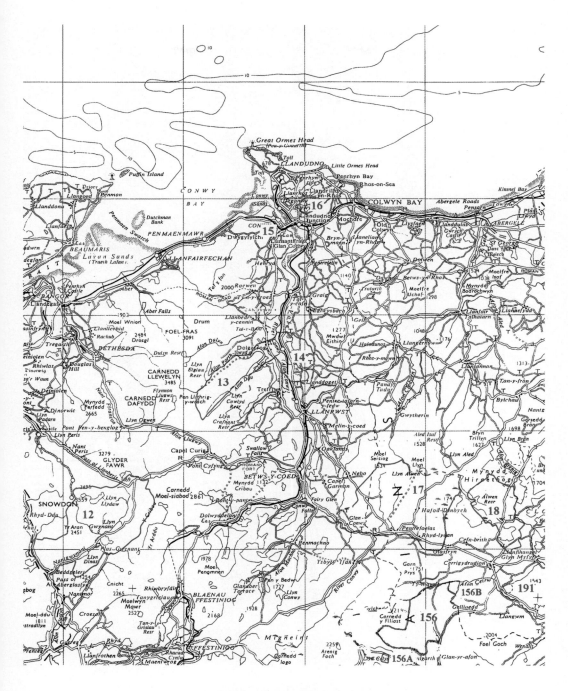

Map III: Cistercian Lands in North Wales.
(Reproduced by kind permission of the Ordnance Survey © Crown Copyright NC/01/001).

Map IV: Cistercian Lands in North-Central Wales (W).
(Reproduced by kind permission of the Ordnance Survey © Crown Copyright NC/01/001).

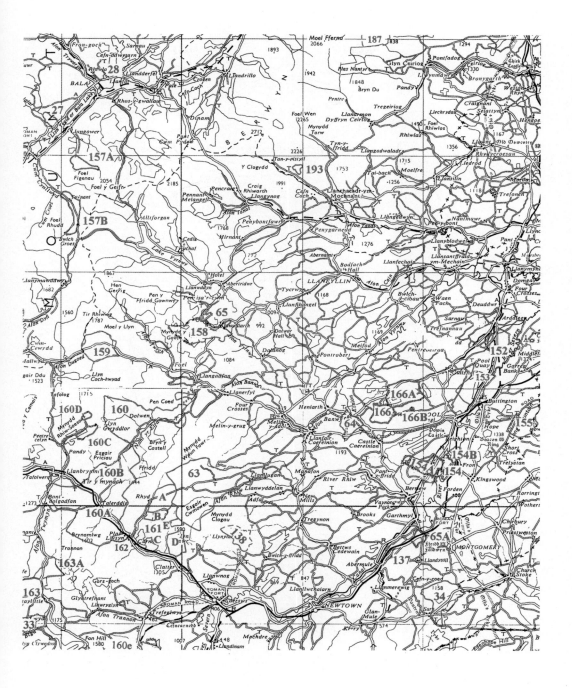

Map V: Cistercian Lands in North-Central Wales (E).
(Reproduced by kind permission of the Ordnance Survey © Crown Copyright NC/01/001).

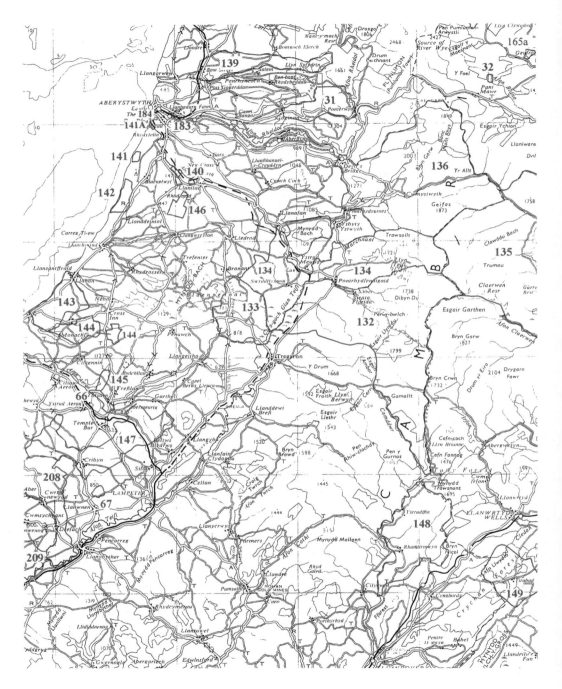

Map VI: Cistercian Lands in South-Central Wales (W).
(Reproduced by kind permission of the Ordnance Survey © Crown Copyright NC/01/001).

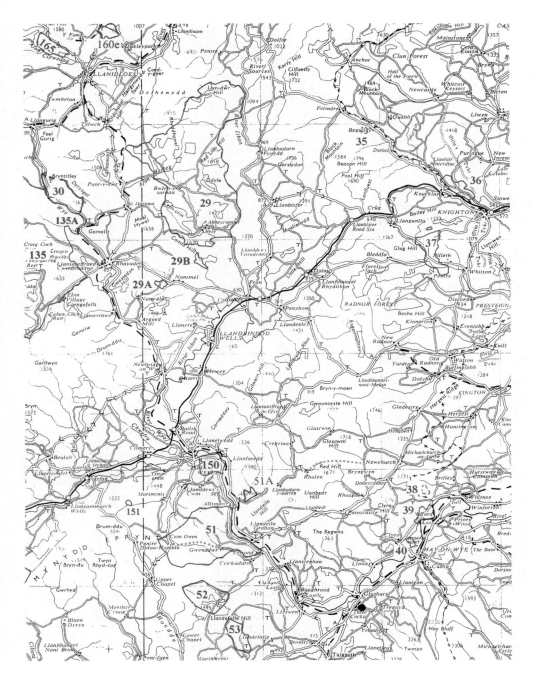

Map VII: Cistercian Lands in South-Central Wales (E).
(Reproduced by kind permission of the Ordnance Survey © Crown Copyright NC/01/001).

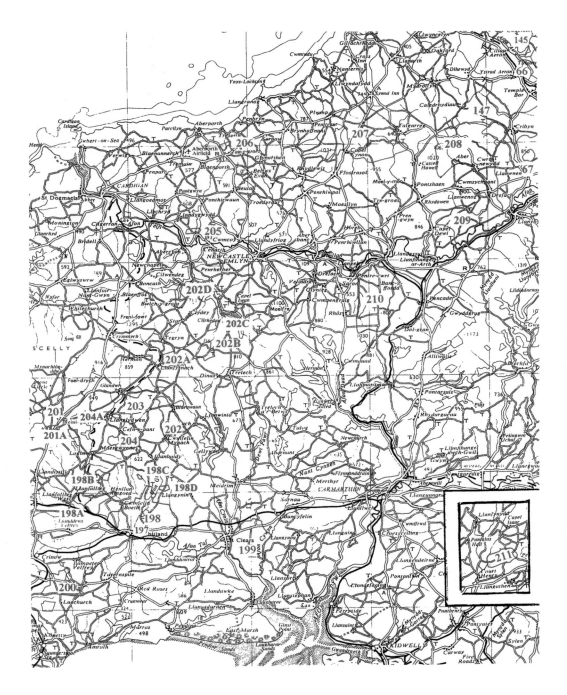

Map VIII: Cistercian Lands in South-West Wales.
(Reproduced by kind permission of the Ordnance Survey © Crown Copyright NC/01/001).

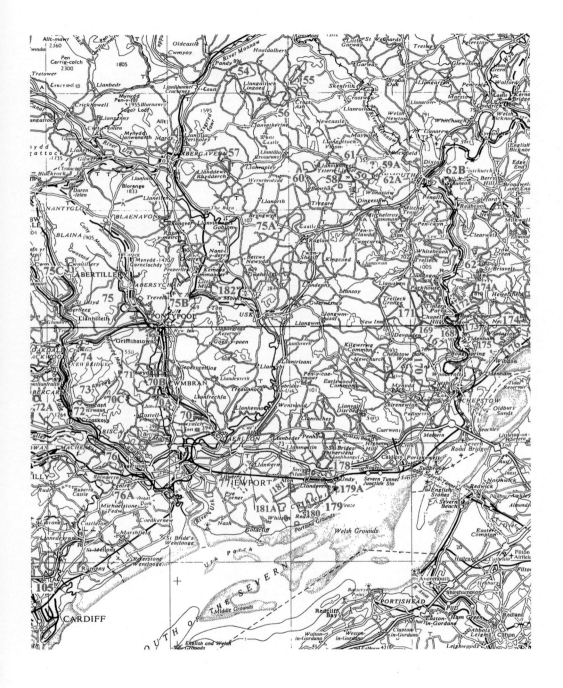

Map IX: Cistercian Lands in South-East Wales.
(Reproduced by kind permission of the Ordnance Survey © Crown Copyright NC/01/001).

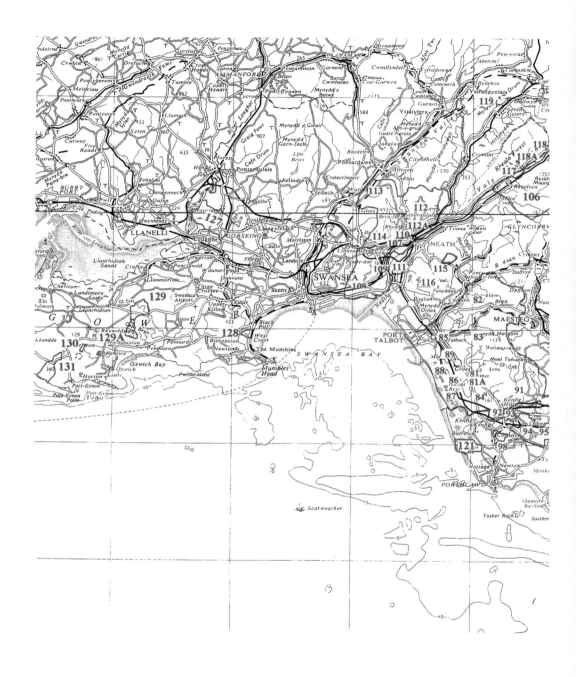

Map X: Cistercian Lands in South Wales (W).
(Reproduced by kind permission of the Ordnance Survey © Crown Copyright NC/01/001).

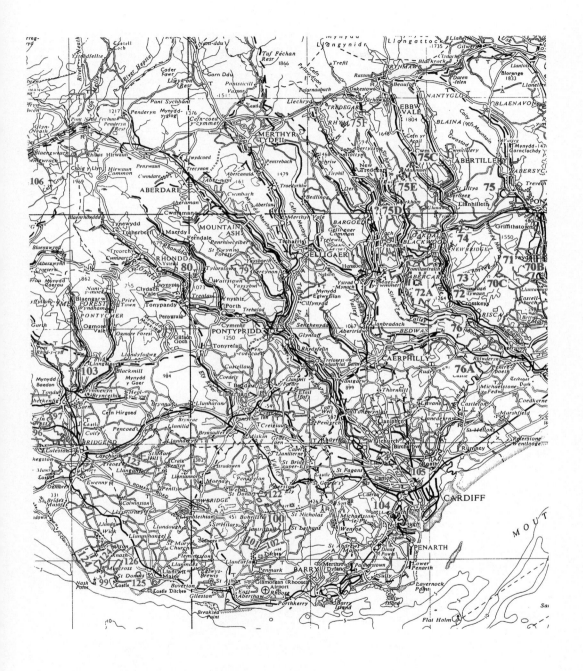

Map XI: Cistercian Lands in South Wales (E).
(Reproduced by kind permission of the Ordnance Survey © Crown Copyright NC/01/001).

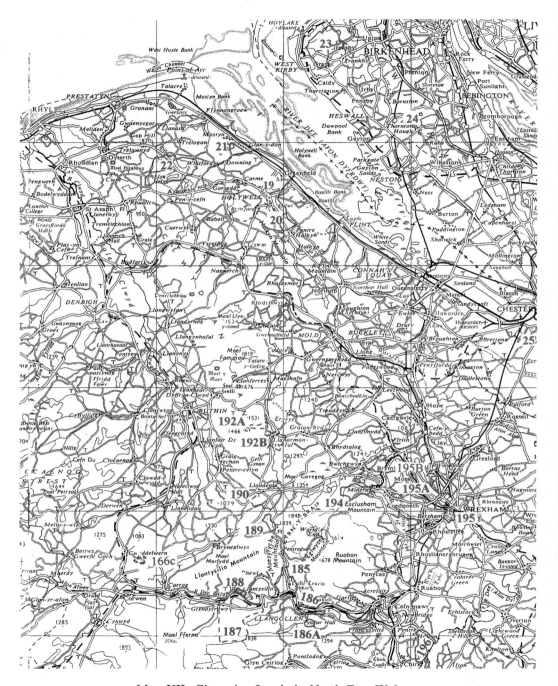

Map XII: Cistercian Lands in North-East Wales.
(Reproduced by kind permission of the Ordnance Survey © Crown Copyright NC/01/001).

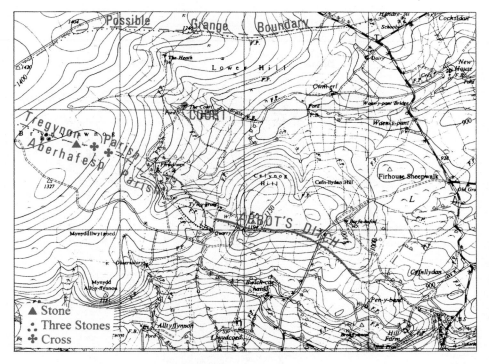

Map XIII-A: Celynog Grange.
(Based upon the Enclosure Award for the parishes of Aberhafesp and Tregynon, Powys, 1815: *Powys Archives* MCC 1, 18. *(Reproduced by kind permission of the Ordnance Survey © Crown Copyright NC/01/001).*).

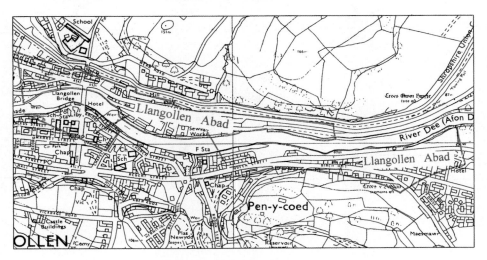

Map XIII-B: Llangollen Abad.
(Based upon the NLW tithe map for the parish of Llangollen. *(Reproduced by kind permission of the Ordnance Survey © Crown Copyright NC/01/001).*)

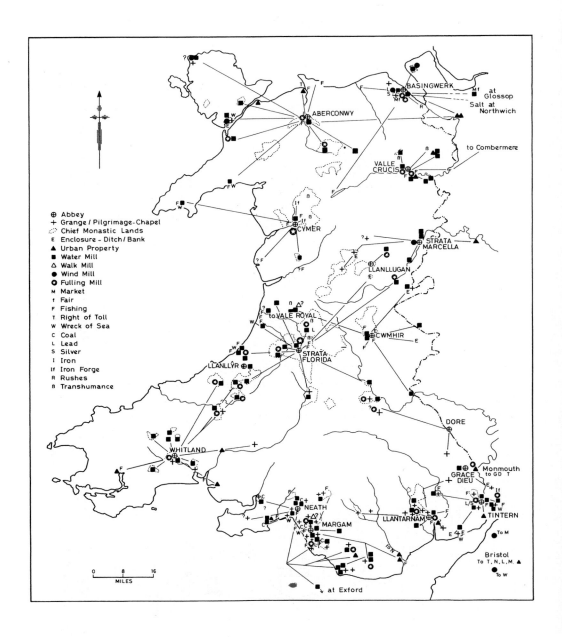

Map XIV: Cistercian Economic Resources in Wales.
(Atlas of Cistercian Lands in Wales, Cardiff, 1990).

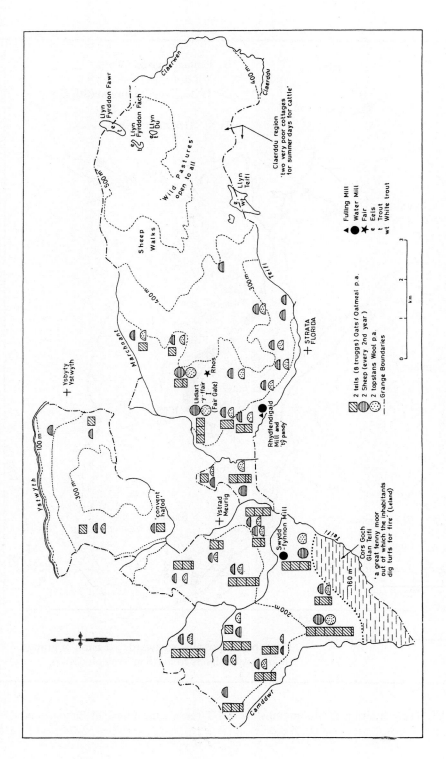

Map XV: Mefenydd Grange, Ceredigion (of Strata Florida). (Based upon NLW, Cwrtmawr MS 873D, the observations of John Leland (c. 1538), and other sources. *Atlas of Cistercian Lands in Wales*, Cardiff, 1990).

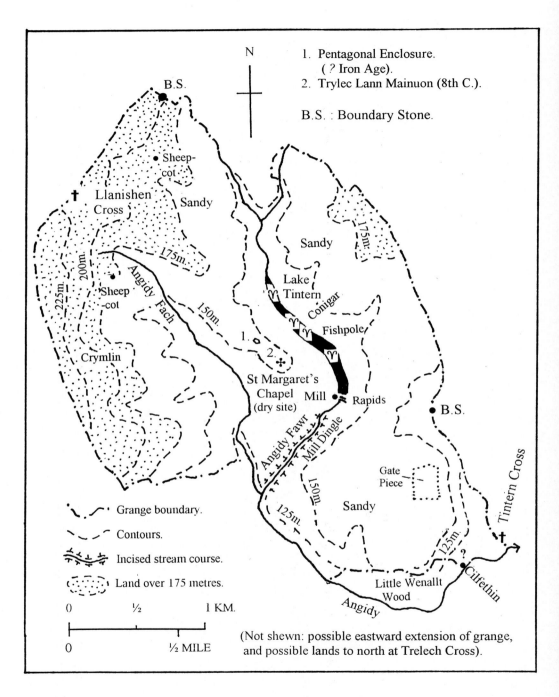

N

1. Pentagonal Enclosure.
   (*?* Iron Age).
2. Trylec Lann Mainuon (8th C.).

B.S. : Boundary Stone.

B.S.

Sheep-cot

Llanishen
Cross

Sandy

175m.

200m

Angidy Fach

Sheep-cot

225m

150m.

Crymlin

1.

2.

St Margaret's
Chapel
(dry site)

Sandy

175m.

Lake
Tintern

Conigar

Fishpole

Mill   Rapids

Angidy Fawr

Mill Dingle

150m.

125m.

Sandy

Gate
Piece

B.S.

Tintern Cross

125m.

Cilfethin

Little Wenallt
Wood

Angidy

Grange boundary.

Contours.

Incised stream course.

Land over 175 metres.

0   ½   1 KM.

0   ½ MILE

(Not shewn: possible eastward extension of grange,
and possible lands to north at Trelech Cross).

Map XVI: Trelech Grange, Monmouthshire (of Tintern): the Physical Background.

subject instead, in respect of 'fornications and adulteries', to 'correction' (perhaps corporal punishment) in the monastic chapter-houses.[49] Margam (1448) could enforce judgement in its lordship of Eglwys-geinor by committing miscreants to imprisonment in Ogmore Castle.[50] An abbot of Strata Florida (1534) placed in irons, and then sent to custody in Aberystwyth Castle, a monk and a layman accused of forging money.[51] Finds at Ystrad Fflur have included a set of manacles.[52] Tintern's gate-house doubled up as a prison for local offenders,[53] and it had a stock at its Woolaston manor.

'Courts baron' came to the fore with the actual sale of land to freeholders within monastic jurisdiction. Such courts were held by Basingwerk – in its moiety of Holywell (1388),[54] Margam – for Hafod-y-porth lordship (1470),[55] and Strata Marcella – at Talerddig.[56] The scope of Llantarnam's court baron was spelt out at the Great Sessions in Newport (1476), and included the power of distraint by its bailiff and the imposition of fines of up to 10s.[57] Whilst there was a technical distinction between 'courts baron' and 'courts leet', the terms probably became interchangeable. At Tintern, however, it was later said (1651), a court baron was customarily kept 'at will' of the lord, a court leet 'at the usual times'.[58]

There is much evidence of the continued enjoyment of jurisdictional rights by the Welsh Cistercians. Edward Charlton's comprehensive charter in favour of Strata Marcella (1420) asserted, in somewhat exaggerated phraseology, that 'from the time of the foundation of the house', not only the monks but also 'all persons within the enclosure', were, in most respects, exempt from presentment at the 'great court of Powys'.[59] Instead, the monastery had its own courts – as at Talerddig, where (later evidence deposed in 1601) it had 'a leet court, view of frankpledge, and a court baron. The inhabitants ... owed no duty to any other court leet or baron'.[60] Few records of Margam's courts exist – those which do tell of another court function – the admission of tenants to their holdings.[61] In their last years, Valle Crucis[62] and Whitland,[63] respectively, appointed their Stewards to hold 'all court leets and hundreds' and as 'keeper of courts'.

Several instances can be cited to show that, for much of the earlier monastic period, the abbatial courts were held at approximately three-weekly intervals, but with, perhaps, far less frequency towards the Suppression. On Margam's manor of Bonvilston, its court leet was held 'from month to month' in the 13th century;[64] in the case of Strata Marcella 'at intervals of three weeks or more'.[65] At Llantarnam, in the 1530s, the court baron was held but twice a year,[66] and the same was true, at the Dissolution, of Strata Florida's court leet in Mefenydd.[67]

The only Cistercian manor in Wales for which an extensive series of court rolls exist, stretching from the early 13th century down almost to the Suppression, is Tintern's manor of Porthcaseg.[68] These suggest a three-weekly interval between courts in the mid-13th century – with *perhaps* no sittings in harvest time,[69] but on average only three or four courts yearly in the 14th and 15th centuries.[70] The court appears to have been held at Porthcaseg itself,[71] where a 'Court House Field' long retained its name.[72] From at least 1402 onwards, the court was held under the presidency of the abbey Steward or his deputy; before that probably of the cellarer –

who continued to have an influential role. On occasion, a jury was employed – as in a land dispute at Landreston (14 February 1340).[73]

The earliest Porthcaseg court rolls (1262–63) reveal something of contemporary life,[74] mentioning Brebelof who had taken a wife without permission, and telling of John Mason and his sons who had badly assaulted Richard of St Briavel's. One absentee from court (in the autumn of 1262) was condoned 'because of the state of the weather'. The courts took note of land disputes between tenants, arranging in one instance a *love-day* at Trelech Grange to allow reconciliation between the contending parties.

From the early 14th century onwards, much business of the court was taken up with the 'entry' of tenants into their holdings *(Chapter 14)*, whilst fines for unlicensed marriages and incontinence *(lairwite)* were prominent in these years.[75] Fines were imposed for petty offences, such as verbal abuse of the monastic community, and the use of a short measure – which was confiscated.[76] In the early 15th century, transgressions included selling bread without licence,[77] cutting greenwood in the abbot's wood,[78] and absence from court, thirty-three men defaulting in 1406 alone.[79]

This was a time of tension effected by the Glyn Dŵr Revolt, which affected the abbey lands badly. Another turbulent period in Wales, the decade of the 1440s, may have been reflected in the affrays (1444, 1447) at the abbey gate and the mill pond.[80] There were also robberies – like the theft of a small boat by night (1448),[81] and even the spiteful diversion of a mill-leat (1445).[82]

From 1400 onwards, Porthcaseg Court laid down from time to time a series of regulations, bye-laws in effect, regarding wage levels, work duties on the demesne, and the behaviour of the inhabitants.[83] As for wages, the rates laid down (1401) were 2d. per day for reapers and 3d. for mowers. If food was not provided and gleaning was not permitted, then an additional 2d. a day was allowed. There was an insistence on a corporate labour effort at harvest time. Abuse of the monastic precinct is implied in the regulation that 'no one shall take a dog into the church or cloister' (1401).[84]

As late as 1528, the court forbade recourse to dice and cards within the manor, the playing of handball at the abbey gate, and the keeping of goats – presumably because of the destruction they could cause. Another improper use of the monastic precinct is suggested by the stipulation that 'no one is to wash any dirty thing, neither clothes nor other corrupt matter, in the stream which runs through the middle of the abbey' – that stone-lined channel is still very much in evidence. The penalty was quite stiff! – a 7s. fine, and this sanction also applied to breach of a neighbourly commandment: 'Thou no may hack neither hew in other man's woods.'[85]

NOTES

1. Lekai L.J. 1977, 450 (XXIII).
2. PRO, E 318/569.
3. *Taxatio Eccl.* 284.
4. Hays R.W. 1963, 109.
5. Williams S.W. 1889, Appx. xi.
6. Cowley F.G. 1977, 247.
7. Hays R.W. 1963, 107.
8. NLW, Badm. Manorial 1571.
9. V.C.H. *Shropshire* VIII (1968) 153, 202–04, 207.
10. *Valor Eccl.* IV, 371.
11. Rudder S. 1779, 844.
12. *Tintern MSS* 64 (No. 2396).
13. *Taxatio Eccl.* 278.

14. NLW, Badm. Manorial 1572, 1574.
15. *Itin. Wm. Worcestre* 57.
16. Once sub-cellarer of the monastery [PRO, E 210/D.5724].
17. *Year Books* (Rolls Ser.) 33/35 Edw.I. (Mich. Pleas, 1306) 306–11.
18. *Cal. Patent R.* 1346, 162–63.
19. Cowley F.G. 1977, 255.
20. *Cal. Charter R.* 1332, 267–69.
21. *Tintern MSS* 67 (No. 2399).
22. Hays R.W. 1963, 114.
23. *Cartae Glam.* II, 413–14.
24. *Cartae Glam.* IV, 1296–97 (MXVII).
25. *Anc. Pet.* 27 (4/165).
26. Owen G.D. 1935, 229 [Noted in 1447]. ['Sergeant': 'attorney'; able to stand in for an absent defendant].
27. NLW, Penrice and Margam Ch. 212.
28. *Valor Eccl.* IV, 371.
29. *Rec. Caern.* 217–18.
30. *Cal. Charter R.* III, 98.
31. Hays R.W,. 1963, 72, 73*n*, 88.
32. *Ibid.* 114. [Presumably they were abbey retainers].
33. UCNW, Porth Yr Aur Add. MS 59.
34. Birch W. de Gray. 1902, 149–50.
35. NLW, Penrice and Margam Ch. 100.
36. Price G.V. 1952, 260.
37. *Cf.* Birch W. de Gray 1897, 352–54.
38. *Cf.* NLW, Badm. Manorial 1641 (of 1303), 1657–58.
39. *Ibid.* 1657, mm. 1r, 9d.
40. *Arch. Camb.* I (1846) 454; RCAHMW, 6 *Merioneth* (1921) 96 (No. 277*n*.)
41. Jones Pierce T. 1950, 32.
42. Williams S.W. 1889, Appx. lxvii–lxviii.
43. *Tintern MSS* 67 (2399).
44. Cowley F.G. 1977, 74, *W Map*, 56.
45. Gloucester City Record Office, Badminton Plan XIX (Photocopy 840).
46. NLW, Penterry parish tithe-map.
47. Hays R.W. 1963, 114.
48. Information, some years ago, of the resident farmer.
49. *Cal. Papal Reg.* V, 164; VI, 74; VII, 290.
50. Birch W. de Gray. 1897, 345.
51. Williams S.W. 1889, Appx. lxxvii–lxxxi; *LP (Hen. VIII)* VII, 477.
52. Williams S.W. 1889, 216.
53. PRO, LR 1/228, f. 6r–d (pencil no. 37).
54. *Chester Recog. Rolls,* I, 25.
55. Birch W. de Gray. 1897, 348.
56. *Exch. Proc.* (2) 273; PRO, E 134/6 James I. Mich. 42.
57. Pugh T.B. 1953, 28, 106; *Cf.* Williams D. H. 1967, 145.
58. NLW, Badm. Manorial 2445, p. 20.
59. Jones M.C. 1868, 298–99, 324–25; *Ibid.* 1871, 324–26; 1873, 352.
60. Williams D.H. 1976b, 184.
61. *Cf.* Birch W. de Gray. 1897, 347–48, 350, 352–53, 357, 359 (1487 to 1536).
62. PRO, E 315/93, f. 207.
63. PRO, SC 6 (Hen. VIII) 4903, mm. 32–33; E 315/104, f. 121d (2nd nos.); 105, f. 100.
64. *Arch. Camb.* 1868, 357.
65. Jones M.C. 1868, 299, 324–25.
66. PRO, SC 6 (Hen. VIII) 2497, m. 2d.
67. Owen G.D. 1935, 228.
68. For an analysis of Tintern's court rolls see: Cowley F.G. 1977, 253–57. Other 15th C. court rolls occur in NLW (Moor Grange) and Gloucestershire R.O. (Woolaston Manor) Badm. Group 2 Deeds.
69. No courts in August–September 1269: NLW, Badm. Manorial 1640.
70. *Cf.* NLW, Badm. Manorial 1654, 1657.
71. *Ibid.* 1575.
72. Gwent R.O. D.412/64.
73. NLW, Badminton 1645.
74. Williams D.H. 1976, 134 (transcribed).
75. Cowley F.G. 255.
76. NLW, Badm. Manorial 1645, mm. 6, 9.
77. *Ibid.* 1657, m. 10r.
78. *Ibid.* 1656, m. 1d.
79. *Ibid.* 1656, m. 1r.
80. *Ibid.* 1657, mm. 6r, 9r.
81. *Ibid.* 1657, m. 9d.
82. *Ibid.* 1657, m. 7r.
83. Williams D.H. 1976, 136 (transcribed).
84. NLW, Badm. Manorial 1654, m. 3r.
85. *Ibid.* 1663, mm. 3r–4d.

CHAPTER 14

ESTATE MANAGEMENT

Much of the early success of the Cistercians in the agricultural sector derived from the careful planning and central control system of their land management, accompanied by the keeping of detailed records. There were changes with the passing of the centuries, like the effective replacement of monastic officials by lay stipendiary officers, and as land was increasingly demised, but until the late 13th century, and perhaps later, a traditional Cistercian pattern operated on the greater part of their lands in Wales.

The Cellarer

The central pivot of Cistercian economy in those days was the monk-cellarer,[1] and whilst his significance may have declined in later years, his position remained one of prime importance within a monastic community. He was its chief business manager, and so it was that Margam's cellarer travelled (in 1207) to King John (at Bradenstoke, Wiltshire), to pay a heavy fine exacted from the abbey.[2] The cellarer of Tintern is on record as performing another function of the office, that of oversight of the granges.

The cellarer of a large house shared the burden with assistants – known as con-cellarers (Dore, 1312)[3] and sub-cellarers (Tintern 1293).[4] Each monastery also had (usually two) 'bursars' or 'treasurers', through whom all monies received by the cellarer and other monastic officials were channelled, or their usage accounted for.[5] Tintern's treasurer in 1412 was a monk, John Dore,[6] though, that same year, the reeve's account for Porthcaseg manor speaks of its 'bursars'.[7] The terms were interchangeable.

The work of the cellarer *vis-à-vis* the treasurers was complementary, and there is evidence of the regard for his role as late as Tudor times – when it was overshadowed by the appointment of a lay Steward. It was not only in the 13th century that (because of the experience they had acquired) cellarers like John de la Warre of Margam (1234) and Walter of Hereford at Tintern (1327) were translated to the abbacies of their houses, but also at least five of Tintern's abbots (elected between 1441 and 1513) had held the post of cellarer immediately before, or within a few years of, assuming the abbacy.[8] The office of cellarer was still an important stepping stone.

Most is known of the activities of the cellarers of Tintern. One (in 1318) was so jealous of his monastery's rights that, with his greyhounds, he came to Llanthony Priory's manor at Alvington – contiguous to land of Tintern, and killed ten of its pigs.[9] It was the cellarer (of 1427) who sold timber towards repairs at Caldicot Castle.[10]

Such diverse duties are reflected in the only two extant cellarer's rolls emanating from the abbey. The first (of 1411–12)[11] tells of the cellarer (John Morris) paying visits not only to Porthcaseg and Woolaston for court-days, but journeying also (on horseback with two companions) to the abbey's manor at Acle, Norfolk, and going on business to Bristol. It notes miscellaneous expenses – including 3s 4d for 2lbs. of pepper, bought for the guest house. It records substantial re-roofing at Woolaston Grange – involving the purchase of 2,000 tiles, a load of limestone, and the hiring of a tiler for four weeks and three days. The cloister roof was also repaired that year. The second roll (1434–35)[12] is less informative.

The leading individual on each grange was a *conversus* styled the 'granger' or 'master of the grange'. This office was held, for example, by Philip Seisil at Llantarnam's Maestir Grange (1204).[13] The very substantial decline in the numbers of *conversi* by the mid-14th century saw the position disappear. There was still a 'master of the grange' (Brother Meurig) at Margam's Llanmihangel in 1358,[14] and the office is mentioned in retrospect at Tintern's Merthyr Gerain in 1388, but, by that time, that grange was under the control of a lay bailiff (William Walter).[15]

The Bailiff[16]

The bailiff, rather than the former granger, now became answerable to the cellarer, and some Tudor-period contracts drawn up on the appointment of bailiffs (by Cistercian houses) survive.[17] One of a bailiff's primary tasks was the collection of rents. This was made plain when John Edwards was appointed 'bailiff or collector of rents' for Valle Crucis in Bromfield and Iâl (1534).[18] The bailiff's duties consequently included the compilation of detailed annual accounts; two of which survive for Tintern's Merthyr Gerain Grange (1387–89).[19] The newly appointed bailiff of Strata Florida's Nant Bau Grange (1528) was obliged to make yearly to the monastery 'a good and faithful account'.[20]

Bailiffs also supervised work done on the demesne,[21] hired labourers and saw to their sustenance,[22] distrained for rents in arrears,[23] and arranged corrodians' perquisites (such as timber rights).[24] Jenkin Morgan, of Llantarnam's Magna Porta lordship, by virtue of his 'bayliship' held the court barons pertaining to the monastery.[25] Some bailiffs in remote areas had widespread territories to oversee – as those of Cymer and Strata Marcella. There is only one known example of a monk-bailiff: John York, who supervised Strata Florida's Abermiwl and Cwmdeuddwr Granges, and continued to do so after the Suppression (1539).[26]

The bailiff was a stipendiary official: Tintern's home bailiff received £3 p.a. (1535)[27] and Basingwerk's £4 p.a. (1536),[28] but not all received as much. The position had its perquisites, which might include residential accommodation (as for certain bailiffs of Margam[29] and Whitland);[30] distinctive clothing – monastic livery perhaps (as 'one tunic like the other servants' accorded Strata Florida's bailiff at Nant Bau; 1528);[31] a grant of land (Tintern's bailiff at Merthyr Gerain inherited eleven acres of meadow which 'the granger had by custom'; 1388);[32] or of tithes (Dore's bailiff in Gwenddwr was granted the greater tithes there; 1529).[33] As the Suppression drew near, and monastic control of their lands became perhaps less directly controlled, the bailiff of Tintern's Woolaston Grange [1530] received one third of it by lease,[34] whilst the bailiff of Strata Florida's Y Dywarchen [1538] demised it outright.[35] In this way, the abbey secured very necessary ready money *(Chapter 6)*, whilst its bailiff (William Voya) ensured his own future.

The Steward

In the later Middle Ages stipendiary lay Stewards took precedence over the cellarers with regard to the manorial courts. In earlier times, Stewards were men of modest rank: local landowners, like John Lovel at Margam (1402)[36] and John ap Wilcock for Tintern (1402).[37] In latter years, the Stewards were frequently (though rarely at Margam)[38] from the wealthier gentry. At Cymer, where no Steward finds mention, the last abbot, Lewis ap Thomas (described as 'a good husband'),[39] perhaps largely managed its estates himself. Aberconwy, by Tudor times, had three Stewards – one each for its lands in Anglesey,[40] Caernarfonshire (a Wynn of Gwydîr)[41] and Denbighshire (Maredudd ap Thomas and his family for nigh on a century).[42]

Several Stewards held several like positions simultaneously, not least Lord Ferrers, Chief Justice of south Wales,[43] who was appointed to six monastic Stewardships – including Whitland (1527),[44] Llanllŷr (1532)[45] and Strata Florida (1533).[46] In the Welsh Border and south Wales, the Herbert family played an influential role. Charles Herbert of Troy was Steward both at Grace Dieu (from 1524)[47] and of Tintern (by 1535).[48] Walter Herbert was appointed 'overseer' of Tintern's Border lands (1531),[49] whilst Thomas Herbert was the abbey's coroner[50] and bailiff of Moor Grange.[51] Another Herbert, George, was the last Steward of both Margam[52] and Neath.[53] The earls of Worcester were Stewards of Tintern's Norfolk lands (from 1514),[54] and of those of Llantarnam (from 1526),[55] as well as of Brecon and Ewenny Priories.[56]

Such Stewards were men of influence and power, which ought to have redounded to an abbey's advantage. This was not always the case; an earl of Worcester interfered with Tintern's fishing rights,[57] whilst William Brereton imprisoned at Holt the erring youthful Abbot of Valle Crucis (1535; *Chapter 5*). They were far from subservient to their monastic 'employers'. A few Stewards were appointed because of family connections, like John Stradling (Steward of Margam, 1459–87) – obviously related to Richard Stradling, cellarer there (1486).[58] Edward Pennant, a close relative of Basingwerk's Abbot, was its last Steward in Holywell.[59] A namesake of the last Abbess of Llanllugan, though not named as Steward, fulfilled that office.[60]

A principal duty of a Steward was to preside over the courts of his abbey. Lord Ferrers was appointed by Whitland as 'Steward in all our courts' (1527),[61] whilst Richard Williams was given 'full power and authority to hold all courts leet and hundreds', pertaining to Valle Crucis (1532).[62] Stewards of consequence, as men of affairs, normally employed deputies to fulfil their role. Thomas Herbert was 'deputy Steward' for Grace Dieu (c. 1524),[63] and, for Valle Crucis, Edward ap Rhys was 'sub-Steward' to William Brereton, Constable of Holt Castle (1535).[64]

The Clerk of Court

This office was fulfilled in Margam's lordship of Hafod-y-porth (from 1531) by John Vaughan and his son, David, with an annuity of 26s. 8d., supplemented by food, drink and stabling at the abbey on court days.[65] David, and his brother Hopkin, may have held a like position at Neath.[66] Courts required a *scribe*, whose usual fee was 2s per year,[67] and parchment for the court rolls: the purchase price of this at Tintern's Merthyr Gerain Grange (1388) was 2d.[68]

The Receiver

Several monasteries, in the last decade before the Suppression when much of their land was being demised, appointed Receivers or 'overseers',[69] who rivalled the Stewards in importance and prestige. At Tintern (Walter Herbert, 1532)[70] and Strata Florida (Richard Devereux, 1538),[71] were near relatives of the abbeys' Stewards. Neath's 'receiver-general' (William Hopkins, 1536)[72] held other monastic positions: he was Neath's bailiff in Gower and Neath,[73] and (from 1537) its forester-general,[74] thus building up a substantial annuity. In 1538, the abbey could not refuse him the lease of its fishing rights in the river Neath.[75] At Whitland, David Nash [a 'batchelor of law'] started his career in the monastery's service as 'adviser and scribe' (1535),[76] and was promoted (1538) to be bailiff, receiver-general and collector of rents.[77] Whitland's dissolution followed a few months later, but David Nash continued in the same capacity for the Crown.[78]

The Receivers were ultimately responsible for the collection of rents and the demising of land. In the last respect, they had considerable discretion. Strata Florida afforded Richard Devereux 'plenary powers', and valuable leases were made after his appointment *(Chapter 6)* – amongst them the grant to himself of Llangurig rectory, but, to be fair, he made a substantial down-payment.[79] David Nash presided over the wholesale carve-up of much of the Whitland estate.[80] After the Suppression, Stewards and Receivers had a ready claim upon their former charges: Strata Florida passed into the hands of the Devereux family,[81] and Tintern went to the Worcesters.[82]

Other Officials

These included *auditors*, like Edmund Turner, of Cardiff, for Tintern's distant Acle manor.[83] He was also, for a time, Neath's Receiver.[84] That house had John Righaun as 'auditor and *recorder*'.[85] Strata Florida's *notary*, John Gwyn, benefited by the demise to himself of the abbey's mill at Ffynnon O'er (1538).[86] The employment of steward, receiver, and sundry other stipendiary officials and servants, contributed to a salary bill which swallowed up nearly one-third of the gross income of Tintern (1535).[87] The proportion in other houses may have been lower (at Cwmhir perhaps only 12%),[88] but it was a situation far removed from the 12th century Cistercian ideals of self-sufficiency and manual labour.

Documentation

Running parallel with the administration of the monastic estates were the safe-keeping of original charters relating to land acquisition and leasing, and the careful compilation of the court rolls and grange accounts, and the accounts relating to the departments of the various religious and secular officials. Unfortunately, very little contemporaneous material regarding the Welsh lands of the Cistercians is extant. Margam is best represented, with some seven hundred deeds surviving, as well as twenty-three *charter rolls* – comprising copies, made chiefly in the 13th century, of original deeds.[89] Many monasteries favoured the copying of their charters and deeds into bound volumes. Such *cartularies* were referred to as a monastery's 'register', or 'register book', or (as at Whitland, 1535) the 'books of holdings'.[90]

In 1248, there was reference to the *Register of the Monastery* of Strata Florida,[91] and, after the Suppression, the tenants of its Dywarchen Grange told how 'the abbot set down [their] public agreement in writing in the Register Book of the monastery'.[92] Later, it seems the work expanded, for note comes (in 1600) of the former 'Register Books' of the abbey.[93] Unfortunately, neither they – nor the *Register of Neath* extant in 1707[94] – have survived. Various individual deeds, largely concerning demises, occur scattered amongst the manuscript collections of the National Library, the Public Record Office, and elsewhere. Noteworthy among them are two 'books' of leases by Dore of lands in Cantref-selyf,[95] and a small late 16th century collection of Cwmhir's leases.[96] Thacker's later surveys (1609) of some of Strata Florida and Whitland's former granges are also of importance.[97]

The position of cellarer was reflected in the *cellarer's rolls*, the office of granger in the *grange accounts*, the office of bailiff in the *reeve's accounts,* and the keeping of courts in the *court rolls* – all noted before. The bailiff's accounts for Porthcaseg, extant for 1392–97 and 1411–12, relate chiefly to rents paid by tenants, but also show the continuance of assarting.[98] One reeve of Strata Florida, of about 1475, used a portable slate talley (excavated to the east of the chapter-house) for recording payments in kind made by the abbey's tenants of Hafodwen.[99]

Whilst it is fortunate that a very small proportion of such accounts and rolls have survived, there is a complete dearth of any financial records for the constituent departments of the great houses: brew-house, guest-hospice, and the like. The loss of some material can be documented as the 'great charter' of Valle Crucis purloined about 1590;[100] the theft of deeds relating to Grace Dieu and its lands about 1615;[101] the suggested destruction by fire during the Civil War of many papers of Tintern stored at Raglan Castle;[102] and the disappearance of the *Register of Neath* kept at St Donat's in 1707.[103] Early 13th century deeds granting lands and rights in north Gwent to Dore, passed (only about thirty years ago) from a defunct Midlands firm to a Kentish dealer, and thus to an American university research library.[104]

The Seal in Cistercian Usage

Major demises, and grants of office and corrody, were accompanied by documentation under seal. A typical example was Whitland's lease of Aberelwyn (12 October 1538):

> In witness whereof to that one part of these indentures remaining with Llywelyn ap Morris, the forsaid abbot and convent have put their seal, and to that other part remaining with the abbot and convent the forsaid Llywelyn hath put his seal; given in the chapter-house. . . .[105]

Few deeds with monastic signatures survive; an exception is the lease by Strata Marcella of Penllyn Grange (1525), attested by its small community in their own handwriting.[106] After the Suppression, some monastic tenants refused to produce their title-deeds, perhaps because they had none. The Crown bailiff of Strata Marcella alleged of Nicholas Purcell's claim to two great pastures that 'he had no such lease, nor could the counterpane of such a lease be found'.[107]

Until the 14th century, the *seal* employed in attesting Cistercian deeds was the abbatial seal.[108] Cwmhir [*c.* 1235] felt constrained to explain that 'it is not the custom of our Order to have a common seal, except the seal of the abbot'.[109] Variance in practice led the General Chapter (1200) to prescribe: (i). That the abbot's seal was not to bear his personal name, and (ii) that the device was to be either an effigy of the abbot holding his staff *(Plate IX: 4)*, or else a cowled wrist with hand clutching the staff *(Plate IX: 1, 2)*.[110] There might be an intermediate stage – as at Margam[111] – the abbot's figure appears at only three-quarters length *(Plate IX: 3)*. From 1257, the figure of an abbot became the compulsory image, the 'hand and staff' device being employed upon the second ('lesser' or 'counter') seal now permitted *(Plate IX: 6)*.[112]

Common seals (like the 'chancery seal' of Tintern)[113] came to be used as a consequence of English statute (Parliament of Carlisle, 1306/07)[114] and papal provision (Benedict XII, 1335).[115] The General Chapter (1335) ordained that these new Cistercian common seals were to be 'made rounded, of copper, and engraved with the image of the Blessed Virgin' *(Plate IX: 7)*.[116] Henceforth, for greater security, the abbot's own name was to be engraved upon his seal *(Plate IX: 5)*.[117] In later centuries, the form of the counter-seal applied to the reverse of impressions of the common seal, varied greatly – like the two-headed eagle used by Abbot Richard Dorston of Strata Florida *(Plate IX: 8)*.[118] A late collection of Cwmhir's leases said, of the common seal used in Abbot Richard Vaughan's time (1516–30), that 'it ought to have upon the backside three small seals, every one of them *v* square'.[119]

Several common seals bore heraldic devices, like those of Margam (three clarions – for its founder, Robert, Earl of Gloucester, and three chevrons – for the Clares, lords of Glamorgan),[120] and of Valle Crucis (checky – the arms of Bromfield and Iâl.)[121] Even the poor house of Cwmhir possessed a seal bearing, at the base, a shield impaling the arms of Burgh and Mortimer, Barons of the March.[122] Four late medieval common seals – as that of Aberconwy[123] *(Plate IX: 7)* depicted an abbot kneeling before the Blessed Virgin Mary. The new seal used by Strata Florida after its restoration (1537) is said to have borne the arms of the king.[124]

Evidence of careful custody, commanded in 1238,[125] 1306[126] and 1335,[127] meant that at Cwmhir (1522) the common seal was:

> Wont to be kept in a chest with two locks, the key of one lock remaining with the abbot, and the other with one of the monks especially appointed for the purpose.[128]

This precaution was intended to guard against theft and any misuse of the seal, the then abbot being said to have used it to make irregular demises. It was later said that there was no common seal during his reign.[129] The last Abbot of Strata Florida was alleged to have made a pretended lease *after* his abbey's suppression, using 'a counterfeit seal, like the convent seal of the monastery'.[130] Theft and misuse of the common seal in times of unrest, against the best interest of an abbey, was known at Strata Florida (1428)[131] and Cwmhir (1442).[132] A common seal might have a working life of two centuries – from its engraving down to the Dissolution – this probably accounts for the poor impressions extant of Cymer's seal, much worn with age.[133]

Three Welsh Cistercian seal matrices are extant: a gilded brass abbot's seal of Grace Dieu, which was altered in the mid-fourteenth century (by the addition in the field of the words ET CONVENT) to become the house's common seal;[134] a fine silver matrix (of 15th century date) of an abbot of Strata Florida, with his personal name struck out – perhaps to allow a successor to use it;[135] and the late 13th century silver matrix of an Abbot William of Neath, found on the foreshore at Aberafan, Port Talbot, in 1999.[136] In the first two instances, the modifications may have been money-saving measures.

NOTES

1. Williams D.H. 1998, 269–71.
2. *Cartae Glam.* II, 312–13 (CCCXIV); *Rot. Claus.* I, 92.
3. Exeter Coll. Oxford, MS 1. ff. 75–78.
4. PRO, E 210/D.5724.
5. Williams D.H. 1998, 271–72.
6. NLW, Badm. Manorial 1575. Earlier (1406-07) he seems to have been its cellarer [NLW, Badm. Deeds (Group 2) 14824.
7. NLW, Badm. Manorial 1574.
8. *Fasti Cist.* passim.
9. PRO, C 115/K.2/6683, f. 94.
10. Birbeck T.T. 1973, 85.
11. NLW, Badm. Manorial 1575.
12. *Ibid.* 1576.
13. BL, Addit. MS 48984, f. 127r. *Cf.* Williams D.H. 1984. II, 256.
14. NLW, Penrice and Margam Ch. 229.
15. NLW, Badm. Manorial 1571. *Cf.* Cowley F.G. 1977, 259.
16. Also referred to, in later years, as 'beadle' at Margam and Neath: PRO, LR 1/228, ff. 81, 108.
17. *E.g:* PRO, E 315/104, f. 31 [Rhys ap William, Margam's bailiff at Resolfen.]
18. PRO, LR 1/213, mm. 6d–7r. *Cf.* NLW, Nanhoron Deed 347 [Ieuan Geoffrey for Aberconwy's lands in Talybolion, Anglesey.]
19. NLW, Badm. Manorial 1571. [For a summary, see: Williams D.H. 1965, 20–24.]
20. PRO, LR 1/228, f. 98d.
21. NLW, Badm. Manorial 1654, m. 3 ['No-one shall work or collect corn outside the lord's demesne, when the bailiff shews that there is work to be done for the lord within it'.]
22. NLW, Badm. Manorial 1571.
23. Pugh T.B. 1953, 28, 106.
24. *E.g:* PRO, SC 6 (Hen. VIII) 2496, m. 7d (Llantarnam), 5142, m. 1 (Basingwerk), E 315/92, ff. 97d–98r (Tintern).
25. PRO, E 315/93, f. 90d; SC 6 (Hen. VIII) 2497, f. 2d; *Cf.* SC 6 (Hen. VIII) 5142, m. 1 (Basingwerk).
26. Williams G. 1962, 368*n*; PRO, LR 1/228, f. 65; LR 6/152/4. He was also remunerated for his 'helps and services' to his brethren [PRO, E 315/102, f. 83; LR 1/228, f. 19.]
27. *Valor Eccl.* IV, 370.
28. PRO, SC (Hen. VIII) 5142, m. 6d.
29. PRO, SC 6 (Hen. VIII) 5155, mm. 13d–14r.
30. PRO, E 315/103, f. 82d.
31. PRO, LR 1/228, f. 98d.
32. NLW, Badm. Manorial 1571.
33. PRO, LR 1/228, f. 16 (transcribed in Williams D.H. 1966, 98); E 315/238, f. 64.
34. V.C.H. *County of Gloucester* X (1972) 106.
35. PRO, LR 1/228, f. 89; SC 6 (Hen. VIII) 4868, m. 1r.
36. Cowley F.G. 1977, 258; *Cartae Glam.* IV, 1186 (DCCCCLVII).
37. NLW, Badm. Manorial 1655.
38. Williams D.H. 1984. II, 258.
39. O'Sullivan J.F. 1947, 120.
40. PRO, LR 1/212, f. 300.
41. Hays R.W. 1963, 174–75.

42. NLW, MS 5908E; PRO, LR 1/212, f. 300.
43. Williams G. 1962, 367.
44. PRO, E 315/105, f. 100; LR 1/228, ff. 61d–62; SC 6 (Hen. VIII) 4903, mm. 32–33.
45. PRO, E 315/104, f. 122 (2nd nos.); E 315/210/54; LR 6/152/2;
46. PRO, E 315/105, f. 100; E 321/44/169; LR 1/228, f. 105d. *Cf.* Owen G.D. 1935, 374–76.
47. *Valor Eccl.* IV, 361. He had also been Steward of Monmouth Priory [PRO, E 315/94, f. 244].
48. *Valor Eccl.* IV, 370; *Monasticon* V, 272.
49. PRO, E 315/95, ff. 133d–134d.
50. *Valor Eccl.* IV, 371.
51. *Worcester Lands* II, 326.
52. PRO, SC 6 (Hen. VIII) 5155, m. 14r.
53. *Valor Eccl.* IV, 351. [He was assisted by Henry Hopkin.]
54. *Valor Eccl.* IV, 370; *Monasticon* V, 272.
55. PRO, E 315/105, f. 19.
56. Williams G. 1962, 367. *Cf. Worcester* Lands I, 43.
57. Williams G. 1962, 405.
58. Birch W. de Gray. 1897, 348, 350, 357–58.
59. *Valor Eccl.* IV, 438.
60. PRO, E 315/104, f. 177d (2nd nos.); SC 6 (Hen. VIII) 5257, m. 1r–2d.
61. PRO, E 315/104, f. 121d (2nd nos.); LR 1/228, ff. 61d–62; SC 6 (Hen. VIII) 4903, mm. 32–33.
62. PRO, E 315/93, f. 207.
63. PRO, E 315/100, f. 37d.
64. *Valor Eccl.* IV, 447.
65. PRO, E 315/91, f. 72d.
66. PRO, E 315/105, f. 37d; LR 1/228, f. 108.
67. *E.g:* PRO, SC 6 (Hen. VIII) 2497, m. 7d.
68. NLW, Badminton Manorial 1571.
69. William Edwards was so termed at Valle Crucis [PRO, E 315/100, f. 1d.]
70. PRO, E 315/95, ff. 133d–134d.
71. PRO, E 315/93, f. 60. [He was Lord Ferrers' son.]
72. PRO, LR 1/228, ff. 83d–84r.
73. PRO, LR 1/229, f. 15r.
74. PRO, E 315/103, f. 2d.
75. PRO, SC 6 (Hen. VIII) 5156, mm. 3d–4r.
76. PRO, E 315/103, f. 82d.
77. PRO, SC 6 (Hen. VIII) 4903, m. 33r.
78. *Augm. Rec.* 28–29.
79. PRO, SC 6 (Hen. VIII) 4868, m. 12r.
80. See Chapter 6.
81. Jones Pierce T. 1950, 33.
82. Williams D.H. 1976, 112.
83. *Valor Eccl.* IV, 370. Richard Goldsmith acted for its Welsh Border lands.
84. *Ibid.* IV, 351. [He was succeeded by William Hopkins in 1536.]
85. Birch W. de Gray. 1902, 153.
86. NLW, Cwrtmawr MS 873D, f. 45. [This lease, moreover, appears to have been a forgery.]
87. *Valor Eccl.* IV, 370–71.
88. Jones A. 1937, 273; Williams D.H. 1976a, 99.
89. 18 of the charter rolls of Margam, containing some 500 entries, are preserved in the National Library of Wales [Penrice and Margam Charters 288–96, 543–46, 2089–2093]. The remainder of the deeds (some 200) are mostly amongst the British Library Harleian MSS. This dual location results from the splitting up of Margam's estates since its dissolution [Birch W. de Gray, *A Descriptive Catalogue of Penrice* and Margam MSS I (London, 1893) iii–v.]
90. PRO, E 315/103, f. 82d.
91. Williams S.W. 1889, 128.
92. PRO, E 112/59/25 (Cardigan), mm. 1–2.
93. *Exchq. Proc.* (1) 95.
94. Lhuyd E. 1707. III, 121, 123–24; *Cf.* Birch W. de Gray. 1902, 34, 151; *Arch.* Camb. 1868, 41.
95. PRO, E 303/5, ff. 88–130 [original deeds], E 315/238, ff. 58–87d [copies.]

96. PRO, LR 2/76.
97. PRO, LR 2/205, ff. 200–217 (Whitland); ff. 216–26 (Strata Florida).
98. NLW, Bad. Manorial 1572, 1574, respectively. *Cf.* Cowley F.G. 1977, 257; Williams D.H 1976, 136..
99. Jones E.D. 1950, 2; Lewis J.M. 1976, 25–26.
100. *Exchq. Proc.* (1) 173.
101. *Star Chamber Proc.* 193, Williams D.H. 1976, 70.
102. *Cf.* Clark A. I (1980) 198.
103. *Arch. Camb.* 1868, 41.
104. They now form: MS Flat (Abbey Dore Collection), Dept. of Special Collections, Spencer Research Library, University of Kansas.
105. PRO, SC 6 (Hen. VIII) 4903, f. 3r.
106. BL, Addit. Ch. 10654; Williams D.H. 1976b, 162–63 *(illus.)*
107. PRO, E 321/19/100.
108. For greater detail, see: Williams D.H. 1993, 16; 1998, 108–11.
109. Beverley Smith J. (1970) 91.
110. *Statuta* I, 487, 251–52 (15, 17); *Cf.* I, 487 (1218/13), 493 (1218/45).
111. NLW, Penrice and Margam Ch. 6, 26, 27, 151.
112. *Codif. Cist.* (2) 297–98.
113. *E.g:* NLW, Badminton Manorial 1663, m. 1 (of 1524).
114. Clay C.T. 1928, 4; Heslop T.A. 1986, 282–83.
115. *Statuta* III, 411 (1335, *bulla* 2), 414–15 (1335, *bulla* 8).
116. *Statuta* III, 437 (1335/2).
117. *Statuta* III, 415 *(bulla 9)*.
118. Carmarthen Record Office, Lort Deed 11/554.
119. PRO, LR 2/76, f. 19d.
120. PRO, Harleian Ch. 75 A.48.
121. PRO, E 326/10141. [The supposed arms of Valle Crucis were: *between three* crosslets fitchy, a lion rampant charged with three bars, armed and langued; Lloyd J.Y.V. V (1885) 153].
122. PRO, E 329/244.
123. PRO, E 42/321; *Cf.* BL, Harleian MS 2038, f. 118 and NLW, Coed Coch MS 870 (Basingwerk); Carmarthen R.O. Lort Deed 11/554 (Strata Florida); Antony House, Cornwall, MS BD 13/102 (Strata Marcella).
124. NLW, Cwrtmawr MS 873D, f. 25. (No known example survives).
125. *Statuta* II, 185 (1238/3).
126. Clay C.T. 1928, 4.
127. *Statuta* III, 437 (1335/2), 441 (1336/1).
128. PRO, C 24/29 (Pt. 2).
129. PRO, LR 2/76, f. 19d.
130. NLW, Cwrtmawr MS 873D, f. 25.
131. Williams S.W. 1889, Appx. xl.
132. *Anc. Pet.* 503 (336/5874).
133. NLW, Dolrhyd Deed 1, Peniarth (Hengwrt) Deed 208.
134. The property of the Society of Antiquaries, it is on deposit at the National Museum of Wales. For its history, see: *Monm. Antiq.* IV (1980) 54. *Cf.* Williams D.H. 1987, 148 (No. 242), 1989, 77 (No. 242a).
135. On display at the National Museum of Wales. *Cf.* Williams D.H. 1993, 25 (D. 24).
136. Now acquired by the National Museum of Wales. *Cf.* Redknap M. 1999, 90.

CHAPTER 15

LAND RECLAMATION and WOODLAND UTILISATION

To ensure self-sufficiency of *food supply*, the 12th century Cistercians practised manual labour, helped by a low-cost labour force (the *conversi*), whilst the acquisition of large estates allowed most abbeys of the Order to become significant economic entities in their own right. In Wales, Cistercian economic life was conditioned by a troubled background, by previous land utilisation, and by relief and climate. When the Cistercians first came to Wales, much of the best land had already been settled[1] – though a fair amount was acquired by gift or purchase, whilst the large tracts obtained of steeply sloping, cooler uplands, encouraged sheep-rearing and wool production.

In the earlier Middle Ages agricultural endeavour was, at times, inhibited by warfare and raids, arson and rustling, and, in later centuries, by periods of misrule and local feuding. The swift diminution of *conversi* numbers (from the mid-13th century) led to progressive transformation of the monastic communities from directly involved farmers to financially interested landlords; a metamorphosis, though, that was never fully completed.

Glimpses of monastic diet can be gained in documentation, as for Tintern which supplied salmon to its daughter-house at Kingswood (1262),[2] sardines, salmon and fresh-water fish to visiting Bishop Swinfield of Hereford (1289),[3] and obtained pigs for itself from Merthyr Gerain Grange (1388).[4] It is clear from poetic evidence (undoubtedly exaggerated) that, still in the late 15th century, the bulk of monastic food came from its own lands. Tudur Aled (d. 1526), having enjoyed the hospitality of Strata Marcella, could praise 'its venison and wild game ... home brewed cider, mead and bragget'.[5] Guto'r Glyn (d. 1493) noted, extravagantly, that 'in the world never has been better lands for food than where grows the corn of the virgin Marcella'.[6] For Valle Crucis, archaeological evidence suggests – for the later Middle Ages when abstinence might be circumvented – 'a solid diet of bread, mutton, salt pork and bacon, cheese, eggs and river fish'.[7] Salt,[8] a medieval necessity, was brought to Margam by ship (1229),[9] obtained as a gift (1261)[10] and as a kind rent (1470);[11] a reminder that much monastic food came from rents in kind, and, indeed, from the rendering of tithes.

Land Reclamation

The marginal nature of Cistercian settlement in parts of Wales meant, very often, that much preparatory work was necessary before intensive agriculture could be undertaken. This was part of the expertise of the White Monks, as their critic, Gerald of Wales, acknowledged: 'Give them a wilderness or forest, and in a few years you will find a dignified abbey in the midst of smiling plenty'.[12] The diminution of the *conversi* in the later 13th century, however, saw some monastic land, once cultivated, revert to waste. There were, for example, no less than two carucates of uncultivated land at Cwmhir's Nant-yr-arian Grange in 1291.[13] The likelihood is that this was secondary waste, rather than wilderness pre-dating monastic occupation.

The Welsh Cistercians sought grants of secondary waste in secular ownership. This was true of Dore (1250) in north Gwent,[14] Basingwerk at Glossop (1290),[15] Margam (1281)[16] and Grace Dieu (1338) – the latter 'bringing back to cultivation' thirty-six acres [14.5 ha.] in the Forest of Dean.[17] The abbeys were involved in land reclamation, including secondary waste, down to at least the mid-14th century. The monastic economy thereafter saw considerable modification, and total reclamation may never have been achieved. 'Waste land' was noted on properties of Tintern (in Chapel Hill, 1438)[18] of Margam (in Hafod-y-porth, 1527),[19] and, shortly after the Suppression, on lands formerly of Llantarnam (at Magna Porta and in Wentsland).[20]

Woodland Utilisation

A medieval woodland supplied not only timber – for building purposes and as fuel, and other forest products – such as honey and nuts, it also afforded scope for pannage – the pasturage afforded to herds of pigs, and for the the hunting of wild game. The Welsh Cistercians, owning as they did large tracts of forest, took advantage of such a varied resource. When Cwmhir leased the whole Forest of Maelienydd from the Mortimers (1357), they gained access certainly to timber but also to *nuts* and *wild honey*.[21] Margam (at Resolfen)[22] and Strata Marcella (in Coed-y-mynach)[23] obtained honey in their woods. Strata Florida may have received it from sea wreck.[24] Tintern sold honey at 'Triket' (1291),[25] whilst Valle Crucis served it to its poetic guests.[26]

Another forest product was *bark* for the monastic tannery. Apart from its own lands, Tintern had rights to bark from part of 'the lower Forest of Went', rendering 2d. per load to the 13th century Earls of Pembroke.[27] The usefulness of monastic woodlands for *pannage* is reflected in manorial records and demises: the tenants in Porthcaseg paid Tintern 2s for this right (1372),[28] whilst Strata Marcella demised two holdings in Tir-y-mynach, the lessees being likewise obliged to pay 'tak[29] for hogs'.[30]

Abbots, like David ab Owain of Strata Marcella (1485–90), who rode to hounds and who put 'prime venison and wild game' on the tables of his guests,[31] must have appreciated the *hunting* facilities of his forests. The monks of Cymer did, centuries before. Llywelyn ab Iorwerth (1209) had granted them 'birds and wild beasts and animals of every kind',[32] but their abbot, in later defending the house's privileges (1348), laid claim to take 'falcons, sparrow hawks, and all other birds and beasts of the forest'.[33] This detailed assertion must indicate Cymer's actual usage of its woodlands in the mid-14th century. Dore had a heronry at its Llanfair Cilgoed Grange.[34] After the death of its poet-sportsman, Sawnder Sîon (d.?late 15th C.), it was regretted that Llantarnam would not have 'the flying of falcons around . . . no greyhounds or steeds'.[35]

The monks of Tintern (1302) had the right to hunt venison in part of Wentwood.[36] Those of Cwmhir, seeking restoration of rights interfered with by Roger Mortimer II, specifically requested of Edward II (*c.* 1322) that they might 'take their venison'.[37] Other indications of monastic hunting can be seen in the presence of 'hunting dogs' with Brother Geoffrey of Tintern at Alvington (1318),[38] and by the fine (16s.) imposed on the monks of Basingwerk (1353) for 'the lawing of their dogs in the Wirral'.[39] Its latter-day abbots had their greyhounds.[40] Red deer formed part of the diet for some at Valle Crucis,[41] and 'venison from the parks on the hillside' was laid before the guests of Neath.[42] There is more than an hint that venison stolen from the royal Forest of Dean was to be found at Tintern's Aluredeston Grange (1270),[43] whilst the abbey's woodward (1291) was said to be 'a notorious poacher'.[44]

Woodland Clearance: Assarting

Valuable as their woodlands were, one of the chief claims to fame of the White Monks lay in the zeal with which, reputedly, they cleared them – often as a necessary concomitant to the preparation of their land for farming, and grants of permission to the monks to fell trees were frequently accompanied by the corollary 'and to bring the land into cultivation'. This was true of licences to fell granted to Dore (for lands in Cantref-selyf; 1241)[45] and to Basingwerk (for Glossop; 1290).[46] An important inducement to assart lay in the privilege of the Cistercians, from 1132 on, of not paying tithes on land newly brought into cultivation *(Chapter 12).*

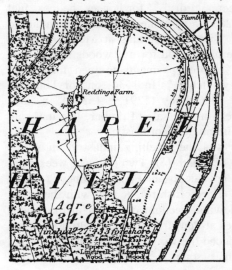

The potential for woodland clearance is demonstrated by many monastic charters, not least those of Tintern.[47] The actuality realised is reflected in place names and documentation. Two granges in Wales were originally (1291) known as 'The grange of the Assart'; one was close to Neath,[48] the other lay in proximity to Tintern *(Fig. 103).*[49] In later years, they were called Rhydding and Ruding *[Redding]* Granges respectively. Other usage of the Middle English word 'ridding' ('clearing') comes on other lands of Tintern, as 'Monks Redding' at Modesgate Grange (in 1476) and at Woolaston (1864).[50]

Records show assarting on the lands of Tintern on a greater or lesser scale down to the early years of the 15th century. The most notable instance comes in the heavy fine (£112 10s 0d) imposed upon the abbey (1282) for clearing 200 acres of royal

Fig. 103: Tintern's 'Grange of the Assart', still reflects woodland clearance. *(Reduced from the O.S. 6" Map [1ˢᵗ Edn.])*

forest without permission. This major assart probably resulted in Ashwell Grange (in the Forest of Dean).[51] West of the Wye, the rolls of Porthcaseg manor reveal a continuance of assarting by tenants of Tintern from 1263 down to 1393 – the process brought increased revenue to the monastery.[52]

Basingwerk, over the century of 1250 to 1350, made considerable assarts in England, especially in the Peak Forest – at least twice without royal leave.[53] As late as 1351, it made 'new ploughings' in the Forest of Wirral.[54] Research involving pollen analysis suggests that, on the lands of Strata Florida, there was extensive deforestation in the late 13th–early 14th centuries[55] – at a time when it was demanded of the abbey for security reasons. Lhuyd (1707) noted that the parish of Newton Nottage, where much land had belonged to Margam and Neath, was 'sometime a forest, as witnesseth ye register of Neath, but now ye barrenest soil of all Glamorgan'.[56]

The clearance of woodland was not only the result of the extension of arable land; it also resulted from the need for building material and fuel. Most monasteries, apart from their own resources, received timber rights on the lands of their patrons. Grace Dieu received royal gifts of timber to help in the rebuilding of the abbey after its burning in 1233. These included twenty trees from the Forest of Dean (1235), four oaks from Grosmont Forest (1240), and two from Skenfrith (1253).[57] That early grange buildings were largely in timber, and the varied usages of such wood, was demonstrated when Dore (1241) was allowed timber in Cantref-selyf 'for building, for fuel, and for making hedges', at its granges at Trawscoed and Wernddyfwg.[58]

Basingwerk (1285) was able, in the commote of Penllyn (Meirionydd) to take what it needed 'of the wood there, both green and dry',[59] for houses, hedges, fuel and other purposes.[60] It built in Glossop (1285) 'a carpentered house, one hundred feet in length and fifteen feet in width'.[61] Tintern's servants at Merthyr Gerain Grange (1388) sought 'in Wyeswood and Bernardswood for dye woods for the new byre'.[62] A later cellarer's roll (1411–12) records payments to men for felling timber, and for carrying wood to the abbey kitchen.[63] In 1536, one of Tintern's stipendiary officers was its wood-cutter.[64] The abbey (1291,[65] 1535),[66] as also Basingwerk (1291),[67] gained a small income from the sale of timber, like that sold (in 1427) to be made into shingles for repairs at Caldicot Castle.[68]

A major consumer of medieval timber was the smelting industry, in which several Welsh Cistercian houses were active *(Chapter 18)*. Two oaks per week were said to be needed for each of the forges of not far distant Flaxley Abbey.[69] When Grace Dieu (1227) bought Penyard Manor (Herefordshire), it was with the privilege of 'disafforestation', a technicality allowing freedom of action in the woods there. The abbey had two or three iron forges at Penyard.[70] Lead smelting at Strata Florida's Cwmystywth Grange certainly reduced the wooded acreage there. Leland (*c.* 1538) noted of the lead smelting there that 'some men supposed that it ceased because the wood is sore wasted'.[71]

Much clearance of monastic woodland was not of the monks' own volition or doing; it was sometimes forced upon them. The need to sustain easy military communications, and maintain law and order, in the years of the Conquest and thereafter, caused Edward I to order certain abbeys in troubled areas to make substantial assarts where his officers prescribed. Basingwerk (1278) had to uproot Gelli Wood (Flintshire) – the job took seven years.[72] Strata Florida was tardy in obeying the instruction given (in 1278) to 'enlarge the passes through its woods' so that they would be safe and open for travellers. The command had to be repeated in 1280,

1284 and 1300.[73] Basingwerk (1280) received a similar demand.[74] Leland summed it up in part, much later, when he noted of the lands of Strata Florida, that 'men for the nonys destroyed the great woods, that they should not harbour thieves'.[75]

Few religious houses did not suffer, at one time or another, from unauthorised encroachments on their woodlands, despite the privileges accorded by their charters. Edward I (1284), for instance, gave Aberconwy immunity from forest law, and forbade the cutting of its timber for the king's works.[76] Margam (*c.* 1240) saw serious depredations made in its forests by the family of Alaythur,[77] whilst the local populace wasted the woods of Cwmhir in Ceri (1252).[78] Llantarnam (1317) saw royal foresters 'sell by force' its woods of Glyn Ebbw and Gelli Ezurnoun.[79] Men felled and removed trees belonging to Neath (1423).[80]

Trespass in the woods of Tintern – by an apparently restless peasantry – was an offence repeatedly mentioned in the early 15th century rolls of Porthcaseg Manor.[81] Some of these encroachments came in the early post-Conquest period – when the monasteries were having to vigorously defend their liberties. Others followed in the wake of the Glyn Dŵr Revolt – when timber was needed for the repair of devastated buildings. Thus, in 1403, the priory of St Clear's was allowed timber from the woods of Whitland – which had taken the wrong side in the Rebellion –'to repair the houses of the priory.'[82]

Monastic tenants often had legitimate rights to timber, though restrictions on cutting might be placed. Tenants of Basingwerk could take 'reasonable firewood out of the great wood';[83] those of Llantarnam could take timber 'for burning, enclosing and building'.[84] Tenants of Cwmhir enjoyed 37½ acres [15 ha.] of unenclosed wood in the hills of Ceri.[85] A much greater area (566 acres [230 ha.] of underwood), was open to the tenants of Strata Marcella in Talerddig, but, as it had never been enclosed, 'the spring thereof was for the most part destroyed'.[86] The potential for such depredation by animals was underlined by Leland, who noted of some of Strata Florida's woodlands that 'goats so bit the young spring that it only grew into shrubs'.[87]

Woodland Conservation

Despite the several factors making for a reduction in their woodland acreage, in the later medieval period the Cistercians adopted a policy of forest conservation. This was shown in the appointment of stipendiary officials to safeguard their woodlands, in the injunctions of manorial courts, and in the restrictions placed upon tenants' timber rights. By the late 13th century, John of Aure was Tintern's woodward at Harthill (Gloucs.).[88] Hywel ap Thomas was its 'keeper' for Bernards Wood (1435),[89] and the abbey had its 'foresters' (1438, 1520)[90] and 'wood-cutter' (1535).[91] Margam had a 'forester' by 1349,[92] whilst, in its closing years, Neath appointed William Hopkins, already its receiver-general as also its 'forester-general'.[93]

Restrictions placed on tenants' timber rights generally asserted that it was only to be 'necessary timber',[94] and the amount cut to be at the deliberation of an abbey's bailiff or forester.[95] Margam allowed only dead wood, not 'green wood', for the repair of local sea defences (1349).[96] Tintern's manorial court for Porthcaseg ordained in one year alone (1528)[97] that timber was not to be felled in the monastery wood without special permission,[98] that depredations were not to be made in the woods of neighbouring fellow tenants,[99] and that goats, presumably because of the damage they might do, were not to be kept in the lordship.

The results of these monastic endeavours at woodland conservation find expression in detailed surveys written into several post-Dissolution Particulars for Leases.[100] Basingwerk had, locally, at least 300 oaks of 60 to 80 years' growth (mostly valued at 6d per tree),[101] whilst Grace Dieu had 200 oaks of 80 and 100 years' age.[102] Llanllugan nunnery, at Hydan, had 160 acres of woodland, one-quarter of which were set with oaks of 60 and 80 years' growth, and which were valued at 3s 4d per acre.[103] This substantial presence of oaks in monastic woods was attested soon after the Suppression, by the felling of 'twenty great oaks' at Llantarnam's Gelli-lâs Grange to build a ship for the navy.[104] No less than 116 oaks (sixteen of them 'great okes') were felled at Maenan *(Aberconwy*; 1540) to repair the Shire Hall in Caernarfon.[105]

Various other records bear witness to this wealth of monastic timber in Tudor times. Woodland was so plentiful in Llantarnam's former Wentsland Manor that, before the coming of the iron industry to Pontypool, it was 'of small or no value'.[106] John Leland (*c*. 1538) was fond of describing it. Most graphic was his account regarding Whitland: 'Bytwixt Cairmardin and Whitland is in no place such plenti of wood as is at Whitland cell, standing in a vast wood as in a wilderness'.[107] He must have been thinking of the local Cardiff Forest, later described (1594) as 'the chiefest wood for timber that Her Majesty hath in the said country'.[108]

Reminders of former Cistercian woodlands[109] still endure in lesser place-names: *Coed-y-mynach* – as in Bleddfa (Radnor) on former land of Cwmhir, at Llansantffraed Cwmdeuddwr – formerly belonging to Strata Florida; and (as 'Monkswood') on Gwent lands once of Tintern; and *Coed-yr-Abad (alias Coed-yr-abbot)* – like those woods so named in Bonvilston (formerly of Margam) and Carno (once the property of Strata Marcella). Halghton Wood (formerly of Valle Crucis) and Ravensnest Wood (once of Tintern) were also previously so known, whilst, south of Tintern's Rogerstone Grange, the term 'Prior's Grove' has become 'Briers Grove'.

Marshland and Drainage

Those abbeys with lands lying next to the Severn estuary and the Bristol Channel found a need – particularly with the continuing post-glacial rise in sea-level – to take protective measures, by banking (to keep sea water out) and ditching (to drain excess water away) their coastal marshlands. One of Tintern's chief holdings in the Caldicot Levels was Moor Grange *(Fig. 104)*, where (about 1245) the monks had leave 'to make a ditch about the boundary of their grange in the moor of Magor, and in the ditch they may do what they will, and the watercourses within and without they may order as they see fit'.[110] This licence gave potential for wild-fowling, whilst the keeper of nearby Aberweythel Mill was ordered to maintain the cut and sluice giving outlet to the Bristol Channel. Mention of the grange water-courses being repaired comes in 1493.[111]

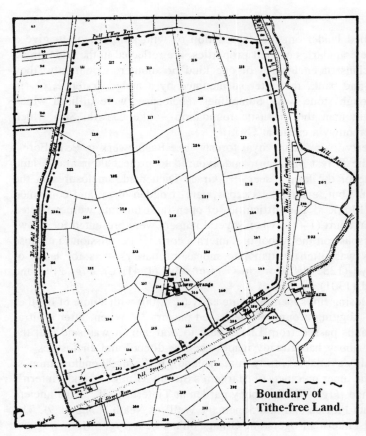

Margam had similar problems, in Afan Marsh, to those of Tintern. Severe inundation by the sea of these coastal lands was reported to the General Chapter (1336),[112] was said to render the land 'habitually sterile' (1383),[113] and to extend 'upwards of four miles' (1440)[114]; despite the banks raised, like a new *walda* in 1213,[115] and the duty laid on the abbey's tenants (at Theodoric's Grange) of maintaining the sea-walls and repairing the woodwork of the 'gouts'.[116] There is plenty of evidence of Margam ditching the marsh – from the early 13th century on,[117] and

Fig. 104: Tintern's Moor Grange, surrounded by reens and protected by embankments: the 'black wall' to the west, and the 'white wall' on the east.
(Reduced from: NLW, Magor parish tithe-map, 1847).

maintenance of ditches was a duty demanded of its tenants at Hafod-heulog Grange (1484).[118] On its tenants at Moor Grange (Cardiff; 1518) was laid the obligation to upkeep 'the sea-walls, weirs, ditches and fences'.[119] At this time too, Neath (1513) saw lands in Gower 'wasted by an inundation of waters'.[120] Water was not the only problem; encroachments by wind-blown sand (which eventually buried the town of Kenfig), wrought such havoc with Margam's lands that it gained the advowson of Aberafan church (1484) in reparation.[121]

Enclosures

Protection of reclaimed land from the depredation of wild animals, or to give a clear indication of the boundaries of their properties, are reflected in the widespread usage by the Cistercians of enclosures of one kind or another. Commonly, they consisted of a ditch and bank, the latter surmounted by a hedge or fence, or, in mountain areas, a rough stone wall. Sometimes, enclosures were utilised which were of earlier origin than the monastic foundation – like Clawdd Seri which enclosed part of Aberconwy's estate at Cwm.[122]

Abbeys with property in, or near, royal forests (like Basingwerk in Peak Forest and Grace Dieu in the Forest of Dean), endeavoured to protect their arable land from 'the free roving of the king's deer'.[123] Grace Dieu made enclosures in the Forest of Dean (1338), but, even so, its crops were 'trodden down and consumed by the king's deer' (1361).[124] The difficulties of open-field farming were reflected at Woolaston manorial court (1406), when several reapers were presented for allowing their beasts to trespass on the Abbot of Tintern's corn.[125] Permission to enclose newly asserted lands was often written into monastic charters – as for lands of Basingwerk in Penllyn (1285),[126] Dore in Cantref-selyf (1241; *Cf. Fig. 2*)[127] and Tintern in Wentwood (1301).[128]

The process of enclosing finds mention quite early (*c.* 1200) with a note of Brother Jewaf of Llantarnam 'digging around' some leased pasture.[129] When, after arbitration (1253) certain lands passed from Llantarnam to Margam, it was said that the monks of the former abbey had already made 'hedges, ditches and enclosures'.[130] Where stone was readily available (rarely in marshland), *walls* might enclose monastic properties – like the inner precincts of Margam's Stormy Grange[131] and Tintern's Merthyr Gerain Grange *(Fig. 95)*, the abbey garden at Tintern itself,[132] the ancient cemetery wall at Strata Florida and the 'Sanctuary Wall' of Neath *(Chapter 9)*. The 'Long Wall' bounded Tintern's Rogerstone Grange on the west *(Fig. 96)*.

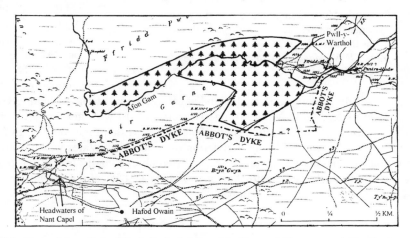

Fig. 105: Strata Marcella's 'Black Dyke' *(after Mr Howard Thomas and Mr Graham Thomas; overdrawn on a reduced version of the 1ˢᵗ edn. 6" O.S. Map).*

Remnants are still to be seen – though rarely surveyed, of enclosures like Clawdd Mynach (marking the northern extent of Neath's Monknash Grange),[133] and the Grange Ditch surrounding Cwmhir's Gwern-y-go Grange.[134] Of especial note are the bank and ditch enclosing Llantarnam's Llanderfel cell *(Fig. 64)*, and the Abbot's Dyke bounding Strata Marcella's Hafod-owain *(Fig. 105)*. This last, called 'the black dyke' *(c.*1185), perhaps because of its peat subsoil, consisted of a 15 ft. wide bank bordered by a ditch of equal width.[135] A well-defined grange enclosure is that protecting Waun-y-capel at Margam's Hafod-y-Porth Grange.[136] Adjacent field-names reflect the substantial remains of a partly stone embankment, presumably of medieval origins, forming the eastern boundary of Dore's Trawscoed Grange (Brecs; *Fig. 2*).

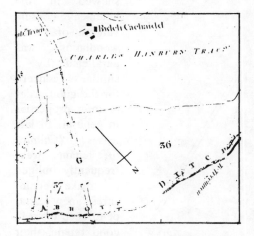

Fig. 106: The Abbot's Ditch, Celynog, Powys. *(Powys Archives, MCC I, 18).*

Evidence of former monastic enclosures comes in legal depositions well after the Suppression. One witness (in 1588–90) told of 'the print of an old ditch, called the "Abbot's Ditch"', at Dolwen in Strata Marcella's Talerddig Manor.[137] Another deponent (in 1608) talked of 'the abbot's ditch and abbot's meares' in Talerddig.[138] The still visible Abbot's Ditch *(Fig. 106)* which formed part of the southern limits of Strata Florida's Gelynog Grange – and, simultaneously, separated the parishes of Aberhafesp and Tregynog – was called (in 1638) 'a two-faced ditch',[139] and, by an Enclosure Award of 1815, 'a double ditch' *(Fig. 106; Map XIII-A).*[140]

Moated Sites

A variety of considerations- drainage, defence, wild animals, stock breeding – may account for the moated sites which have been observed at certain Cistercian granges – as at Caerwigau and Roath Dogfield, Cardiff (formerly of Margam),[141] and Tintern's Aluredeston Grange.[142] Very striking is the enclosure at Cwmhir's former Mynachty in Radnorshire, fed by a tributary of the river Lugg. Within the main enclosure, measuring some 110 x 55 metres with a four-metre wide moat, a small inner enclosure contains building foundations *(Fig. 107;* Plate XII-C). This may be the site of Cwmhir's Treburvaugh Grange.[143]

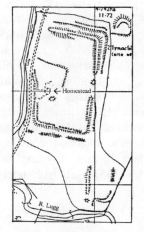

Fig. 107: Mynachdy, Powys. *(1st edn. 6" O.S. Map).*

At Tintern's Grangefield in the moor of Redwick, an outer ditched enclosure (*c.* 40 x 55 m.) stood around a smaller inner enclosure (*c.* 20 x 25 m.) on a slightly different orientation. It drained into the adjacent reen, leading 2 km. south to the Severn estuary.[144]

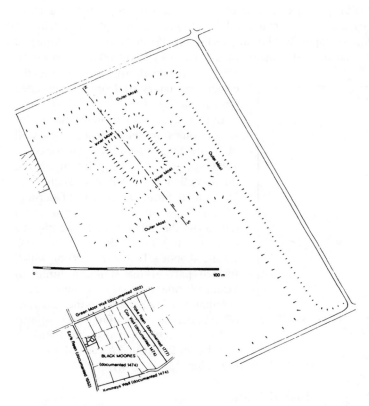

Fig. 108: Double Moated Enclosure, Grangefield, Redwick, Monm. *(S. Rippon; Monm. Antiq. XII: 1996).*

Maintenance of Enclosures

The interest which the Cistercians showed in the latter-day conservation of their woodlands was paralleled by a similar concern for the good order of their properties in general. In late leases *(Chapter 6)*, tenants were frequently obliged to make enclosures anew, and/or to keep them in good repair, their monastery often helping them with rights of hedgebote.[145] A tenant of Basingwerk (1498) had to enclose his holding 'With bushes, ditches and hedges, within four years';[146] a lessee of Strata Florida (1537) was to 'build, dig, and maintain in good order, a hedge and ditch between his land and the demesne of the abbey'.[147] On 1 October 1528, Tintern's manorial court of Porthcaseg gave all landholders one month to 'close their hedges' fronting the monastic demesne.[148] Even at this late stage, Basingwerk (1535) itself had 'lately made a new close in the mountains'.[149]

After the Suppression

Despite the centuries-old process of enclosing, much monastic land – especially coastal and mountain pastures – remained unenclosed when the Dissolution came. Later secular owners, trying to improve these properties, met resistance from tenants claiming common rights. New hedges and ditches made at Neath's former properties of Cwrt-y-carnau (1577)[150] and Coed Ffranc (1581)[151] were forcibly demolished by aggrieved parties. At much the same time, 'to make it more profitable', Sir Rowland Hayward 'ditched and trenched' the 400-acre [160 ha.] pasture of Gwern Valley (formerly of Strata Marcella). Alas! at five o'clock one morning some fifty disguised persons, with 'shovels, mattocks and other like weapons', broke down the new enclosures.[152] A precursor of the Rebecca Riots?

Boundary Marks

Stones were placed to mark the northern boundary of land granted to Margam (about 1190),[153] and the setting up of 'boundary marks' was part of a settlement between Margam and Neath (1249).[154] By 1519, a 'mear stone' had been set up to mark 'the new marsh' adjacent to Margam's Llanfugeilydd Grange.[155] A standing stone denoted the western limits of Neath's Walterstone Grange in Gower *(Fig. 109a),*[156] whilst a *wayside cross* may have stood on the northern boundary of its Gelligarn Grange.[157] The south-west boundary of Strata Florida's Celynog was marked by two crosses, as well as the 'Three Stones'*(Map XIII-A).*[158] Tintern's Trelech Grange lay between Llanishen Cross (on the west; *Fig. 109b*) and Tintern Cross (on the east); both crosses stood on monastic land and were very probably erected by the monks themselves. A mear stone (hardly discernible in 1677) separated the grange from the parish of Trelech *(Map XVI).*[159] Three boundary stone sites can be identified at the abbey's Rogerstone Grange *(Fig. 96)*. Aerial photography suggests boundary stones on the western border of Llanfihangel Llantarnam parish.[160] Densest west of the abbey's Llanderfel cell, they may derive from monastic concern to delimit clearly their property.

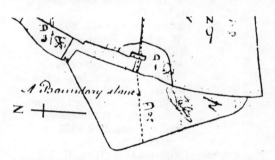

Fig. 109a: Boundary Stone at the western extremity of Neath's Walterstone Grange: SS 507899. *(From a Map by John Williams of Thomas Talbot's Estate (1785), held by the West Glamorgan Archive Service, D/D P 813; (a later tracing is D/D P 822).*

Fig. 109b: Llanishen Cross, Monm. *(NLW, Badminton Plans, Vol. 5 (1765):* ST 477029.

NOTES

1. Cowley F.G. 1977, 70.
2. *Kingswood Docs*. 216.
3. Stevens B.J. 10; *Bishop Swinfield's* Household Roll (Camden Soc. LIX: 1854, 62).
4. NLW, Badm. Manorial 1571.
5. Williams G. 1962, 380.
6. *Mont. Collns*. VI, 358; Price G.V. 1952, 271.
7. Barker, G. in Butler L.A.S. 1976, 123.
8. See also Chapter 18.
9. *Cal. Close R.* 1229, 203.
10. *Cartae Glam*. II, 648–49 (DCXIV).
11. Birch W. de Gray. 1897, 348.
12. King A. 1954, 3.
13. Cowley F.G. 1977, 261.
14. *MSS in BM* III, 711.
15. Jones A. 1933, 174.
16. *Cartae Glam*. III, 835.
17. *Cal. Fine R.* 1338, 65.
18. NLW, Badm. Manorial 1657, m. 2d.
19. Birch W. de Gray. 1897, 357.
20. PRO, LR 2/84, f. 108d; SC 6 (Hen. VIII) 2497, m. 3r.
21. Cole E.J. L. 1964, 32.
22. PRO, SC 6 (Hen. VIII) 5155, m. 3d. *Cf.* (for Neath) Birch W. de Gray. 1902, 62.
23. *Augm. Rec.* 463.
24. Williams S.W. 1889, 147.
25. *Taxatio Eccl.* 282b.
26. Price G.V. 1952, 164.
27. *Cal. Charter R.* 1307, 99.
28. NLW, Badm. Manorial 1652, m. 1r.
29. 'Tack': a due for pannage.
30. *Augm. Rec.* 463.
31. Williams G. 1962, 380; Lloyd H.W. 1879, 33.
32. *Llywelyn's Ch.* 56.
33. *Rec. Carn.* 199.
34. PRO, SC 6 (Hen. VIII) 7319, m. 10r (where 'herenshawys').
35. Alphonse Sr. T. 1979, 89.
36. *Cal. Charter R.* 1307, 105–06.
37. *Anc. Pet.* 55; PRO, SC 8/40/1972.
38. PRO, C 115/K.2/6683, ff. 93b–95b.
39. *Black Prince's Reg.* III, 118 (It is difficult to understand why, as 'lawing' meant disabling a dog).
40. Owen E. 1920, 54–55.
41. Butler L.A.S. 1976, 122.
42. Rhys Phillips D. 1925, 658–60.
43. PRO, E 32/28, 29 (Kind info. of Dr Cyril Hart).
44. Wood J.G. 1936, 214; Bazeley M.L. 1910, 265.
45. *Cal. Charter R.* 1241, 260.
46. *Ibid*. 1290, 373.
47. *E.g: Cal. Charter R.* III, 106.
48. NGR: SS 747989. The name of its Cwrt *Sart* grange had a like derivation.
49. NGR: ST 532994.
50. VCH, *County of Gloucester* X (1972) 110.
51. Bazeley M.L. 1910, 258.
52. As in NLW, Badm. Manorial 1639 (at Porthcaseg Court, 3 April 1263): 'Nawar takes a certain measure of land *which he has cleared without leave* ... and he gives 2/-, and one halfpenny annually *from the increased revenue*'. See, too: 1572 (of 1392–93).
53. Williams D.H. 1984. II, 272.
54. *Black Prince's Reg.* III, 49–50, 118.
55. Moore P.D. 1968, 1009; 1969, 374–75; Turner J. 1964, 83.
56. Lhuyd E. 1707. III, 124.
57. *Cal. Close R.* 1235, 44; 1240, 185; 1253, 11.
58. *Cal. Charter R.* 1241, 261.
59. Timber rights were sometimes restricted to dead wood: Williams D.H. 1998, 316, 318.
60. *Cal. Charter R.* 1285, 290.
61. Kerry C. 1893, 73–74. The abbot defended his rights in Peak Forest personally at the Pleas of the Forest held in Derby at Michaelmas, 1285.
62. NLW, Badm. Manorial 1571.
63. *Ibid.* 1575.
64. *Valor Eccl.* IV, 370.
65. *Taxatio Eccl.* 282b.

66. *Valor Eccl.* IV, 370.
67. *Taxatio Eccl.* 262.
68. Birbeck T.T. 1973, 85.
69. Bazeley M.L. 1910, 272.
70. *Rot. Litt. Claus.* II, 183; *Cal. Charter R.* I, 3 (and *Corrigenda* xiv).
71. *Itin. J. Leland* III, 123.
72. *Cal. Patent R.* 1278, 256; *Cal. Chancery R.* var. 186–87, 301–02; Jones A. 1933.
73. *Cal. Chancery R. var.* 171, 184, 293; *Cal. Patent R.* 1300, 499.
74. *Cal. Chancery R. var.* 187.
75. Williams S.W. 1889, Appx. iii.
76. Hays R.W. 1963, 72.
77. Birch W. de Gray, 1902, 71.
78. *Cal. Close R.* 1252, 143; 1254, 20.
79. *Anc. Pet.* 200–01 (119/No. 5948); Bradney J.A. III: Pt. 2 (1923) 225.
80. Birch W. de Gray. 1897, 341.
81. NLW, Badm. Manorial 1656.
82. *Cal. Patent R.* 1403, 298.
83. Owen E. 1920, 49.
84. PRO, E 315/104, f. 106d; SC 6 (Hen. VIII) 2497, m. 7d.
85. Morris E. R. 1893, 84.
86. PRO, E 318/Box 9/349; *Cf. Arch.* Camb. 1881, 215 (for Basingwerk)..
87. Williams S.W. 1889. Appx. ii.
88. Bazeley M.L. 1910, 257.
89. NLW. Badm. 1576. [Fig. 96].
90. NLW, Badm. Manorial 1657, m. 1d; PRO, E 315/92, f. 97d.
91. *Valor Eccl.* IV, 371.
92. Birch W. de Gray. 1897, 312.
93. PRO, E 315/103, f. 2d; SC 6 (Hen. VIII) 5156, mm. 3d–4r.
94. *E.g:* PRO, E 315/417, f. 7r.
95. *E.g:* PRO, E 315/104, f. 106d; E 315/92, f. 97d.
96. Birch W. de Gray. 1897, 311–12.
97. NLW, Badm. Manorial 1663, mm. 3–4.
98. 'As well to burn in houses as to make poop sails'.
99. 'Thou may no hack neither hew in other men's woods'.
100. Williams D.H. 1984. II, 276–77.
101. *Arch. Camb.* 1881, 215.
102. PRO, E 318/Box 13/569.
103. PRO, E 318/Box 9/349.
104. *Augm. Rec.* 132; *Cf. Early Chancery* Proc. 241.
105. Owen E. 1917, 82, *Cf.* 86.
106. PRO, E 134/13 Jas. 1/Mich.16 (Monmouth).
107. *Itin. J. Leland* III, 115. *Cf.* 71, 81.
108. PRO, E 310/34, f. 208.
109. For grid references: Appendix III (*Inventory*). For more examples: Williams D.H. 1984. II, 277.
110. *Cal. Charter R.* III, 104–05.
111. NLW, Badm. Deeds (Group 2) 14482.
112. Birch W. de Gray. 1897, 305.
113. O'Sullivan J.F. 1947, 123.
114. Birch W. de Gray. 1897, 343.
115. *Ibid.* 230, *Cf.* 311.
116. Gray T. 1903, 166; *Arch. Camb.* 1867, *Cartae Glam.* IV, 1267–68 (of 1349).
117. NLW, Penrice and Margam Ch. 2028; *Cf. Cartae Glam.* VI, 2209 (mention, in 1519, of 'the monks' ditch' and 'the monks' wall' at Margam's Llanfugeilydd Grange).
118. Birch W. de Gray. 1897, 349.
119. PRO, SC 6 (Hen. VIII) 5155, m. 9d; *Cf.* Cardiff Rec. I, 204–05.
120. *Episc. Reg.* II, 791.
121. Birch W. de Gray. 1897, 320–21.
122. *Welsh Assize R.* 301.
123. Cox J.C. 1905, 158.
124. *Cal. Fine R.* 1338, 65; *Cal. Patent R.* 1361, 11.
125. NLW, Badm. Deeds (Group 2) 14824.
126. *Cal. Charter R.* 1285, 90.
127. *Ibid.* 1241, 261; *Mon. Angl.* V, 556.
128. *Cal. Charter R.* III, 105–06.
129. BL, Addit. MS 48984 (fly-leaf).
130. Birch W. de Gray. 1897, 266–67.
131. Plan by R.E. Kay; Spurgeon and Thomas in RCAHMW, *Glamorgan* III: Pt. 2 (1982) 283 (MG 31).
132. NLW, Badm. Manorial 1657, m. 2d.
133. Called the 'monken dych' in

1567: Glam. Archives CL/Deeds I/34.

134. Jones M.C. 1893, 82–83, 86; RCAHMW I (*County of Montgomery*; 1911) 58 (No. 291).

135. Kind info. of Mr Graham Thomas.

136. RCAHMW, *Glamorgan* III: Pt. 2 (1982) 277 (MG26).

137. NLW, Powis Castle Deed 10250, f. 12; *Cf.* PRO, E 134/33 Eliz. Hilary 16 (Montg.).

138. PRO, E 134/6 James I, Mich. 42.

139. Williams S.W. 1889, 139; *Cf.* RCAHMW, I (*Montgomeryshire*; 1911) 175 (No. 896); Morris E. R. 1876, 306–14; 1898, 75–83.

140. Powys Archives (Llandrindod), MCC I, 18.

141. RCAHMW, *Glamorgan* III: Pt. 2 (1982) 76–78, 94–96 (MS 6), 113–14 (MS 13).

142. Ormerod G. 1861, 94; *Cf.* Gloucs. City Rec. Office D. 726/3, pp. 275d–279. For a possible moated site at Llantarnam's Bryngwyn Grange, see: Glamorgan-Gwent Archaeol. Trust. *Annual Report* (1978–79) 64–74.

143. RCAHMW, III (*County of Radnor*; 1913) 96 (No. 376); NLW MS 13453A, p. 134.

144. Williams D.H. and Rippon S. 1996, 46–48.

145. Williams D.H. 1984. II, 282.

146. Jones A. 1933, 177; Owen E. 1920, 50.

147. Owen G.D. 1935, 150–51.

148. NLW, Badm. Manorial 1663, m. 4d.

149. PRO, LR 1/212, f. 10; Hawarden R.O. Mostyn of Talacre Deed 197.

150. PRO, STAC 5/P.4/4(19).

151. PRO, STAC 5/C.24/15(24).

152. PRO, STAC 5/H.76/17(17); Owen G.D. 1972, 89–90.

153. *Episc. Acts* II, 670 (L. 208).

154. Birch W. de Gray. 1902, 76.

155. *Cartae Glam.* VI, 2209 (MDX).

156. Toft L A. 1988, 147.

157. RCAHMW, *Glamorgan* III: Pt. 2 (1982) 262 (MG 16).

158. Powys Archives (Llandrindod), MCC I, 18

159. Bradney J.A. 1904-, II: Pt. 2 (*Hundred* of Trellech; 1913) 132–33.

160. Williams D. H. 1990, 141 (Pl. 60c, deriving from British Coal).

CHAPTER 16

ARABLE AND PASTORAL FARMING

Cultivation

Tillage of the monastic estates finds only scanty contemporaneous references, and yet it was a basic activity, clearly implied by the estimated carucates of ploughland listed in the *Taxatio Ecclesiastica* (1291). The figures for Margam [53^1/$_2$] and Neath [40],[1] which then led the way, are impressive, and, using a modest equivalent of 80 acres per carucate, would give those abbeys 1700 hectares [4,200 acres] and 1300 ha. [3,200 a.] respectively. Whilst the largest of Whitland's granges contained only 4^1/$_2$ carucates, some of the farms of Margam and Neath could boast 8 to 10 carucates.[2] The individual fiscal value of a carucate varied, for reasons not always apparent. Whilst three of Tintern's granges (Merthyr Gerain, Rogerstone and Ruding) saw each carucate valued at £1, the six carucates at another (Trelech) were only worth 6s 8d. apiece.[3]

All granges practised, of necessity, a mixed economy, but, even so, some were predominantly arable farms and the 'bread-baskets' of their monasteries. Llantarnam's Pwl-pan Grange with 12 carucates ascribed (1291) and Strata Marcella's home grange (7 carucates) were clearly amongst these.[4] Abbeys sited in mountainous areas obtained granges more favourable for cultivation at some distance away – like the Llŷn properties of Cymer, the Lugg, Teme and Wye valley lands of Cwmhir, and the coastal farms by Cardigan Bay of Strata Florida. Despite their arable potential, in years of bad weather, corn might have to be bought – as by Margam (for the starving peasantry in 1189),[5] and by Neath (in England in 1234).[6]

Glimpses of monastic farming are rare – like the note of the monks of Cwmhir reaping corn on their Carnaf and Gabalfa Granges (1231),[7] and those of Tintern ploughing, 'at his request, and not of any duty', the local lands of Richard de Clare (6th Earl of Gloucester; 1230–62).[8] Cultivation of corn is also evidenced, for Tintern (1535), by its distribution at the abbey, and on its granges, by way of alms. The monastery numbered amongst its stipendiary officials its 'grain receiver'.[9] Poets bore witness to 'the wheat land' of Strata Marcella,[10] and 'the white bread' of Maenan.[11]

Cultivation might well be assisted by marling or liming the soil. Margam, early on, received a grant of marl in Kenfig,[12] and Neath in Marcross.[13] Lhuyd (1707) remarked that land given to Neath in Newton Nottage was 'by ye monks so manured that it was brought to tillage'.[14] For Ashwell Grange, Tintern could take lime in Tidenham.[15] Its servants at Merthyr Gerain Grange (1388) spread manure.[16] The very sandy soils of its Trelech Grange also probably needed improvement *(Map XVI)*. The labour services expected of tenants on Strata Florida's Y Dywarchen Grange in post-Suppression times, and presumably in monastic days also, included 'the casting of dung'.[17] When William Franklin (1258) mortgaged an acre of land to Margam, he was entitled to redeem it on returning the mark paid him, 'and the cost of betterment'; clear indication that the monks intended to 'improve' the land so acquired.[18]

The damp and cool upland nature of much of Wales meant that *oats* were significant on all the granges of Strata Florida, and loomed large amongst the kind rents paid by its tenants *(Fig. 77)*,[19] as also by the tenants of Cwmhir in its home manor of Golon – situated entirely above 250 m.[20]

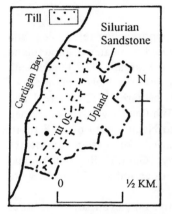

Fig. 110: Morfa Bychan Grange. [The Physical Background].

Particular brands of oats, of low quality and probably for fodder, were the 'hors ottes' and the 'horschettes' grown by some of the tenants of Margam[21] and Llanllŷr,[22] respectively. *Wheat* and *barley* were restricted to more favourable lands. Both were important (despite the dolomitic soils) at Merthyr Gerain Grange (Tintern; 1388,[23] 1539),[24] whilst wheat was a substantial commodity at the 'bread baskets' referred to above.[25] *Rye* was another monastic crop.[26] Morfa Bychan and Morfa Mawr Granges, adjacent to the sea, had the mildest and driest weather and longest growing season of all Strata Florida's granges, and consisted in part of raised beaches bearing relatively fertile boulder clay soils.

Milling

Grain production by the Cistercians was reflected in their interest in the medieval milling industry *(Map XIV)*. The possession of mills, except for their own use, was early abjured by the White Monks,[27] but, by the close of the monastic period, the Welsh abbeys owned nearly ninety water-mills in the Principality and the immediate Border, together with a few walk-mills and wind-mills. Neath, Strata Florida and Whitland had ten or so water mills apiece. A few mills were granted in early days (as that at Talybont to Aberconwy).[28]

Evidence of monastic mill building stretches from the construction of Llantarnam's Maes-tir Mill (1204)[29] through to 1305 – when Aberconwy built a mill at Rhedynog-felen, diverting the Gwyleth stream in the process,[30] down to the abbacy of Thomas Pennant at Basingwerk (1481–1521). Gutun Owain told, in exaggerated fashion, how Pennant: 'With mills has filled every available glen and hill'.[31] Even the decadent Strata Marcella (1536) had a mill at its home manor said to be 'newly built'.[32]

In Tudor times, renewed interest in milling is reflected by several abbeys – like Cymer (at Maes-y-poeth),[33] Dore (at Gwenddwr),[34] and Strata Florida (at Blaenaeron),[35] demising land for layfolk to build mills upon. Whilst a number of Cistercian mills were demised well before the Suppression – as that of Tintern at Merthyr Gerain by 1303,[36] others were retained 'in the abbot's hands', like that of Llantarnam at Abercarn (1536).[37]

Late leases reveal something of the mechanism and waterworks of the monastic grinding mills. Margam, in leasing Garw Mill, with 'a course of water sufficiently to drive the mill, and a pond', expected the lessee to keep it in good order, and 'able to grind and shell all manner of corn'.[38] Whitland (1538), demising its home mill at Hên Dy Gwyn, provided the tenants with the necessary 'mill stones, wheels, ronge, cog, trowys, mill brasys and royffe walls'.[39] Tintern's Angidy Mill (1525) had its dam, flood-gate, water-course, mill-stone and hammer;[40] its mill on Trelech Grange stood by the Angidy brook, at a point where rapids created a natural fall of water *(Map XVI)*. Basingwerk's 'nether walk mill' had its 'stock, water-works, and ansel house'.[41]

The miller generally lived on the premises or close by,[42] so, Strata Florida (1533), demising its Fulbrook Mill, envisaged 'a place for erecting a small chamber in the confines or boundaries of the mill'.[43] Also adjacent to the mill was 'the place for winnowing the corn' (as at Strata Florida's Pyran Mill – 1524),[44] still noticeable at Cwmhir's Nant-yr-arian Grange and Margam's Hafod-y-porth Grange.

A water-mill and its 'poor relation', the fulling or 'tucking' mill, were often proximate, using as they did the same water-supply. Margam's mills in Llanfeuthin *(Fig. 112)*, the corn 'monkynmill' and the fulling 'tokyngmill', both lay on Nant Llancarfan.[45] At Fulbrook, Strata Florida owned 'one mill for all kind of corn, and the other for the fulling art'.[46] Basingwerk's immediate complex included the 'upper' and 'nether' corn mills, and two fulling mills; all four shared the same source of motive power.[47] Similar proximity of 'hen felin' (old mill) and 'pandy' (fulling mill) is to be observed elsewhere[48] – as on properties of Aberconwy (at Voelas),[49] of Llantarnam (at Magna Porta),[50] and of Whitland (at Rhuddlan Deifi).[51]

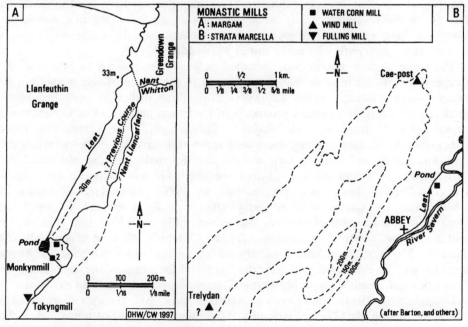

Fig. 111: Some Welsh Cistercian Mills.

A reliable water-supply was essential, and traces of former monastic mill leats are still to be seen – as at Strata Florida's Aberduhonw Grange. At Tintern's Rogerstone Grange *(Fig. 96)*, a relatively small catchment area meant that the corn mill received water from several sources. The principal leats derived from springs in the west, and by diversion from a south-flowing stream to the east of the grange.[52] At the abbey's Trelech Grange *(Map XVI)*, a natural, once lake-filled, depression probably ensured a regular flow of water. To service its Talybont Mill, which lay a little distance from Gelliniog Grange, Aberconwy received 'the water and ditch of Sarn-y-felin'.[53] In Hiraethog, the monastery paid a water rate of 4s. to the Crown (1493) for 'use of water at Llanfair Mill'.[54]

Several Cistercian water-mills were referred to as 'the abbot's mill', but some bore names relating to a monastery or a grange, like the 'Monkynmill' (of Margam in Llanfeuthin) and the 'Court Mill' (of Whitland in Maenor Forion). Others gained their nomenclature from the adjacent stream, like Margam's Garw Mill (in Llangeinor), and its 'Fredulles Mill' (in Hafod-y-porth, after the Ffrwdwyllt). Whitland's 'Milliner Grymm' (in Llanwinio) derived its name from the early grange of Cilgryman.

From the early 13th century onwards, the monastic mills became a source of revenue initially prohibited by the rules of the Cistercian Order. This was inevitable with the growth of a tenantry, whose obligations usually included 'suit of mill'. Indeed, in 1224, the Earl of Pembroke confirmed to Tintern not only its possession of Angidy Mill, but also the right of grinding his local corn, and that of his men.[55] After the Suppression, it was said that at Llantarnam's home mill 'all tenants of the abbey, and all other resiants adjoining, time out of mind, have used to grind all their corn'.[56] There are many such examples – as for Margam's tenants in Bonvilston who owed 'suit of multure' at Llanfeuthin Mill,[57] and Strata Florida's tenants in Cwmystywth who made suit at Pyran Mill.[58]

The value of 'suit of mill' was indicated in late leases granted by Whitland. At Crugerydd Mill, each tenant had to pay a toll to the lessee of one bushel out of every twelve ground;[59] at its Llanwinio Mill, three dishes of corn had to be rendered for every two bushels ground.[60] In 1615, and perhaps in earlier monastic times, 'suit of mill' at Vale Royal's 'Parson's Mill' at Llanbadarn Fawr (Aberystwyth) entailed grinding one's corn at the mill, carrying timber to repair the mill, and cutting and carrying turfs and the like 'for making of the mill pond'.[61]

A few former Cistercian mills, heavily restored, are now domestic dwellings – like Llanllugan's home mill (as recently as 1976), and Margam's mills in Llanfeuthin. Its Cryke Mill is today largely a folly erected in 1830–35. Occasionally, a later wheel survives – as at Strata Florida's Nant Bau Mill, or the outline of the wheel emplacement – as at Cwmhir's Nant-yr-Arian Mill. At Tintern's Merthyr Gerain Mill, a solitary mill-stone lies hidden in a hedge; at Strata Floridas's Rhyd Fendigaid Mill only rough ground indicates its site. The medieval foundations of Neath's Melin Mynach at Gorseinion have lately been excavated.[62]

Dilapidations affected mills even in monastic days. Aberconwy's Cornwy Llys Mill was 'broken' in 1291.[63] Two mills of Whitland were 'out of repair' when the Suppression came (1539).[64] Much more recently, some former mills have been demolished on safety grounds (as Tintern's Rogerstone Mill, about 1976), or to provide land for building purposes (like Whitland's Llanwinio Mill in 1976). Some mill sites are now only traceable by place-names – like *hen felin* – on large scale maps, or field-names – such as *cae felin* – on tithe and estate maps.

In not a few cases, the phenomenon of 'industrial inertia' has meant that other forms of industry have replaced the original corn-milling, or, at least, utilised the same water force. This was true of the Elizabethan brass mills at Tintern, and of the late 18th century copper and brass mills near Basingwerk.[65] Light industry still occupies the sites of Neath's Melin Mynach on Cwrt-y-carnau Grange (the Gorseinon Packaging works), of Llantarnam's Maes-tir Mill (a plastic coating works), and of Margam's Garw Mill (Ofrex Engineering Ltd.).

Wind-mills

A few Cistercian abbeys possessed wind-mills, where the situation in exposed localities favoured their erection.[66] Aberconwy owned one or two in maritime positions in Anglesey, and Basingwerk three or four overlooking the Dee Estuary – in Holywell and in the Wirral. In the late 17th century, Aberconwy's 'towre melyn wynt' at Rhuddgaer was converted into a dower-house.[67] Strata Marcella had one, if not two, wind-mills on low hills overlooking the Severn flood-plain. Both are remembered in their field-name of *Cae post*; the one (at Trelydan) having been blown up in 1916 – to allow road construction.[68] A possible Cistercian spread of post-mills – where the mill revolved on a central post to face the wind – has been argued.[69]

Barns and Granaries

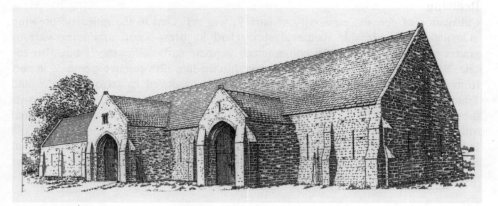

Fig. 112: Monknash Grange Barn (reconstruction).
(Crown copyright: Royal Commission on the Ancient and Historical Monuments in Wales, 1982).

Barns also indicate the significance of arable farming. Strata Florida had a barn of note at Aber-miwl (1263);[70] that at Morfa Bychan is now a caravan camp club house. Llantarnam may have had a barn at St Dial's,[71] but the ruined barn at the monastery site may be post-dissolution in date.[72] The keeper *(preceptor)* of Tintern's granary at Merthyr Gerain (1388) spent 6d on food for men who had caught a thief and held him overnight.[73] Lhuyd (1707) noted Whitland's barn at Maenor Forion.[74] The outstanding stone-walled Cistercian barn in Wales was at Neath's Monknash, measuring (internally) 64.4 m x 10.4 m.[75] Former barn sites are suggested by the Welsh place-name, *ysgubor* – as adjacent to Cwmhir's Mynachty-poeth,[76] and as occurring in Ysgubor-cwrt ('Skybbercourt' ['the Court Barn'] of Llantarnam)[77] and, formerly, in Ysgubor Fawr (the 'Great Barn' of Strata Marcella, now Dyer's Farm, Pool Quay).[78]

Gardens and Orchards

Horticulture had its place on the estates of the Cistercians. Tintern had a 'great orchard' at the abbey,[79] whilst it allegedly hanged a man at Woolaston (*c.* 1200) for stealing its apples there.[80] Cymer had no less than three orchards on site;[81] at Neath there was a meadow called 'Prior's Orchard'.[82] Guto'r Glyn (*d.* 1493) praised the provision of fruit for the guests at Valle Crucis; 'A thousand apples for dessert . . . grapes, the *fruit of orchards'*.[83] Might viticulture have been attempted on the terraced slopes at both Dore's Gwenddwr[84] and Llanfair Granges? – those at the latter had a southerly aspect *(Fig. 94)*. Tudur Aled referred to 'Aberconwy, field of vines'.[85] For vegetables, Tintern had two gardens at the abbey, one being termed 'the lesser'. It lay west of the monastery, between the Angidy and Talbot brooks.[86] Gardens were found, too, on granges – like Margam's Llanfeuthin (1291),[87] as well as at Tintern's Rogerstone (1291)[88] and Merthyr Gerain (a walled garden; 1388).[89]

Brewing

Cultivation of cereals, especially of barley, was reflected in the monastic brewing industry. Every sizeable medieval abbey had its brew-house producing various grades of ale, useful for the communities at their daily 'drinkings', but also for sale.[90] The troubles with the Welsh *conversi* in the late 12th century stemmed in part from excessive consumption of beer.[91] Margam produced its 'strong beer'[92] and Tintern its 'better beer',[93] but it also had 'dregs' left over, once stolen from its brewery (1445).[94] There was poetic praise for the 'home brewed cider, mead and bragget' of Strata Marcella (*c.* 1490).[95] Basingwerk sold beer in Holywell (1347).[96] In their last decades, if not long before, a 'tavern-house' stood at Llantarnam's Pen-rhys cell,[97] and an ale-house within the precincts of Strata Florida,[98] whilst grain for malt was ground in the mills of Vale Royal and Whitland.[99]

Mixed Farming

There were Cistercian granges in Wales on which arable farming predominated, and others where the key-note was pastoralism. In other words, there was a mixed economy *within the total economy of individual abbeys*. This specialisation was possible because most monasteries came to acquire lands with a variety of conditions of relief, soil and weather. [This mixed economy was demonstrated when (about 1310) Tintern was able to help restock the garrison of Chepstow Castle with wheat, oats, oxen, pigs and sheep].[100] Further, there was a mixed economy, to a greater or lesser extent, *within the bounds of every individual grange*. This was enhanced by many a grange including markedly different aspects of slope, soil, and even altitude, within its borders. All this (as well as the medieval needs of a self-sufficient society) contributed to a mixed agricultural economy.

Monasteries sited in upland areas – like Cwmhir, had properties which were largely oat-producing and pastoral (like its Golon Manor), but, as noted before, had their 'bread-baskets' in more favourable areas, often at some distance – like Cwmhir's Gabalfa Grange by the river Wye. Aberconwy balanced the produce from sheep-rearing mountainous areas – like Nanhwynan, with arable land and meadow (for cattle) at lowland granges – such as Bodgedwydd and Creuddyn. There might be differentiation between the pastoral products of granges, kind-rents yielding to Whitland wool and lambs from Maenor Forion and Rhuddlan Deifi, but much cheese from Iscoed and Castell Cosan, both closer to the abbey *(Fig. 78)*.[101] There was varia-tion in cereal products on the lands of Margam, some granges being more important for kind-rents of wheat (like Llangewydd), others for barley (as Whitecross).[102]

Cymer's grange at Neigwl in Llŷn (1350) returned a variety of kind rents: wheat, oats, pigs, butter, cheese, herrings.[103] Cwmhir's Gabalfa Grange (1387) returned rents of wheat, but also had some 250 sheep.[104] The remaining demesne lands of Tintern at Woolaston Grange (1536) possessed '12 oxen, 2 wains, 2 sound ploughs, 2 ox harrows, 2 pairs of horse harrows, with all manner of materials for husbandry; 4 cows, 1 bull, 1 boar, 1 sow, 6 piglets, 1 gander, 2 geese, 1 cock, 4 hens'.[105] Diversity indeed!

One of the clearest examples of differentiation of production within a grange was Mefenydd Grange, Strata Florida's leading property *(Map XV)*. A mixed economy (though no wheat) held sway in the western part of the grange – with the cultiva-tion of oats taking place up to about 250 metres, but with sheep rearing and wool production completely dominant in the steeper, higher, cooler and damper eastern section.

Merthyr Gerain Grange, Monmouthshire

This important grange of Tintern *(See p. 202 and Fig. 95)*, is almost the only Welsh Cistercian grange with detailed annual accounts to survive,[106] and then for two years only (1387–89). The accounts give a vivid picture of the agricultural life there, after the hey-day of the *conversi*, but whilst the grange – supervised by a bailiff and a few other full-time servants – was still under the direct control of the abbey. The bailiff's authority extended to detached abbey lands lying further south and south-west, as in the pastures of Broadmead and Llandevenny.

Many other labourers were hired to work on the demesne lands as occasion demanded, as in times of ploughing, sowing, hoeing – 124 labourers on one day alone, harvesting and threshing – the latter sometimes performed by women. Wages were not high, and varied according to the occupation performed: 1d. per day for ploughing (perhaps a relatively short autumn or spring day), 1½d. for spreading manure, 2d. for harvesting, and 4d. for making hay-stacks in the autumn. Food, including beer, was frequently provided for the workers 'lest they go from the field to their own'. There was sensible management!

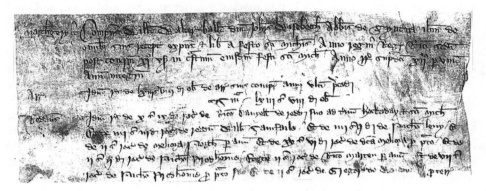

Fig. 113: The commencement of the Merthyr Gerain Grange Accounts (1387) – telling of rents received by the bailiff.   *(National Library of Wales, Badminton Manorial 1571).*

The accounts show an annual production of over 30 qtrs. of wheat and barley, mostly retained for the monks' own use, but with some kept for seed or sale. Whilst some stock was also sold, there is specific mention of ten pigs being slaughtered and sent to the abbey. There was expenditure on machinery; the mending of 'iron ploughs' and the greasing of wagons. The grange lands were now mostly leased out, and a considerable part of the income was derived from the rents payable. Leaving aside produce allocated directly to the monastery, the financial value (of receipts over expenses) was negligible.

Miscellaneous expenses included: salt bought for the servants, and bread and beer for a visit by the abbot; and wages to servants bringing in turfs for use on festival days. The old byre was being repaired, and a chamber made therein for the keeper, who used candles in wintertime. A new (thatched) byre was being constructed, and a key bought for its door. The gate of the sheep-cot and the stable roof were being repaired; the hen-house and the vaccary thatched. All this emphasises the mixed economy of any grange.

Pastoral Farming

In the late 12th and the 13th centuries, pastoralism may have formed the mainstay of Cistercian economy in Wales. Flocks ran into very large numbers, and – as at Basingwerk[107] and Strata Florida[108] – were under the care of monastic 'keepers', responsible *conversi* appointed to this task. Animal rearing remained important throughout the Middle Ages. Margam (1336) 'relied for support mostly' upon its animals;[109] a tenant of Strata Florida (at Blaenaeron, 1504) was 'not to plough his holding';[110] to the very end, Strata Marcella retained its 400-acre [160 ha.] Gwern Valley pasture 'only for cattle kept for the provision of the monastery'.[111] Most granges had a mixture of animals, like Dore's Llyncoed (Gwent; *c.* 1230): 'oxen, cows, sheep and pigs',[112] but on the more mountainous granges sheep, nimble of foot, presumably predominated.

In earlier monastic days, animals and their produce might be used in barter. Cows and lambskins formed part of the payments made by Margam and Neath in obtaining quitclaims and leases of land, whilst (as late as 1255) two cows were included in the price Strata Florida paid for its great bell.[113] In later centuries, there was a cut-back in the direct control of Cistercians over their pastures, pasture land even being sold – as by Cymer (1291)[114] and, at Merthyr Gerain (1388), by Tintern.[115]

A pastoral economy was not without its difficulties and hazards – as for Margam, the local Welshry (1223–24) killing hundreds of its sheep,[116] and a 'terrible mortality' affecting its animals (1336).[117] Rustling was not uncommon, and in times of national disturbance or local feuds, or contentions for an abbacy, Basingwerk (1282),[118] Grace Dieu (1396)[119] and Strata Florida (1428)[120] so suffered. Pasture rights formed the basis for disputes between monasteries and neighbouring landowners, or even between abbeys themselves *(Chapter 1)*.

The basis of the White Monks' pastoralism lay in the considerable acreages of upland which they possessed, and their extensive rights of common of pasture beyond their own properties. Amongst Aberconwy's mountain pastures were around 12,000 acres [nearly 5,000 ha.] on the slopes of Snowdon,[121] whilst Strata Marcella in Talerddig had 2,000 acres [800 ha.] in Trefegwlys parish alone.[122] Leland (*c.* 1538) told how 'all the mountain ground between Alan[123] and Strata Florida belongeth to Strata Florida, and is almost for wild pastures and breeding ground'. He added that its pastures were free to its tenants.[124]

Strata Marcella's lands at Capel Dolwen, outside the Abbot's Ditch, 'did lie open, and were used as commons by the neighbours'.[125] Valle Crucis had 'thousands of acres of limestone grazing' on the Llandysilio, Maesyrychen and Ruabon Mountains'.[126] Litigation concerning Cwmhir's former extensive sheep-walks in Cwmbiga Grange (1585) centred, in part, on whether the grange could sustain 2,000 sheep or under 1,000.[127] An indication of the potential numbers involved.

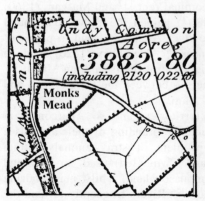

Fig. 114: Monks Mead, Undy, Monm. (*1ˢᵗ edn. 6" O.S. Map, reduced*).

Mountain pastures were the most extensive, but they were not the only ones to be had. Basingwerk had grazing rights (from 1289) on Saltney and Hawarden Marsh,[128] while Strata Florida's Cwmystwyth Grange included a portion of the ill-drained Rheidol flats. Several monasteries had valuable pastures adjacent: Strata Marcella[129] and Whitland,[130] their 'Great Meads', Neath, its Cadog's Mead;[131] Tintern, its pastures of Abbot's Ham, Layton Field, Passage Mead and Plumweir Mead.[132] Leland noted of Grace Dieu, sited on the narrow Troddi flood-plain, that 'veri good pastures be about this place'.[133] Margam, Llantarnam, Neath and Tintern all had substantial pastures, sometimes encapsulated in the name of Moor Grange on the coastal marshes next the Bristol Channel. Margam had (confirmed about 1248) the right to pastures between the Taff and Ely rivers at Cardiff, paying 1d yearly for every ten sheep, and another 1d for every two head of cattle, so grazing.[134] Tintern's meadows in the Caldicot Levels included several detached properties, one – in the parish of Undy – was known as Monks Mead *(Fig. 114)*, corrupted in modern times to 'Monkey Mead'.[135]

Meadow and pasture meant *hay-making*, reflected in the accounts of Tintern's Merthyr Gerain Grange, which (1389) had sold five *crosses* of fodder.[136] The importance of hay was shown in post-Suppression troubles at a holding on Strata Florida's former Blaenaeron Grange, when ten loads of hay were set on fire, and another ten thrown into the River Camddwr.[137] As winter cattle feed, Valle Crucis may have utilised oak foliage from its local woods.[138]

Most monasteries enjoyed *common of pasture* outside their own lands.[139] Such a right was generally on unenclosed land, it might not be exclusive, and could have restrictions placed upon it. Cwmhir (1314), granted rights of common in Maelienydd, had to leave 'a sufficiency of open common and pasturage for the lord's beasts'.[140] Strata Marcella had common rights throughout Arwystli and Cyfeiliog, save where Cwmhir and Cymer had privileges.[141] The upshot was that Cwmhir and Strata Marcella had grazing as far distant from the monasteries as Pumlumon (Plynlimon). Strata Marcella had further rights in Powys and in Mochnant, but with reservations in favour of the Knights Hospitaller.[142] Margam, Neath and Llantarnam had rights in the mountains of south Wales, the conflict of interests leading to some of the disputes noted before *(Chapter 1)*.

Pastoralism was perhaps at its zenith in the 13th century, but its significance continued thereafter. The rights of common traceable in the charters of Strata Marcella (from 1201)[143] and of Strata Florida (from 1202)[144] find their place in the respective confirmatory charters of 1420[145] and 1336.[146] A continued search for new pastures in the 14th century saw Whitland (1303) lease pasture in the Prescelly mountains (Pembrokeshire) for what became a nominal rent,[147] and Margam (1360) granted rights in Cefn Cribwr.[148] Margam (1304) gained the right to impound animals found in the embankments south of the river Afan – but had to pay 1/2d. per animal towards the upkeep of the sea defences.[149] The abbey (1420) – which by the early 13th century had obtained substantial pasture rights in Afan Marsh,[150] lost a case concerning certain common lands there – between the King's Wall and the Welsh Wall – in favour of the burgesses of Afan.[151]

Mountain grazing lands were broad, open territories, and so Aberconwy at least,[152] as also Strata Florida's tenants,[153] found the branding of their animals a necessity. Local agreements dealt with the problem of stray animals. Strata Marcella's tenants in Penllyn (at Cwmllwyd and Cwmhyfed) used 'to hunt and chase away' any strange cattle straying on to monastic land, whilst neighbouring residents did likewise, but in the reverse direction.[154] Rivers frequently formed the boundaries between the grazing areas of different monasteries. The Rhondda Fawr separated Llantarnam's sphere of influence from that of Margam;[155] and, as a result

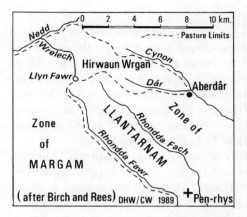

Fig. 115: Pasture rights of Llantarnam and Margam Abbeys.

of arbitration, a headwater of the Rheidol delineated the Pumlumon pastures open to Cwmhir from those of Strata Marcella.[156]

Rights of Way

Way-leave was essential to any monastic economy, not just for the movement of stock, but also for the transport of grain, food and minerals. Amongst the several grants made were those by Gilbert de Clare (1289) to Neath – 'The easements of public ways', between the abbey and Briton Ferry and Swansea;[157] and by Thomas of Afan to Margam (1349): 'Ingress and egress for its carriages from Resolfen to the abbey'.[158] Tintern had 'free access to its meadows' – some of which lay in detached portions in the Caldicot Levels.[159] Dore – to meet its interests in Cantref-selyf[160] – had the right of passage along 'the way above the Wye going from Llyswen to Builth' (early 13th C.),[161] and by 'that footpath which leads from Nanteglwys to Gwenddwr' (1271).[162]

Cattle Rearing

In the 13th century, cattle may have been as important as sheep, especially in the remoter abbeys of mid-Wales, perhaps unable to participate as fully in the wool trade as the Border houses.[163] At any rate, the *Taxatio* (1291) computes 428 cattle on the lands of Strata Florida as compared to 1,327 sheep, and for Cwmhir (in Ceredigion alone) 128 cattle compared to 300 sheep.[164] Cattle had a varied usage – for meat, milk, hides, haulage and ploughing. Specific additional pasture rights allowed Margam to graze on Cefn Cribwr '50 oxen, 30 cows, 40 steers and heifers',[165] whilst Tintern received pasture 'in the park of Mynydd-y-gaer *(Fig. 96)* for the oxen of the seven ploughs belonging to its Rogerstone Grange'.[166]

Tanning, and the preparation of *hides*, were a corollary of cattle rearing. Tanneries are on record at both Margam and Tintern (1291).[167] The latter's – later called *La Tanhouse* (1535)[168] – was accorded a cheap and plentiful supply of bark,[169] lodged perhaps in the 'bark-loft' (1568) within the precincts of the abbey.[170] Cistercian participation in the significant export of hides from Wales in the Middle Ages may be suggested by the case of a worldly-wise *conversus* of Neath (1205), who cancelled the sale of hides to Quincy Abbey (Yonne, France) in favour of a better deal elsewhere.[171] One use of hides was in the burial of the dead: the body of a 13th century (non-monastic) dignitary, laid to rest at Tintern, was sewn up in an ox hide prior to interment.[172]

Dairying

Dairying was significant on low-lying granges, like those of Whitland which yielded rents of cheese (1536; *Fig. 72*).[173] Butter and cheese were amongst the produce of Cymer's Neigwl Grange (Llŷn; 1350).[174] A hint of dairying comes in 'the fifteen cows called the *heyfords*' owned by the nuns of Llanllŷr. Were they a dairy herd? [A later record (1539) refers to them as 'the heifers'].[175] It is worth noting that milk production is still carried on at Llanllŷr House. Archaeological evidence suggests that a high proportion of Valle Crucis' cattle were dairy cows.[176] It had an important 'vaccary and dairy house', its *efenechtid* in Llandysilio-yn-Iâl.[177]

Vaccaries are noted among the possessions of several abbeys, particularly in mid-Wales. They included that of Aberconwy at Llyn Cymer in Cerrig-y-drudion,[178] and of Strata Marcella at Pennant-tigi in Mallwyd. The value of the latter is shown by the persistence of the monks in endeavouring to repossess it, after its confiscation by Prince Llywelyn ap Gruffydd.[179] Cymer's home vaccary lay by its cemetery,[180] that of Tintern was placed between the abbey garden and the Angidy brook.[181] Morgan Gam (*c.* 1230), demising pasture in Afan to Margam, allowed the monks a suitable site 'to make a house for the work of their cattle'. This may have been the vaccary at Melis Grange.[182] This list is by no means exhaustive.

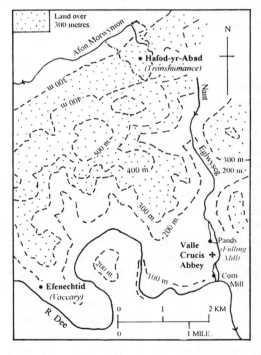

Fig. 116: The Pastoral Locality of Valle Crucis [*Mills: Pratt D. 1997*].

Transhumance

The hilly terrain probably led the medieval Cistercians to share in the prevailing Welsh custom of transhumance – the upward movement in summer of flocks, accompanied by their shepherds, to find fresh and cool pastures.[183] The place name *hafod* ('summer dwelling') occurs at least eight times on the mountain pastures of Strata Florida, including *hafod-yr-abad* ('the abbot's *hafod*') in Cwmystwyth Grange, and *hafod-y-gofaint* ('the convent *hafod*') on Mefenydd Grange. The English equivalent of *hafod* comes in 'the summer house' belonging to a tenant of Strata Florida on its Y Dywarchen Grange.[184] John Leland noted, in the Claer-ddu region, on, or near, lands of Strata Florida: 'Two very poor cottages for summer days for cattle'.[185]

The term *hafod* appears to have been synonymous in Caernarfonshire with 'vaccary',[186] but it may not be conclusive proof of transhumance in all cases. It also came to denote the cottages tenants had the right to erect on the wastes appurtenant to their holdings.[187] It is, however, very often a likely pointer, as was the grant to Valle Crucis of 'summer pasture' in the Minera Hills.[188] Stock movement is also indicated by varying depositions concerning Cwmhir's former Cwmbiga Grange (1585): one alleging that the grange sustained only 30 kine in winter, but 400 in summer.[189]

Both Welsh and English terms occur on former lands of Cymer: Hafod Newydd in Llanfachreth; a field, *Cae summerhouse* (1794), pertaining to Hengwrt;[190] and, near Brynllyn on its Cwmkedrin Grange, an isolated 'cottage or dairy house for summer' (1548).[191] The term *hafod* occurs six times on Aberconwy's former Nanhwynan Grange, and occasionally on lands of Strata Marcella (Hafod Owain, Talerddig) and of Valle Crucis (Hafod-yr-abad, Llandysilio; *Fig. 116*).

Other Stock

Pigs find frequent mention in the grange and manorial accounts of Tintern. It had a piggery in Porthcaseg Manor,[192] and pigs formed part of the stock sent as food to the abbey from its granges.[193] Useful as a source of lard, as well as of meat, they were kept at Valle Crucis throughout its history,[194] and were numbered amongst the stock of Dore's Llyncoed Grange (1230–68),[195] and of Cymer's Neigwl Grange (1350).[196] The importance of pannage rights has been noted *(Chapter 15)*.

Goats were listed amongst the animals of several abbeys by the *Taxatio* (1291), which credited Llantarnam with forty-six.[197] Destructive animals, damaging the woodlands of Strata Florida,[198] they were prohibited from Tintern's Porthcaseg Manor (1528).[199] One of Whitland's tenants (at Blaen-gwyddno) had 'mountain goat's ground' appurtenant to his holding.[200] *Chickens* are evidenced in the kind rents paid by tenants to Strata Florida,[201] Strata Marcella[202] and Whitland.[203] Merthyr Gerain Grange (Tintern) had its hen-house.[204]

Rabbits abounded in the free warren granted to Margam (in its nearby Burrows, between the Afan and the Kenfig).[205] On their demesne lands, right of warren was also accorded to Basingwerk,[206] Strata Florida[207] and Tintern.[208] The related term *Conygarth* (or similar) occurred on lands of Basingwerk (in Wirral; 1536),[209] and of Tintern (near the abbey; 1506; and on Trelech Grange, 1765).[210]

The keeping of *doves*, an important source of food in winter-time, and of dung for manure,[211] is reflected by the still visible remains of monastic dovecots at Neath's Gelli-garn and Monknash Granges *(Fig. 92; Plate XII-A)*.[212] Both 'colver-houses' were noted in the first post-Suppression accounts (1539).[213] Grace Dieu had a dove cot adjacent to its Osbaston Mill,[214] and one stood within the abbatial complex at Tintern *(Fig. 50)*.[215] John Aram (1779) marked a 'Dove House' close to the site of Llantarnam (1779),[216] whilst Nant *Colomendy* at Whitland *(Fig. 8)* suggests a dove cot there.[217]

Horse Rearing

Horses were a very necessary adjunct of medieval times, for travel and hunting – like those of Basingwerk,[218] and for haulage. Amongst noted Cistercian studs in the 13th century were those of Grace Dieu,[219] Margam, Neath[220] and Strata Florida.[221]

(Might the later, noted horse fairs at Ffair Rhos, close to the abbey and on its former land, have had their origin in monastic times?) Cwmhir had 26 mares at Nant-yr-arian Grange alone (1291);[222] Tintern was granted, for a time, pasture for forty mares with their foals in the Forest of Dean (1234).[223] The shoeing of horses, and the repair of the stable roof, were among the expenses noted in its Merthyr Gerain Grange accounts (1389),[224] whilst one of the abbey's stipendiary officials was its 'Keeper of the Horses' (1535).[225] Lesser employees, like grooms, probably occupied the 'room in the stable' at Whitland (1539).[226]

The value placed upon horses was demonstrated by the Welsh princes expecting a tribute of two horses annually from Basingwerk. Prince Gwenwynwyn (1190) expected to be supplied with 'two colts of its superior breed' – possibly a Spanish strain introduced into Powys about that time.[227] Colts and mares were stolen from Basingwerk's home stud during the Conquest (1282).[228] Horses might be sold (one fetched Margam 5s; early 13th C.);[229] or used in barter: Margam gave two horses – valued at £2 and £1 6s 8d – in part payment for the fee of Llangewydd (1202).[230] Abbots riding abroad did so on horseback: one abbot of Aberconwy (1489) was thrown from his horse and killed;[231] the last abbots of Cwmhir and Strata Marcella (1536–37) rode to London in connection with the surrender of their monasteries. Often on horseback, visiting the granges, was an abbey's cellarer, like cellarer Morris of Tintern (1412) travelling with a party of three horses to its Acle Manor (Norfolk).[232]

Sheep Rearing

The Welsh Cistercians were as great sheep farmers and wool producers as their counterparts elsewhere in north-west Europe, especially those abbeys close to communication routes. The value set by the White Monks upon their sheep is reflected in the gift of twelve animals made by Basingwerk to Vale Royal (1330) in the year of the consecration of its church.[233] The numbers of sheep given in the *Taxatio* (1291) run into four figures for Margam (5,285), Neath (4,897), Tintern (3,264), Basingwerk (2,000 in Penllyn alone), Strata Florida (1,327) and Whitland (1,100). The last was one of the remoter houses where dairying was more significant. These figures may, in fact, represent a recovery stage after the troubles of the Conquest and, in Glamorgan, the effects of scab a decade before.[234] Caution must be applied in adducing the evidence of medieval surveys; the poll tax return of 1379, for example, still credits Strata Florida with 1,327 sheep – copying the figures given over ninety years previously.[235]

In the earlier monastic period, experienced *conversi* like William (1261) and Walter (1291) of Tintern, were numbered amongst the shepherds of that abbey.[236] At Strata Florida, brothers Madog and Anian were 'masters of the sheep and cows'.[237] As the numbers of *conversi* decreased, paid shepherds were employed – as Richard Blyth at Tintern's Rogerstone Grange (1412).[238] It has been asserted, but the evidence is not transparent, that Margam's shepherds had the help of dogs imported from Brittany in Tudor times.[239] By the time of the Suppression, when much monastic land had been demised, the size of flocks directly administered from a monastery had greatly decreased, and, therefore, the *Valor* (1535) fails to record any 'masters of flocks' amongst the stipendiary officers of abbeys like Tintern.

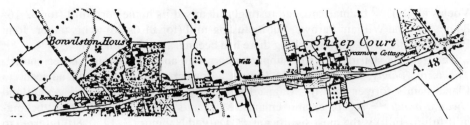

Fig. 117: Margam's former sheep-fold, Bonvilston Manor. *(1ˢᵗ edn. 6" O.S. Map).*

The care given to sheep-rearing is also evidenced by many documentary notes of monastic 'sheep-cots', 'sheep-folds' or 'sheep-houses', like those of Margam at Bonvilston,[240] of Neath at Cwrt Herbert,[241] and on six of the properties of Tintern – including Aluredeston (its gates vandalised in 1318),[242] Merthyr Gerain (its gate being repaired in 1388),[243] and Porthcaseg (demised in 1524).[244] Ordnance Survey maps still mark old sheep-cots on other properties of Tintern – Modesgate, Rogerstone and Trelech Granges. In order to retain a certain degree of control over its flocks, Margam excepted the sheep-fold when it demised Hafod-y-porth (1470)[245] and Llangewydd (1517)[246] Granges. Sheep-cots could be of some size, like Dore's 'great house called Sheepcote' in Trawscoed (Brecs., 1536).[247] Later evidence (1790) told of Cwmhir pasturing its sheep on Llechelwyddan Common (Cefnllys), and having 'a sheepcot standing thereon, the walls of stone ... a large building ... it hath seven doors'.[248]

Sheep-rearing was also reflected in kind rents of wool, like those rendered by Strata Florida's tenants at Hafodwen (19 topstans yearly, valued at 1d each) and of Blaenaeron (22 topstans [1 topstan = 5 kg./11 lbs].[249] What may have been commuted collective wool rents was called the 'custom wool', *gwlan y menythe*, derived jointly from the abbey's Anhuniog, Blaenaeron, Cwmystwyth, Mefennydd and Pennardd Granges. Demised in 1536 for a down payment of £30,[250] it fetched a sale price of double that thirty years after the Dissolution.[251] Wool rents were also important to Whitland; Maenor Forion Grange alone supplying it 96 fleeces annually.[252]

Fulling Mills

Whitland and Strata Florida accounted for one-third of the twenty-seven recorded Cistercian fulling-mills in Wales and the Border; four of them lying in the cloth-making Teifi valley. To what extent the monks, early on, shared in this industry is unknown,[253] but, in later years, the mills were primarily a source of income. Grace Dieu, for example, demised its fulling-mill at Osbaston (Monmouth) in 1486,[254] and Strata Florida its mill at Blaenaeron in 1533.[255] The income derived by leasing out a fulling-mill was much less than for a corn-mill; it was very much the 'poor relation'. Cymer's fulling-mill brought in only 1s. 8d. yearly in rent,[256] whilst Whitland's fulling-mill at Hen Dy Gwyn was demised for one-third the rent paid for its corn-mill there.[257] This did not deter some abbeys from allowing tenants to erect new fulling-mills in Tudor times[258] – as Margam at Hafod-heulog (1484)[259] and Aberconwy at

Voelas (1502).[260] Llantarnam, interestingly, demised its home corn-mill (for £2 16s 8d p.a.) to one William Parowe, but its fulling-mill (for £1 6s 8d) to his father, John Parowe. By the Dissolution, milling there had became a family concern![261]

The frequent sharing of water-supply by corn-mill and fulling-mill has been noted. The term, *pandy*, often precisely locates a former fulling-mill, and adjacent to Llantarnam's former mill (at Magna Porta) were lands termed *Kayre pandy* and *Gwan a pandi*.[262] As for extant remains, Margam's 'tokyngmill' (i.e. its 'tucking-mill/fulling-mill') is the most significant.[263] Dafydd Nanmor (*fl.* 1450–80) referred to weaving on the loom of Strata Florida,[264] and Margam had its tailor's shop (1518 – when probably demised).[265] Tintern's tailor, by 1535, was a stipendiary servant, and the abbey incurred no small expenditure on robes for the community.[266] There is no evidence that, in its latter years, the monastery produced any cloth.

NOTES

1. *Taxatio Eccl.* 282–84.
2. Cowley F.G. 1977, 82.
3. *Taxatio Eccl.* 282b.
4. *Taxatio Eccl.* 281b, 289b.
5. Cowley F.G. 1977, 82.
6. *Cal. Patent R.* 1234, 69.
7. *Cal. Close R.* 1231, 547.
8. *Cal. Charter R.* 1307, 103–04.
9. *Valor Eccl.* 370.
10. Jones M.C. 1873, 358.
11. Richards R. 1959, 244.
12. Birch W. de Gray. 1897, 186 (of 1245).
13. Glamorgan Archives, CL/Deeds 1 / 2; *Neath Deeds* 205–06.
14. Lhuyd E. 1707. III, 124.
15. *Cal. Charter R.* III, 104–05.
16. NLW, Badm. Manorial 1571.
17. *Exchq. Proc. (2)* 96.
18. Birch W. de Gray. 1897, 190.
19. *Cf.* [for Aberduhonw Grange] NLW, tithe-map, parish of Llanddewi'r-cwm (Brecs.).
20. PRO, SC 6 (Hen. VIII) 5412.
21. PRO, SC 6 (Hen. VIII) 5155, m. 13d.
22. PRO, E 315/201, f. 54d.
23. NLW, Badm. Manorial 1571.
24. PRO, LR 6/152/4.
25. *Cf. Lleyn Accts.* 273; *Cal. Inq. Misc.* VI, 107 (No. 228).
26. *Exchq. Proc. (2)* 252.
27. Lekai L.J. 1977, 450 [XXIII], 459 [XV].
28. Hays R.W. 1963, 18, 21.
29. BL, Addit. MS 48984, f. 127r.

30. Hays R.W. 1963, 89.
31. *Arch. Camb.* 1846, 111.
32. Jones M.C. 1869, 95; *Cf.* Barton P.G. 1999, 77.
33. PRO, LR 1/213, f. 271.
34. PRO, E 315/50, f. 176.
35. PRO, SC 6(Hen. VIII) 4868, m. 5d.
36. NLW, Badm. Manorial 1641.
37. PRO, SC 6 (Hen. VIII) 2497, mm. 6–7.
38. PRO, LR 1/228, f. 158.
39. PRO, LR 1/228, ff. 182d–183. *Cf.* PRO, SC 6 (Hen. VIII) 4903, m. 5r ['Milliner Grymm';] Owen G.D. 1935, 22 [Aberelwyn Mill].
40. NLW, Badm. Manorial 1663, m. 1d.
41. PRO, LR 1/212, f. 144; 213, f. 230d.
42. NLW, Cwrtmawr MS 973D, p. 45.
43. *Ibid.* p. 33.
44. *Ibid.* p. 20.
45. For their names, see: PRO, SC 6 (Hen. VIII) 5155, m. 9r.
46. NLW, Cwrtmawr MS 873D, p. 33.
47. PRO, SC 6 (Hen. VIII) 5142.
48. NLW, Cwrtmawr MS 873D, p. 45 (Strata Florida's 'ty pandy' at Pont Rhyd Fendigaid).
49. Heald G.O. 1976, opp. 211 (illus.).
50. BL, Harleian MS 606, f. 149.
51. PRO, LR 1/228, ff. 182–83.
52. Williams D.H. 1999, 27–29.
53. Hays R.W. 1963, 18.
54. *Ibid.* 115n.
55. *Mon. Angl.* V, 268.

56. *Augm. Rec.* 132.
57. PRO, SC 6 (Hen. VIII) 5155, m. 9r.
58. *Exchq. Proc. (2)* 94.
59. Owen G.D. 1935, 225.
60. PRO, C 1/1397, m. 13.
61. *Exchq. Proc. (2)* 102.
62. *Pers. comm.*
63. Hays R.W. 1963, 109.
64. PRO, SC 6 (Hen. VIII) 4903, m. 33d.
65. Manley J.F. 1977, 47.
66. See Map 2 and Appendix 3.
67. *Cf.* Hays R.W. 1963, 190; Jones H.L. 1846, 317.
68. Barton P.G. 1996; Jones M.C. 1868, 306; 1873, 376; Davies A.S. 1930, 153–54.
69. Hodges H. 1975, 32–33.
70. Williams S.W. 1889, 143.
71. Monmouthshire County Council, *County Treasures Survey* 1972; info. of Mr Bryn Daniel.
72. Postulated by Mr A.G. Mein.
73. NLW, Badm. Manorial 1571.
74. Lhuyd E. 1707, III. 77.
75. RCAHMW, *Glamorgan* III: Pt. 2 (1982), 263 (xi).
76. Williams D.H. 1976a, 92.
77. Williams D.H. 1976, 90.
78. RCAHMW, I (*County of Montgomery*, 1911) 41 (No. 205).
79. PRO, E 315/398, f. 1r.
80. *Walter Map* 56.
81. PRO, E 315/201, f. 4.
82. PRO, SC 6 (Hen. VIII) 5156.
83. Price G.V. 1952, 164.
84. Suggestion during site talks at Cwmhir (1969) by the late Mr Onfel Thomas, F.S.A. of Builth Wells.
85. *Welsh Verse* 67. .
86. NLW, Badm. Manorial 1657, m. 2d. ['the minor garden' 1438].
87. *Arch. Camb.* 1867, 317.
88. *Taxatio Eccl.* 282b.
89. NLW, Badm. Manorial 1571.
90. Williams D.H. 1998, 206, 245.
91. *Statuta* I, 191, 199 (1195/66, 76; 1196/8–9).
92. *Cartae Glam.* III, 1132; *Cf.* Birch W. de Gray. 1897, 261; O'Sullivan J.F. 1947, 112 [Margam's ale-presses].
93. PRO, E 315/92, ff. 97d–98r.
94. NLW, Badminton Manorial 1657, m. 7r.
95. Williams G. 1962, 380.
96. *Flint Accts.* 19.
97. PRO, SC 6 (Hen. VIII) 2497; *Rec. Augm.* 141.
98. Williams S.W. 1889, 169.
99. *Exchq. Proc.* (2) 102, 111.
100. *Anc. Pet.* 525 (327).
101. Owen G.D. 1935, 193–97.
102. PRO, SC 6 (Hen. VIII) 5155, m. 13.
103. *Lleyn Accts.* 273.
104. Cowley F.G. 1977, 261.
105. PRO, E 315/398, f. 1.
106. NLW, Badm. Manorial 1571, originally transcribed for the author by Dr. C.H. Talbot, and summarised in Williams D.H. 1965, 20–24.
107. *Taxatio Eccl.* 289.
108. Williams S.W. 1889, 120; Appx. xvii.
109. Birch W. de Gray. 1897, 305.
110. NLW, Cwrtmawr MS 873D, p. 31.
111. PRO, STAC 5/H.76/17(17).
112. Kansas 1/1.
113. Cowley F.G. 1977, 84.
114. Richards R. 1959, 248.
115. NLW, Badm. Manorial 1571.
116. Cowley F.G. 1977, 83.
117. Birch W. de Gray. 1897, 305.
118. *Flint Pleas* 2.
119. *Cal. Patent R.* 1398, 362.
120. *Anc. Pet.* 235 (139); Williams S.W. 1889, Appx. xl.
121. Hays R.W. 1963, 12–13; Lloyd J.E. II (1939) 601.
122. Williams D.H. 1976b, 185.
123. Afon Elan, ten miles [16 km.] to the east of the abbey.
124. Williams S.W. 1889, vi–vii; Giraldus noted its Teifi-side pastures [*Journey through Wales* 227].
125. PRO, E 134/33 Eliz. Hilary 16 (1591).
126. Butler L.A.S. 1976, 120.
127. PRO, STAC 5/H.66/33.
128. Lloyd J.Y.W. 1873, 60–61; NLW, Bettisfield Deeds 1529, 1623.
129. PRO, SC 6 (Hen. VIII) 5260; *Mont. Collns.* 1869, 403; 1873, 370. (It was 34 acres [14 ha.] in extent).

130. PRO, SC 6 (Hen. VIII) 4903, m. 1r.
131. PRO, LR 1/228, ff. 82d–83r.6
132. NLW, Badm. Manorial 1524, mm. 41–42; PRO, E 315/398, m. 1r.
133. *Itin. J. Leland* III, 50.
134. Birch W. de Gray. 1897, 236, 260.
135. NLW, Undy parish tithe-map.
136. NLW, Badm. Manorial 1571.
137. *Exchq. Proc. (1)* 89.
138. Butler L.A.S. 1976, 121.
139. *Cf.* Williams D.H. 1988. II, 298–99.
140. Banks R.W. 1888, 213, 216.
141. Banks R.W. 1888, 207–09; Jones M.C. 1873, 353–54.
142. Jones M.C. 1873, 354; *Mont. Collns.* LI, 176 (No. 19).
143. Williams D.H. 1976b, 189.
144. Williams S.W. 1889, 120.
145. Jones M.C. 1873, 353–54.
146. Williams S.W. 1889, Appx. lvii; *Cal.* Charter R. 1336, 382–86.
147. Owen G.D. 1935, 164; Cowley F.G. 1977, 265.
148. *Cartae Glam.* VI, 2380 (MDCXLVI).
149. *Catal. Penrice* I, 64–4 (Ch. 190).
150. Williams D.H. 1984. II, 299.
151. *Cartae Glam.* IV, 1483–84 (MCXIII).
152. Hays R.W. 1963, 22.
153. Owen G.D. 1935, 163.
154. PRO, E 178/5113; *Cf. Cartae Glam.* III, 979; VI, 2306 (MDLXXXV); Ruthin R.O. DD/WY/6233: for an agreement reached by Valle Crucis.
155. Birch W. de Gray. 1897, 174; 1902, 62.
156. Jones M.C. 1872, 117.
157. *Cartae Glam.* V, 1685; Birch W. de Gray. 1902, 82. *Cf. Episc. Acts* I, 361.
158. *Arch. Camb.* 1867, 37; Birch W. de Gray. 1897, 313.
159. *Cal. Charter R.* 1307, 104.
160. *Ibid.* 1241, 261.
161. *Mon. Angl.* V, 554.
162. BL, Harleian Ch. 43. A 71.
163. Cowley F.G. 1977, 85; Donkin R.A. 1962, 33; *Cf.* Butler L.A.S.B. 1976, 118.
164. *Taxatio Eccl.* 276–77. The figures

for Cymer and Strata Marcella [pp. 289b, 292b–293] are suspect.
165. *Catal. Penrice* IV, 167 (Ch. 2067).
166. *Tintern MSS* 2399 (67); *Cf. Cal. Inq.* Post Mortem IV, 294 (No. 434).
167. *Taxatio Eccl.* 284 (M), 282b (T).
168. *Valor Eccl.* IV, 370.
169. *Cal. Charter R.* 1307, 99.
170. NLW, Badm. Manorial 1524, m. 42r.
171. *Statuta* I, 310 (1205/14).
172. Hemp W.J. 1938, 131–33 (illus.).
173. PRO, SC 6 (Hen. VIII) 4903, mm. 4r, 9d, 19d.
174. *Lleyn Accts.* 273.
175. PRO, LR 6/152/2, 4; LR 6/152/3 [of 1538] calls them: 'The young *[iuvenum]* cows called the heyfords'.
176. Butler L.A.S. 1976, 121.
177. Pratt D. 1997, 24, 62 [*n*11].
178. Hays R.W. 1963, 106.
179. *Cal. Inq. Misc.* II, 182 (No. 732).
180. PRO, LR 1/213, f. 119d.
181. NLW, Badm. Manorial 1657, mm. 2d, 3d; *Cf.* 1571 [a thatched vaccary on Merthyr Gerain Grange].
182. 8; Gray T. 1903.
183. Bowen E.G. 1950, 36.
184. *Exchq. Proc. (2)* 95–96; it was on the land of Ty-llety-Ievan-hên.
185. Williams S.W. 1889, Appx. iv.
186. *Sheriff Caerns.* 149–50.
187. Owen G.D. 1935, 163.
188. Price G.V. 1952, 63 (215a. : 87 ha.); RCAHMW, 4 (*County of Denbigh*, 1914) 160. The area now forms a detached portion of Esclusham Above: Palmer A.N. 1890. IV, 198.
189. PRO, STAC 5/H.66/33.
190. UCNW, Nannau-Hengwrt MSS 677–78.
191. *Augm. Rec.* 429.
192. NLW, Badm. Manorial 1572 (of 1393).
193. *Ibid.* 1571 (of 1388).
194. Butler L.A.S. 1976, 122.
195. Kansas 1/1.
196. *Lleyn Accts.* 273.
197. *Taxatio Eccl.* 285.
198. Williams S.W. 1889. Appx. iii.

199. NLW, Badm. Manorial 1663, m. 3d.
200. PRO, LR 2/206, f. 224.
201. Williams S.W. 1889, 148.
202. PRO, SC 6 (Hen. VIII) 5260, m. 2d.
203. PRO, SC 6 (Hen. VIII) 4903.
204. NLW, Badm. Manorial 1571.
205. *Cartae Glam.* IV, 261; Birch W. de Gray. 1897, 310; Gray T. 1905, 102.
206. Pennant T. 1796, 199; Hays R.W. 1971, 123 (in Co. Flint).
207. Williams S.W. 1889, 148 (in counties of Cardigan and Carmarthen).
208. *Cal. Charter R.* 1307, 106 (in Wentwood); 1325, 477 (at Acle Manor, Norfolk)..
209. *LP (Hen. VIII)* XV, 561 (No. 1032).
210. NLW, Badm. Manorial 1568; (Map Room) Badminton Plans, Vol. 5.
211. Info. of the late Mr G.C. Boon.
212. RCAHMW, *Glamorgan* III: Pt. 2 (1982) 260 (MG 16), Fig. 143 and Pl. 42: Gelli-garn; 263 (MG 17), 265 (Fig. 145): Monknash.
213. PRO, SC 6 (Hen. VIII) 5156, m. 1r.
214. *Grace Dieu Docs.* 190.
215. Robinson D.M. 1995, 68.
216. Pontypool Estate Plan, consulted by permission of Mr (now Sir) Richard Hanbury Tenison.
217. James T. 1978, 71.
218. Owen E. 1920, 54–55.
219. Bazeley M.L. 1910, 250.
220. *Cartae Glam.* I, 30.
221. Cowley F.G. 1977, 83 (quoting Giraldus Cambrensis).
222. *Taxatio Eccl.* 277.
223. *Cal. Close R.* 1234, 538; *Cal. Patent R.* 1234, 74.
224. NLW, Badm. Manorial 1571.
225. *Valor Eccl.* IV, 371.
226. Owen G.D. 1935, 362.
227. Thomas D.R. 1886, 118; Lloyd J.Y.W. 1876, 234; *Cf. Cal. Inq. Misc.* I, 392 (No. 1357); Jones A. 1933, 173.
228. *Cal. Inq. Misc.* I, 379 (No. 1302).
229. *Catal. Penrice* IV: 1, 134 (Ch. 1980.)
230. *Ibid.* Ch. 62.
231. *Letters to Cîteaux* 127–30 (No. 64).
232. NLW, Badm. Manorial 1575.
233. Donkin R.A. 1978, 87–88.
234. Cowley F.G. 1977, 86–87.
235. Williams G. 1962, 174.
236. BL, Arundel MS 19, f. 33d.
237. Williams S.W. 1889, 120–21, xvii.
238. NLW, Badm. Manorial 1575.
239. By M.C. Harris in: *Country Life*, 27 December 1973, p. 2173.
240. Birch W. de Gray. 1897, 138. At Grangetown (Cardiff) it constructed a sheep-cot in the late 13th century: NLW, Penrice and Margam Ch. 295.
241. Birch W. de Gray. 1902, 82.
242. PRO, C 115/K.2/6683, ff. 93–95.
243. NLW, Badm. Manorial 1571.
244. *Ibid.* 1663, m. 1; *Cf.* 1659, m. 1. [It stood near Stow Weir Meadow, towards Ruding Grange].
245. Birch W. de Gray. 1897, 348.
246. NLW, Penrice and Margam Ch. 5069.
247. Williams D.H. 1976, 38.
248. Banks R.W. 1888, 214.
249. Williams S.W. 1889, 177; Appx. xci, xcvii *et seq.*
250. *Ibid.* Appx. ciii.
251. Owen G.D. 1935, 192–93.
252. PRO, SC 6 (Hen. VIII) 4903, mm. 16–20.
253. *Cf.* Cowley F.G. 1977, 85.
254. PRO, SC 6 (Hen. VIII) 2496, m. 1d; *Grace Dieu Docs.* 190.
255. NLW, Cwrtmawr MS 873D, 33; PRO, SC 6 (Hen. VIII) 4868, m. 5d. [It appears to have been built in order to be demised].
256. PRO, E 315/201, f. 4.
257. PRO, LR 1/228, ff. 182–83.
258. *Arch. Camb.* 1846, 111.
259. Birch W. de Gray. 1897, 349.
260. NLW, Cernioge Deed 48.
261. BL, Harleian MS 606, f. 149; PRO, SC 6 (Hen. VIII) 2497, m. 2r.
262. *Ibid.*
263. RCAHMW, *Glamorgan* III: Pt. 2 (1982) 293 (MG 38); Williams D.H. 1990, 134 (Pl. 52).
264. *D. Nanmor* 74.
265. Birch W. de Gray. 1897, 355.
266. *Valor Eccl.* IV, 371.

CHAPTER 17

HOME AND OVERSEAS TRADE

A surplus in production of some commodities, together with a need to import vital necessities (like salt and wine), and an ability to earn revenue, led to considerable buying and selling by the White Monks.

The Wool Trade

The overseas export of wool emanating from Welsh Cistercian flocks can be traced practically throughout the 13th century, commencing with the licence given by King John (1212) to Strata Florida 'to sell its wool beyond sea for three years'.[1] Such leave had frequently to be sought on account of changing political conditions *vis-à-vis* France.[2] There is no further knowledge of the wool trade of Strata Florida, but at this time Whitland also was producing wool for sale – where is unclear.[3]

Down to the early 1270s, most wool exports were to Flanders – as the sales by Margam to merchants of Ghent (1250, 1252),[4] and of Douai (1271).[5] In two years at least, the wool was impounded by the Crown, at Bristol (1250) and Southampton (1271); the points of export. In other years, it perhaps went securely on its way.[6] An experienced monk acted as an abbey's wool-merchant: like Richard of Margam (1250) and Thomas de Haneworth for Tintern (1272).[7] From the late 13th century on, trade with Italian merchants became increasingly to the fore, like the merchant of Lucca (1277) carrying to Chester 'twenty sacks of wool bought from Aberconwy'.[8] Dore's many sheep in Cantref-selyf and north Gwent will have assisted that abbey's well-documented exports to both Flanders (1272–76) and Italy (1303–34).[9]

The home trade in wool by Basingwerk can be documented throughout most of the 14th century, with known sales to: a merchant of Chester (William of Doncaster, for nearly £50 in 1314);[10] to the Prince of Wales (who in 1347 sought the abbey's 'excellent wools', but wanted them cheaply and with payment delayed);[11] and to a citizen of London (1362).[12] In the later 14th century, monastic profits in the wool trade were reduced by marcher lords engaging in large-scale sheep rearing, by royal taxation, by the setting-up of the Staple, and by the emergence of other middle-men.[13]

An imperfect picture of Cistercian wool production is afforded by Pegolotti's late 13th century list of wool-exporting monasteries.[14] It is not clear whether the list gives the total clip available for sale, or only that sold to a particular merchant of the Bardi. It may have been compiled in the wake of troubles from scab and war, so, important though it is, it must be treated comparatively rather than quantitatively.

The list suggests that, apart from Cwmhir (or Cymer) and Valle Crucis, all the Welsh abbeys were wool exporters. Five are listed as providing 15 sacks or more – each sack containing about 340 lbs. [150 kg.]. Tintern stands out; its best wool, while much less in quantity than that of the Yorkshire abbeys (Fountains produced 76 sacks) was much better in quality, fetching as it did the highest price of British monastic wool: 28 marks per sack. Its only equals were Dore, and Stainfield nunnery in Lindsey.

When Margam exported 42$^{1}/_{2}$ sacks (1250) to Flanders, at least one sack of coarse wool was included,[15] but when Pegolotti compiled his list Margam was not making 'either medium or inferior wool'. Llantarnam did, at this time, produce rather coarse wool. Pegolotti's figures suggest that, from the sale of wool abroad, Margam received about £167, and Tintern about £150 p.a. These were no mean sums, not directly taken into account in the *Taxatio* (1291). Another list, emanating from Douai, assesses the value of wool from Margam at £50, and from Neath at £45 – but these figures may reflect sales to Flanders.[16]

Trading Privileges

Monastic trade was facilitated by several factors, including: way-leaves, toll exemptions, hospices and warehouses in ports and towns, the possession of ships amd harbours, and the ability to hold markets and fairs.[17]

Quittance of toll, passage and pontage, through all his dominions, was granted by Henry II (1154–89) to Aberconwy,[18] Margam,[19] Neath[20] and Strata Marcella;[21] and, additionally, by King John (1199–16) to Strata Florida[22] and Whitland.[23] Henry III confirmed some of these rights.[24] Restrictions might be written in: as for Strata Marcella (1200) – London was excepted, and only the monks' own goods were covered.[25] The rights of Cwmhir, likewise granted at a time of warfare (1232), were conditional upon the goods traded not falling into the hands of the king's enemies.[26]

Overseas trade was aided by Henry I (in respect of Tintern)[27] and Henry II (in the instance of Margam),[28] absolving those abbeys from any tolls at the ports of Dover, Estreham, Hastings, Southampton, Barfleur and Dieppe. At home, Aberconwy[29] and Neath[30] could trade freely with ships putting in on their lands.

Local rights for Basingwerk included freedom from toll in the earldom of Chester (granted by Earl Ranulf shortly after its foundation), and in the four Cantrefs (given by Princes Llywelyn and David ab Iorwerth);[31] for Margam, freedom from tolls 'in buying and selling all manner of merchandise', in the Gower lands of William de Braose,[32] and freedom from tolls in the 'boroughs' of Earl William of Pembroke in Wales and Ireland;[33] for Strata Marcella, freedom from toll in Edward Charlton's lordship of Powys (1420), 'for the buying of beasts and victuals for their own use'.[34] This last privilege explains why later occupiers of the manor of Strata Marcella Abbot were absolved from payment of tolls at Welshpool Market.[35] Tenants of Valle Crucis' former lands in Wrexham were quit of toll at Wrexham Market.[36]

Urban Property *(See Map XIV)*

From the twelfth century on, holdings in towns and ports were important to the Cistercians, as accommodation for monks and *conversi* on business, as offices for the transaction of trade, and as warehousing for the storage of goods. Bristol was extremely important to the south Wales monasteries. Llantarnam,[37] Margam,[38] Neath,[39] Tintern[40] and Whitland[41] were all free from toll there; later confirmation of some of these rights traces monastic trade in Bristol down to the mid-15th century.

Margam, however, exchanged all its property in Bristol and Gloucestershire (between 1484 and 1486) with Tewkesbury Abbey, in return for a grant of tithes.[42] Its holdings in the port had been considerable, and included (at varying dates): property within the Castle bailey – by 1153, six years after the abbey's foundation;[43] buildings and land in Smale Street and near St Augustine's cemetery, as well as St Milburga's hermitage. In the early 13th century, Margam acquired a stall in the Market, and two stalls in Goldsmith's Place.[44] It may be because of such contacts that several of Margam's monks were Bristol men *(Fig. 55)*.

Tintern, which early on sold land by the river Frome in Bristol,[45] had a messuage on Redcliffe Street (the merchants' quarter, 1242),[46] two shops in St Ewen's quarter (1312),[47] and a tenement called Hilary Pal*marina* (1512).[48] The abbot was a member of the Bristol Staple,[49] and his monks had free passage on the Beachley–Aust ferry.[50] Llantarnam, too, had land in the port;[51] Neath, land near St Augustine's Abbey[52] and a house in Snowne Street,[53] and Whitland, property in nearby Bedminster.[54] The need for a place to reside when 'in town' was demonstrated by a taxation of Bristol in 1313. One inhabitant, Alice of Godeshall, had to pay tax 'in respect of her house, in which stay various people, namely the abbot of Neath, the abbot of St Augustine's, and the church of St Werburgh'.[55]

Cardiff was also a port of prime importance to the Cistercians. Earl William of Gloucester (d. 1183) gave the monks of Margam (prior to 1166),[56] and to Neath, houses in the city for them 'to have harbouring there'.[57] Margam soon came to have other properties in Cardiff – as in Cabelle Street, Mill Street and St Mary Street ('near the river Taff').[58] Neath, in a deal with Gilbert de Clare (1289)[59] not entirely to its own advantage,[60] came to own hundreds of burgages in Cardiff – with thirty-six in St Mary Street alone, and others in Barry Lane, High Street, St John's Street, and elsewhere. The whole of Neath's holdings were demised to Sir John Tyrrell for £15 p.a. (1485), and then to Laurence Buller for only 10 guineas (1529).[61]

The numerous other properties of Neath included 220 or so burgages in Cowbridge, leased out to James Turberville in 1504.[62] Margam had urban property in Kenfig (giving its name to 'Monk's Street'),[63] whilst Tintern's holdings included several houses in Chepstow.[64] Whitland owned burgages in New Carmarthen (in Spilman Street) and Haverfordwest (in Fryer Street) – a port where the abbey had fishing interests.[65]

Both Aberconwy[66] and Basingwerk[67] had properties in Chester – a centre for their wool trade, whilst Strata Marcella (1225) had three shops in Shrewsbury market-place.[68] Valle Crucis had two urban manors: Llangollen Abbot *(Map XIII-B)* and Wrexham Abbot – the latter including a court-house and a mill. Of sixteen of the tenements in Wrexham, it was later said (1589) that 'there hath hitherto been good hospitality kept for the relief of the poor near there about'.[69]

Ships and Shipping

Monasteries situated in riverine and marine locations commonly had their own harbours and boats. Margam (1189) sent a ship to Bristol to obtain corn for the starving;[70] in 1229, 1234 and 1246,[71] its vessels were trading in Devon, Bristol,

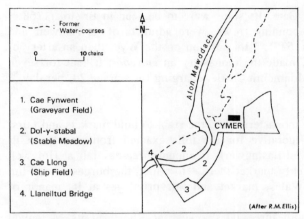

Fig. 118: Based on NLW, *A survey of the several estates in the county of Merioneth belonging to Griffith ap Howell Vaughan, Esqr.*(1794).

Key on map:

1. Cae Fynwent (Graveyard Field)
2. Dol-y-stabal (Stable Meadow)
3. Cae Llong (Ship Field)
4. Llanelltud Bridge

(After R.M.Ellis)

Former Water-courses

0   10 chains

-N-

Afon Mawddach

CYMER

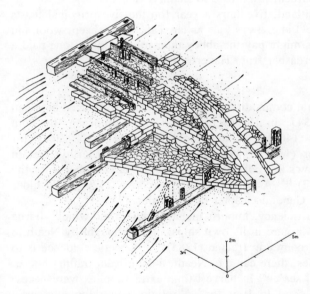

Fig. 119: Woolaston Grange Quay, Upper Section. *(Isometric drawing, M.G. Fulford et al., Trans. Bristol and Gloucs. Archaeol. Soc. 110: 1992).*

and Somerset, respectively. It carried produce from its Whitecross Grange coastwise to the abbey.[72] Neath (which, in 1235, had a vessel called the *Hulc*),[73] had two boats commandeered by the Duke of York (*c.* 1410).[74] Ships visited Neath town and abbey to do trade (1521),[75] and there is note (1534) of the abbey's 'key *(quay)* wall'.[76]

Freedom from customs for its ships was claimed by Aberconwy in the *Quo Warranto* Proceedings (1348),[77] whilst, in the time of the Glyn Dŵr Revolt (1406) the monastery lost 'a boat, with its tackle'.[78] Cymer's boats (noted in the 14th C.)[79] must have been imperative for communications with its Neigwl Grange in Llŷn. Close to the monastery *(Fig. 118)* are the sunken and marshy Cae Llong *(Ship Field)* and Dol Stabal *(Stable/Staple Meadow* – the latter interpretation might reflect trade).[80] Strata Florida may have had a port at Aberarth on the Ceredigion coast.[81]

Recently uncovered and recorded has been a mid-12th century stone and timber harbour, capable of taking sea-going vessels as well as river craft, at Tintern's Woolaston Grange by the Severn Estuary *(Fig. 119)*.[82]

Tintern could easily be reached by boats sailing on

the river Wye up to its Water Gate. Its ships were to be seen in Bristol (1268,[83] 1453[84]), whilst smaller craft, conning trows, were adjuncts of its Ashweir and Stoweir fisheries on the Wye (1527).[85] Its position on the Wye, then an artery of trade for upstream Monmouth, made the monastery an *entrepôt*; it kept for seven days (1258) wine in transit to Monmouth Castle, charging for storage 2d. per day.[86]

Markets and Fairs

Local trade was assisted where monasteries had the right to hold markets and fairs, but these were perhaps most lucrative for the tolls exacted from secular stall-holders. Edward I (1292) allowed Basingwerk an annual three-day fair at Holywell (over Trinity-tide),[87] and a weekly market there – to which the burgesses of Flint took exception, and, outside Wales, market and fair privileges at its manor of Glossop (1290).[88]

Strata Florida is credited with three fairs a year at Rhos, on its Mefenydd Grange, mainly for the sale and purchase of horses and cattle.[89] Taking place over the feasts of St James, the Assumption, and Holy Cross, some late Tudor records omit to ascribe the Rhos fairs to the abbey.[90] It gained but little revenue from 'all fairs and markets' at Talsarn Green, proximate to Llanllŷr nunnery.[91]

Under the patronage of Whitland, five fairs a year (on the five principal feasts of the Blessed Virgin) were held at Eglwys Fair ar lan Taf, when sheep, wool and corn were traded. Stall-holders might pay the abbey their tolls in kind, 'one paid a penny-worth of apples, a haberdasher from Haverfordwest a felt hat'.[92]

Other Trade

Monastic trade embraced several commodities; the sale of abbey-produced beer can be traced for Basingwerk (1347, in Holywell),[93] and, in Glamorgan, by both Margam (1450)[94] and Neath (1468).[95] Tintern sold honey (1291),[96] stock for replenishing Chepstow garrison (1307),[97] vegetables and grain at Merthyr Gerain Grange (1388),[98] calves and cows at Ruding Grange (1411),[99] and timber – for the repair of Caldicot Castle (1427).[100] A *conversus* of Aberconwy (1205) sold hides in a way which displeased the General Chapter of the Order.[101]

Despite the hoped for self-sufficiency, imports included salt[102] and wine[103] borne (presumably from Bristol) to Margam in its own ships; corn – bought by Neath in England (1234)[104] and by Aberconwy in Ireland (1283).[105] If poetic evidence is to be believed then, in Tudor times, there came to Neath, a significant trading house, 'all kinds of wine by land and sea'.[106] In harvest-time extra supplies were necessary: Cwmhir (1231) buying food in Hay for its religious working at nearby granges,[107] whilst Tintern bought beer for its hired workers at Merthyr Gerain (1388) and Woolaston Granges (1412).[108]

From the early 15th century onwards, as its own directly managed economy declined, and the increasing number of tenants in its neighbourhood set up shops and stalls, Tintern jealously guarded its sole rights of buying and selling on its lands.[109] The abbey granted licences to tenants who might wish to sell various commodities, usually for a fee of 6d, but in the case of beer this was increased to

1s.[110] The manorial court-rolls tell in 1442, *inter alia*, of William Vaughan permitted to sell 'bread, beer and other necessaries', and of Richard Gruffydd and Hywel Roger having leave 'to erect and hold a stall within the gate of the abbey, and sell meat'.[111] One tenant's surname was *'beremaker'* (1443).[112] One of the last tenants of the Angidy Mill (1525) was allowed to sell bread and beer, as well as do his grinding.[113]

The abbey's Porthcaseg court regulated the local traders, fining, for example, one person (in 1444) 2s. for holding a 'fulstall' within the abbey gate, contrary to regulations.[114] One of the last recorded courts (in 1528) ordered that 'every butcher, and anyone who sells victuals, shall remain in the place granted to them beforehand *by deed'*.[115] This indicates the seriousness with which the monastery supervised its tenantry, and suggests that some traders wanted to move their stalls so as to increase their takings. As for the monastery, it gained a small addition to its annual income from the entry fines and yearly rents paid by these local shop-keepers.

NOTES

1. Williams S.W. 1889, Appx. xix. (It was to be the monks' own wool, not wool handled on behalf of another party).
2. Williams D.H. 1998, 357–58.
3. Cowley F.G. 1977, 86, 122.
4. *Cal. Close R.* 1250, 304, 314. , *Cf.* 239; *Cal. Patent R.* 1252, 166.
5. *Cal. Patent R.* 1271, 526.
6. It is usually only when such interception took place, that we learn of the trade.
7. *Cal. Patent R..* 1272, 703; *Rot. Hund.* I, 176 (Tintern trading wool in 1276).
8. *Cal. Patent R.* 1277, 235.
9. Williams D.H. 1976, 49–59; 1998a, 35–36.
10. *Chester Deeds* 155–56.
11. *Black Prince's Reg.* I, 81–82, *Cf.* 137–38, 145; Williams G. 1962, 142.
12. NLW, MS 8942E.
13. Cowley F.G. 1977, 236.
14. Pegolotti F.B. 1936, 261–63.
15. *Cal. Close R.* 1250, 304, 314.
16. Cowley F.G. 1977, 88–89.
17. Williams D.H. 1998, 385–97.
18. Hays R.W. 1963, 21, 40–41.
19. *Penrice* I, 6 (Ch. 12).
20. *Cartae Glam.* I, 139 (CXL).
21. Jones M.C. 1871, 308.
22. Williams S.W. 1889, Appx. xix.

23. *Carmarthen Charters* 79–80: *Cf.* [for other houses] Hays R.W. 1963, 21; Birch W. de Gray. 1897, 177.
24. *Cal. Charter R.* 1232, 155, 171; *Cal.* Patent R. 1247, 504; 1318, 163.
25. Jones M.C. 1871, 293.
26. *Cal. Charter R.* 1232, 155; *Cf. Cal. Patent R.* 1318, 163.
27. *Cal. Charter R.* 1307, 88.
28. *Penrice* IV, 173 (Ch. 2089–5); *Cartae Glam.* VI, 2270–71 (MDXLIX).
29. Hays R.W. 1963, 21–22; *Cal. Charter R.* 1332, 269.
30. Trott C.D.J. 1946, 17; Phillips D.R. 1925, 611–12.
31. Jones A. 1933, 171–73; O'Sullivan J.F. 1947, 25–26; *Cal. Charter R.* 1285, 90.
32. *Cartae Glam.* III, 1081–82; *Cf.* II, 421; Birch W. de Gray. 1897, 313–14; Llewellyn R.W. 1898, 144.
33. *Cartae Glam.* I, 201–02 (CXCV).
34. Jones M.C. 1868, 299.
35. *Ibid.* 326.
36. Price G.V. 1952, 82.
37. *Cal. Inq. Misc.* I, 43 (No. 125).
38. Birch W. de Gray. 1897, 39.
39. *Ibid.* 1902, 49.
40. *Little Red Book* I, 235.

41. *Ibid. II, 199.*
42. Birch W.de Gray. 1897, 350.
43. *Ibid.* 23, 37, 40, 52; *Cf.* 202–04; *Cartae* Glam. I, 126, 166.
44. Birch W. de Gray. 1897, 203–04; *Cartae* Glam. III, 881–82, 891–92.
45. St Aug. Ch. 298–99 (No. 472).
46. *Cal. Charter R.* 1242, 272.
47. *Trans. Bristol and Gloucs. Archaeol.* Soc. XIX (1895) 232.
48. *Compotus R.* 156–57; *Cf. Cal. Patent R.* 1550, 267–68.
49. Carus Wilson E. 1933, 187.
50. *Cal. Charter R.* III, 88, 97.
51. PRO, E 210/D.5836.
52. *St Aug. Ch.* 366–67 (No. 572).
53. PRO, SC 6 (Hen. VIII) 5156, m. 9d.
54. *Cal. Patent R.* 1315, 348.
55. *Bristol Tallage* 230.
56. Birch W. de Gray. 1897, 42.
57. *Ibid.* 1902, 49.
58. *Ibid.* 1897, 206–07; *Cartae Glam.* IV, 1280–81.
59. Birch W. de Gray, 1902, 81; Williams G. 1962, 357; *Cardiff Rec.* I, 265.
60. Cowley F.G. 1977, 247.
61. PRO, LR 2/233, f. 21; *Cal. Patent R.* 1488, 218.
62. PRO, LR 2/233, f. 28.
63. Llewelyn R.W. 1898, 144–46; *Catal.* Penrice I, 7, 148 (Charters 14, 386).
64. NLW, Badm. Manorial 1524, m. 44d; 2445, pp. 15–16.
65. *Augm. Rec.* 265, 507.
66. Hays R.W. 1963, 110–11.
67. Owen E. 1920; *Mon. Angl.* V, 264.
68. *Shrewsbury Cart.* 146, 149, 161.
69. *Exchq. Proc. (1)* 149, 177.
70. Cowley F.G. 1977, 82.
71. *Cal. Close R.* 1229, 203; 1234, 360; 1246, 430.
72. Gray T. 1905, 90.
73. *Cal. Patent R.* 1235, 108.
74. *Anglo-Norman Pet.* 39.
75. Phillips D.R. 611–12; Trott C.D.J. 1946, 17.
76. PRO, SC 6 (Hen. VIII) 5156, m. 3d.
77. *Rec. Carn.* 144.
78. Hays R.W. 1963, 131*n*.
79. *Rec. Carn.* 200.
80. Ellis T.P. 1927, 4; 1928, 39; *Nannau* MSS 677–78.
81. Williams S.W. 1889, 107–08.
82. Fulford M.G. 1992, 101–21.
83. *Cal. Inq. Misc.* I, 119.
84. *Itin. Wm. Worcestre* 226.
85. NLW, Badm. Manorial 1663, m. 4r.
86. *Aberg. Accts.* 17.
87. *Flint Accts.* 174; *Black Prince's Reg.* III, 115; *Chester Recog. R. (36).*
88. *Cal. Charter R.* 1290, 372; Jones A. 1933, 174–75.
89. Owen G.D. 1935, 215–16; Pierce Jones T. 1950, 30–31; Jones J.E.J. 1981, 12–13.
90. *Augm. Rec.* 237–38; *Exchq. Proc. (1)* 91.
91. NLW, *Cal. Crosswood Deeds* 51–52.
92. Owen G.D. 1935, 216–17; *Cf. Exchq.* Proc. (1) 120.
93. Jones A. 1929, 19.
94. Birch W. de Gray. 1897, 346, 348.
95. *Ibid.* 1902, 137–39.
96. *Taxatio Eccl.* 282b.
97. *Anc. Pet.* 525.
98. NLW, Badm. Manorial 1571.
99. *Ibid.* 1575.
100. Birbeck T.T. 1973, 85.
101. *Statuta* I, 310 (1205/14).
102. *Cal. Close R.* 1229, 203.
103. Evans A.L. 1958, 91.
104. *Cal. Patent R.* 1234, 69.
105. *Cal. Chanc. R. var.* 269.
106. Phillips D.R. 1925, 658–60, Williams G. 1962, 380.
107. *Cal. Close R.* 1231, 547.
108. NLW, Badm. Manorial 1571, 1575.
109. Williams D.H. 1984. II, 319.
110. NLW, Badm. Manorial 1663, m. 1d.
111. *Ibid.* 1657, mm. 2d, 6r, 10d.
112. *Ibid.* 1657, m. 5d.
113. *Ibid.* 1663, m. 1d.
114. *Ibid.* 1657, m. 6r (*?* for 'fore-stall').
115. *Ibid.* 1663, m. 4d.

CHAPTER 18

FISHING AND INDUSTRY

Fisheries *(See Map XIV)*

Perpetual abstinence from flesh-meat was strictly enjoined in the early history of the Cistercian Order (the sick only being excepted), and this practice was generally well observed until the early 14th century. Even when meat did come to be eaten in a special refectory set aside for this purpose, particularly after an enabling statute of the General Chapter in 1481, abstinence remained a significant element, especially in the seasons of Advent and Lent, when, in many monasteries, herrings were common fare.[1]

In Wales, monastic possession of both maritime and inland fishing rights meant a variety of produce – including herrings, eels, trout and salmon, and, where necessary, inland abbeys constructed their own fish-ponds. The importance of fishing to a great house like Tintern, was demonstrated in the post held by a monk or *conversus* (John of Walweir; 1320) as 'guardian of the fisheries',[2] as well as in the £6 p.a. expended in the closing years on the wages of the abbey's secular fishermen.[3] Tintern's situation by the salmon-rich river Wye was reflected when 'a young man of Tintern' took salmon to its daughter abbey at Kingswood (Gloucs; 1262).[4] A gravestone (of John Wilfred), yet to be seen at the abbey, is engraved with salmon and trout.

The Fisheries of Tintern

Tintern possessed rights in several Wye weirs, though the exact number varied through its history *(Fig. 102)*, as sometimes did their names. Early granted Alfsweir, Plumweir, and Stoweir, these were exchanged (about 1150) for a share in Walweir, Halfweir and Badingsweir[5] – yet in 1224 Plumweir, and in 1527 Stoweir, were back in the hands of the abbey.[6] Early Ordnance Survey maps mark a 'piscatory' near Tintern *(Fig. 120)*;[7] this was in fact the former Stow Weir House (of 1763).[8] In 1839, it was 'a vivid ruin by the water side'.[9] About 1246, Tintern was granted half of Ashweir with timber to maintain it.[10] Later (1460), it freely demised that portion of Ashweir 'nearest the Welsh side', to its former cellarer, Walter Gethin, and two layfolk – a sort of limited company![11]

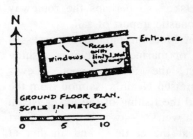

Fig. 120: Stow Weir 'Piscatory'. *(Crown copyright: Royal Commission on the Ancient and Historical Monuments of Wales [Ordnance Survey Archaeological Record Card]; N.V. Quinnell, 1957.*

The grant of Bigsweir to Tintern by Edward II (1326) reduced the profits of the Forest of Dean by 25s.[12] Tintern (by 1330) also owned Ithelsweir,[13] where (in 1397) with contrivances called 'wiles', it was accused of catching young salmon 'in defiance of the king and the statute'.[14]

The Wye fisheries were a cause of friction, particularly in the 14th century. There was a reluctance of local people and tenants given their use to pay the rents due – sometimes for years,[15] but the most notable incident occurred about 1330. Abbot de Camme caused several of the weirs to be raised – by five or six feet, thus impeding navigation, and especially affecting the passage of vessels laden with wines and food for the Earl of Lancaster's castle at Monmouth. When the bailiff and Steward of St Briavel's Castle were sent to lower the weirs, they were assaulted by a monk-led group of locals.[16]

Fishing in the Wye saw the employment of conning trows (as Ashweir and Stoweir, 1525),[17] and of corrock nets – like one lying between Stoweir and Plumweir, 1491).[18] Another fishery of Tintern lay between the Angidy mill-pond and the Wye (1438).[19] In the Severn Estuary, Tintern had fishing rights up to the middle of the river adjacent to its Woolaston and Moor Granges.[20] At Woolaston, a latter day tenant of the abbey was permitted 'to make puttes and engens in the river of Severn'.[21] For the purposes of fishing at its somewhat distant Estavarney Grange, Tintern made a weir and 'backwaters' in the river Usk.[22]

Fig. 121: Llantarnam's outlet to the river Usk.

The river Usk was also important to Llantarnam which, by 1383, enjoyed the lease of 'the Ceyne', a fishery at Tredunnock.[23] After the Suppression, Llantarnam was said to have had fishing rights in the Usk every ninth day.[24] It also had the fishing of the Afon Lwyd from Pontnewydd down to its confluence with the Usk.[25] A narrow strip of the parish of Llantarnam extended to the Usk, forming a land corridor for the monastery to the river *(Fig. 121)*. Might this access to the Usk have been for fishing purposes? In the 19th century, a salt-house and salt wharf stood east of the inlet off the Usk,[26] so perhaps the routeway was for the monastic import of salt.

Like Tintern, Margam and Neath possessed a combination of marine and riverine fishing rights. Whilst the Tudor poet, Lewis Morgannwg, praised Neath's 'salmon from the ocean',[27] it had the fishing of the lower Neath river[28] and of Crymlyn Bog,[29] and (1291) of seven weirs[30] – two of them at Cwrt Betws,[31] one (in the Tawe) at Swansea ferry near the castle,[32] and another at Kilvey.[33] Margam had, from its foundation,[34] the fishing of the Afan stream (salmon, gillings and sewin),[35] and of Kenfig Pool (a sand-dune impounded lagoon)[36] – but it knew instances of large-scale poaching, as in 1365 when it had to go to the County Court in Cardiff to regain possession of those fisheries.[37] Margam also had fishing rights in the rivers Ely[38] and Taff at Cardiff[39] – the latter originally a perquisite of Pendâr Abbey.

In west Wales, Whitland was served by adjacent fish-ponds,[40] by a weir in the Towy at its St Leonard's Chapel, St Ishmael's,[41] and had fishing rights at Haverfordwest each Friday and Friday night. In central Wales, Strata Florida, almost from its foundation,[42] had the right to fish in Cardigan Bay offshore from its properties of Morfa Ankar, Morfa Bychan and Morfa Mawr.[43] Both Strata Florida[44] and Vale Royal (as rector of Llanbadarn)[45] had fisheries in the Ystwyth at Aberystwyth, where herrings were the principal catch.[46] John Leland (*c.* 1538) vividly described the inland fisheries of Strata Florida, ascribing a dozen

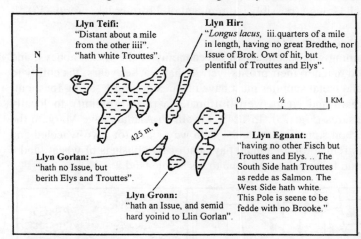

Llyn Teifi:
"Distant about a mile from the other iiii".
"hath white Trouttes".

Llyn Hir:
"*Longus lacus*, iii.quarters of a mile in length, having no great Bredthe, nor Issue of Brok. Owt of hit, but plentiful of Trouttes and Elys".

N

425 m.

Llyn Gorlan:
"hath no Issue, but berith Elys and Trouttes".

Llyn Gronn:
"hath an Issue, and semid hard yoinid to Llin Gorlan".

Llyn Egnant:
"having no other Fisch but Trouttes and Elys. ... The South Side hath Trouttes as redde as Salmon. The West Side hath white. This Pole is seene to be fedde with no Brooke."

0 ½ 1 KM.

Fig. 122: John Leland's comments on the Teifi Pools, 4¹/₂ km. ENE of Strata Florida.

or so natural lakes yielding eels and trout to the monastery – principally the Teifi Pools *(Fig. 122),*[47] in which, an ancient tradition had it, beavers also once lived.[48]

Cymer fished chiefly in the lower Mawddach ('the water of Cymer', *Fig. 7*) and at Neigwl Grange in Llŷn. The former consisted of two sections: the 'nether fishery' downstream from the abbey, and the 'upper fishery' upstream to Llyn Penmon.[49] The sea fishery and a weir at Neigwl[50] provided herrings, which led Prince David (1280) to include one *mease* of these (perhaps about 500 fish) in a rent he wished to exact from the monks.[51] Based upon Llywelyn's charter (1209), Cymer (1348) asserted its right to fish 'in all its rivers, ponds and waters, and in the havens and shores of the sea'.[52]

Other maritime houses were Aberconwy (originally) and Basingwerk. The former owned that part of the Menai Straits adjacent to its Gelliniog Grange (Anglesey), had fishing in the Conwy up to Abergyffin,[53] and, in the same river, a weir (the 'Warles') at Maenan.[54] There were also rights (until 1348) in the Dwyfach and Dwyfor rivers.[55] One abbot bought fishing nets at Chester (1258).[56] Basingwerk had a weir at West Kirby (Wirral),[57] was granted by Prince David (1240) a fifth part of the catch at Rhuddlan,[58] and had the fishing (though no salmon)[59] in Lake Tegid which it owned.[60]

Inland monasteries were less fortunate. Valle Crucis depended upon an adjacent large stank, and weirs in the Dee – like those at Llangollen and at Overton[61] – where, from its foundation, it had the right to fish weekly 'from vespers on Sunday until Monday morning'.[62] Marine fish were imported; the remains of a large cod (dating from the abbey's earliest years) have been excavated on site.[63] Fish-ponds played an important role at Cwmhir (perhaps at Fishpools Farm, 3 km. north-west of the monastery);[64] Grace Dieu (a 'Fishpool Meadow' forming part of the home demesne),[65] Dore's Llanfair Cilgoed Grange (a descending series of four; *Fig. 94*), and at Tintern's Trelech Grange (possibly the remnant of a former lake; *Map XVI*).[66]

Mineral Working *(See Map XIV)*

While it is true that mining was secondary in the economy of the Welsh abbeys, and cannot have contributed much to their profits, yet, in their earlier years, the ability to obtain their own fuel and metal supplies must have meant a domestic saving for them. In south Wales, Margam and Neath were fortunate in their proximity to locally outcropping Coal Measures *(Fig. 73)*. In 1249, Owain ab Alathur gave Margam the right to dig 'all the carbon stone' in his lands, with way-leave for 'two-wheeled and four-wheeled carts', in return for an annual payment of five bushels of wheat, and a promise of compensation for any damage done to his arable land.[67]

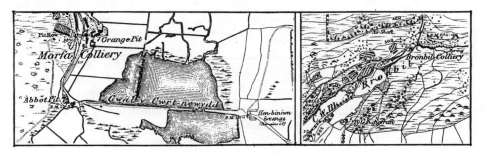

Fig. 123, left: the Coal Measures stretch west of Margam into the Bristol Channel; the term 'Grange Pit' could be modern, taken from the adjacent New Grange, but the term 'Abbot Pit', may well date from medieval times; *right:* a coal mine is noted at Bronbil just after the Suppression. *(Reduced from the 1st edn. O.S. Map).*

Margam's pits included those in Cefn Cribwr – very much an entity at the time of the Suppression,[68] on the boundary of Penhydd Waelod grange,[69] and, on the lands of Hafod-y-porth Grange, 'sea-coal' towards the estuary of the Ffrwdwyllt.[70] When, in the 1950s, the National Coal Board surveyed for possible new drift working on Aberbaiden Mountain, it seemed the coal had been taken by Margam centuries before. Neath's three pits in Gower, yielding 'pit-coal, stone coal, and sea-coal', at Grange (West Cross), Tir-y-abad (Gorseinon; *Fig. 99*), and at Oystermouth (Gower's Cross), were 'upholden with timber' (1577).[71] It is *possible* that Basingwerk mined coal at Coleshill,[72] and Llantarnam at Llanderfel.[73]

The Carboniferous Limestone fringe south-west of Margam *(Fig. 73)* gave that abbey both *lead* and *iron* ores, metals which were very useful in 13th century monastic building. In the mid-13th century, Margam had local mining rights with way-leave, and actively prospected for further supplies of these ores in Corneli.[74] One grant was effective 'as long as the mineral holds out'[75] – indicating the exhaustible nature of all ore deposits. In the Forest of Dean, Tintern was smelting iron from 1141[76] to at least 1268.[77] In the mid-15th century, it was extracting *silver* from lead within its outer court.[78] Grace Dieu was permitted by Henry III (1227) to mine 'as much (iron) ore as necessary' for its two itinerant forges at Penyard (Herefordshire), but it sold that manor in 1267, and presumably ceased smelting there.[79]

Prince Llywelyn's charter for Cymer (1209) had allowed it to take 'stones of whatever kind, metals and treasures'.[80] That it actively pursued mining and smelting is clear from a later abbot's claim (1348) to be able to take, 'for his work', materials which 'can be reduced to another state'.[81] Its forge at Trawsfynydd was in the hands of the Crown in 1392, when it produced 82 'dozen' of iron.[82] The abbey may also have had a forge in Llanfachreth.[83] In north-east Wales, Earl Ranulf (d. 1153) gave Basingwerk 'the manor of Fulbrook, on which there are silver deposits', but there is no tradition of the abbey profiting from them.[84] Nearby, Vale Royal Abbey (1291) mined lead in Englefield, at a time when its new monastery was being built.[85]

Early on (1198), Strata Marcella obtained lead-mining potential with its purchase of Cwm Llwyd, 'with all its utilities, above the same land and *below* it',[86] but most is known of Strata Florida's great lead mine at Briwnant in Cwmystwyth.[87] Leland (1538) wrote that it had ceased working, perhaps because 'the wood is sore wasted'[88] – in other words, fuel was lacking. Demised by the Crown in Elizabethan days, the lessee was permitted to dig 'pits and shafts', and have rights of 'way-leave and stay-leave for his carts, in the same way as did the abbot'.[89]

As with corn milling, so too *industrial inertia* has meant that former Cistercian smelting centres are occupied still today by heavy industry. This may have been reflected in the early wire works of Tintern's Angidy valley (1566),[90] whilst an iron forge at Whitland (1636) probably used the already existing mill and water facilities there.[91] The best tribute to monastic metallurgy comes in the modern nomenclature of the Neath Abbey Ironworks, and of the Abbey Steel Works, Port Talbot.

Stone quarrying was commonplace, especially for church and cloister construction *(Chapter 7)*. A quarry (probably belonging to Tintern) at Merthyr Gerain (1286), supplied 69 'great free-stones' for building purposes at Llangybi Castle,[92] whilst Grace Dieu (1306) had a 'quarry of stone' to enclose its park of T. (perhaps Trivel).[93]

Salt, brought in by ship to Margam, could be obtained by Basingwerk from its own pits in the Cheshire salt-field at Middlewich and Northwich.[94] In medieval days, it was essential for preserving winter slaughter meat.

Peat and *turf* formed an important medieval fuel supply. Strata Florida owned much of Cors Goch Glan Teifi (Tregaron Marsh), which, Leland noted, was 'a great fenny moor out of which the inhabitants dig turfs for fire'.[95] In one late lease, of the holding of Tydyn-y-gorsse, the turbary was excepted, being 'in the disposition of the abbot'.[96] Turfs featured more than once in post-Dissolution disputes concerning former Cistercian lands. One such (in 1611) centred upon the cutting of 10,000 turfs at Gofolion in Rhydcriw, a holding once belonging to Cymer.[97]

Wreck of Sea

The right to claim 'all and singular the goods which by shipwreck or tempest of the sea ... shall happen to be upon any lands of the monks',[98] was enjoyed by Aberconwy,[99] Neath,[100] Tintern,[101] Margam and Strata Florida, but, in the case of Cymer, was restricted to its own cargoes only, and that subject to inquest by two jurors.[102] Strata Florida's right to wreck, granted by Cynan ap Maredudd (1294) was confirmed as late as 1426. The charter indicates the variety of goods which might accrue, including 'wine, honey, corn, fish, precious stones, jewels ...'.[103] In the early 14th century, Margam's right to offshore wreck was twice (unsuccessfully) challenged; in 1333, it therefore gained a boat, three bales of wool, a coffer and a cask.[104] Its privilege of wreck endured to the Dissolution, and then passed to the Mansel family.[105]

NOTES

1. Lekai L.J. 1977, 370–71; Williams D.H. 1998, 245–46, 364.
2. *Reg. Ade de Orleton* 256–57.
3. *Valor Eccl.* IV, 370.
4. *Kingswood Docs.* 216.
5. 'Badings' = 'baited hooks for catching fish', – perhaps the later Hook Weir: Wood J.G. 1936, 209, 213.
6. *Cal. Charter R.* III, 98–98; *Close R.* 1336, 578; *Patent R.* 1326, 332; *Mon. Angl.* V, 268. In more modern mapping, they have been referred to as 'Plumb' and 'Stone' Weirs. At Plumbweir, Malmesbury Abbey had rights: PRO, SC 6 (Hen. VIII) 3986. Tintern also leased, certainly for a time (1291), Brockweir from Monmouth Priory.
7. NGR: ST 535985. For another plan, see: PRO, MPE 926 (of 1843).
8. NLW, Badminton Plans, Vol. 2, No. XX.
9. Thomas W.H. 1839, 18; *Cf.* Beattie W. 1844, 104.
10. *Cal. Charter R.* 1307, 104.
11. NLW, Badminton Manorial 1657, m. 14d. (This practice of a religious leading lay-folk in the almost autonomous administration of monastic assets, found its parallel elsewhere: Williams D.H. 1998, 297).
12. *Cal. Charter R.* 1341, 191.
13. BL, Campbell Charter III, 10: *MSS in* BM III, 622.
14. *Gloucs. Peace Rolls* 158.
15. *Reg. Adam de Orleton* 256–57.
16. *Cal. Inq. Misc.* II, 339; *Close R.* 1331, 370–71 1334, 304-05; *Patent R.* 1331, 201.
17. NLW, Badm. Manorial 1663, m. 4r.
18. NLW, Badm. Deeds, Group 2, 14480.
19. NLW, Badm. Manorial 1657, m. 2d.
20. *Cal. Charter R.* III, 104; *Mon. Angl.* V, 268.
21. *Chepstow, Tintern MSS* 1496.
22. *Mon. Angl.* V, 269.
23. *Cal. Close R.* 1383, 343; perhaps the later 'Sines' pool (NGR: ST 389939) – info. of Mr Geoff Mein.
24. *Augm. Rec.* 141.
25. PRO, STAC 5, M55/7; SC 6 (Hen. VIII) 2497, m. 9d.
26. Llanfihangel Llantarnam parochial tithe-map.
27. Birch W. de Gray. 1902, 140.
28. PRO, SC 6 (Hen. VIII) 5156, mm. 3d–4r.
29. Birch W. de Gray. 1902, 42.
30. *Taxatio Eccl.* 282.
31. PRO, SC 6 (Hen. VIII(5156, m. 8d.
32. *Cartae Glam.* II, 477; Birch W. de Gray. 1902, 69; Robinson W.R.B. 1967, 194.

33. PRO, SC 6 (Hen. VIII) 5156, m. 8d.
34. *Catal. Penrice* I, 1 (Charter 1).
35. *Cartae Glam.* V, 1771.
36. *Ibid.* IV, 1312–13.
37. *Ibid.* IV, 1312–18; Birch W. de Gray. 1897, 317–19.
38. Birch W. de Gray. 1897, 123.
39. *Catal. Penrice* I, 10 (Charter 23).
40. James T. 1978, 71 *et seq.*
41. PRO, SC 6 (Hen. VIII) 4903, m. 23; Rees W. 1953, 199; Evans G. 1915, 130.
42. Williams S.W. 1889, Appx. xiii, lxiii; Bowen E.G. 1950, 37.
43. PRO, E 315/103, f. 111.
44. Williams S.W. Appx. lxxi.
45. *Exchq. Proc. (2)* 102.
46. PRO, E 315/103, f. 111.
47. Williams S.W. 1889, Appx. v–vi.
48. Defoe D. II (1962) 58–59.
49. *Augm. Rec.* 122–23, 443; PRO, LR 1/212, f. 214.
50. *Rec. Carn.* 218.
51. Hays R.W. 1963, 75.
52. *Rec. Carn.* 199.
53. Hays R.W. 1963, 12.
54. UCNW, Mostyn (Bangor) Deeds 1281.
55. Hays R.W. 1963, 14; *Cf.* 16–17, 75.
56. *Ibid.* 51.
57. PRO, SC 6 (Hen. VIII) 5543, m. 4d.
58. Jones A. 1933, 173.
59. *Journey through Wales*, 198.
60. *Cal. Charter R.* 1285, 290.
61. Price G.V. 1952, 31–32, 81, 246–47.
62. *Anc. Pet.* 455.
63. Butler L.A.S. 1976, 122.
64. Thomas D. 1998, 7–8.
65. Williams D.H. 1976, 68.
66. NLW, Badm. Manorial 1704, mm. 2–4.
67. Birch W. de Gray. 1897, 257.
68. *Ibid.* 360, 362; *Cf. Augm. Rec.*415; PRO, E 315/201, f. 37.
69. *Ibid.* 355–56.
70. *Ibid.* 354.
71. *Augm. Rec.* 414–15, 417; PRO, SC 6 (Hen. VIII) 5156, m. 1r.
72. Jones A. 1933, 170.
73. Open-cast activity here in 1634: Rees W. 1968. I, 107.
74. Birch W. de Gray. 1897, 192, 266, 274.
75. *Ibid.* 192.
76. *Cal. Charter R.* III, 96.
77. *Cal. Inq. Misc.* I, 120 (No. 354).
78. Courtney P. 1989, 125.
79. *Rot. Litt. Claus.* II, 183, 185.
80. *Llywelyn's Charter* 56.
81. *Rec. Carn.* 199; *Arch. Camb.* 1873, 170.
82. PRO, SC 6/1203/2.
83. RCAHMW, *Merioneth* (1921) 106; Schubert H.R. 1957, 129 (*n.* 1).
84. *Cal. Charter R.* 1285, 89.
85. *Cal. Patent R.* 1283, 82; VCH, *Chester* III (1980) 157.
86. *Strata Marcella Ch.* 161–62 (No. 19).
87. *Augm. Rec.* 228–29.
88. *Itin. J. Leland* III, 123.
89. PRO, E 315/155, f. 3.
90. Courtney P. 1991, 150.
91. James T. 1978, 71.
92. *Arch. Camb.* 1956, 104.
93. *Year Books* (Rolls Ser.) XXXI (33/35 Edw. I) 330.
94. Owen E. 1920, 57; Wrottesley G. 1906, 336, 339; *Chester Recog. R.* (36) 25.
95. Williams S.W. 1889, Appx. iii.
96. PRO, LR 1/228, f. 151.
97. *Exchq. Proc. (2)* 231; Cf. *(1)* 89.
98. Williams S.W. 1889, Appx. xvii.
99. Hays R.W. 21; *Cal. Charter R.* 1332, 268.
100. Birch W. de Gray. 1902, 49, 58–61.
101. *Cal. Charter R.* III, 104-05.
102. *Rec. Carn.* 199; *Llywelyn's Ch.* 52, 58.
103. Williams S.W. 1889, 147; Appx. lvii–lxxiv.
104. Birch W. de Gray. 1897, 296, 303–04.
105. *Star Chamber Proc.* 82–83; Rees W. 1957, 178–80.

CHAPTER 19

TITHES AND APPROPRIATED PARISHES

The fundamental document of the Cistercian Order, the *Charter of Charity*, absolutely forbade the White Monks to receive tithes, for they were intended to live solely by the fruits of their own labour. This ideal was rather short-lived, and resistance to the reception of tithes was perhaps affected by the incorporation of other religious orders, like the congregation of Savigny (1147) who did accept them.[1] Before the 12th century came to its close, the Welsh Cistercians were beginning to receive parish churches and their greater tithes, and were castigated for so doing by Giraldus Cambrensis.[2]

Nearly eighty parishes in Wales were appropriated to Cistercian abbeys *(Fig. 124)*, Cwmhir alone had none. At first, tithes were a source of food, of 'hidden income'; later, demised, they became a source of cash. With other revenues from their parishes, tithes formed the 'spiritualities' of an abbey, accounting for almost three-quarters of the gross revenue of Valle Crucis and over one-third of that of Cymer.[3]

The income and tithes appropriated parishes brought in motivated monasteries to seek their acquisition in times of financial hardship (thus Margam sought Aberafan),[4] of natural disasters – like floods (so Neath appropriated St Donat's),[5] of a heavy burden of charity and hospitality (Tintern therefore acquired Woolaston),[6] and when extra resources were needed to further building work (for this Valle Crucis acquired Wrexham).[7] It helped if an abbey had a generous benefactor, like Prince David (1240) giving Holywell church to Basingwerk,[8] or, indeed, a Cistercian bishop, like Cadogan of Bangor (1215–36) confirming Llangurig to Strata Florida.[9]

The process of appropriation could be both lengthy and costly, so much so as to delay any real benefit.[10] The first step was to obtain the advowson of the benefice and then await the voidance of the cure. Approval to appropriate was required from the diocesan bishop and his chapter, with confirmation from both king and pope. Each stage might cost substantial sums of monies, and there might be litigation by injured parties. The deed accomplished, the monastery, now rector of the church, had to maintain the chancel and find housing and stipend for the new vicar and his successors. There might be customary dues to pay to the bishop and his archdeacon, whilst the possession of spiritualities qualified an abbot to be called upon as a collector of clerical tenths and subsidies *(Chapter 3)*.

The necessary steps can be traced in Wales. Neath was granted the advowson of St Donat's in 1341, the appropriation received papal blessing in 1344 and royal confirmation in 1346.[11] Margam's appropriation of Afan church (papal approval in 1383, royal confirmation in 1384) was certified (in June 1385) by the archdeacon of Llandaff, the way having been paved by the resignation of the rector.[12] Llanbadarn Fawr fell into Vale Royal's lap partly because of the consecration of its rector, Robert Stretton, as Bishop of Coventry and Lichfield (1360). Unfortunately, Innocent VI's death briefly delayed proceedings.[13]

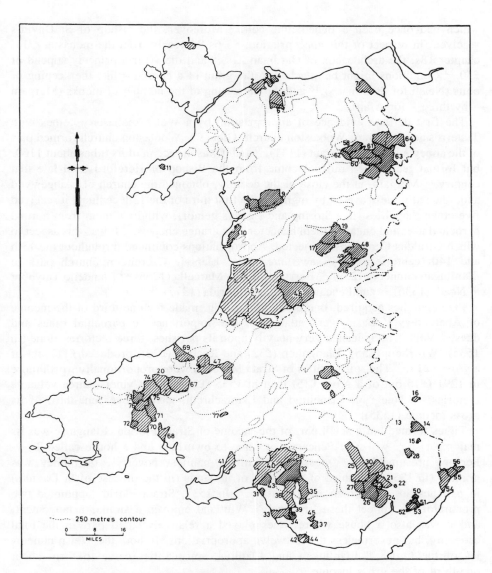

Fig. 124: Welsh parishes appropriated by the Cistercians.
(The number of each parish relates to the number recorded in Appendix III [Inventory]).

The matter of cost varied. Margam's acquisition of Afan church was only obtained 'at great expense from the Holy See',[14] for there will have been a contribution to the papal coffers, and the expenses of travel to Rome, or the engagement of representatives there. Vale Royal paid no less than 1,000 marks to Gloucester Abbey (1398) in return for the latter surrendering its rights in Llanbadarn church, which had once been a Benedictine cell.[15] Moreover, the bishop of St David's received, in respect of this appropriation, £3 6s 8d yearly from the monastery, his chapter 18s, the archdeacon of Cardigan 21s,[16] and the vicar a princely stipend of £20.[17] Conditions might be attached to the grant of a church – like the keeping of obits (Neath for St Donat's),[18] and the increasing of the number of monks (Margam – by three – for Afan).[19]

The first definite evidence of appropriation by a Welsh monastery comes with Tintern's acquisition of Woolaston church (Gloucs.). Woolaston church formed part of the abbey's foundation grant (1131),[20] and it was in receipt of its tithes about 1160, but formal recognition did not come from the Bishop of Hereford until late that century.[21] Margam, at the close of the century, obtained the church of Llangewydd and, allegedly, destroyed it by night. In the first third of the 13th century, it received five other chapelries (like Stormy and Eglwys-geinor), withdrew them from normal parochial use, and engaged them henceforth as grange chapels.[22] It was this aspect to which Giraldus Cambrensis objected. Appropriations continued throughout the 13th and 14th centuries. They saw, *inter alia*, Llanfair Caereinion church pass to Llanllugan nunnery (1239),[23] Berriw to Strata Marcella (1265),[24] Llandeilo Talybont to Neath (1336),[25] and Pencarreg to Strata Florida (1377).[26]

Five churches acquired, one being Llanbadrig, made for one-third of the income of Aberconwy.[27] Basingwerk attached a like importance to parochial tithes and dues.[28] Valle Crucis leaned very heavily upon its parishes; three rectories alone (in 1535): Wrexham (£55), Llangollen (£32) and Ruabon (£30), produced £117 out of a gross £214.[29] The spiritualities of Strata Marcella were proportionally worth more in 1291 (£16 out of a gross £35) than in 1535 (£22/87).[30] Cymer's three valuable rectories – Llanegryn, Llanelltud and Llanfachreth, gave it over one-third of its gross income (1535).[31]

Tithes formed but a small part of the income of Strata Florida. Llangurig was its major parish,[32] whilst at Pencarreg it came to own land and a house called Ty-y-Person, presumably the vicarage.[33] Citing 'manifest poverty', the abbey was granted (in 1339) one-third of the tithes of its lands (in the diocese of St David's) in parishes not of its own appropriation.[34] In 1537, Strata Florida appointed two procurators to collect these 'tryanes'.[35] Whitland enjoyed a similar arrangement, and it was also a house where tithes played a relatively small part in the total economy, but nevertheless it had twelve appropriations. In both the Welsh nunneries of the Order,[36] Llanllugan and Llanllŷr, spiritualities came to form about one-third of the gross income.

The most outstanding single appropriation in Wales was that of Llanbadarn Fawr, with its ten dependent chapels (like Aberystwyth and Llanafan), by the Cheshire abbey of Vale Royal.[37] It brought an annual return of no less than £120 (equivalent now to £36,000).[38] Effectively, it was the gift of the Black Prince, made partly because of the need to finance the rebuilding of the church nave at Vale Royal, destroyed in a great storm (19 Oct. 1359).[39] Although episcopal, royal and papal approval was received for the gift (1361–62),[40] Gloucester Abbey, of which Llanbadarn had once been a cell, later objected. The case came before the Council in Chancery (1381),[41] eventually, royal approval of the appropriation was reiterated (1399),[42] but the cost of 1,000 marks 'for the ransom of the church', led to divisions in the community at Vale Royal.[43] In the mid-15th century, the abbot complained of the treatment he and his agents received in Wales.[44]

In south Wales, tithes and the income of tithe-barns contributed £70 towards Margam's gross income of £190 (1535).[45] Its eight churches included Llangewydd, first leased from its priest, William, in 1188, then abjured by his successor, Riuan, about 1195, in favour of the monks, and finally destroyed by them;[46] its site now commemorated in the field-name, *Cae'r Hen Eglwys*.[47] Two of its churches, Kenfig (1206)[48] and Newcastle (1265), were leased from Tewkesbury Abbey. The rent for the latter rose from £15 13s 4d to £23. In 1336, it was agreed that it could be increased or decreased 'according to the variations of times and years'.[49]

Neath received substantial income from the rectorial tithes of about six churches, including Cadoxton (Llangatwg-iuxta-Nedd). Surprisingly, the latter – whilst listed in the *Taxatio* of 1291 – finds no mention in the *Valor* of 1535,[50] undoubtedly, an oversight. In Gwent, Llantarnam's possession of Basaleg church, with its dependent chapelries – like Mynyddislwyn, indicates that the monastery had long absorbed the possessions of Basaleg priory, a Benedictine cell of Glastonbury, probably early in the 13th century.[51] Grace Dieu's principal appropriation – perhaps not received until after 1291 – was Skenfrith.[52] It leased the tithes of its home chapelry, Treurgan, from the chapter of Llandaff.[53]

Apart from Woolaston, Tintern had the churches of Lydd in Kent and Halvergate in Norfolk – the last by gift of Earl Roger Bigod (1301),[54] and, in Gwent, the church of Magor, originally leased from the Italian abbey of Gloria in the diocese of Anagni.[55] It paid small annual pensions for other tithes, as 5s to Goldcliff priory for Porton church; the latter's value was small, its parish partly washed away by the sea. Tintern also received 'Lammas tithes', worth £2 yearly.[56]

Appropriated churches were normally served by vicars presented to the diocesan bishop by the monastery concerned, assisted by stipendiary chaplains. This right of patronage became a cause of dispute between Valle Crucis and Bishop Anian II of St Asaph (about 1275), since the abbey (as sometimes other houses) preferred, in the majority of its churches, to appoint only chaplains rather than perpetual vicars – the latter having far greater rights.[57] Aberconwy (1284) was expected to appoint three chaplains to serve Aberconwy parish church: one Welsh and two English.[58] If a monastery failed to nominate, as did Tintern once in the case of Woolaston (1252), it lost its right of patronage for that turn.[59]

The ordination lists of episcopal registers (those for Hereford are mostly extant) show the frequent presentation of candidates on the 'title' of a monastery. These newly ordained served as chaplains, undoubtedly rising to incumbencies in due course. Monastic letters of presentation under seal are extant for, amongst others, Matthew Harding, presented for ordination as acolyte by the abbot of Llantarnam in 1465,[60] and for Hugh Gruffydd, sponsored by the abbot of Basingwerk in 1533.[61] The Hereford registers record several presentations by Tintern to the vicarage of Woolaston.

A detailed agreement might be drawn up at the time of an appropriation, laying down specific conditions of stipend and housing for the incumbent. Margam, on receiving the church of Newcastle, was obliged to supply the vicar with a court and house, 'sufficient according to the judgement of local men'.[62] Neath allocated a house and lands by St Donat's church for the vicar there.[63] The vicar of Magor (Gwent), however, paid Tintern 6d rent for 'the rectory by Magor cemetery';[64] this may be the ruined house there called 'the procurator's house'.[65] Stipends varied, and most incumbents were not as fortunate as the vicar of Llanbadarn with his £20 per year. One of the poorest was Tintern's vicar at Woolaston: his stipend of £2 p.a., fixed in 1274, remained unchanged in 1535.[66] In 1385, the Bishop of Hereford sequestrated the living because the stipend had not been paid.[67]

Fig. 125: The initials of William of Stratford, Abbot of Vale Royal, at Llanbadarn Fawr church.
(W. Gwyn Thomas; Arch. Camb. 1978).

As rector, the monastery owning a church had the duty to maintain the fabric of the chancel. Abbot William of Stratford of Vale Royal rebuilt the east end of Llanbadarn Fawr in the late 15th century, leaving his name (*Fig. 125*) engraved in the stonework.[68] A century before, an episcopal visitation (1397) shows Tintern to have somewhat neglected Alvington church (Gloucs.): the chancel windows were broken, and the chancel was 'defective in its tiling and ceiling'.[69] When appropriated churches and tithes came to be demised, the lessees were obliged to keep the chancels in good repair. Margam (1522) demanded this duty of those who sought the chapels of Laleston and Tythegston.[70]

Lessees, both before and after the Suppression, also had to maintain the incumbent or chaplain. Dore (1530), granting layfolk the reversion of the advowson of Gwenddwr (Brecs.), allowed them to appoint a priest, but first they were to 'present him to the abbot and convent, as to his ordinary, who shall admit him to ye cure'.[71] Later Crown lessees occasionally employed ousted monks to serve their former chapels: this was true of John York officiating at Strata Florida,[72] and of John Didbroke – still serving Dore's Llanfair Cilgoed chapel thirty-four years after the Dissolution.[73]

Glimpses can be caught of the nature of the greater tithes forming the chief perquisites from appropriated parishes. Those of Ruabon, pertaining to Valle Crucis, included 'corn, hay, eggs, hemp and flax, geese and pigs'.[74] Grace Dieu's tithes from Skenfrith, paid in kind as late as 1542, consisted then of two horse-loads of wheat, twelve horse- and two wagon-loads of barley, two loads of beans, and seven loads of oats.[75] Lesser tithes went to the vicar, but at Gwenddwr (1529) Dore made provision that 'if the abbot be willing to have the tithing lambs, the vicar shall see them to him for his money before any other man'.[76] Payment of tithes in kind necessitated concomitant barns for storage purposes. Margam had at least five: in Llangynwyd, Kenfig, Laleston, Glyncorrwg and Penllin.[77]

The possession of tithes was a highly prized asset, and not infrequently a matter of contention.[78] Tintern had a lengthy dispute with Llanthony Prima regarding Alvington chapel (Gloucs.); it extended, intermittently, from about 1160 to 1318 when Llanthony renounced its claim to the chapel.[79] The tithes arising from lands of Margam at Llanfeuthin occasioned a dispute with Gloucester Abbey – as Rector of Llancarfan (1262, 1322).[80] An extreme example of Cistercian partiality to tithes came in an alleged raid (about 1300) by an abbot of Strata Marcella, who, attended by his retainers and 'with horses and arms and banners displayed', forcibly took tithes belonging to Chirbury Priory.[81] Interest in tithes persisted to the Suppression: Nicholas Pennant, the last abbot of Basingwerk, was accused of causing his prior, and various relatives and friends, to steal the tithe of oats belonging to his vicar in Holywell.[82]

In latter years, perhaps because of the difficulties of collection, tithes might be farmed out just as a monastery might demise its lands.[83] Strata Marcella leased out its churches of Betws (1492–1517)[84] and Berriw (1529),[85] though three valuable rectories of Cymer were still 'in the hands of the abbot' at the Suppression.[86] To help raise money to avoid closure, Whitland farmed out all its twelve parishes within the space of two months (October–November 1538).[87] The recipients might be people of local influence (like Jenkin Morgan of Caerleon receiving several churches from Llantarnam),[88] or there might be a degree of nepotism (as when Abbot Pennant of Basingwerk demised two sets of tithes to his brothers, David and John).[89] After the Dissolution, these leases could cause contention as to the rightful owner: at Llantarnam Lettice Morgan competed with Jenkin Morgan for their possession.[90] Berriw church was said to have been demised to Nicholas Purcell by Strata Marcella in an irregular fashion.[91]

NOTES

1. Lekai L.J. 1977, 66, 450, 759.
2. Cowley F.G. 1977, 181.
3. PRO, SC 6 (Hen. VIII) 5222–23, 5259.
4. Birch W. de Gray. 1897, 321.
5. *Ibid.* 1902, 132–33.
6. Cowley F.G. 1977, 185.
7. Price G.V. 1952, 68–71.
8. *Arch. Camb.* 1846, 107–08.
9. Cowley F.G. 1977, 185; but *cf.* O'Sullivan J.F. 1947, 13, for its donation by Hywel ab Ieuan [*d.* 1185].
10. Desmond L.A. 1975, 246–47.
11. Birch W. de Gray. 1902, 30–33; *Cal.* Papal L. (Pet.) I, 62; the abbot of 1341 was a native of the parish, and will have known the grantor, Edward Stradling.
12. *Cartae Glam.* IV, 1350–51, 1358, 1366–67; matters were helped by

the bishop of Llandaff being the king's confessor.
13. *Cal. Papal Reg. (L)* IV, 88; the bishop of St David's acted 'with the consent of his chapter'.
14. *MSS in BM* III, 555 (No. 852).
15. Lewis F.R. 1938, 29–30.
16. *Cal. Papal Reg. (L)* IV, 88.
17. *Exchq. Proc. (2)* 103.
18. Birch W. de Gray. 1902, 132.
19. *Ibid.* 1897, 320.
20. *Cal. Charter R.* III, 97; VCH, *Gloucester* X, 115.
21. Cowley F.G. 1977, 185.
22. *Ibid.* 182–83; *MSS in BM* III, 568 (945).
23. *Mont. Collns.* XVI (Gittins E.P.) 347–48.
24. Jones M.C. 1870, 122 *et seq.*
25. Birch W. de Gray. 1902, 130–33; *Anc.* Pet. 404; *Cal. Papal Reg.*

(*Pet.*) I, 40.

26. *Cal. Patent R.* 1377, 14.
27. Hays R.W. 1963, 116–19.
28. Jones A.J. 1933, 171–72, 175.
29. Price G.V. 1952, 31, 66–81.
30. Williams D.H. 1976b, 188–89.
31. *Valor Eccl.* IV, 426; PRO, E 315/201, f. 12; SC 6 (Hen. VIII) 5222.
32. Williams S.W. 1889, 111; *Cal. Papal Reg.* (*L*) I, 558–59.
33. RCAHMW, *Carmarthenshire* (1917) 235 (No. 695).
34. Williams S.W. 1889, Appx. lii–liv.
35. NLW, Cwrtmawr MS 873D, p. 13.
36. Cowley F.G. 1977, 186; PRO, LR 1/228, f. 129d.
37. *Anc. Pet.* 360; *Early Chanc. Proc.* 37; *Exchq. Proc.* (*2*) 123.
38. Bevan W.L. 1888, 103.
39. Lewis F.R. 1938, 24–25.
40. *Ibid.* 27–29.
41. *Anc. Pet.* 359–60.
42. Lewis F.R. 1938, 32; *Cf.* 29–30..
43. PRO, E 326/8648.
44. Lewis F.R. 1938, 33.
45. *Valor Eccl.* IV, 351.
46. *Cartae Glam.* I, 200–01, 206–07; Cowley F.G. 1977, 182.
47. NGR: SS 875809.
48. Llewellyn R.W. 1898, 145.
49. Randall H.J. 1955, 20; Birch W. de Gray, 1897, 343–44.
50. Williams D.H. 1984. II, 339.
51. *MSS in BM* III, 710 (No. 20406).
52. *Cal. Patent R.* 1291, 451; *Augm. Rec.* 137, 140–41.
53. *Valor Eccl.* IV, 361.
54. *Cal. Patent R.* 1307, 530–31, *Valor Eccl.* IV, 370.
55. *Cal. Close R.* 1385, 638; *Patent R.* 1442, 85–86.
56. *Valor Eccl.* IV, 370–71.
57. Price G.V. 1952, 78–79; *Arch. Camb.* 1868, 156.
58. Hays R.W. 1963, 66, 117–18.
59. *Cal. Papal Reg.* (*L*) I, 288; VCH, *Gloucester* X, 115.
60. NLW, LL/0/4131.
61. Hawarden R.O. D/PT/995.
62. Randall H.J. 1955, 20.
63. Birch W. de Gray. 1902, 133; *Cal. Papal Reg.* (*L*) VI, 62.
64. NLW, Badm. Manorial 1571 (of 1388); *Cf.* NLW, Barnard Deed 5, Tredegar Park Deeds, Box 58 (No. 65).
65. Thomas H.J. 1992, 31–34.
66. VCH, *Gloucester* X, 115; *Valor Eccl.* IV, 370–71.
67. *Reg. J. Gilbert* 89.
68. Thomas W.G. 1978, 127–29.
69. Bannister A.T. 1929, 449–50.
70. PRO, LR1/228, f. 88; SC 6 (Hen. VIII) 5155, mm. 7d; *Exchq. Proc.* (*1*) 210.
71. PRO, E 303/5/96.
72. PRO, LR 1/228, f. 65d.
73. Jones J. 1997, 89 (No. 28).
74. Price G.V. 1952, 73.
75. *Augm. Rec.* 137.
76. PRO, E 303/5/96.
77. PRO, E 315/417, ff. 5d–6r; LR 1/228, f. 88; SC 6 (Hen. VIII) 5155, m. 7d; *Augm. Rec.* 421; *Valor Eccl.* IV, 351.
78. Williams D.H. 1984. II, 345.
79. *Ibid.* 1976, 127–28.
80. Cowley F.G. 1977, 242.
81. *Anc. Pet.* 492.
82. Owen E. 1920, 66.
83. Williams D.H. 1984. II, 345–47.
84. PRO, LR 1/213, f. 137d.
85. Williams D.H. 1976b, 178, 188.
86. PRO, SC 6 (Hen. VIII) 5222.
87. PRO, SC 6 (Hen. VIII) 4903.
88. *Augm. Rec.* 134–35.
89. Owen E. 1920, 64.
90. *Augm. Rec.* 134–35.
91. Williams S.W. 1891, 29–30; *Augm. Rec.* 151.

Chapter 20

DEMISE OF MONASTIC LAND

As monasteries aimed, in the 13th century, at making their land management more efficient, and especially as direct cultivation lessened with the diminution in *conversi* numbers, there was an increasing incidence of land demise by the Cistercians. This was accelerated in the 14th century by the decision of Boniface VIII (1302) to allow the tithe-free lands of the White Monks to retain the *status quo* even if demised, and by the Black Death – with its consequent labour shortage and concurrent social change.[1]

The General Chapter attempted to regulate the process, but in such a way as to leave many loopholes. In 1208, it allowed poor land, or land not able to be cultivated, to be demised for half the produce, or in any other way. In 1220, 'less useful' land could be farmed out, and, a few years later (1224), general permission was given – providing it had the consent of a monastery's father-abbot and of the community.[2] As early as 1203, Innocent III, in a bull granted to Margam, insisted that the consent of 'at least the larger and wiser part of the [monastic] chapter' was essential.[3] Even by the close of the 12th century, Margam had demised several small plots of land in Kenfig.[4]

Some major *outlying* possessions leased outright, at a relatively early date, included Strata Florida's Y Dywarchen Grange (by 1291),[5] and Cwmhir's Carnaf-Gabalfa complex (by 1387).[6] Control might be kept of most granges, but within them (as at Tintern's Merthyr Gerain by 1388)[7] much land had been alienated, though some demense retained. The consequence was that, by around 1400, little remained in Wales to distinguish Cistercian from Benedictine economy.[8]

An unusual lease occurred (December 1351) when, possibly as a consequence of the Black Death, Dore demised all its lands in Cantrefselyf (Brecs.) for ten years for a return of 40 marks per year. The lessees were a five-man company, headed by two monks, whilst three laymen completed the 'board of directors'.[9] It was a move which had its parallel elsewhere,[10] but it was not in accordance with the early emphasis of the *Charter of Charity*: 'In raising our animals and cultivating our lands, we are not to have joint dealings with laymen, such as giving or receiving shares or profits'.[11]

There were instances of improper and mischievous demising of monastic land – such as occasioned by Abbot John ap Rhys of Strata Florida which led to the undoing of Cymer (1443),[12] and by Abbot Richard Vaughan of Cwmhir (1516–30) who, perhaps under pressure from influential lay-folk, irregularly demised three granges.[13]

More legitimately, from the 15th century on, a succession of properties – often lying at some distance from their parent abbey – were farmed out, though it is not clear whether the leases were new, or were entered upon after the expiry of the previous holder's tenure.[14] They included the demise of Sker Grange by Neath (1467),[15] of Glossop Manor by Basingwerk (1484),[16] and of Celynog Grange by Strata Florida (1521),[17] to name but a few. The rapid acceleration of leasing in the last years of Cistercian life has been noted *(Chapter 6)*.

Even where land remained 'in the abbot's hands', it was largely farmed by tenants under the supervision of a bailiff *(Chapter 14)*. The result was that, by the Suppression, Cwmhir's home manor of Golon was split into 75 holdings,[18] and Llantarnam's Wentsland-Bryngwyn into 55 portions.[19] Demising intruded even into the immediate confines of a monastery: at Strata Florida (1534), John ap Dyo had a house 'within the precinct of the monastery';[20] likewise, at Cwmhir (1537), a rent of 3s. 4d was received for 'one parcel of land within the precinct of the monastery'.[21]

At the Dissolution, two of Strata Floridas's granges (Abermiwl and Cwmdeuddwr) were, unusually, supervised by a monk-bailiff.[22] At Tintern also, two granges (Moor and Rogerstone) remained under the control of its bailiffs, but Moor had lately been 'restored to the abbot's own use'.[23] Neath retained Cwrt Betws and Cwrt Herbert under its control.[24] Even when a grange was demised outright, some demesne might be retained:[25] Margam, leasing its Moor Grange (Cardiff, 1517) reserved two acres of hay.[26] Would be tenants did not always appreciate marginal land: one holding of Strata Florida (1539) lay unoccupied 'because it was in the hills and no one wished to live on it!'.[27]

Land was held under several forms of tenancy. Glanmor Williams has shown the importance of copyholders on the properties of Llantarnam (186), Margam (115) and Neath (68).[28] Eleven tenements of Neath in Gelligarn were 'never letted, but only by copy of court roll' (1540).[29] On the death (in 1524) of Tintern's tenant of the Sheephouse in Porthcaseg, 'there came Catherine, his widow', to the manorial court, displaying a 'copy' of the tenancy.[30] Seventy-one of Margam's copyholders held *per virgam*, and in perpetuity; a relic of the former virgaters, villeins rendering services in proportion to their holdings. Others held their land for 'three lives'.[31] Leaseholders were more important at Strata Florida (175) and Whitland (138).[32] In their late leases, a term of ninety-nine years was common;[33] at Margam seventy years only was known,[34] at Strata Florida's Y Dywarchen Grange but ten.[35]

On demising land, care might be taken to delimit its exact bounds. When, in 1519, the borders of the holding of one of Margam's tenants were confirmed by a twelve-man jury, the Book of the Gospels was carried round them in accordance with 'the custom of the manor'.[36] A lease by Tintern (1493) was delimited by reference to adjacent holdings; one granted by Neath (1534) had as reference points 'the wall that cometh from the Key *(quay)* and the way that cometh from the abbey'.[37]

Entry fines (sometimes called 'relief')[38] were payable – at the manorial court – on assuming a monastic holding, rents thereafter to the bailiff or reeve.[39] At Tintern, entry fines were about three times the annual rental, even greater. John Whitmyll, in 1506, paid down £1 13s 4d, but his annual rent was only 2s.[40] At Strata Florida's Y Dywarchen, tenants paid 'double the rent in fine', a payment colloquially called 'Beverage'.[41] Entry fines might be paid, in part at least, in kind. Nicholas le Whyte paid Tintern (1312) two gallons of wine, and a 1s rental thereafter.[42] John Mason (1454) gave a salmon.[43] Tintern's tenants at Landreston (St Pierre) paid a collective 'recognizance' of one mark on the accession of a new abbot;[44] certain of Strata Marcella's tenants paid 'myze' upon an abbot's death.[45]

On the death of a tenant, *heriot* was payable by some monastic lessees – though not all.[46] Heriot might also be payable from the chattels of anyone dying on the property, strangers included (as at Llantarnam's Bryngwyn Grange, 1496),[47] and if a holding passed out of one tenant's hands into the possession of another ('on decease or alienation', as was the custom at Strata Florida's Anhuniog Grange).[48] Heriot consisted, customarily, of yielding to the abbey the 'best beast' of the deceased (Margam, 1516;[49] Strata Florida, 1524).[50] It might be a sheep[51] or a ram[52] or a horse,[53] or it might be commuted to a pecuniary payment.[54]

In west Wales, especially, certain customary payments dating from pre-monastic times were also owed by certain tenants.[55] The chiefest of these was a heavy burden known as *'comortha'*: 'a fine payable every third year over and beside the annual rent'.[56] The total value of 'comortha' to Strata Florida averaged nearly one-third of its income from landed property in those years when it fell due.[57] From tenants on its Anuniog-Morfa Mawr and Hafodwen Granges, Strata Florida received an annual tribute in kind, *'exania'*, bringing it from those properties (perhaps at Christmas) 88 pullets and 180 capons, respectively.[58] Other of its tenants yielded tributes called 'custom wool' and 'mountain silver' – the latter a payment for grazing rights.[59]

The General Chapter of the Order (1208), in permitting leasing, had envisaged that tenants would pay their rent in kind 'for half the produce'.[60] Payment in kind in Wales – where it was by no means a novel practice – probably never achieved this dimension, and money rents were often sought from the outset. Payments in kind, as time passed, were often commuted to money rents, but some survived through until the Suppression.

At that time (1539), the tenants of Strata Florida's lands in Ceredigion rendered to the abbey approximately 90 teils of oats [1 teil = about 5½ bushels], 300 teils of oatmeal, several hundred truggs of corn, 450 capons and pullets, about 120 topstans of wool, and, every second year, 120 sheep *(Fig. 77; Map XV)*.[61] No small return! In addition, Morfa Mawr gave eggs, white bread and 'blade corn',[62] and, from three granges close to the abbey, came 'black oats' for horse fodder – a tribute known as 'cylch march'.[63] A similar picture can be painted for Whitland *(Figs. 78, 98)*.

Margam, too, received a variety of produce. Its early rents expected in kind included 1 lb. of pepper (for lands in Kenfig; early 13th C.),[64] and 1 bushel of 'white salt' (for a tenement in Bristol, 1261).[65] Later, it was to demise Hafod-y-porth Grange (1470) for 10 marks and a crannock of salt yearly,[66] whilst four other granges still rendered appreciable quantities of wheat and barley.[67] Amongst other rents payable to Welsh Cistercian houses were: salt to Basingwerk from its pits in Northwich,[68] corn to Cymer from Neigwl,[69] and oats and oatmeal to the nuns of Llanllŷr.[70]

The decrease in the last decades in monastic vocations, and hence of mouths to feed, probably spurred on an increasing commutation of kind rents into money payments.[71] In the case of Margam's Afan fisheries, commutation was allowed at the rate of 8d per salmon, 4d per gilling, and ½d per sewin (1532).[72] Rents in kind, though, continued to be paid until the Suppression by certain tenants of Margam (as wheat and barley for Tanglwyst Grange),[73] of Basingwerk ('clean and winnowed wheat' for Caldy Grange),[74] and of Tintern (110 qtrs. of wheat being unpaid from Merthyr Gerain's tenants when the Dissolution came).[75]

Labour services of one kind or another formed part of the conditions attaching to several tenancies, but they do not appear to have been a heavy burden, being limited, usually, to three or four days a year at most.[76] Carriage duties included the porterage of iron and salt from Carmarthen to Strata Florida by its tenant of Hafodwen (a southerly grange conveniently situated for this task), whilst its lessee of Y Dywarchen (also in a suitable position) had the obligation to bring to the monastery herrings and imported wine from Aberystywth.[77] At Tintern's Merthyr Gerain and Moor Granges (1388, 1412), rents were, in part or whole, foregone in return for the carting of the demesne corn.[78]

Customary services, in seasonal times of especial agrarian need, included over 150 man-days of work all told on three granges of Whitland.[79] Strata Florida's tenants at Y Dywarchen were obliged to spend a day ploughing, a day casting dung, and a day in reaping.[80] It expected such duties also at Morfa Mawr, but, in course of time, allowed commutation for cash payments on three granges.[81] So, too, did a latter day abbot of Valle Crucis, as some of his tenants in Halghton lived up to 'five miles from the grange', and had to be rebuked 'for coming so late to work'. Individual payments of $10^{1}/_{2}$d each were expected of them.[82]

The building and/or maintenance of property was another condition sometimes written into monastic leases.[83] Basingwerk's lessee of forty acres at Overleigh (Cheshire, 1482) was to build upon it 'a house of two bays and two cross-chambers', the abbey providing the timber required.[84] Tintern obtained a villein's promise (at its Porthcaseg Court, 1263) that he would rebuild the house he had allowed to fall into ruin.[85] A tenant of its Moor Grange (1493) was presented at court for not repairing her barn.[86] Basingwerk expected a tenant of a nine acre holding at Calcot (1498) to enclose it within four years,[87] whilst Margam demanded that its lessee of Cibwr Grange (Cardiff; 1525) 'uproot and destroy all briars and thorns in the meadows'.[88]

When Cymer demised Garth Bleddyn in Nannau (1534), the tenant had to perform unspecified 'customs of ancient usage'.[89] A frequent condition of tenancy on the lands of Strata Florida forbade lessees 'to bring up the offspring of any great man without licence'.[90] Late leases sometimes sought *yearly* hospitality: the last lessee of Margam's Whitecross Grange had to provide the community with a meal;[91] Basingwerk's lessee at Overleigh (1482) had to provide overnight sustenance for the abbot and eight persons, and the holder of its Caldy Grange (1535) an 'abbot's feast' – its 'stewards, tenants and servants dinner'.[92]

Another 'custom of ancient usage' was the tendering of a marriage tax, *lairwite*. Fines for unlicensed marriages were prominent in Tintern's Porthcaseg court in the 1340s.[93] Lairwite was valued at 5s (as much as the annual rental) on one holding of Strata Florida in Cwmystwyth (1530).[94] Lastly, tenants had the obligation, described before, to pay suit of court and mill *(Chapters 13, 16)*. Tenants who defaulted on paying their rent, or withheld the services due, were liable to have their goods distrained or to be forced to leave their holding. Further, there was generally a prohibition against alienation without permission. Tintern (1506) forbade one tenant 'to transfer the property to anyone without the lord's leave, under pain of forfeiture'.[95]

Tenants had their duties and obligations, but they also had their 'perks'. There were rights of firebote, hedgebote and housebote for those holding land of several abbeys *(Chapter 15)*. Basingwerk's local tenants had pannage 'in the hill above the Long Meadow in the Greenfield'.[96] Strata Marcella's tenants had common of pasture on the waste grounds of Arwystli and Cyfeiliog.[97] The tenants of Margam in Eglwys-geinor were quit of all secular exactions, especially of ecclesiastical taxation.[98] Concern for their rights of pasture at Cwrt-y-carnau and of timber from Coed-ffranc, led former tenants of Neath to riot when (about 1577–81) these ancient privileges were threatened.[99]

The foregoing paragraphs have tried, imperfectly, to trace something of the accelerating transformation of Cistercian agrarian economy from the 13th century onwards. There was a huge difference between the *conversi*-manned granges of the 12th century and the *de facto* manorialism of bailiffs and tenants practised in the 16th. To an extent, the change was forced upon the monasteries with changing circumstances – particularly a growing lack of vocations to their especial way of life.

NOTES

1. Cowley F.G. 1977, 242–43, Lekai L.J. 1977, 306-09.
2. *Cf. Statuta* I, 14–15 (1134/IX), 309–10 (1205/13), 346 (1208/5), 427–28 (1214/54, 58), 448 (1215/64), 616 (1220/5); II, 31–32 (1224/10).
3. Birch W. de Gray. 1897, 173.
4. *Catal. Penrice* I, 11 (Charter 26).
5. Cowley F.G. 1977, 241*n*.
6. *Cal. Inq. Misc.* VI, 107.
7. NLW, Badm. Manorial 1571.
8. Cowley F.G. 1977, 269.
9. PRO, DL 25/1285, 1346.
10. As in Tintern's demise of a fishery in 1460 *(Chapter 18)*.
11. Lekai L.J. 1977, 449.
12. *Anc. Pet.* 503; *Cal. Patent R.. 1453*, 65.
13. PRO, C 24/29 (Pt. 2).
14. Williams D.H. 1984. II, 349–50.
15. RCAHMW, *Glamorgan* III: Pt. 2 (1982) 254.
16. Jones A. 1933, 177.
17. PRO, LR 1/213, f. 373.
18. PRO, SC 6 (Hen. VIII) 5412.
19. Bradney J.A. I: Pt. 2 (1906) 463–65.
20. Williams S.W. 1889, Appx. lxxviii.
21. PRO, SC 6 (Hen. VIII) 5412, m. 1r.
22. Williams G. 1962, 368*n*.
23. *Valor Eccl.* IV, 370.
24. PRO, SC 6 (Hen. VIII) 5156, m. 1r.
25. Williams D.H. 1984. II, 351.
26. *Cardiff Rec.* I, 204; Birch W. de Gray. 1902, 150.
27. Owen G.D. 1935, 182.
28. Williams G. 1962, 361–62.
29. Birch W. de Gray. 1902, 150.
30. NLW, Badm. Manorial 1659, m. 1r.
31. Jones A. 1937, 275.
32. Owen G.D. 171; Williams G. 1962, 362.
33. PRO, SC 6 (Hen. VIII) 4868, 4903.
34. Birch W. de Gray. 1897, 352–54.
35. *Exchq. Proc. (2)* 104.
36. Birch W. de Gray. 1897, 355–56.
37. Williams D.H. 1984. II, 352.
38. *E.g:*. Badm. Manorial 1657, m. 2d.
39. *Ibid.* 352–53.
40. NLW, Badm. Manorial 1658.
41. *Exchq. Proc. (2)* 104.
42. *Ibid.* 1642.
43. *Ibid.* 1657, m. 12d.
44. *Ibid.* 1657, m. 14d (21 May 1460).
45. *Mont. Collns.* XXII, 216.
46. Williams D.H. 1984. II, 354–55.

47. PRO, E 315/104, f. 106d.
48. PRO, LR 2/206, f. 218.
49. Birch W. de Gray. 1897, 354.
50. NLW, Cwrtmawr MS 873D, f. 3.
51. *Cartae Glam.* VI, 2391.
52. Birch W. de Gray. 1897, 357.
53. NLW, Badm. Manorial 1659, m. 1r.
54. PRO, SC 6 (Hen. VIII) 2496, m. 1d.
55. Williams D.H. 1984. II, 354–55.
56. PRO, E 321/14/16.
57. *Cf.* PRO, SC 6 (Hen. VIII) 4868.
58. Owen G.D. 1935, 208.
59. Jones A. 1937, 277.
60. *Statuta* I, 346 (1208/5).
61. Jones A. 1937, 282; *Cf.* Owen G.D. 1935, 189–200.
62. NLW, Cwrtmawr MS 873D, f. 29.
63. Jones A. 1937, 278; Williams S.W. 1889, 177–78; PRO, SC 6 (Hen. VIII) 4868, m. 2r.
64. Llewellyn R.W. 1898, 144.
65. *Cartae Glam.* II, 648–49.
66. Birch W. de Gray. 1897, 348.
67. Williams D.H. 1984. II, 357.
68. Jones A. 1937, 278.
69. *Valor Eccl.* IV, 426; PRO, E 315/201, f. 4; *Cf.* E 310/36/219, f. 24; *Augm. Rec.* 288; *Exchq. Proc. (1)* 47.
70. PRO, LR 6/152/1–4.
71. Williams D.H. 1984. II, 357–58.
72. Birch W. de Gray. 1897, 358.
73. *Ibid.* 353.
74. Owen E. 1920, 54.
75. PRO, LR 6/152/4, m. 10r.
76. Williams D.H. 1984. II, 358–59.
77. NLW, Cwrtmawr MS 873D, ff. 55, 63.
78. NLW, Badm. Manorial 1571; Williams D.H. 1965, 21–22.
79. PRO, SC 6 (Hen. VIII) 4903 *passim.*
80. *Exchq. Proc. (1)* 91, 96.
81. Owen G.D. 1935, 202; PRO, SC 6 (Hen. VIII) 4868.
82. NLW, Chirk Castle Deed F.12, 897.
83. Williams D.H. 1984. II, 359–60.
84. Owen E. 1920, 58.
85. NLW, Badm. Manorial 1639.
86. NLW, Badm. Deeds, Group 2, 14482.
87. Owen E. 1920, 50; Jones A. 1933, 177.
88. *Cardiff Rec.* I, 204–05.
89. NLW, Dolrhyd Deed 1.
90. NLW, Cwrtmawr MS 873D. ff. 4, 8, 10 (leases of 1527–34).
91. Gray T. 1905, 90 (*'jentaculum'*).
92. Owen E. 1920, 54–55, 57–58.
93. Cowley F.G. 1977, 255; Williams D.H. 1984. II, 360.
94. NLW, Cwrtmawr MS 873D, f. 20.
95. NLW, Badm. Manorial 1657, m. 2d; *Cf.* Ibid. 1658; Birch W. de Gray. 1897, 348; PRO, E 315/104, f. 106d..
96. Owen E. 1920, 49.
97. *Exchq. Proc. (2)* 273.
98. Birch W. de Gray. 1897, 345–46.
99. PRO, STAC 5/C.24/15 (24).

CHAPTER 21

CISTERCIAN STUDIES[1]

In the last fifteen years, there has been a flowering of Welsh Cistercian studies, most of which have been referred to in the foregoing chapters. Geophysical surveys have taken place at Cwmhir,[2] Grace Dieu,[3] Strata Marcella[4] and Whitland *(Fig. 126)*.[5] Excavations have taken place at the emplacement of Neath's Gorseinon mill,[6] in the outer court of Tintern,[7] and at its Woolaston Grange quay.[8] Due to the enthusiasm of the individuals concerned, a 'Cistercian Trail' has emerged in Wales,[9] and the 'Monks' Trod' between Cwmhir and Strata Florida is regularly walked.[10] Very importantly, a new series of illuminating guides to the Cistercian monuments of Wales has been issued by Cadw: Welsh Historic Monuments.[11]

Whitland Abbey Landscape Survey *(Fig. 126)*
Following on from earlier work by Mr Terrence James, the complex of earthworks chiefly associated with the monastic water-system, was surveyed by Archaeoleg Cambria in 1999, and includes fishponds, supply and drainage channels, and the possible diversion of the Afon Gronw (shown as the early course). The features were partly reused by the nearby ironworks, operative in the 17th and 18th centuries. The boundary of an outer precinct may have dictated and been preserved by the pre-1830 roadway and the linear earthwork which preserves its line between the two northernmost ponds. The presence of two gateways, which feature strongly in local tradition, may be confirmed by physical evidence.

The remainder of this chapter is mostly concerned with the history of Cistercian studies in Wales, prior to the immediate present.

The Tourist
The travelling antiquary is nothing new: William Worcester visited and made valuable notes on Tintern in 1478, whilst John Leland took in several Cistercian abbeys on his peregrination fifty years later. The Romantic Movement of the latter half of the 18th century awakened a new interest in the monastic ruins of Wales.[12] Tintern became both fashionable and commercialised, aided by its clearance and landscaping (using over one hundred workmen)[13] by the 5th Duke of Beaufort – though one writer called him 'a vandal'. His Grace had 'conceived the pious design of restoring the church. Happily, heaven took him to itself before he had time to execute it'.[14] Other landlords, like Thomas Wilson at Cwmhir (1824)[15] and Henry Yelverton at Whitland (1837),[16] followed the ducal example and spruced up their monastic sites.

Tourists came to Tintern by river boat, either from Bristol via Chepstow, or down the Wye from Ross, in specially equipped pleasure craft. Early visitors (late 18th century on) were met by 'a number of poor, miserable inhabitants' seeking alms.[17]

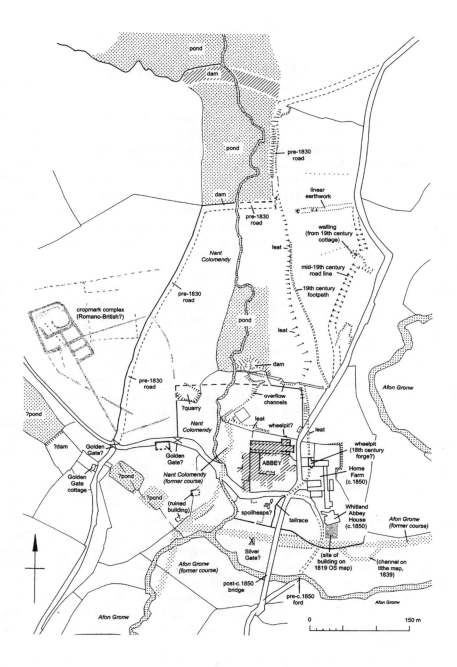

Fig. 126: Whitland Abbey and associated features.
(Courtesy of Mr Neil Ludlow, Archaeoleg Cambria).

Barber (1803) was shown around Tintern by 'an old woman, bent nearly double'.[18] One visitor was King Frederick Augustus of Saxony (1848);[19] one custodian, 'always unremitting in his attention to visitors', was a Mr Payne (1861).[20]

At other abbeys, a flood of visitors came during and in the wake of archaeological excavations. For those coming to Strata Florida, following upon the work of Stephen Williams (1887–88), cheap return tickets were issued by the Manchester and Milford Railway, though not on Pontrhydfendigaid Fair Days![21] During the excavation Stephen Williams directed at Strata Marcella (1890), on Sunday afternoons, a day of rest for the diggers, numerous tiles were purloined from the site.[22] Valle Crucis was under the care of a lady custodian by at least 1846; her visitors included Mr Gladstone. Closed to the public on Sundays, there were those who would clamber over the wall, and once, in August 1858, a policeman was brought to keep unwanted people out![23]

Tintern was immortalised when William Wordsworth penned his *Lines Written a Few Miles above Tintern Abbey* (1798). He had visited Tintern before (1793), as had J.M.W. Turner (1792, 1795, 1798) who left to posterity several water-colours of the abbey, some showing the tools of conservation – a rake, a barrow, a roller.[24] Artists depicted features which have since disappeared: notably, Grimm's view of the vaulted interior of Margam's chapter-house (1777; *Frontispiece*) – its roof collapsed but twenty years later;[25] and the Buck brothers' print of Cymer (1742) – showing a double storey of lancet windows at the east end of its church.[26] Nichols' watercolour of the great gate of Tintern (1822) indicated its former strength and size *(Plate XI-B)*.[27]

Excavations

Incentive for excavation stemmed from the emergence of learned societies, and the predilections of interested (sometimes wealthy) individuals. The first excavation at Strata Florida (6–8 Sept. 1847) took place to reveal its foundations to members attending the first Annual Meeting of the Cambrian Archaeological Association nearby in Aberystwyth.[28] Clearances at Neath were made to show the tile pavements there to, again, members of the Cambrians on field visits in 1861 and 1886.[29]

A member of the party viewing Strata Florida in 1847 was Viscount Dungannon. Four years later, with Watkin Wynne (of Oswestry, and, later, Peniarth) he conducted a year long clearance at Valle Crucis.[30] Hugh Owen, the next investigator at Valle Crucis (1885–1900), remembered visiting it during Dungannon's work.[31] E.V. Collier, who led excavations at Whitland (1926–27), took measurements at Strata Florida during Stephen Williams' work there.[32] In all these early excavations, vast quantities of rubble, soil and vegetative growth, had to be removed before satisfactory results could be achieved.[33]

Stephen Williams was, without doubt, 'the father of Cistercian archaeology in Wales'.[34] A railway surveyor-turned-land agent, domestic and ecclesiastical architect, antiquarian, territorial officer, and county surveyor of Radnorshire (1864–99), he directed major excavations at Strata Florida (1887–88), Strata Marcella (1890) and Talley (1892–94), and less substantial exploration at Cwmhir (1889, 1894). Though his work was criticised in his own day, and although geophysical survey has shown the church of Strata Marcella not to be as long as he postulated, yet he did much to further knowledge of those sites.

Williams published what was, for its time, a classic work: *The Cistercian Abbey of Strata Florida*; a copy found its way to Balmoral Castle, and it was reviewed even in *The News of the World*. The emergence of Welsh periodicals, notably *Archaeologia Cambrensis* (1846–) and the *Montgomeryshire Collections* (1868–) facilitated the publication of excavation reports, whilst other works of note included the Reverend Henry Hey Knight's *Specimens of Inlaid Tiles from Neath Abbey* (1850: *Fig. 43*)

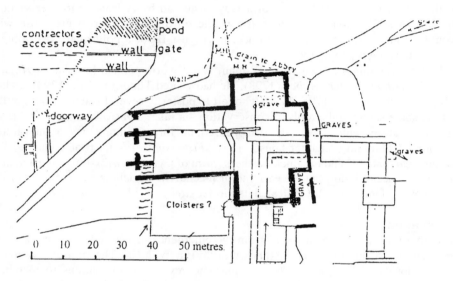

Fig. 127: Llantarnam Abbey Church: postulated plan. *(A.G. Mein).*

Towards the close of the 19th century, Thomas Blashill postulated the position of the Norman church of Tintern *(Fig. 31)*,[35] whilst Vaughan Hughes conducted (sharply criticised) work at Basingwerk.[36] After the Great War, Glen Taylor worked at Neath,[37] Kendrick at Maenan,[38] Clapham and Wheeler, and then Collier, at Whitland.[39] In recent decades L.A.S. Butler has carried out important excavations at both Maenan and Valle Crucis, one of them in partnership with D.H. Evans.[40] An exploratory excavation has perhaps pin-pointed the final site of Grace Dieu,[41] Geoff Mein has recovered part of the plan of Llantarnam *(Fig. 127)*,[42] and Dilwyn Jones may have located the monastic kitchen at Margam.[43]

Finds

The objects excavated on Welsh Cistercian sites have been varied. Sculptured stonework and pottery fragments have been noted in earlier chapters. Not surprisingly, several papal leaden *bullae* have been found.[44] Durable objects, they have lasted whilst the charters to which they were attached have perished. A concentration of papal *bullae* in the immediate neighbourhood of Llantarnam *(Fig. 128)* might suggest a concealment of charters in the difficult weeks leading up to the Suppression, whilst the personal seals discovered perhaps indicate the presence of travellers, and others, using the monastic guest-house.

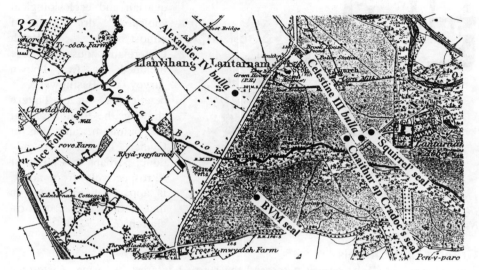

Fig. 128: Llantarnam: Locations of Seals.
(Plotted on the 1ˢᵗ edn. 6" O.S. map, with assistance from Dr J.P. Davis.).

Medieval coins have been unearthed at most Cistercian sites. Hoards have been found at Cwmhir: thirteen *deniers* dating from the reigns of Henry II (1154–89) and Richard I (1189–99), issued in their capacity as Dukes of Aquitaine;[45] a mile west of Grace Dieu: nine or more gold coins, ranging in date from Edward IV (1461–83) down to 1536–37, it is possible they were hidden to avoid confiscation at the closure of the abbey;[46] beneath the floor of the west range of Neath: 166 English pennies, dating from 1325–27, perhaps their concealment was connected with the hue and cry in the vicinity at the time of the pursuit of Edward II, who stayed at Neath before his capture nearby in November 1326.[47]

Plans and Surveys

Whatever the limitations of the early investigators may have been, they did uncover much which had lain hidden for generations, and thus enabled plans to be drawn of the abbey churches and, sometimes, the conventual buildings. John Carter (1748–1817), said to be 'rather irascible in temper and a quarrelsome man',[48] produced plans and sketches at Margam *(Fig. 49)*[49] and Tintern.[50] The Reverend John Parker, Vicar of Llanyblodwel, Salop,[51] made many drawings of ecclesiastical edifices in Wales. Executed in the 1840s and 1850s, they included plans of Strata Florida *(Fig. 44)* and of Valle Crucis.[52]

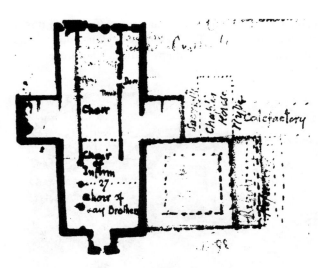

Fig. 129: Walcott's Plan of Cymer (c. 1870).
(By permission of the British Library, Addit. MS 31,380, No. 80).

Prebendary Mackenzie Walcott of Chichester (*c.* 1870), described as being 'always at work on anti-quarian and ecclesiological subjects',[53] drew plans of almost all the Welsh Cistercian houses. These included the first known survey of Basingwerk, a detailed lay-out of Tintern showing the foundations of the pulpitum, and one of Cymer. This last, roughly done, perhaps in a hurry or retrospectively from notes, is apparently erroneous in that it depicts a cruciform church *(Fig. 129)*.[54]

Granges and Chapels

The close of the 19th century witnessed the start of interest in former Cistercian granges and pilgrimages centres.[55] Thomas Gray (about 1898) brought to light the Grange of Theodoric buried in coastal sand near Margam,[56] whilst Colonel Llewelyn Morgan (1899) described the remains of Neath's Cwrt-y-carnau Grange chapel.[57] Just before the Great War[58] (with further exploration after World War II),[59] the site of Llantarnam's Penrhys cell was excavated by the Rhondda Naturalists' Society.

The Great War past, George Hammond excavated Neath's chapel in Coed-ffranc. The work was visited (1924) by members of the Neath Antiquarian Society, trav-elling by train to Jersey Marine Station. The *Cambrian Daily Leader* reported that their arrival 'brought out the greater part of the inhabitants'.[60] More recent work (mostly noted in preceding pages) has included an excavation by John M. Lewis at Neath's Cwrt Betws (1956),[61] and, with Bernard Knight, an examination of burials at Margam's Llanfeuthin manor.[62] Norman Parkes and Peter Webster have explored Tintern's Merthyr Gerain Grange (1971–72).[63]

Space precludes mention of all such endeavours, but by no means least have been the contributions by W.E. Griffiths, C.J. Spurgeon and H.J. Thomas to the *Inventory* for Glamorgan of the Royal Commission on Ancient and Historical Monuments in Wales (1982), which contains substantial sections relating to the granges of Margam and Neath.[64]

There remains to be noted the sterling work of the late Mr Richard E. Kay, a member of the Woolhope Club, who, for almost sixty years, was a seasoned observer and prodigious recorder of historic sites, working in earlier years with the

Reverend Mr Porter.[65] Two years before he died, Mr Kay deposited his thirty-nine field notebooks, spanning the years from 1936 to 1993 and containing much Welsh material, at the Ancient Monuments Record of the Royal Commission (Aberystwyth). Mr Kay was always of the greatest assistance to the present author, a kindness reflected in several of his plans which appear in this volume.

The Historian

It is impracticable to record the names of all those gone before us (like Walter de Gray Birch of the British Museum, and Edward Owen of the India Office) who have contributed so much to Welsh Cistercian studies in the past, but they are cited in the Bibliography.[66] The works of Birch,[67] and of the late Leslie Evans,[68] regarding Margam, have recently been republished. The author is very much aware that 'other men laboured, and ye are entered into their labours' (St John 4:38). He is conscious of the encouragement that present authors, with like interests, have given him; notably Sir Glanmor Williams, Dr Fred Cowley, Dr David Robinson and the late Mr Leslie Evans.

Our cumulative knowledge of Cistercian history in Wales is but a small fragment of the whole truth. Even Churchyard, writing but fifty years after the Suppression, in his *Worthines of Wales* (1587)[69] had to confess, concerning Tintern, that it was:

> As old a sell, as is within that land,
> Where divers things, hath bene right worthie note,
> Whereof as yet, *the troth I have not gote*.

Would that we could be like the 5th Earl of Worcester who, visiting Strata Florida, met: 'A woman aged one hundred, who described to him the lives of the monks, their Order of Services, habits and customs'.[70]

NOTES

1. See especially: Courtney P. and Gray M. 1991, Knight J.K. 1977, Robinson D.M. 1995, 1997; Thomas R. Gwyn 1976, Williams D.H. 1995.
2. By the Clwyd-Powys Archaeological Trust (David Thomas), in conjunction with Cadw (Dr S Rees).
3. Phillips N. and Hamilton M. 2000, 50–54.
4. Williams D.H. and Arnold C.J. 1992, 94.
5. By Archaeoleg Cambria.
6. Cardy C. and Gibbs M. 1995, 26–27.
7. Courtney P. 1989, 99–143.
8. Fulford M.G. *et al.* 1992, 101–27.
9. Organised by Dr Madeleine Gray.
10. Inspired by Dr John Davies and others.
11. In the time of Dr David Robinson as publications editor.
12. Knight J.K. 1977, *passim*.
13. Heath C. 1801, unpaginated.
14. Taylor J. 1869. II, 77.
15. Rees W.J. 1849, 241–51.
16. Collier E.V. 1925, 63–64.
17. Evans J. 1810, 160.
18. Barber T. 1803, 147; *Cf.* Courtney P. 1991, 153.
19. Taylor J. 1869. II, 77.
20. *Monmouthshire Merlin*, 8 June 1861, 5.
21. Robinson D.M. 1992, 21.
22. Jones M.C. 1891, 158*n*.
23. Thomas R.G. XXXX 230.

24. Tate Gallery, Turner Bequest; *Cf.*
     Robinson D.M. 1995, 22–23.
25. Wyndham H.P. 1781, 34.
26. Buck S. and N. 1742. III, No.
     49; NLW (Maps and Prints), PB
     755 (63/2).
27. In private hands.
28. *Arch. Camb.* VII (1852) 361–62.
29. *Ibid.* 1861, 345, 347.
30. *Arch. Camb.* VII (1852) 277–78;
     Williams S.W. 1889, 183.
31. Price G.V. 1952, 202.
32. *Trans. Carmarthenshire Antiq.*
     Soc. XIX (1926) 58, XX (1927)
     85.
33. Williams D.H. 10.
34. For Williams, see: Fenn R.W.D.
     and Sinclair J.B. 1989, 116–33;
     Williams D.H. 1992, 55–94;
     Ibid. 1999a, 116–42.
35. Blashill T. 1881, 106-07.
36. *Arch. Camb.* 1891, 127.
37. Taylor A.J. 1947, 145.
38. Butler L.A.S. 1963, 31–32;
     RCAHMW, *Caernarfonshire* I
     (East), 1.
39. *Arch. Camb.* 1921, 205-09;
     Trams. Carmarthenshire Antiq.
     Soc. XIX (1926) 63–65.
40 . Butler L.A.S. 1963, *Ibid.* 1982;
     with D.H. Evans 1980.
41. *Monm. Antiq.* III: Pt. 1
     (1970–71) 55–58.
42. Pers. comm.
43. *Arch. in Wales* 16 (1976) 84.
44. Williams D.H. 1984. II, 364.
45. *BSFN* 1978, 372–74; info. of Mr
     E. Besly.
46. *Monm. Antiq.* I (1961–64) 40–41;
     Lewis J.M. 1976, 31.
47. Lewis J.M. 1976, 26–27; *British
     Numismatic Jnl.* XXVIII, 294–98,
     555–59.
48. *DNB* IX, 200-01; *Arch. Camb.*
     1896, 172–74.
49. BL, Addit. MS 29940, f. 68.
50. *Ibid.* ff. 132–53.
51. *Arch. Camb.* 1860, 317.

52. NLW, Dept. of Maps and Prints,
     P. 556 *(Parkers' Drawings,* II).
53. *DNB* LIX,11.
54. BL, Addit. MS 31370 (Walcot's
     Topographical Drawings IX) Nos.
     6 and 7 (Tintern); MS 31380 (XI)
     Nos. 61 (Basingwerk), 72
     (Margam), 80 (Cymer).
55. Williams D.H. 1995, 17–20.
56. Gray T. 1905, 95–103.
57. Morgan W. Ll. 1899, 9–19.
58. *Arch. Camb.* 1913, 144–45;
     1914, 360.
59. Info. of the late Mr Gruffydd
     Jenkins of Bargoed. Excavation
     was in 1947–48.
60. Royal Institution of S. Wales,
     *Eighty-Ninth Report of the
     Council* (1923–24) 7, 31;
     Hammond G.B. 'Chapel of St
     Margaret's, Coed Franck: Notes
     on the Excavations': *Ninety-First
     Report of the Council* (1925–26)
     27–30.
61. Info. of Mr John Lewis, who has
     deposited the relevant notes in the
     Dept. of Archaeology and
     Numismatics, National Museum
     of Wales.
62. *Arch. Camb.* CXXII (1973)
     147–53.
63. *Ibid.* CXXIII (1974) 140–54.
64. Vol. III: Pt. 2 (1982): *Medieval
     Non-defensive Secular
     Monmuents,* 245–97.
65. *Cf. Monm. Antiq.* XVI (2000) 44.
66. See: Williams D.H. 1984. II,
     366–67.
67. Swansea: West Glamorgan
     Archive Service, 1997.
68. Port Talbot Historical Society,
     1996.
69. Quoted by J.K. Knight, in:
     Severn and Wye Review II; ii
     (Winter, 1972) 39.
70. Durant H. 1966, 65 (quoting
     Thomas Bayly, *Worcester's
     Apophthegmes* (1650) Apop. 17.

CHAPTER 22

THE CISTERCIANS TODAY

Cistercian life in Wales has again found a home in the Principality. Monks and nuns of the Strict Observance (sometimes called 'Trappists') live and worship on the island of Caldey, and at a site quite close to the former abbey of Whitland, respectively.

Abbey of Our Lady and St Samson, Caldey Island/Ynys Bŷr, Pembrokeshire.[1]

Caldey is an island (extra-diocesan and extra-parochial) with a long monastic tradition: a Celtic monastery, with St Samson as one of its early abbots; a medieval cell of St Dogmael's (Tironian) abbey – its remains now forming St Illtud's Priory; and, from 1906 to 1928, a Benedictine house (first Anglican, then Roman Catholic). The present Cistercian foundation was made from the Belgian abbey of Scourmont in 1929, and was raised to the status of an abbey in 1959. A Norwegian monk (John Gran) received episcopal ordination as bishop of Oslo in 1963, and the monastery celebrated its golden jubilee with the consecration of its new high altar in 1979 *(Plate XVI-A)*.

The Cistercian community has known tribulation: police suspicion of a largely foreign community during the 1930s; challenges regarding the rights of the religious as proprietors of the island; the conscription (during World War II) of several Belgian monks to serve in non-combatant roles in their country's army; and an accidental fire in 1940 which destroyed the library and necessitated the rebuilding of the church.

Being on an island brings its own inherent problems, now mostly solved. A submarine electricity cable (1965, renewed 1981) largely obviates the former need to manhandle over 100 tons each year of coal on the beach; a radio-telephone link (1951) replaced the submarine telephone cable which snapped in a storm (1938). With grant aid (1990s) the landing stage has been very much upgraded. In years gone by, a long dry summer could spell severe water shortage, but this has been solved by the drilling of a large borehole and the installation of two huge tanks underground.

The principal and lasting difficulty has been the recruitment of vocations. The founding community was Belgian to a man. English recruits were soon attracted but, with the exception of a few – like the legendary Brother Thomas (professed 1934), many did not persevere. There were occasions, as in 1936 and 1948, when the future of Cistercian life on Caldey seemed very uncertain. There is difficulty in recruiting Welsh vocations from a Principality where both the Roman Catholic and Anglican Churches are minority bodies, but vocations now seem to be improving significantly.

Over the last eighty years, Cistercian economy on Caldey has rung the changes, but the Trappists have succeeded where the Benedictines failed. At the outset, in 1929, they were busy clearing the fields of stones as prelude to the cultivation of hay and oats. Economic self-sufficiency was reached in 1959, and has successively involved exports some time since abandoned. In the mid-1950s, some 8,000 table chickens, 150 pigs and 30 bullocks were sent across to the mainland. From the

1960s, the monastery's dairy underpinned the sales in the tea-room of items like ice-cream, cheese-cake, chocolate and yoghurt. Unfortunately, the dairy has latterly been forced to close, a consequence of labour costs and European Community regulations. A prime beef herd is still maintained, and island-produced shortbread and chocolate sold. Self-sufficiency is also aided by the home baking of bread, while the novices produce vegetables for the community's needs.

The best-known Caldey industry is the manufacture of perfume, partly based on island gorse, it has a substantial output, with local sales and a mail-order department. As one researcher noted in its early days, making perfume 'is not affected by delays, can be made and sold at all seasons, and does not call for the employment of many men'.

Fundamental to the island economy is tourism; poor weather in summer can bring problems, but on sunny days large numbers of visitors may be found on Caldey at the peak of the tourist season. Apart from the tea-room, there is a post-office (with its own postal imprint) -cum-museum (displaying prehistoric artefacts found by Brother James) -cum-art gallery (exhibiting paintings by the former monk-artist, Peter Anson), souvenir shop, and a Video Interpretation centre – where a film of the monks' daily life can be seen. Visitors (who come to and fro on the vessels of the 'pool' of Tenby boatmen) can repose on the beach of Priory Bay, or enjoy the guided walks provided. The post-office has recently gone on-line.

Most important of all, Caldey plays an invaluable role in the spiritual and ecumenical life of Wales, not only by the presence of an intercessory, contemplative community, but also by making retreat accommodation available for up to some 750 guests annually. The tourists, too, are able to receive Holy Communion, and obtain counselling and absolution, and few could fail to leave the island untouched by what they see and witness. Caldey is like a beacon-light off the coast of Wales!

Holy Cross Abbey/Abaty'r Groes, Whitland, Carmarthenshire

A welcome addition to the religious life of Wales, has been the move (in 1991) of the Cistercian nuns (of the Strict Observance) of Holy Cross Abbey, Stapehill, Dorset (established from France in 1802), to a property just outside the town of Whitland (Carms., *Plate XVI-B*). The sisters came, unaware of how close they would be to the medieval abbey of Whitland. Here again are signs of life and vocations, as the nuns provide a service to the Church – making altar breads, providing a retreat centre, and practising ecumenism (greeting regularly the local vicar and his congregation). For the time being, at least, the community has foregone a precinct wall so as to be more approachable by the local populace, few of whom are Roman Catholics.

---

1. The story of Caldey is well told in: Anson P.F, *The Benedictines of Caldey* (London, 1940); Ibid. *Abbot Extraordinary* (London, 1958); Day, E. Hermitage *et al.*, *The Benedictines of Caldey Island* (Caldey Abbey, 1907; reprint, Quidenham, 1980); Done Bushell W., 'Caldey: An Island of Saints' (*Archaeologia Cambrensis* 1908, pp. 237–60); Howells R(oscoe), *Total Community* (Tenby; 2nd. edn. 1982); Ibid. *Caldey* (Llandysul, 2nd. edn. 1996); Maitland, (Dom) B(ede), OSB, typescript thesis (1956) for the Cambridge Geographical Tripos; and the guide-books available on the island.

KNOWN ABBOTS

Aberconwy

1258	Anian.
1278–81	Maredudd.
1284–1301	David.
1303	Tudur.
c. 1320–40	Ieuan ap Rhys.
1344	Clement.
1345–56	Cynfrig.
1379–98	John.
1406–09	Hywel ap Gwilym.
1428	John ap Rhys.
1431	David.
? –1478	Reginald.
1482–88	David Wynchcombe.
1490	John.
1491–1501	David Lloyd *(perhaps also in 1489)*.
1503–13	David ab Owain.
1513–26	Geoffrey Kyffin.
1528	Hugh ap Rhys.
1529–35	Geoffrey Johns.
1535–37	Richard ap Rhys (*al.* Price).

Basingwerk

c. 1152–55	Gilbert of Louth Park.
1177	Matthew.
1192	Robert.
1198	W...
early 13th C.	Geoffrey.
c. 1220	A...
1226	Simon.
1256	John.
ante-1282	German.
1282–87	Hugh.
1289	*?* Ernald.
1311–29	William.
1336–45	Richard de Kokenfield.
1351–59	Ralph.
1362	Richard.
1394–1405	Henry.
1430–54	Henry Wirral.

1465–76.	Richard Kirkby.
(1466	Edmund Thornebar).
1481–1522	Thomas Pennant.
1525–36	Nicholas Pennant.

Cwmhir

1184	Meurig.
c. 1190	Canawg.
c. 1200	Rhiryd.
c. 1215–22	Gwrgenau.
1226	A...
c. 1241	Philip.
1260–61	Gruffydd.
1276–97	Cadwgan ab Ieva.
1475–90	Owain ap David.
1490–91	Owain Ellis (*? the same*).
1491–94	Humphrey.
1499–1508	Thomas.
–1516	William Jones (*al.* Johns).
1516–30	Richard Vayn.
1532–34	Geoffrey Davis.
1535–37	John Glyn.

Cymer

1209	Esau.
1274–81	Llywelyn.
1284	Cadwgan.
1343	Philip.
1398	John Loncastell.
1441–42	John ap Rhys.
1442–43	John Cobbe.
1443–44	Richard Kirkby.
c. 1443–	John Cobbe.
1474	John.
1481	William.
1482–87	John Stratford.
1487–91	William.
1494	Gruffydd goz.
1495–96	David Wynchcombe.
1499	Richard.
1499–1506	Gruffydd (*al.* Geoffrey).
1514–16	David Ffloyd.

? 1521–25	John (*?* Glyn).
? 1517–37	Lewis ap Thomas.

Grace Dieu

1236	John.
? 1240	Walter.
1246	Roger.
1267	William.
1281	Warin.
1306	A...
1337	Walter.
1350	Robert.
ante-1383	John Wysbeche.
1427	*?* Richard Moyne.
1447	Richard Clifford.
? 1451	Roger of Chepstow.
1473–84	John Mitulton.
1486–95	Richard Dorston.
1508	Thomas Philpott.
1515–17	Stephen Green.
1530–32	John Rowthwell (*al.* Buildwas).
1533	William Ipsley.
1534	Thomas Perpin.
1534–36	John Gruffydd.

Llantarnam

c. 1205	Walter.
1227	Cynfrig.
1279	Anian.
1313	Gruffydd.
mid-14th C.	David.
1377–1400	John ap Gruffydd.
1400–05	John ap Hywel.
1431–62	Stephen (*?* Went).
1465	William Nunam.
1476–96	John.
1507–33	Morgan Blethyn.
1533–36	Jasper ap Roger (*al.* Thomas).

Margam

1147–53	William of Clairvaux.
1153–55	Andrew.
? late 12th C.	John.
c. 1166–88	Cynan.
1196–1203	Roger.
1203–13	Gilbert.

1213–37	John of Goldcliff.
1237–50	John de la Warre.
1250–67	Thomas of Portskewett.
c. 1270	Gilbert II.
c. 1305	Roger II.
1307–08	Thomas.
c. 1312–26	John de Cantelo.
1338–59	Henry.
1366–85	John.
–1413	John.
1413–	David.
1415–23	William Meyrick.
1425	John Hamlyn.
? 1441	William.
1441–60	Thomas Franklin.
1468–87	William Corntown.
1487–94	John Hopkin.
c. 1497	*?* Thomas.
1500–17	David ap Thomas ap Hywel.
1517–28	John Gruffydd.
1529–36	Lewis Thomas.

Neath

1129–45	Richard.
1150–69 (*?* 73)	Ralph.
1170–*c.* 93	Walter.
1201	Abraham.
–1218	Clement.
1218–	Gervase.
–1245	Richard.
c. 1245–53	Robert.
1266–89	Adam of Carmarthen.
1322	David.
1326–41	William of St Donat's.
1358–60	Thomas.
1401	John Nicholl.
1421–23	Leysan.
1424–41	Thomas Franklin.
1450–51	John ap Hywel.
1468	Robert.
1502-07	John.
1510–39	Lleision ap Thomas.

(*variant dating:*
1423	John).

Strata Florida

1164–85	David.
1185–88	Seisil.
c. 1199–1200	Dyniawal (Deiniol).
–1203	*?* Cadwgan.
1225	Cedifor.
1226	P...
1227	*?* Dolphin.
1248	Gruffydd.
1268	Joab.
1278–80	Philip Goch *(13th abbot).*
1280–94	Anian Sais *('the Englishman').*
1299	John
1336–38	Maredudd Bool.
1344–80	Llywelyn Fychan.
1385	*?* Richard Vaughan.
1407	Richard ap Gruffydd.
1427	John.
1430–36	Richard.
1436–41	Rhys.
1442–43	William Morris.
	(John ap Rhys intrudes).
1444–86	Morgan ap Rhys.
1487	William Marlow.
–1495	John.
c. 1495–1500	Dafydd ab Owain.
1501	John.
c. 1509–13	Richard Dorston.
1516–39	Richard Talley.

Strata Marcella

c. 1173	*?* Enoch.
1176–83	Ithel.
1183–98	Gruffydd.
1199–1201	Philip.
1201	J...
1215	David.
1234	Ieuaf (Joab).
? 1227–48	Goronwy.
1271–78	James.
1281	Edeneweyn.
1284	C...
1286	H...
–1332	Gruffydd.
1333–	Matthew.
1367	William.
1377–96	David.

1406	John.
1485–90	Dafydd ab Owain.
1492	Lewis.
1496	Maurice ab Ieuan.
1496–1513	David Wynchcombe.
1515	Lewis ap Thomas.
1517–25	David Ffloyd.
1527–36	John ap Rhys (Price; *al.* Goyddvarche).

Tintern

1148–57	Henry.
1169–88	William.
1188–	Vido.
1232–45	Ralph.
1253	J...
1267–77	John.
1294–*?* 1305	Ralph.
1305–20	Hugh de Wyke.
1321–27	Walter of Hereford.
1330–31	Roger de Camme.
1333	Walter.
1340–42	Gilbert.
1349–75	John.
1387–1407	John Wysbech.
1411	John *(? the same).*
1413–37	John Cherville *(al.* Charefield).
1438–41	Robert Acton.
1442–55	John of Tintern.
1456–59	Thomas Monmouth.
1460–86	Thomas Colston.
1487–93	William Kere.
1493–1506	Henry Newland.
1513–17	Thomas Morton.
1521–36	Richard Wyche.

Valle Crucis

1200	Philip.
1207	David.
c. 1210–22	John.
1226	M...
1227–34	T...
? 1240	Adam Vras.
1247	Madog.
1251–54	Anian ap Maredudd.
1270	Gervase.
1275–84	Madog.

c. ? 1296	Hywel.
1330–44	Adam (al. Atha, Adas).
1409–33	Robert of Lancaster.
1438–48	Richard Mason.
(1450	? David).
1455–61	John ap Richard (Sîon ap Rhisiart).
1480–1503	Dafydd ab Ieuan ab Iorwerth.
1503–? 27	John Lloyd (Sîon Llwyd).
1528–35	Robert Salisbury.
1535–36	John Durham (al. Deram, Heron).

Whitland

–1147	? Morfran.
c. 1166–76	Cynan.
1184	Rhydderch.
1188	John.
ante-1198	Richard.
c. 1193–1202	Peter.
1203–15	Cadwgan.
1226	Hoedlew.
1279–1300	Llywelyn.
1345	Richard.
1352	Hywel Seys
1399	Lewis Dew.
1433–43	David ap Rhys.
1469–91	Maurice ab Ieuan.
1491–? 1527	Thomas ap Rhys.
1527–39	William Vayn (al. Thomas).

Abbesses:

Llanllugan

late 13th C.	Erdoduel.
1524–36	Golybright vergh Llywelyn ap Johns (? al. Rose Lewis).

Llanllŷr

1284	E...
c. 1460–1500	Anne.
1488	Margaret.
1532–37	Elizabeth Baynham (al. Bonham).

Caldey
Abbots:

1959–80	James Wicksteed.
1984–96	Robert O'Brien.
1999–	Daniel van Santvoort.

Conventual Priors:

1934–42	Aelred Lefevre.
1946–54	Albert Derzelle.
1954–59	Eugene Boylan.

Superiors ad nutum:

1929–30	Andrew Garcette.
1930–34	Aelred Lefevre.
1954	Godefroid Belorgey.
1980–84	Robert O'Brien.
1996–97	Robert O'Brien.
1997–99	Daniel van Santvoort.

Whitland
Abbess:

1991–	Mother Catherine Priest.

APPENDIX 2
COMPARATIVE VALUES

	1291 Taxatio[1] Ecclesiastica	c. 1355 Cistercian[1] Tax Book	1400 Subsidy for[5] Cistercians at Oxford	1521 Subsidy for[6] General Chapter	1522 Loan for[7] French War	1535 Valor[8] Ecclesiasticus	1536–9 First Ministers' Accounts
Aberconwy	£ 76 15s. 8d.	£24	£1 10d. 0d.	13s. 4d.	£40	£179 10s. 0d. *(56 8s. 10d.)*	£169 1s. 9d.[9] *(52 6s. 8d.)*
Basingwerk	£ 68 8s. 0d.	£16 +	£1 6s. 8d.	£1 0s. 0d.	£40	£157 15s. 2d. *(44 8s. 0d.)*	£163 7s. 11d.[10] *(46 1s. 8d.)*
Cwmhir	£ 35 12s. 0d.[2]	£32	£1 6d. 8d.	3s. 4d.	– – –	£ 28 17s. 4d. *(– – –)*	£ 40 8s. 1d.[11] *(– – –)*
Cymer	£ 28 8s. 3d.[3]	£17 ?	£1 6s. 8d.	6s. 8d.	(– – –)	£ 58 15s. 4d. *(19 1s. 8d.)*	£ 67 4s. 10d.[12] *(26 15s. 0d.)*
Grace Dieu	£ 18 5d. 10d.	£13 15s. 0d.	13s. 4d.	3s. 4d.	– – –	£ 26 1s. 4d. *(5 1s. 4d.)*	£ 36 18s. 8d.[13] *(3 0s. 0d.?)*
Llantarnam	£ 44 15s. 0d.	£24	£1 6s. 8d.	10s. 0d.	£66 13s. 4d.	£120 3d. 2d. *(42 0s. 9d.)*	£144 19s. 6d.[14] *(17 8s. 8d.)*
Margam	£255 17s. 4½d.	£34	£2 6s. 8d.	£1 0s. 0d.	£40	£188 14s. 0d. *(37 13s. 4d.)*	£245 14s. 7½d.[15] *(42 6s. 8d.)*
Neath	£235 8s. 1d.	£16 13s. 4d.	£2 6s. 8d.	£1 6s. 8d.	£40	£150 4d. 9d. *(12 11s. 8d.)*	£184 15s. 10d.[16] *(16 5s. 0d.)*
Strata Florida	£ 50 15s. 8d.	£24	£1 16s. 8d.	£1 6s. 8d.	£40	£122 6s. 8d. *(22 0s. 0d.)*	£290 1s. 4d.[17] *(18 8s. 8d.)*
Strata Marcella	£ 35 14s. 10d.	£33	£1 3s. 4d.	6s. 8d.	– – –	£ 73 7s. 6d. *(22 5s. 0d.)*	£ 70 16s. 10d.[18] *(13 0s. 0d.)*
Tintern	£128 9s. 8d.	£22	£2 13s. 4d.	£1 6s. 8d.	£66 13s. 4d.	£256 13s. 6½d. *(55 4s. 4d.)*	– –[19]
Valle Crucis	£ 91 8s. 0d.	£32	£1 6s. 8d.	13s. 4d.	£66 13s. 4d.	£214 3s. 5d. *(152 16s. 5d.)*	£201 18s. 11d.[20] *(143 10s. 4d.)*
Whitland	£ 44 15s. 4d.	£30	£1 16s. 8d.	£1 0s. 0d.	– – –	£153 17s. 2d. *(22 5s. 9d.)*	£177 8s. 3d.[21] *(5 13s. 0d.)[22]*

Notes/References :

1 : gross value, incl. spiritualities and stock.
2 : incomplete evidence, therefore an under-estimate.
3 : spiritualities uncertain, therefore an under-estimate.
4 : *Cistercian Tax Book* (1979); medium values employed.
5 : R.C. Fowler in *Engl. Hist. Review*, XXIII (1908), pp.84–5.
6 : *Letters to Cîteaux*, 262–63.
7 : LP III, pt.2, p.1047 (no. 2483).
8 : gross value; value of spiritualities shown in bracketed italics beneath.
9 : PRO, *SC* 6 (Hen. VIII) 4972.
10 : ibid. 5142.
11 : ibid. 5412.
12 : ibid. 5222.
13 : ibid. 2496.
14 : ibid. 2497.
15 : ibid. 5155.
16 : ibid. 5156.
17 : ibid. 4868.
18 : ibid. 5259.
19 : no comparable figures available.
20 : *SC* 6 (Hen. VIII) 5543.
21 : ibid. 5903.
22 : only Llanfihangel Abercywyn, one of several appropriations noted, therefore an under-estimate.

APPENDIX 3

INVENTORY OF PROPERTY

(The enumeration corresponds to that on Maps I–XII, XIV, the sections on Economic Resources relates to Map XIV, and the lists of Appropriated Churches to Fig. 124).

Aberconwy

1. *Cornwy Llys Grange:* Mynachdy (SH 309923); church site on Bryneglwys (SH 293925) may indicate cleared/deserted village; **2.** *Ucheldref* (SH 349874); **3.** *Gwaunydog* (SH 367884); **4.** *Tre Feibion Maelog* (SH 359859); **5.** *Bodgedwydd Grange* (SH 363714; *'cwyrtai':* SH 374727); **6.** *Penmynydd;* owned half the township; former 'mynachty' may be Plas Penmynydd [SH 496752]; **7.** *Gelleiniog Grange (Fig. 74c)* with *Cyfydd Grange:* 'cwrt' and chapel at Quirt (SH 458649), 'Pont-mynach' nearby (SH 455668), windmill [Y Tŵr; SH 446643] converted into dower house in late 17th C; **8.** *Rhedynog-felen:* first abbey site (1186–c. 1190), at perhaps SH 461574, or at Hen Gwrt (SH 453573); **9.** *Cwm:* 'mynachty' (SH 441457), lands partly bounded by Clawdd Seri; **10.** *Nant Call Grange* (SH 478467); **11.** *Ffriwlwyd Grange:* 'Llawr mynachty' (SH *c.* 458384), grange lost by exchange in 1350. Capel Galltcoed (prob. non-monastic) lies to north of grange; **12.** *Nanhwynan Grange (Fig. 19)*: extensive mountain pastures, Hafod-y-llan [SH 629513], Hafod-y-porth [SH 609947]; **13.** *Ardda-Darllas Grange*: incl. ownership of half of Llyn Cowlyd [SH 727624]; **14.** *Maenan township (Fig. 10):* abbey site (1284–1536; SH 789656), immediate demesne formed the extra-parochial area of 'The Abbey'. Woodland held in Eglwys-bach; **15.** *Aberconwy:* second abbey site (*c.* 1192–1284; SH 782776); **16.** *Creuddyn Grange:* lands here largely lost (1284) in exchange for Penmynydd, but some later returned – incl. a quarter of the vill of Bodysgallen. [N.B: Tithe-map gives 'old abbey', where O.S. plots 'bishop's palace', SH 761829]; **17.** *Hiraethog Grange*: Cwrt-y-llan [SH 905516], Cernioge [SH 906504] – probably its early 'Karennok' Grange]. N.B: Bryn-yr-eglwys' occurs at SH 873523 (close to abbey mills). Abbey also owned Llanfair-isaf [SH 828527]; **18.** *Tir-yr-abad Uchaf:* 'Hafod-y-llan uchaf' [SH 951537], 'isaf' [SH 957532]. (Minor properties included a field in Llanfaes, Anglesey).

Economic Resources: Grange and other chapels: Quirt (SH 458649), ? Llanfair-isaf (SH 825527), Capel y Foelas (SH 893925); *Water-mills:* Cornwy Llys (SH 316926), Tre Fraint (moiety, SH 523728), Tal-y-bont (SH 449667), Rhedynogfelen (? SH 466583), Maenan (SH 794657 and ? 789654), Foelas (SH 873516), Llyn y Cymer: ? Pentre (SH 972524), Tŷ Brith (Llanfair), Ffriwlwyd (SH 439375); *Wind-mills:* Rhuddgaer (SH 446643), ? Cornwy Llys (SH 311928); *Fulling-mills:* Ardda (SH 773663), Foelas (SH 873516), Rhedynogfelen (?SH 446643); *Fisheries*: at Ffriwlwyd – in the Dwyfach and Dwyfor (until 1348); in the Conwy – at Degannwy and at Maenan (the 'Warles'); leases Trefriw fishery (*c.* 1355); fishing perhaps also in Llyn Cowlyd, and possibly a coastal weir at Llandrillo-yn-Rhos (SC 842809); *Turbary:* at Penmynydd, Angl., *Vaccaries:* At Trekedewe' in Hiraethog, and at Llyn Cymer in Tir-yr-abad Uchaf; *Wreck of Sea:* in Menai, off Gelliniog Grange; *Right of Toll:* In Conwy estuary, perhaps short-lived; *Urban Property:* in Bangor, Chester, Conwy.

Appropriated Churches/Tithes: **1**. Llanbadrig (SH 376947), **2**. Dywgyfylchi (SH 737773), **3**. Conwy (SH 781776), **4**. Eglwys-rhos (SH 793804), **5**. Eglwys-bach SH 803705), **6**. Maenan towship.

Basingwerk

19. *Lordship of Greenfield* alias *Fulbrook:* abbey site (SJ 196775; *Figs. 24, 74a*), proximate 'court green'; in Holywell, three granges: Home Grange, Middle Grange, Over or Higher Grange (SJ 173762); earlier grange names incl.: Fulbrook, Sovereign (1285) and Beggesburch (1291); woodland incl. Kingswood and Great Wood (SJ 186782); **20.** *Calcot:* (SJ 168740), substantial lands here, if not whole township; **21.** *Merton Abbot* (SJ 157778); **22.** *Tre'r Abad, Gelli Grange* and *Hendre Mynach:* (SJ 108786, 128782, 097771, respectively); **23.** *Caldy Grange (Fig. 74d):* 'grange' (SD 219870) with Grange Wood to east; property (demised in 1330) incl. 'grange of Hall' (SD 223869), abbey owned township of Grange, and, eastern border, property at Newton-cum-Larton (*c.* SD 236870) and the Rake House (SD 233877); **24.** *Thornton Grange* (SD 315814); **25.** *Lache Grange (Fig. 18):* uncertain bounds (*c.* SJ 399649), incl. Netherlech (SJ 407648); **26.** *Cwmtylo* (SH 849342); **27.** *Gwernhefin Grange (Figs. 21, 74b):* (SH 893328); **27a.** *Boch-y-rhaiadr Grange (Fig. 20):* (SH 847396); **28.** *Penmaen:* uncertain bounds, now in estate of Plas-yn-Penmaen, incl. Cwm Tir yr-mynach (*c.* SH 913428).

Economic resources: Grange and other chapels: Tre'r-abad (SJ 104779) four 'capel' field-names on tithe map; Gelli (SJ 128782, *Plate XIII-A*); *?* Over Grange (SJ 173762); St Winefride's pilgrimage chapel, Holywell, with well (SJ 185763); *Tithe-barn:* in Coleshill; *Water-mills:* in Greenfield, 'upper' [SJ 186763] and 'nether' corn mills, close to abbey on Holywell stream; *Wind-mills:* Holywell (*?* SJ 191758), two in Wirral (SD 222687 and *?* 242881); *Fulling-mills:* two in Greenfield, the 'lower' was two closes distant from the 'nether' corn mill; *Conyger:* at Caldy Grange; *Fisheries:* stank by abbey; in Clwyd (at Rhuddlan), Dee (presumably); Llyn Tegid (Lake Bala), and at West Kirby (Wirral); *Coal-mine:* in Coleshill (leased from Crown); *Lead and silver mines:* poss. worked in Carboniferous Limestone west of Holywell; *Rushes:* in Saltney Marsh; *Salt-pits:* in Middlewich and Northwich (Cheshire); *Markets and Fairs:* Holywell (Flints.), Charlesworth and Glossop (Derbys.); *Urban property:* in Chester, Flint, Holywell, and Shrewsbury (1295).

Appropriated Churches: **7.** Holywell (SJ 185763), Betws-'meynogan' (*?* Abergele) lost to abbey by early 13th C.

Combermere: fishery rights, and land, in Overton (SJ 354421).

Cwmhir

29. *Golon Manor (Fig. 76):* abbey site (SO 055711), poss. earlier site, Tŷ Faenor (SO 071711), detached lands: **29a.** *Nantymynach* (SO 014662), **29b.** *Rhymney* (SO 049680); **30.** *Dolhelfa Grange:* (SN 927738) barn is oldest feature; **31.** *Nant-yr-arian Grange* (SN 715813; important pastoral property *(Fig. 71)* more extensive than present farm; **32.** *Esgair-maen* and *Mynachlog* (*c.*SN 860840); **33.** *Cwmbuga Grange* (SN 859892), important for transhumance; **34.** *Gwern-y-go Grange (Fig. 100):* SO 222919; held with lands in Brompton, Churchstoke and Foxton; **35.** *Cwmbugail* (SO 182796) ascription of Prof. Wm. Rees; **36.** *Mynachdy-poeth Grange* (SO 255747), Ysgubor)SO 268744) – where two ponds on tributary of Teme; **37.** *Treburvaugh Grange (Figs. 85, 107):* Mynachty (SO 229697), tradition of burials at more southerly 'mynachdy' (SO 235694), 'coed-y-mynach' (SO 250672). 'Thlayan-wyddan' and 'Blakenhavoe' Granges (noted in 1297) perhaps in this area; **38.** *Lands in Brilley:* uncertain location, stretched towards Michaelchurch; **39.** *Gabalfa Grange* (*c.*SO 236460); **40.** *Carnaf Grange:* 'tir-y-mynach' (SO 225434). Did Court Farm relate ? (SO 213433).

Economic resources: Grange and other chapels: Gwern-y-go (S Michael; SO 222919); *Enclosures:* at abbey (SO 056711, 065726), Grange Ditch (SO 222920), Mynachty (SO 230697; *Plate XII-C*); *Water-mills:* Home Mill (SO 056710), Guellanissa (in Golon), Gwern-y-go (SO 212923), Gabalfa (SO 242467), Nant-yr-arian (SN 715813) – leat and winnowing area traceable (*Plate XIV-B*); Melin Biscuant (*?* SO 116566); a mill leased in Clun Welshry; *Fisheries:* Fishpool Farm (SO 044725, dam: 043729), Cefn-pawl ("Monks' Pool" in 1820s) SO 067706; *?* Bwlch-y-sarnau (SO 030747), *?* Llyngwyn (SO 012649), weir in Dôl-fawl (*c.* SO 262740); *Sheepcot:* Llechelwyddan (location lost). (No appropriated church or urban property known).

Cymer

41. *Abbey and Home Grange (Figs. 7, 118);* abbey site (SH 722195), 'old court' (Hengwrt, SH 718188 – perhaps the Curcy or Quirtas Grange noted in 1791); indicative field-names: Cae Llong ('ship field'; SH 722192), Dôl-y-stabal ('stable/staple meadow', SH 718194); **42.** *Abereiddon, Esgaireiddon and Hafod Newydd Granges:* Abereiddon (SH 800219, Hen-gwrt-uchaf today); Esgaireiddon lay to east; Hafod Newydd is Cae'r-dynyn now (SH 829245); Pistyll Hen-fynachlog (SH 807231); **43.** *Brynbedwen Grange:* (SH 817220); **44.** *Cwm Cedryn Grange:* isolated holdings, Cwmhesgin (SH 787296), Bryn-llin (SH 772298), Gwynfynydd (SH 732284); Dôl-y-mynach, (SH 736313); important pastoral property: licence to graze sixty cows at Y Feidiog (*c.* SH 780230*)*, 'hafod' at Craig-y-Dinas (noted 1292; SH 788297), 'dairy-house for summer, set in a moorish valley', pertained to Brynllin in late medieval times; **45.** *? Cyfeiliog Grange:* incl. Cwm Celli (SH 790101), Esgairneiriau (SH 786096), Cwmygerwyn (SH 802107) and Llwydiarth (SH 779103); **46.** *Cwmcadian Grange:* (SH 744061); **47.** *Gellisarog Grange:* (*c.* SH 593076), isolated holdings stretched from Rhyd-cryw *c.*SH 630100) to Dysynni estuary, and incl. Bodowen (SH 586056), Nant-y-cynog (SH 584041), Cae'r Abad (SH 598056), Cae'r Mynach (SH 602074), and Rhydygarnedd (SH 590026) – giving abbey a base on estuary. Cymer *may* have owned other lands, like Nantymynach (SH 644048), but there is no conclusive proof that Hendre Mynach (SH 608167), Cil-mynach (SH 610165), Bryn-mynach (SH 610164) and Tŷ-mynach (SH 607168) belonged to the abbey; **48.** *Neigwl Grange:* perhaps centred on Neigwl Uchaf (SH 260299), and incl. Rhos (SH 257293) and Gelliwig (SH 258302); ²/₃ of Neigwl township became extra-parochial; *?* landing stage at Y Penrhyn Rhiw (*c.* SH 239280); **49.** *Ceidio:* owned half the township: Ceidio (SH 284381), Plas yng Ngheidio (SH 291389); **50.** *Mynachty:* (SH 235319), with Tŷ Ruttan (where field-names of 'cae mynach' and 'llain mynach' at SH 234322).

Economic resources: Water-mills: Cymer, Pentre (SH 722192), Neigwl (*?* SH 260299), Melyn Gorys (*?*SH 752048); in 1500, Cymer demised land at Maes-y-poeth (locn. unknown) for building anew the mill there; *Fulling-mill:* 'pandy' (SH 734192); *Fisheries:* Neigwl (locn. of weir unknown), 'water of Cymer' (in Mawddach estuary); *perhaps* in Dysynni at Rhydygarnedd (SH 590026) and in Llyn Cnwch (SH 737207); *Lead mine: possibly* at Gwynfynydd (SH 732284); *Iron forge:* in Trawsfynydd (locn. unknown), and possibly at Dôl-y-clochydd (SH 731213); *Transhumance:* suggested by later mention of 'summer-houses' pertaining to Hengwrt (SH 733196) and Brynllin (SH 772298), and a 'hafod' at Craig-y-Ddinas (1292; SH 788297); a vaccary also at abbey (next the cemetery); *Urban property:* possibly in Dolgellau, where Hengwrt had a holding in 1794.

Appropriated Churches: **8.** Llanelltud (SH 717196), **9.** Llanfachreth (SH 754225), **10.** Llanegryn (SH 602054), **11.** Ceidio (SH 288382).

Dore

51. Gwenddwr Grange: 'cwrt' (SO 072461), chapel (SO 065432, St Dubricius today); **51a.** *Tir-y-Court* (Aberedw): (SO 091479, Court Farm today); **52.** *Nant Eglwys* alias *Llan Eglwys:* (SO 062386), 'Nant Mynach' (SO 061396); a 'pont-mynach' was noted in Cantref-selyf in 1268; **53.** *Trawscoed Grange (Fig. 2):* site of a late 12th C. abbey reduced to grange status, lands came to incorporate Wernddyfwg (SO 077360), formerly a separate grange; **54.** *Llyncoed Grange:* (SO 360222), 443 acres tithe-free, 'Campston Grange' today; **55.** *Cold Grange:* (S) 409222) – Grace Dieu had land of same name; **56.** *Llanfair Cilgoed Grange (Fig. 94):* foundations of cell with chantry chapel, earlier a Celtic hermitage (SO 391193); traces of terraces, ponds, courtyard wall; an aviary here; **57.** *Morlais Grange:* 'mynachty' (SO 343141).

Economic resources: Grange and other chapels: Llanfair Cilgoed (and chantry; SO 391193); Gwenddwr (later parochial; SO 064433); in 1360–69, Dore had use of St Noye's chapel, Blackbrook (parochial, where a holy well; SO 430210); *Water-mills:* two or three in Cantref-selyf, perhaps at: Gwenddwr (SO 072461), Wernddyfwg (SO 074356) and Nant Eglwys (SO 062386); *Fulling-mills:* two in Cantref-selyf, of uncertain locn., *Enclosure of note:* bank forming eastern border of Trawscoed *(Fig. 2); Fishery and Aviary:* Llanfair Cilgoed (S) 391193; *Fig. 94); Sheepcot of note:* Trawscoed (locn. lost).

Grace Dieu

58. *Treurgan/Parc Grace Dieu (Figs. 11 and 101):* incl. 1st abbey site (*c.* SO 447133): court, cemetery, barn and close called 'old abbey' sited 'in lordship of Raglan'; proximate is 'Parlour Farm' (SO 443121) – where tradition has it monks could talk and do business; **59.** *Hendre:* incl. 2nd abbey site (*c.* SO 451132), deeply buried beneath alluvium, 'abbey bridge' (SO 448134), 'old hendre' (SO 463126); Troddi stream apparently straightened, former water-courses traceable; **59a.** Extra-parochial area marked *'Cold Grange'* on tithe map; **60.** *Penrhos Grange:* (SO 416136); **61.** *Crug-yr-onnen Grange:* Court Farm (SO 436142), incl. Longbridge Meadow (434139) probably pertained to abbey; **62.** *Stowe Grange:* SO 562062, held with nearby lands of Wyegate (*c.* SO 552062) and Langeford; **62a.** *Coed-ythan Grange:* locn. lost, perhaps adjacent to Old Bailey Pit (SO 482131); **62b.** *Beaulieu Grange:* (SO 534125), held with Broadstone (SO 537122). (Grace Dieu also held from 1227–1337, the manor of Penyard, Herefs).

Economic resources: Grange and other chapels: In Parc Grace Dieu (where 'Little Chapel Meadow' on west bank of Troddi); at Stowe Grange (and chantry; SO 562062), called 'the Free Chapel of St Briavel's (*c.* 1350), – burials discovered in 1912; a chantry chapel in Monmouth Castle (from 1357 until at least 1462); in Trivel Wood (parochial; *c.* SO 436332 – where later stood Park Hall); *Water-mills:* near abbey, perhaps at 449134 or 443143 (where 'Cae felin'); *Fulling-mill:* at Osbaston, Monmouth (locn. unknown), attached to it was a workshop *('fabrica'); Iron forge:* at Penyard (Herefs.) 1227; *Dovecot:* at Osbaston (by fulling-mill); *Urban property:* in Grenars Street, Monmouth.

Appropriated Churches/Tithes: **14.** Skenfrith (SO 456203); **15.** Treurgan (SO 447133) – leased from Llandaff Cathedral Chapter; **16.** Trivel (*c.* SO 436332).

Llanllugan

63. *Manor of Llanllugan*: nunnery site (SJ 058023; *Fig.4*), Court Field adjacent; **64.** *Hydan Grange:* prob. early site of nunnery; prob. at Hydan Uchaf (SJ 1470700; lands incl. Ty'n

Gwilym at Nant-fforch (SO 147062); **65.** *Cowny:* eight holdings here; **65a.** *Court Coldmore* (SO 199976); at some stage this passed into the hands of Chirbury Priory. (In the 13th C., land was also held in Wigmore, Herefs.).

Economic resources: Water-mills: at Llanlllugan (SJ 057022 – 'lower mill', 043015 – 'upper mill', ? 055017 – 'middle mill') and Hydan (? SJ 147070); *Fulling-mill* – also at Hydan.

Appropriated Churches: **17.** Llanllugan (SJ 058023), **18.** Llanllwchaearn (SO 107919), **19.** Llanfair Caereinion.

Llanllŷr

66. *Llanllŷr:* abbey site (SN 543561; *Fig 5)*, burials adjacent; **67.** *Moelfre Grange:* several 'moelfre' place-names in area, might be SN 535487; **68.** *Glanrhiwfallen Grange:* (SN 559956), bounds uncertain; **69.** *Crug-y-saeson Grange:* ascribed by Prof. Wm. Rees to SN 543634; *Other Lands* – listed in 1291, but not identifiable with certainty, include: *Sennonlen Grange* (? at Llainyffynnon, SN 517334), *Llanhirmoel*, and *Castell Hewyn Grange* (? at Castell Hywel, SN 528590); nunnery also owned lands in Llanybydder parish.

Economic resources: Chapel: ? at Lloyd Jack (SN 528562), *Water-mill:* Llanllŷr (SN 544561). *Appropriated Church:* **20.** Cenarth (SN 271561).

Llantarnam

70. *Magna Porta Manor:* abbey site (ST 312929; *Fig. 126)* – burials found; *Cefn-mynach Grange* (Pentre-bach, ST 285921) *?* first site of abbey in former 'parish of Dewma'; St Dial's (ST 285953) had some connection with the abbey; land also owned in Caerleon; **70a.** *Ysgubor Grange:* (now Court Farm, ST 303936); **70b.** *Gelli-las Grange* (now the Grange Industrial Estate, ST 297953); **70c.** *Dorallt Grange* (ST 266940) – also in Henllys parish was 'coitca mynachlog' (*c.* ST 258943); **71.** *Llanderfel cell, pilgrimage chapel and tavern:* (ST 264953; *Fig. 64)*, marked bounding enclosure; **72.** *Trefcarn Grange* with chapel (at former Chapel Farm, ST 216938, *Fig. 85)*, burials found (ST 216937); 'pont-mynach' adjacent; site now of an industrial estate and school; **72a.** *in Mynyddislwyn:* abbey owned much of parish, as also land and mill at Penmaen; **73.** *Rhyswg Grange:* Rhyswg Fawr (ST 227946); **74.** *Cilonydd Grange:* (ST 228972), 'Cae Capel' *alias* 'Cae Eglwys' (ST 229973); **75.** *Wentsland and Bryngwyn Manor:* stretching west into the mountains, with detached portion towards Raglan; included 'Wentsland' (SO 272006), mill at Hafodyrynys (ST 223989); manor incl.: **75a.** *Bryngwyn Grange* alias *Tir-y-Mynach:* 'tre mynach' (SO 398083) with earthworks (SO 400084), Wern-y-cwrt' (SO 393088), Chapel Farm (SO 398092); **75b.** *Mynachdy'r-waun Grange:* 'mynachdy' (SO 314026), 'court' (SO 305012); **75c.** *Arail Grange:* (SO 212031); **75d.** Possible sites holdings might include Cwrt Coch, Aberbargoed (ST 156999) where mill; **75e.** *Manmoel:* (SO 179031) chapel, court, mill; **75f.** *Blaen Rhymney Grange:* centred on Blaentyswg: SO 131076 – identified by M. Gray, further south is 'Tir-cwrt' (SO 161038); **76.** *Maestir Grange:* the modern 'pont-y-mister', occupied by a Plastic Coating Works today; unidentified is 'Mahenel Grange' of same period; **76a.** *Mynachty* (ST 246863), marked on 1st edn. 6" OS map as 'Site of Priory', poss. site of Basaleg Priory, subsumed into lands of Llantarnam; Mynachty Wood adjoins (eastern portion of present Park Wood); **77.** *Pwl-pan Grange:* (ST 355877), where chapel and burials; Goldcliff Priory also had a manor in Pwlpan, perhaps at Hartridge Farm; **78.** *Llys Tal-y-Bont Grange:* 'mynachty' (SO 168789), site now of Mynachty Housing Estate; **79.** *Mynachdy:* (SO 049951) to north of the Ffrwd, with

Capel Fynachlog (SO 048943) to south: possible site of Pendâr Abbey; **80.** *Pen-rhys (Fig. 59):* pilgrimage chapel (ST 001946) and well; cell attracted settlers, Leland (*c.* 1538) referred to 'Penrise village'.

Economic resources: Grange chapels: Gelli-las (St Bridget, ST 297953), Trefcarn (ST 216938), Cilonydd (ST 229973), Pwl-pan (ST 355877), Mynachty (ST 048943), Bryngwyn (SO 398092); *Pilgrimage chapels:* Llanderfel (ST 264953) with tavern; Pen-rhys (ST 001946) with holy well; *Enclosures of note:* Llanderfel (ST 264953), Bryngwyn (SO 398086, 400084; poss. moated site, SO 394086); *Barns of note:* Home Grange (ST 312930), Cilonydd (ST 228972) – both may be post-monastic, but not certainly so; *Water-mills:* Maestir (ST 242898; built 1202), Home (ST 308932), Abergwyddon (ST 214949), Hafod-yr-ynys (ST 223988), ? Bryngwyn (poss. connected with a dam at SO 398086), Melin Penmaen (? just N. of Croes-penmaen, ST 197989), 'Melin van Howell' (very probably Manmoel Mill [SO 179031, but note that 'Cae'r dan'r Heol' occurs at SO 144031 – now in New Tredegar), Melin Brynam, perhaps on the Nant Brynar, Pontllanffraith (mill-site at SO 182957), mills held with the 'mansion house' of Abercarn might have included Abergwyddon Mill *(supra);* other possible monastic mill sites in Abercarn area: Cwmcarn Mill (SO 236934) or at site of Abercarn House (SO 217958); *Fulling-mills:* Abbey (ST 308932, the later 'tuck-mill'), at Abercarn (perhaps the mill and 'pandy' at Gelligroes – ST 177948); *Fisheries:* in Afon Llwyd, downstream from Pontnewydd to its confluence with the Usk ('Aberavon fishery'); fishing rights in Usk, esp. at Tredynog (the 'Ceyne', ? ST 389939); fish-ponds at Bryngwyn (SO 398002); ? 'stew' at abbey; *Coal-mine:* potential at Llanderfel (ST 264952), where 17th C. opencast working; *Urban property:* in Bristol and Caerleon.

Appropriated Churches/Tithes: **21.** Llanfihangel Llantarnam (ST 307931); and, *tithes from its own lands only,* in: **22.** St Gwnog ('Quencoke Chapel', ST 337929); **23.** Henllys (ST 267911); **24.** Basaleg (ST 277871), and its former dependent chapels: **25.** Bedwellte (ST 166003), where St Sannan's well (ST 168001); **26.** Machen (ST 227881); **27.** Mynyddislwyn (ST 193939); **28.** Bryngwyn; **29.** Trefethin, and **30.** Llanhiledd.

Margam *(See especially: RCAHMW, Glamorgan III: Pt. 2 (1982) pp. 266–297.)*
81. *Margam Abbey:* abbey site (SS 802863), outside gate was secular infirmary and 'the hamlet *without the walls' (Fig. 68);* pre-monastic 'cemetery without the gate'; remains of assumed holy well ('monks' bath', SS 803869); foundation estate extended south-eastwards *(Fig. 73);*
81a. *Cwrt-y-defaid:* (? al. *Llanfugeilydd Grange;* SS 801856); **82.** *Penhydd Grange:* (SS 806931), field names of 'Cae Cwrt' and 'Cae Capel' at Penhydd Fawr; **83.** *Hafod-y-porth Grange:* (SS 80899) lent its name to abbey lordship; **84.** *Notteschecourt Grange:* (SS 803847, 'Notch Coarton) formerly near Nynnid – where remains of a chancel arch and Early Christian stones found, 'cwrt-bychan' (SS 805846); Lhuyd (1707) noted Margam as having a grange at 'Eglwys Newydd'; alternative site of this grange is Nottage Court (SS 821782), where Margam received lands in 1452, and where is a tradition of chapel and burials; **85.** *Melis Grange:* 'cwrt ucha' (SS 767896; ? the 'Batchie Grange' of 1291), 'cwrt isaf' (SS 765897); site now bears railway lines, street-name commemorates the court; **86.** *New Grange* alias *Middle Burrows Grange:* (SS 782896; Hen Biniwn latterly; *Figs. 79, 88):* some remains preserved near strip mill of steel works, field-name of 'cae mynach', grange approached by paved cause-way, Heol y Deiliaid; **87.** *Morfa Mawr:* (SS 776848), demolished 1976, described as a grange by R.E. Kay; **88.** *Theodoric's* (al. *Terrys) Grange:* (SS 769848): former hermitage granted to Margam. *c.* 1188; besanded after Suppression, levelled for steelworks 1949; **89.** *Whitecross*

Grange al. *Groeswen:* (SS 781883), now demolished; **90.** *Granges of uncertain location: Ynys Afan* (*? c.*SS 798944), *Kenfig Grange* (long besanded), *Gardin Grange* (perhaps in Laleston), *Moyl Grange* (*?* ST 054734), *Orchard Grange* (*?* at Castleton in St Athan, ST 024683); **91.** *Hafodheulog Grange:* (SS 841846), outlier at Hendre Iago (SS 850847); **92.** *St Michael's Grange:* 'Llanmihangel' (SS 841846), Maltese Cross (of *c.* 1100) found here, incl. 'portland' in Kenfig; **93.** *Lands in Y Pîl (Pyle):* substantial tithe-free area north of Marlas-Kenfig road; **94.** *Stormy Grange:* (SS 847813); by 1518, divided into grange proper and 'cwrt-bychan'; **95.** *Horegrove Grange:* (SS 859812), no medieval remains, approached from west by a sunken track; **96.** *Llangewydd Grange:* (SS 872814) to SW of Court Farm, necessitated clearance of vill and church of Llangewydd (*c.* 1202–18); **97.** *Court Colman:* (SS 884819), may have had different older name; **98.** *Tŷ Tanglwst Grange:* (SS 822808), extended to the chapel of Corneli, field-names incl. 'Monkland' and 'Cae'r Bakehouse' (next to homestead), woodland held at Old Ballas (SS 831806); **99.** *Lands in Marcross Berrow:* extent uncertain, 'Cae'r Eglwys' (*c.* SS 917682); **100.** *Bonvilston Manor:* incl. demesne at Newdown, the Longge, Coed-yr-abad (*c.* ST 071732, now cleared), 'Sheep's Court' (ST 071742, *Fig. 117*), lands held in adjacent Turbernesdown; in 13th C. abbey held Caerwigau (ST 056753); **101.** *Llanfeuthin Manor:* (ST 051714), formation of grange meant displacement of people of Bradington, a Celtic ecclesiastical site, lands incl. a 'great close' (1519) and 'monkyncom' *al.* 'tre'r-reghen' (17th C.); **102.** *Greendown Grange:* (ST 062725, where long-house/barn today); **103.** *Eglwys-geinor:* in angle between Garw and Ogmore rivers; abbey's 'lordship' here perhaps comprehended two initial granges: Garw (*?* SS 905867) and Eglwys-geinor (*?* SS 925879, where Tŷ Cae'r Abbot); incl. Hen-llys (*c.*SS 920884); **104.** *Moor Grange* (Cardiff): lends its name to Grangetown, Grange Farm survives in Clive Street (ST 176749); **105.** *Cibwr Grange* (Cardiff): (ST 178779), farm demolished in 1899, later *alias* of Heath Grange; may have been the 'manor' in Roath Dogfield granted abbey *c.*1190; incl. Crwys-bychan (ST 180784) now site of Gladstone Road schools, 'Cae Abbot' occurs (ST 198781); **106.** *Resolfen Grange:* extensive mountain area, occupied by Earl of Gloucester (1291–1329) and exchanged for manor of Newton Nottage (1452); site of grange buildings nucleus changed *c.* 1185; but for how long and to what extent is unknown. *Other lands* held in: Dinas Powis and Llancarfan, and in Gloucestershire (until exchanged *c.* 1485) at Olveston, Saltmarsh and Tockington (*Ostbridge Grange,* ST 575856).

Economic resources: Grange and other chapels: Capel Mair (SS 801865), within a seemingly circular enclosure, burials found, had later recusant use, holy well (Ffynnon Mair); Penhydd (SS 806931), chapel here by 1234; Hafod-y-porth (SS 801899), field-name of 'Waun-y-capel' south of farmhouse, chapel marked by Speed (1610) and, less certainly, on Admiralty chart (1859), burials here; St Thomas, Melis, sited at either the 'hen gapel' at Cwrt Ucha, (SS 767896) or near the Dry Dock (where 'Plattau yr Hen Eglwys'), demolished 1900, burials and portions of Early Christian stones found; St Theodoric's (SS 769863), foundations remain; Capel-y-trisant, Hafodheulog, (SS 841846), in Margam's hands by 1217, previously a parochial chapel, sited on platform cut in hillside at *c.* 175 metres; St Michael's (SS 816829), no remains save two portions of window cusps; Stormy (SS847813), received early 13th C., previously parochial, foundations visible; Llangewydd, two chapels in 1239 (*c.* SS 872814), one inside and one without the court of the grange; St Meuthin's (ST 051714) built *c.* 1190, but inheriting Celtic site with cemetery; Resolfen, where old chapel (*?* SN 820618) gave way – with change of court site about 1185 - to new chapel (*?* SN 848023 – where 'Cae Capel'); Eglwys Nynid (SS 803847) where chancel arch and Early Christian stones found; *?* at Caerwigau – where 'Chapel Close' (SS 968752) and 'Dwyr Capel' (ST 065752); *Enclosures of note:* at Hafod-y-porth (SS 801899), sea-walls/banks/

ditches at Melis and New Granges', *?* Caerwigau (moated enclosure, ST 056753); *Tithe and other barns:* in Kenfig, Laleston, Bonvilston, Llangeinor, Pen-llin, Hafod-heulog, Hafod-y-porth, and at St Michael's Grange (the latter over 30m. in length); *Water-mills:* Cryke (SS 802864, where mock folly); 'Fredulles' on Ffrwdwllt (SS 790898) – it, or fulling mill, may be the 'New Mill' of 1520; Hafodheulog (*c.* SS841846); Llanmihangel (SS 818824, fulling adjacent); Llangewydd (SS 870814); 'Monkynmill', Llanfeuthin (056713), fulling nearby *(Fig. 111)*; Garw (SS 914877, site of Ofrex Engineering Ltd.); Resolfen (SN 831015 or 822020); *?* Caerwigau (ST 056755); Ostbridge (SO 575856); *Walk-mill:* possibly at Hafod-y porth (SS 801899); *Wind-mill:* at Tockington, Gloucs. (lost by exchange *c.* 1485); *Fulling-mills:* Sheep's Mill (SS 801856), 'Fredulles' (SS 790898), Llanmihangel (ST 819823), 'Tokyngmill', Llanfeuthin (SS 055712); *Sheepcots of note:* at Hafod-y-porth, Bonvilston *(Fig. 117)*, Llangewydd, Stormy, Grangetown (Cardiff); *Fisheries:* in river Neath (at Resolfen), in Afan (where salmon, sewin, gillings), in Kenfig Pool [SS 797815], in Cardiff area (in rivers Ely and Taff); *Coal-mines (Fig. 123):* at Cefn Cribwr and Bronbil (not clear whether one or two pits; old workings at Brombil - where pit was on 'Cefn Kewske – at SS 787880, 'Cefn Cribwr' possibly *c.* SS 823833); at Penhydd-waelod (on Gorse Moor, and marked by two stones), in lower course of Ffrwdwyllt ('sea-coal') – 'Abbot's Pit' marked on former shoreline west of New Grange *(Fig. 123)*; *?* at Aberbaiden (NCB suggestion of 1950s);. *Iron and lead-mines:* in Corneli, perhaps at Tŷ Tanglwst; *Wreck of sea:* on coastal lands. e.g. of Hafod-y-porth lordship; *'Honey stocks':* in Resolfen between rivers Clydach and Gwrach; *Roads:* linked abbey to Llangynwyd, approached abbey gate, led to New Grange (paved causeway of Heol y Deiliaid); *Urban property:* at Bristol (in Smale St., Goldsmith's Place, Castle Bailey, and near St Augustine's Abbey), Cardiff (in West St., Cabelle St., St Mary St., and in Roath by bridge called 'pontlike'), and in Cedweli, Kenfig (where 'Monks' Street') and Neath.

Appropriated Churches/Tithes: **31.** Aberafan (*c.* SS 755900), **32.** Glyncorrwg (SS 870056), **33.** Kenfig (SS 801824 – by lease from Tewkesbury Abbey until *c.* 1485), **34.** Laleston (SS 867798), **35.** Llangeinor (SS 924879), **36.** Llangynwyd (SS 857888), **37.** Pen-llin *alias* Llanfrynach (SS 979888), **38.** Resolfen (*c.* SN 848023), **39.** tithes of parish of Newcastle Hundred (mostly by lease from Tewkesbury Abbey until *c.* 1485). Also held Olveston, Gloucs. (*c.* 1309), and the advowson of Bonvilston.

Neath *(See especially: RCAHMW, Glamorgan III: Pt. 2 (1982) pp. 251–265).*
107. *Neath Abbey (Fig. 8):* abbey site (SS 738973), gatehouse (737976 – immediately ESE of school in New Road), quay by river Neath, Lhuyd (1707) noted: 'A great stone at ye mouth of an old vault'; **108.** *Coed-ffranc Township:* Cwrt Llan Margaret (*?* SS 705942, with chapel and holy well, *Fig. 61*); **109.** *Cwrt Betws:* grange (SS 723956) with chapel; ('betws'), late-medieval pottery found (1956), traces of paving on road leading to grange; **110.** *Cwrt Herbert* alias *'Tetteberne' Grange:* (SS 743977) now demolished; **111.** *Cwrt Sart:* (SS 740956) now a housing area and lending its name to local school; **112.** *Blaenhonddan Township:* incl. **112a:** *Rhydding* alias *Assart Grange* (SS 751988); **113.** *Ynysymwn Township:* 'Ynysymwn Uchaf' (SN 714024); **114.** *Dyffryn Clydach Township:* incl. Cwrt-rhyd-tir (SS 734985, Longford Court today) and Cwrt-y-clafdy (the secular infirmary, SS 725977), **115.** *Cefn Saeson Grange:* (SS 776965); **116.** *Hendre Hertfotte Grange:* unlocated, but in Neath Citra/Baglan/Briton Ferry, [NB: 'Cefn-cwrt', SS 750939]; **117.** *Rheola Grange:* (*c.* SN 838042); Nos. 117-120 were lost, either to the Welshry or Gilbert de Clare, about 1280; **118.** *Aberpergwm Grange: ?* 'cwrt' and 'cae capel' at SN 868061; **118a.** *Pwllywernen*

Grange: c. SN 860055 (where Pwll-faron today) or SN 857051 – where now is Maes-gwyn; **119.** *Crynant Grange:* (*c.* SN 791047); **120.** *Blaendulais Grange:* locn. uncertain, (*? C.* SN 833098); **121.** *Sker Grange:* (SS 795798) bought from Margam *c.* 1175, substantial extra-parochial area, blocked gateway and barn may be partly medieval, field-names incl. 'Abbot's Close'; abbey also had land in Corneli, and at least 10 acres in Newton Nottage ('Tir Abbot'); **122.** *Lands at Pendeulwyn:* (*c.* ST 060766); **123.** *Gelli-garn Grange:* grange was close by the now uninhabited 'cwrt' (SS 957784), major property with chapel, mills, barn; a wayside cross stood close to northern grange boundary (SS 960785); **124.** *Monknash Grange:* (SS 919705), the most outstanding grange site in Wales *(Fig. 93, Pl. XII-A)* comprehending some 840 acres (340 ha.), chapel, mills, dovecot, etc., Ffynon Fair (SS 906701) and Ffynon Mari (SS 916705) may have been early holy wells, lands prob. incl. Lower Monkton (SS 926711) and 'cwrt-y-mynach' (SS 914716), both in Wick parish; **124a.** *Marcross Grange:* (SS 926694), one unit with Monknash by the Suppression; **125.** *Tir-yr-abad: ?* the tithe-free area (in Llantwit Major) around SS 956687, Neath's lands there were called 'the abbot's rents' (1536), 'a little manor, Rysoulen' (1707); **126.** *Capel:* (SS 937691), four carucates in 1291; **127.** *Cwrt-y-carnau Grange (Fig. 99):* (SN 573004) chapel, mill, mine; **128.** *Grange* (West Cross, Swansea): (*c.* SS 616899 – where TA Centre now), mine; **129.** *Cillybion Grange:* (SS 517913), abbey's manor extended to the Welsh Moor, field-name of 'Llanhywel' (SS 529915); **129a.** *Walterstone Grange:* (nucleus at SS 510896 or 514895), abbey came to own whole vill, but original grange [tithe-free] was southern strip – marked at western extremity by a boundary stone (SS 507899, *Fig. 109a*); **130.** *Berry:* (SS 472879), bounds uncertain, several parcels here tithe-free, perhaps connected with **131.** *Paviland Manor:* (SS 445865), with other proximate lands at Monksland (SS 458877).

Economic resources: Grange and other chapels: Betws (SS 723956), Capel (*?*SS 937691), Gelli-garn (SS 959785), Monknash (*?* SS 919705 – possibly not the present nearby church, licensed for the sacraments in 1607; another (deserted) church site occurs at SS 913697); Sker (*?*SS 796799, tradition of chapel – of later recusant use – in building called Tŷ'r-ychen), St Margaret's with holy well (SS 705940), St Michael's, Cwrt-y-carnau (SS 572004, by the Loughor estuary; *Fig. 90*), St Giles in Neath Castle (temp. in 12th C.); less certain: Aberpergwm (SN 868061, where 'cae capel'), Crynant (*c.* SN 791047 – in 1707 two chapels here, 'ucha' and 'isa', but no certainty as to their monastic provenance), Morfa (SS 749979); *Enclosures of note:* the 'sanctuary wall' at the abbey, perhaps the precinct enclosure, noted in 1536 and 1707; banks, etc. at Cwrt Herbert (SE of grange), Gelli-garn (on two sides, a leat which never dries out), Marcross (rectilinear enclosure encompasses much of grange) and Monknash Granges (central 20 acres delineated by pentagonal enclosure, grange bordered on north by now diminutive Clawdd y Mynach; *Tithe- and other barns:* at Gelli-garn Grange (*?* the abbey's tithe-barn noted in St Mary Hill parish; at grange site, stone-walled enclosure may be granary foundations), Marcross and Monknash Granges (at latter, granary of 64 metres length), and possibly at Sker and Lower Monkton; *Water-mills:* Cwrt Betws (SS 723956), Clydach Mills ('lower': SS 738981, and 'higher': SS 739989); Cwrt-y-carnau (Melin Mynach, SS 593988, excavated 1994/95, site now of light industry), Gelli-garn (*?*SS 957784, 949792), Marcross (*?*SS 916685), Monknash (SS 908702), Pendeulwyn (ST 060766), West Cross (*?* SS 612985), and perhaps another in the Swansea area; *Wind-mill: ?* at Monknash (where 'Mill Farm', SS 917705); *Fulling-mill:* at Gelli-garn (*c.* SS 949792); *Sheepfold of note:* lying at Cwrt Herbert, 'between the abbey and the castle of Neath'; *Dovecots:* remnants of the 'colver-houses' noted in 1539, still visible at Gelli-garn (SS 957784) and Monknash (SS 921705); *Fisheries:* 7 weirs listed in 1291, perhaps incl. fisheries in Crymlyn Bog (*c.* SS 695950, where potential fishing also offshore) and from thence to river Tawe, two weirs in Tawe (one being near Swansea Castle and 'the passage of Swansea', the other close to 'Abermemroth'), a 'monk-weir' noted at Cilfai (1539), two weirs at Cwrt Betws, another possibly at Marcross, a fish-pond at Gelli-garn, also early fishing rights at Briton Ferry; *Coal-mines:* 3 in lordship of Gower: at Cwrt-y-carnau (SS 595993), at West Cross (SS 612985) and in Oystermouth (at Gower's Cross); another at Cwrt Herbert, and potential at Cwrt Betws; *Urban property:* at Bristol (in Snowne St.), Caerleon, Cardiff (in High St., St John's St., St Mary St., Barry Lane, Orchard St., etc.), Cowbridge (where 220 burgages).

Appropriated Churches/Tithes: **40.**Llangatwg Nedd (Cadoxton, SS 75986?, with dependent chapels *(supra)*, **41.** Llandeilo Tal-y-bont (SS 030584), **42.** Monknash (SS 921705), **43.** Castell-Nedd (Neath, SS 753976), **44.** St Mary Hill (SS 957793), and, prior to an exchange (about 1290), Cilybebyll.

Strata Florida *(Ystrad-fflur)*. *(See especially: G.D. Owen [1935] 10–27)*
132. Pennardd Grange: 1st abbey site ('hen fynachlog', SN 717645; *Fig. 12*), 2nd abbey site (SN 719644; *Fig. 66*) – where tithe-free area between rivers Teifi and Glasffrwd; **133.** *Blaenaeron Grange:* 'mynachty' occurs (SN 637628), incl. early 'grange called Castell Flemish' (noted in 1184; SN 654632); **134.** *Mefenydd Grange (Fig. 87, Map XV):* 'hafod-y-gofaint' ('convent hafod'; SN 701690); O.S. marks 'Carreg Bwlch Mynnachlog' (SN 777709); **135.** *Cwmteuddwr Grange*: large area of common pasture with isolated holdings; grange centre perhaps around Llanmadog (SN 939656), nearby were Coed-y-mynach (SN 945666) and Capel Madog (SN 939658 – in field opposite Elan Valley Hotel) **135a.** *Nannerth Grange:* (SN 947716); **136.** *Cwmystwyth Grange:* several hafod names, e.g. 'Hafod-yr-abad' (locn. lost); **137.** *Aber-miwl Grange (Fig. 22);* 'court' at SO 158944; **138.** *Celynog Grange (Map XIII-A):* 'court' (SO 045981), perhaps 'yr hen Gelynog', lands incl. Bwlch-cae-haidd (SO 052964); **139.** *Y Dywarchen* alias *Tir-y-mynach* alias *Doverchen Grange:* 'cwrt' (SN 646846, lands incl. Lletty-evan-hen (SN 685848) with its 'summer-house'; **140.** *Aber-mad:* lands touched on river Ystwyth, mill (SN 5498763), incl. Pentrellyn (*c.* SN 613750); **141.** *Morfa Bychan (Fig. 109):* (SN 566771), demolished old house contained a gothic-style doorway; **141a.** *Allt Wen* and *Morfa Ankar: c.* SN 577797 and 580800, respectively; land at mouth of Ystwyth; **142.** *Mynachty Graig:* (SN 558747); **143.** *Morfa Mawr Grange (Fig. 19):* (SN 504656); **144.** *Anhuniog Grange:* 'mynachty' (SN 504620); **145.** *Gwrthwynt Grange* alias *Tryane Grange:* (SN 533579); **146.** *Trefaes Grange:* (SN 602730), 'Allt-y-mynach (SN 608749); **147.** *Hafodwen Grange:* 'maes-mynach' (SN 519506), Capel St Silin and graveyard (no visible remains, SN 517509); **148.** *Nant-bau Grange* alias *Rhandir Abad (Fig. 97):* nucleus may have been in Ystrad-ffin, where Capel Peulin (SN 788471), 'bron-y-cwrt' (SN 569449); **149.** *Llandulas* alias *Tir-y-abad:* 'tyr abad' (SN 874416), incl. early property of Cefn Ioli (SN 886407), 'Spite Inn Farm' (SN 863410); **150.** *Aberdihonw Grange (Fig. 15);* (SO 063507), granted in 1202; 'grange wood' (?SO 057508), ferry across Wye found mention in 1615; **150.** *Cae'r Mynach:* (SN 984471), and other lesser unknown lands in Breconshire.

Economic resources: Grange and other chapels: Capel Madog (SN 939658; *Fig. 92*); Capel Peulin (SN 788471), 'bron-y-capel' occurs in Blaenaeron Grange (*temp.* Eliz. I), 'bryn-y-capel' in Mefenydd Grange (SN 729682), Capel St Silin in Hafodwen Grange (SN 517509), abbey early owned 'Y rhiw y capel' abutting on Cardigan Bay; *Water-mills:* Pontrhydfendigaid (SN 731666), Aberdihonw (SO 062507; leat traceable, 'place for winnowing' noted in 1532), Aber-mad (SN 598763), Y Dywarchen (SN 645846), Fulbrook (SN 668626), Hafodwen (SN

515509), Llanddewi Aberarth (SN 480638), Morfa Mawr (SN 504657), Nant-bau (SN 774446, wheel traceable), Pyran (?SN 775746) had adjacent 'the place for winnowing the corn' [1524], Swydd-fynnon (SN 694662); *Fulling-mills/'ty pandys':* Pontrhydfendigaid (SN 731666), Fulbrook (*c.* SN 669626), others of uncertain location incl. one in Anhuniog Grange and another in Dolforwyn; *Enclosures of note:* cemetery of Strata Florida ('meanly walled with stone', 1538), perimeter of Ffair Rhos – broken by gateways of Llidiart-y-ffair (SN 736681) and Borough Gate (SN 736678), Abbot's Ditch at Celynog, where also boundary marks, *Fig.* 106), and wall along Carreg Bwlch Mynachlog; *Barns of note:* Aber-miwl (*c.* SO 158944, 'great barn' of 1263), Morfa Bychan (SN 565711, now club of caravan park), Hafodwen (SN 516509), Y Dywarchen (SN 646846); *Fisheries:* Teifi Pools *(Fig. 122)* and other neighbouring lakes, like Llyn Fyrddon Fawr (SN 800707), listed in S.W. Williams 1889, v–vi; coastal fisheries along Cardigan Bay (as at Aberarth and Morfa Ankar); *Lead-mine:* Briwnant (*c.* SN 795740), potential elsewhere; *Fair:* Ffair Rhos (SN 739680), dubious ascription of a fair at Talsarn (SN 546653); *Wreck of sea:* along shores of its Cardigan Bay lands.

Appropriated Churches: **46.** Llangurig (SN 908799), **47.** Pencarreg (SN 535450) manse was 'Tŷ-y-person', and abbey owned land called 'mynachlog'.

Strata Marcella *(Ystrad Marchell) (See especially: G.C.G. Thomas, The Charters of the Abbey of Ystrad Marchell [Aberystwyth, 1997]).*
152. Tir-y-mynach alias Manor of Strata Marcella Abbot *alias* Major: incl. 'grange' (SJ 246156), Ysgubor Fawr grange (SJ 253117, now Dyer's Farm), a 400-acre great pasture in Gwern valley (probably Gwern Fele, SJ 2614), with lands also in Berriw and Buttington; **153.** *Abbey Grange (Fig. 28):* abbey site (SJ 251104) where later a farm-house, perhaps on line of cloister; a 38-acre 'great mead', Coedymynach (*c.* SJ 245108 – honey) and Goleugoed (*c.* SJ 2714 – pannage), 7 carucates arable; **154.** *Trehelyg:* (*c.* SJ 21033, lands unlocated) with Wernllwyd (SJ 204028); **154a.** *Ystradelfeddan Grange* (bounds uncertain), **154b.** *Tyddyn-prid;* **155.** *Rhosgoch Township:* where Monksfield (SJ 295087), held from 1229, perhaps with the immediately adjacent detached portion of Wollaston, its 'manor' in Wollaston; also held Bronrotpol (where Plas-y-cwrt, SJ 316126); **156.** *Bala-Penllyn Grange:* vaccary at Cwmhesgin (SH 882419), **156a.** *Coed-y-mynach* (SH 866406 – now largely submerged beneath Llyn Celyn), **156b.** *Cwm-main* (SH 925467); **157.** *Pennant-tigi:* where a vaccary in 1324, 'uchaf' occurs at SH 813162; *Lands in Edeyrnion:* **157a.** *Cwm Hyfed* (SH 903297), **157b.** *Cynllwyd* (*c.* SH 906262); **158.** *Coed-llyn:* (*c.*SJ 022153) with lands at Cuddigl (SJ 018162) and Llogell (SJ 032154), all forming part of 160 *infra;* 'cae'r-y-mynach' (SJ 034149), 'rhyd-yr-abadau' (SJ 049141) at Cyffin: tradition of a monastic cell (? at Cyffin Fawr, SJ 038141); **159.** *Perfeddgefn:* incl. Dol-y-maen (SH 942137); **160.** *Tir-y-Mynach (Fig. 75):* manor comprehending lands in 11 parishes, incl. 161-165: **160a.** *Talerddig* (SH 931002) where abbey courts held, **160b.** *Hafod Owain* (SH 928027, granted 1190), **160c.** *Esgair-gelynen:* (SH 916060), **160d.** *Clegyrnant:* (SH 922076), *?* **160e.** *Bwlchllyn: ?* SN 972883); **161.** *Tir Abad:* part of No. 160, incl. **161a.** *Cwm Arannell:* (SN 976991), **161b.** *Y Bedwosed:* (SN 972987), **161c.** *Rhiw Caenesied:* (*c.*SN 972964), **161d.** *Pantygesail* (SN 989972), **161e.** *land east of Blaengwm:* (*c.*SN 995987); **162.** *Blaen Carno* (SN 944941) and *Llysyn* (*c.*SN 956974); **163.** *Lands in Trefeglwys:* over 2,000 acres [800 ha.] incl. Aberbachog (SN 881926), Dol-gwyddol (SN 883923), Llywyn-y-gog (SN 875919), Felin Newydd (SN 875927), and Nant-yr-hafod (SN 874913), **163a.** *Bodreiswal* (SN 884944); **164.** *Mynachty:* (SN 789955), with lands at Hengwm (SN 781948) and Cwmbir (SN 785951); **164a.** *Rhosgwidol:* (SN 839977) bought in 1199; **165.** *Penwar:* (*c.* SN 925868), with Bryntail (SN 919871) and Pen-y-

clun (SN 930874); **165a.** *Brithdir* (SN 894857); **166.** Lands in *Moydog* ('fawr', SJ 168079, tithe-free land at SJ 159085), Hengwm (SJ159071), **166a.** *Trefnant Mynach* (SJ 185092), **166b.** Lands in *Gaer* (*? c.* SJ 187084); **166c.** *Esgyn Gaenog:* (SJ 089460).

Economic resources: Grange and other chapels: Capel Dolwen (SH 977075), Capel Maine, Talerddig (*c.* SH 931002); *Pilgrimage shrine:* of Holy Cross in the abbey; *Enclosures of note:* Abbot's Ditch, described in 1588 as 'the print of an old ditch' coming from Dolwen and passing between Brynmawr and Llidiart-y-dallva (perhaps *c.* SO 980070), and Abbot's Dyke (early termed 'the black dyke') near Hafod Owain (*Fig. 105*); *Water-mills:* Home Mill (SJ 254111), Guilsfield (Cegidfa) Mill ('the mill of Kagigway', SJ 217116), another mill in Tir-y-mynach described in 1536 as 'newly-built', *?* Talerddig Mill (SH 929001), a mill of the Moydog group of lands – perhaps Trefnant Mill (SJ 172037); *Wind-mills:* Cae-post (SJ 252122 – identifed by P.G. Barton), *?* Trelydan (SJ 222092); *Fisheries:* early rights – perhaps not long sustained – in the Dyfi (*c.* SH 800031), and at old Aberystwyth and Llanbadarn; *Lead-mining potential:* at Rhosgwidol (SN 839974), Bryn Tail (SN 917869) and Pen-y-clun (SN 933876); *Urban property:* 3 shops in Shrewsbury Market Place (1225).

Appropriated Churches: **48.** Berriw (SJ 187008), **49.** Betws Cedewain (SJ 123968).

Tintern
167. *Porthcaseg Manor (Figs. 81, 102):* abbey site (ST 531999, *Figs. 6, 29, Plate I*), within precincts were brew-house, bake-house, guest-hall (*Fig. 58*), stables; a chamber over abbey parlour (inner gate); later note (1568) of laundry-house, pantry-house, bark-loft; precinct wall (vestiges remain) broken by the Great Gate (*Plate XI-B*, with its garret gaol) and the Water Gate; ferry across Wye (Passage Meadow was here); Abbey Cross stood by road leading to Tintern village; paths converging on Great Gate included the Stony Way and the Long Way; the 'great orchard' touched upon Plumweir Mead; at Porthcaseg itself (ST 524982) occurs 'Court House Field'; manor included Nos. 168–170; **168.** *Ruding Grange (Fig. 103):* (ST 532994), literally 'Assart Grange'; a former drainage system of stone-filled trenches, old land drains and open ditches has been noted here; **169.** *Secular Firmary Grange (Fig. 65):* (*c.* ST 521999, where 'firmary grove'), referring to the external infirmary of the abbey; 'chapel meadow' occurs close to Penteri House (ST 522997); **170.** *Rogerstone Grange (Fig. 96):* (ST 506966), important arable property, stretched south to include Bernardswood, and touched upon Cophill (ST 508947) and Howick (ST 502956 – where abbey owned 'Y Stable'); lands also held at St Wormet's and 'Landreston'; **171.** *Trelech Grange alias Cilfethin (Map XVI):* (ST 492017), a Celtic site with prehistoric antecedents, field-names incl. Chapel Meadow and Bakehouse Meadow, grange delimited by boundary stones and wayside crosses, lands also held in adjacent Llanishen; **172.** *Brockweir Grange:* (SO 540012), some Tudor architectural remains; **173.** *Modesgate Grange:* (SO 551006 – Madgett today), formerly a detached portion of Woolaston parish, 'chapel mead' occurs (ST 554006); **174.** *Woolaston Manor:* included Nos. 172–173, 174a–177; **174a.** *Harthill Grange:* (SO 546027), largely extra-parochial, abbey owned Hartshill Wood, now largely cleared; **175.** *Ashwell* (*?* alias *Halishall) Grange:* (ST 574987); **176.** *Woolaston Grange (Fig. 119, Plate VI-C):* (ST 588983), chapel, mill, etc., wreck of sea and fisheries; harbour lately excavated; **177.** *Aluredeston Grange:* (ST 596994): no visible remains save earthworks, but chapel, mills, byre, bake-house, etc., **178.** *Merthyr Gerain Grange (Fig. 95):* (ST 427884), 'Upper Grange' today; in parish of Merthyr Gerain *alias* Salisbury; granary, byres, stable, etc., recent survey shows stone-wall enclosures broken by gate-ways; **179.** *Moor Grange (Figs. 84, 104):* (ST 428855), 'Lower Grange' today; **180.**

Broadmead: (*c.* ST 400838), much pasture owned here; **181.** *Greenmoor:* (*c.* ST 395587): extra-parochial pasture area; **181a.** *Grangefield (Fig. 108, Plate XII-B):* (ST 389849): double moated enclosure, within the inner enclosure formerly stood a boundary stone; **181b.** *Other lands in Redwick and Undy:* a 'New Grange' finds mention in 1572 (this may have been 181a); detached holdings incl. land by Redwick cemetery and 'Monks Mead' in Undy (ST 436864, *Fig. 114*); **182.** *Estavarney Grange* alias *Monkswood:* (SO 353032. Other detached lands included 'Tintern's Lugg' by the Olway Brook (SO 403019, *Fig. 82*). Tintern's most valuable manor was far afield, in Acle (Norfolk).

Economic resources: Grange and other chapels: at Moor Grange (now built over), Trelech Grange (inherited an 8th C. Celtic church, 'Lann Mainuon', chapel heavily restored and is parish church today); Estavarney (to east of present farm, *Fig. 91*), Rogerstone Grange (dedicated to St John, sited perhaps by precinct wall), Modesgate Grange (where 'chapel mead', SO 554006), Woolaston Grange (ST 587983 – *Plate XIII-B*, had an undercroft, now demolished apart from an arch), Aluredeston Grange; St Andras Church, Chapel Hill (ST 531999, now a ruin), St Anne's Gatehouse chapel (ST 532199, in private hands), Secular Infirmary chapel (by Penteri House perhaps, where a 'chapel meadow'); *Holy well (Fig. 63):* St John's Well, Rogerstone Grange (ST 506969, site of Chepstow Waterworks); *Water-mills:* Angidy (SO 530002), 'Sondmulle' in Tidenham (location unknown), Aluredeston (*c.* ST 596994), Brockweir (SO 546014), Merthyr Gerain (ST 429891, mill-stone lately in hedge), Rogerstone (SO 506967 *[Plate XIV-A]*, now demolished, pond served by several leats), Trelech (SO 496014, at end of post-glacial lake and at break of slope caused by rapids), Woolaston (SO 588984, a 'Clap Mill' noted at this grange in 1488); *Fulling-mills:* Angidy (perhaps *c.* SO 530002), Aluredeston (*c.* ST 596994), another suggested at Raglan (by NLW, Badminton Deeds 15732, 1578); at 'Triket' (1291) – perhaps the Angidy area – there was a *tannery* and *timber* and *honey* were sold; *Moated enclosure:* Grangefield (*q.v.*); *Medieval roads:* Stony Way and Long Way led to abbey gate-house, tenants had duty of upkeep of roads at Trelech (where paving remained in 19th C.) and Rogerstone Grange (like its 'lodeway'); *Sheepcots of note:* at Trelech Grange (*Map XVI*), Modesgate Grange (ST 549997), Woolaston Grange (ST 588983), and close to Stow Weir Meadow, near Ruding Grange; *Fisheries:* for salmon especially) in Wye at Ashweir (SO 529003), Brockweir (SO 539012), Ithelsweir (SO 531031), Plumweir (ST 538996), Stow Weir (ST 536985; *Fig. 120*) and Walweir (ST 539979) – number owned varied throughout the Middle Ages; offshore fishing rights at Moor and Woolaston Granges (at latter was 'Tinternespulle'), also owned 'Gale Pool' (in Tidenham parish); fishing also in Usk at Estavarney and in Angidy (by mill); a notable stank (the former marsh of Lake Tintern) at Trelech Grange (*Map XVI*); *Iron-mine and forge:* in Forest of Dean, in St Briavel's parish; *Lead and silver works:* seemingly in abbey precinct by 15th C; *Wreck of sea:* adjoining Woolaston and Moor Granges; *Urban property:* in Bristol (in Fisher's Lane, Redcliffe Street), Chepstow, Monmouth (in Monnow Street).

Appropriated Churches/Tithes: **50.** Merthyr Gerain *alias* Salisbury (precise site uncertain); **51.** Magor (ST 425870 – could the 'rectory by Magor cemetery' noted in 1388 be the later so-called 'procurator's house'?); **52.** Porton (*c.* ST 389826 – now lost by coastal erosion); **53.** Redwick (ST 412841); **54.** Tidenham (ST 556959); **55.** Woolaston (ST 587993 – almshouse endowed close by in latter years of abbey); **56.** Alvington (SO 603007). Hewelsfield church may have belonged to the monastery, whilst the former parish of Porthcaseg, whose tithes once belonged to St Kingsmark Priory, was largely assimilated into Tintern's property. Further afield, the abbey had the valuable rectories of Halvergate (Norfolk) and Lydd (Kent).

Vale Royal *(See especially: F.R. Lewis (1938) 16-38)*
183. Land in Llanbadarn Fawr (Aberystwyth): owned Parson's Mill, and house called 'Creklewe' – perhaps the manse.
184. At *Aberystwyth* – a herring fishery.

Appropriated Church: **57.** Llanbadarn Fawr (SN 599810), with its dependent chapelries of Llangynfelyn, Llanfihangel Genau'r-glyn (*alias* Castell Gwalter), Aberystwyth, Llanfihangel-y-Creuddyn, Llanilar, Llanychaearn, Llanafan, Gwnnws and Llangwyryfon.

Valle Crucis *(See especially, Pratt D. 1997, pp. 4, 20-24, 46-55)*
185. Valle Crucis alias *Llanegwest (Figs. 25, 116):* abbey site (SJ 204442), proximate Home Grange, another grange may have been sited at Trevor Mills (SJ 261413); **186.** Manor of *Llangollen Abad (Map XIII-B)*; **186a.** *Tirabad:* incl. 'Baketon' Grange (SJ 217411), and lands of Pengwern Hall Estate (SJ 224421), where perhaps another grange; **187.** Mwstwr Grange: centred perhaps on Plas Isaf (SJ 164421 – where tithe-free lands, abbey owned half township; **188.** *Efenechdy:* (SJ 166434); **189.** *Hafod-yr-abad:* (SJ 188486), like Nos. 190, 192, lies close to river Alun; an enclosure, possibly a grange site, occurs at Hen Eglwys (SJ 177485); **190.** *Buddugre'r Abad Township* alias *Bodigre'r Abbot:* 'Cwrt'r Abad' (SJ 192518); lands incl. Cefn Du (SJ 191510) perhaps a remnant of the abbey's 'great pasture in Yale' of this name; **191.** *Moelfre-fawr:* (c. SJ 958472) bounds unknown; **192a.** *Banhadlan:* (SJ 181567), ? the 'Bodhang' Grange of 1291; **192b.** *Creigiog Grange:* at Creigiog Uchaf (SJ 193553), bounds uncertain, name 'abbey-lands' persists; **193.** *Gwernfeifod Grange (Fig. 22):* (SJ 094290), in this parish (Llanrhaeadr-ym-Mochnant) are tithe-free fields: 'Maesydd yr Abad'; **194.** *Hafod, etc.:* (SJ 257515) incl. area of Park Farm and Lower Park Mine, 215 acres (87 ha.) summer pasture; **195.** *Wrexham Abbot:* 'Court' (SJ 328492), near which is an earthwork; valuable manor, abbey also held **195a.** *Stansty Abbot* alias *Stansty Isaf:* 'grange' (SJ 331518), and **195b.** *Lands in Acton:* 'grange' (SJ 331518); lands also held in Bersham and Northcroft; **196:** *Halghton Manor:* 'court' (SJ 316393). Other lands, of uncertain location, in Meifod, Overton and Glyntraean ('maes mynach'). OS maps mark a 'grange' in Llanynys (SJ 106609) but its ownership is not known.

Economic resources: Grange chapels: tradition of an old chapel at Creigiog Grange, 'Hen Eglwys' occurs west of Hafod-yr-abad; *Water-mills:* Home Mill (SJ 205436), and at Buddugre'r Abad, Halghton (SJ 316435), Llangollen Abad (SJ 216420), Wrexham (SJ 331502); *Fulling-mills:* Home (SJ 203444), and, perhaps, at Halghton (SJ 323431); *Fisheries:* abbey stank, three 'cruez' in river Dee, in Dee also at Llangollen – above the bridge (SJ 214422), weekly rights at Overton Weir (SJ 354421; *Fig. 23*); *Mining:* potential, but no evidence of usage; *Urban property:* abbey's manors in Llangollen and Wrexham (where was 'Abbot's Street').

Appropriated Churches/Tithes: **58.** Bryneglwys (SJ 145473), **59.** Chirk (SJ 291376), **60.** Llandysilio-yn-Iâl (SJ 194436), **61.** Llangollen (SJ 217419), **62.** Llansanffraid Glyndyfrdwy (township of Llan, SJ 111435), **63.** Ruabon (SJ 302439), **64.** Wrexham (SJ 335502), **65.** 'Resolen' township, in or near Wrexham.

Whitland *(See especially, G.D. Owen [1935] 53-67)*
197. Hendy-gwyn: chapel (SN 201162), mills, fair; **198.** *Iscoed Grange:* final abbey site (SN 208182; *Fig. 126*), demesne incl. 'great mead', 'parkedyn' and 'the little gate'; grange incl. the valuable 'Cardiff Forest' (SN 224166); **199.** *Ystlwyf Grange:* 'lower court' (SN 304148), 'parc-yr-abad' (SN 311165), lands of Pant-dwfn (SN 289152) were tithe-free; **200.**

Blaengwyddno Grange: Upper Blaengwyddno, termed 'Grange' today (SN 149123); **201.** *Llwynrebol Grange:* (SN 132261); **202.** *Castell Cosan Grange:* diffuse grange, with lands in nine parishes, it included the early granges of Blaenpedran, Cilgryman and Nantweirglodd; place-names incl. 'crug-y-mynach' (SN 221333) and 'spite' (SN 228324); Lhuyd (1707) noted the hamlet of 'cwrt' (SN 144215) where some 'Christian stones'; **202a.** *Nantweirglodd Grange:* (SN 231322), abbey perhaps owned whole hamlet of 'Tave Llangenau';**202b.** *Blaenpedran Grange (Fig. 83):* 'Cae'r mynach' (SN 265326), 'Clynmynach' (SN 266323); earthworks marked 'Parc y Beddau' ('field of graves', SN 260317); **203.** *Aberelwyn*: in Castell Cosan, held land here extending from mill (SN 197287) to (in 1536) 'St Selbyn's Well'; **204.** *Dyffryn Tawe Grange (Fig. 86):* 'cwrt mawr' (SN 201253) – where site of mill/fish pond and greenway, 'cwrt-bach' (SN 201251); **205.** *? Pen-fai:* abbey may have owned Pen-fai (SN 252425), and certainly Bronclud (locn. lost); **206.** *Blaensaith:* (SN 280501), with Esgair-eithin (SN 284504); **207.** *Crugerydd Grange:* 'mynachlog' (SN 415521), 'llawr-cwrt' (SN 415501); land also reputedly held at Sinod (c.SN 404543); **208.** *Tir Newydd Grange:* 'court' (SN 496483); **209.** *Rhuddlan Deifi Grange*: early nucleus may have been at Crug-y-whil (SN 487429), possibly a chapel here; **210.** *Maenor Forion Grange (Fig. 98):* 'cwrt' (SN 394388), noted by Lhuyd (1707) as a 'place of diversion' for the abbot in summer; **211.** *Llanfihangel Cilfargen:* grange or 'lordship' here; **212.** *St Leonard's Chapel:* locn. uncertain (*?* The Priory, SN 388071), stood by the Tywi in the lordship of Cedweli and in 'the fforrenry of St Ishmael's' (1609), and was held with 20 acres [8 ha.] of land.

Economic resources: Grange and other chapels: Capel Mair, Dancapel, with well (SN 404381) – burials found by cowshed and in field to south; Eglwys Fair Lan Tâf (SN 201162), St Leonard's by the Tywi (*?* a former leper hospice), *?* a chapel at Ystwyth, *c.* SN 299163; *Barns:* perhaps at Ysgubor-fawr (SN 209175); *Water-mills:* Home Mill *(Fig. 8),* Hendy-gwyn (SN 204165), Cwmfelin Mynach – Cilgryman Mill *al.* Milliner Grymm *al.* Llanwinio Mill (SN 228247) – demolished 1976, Blaengwyddno (SN 150123), Crugerydd (SN 419501), Dyffryn Tawe (SN 201253) – signs here of stank or mill-pond, Aberelwyn (SN 197287), Llwynrebol (SN 130262) – signs of pond and leat remain, Maenor Forion (SN 390389) – leat traceable, Nantweirglodd (SN 227322), Rhuddlan Deifi (SN 493431), Tir Newydd (SN 491489), Ystlwyf (?SN 304448), abbey also owned a mill (sold by last abbot) – perhaps a wind-mill – at Bedminster, Bristol; *Fulling-mills:* Hendy-gwyn (SN 204165), Maenor Forion (SN 390389), Rhuddlan Deifi (SN 493432), Tir Newydd (?SN 491489), and another of uncertain location; *Fisheries:* fish-ponds adjacent to abbey *(Fig. 8),* 'cored-y-abad' at St Leonard's in Tywi, and weekly rights in the Cleddau at Haverfordwest; *Fair:* Eglwys Fair Lan Tâf (SN 201162), five times a year on specified feasts of Our Lady; *Urban property:* in Haverfordwest (in The Friars) and in New Carmarthen (in Spilman Street); *Holy wells:* Ffynnon Fair (SN 403382), Ffynnon Cwm Blumen (NW of abbey) was reputedly a healing well.

Appropriated Churches: **66.** Llanwenog (SN 494456), **67.** Llangeler (SN 375393), **68.** Llanfihangel Abercywyn (SN 302133) – five 'pilgrim stones' in cemetery, **69.** Llandysiliogogo (SN 363575), **70.** Llanboidy (SN 217232), **71.** Llanwinio (SN 261264), **72.** Henllan Amgoed (SN 179201), **73.** Llanfyrnach (SN 221312), **74.** Clydai (SN 251355), **75.** Cilrhedin (SN 279349), **76.** Eglwys Fair a Churig (SN 202263), **77.** Llanfihangel Cilfargen (SN 573241); E.T. Lewis ascribed Ludchurch and Merthyr (Carmarthen) to the abbey, while Ecton (1754) attributed also 'Egermond Curacy'.

BIBLIOGRAPHY

Abbreviations

BL	British Library.
HCA	Hereford Cathedral Archives.
NLW	National Library of Wales (Aberystwyth).
NMW	National Museum of Wales (Cardiff).
RCAHMW	Royal Commission on Ancient and Historical Monuments in Wales (Aberystwyth).
UCNW	University College of North Wales Archives (Bangor).
DNB	Dictionary of National Biography.
HMSO	His/Her Majesty's Stationery Office.
VCH	Victoria County History.
Arch. Camb.	Archaeologia Cambrensis./
Arch. in Wales	Archaeology in Wales.
BBCS	Bulletin of the Board of Celtic Studies.
BSFN	Bull.-Soc. Francaise de Numismatique.
Carms. Antiq.	The Carmarthenshire Antiquary.
Monm. Antiq.	The Monmouthshire Antiquary.
Mont. Collns.	The Montgomeryshire Collections.
NLW Jnl.	National Library of Wales Journal.
Trans. Caern. Soc.	Transactions of the Caernarfonshire Historical Society.
Trans. Radn. Soc.	Transactions of the Radnorshire Society.
Y Cymm.	Y Cymmrodor.

Primary Sources

Aberg. Accts. Roderick A.J. and Rees W. (edit.), 'Accounts of Abergavenny Lordship', *Publns. South Wales and Monm. Record Soc.* IV (1957).

Anc. Corr. Edwards J.G. (edit.), Calendar of *Ancient Correspondence concerning Wales* (Cardiff, 1935).

Anc. Pet. Rees, W. (edit.), *Calendar of Ancient Petitions relating to Wales* (Cardiff, 1975).

Ann. Camb. Williams, J. ('Ab 'Ithel'. (edit.), *Annales Cambriae* (Rolls Ser., London, 1860).

Ann. Mon. Luard H.R. (edit.), *Annales Monastici* (Rolls Ser., London, 1864–69).

Augm. Rec. Lewis E.A. and Conway Davies J. (edit.), *Records of the Court of Augmentations relating to Wales and Monmouthshire* (Cardiff, 1954).

Autobiog. GC. Butler H.E. (edit.), *The Autobiography of Giraldus Cambrensis* (London, 1937).

Bart. Cott. Luard H.R. (edit.), *Bartholomaei de Cotton: Historia Anglicana* (London, 1859.

Biog. Reg. Oxford. Emden A.B. (edit.), *Biographical Register of the University of Oxford (1501–40)* (Oxford, 1974).

Biog. Reg. Oxford (1). Emden A.B. (edit.), *Biographical Register of the University of Oxford to A.D. 1500* (Oxford, 1957–).

Black Prince's Reg. *Register of Edward the Black Prince* (HMSO., 1930).

Book of Prests: Fryde E.B. (edit.), *The Book of Prests of the King's Wardrobe, 1294–5* (Oxford, 1962).

Bristol Tallage: Fuller E.A., 'Tallage of 6 Edward II', *Trans. Bristol and Gloucs. Archaeol. Soc.* XIX.

Bromfield Extent: Ellis T.P., 'The First Extent of Bromfield and Yale, 1315', *Cymm. Rec. Soc.* XI (1924).

Brut (1941): Jones T. (edit.), *Brut y Tywysogyon, Peniarth MS 20* (Cardiff, 1941).

Brut (1952): Jones T. (edit.), *Brut y Tywysogyon* (Peniarth MS 20 version; Cardiff, 1952).

Brut (1955): Jones T. (edit.), *Brut y Tywysogyon* (Red Book of Hergest; Cardiff, 1955).

Cal. Chancery R. var.   Calendar of various Chancery Rolls (HMSO, 1912).

Cal. Charter R.   Calendar of the Charter Rolls (HMSO, 1903–).

Cal. Close R.   Calendar of the Close Rolls (HMSO, 1902–).

Cal. Fine R.   Calendar of the Fine Rolls (HMSO, 1911–).

Cal. Inq. Misc.   Calendar of Inquisitions Miscellaneous (Chancery) (HMSO, 1916–).

Cal. I.P.M., Calendar of Inquisitions Post Mortem (HMSO, 1904–).

Cal. Papal Reg.   Calendar of Entries in the Papal Registers relating to Great Britain and Ireland (HMSO, 1893–).

Cal. Patent R.   Calendar of the Charter Rolls (HMSO, 1901–).

Cardiff Rec. Matthews J. H(obson) (edit.), *Records of the Ciounty Borough of Cardiff* (Cardiff, 1898–1911).

Carmarthen Charters: Daniel-Thyssen J.R. and Evans, A.C. (edit.), *Royal charters and historical documents relating to .. Carmarthen* (Carmarthen, 1876).

Cartae Glam. Clark G.T. (edit)., *Cartae et alia Munimenta quae ad Dominium de Glamorgan pertinent* (Cardiff, 1910).

Catal. Penrice: Birch W. de Gray 1893. *A Descriptive Catalogue of Penrice and Margam MSS* (London, 1893–95).

Chepstow, Tintern MSS: Wood J.G, *Chepstow, Tintern, . . . Documents* (Newport Reference Library).

Chester Deeds: Taylor H, 'On Some Early Deeds . . .', *Jnl. Chester and N. Wales Arch. and Hist. Soc.* N.S. VI (1899).

Chester Recog. R.   Chester Recognizance Rolls, PRO Deputy Keeper's Reports: (1) 36th 1875], (2) 37th (1876), (3) 39th (1878).

Chron. Adae de Usk: Thompson E.M. (edit.), *Chronicon Adae de Usk* (London, 1904).

Chr. Bury St. Edmund's: Gransden A. (edit.), *The Chronicle of Bury St. Edmund's* (London, 1964).

Chr. Maiora: Luard H.R. (edit.), *Chronica Majora* (London, 1872–80).

Chr. R. Wendover: Hewlett H.G. (edit.), *Chronica Rogeri de Wendover* (London, 1868–71).

Compotus R. Beachcroft G. and Sabin A., 'Two Compotus Rolls of St Augustine's Abbey', *Bristol Record Soc.* IX.

Councils: Haddan A.W. and Stubbs W. (edit.), *Councils and Ecclesiastical Documents relating to Great Britain and Ireland* (Oxford 1869–78).

Cronica de Wallia: Jones T. (edit.), 'Cronica de Wallia', *BBCS* XII (1946).

Cwmhir Charter: Charles B.G., 'An Early Charter of Abbey Cwmhir', *Trans. Radn. Soc.* XL (1970).

D. Nanmor: Roberts T. and Williams I., *The Poetical Works of Dafydd Nanmor* (Cardiff, 1923).

De Invect. Davies W.S. (edit.), 'Giraldus Cambrensis : De Invectionibus', *Y Cymm.* XXX (1920).

Early Chanc. Proc. Lewis E.A., *An Inventory of Early Chancery Proceedings concerning Wales* (Cardiff, 1937).

Eccl. Charters: Hunter J. (edit.), 'Charters relating to Ecclesiastical Affairs', *Ecclesiastical Documents* (Camden Soc. 1840).

Episc. Acts: Conway Davies J. (edit.), *Episcopal Acts relating to Welsh Dioceses* (Cardiff, 1948).

Eulog. Hist. Haydon F.S. (edit.), *Eulogium Historiarum* II (Rolls Ser., 1860).

Exchq. Proc. (1): Jones E.G., *Exchequer Proceedings concerning Wales* (Cardiff, 1939).

Exchq. Proc. (2): Jeffreys Jones T.I., *Exchequer Proceedings concerning Wales In Tempore James I* (Cardiff, 1955).

Faculty Off. Chambers D.S (edit.), *Faculty Office Registers, 1534–1549* (Oxford, 1966).

Fasti Cist. Williams D.H. (edit.), 'Fasti Cistercienses Cambrenses', *BBCS* XXIV : Pt. 1 (May 1971); Pt. 2 (May 1973).

Flint Accts. Jones A., 'Flintshire Ministers' Accounts, 1301–1328', *Flintshire Hist. Soc. Publn.* 3 (1913).

Flint Pleas: Edwards J.G. (edit), 'Flint Pleas, 1283–85', *Flintshire Hist. Soc. Publn.* 8 (1921).

Flores Hist. Luard H.R. (edit.), *Flores Historiarum* (Rolls Ser., 1890–).

Gervase: Stubbs W. (edit.), *Gervase of Canterbury : The Historical Works* (Rolls Ser., 1879).

Gir. Camb. Brewer, J.S. *et al.* (edit.), *Giraldus Cambrensis, Opera* (Rolls Ser. London, 1869–).

Gloucs. I.P.M. various editors, *Abstract of Gloucestershire Inquisitiones Post Mortem* (London; British Record Soc. 1893–1914).

Gloucs. Notes and Queries: various editors, *Gloucestershire Notes and Queries* (reprinted from *The Stroud Journal*; London, 1881–).

Gloucs. Peace Rolls: Kimball E.G., 'Gloucestershire Peace Rolls', *Trans. Bristol and Gloucs. Archaeol. Soc.* LXII (1940).

Grace Dieu Docs. Owen E. (edit.), 'Documents relating to the dissolved monastery of Grace Dieu', *S. Wales and Monm. Rec. Soc. Publns.* II (1950).

Hist. Works: Wright T., *The Historical Works of Giraldus Cambrensis* (London, 1905).

Hist. Hen. VII: Campbell W., *Materials for a History of Henry VII* (Rolls Ser., 1873–77).

Hockaday Abst.: Hockaday Abstracts (Gloucester Public Library).

Itin. Gir. Camb. Hoare R.C. (edit.), *The Itinerary of Archbishop Baldwin through Wales, A.D. 1188, by Giraldus de Barri* (London, 1806).

Itin. J. Leland: Smith L.T. (edit.), *Itinerary of John Leland* (Centaur Press, 1964).

Itin. Wm. Worcestre: Harvey J.H. (edit.), *William Worcester, Itineraries* (Oxford, 1969).

John of Salisbury: Millor W.J. and Butler H.E. (edit.), *The Letters of John of Salisbury* (London, 1955)

Journey through Wales: Thorpe L., *The Journey through Wales: Gerald of Wales* (Penguin, 1978).

Kansas: MS Flat (Abbey Dore Colln.), Spencer Research Library (Dept. of Special Collections), University of Kansas.

Kingswood Docs. Perkins V.R., 'Kingswood Monastery', *Trans. Bristol and Gloucs. Archaeol. Soc.* XXII (1899).

Lanercost Chr. Maxwell H. (edit.), *The Chronicle of Lanercost* (Glasgow, 1913).

Letters to Cîteaux: Talbot C.H. 1967., *Letters from English Abbots to Cîteaux* (Camden Soc. 4th Ser. No. 4; Royal Hist. Soc. 1967).

Letters from Ireland: O'Dwyer, B.W. (edit.), *Stephen of Lexington: Letters from Ireland* (Kalamazoo, 1982).

Letters Inn. III: Cheney C.R. and M.G., *The Letters of Pope Innocent III* (Oxford, 1967).

Liber Land. Evans G. and Rhys J. (edit.), *The Book of Llan Dâv* (Oxford, 1893).

Lit. Cant. Sheppard J.B. (edit.), *Literae Cantuarensis* (Rolls Ser., 1899).

Litt. Wallie: Edwards J.G. (edit.), *Littere Wallie* (Cardiff, 1940).

Little Red Book: Bickley F.B. (edit.), *Little Red Book of Bristol* (Bristol, 1900).

Lleyn Accts. Jones Pierce T. (edit.), 'Lleyn Ministers' Accounts, 1350-1, *BBCS* VI (1933).

Llywelyn's Charter: Williams-Jones K., 'Llywelyn's Charter to Cymer Abbey in 1209', *Jnl. Merioneth Hist. and Rec. Soc.* III: Pt. 1 (1957).

LP (Hen. VIII): Letters and Papers, Foreign and Domestic, of the Reign of Henry VIII (2nd edn., HMSO, 1920-).

Merioneth Sub. Jones F., 'The Subsidy of 1292', *BBCS Studies* XIII (1950).

Mon. Angl. Dugdale W. (edit.), *Monasticon Anglicanum* (London, 1846 edn.).

Monm. Rec. Matthews J. Hobson., *Monmouth Records* (In Monmouth Local History Centre).

MSS in BM: Owen E., (edit.), *A Catalogue of the Manuscripts relating to Wales in the British Museum* (London, 1900-22).

Munimenta Acad. Oxon. Anstey H. (edit.), *Munimenta Academica* (London, 1868).

Neath Charters: Lewis D., 'Notes on the Charters of Neath Abbey', *Arch. Camb.* (1887).

Neath Deeds: Foster A.G. 'Two Deeds relating to Neath Abbey', *Publns. S. Wales and Monm. Record Soc.* II (1950).

Opera G.C. Brewer, J.S. *et al.* (edit.), *Giraldus Cambrensis, Opera* (Rolls Ser., 1869-91).

Orig. Ch. Hunter J., 'Original Charters of the Family of De La Roche', *Arch. Camb.* 1852.

Orig. Cist. Janauschek L., *Originum Cisterciensium* (Vienna, 1877).

Orig. Lett. Ellis H. (edit.), *Original Letters* II (London, 1827).

Polychron R. Higden: Babington C. (edit.), *Polychronicon Ranulphi Higden* I (Rolls Ser., London, 1865).

Rec. Caern. Ellis, H. (edit.), *Record of Caernarvon* (London; Record Commn. 1838).

Rec. Ward.: Byerly B.F. and C.R., (edit.), *Records of the Wardrobe and Household, 1285-1286* (HMSO; 1977).

Reg Aberconway: Ellis H. (edit.), 'Register of Aberconway', *Camden Miscellany* I; 1847).

Reg. R. Beauchamp: Bannister A.T. (edit.), *The Register of Richard Beauchamp* (Cantilupe Soc., Hereford, 1917).

Reg. C. Bothe: Bannister A.T. (edit.), *The Register of Charles Bothe* (Hereford, 1921).

Reg. Cancell. Oxon. Salter H.E. (edit.), *Registrum Cancellarii Oxon.* (Oxford Hist. Soc., 1930-31).

Reg. J. Catterick: Swanson R.N. (edit.), *The Register of John Catterick* (Canterbury and York Soc., 1990).

Reg. T. Charlton: Capes W.W. (edit.), *Register of Thomas Charlton* (Hereford, 1912).

Reg. W. Courtenay: Capes W.W. (edit.), *Register of William de Courtenay* (Hereford, 1913).

Reg. E. Foxe: Bound up in *Reg. C. Bothe* (q.v.).

Reg. J. Gilbert: Parry J.H. (edit.), *The Register of John Gilbert* (Hereford, 1913).

Reg. R. Mascall: Parry J.H. (edit.), *The Register of Robert Mascall* (Hereford, 1916).

Reg. R. Mayew: Bannister A.T. (edit.), *The Register of Richard Mayew* (Hereford, 1919).

Reg. T. Myllyng: Bannister A.T. (edit.), *The Register of Thomas Myllyng* (Hereford, 1919).

Reg. Ade de Orleton: Bannister A.T. (edit.), *Register of Adam deOrleton* (Hereford, 1907).

Reg. J. Peckham: Martin, C.T. (edit.), *Registrum Epistolarum Fratris Johannis Peckham* (London, 1882-85).

Reg. Th. Spofford: Bannister A.T. (edit.), *The Register of Thomas Spofford* (Hereford, 1917).

Reg. Simon de Sudbury: Fowler R.C. (edit.), *Registrum Simon de Sudbiria* (Canterbury and York. Soc., I (1916), II (1938)).

Reg. J. Trefnant: Capes W.W. (edit.), *The Register of John Trefnant* (Hereford, 1914).

Reg. J. Trillek: Parry J.H. (edit.), *The Register of John de Trillek,* (Hereford, 1910).

Rot. Chart. Hardy T.D. (edit.), *Rotuli Chartarum* (London, 1837).

Rot. Hund. Illingworth W. (edit.), *Rotuli Hundredorum* (London, 1812–18).

Rot. Litt. Claus. Hardy T.D. (edit.), *Rotuli Litterarum Clausarum* (London, 1833, 1844).

Rot. Litt. Patentium: Hardy T.D. (edit.), *Rotuli Litterarum Patentium* (London, 1835).

RSB: Parry D (edit.), *Households of God: The Rule of St Benedict* (London, 1980).

Salisbury MSS: *Calendar of the Manuscripts of the Marquess of Salisbury* (Historical Manuscripts Commission London, 1883).

Scoti-Chron. Goodall W. (edit.), *Joannis de Fordun Scotichronicon* II (Edinburgh, 1793).

Sherifff. Caerns. Waters W.H. (edit.), 'Account of the Sheriff of Caernarfon for 1303–1304' (*BBCS* VII: Pt. 1; Nov. 1933).

Spec. Duorum: Lefèvre Y. and Huygens R.B.C. (edit.), *Speculum Duorum* (Cardiff, 1974).

St Aug. Ch. Walker D. (edit.), *The Cartulary of St Augustine's Abbey, Bristol* (Bristol and Gloucestershire Archaeol. Soc, 1998).

Star Chamber Proc. Edwards, I. ab Owen (edit.), *A Catalogue of Star Chamber Proceedings relating to Wales* (Cardiff, 1929).

Statuta: Canivez J.M. (edit.), *Statuta Capitulorum Generalium Ordinis Cisterciensis* (Louvain, 1933–41).

Strata Marcella Ch. Thomas G.C.G. (edit.), *The Charters of the Abbey of Ystrad Marchell* (Aberystywth, 1997).

Taxatio Eccl. *Taxatio Ecclesiastica Angliae et Walliae ...* (London, 1802).

Tax Book: Johnsen A.O. and King P., *The Tax Book of the Cistercian Order* (Oslo, 1979).

Thesaurus: Martene E. and Durand U., *Thesaurus Novus Anecdotorum* I (Paris, 1717).

Tintern MSS: Wood J.G. (coll.), *Tintern Abbey – Charters and Other Documents* (Newport [South Wales] Reference Library).

Valor Eccl. Valor Ecclesiasticus temp. Hen. VIII ... (London, 1810–34).

Visit. Wales: Siddons M.P. (tr. and edit.), *Visitations by the Heralds in Wales* (London, 1996).

Walter Map: James M.R. (edit.), *Walter Map's 'De Nugis Curialium'* (Cymmrodorion Record Ser. IX; 1923).

Welsh Assize R. Conway Davies J (edit.), *The Welsh Assize Roll* (Cardiff, 1940).

Welsh Memo. R. Fryde N (edit.), *List of Welsh Entries in the Memoranda Rolls, 1282- 1343* (Cardiff, 1974).

Welsh Verse: Conran A., *The Penguin Book of Welsh Verse* (Harmondsworth, Mx., 1967).

West Wales Wills: Green F. (edit.), 'Early Wills in West Wales', *West Wales Historical Records* VII (1917–18).

Worcester Lands: Robinson W.R.B., 'Lands of Henry, Earl of Worcester', I: *BBCS* XXV: Pt. 2 (May 1973), II: *BBCS* XXV: Pt. 3 (Nov. 1973).

Secondary Sources

Adams J. 1981: 'Masons and their Marks at Margam Abbey', *Trans. Port Talbot Hist. Soc.* III: No. 2.

Alphonse, Sr. T. 1979: *Llantarnam Abbey* (cyclostyled, Llantarnam).

Auvry D.C. 1896: *Histoire de la Congrégation de Savigny* (Paris).

Bachellery E. 1950: *L'Oeuvre Poetique de Gutun Owain* I–II (Paris).

Banks R.W. 1873: 'On the Welsh Records in the Time of the Black Prince', *Arch. Camb.*

Banks R.W. 1880: 'The Grange of Cwmtoyddwr', *Arch. Camb.* (1880).

Banks R.W. 1888: 'Notes to the Account of Cwmhir Abbey', *Arch. Camb.* (1888).

Bannister A.T. 1927: 'Miraculous Happenings at Dore', *Trans. Woolhope Field Club* XX.

Bannister A.T. 1929: 'Visitation Returns', *English Historical Review* XLIV.

Barber J.T. 1803: *Tour through South Wales* (London).

Barton P.G. 1996: 'The Windmill of Strata Marcella', *Mont. Collns*. 84.

Barton P.G. 1999: 'A History ... of Montgomeryshire water corn mills', *Mont. Collns*. 87.

Baskerville G. 1927: 'The Dispossessed Religious of Gloucestershire', *Trans. Bristol and Gloucs. Archaeol. Soc*. XLIX.

Bazeley M.L. 1910: 'Forest of Dean', *Trans. Bristol and Gloucs. Archaeol. Soc*. XXXIII.

Beattie W. 1844: *Castles and Abbeys* (London).

Bell H.I. and D. 1942: 'Dafydd ap Gwilym: fifty poems', *Y Cymmr*. XLVIII.

Bell M. 1933: *Wulfric of Haselbury*, Publns. Somerset Rec. Soc. XLVII.

Bernard F. 1967: *L'Abbaye de Tamié : Ses Granges* (Grenoble).

Bevan W.L. 1888: *St. David's* (S.P.C.K., London).

Beverley Smith J. 1963: "The 'Cronica de Wallia' and the Dynasty of Dinefwr", *BBCS* XX: Pt. IV (Nov. 1963).

Beverley Smith J. 1970: 'The Middle March', *BBCS* XXIV: Pt. 1 (Nov. 1970).

Beverley Smith J. 1971: 'The Kingdom of Morgannwg', 'The Rebellion of Llywelyn Bren', 'Lordship of Gower', 'Lordship of Senghennydd', *Glamorgan County History* III.

Beverley Smith J. 1999: 'Cymer Abbey and the Welsh Princes', *Jnl. Merioneth Hist. and Rec. Soc*. XIII: Pt. 2.

Birbeck T.T. 1973: *Sword and Ploughshare* (Chepstow).

Birch W. de Gray. 1897: *A History of Margam Abbey* (London).

Birch W. de Gray. 1902 *A History of Neath Abbey* (London).

Blashill T. 1881: 'The architectural history of Tintern Abbey', *Trans. Bristol and Gloucs. Archaeol. Soc*. VI.

Blashill T. 1883: 'Abbeydore', *Trans. Woolhope Nat. Field Club*.

Bond J. 1999: 'The Location and Siting of Cistercian Houses', in Gray, M. and Webster, P.V. (edit)., *Cistercians in Wales and the West* (forthcoming).

Bowen E.G. 1950: 'Monastic Economy of Strata Florida', *Ceredigion* I.

Bowen E.G. 1969: *Saints, Seaways and Settlements* (Cardiff).

Bradney (Sir) J.A 1904-: *A History of Monmouthshire* (London).

Brakspear H. and Evans M. 1910: *Tintern Abbey* (HMSO).

Bridgeman G.T.O. 1868: 'The Princes of Upper Powys', 'Welsh Lords of Kerry', *Mont. Collns*. I.

Bryan A. 1999: 'Aberconwy Castle', *Trans. Caern. Hist. Soc*. 60.

Bryant A. 1970: *The Age of Chivalry* (London).

Buck S. and N. 1742: *Buck's Antiquities* (London).

Butler L.A.S. 1963: 'An Excavation at Maenan, 1963', *Trans. Caern. Hist. Soc*. XXIV.

Butler L.A.S. 1976: 'Valle Crucis Abbey: An Excavation in 1970', *Arch. Camb*. CXXV.

Butler L.A.S. 1976a: *Neath Abbey* (HMSO).

Butler L.A.S. 1980: (with Evans D.H) 'The Cistercian Abbey at ... Maenan: Excavations in 1968', *Arch. Camb*. CXXIX.

Butler L.A.S. 1981: 'The Boundaries of the Abbey of Aberconway at Maenan, Gwynedd', *Arch. Camb*. CXXX.

Butler L.A.S. 1982: 'The Cistercians in Wales (Sites)', in Chauvin B (edit.), *Mélanges à la Mémoire du Père Anselme Dimier* III: Pt. 5 (Pupillin, France).

Butler L.A.S. 1984: 'Neath Abbey: The Twelfth-Century Church', *Arch. Camb*. CXXXIII.

Cardy C. and Gibbs M. 1995: 'The Lewis Family of Gorseinon', *Report of the West Glamorgan County Archivist, 1994–1995*.

Cartwright J. 1997: 'The Desire to Corrupt: Convent and Community in Medieval Wales', in D. Watt (edit.), *Medieval Women in their communities* (Cardiff).

Carville G. 1979: *Norman Splendour : Duiske Abbey* (Belfast).

Carus Wilson E. 1933: 'Overseas Trade of Bristol', in E. Power and M. Postan, *English Trade in the Fifteenth Century* (London).

Castora J.C. 1997: 'The Cistercian Order as portrayed in the *Speculum Ecclesiae* of Gerald of Wales', *Analecta Cisterciensia* LIII.

Charles Edwards T. 1971: *Saint Winifred and her Well* (Catholic Truth Soc.).

Clancy J.P. 1965: *Medieval Welsh Lyrics* (London: New York).

Clark A. 1980: *The Story of Monmouthshire* (Llandybie).

Clay C.T. 1928: 'Seals of Religious Houses of Yorkshire', *Archaeologia* LXXVIII.

Chidgey P. 1962: *Our Lady of Penrhys* (Catholic Truth Soc.).

Cochrane R. 1892: Plan in P. O'Leary, 'Notes on the Abbey of Graigmanagh', *Jnl. Royal Soc. of Antiquaries of Ireland* XXII.

Cole E.J.L. 1964: 'Maelienydd': 30–31 Edward III', *Trans. Radn. Soc.* XXXIV.

Colker M.L. 1992: 'The Margam Chronicle', *Haskins Soc. Jnl.* 4.

Collier E.V. 1925: 'Whitland Abbey Excavations', *Trans. Carmarthenshire Antiq. Soc.* XIX.

Conbhuí.S.Ó. 1958: *The Story of Mellifont* (Dublin).

Conway Davies J. 1947: 'Giraldus Cambrensis, 1146–1946', *Arch. Camb.*

Coulton G.G. 1960: *Medieval Village, Manor or Monastery* (New York).

Courtney P. 1989: 'Excavations in the Outer Precinct of Tintern Abbey', *Medieval Archaeology* XXXIII.

Courtney P. and Gray M. 1991: 'Tintern after the Dissolution', *BBCS* XXXVIII.

Cowley F.G. 1963: 'The Besanding of Theodoric's Grange', *Arch. Camb.* CXII.

Cowley F.G. 1967: 'Cistercian Economy in Glamorgan', *Morgannwg* XI.

Cowley F.G. 1967a: 'Neath versus Margam', *Trans. Port Talbot Hist. Soc.* I.

Cowley, F.G. 1977: *The Monastic Order in South Wales, 1066–1349* (Cardiff).

Cowley F.G. 1998: 'Margam Abbey to 1349', *Morgannwg* XLII.

Cox J.C. 1905: *The Royal Forests* (London).

Coxe W. 1801: *A Historical Tour through Monmouthshire* (London).

Craster O.E. 1956: *Tintern Abbey* (HMSO).

Cummings R. 1974: 'Ystrad and Penrhys', *Glamorgan Historian* X.

David C. 1969: *St Winefride's Well: A History and Guide* (Slough).

Davies A.S. 1930: 'The Windmill of Trelydan', *Mont. Collns.* XLI.

Davies E. 1980: 'Hafod, Hafoty and Lluest', *Ceredigion* IX: Pt. 1.

Davies H.R. 1942: *Records of the Conway and Menai Ferries* (Cardiff).

Davies J. and Waters R. 1992: *Strata Florida Abbey: Geology of Architectural Fragments* (MS Report).

Davies J.C. 1945: 'A Papal Bull of Privileges', *NLW Jnl.* IV.

Davies J.H. 1999: *Abbey Cwmhir in Radnorshire* (Abbey Cwmhir Heritage Trust).

Defoe D. 1962: *A Tour thro' the whole Island of Great Britain* (London; 1962 edn.).

Desmond L.A. 1971: 'The Statute of Carlisle', *Studies in Medieval Cistercian History*, edit. O'Callaghan J.F. (Cist. St. Ser. 13; Shannon).

Desmond L.A. 1975: 'Appropriation of Churches', *Analecta S.O. Cist.* XXXI (1975:2).

Dimier A. 1964: *Les Moines Bâtisseurs* (Paris).

Dineley T. 1684: *The Official Progress of the First Duke of Beaufort through Wales* (edit. R.W. Banks; London, 1888).

Dodd A.H. 1957: *A History of Wrexham* (Wrexham).

Donkin R.A. 1957: 'Site Changes of Medieval Cistercian Monasteries', *Geography* XLIV: Pt. 4.

Donkin R.A. 1962: 'Cattle on estates of Cistercian monasteries', *Econ. Hist. Review* XV.

Donkin R.A. 1963: *The Cistercian Order in Medieval England : Some Conclusions*, (Trans. and Papers, Inst. British Geographers, No. 33).

Donkin R.A. 1978: *The Cistercians* (Pontifical Institute, Toronto).

Donovan E. 1805: *Descriptive Excursions through South Wales and Monmouthshire* (London).

Dunn E. 1967: 'Owain Glyndwr and Radnorshire', *Trans. Radn. Soc.* XXXVII.

Durant H. 1966: *Raglan Castle* (Pontypool).

Ecton J. 1754: In Browne Willis (edit.), *Thesaurus Rerum Ecclesiasticarum* (London).

Edwards D.A.W. 1976: 'Llanderfil, A Study in Continuity', *Monmouthshire Medley* I, edit. R. Nichols (Risca).

Ellis T.P. 1927: 'Merioneth Notes', *Y Cymm.* XXXVIII.

Ellis T.P. 1928: *The Story of Two Parishes: Dolgelly and Llanelltyd* (Newtown).

Ellis T.P. 1936: *Welsh Benedictines of the Terror* (Newtown).

Evans A. 1979: 'Resolfen Churches and Chapels', *Trans. Neath Antiq. Soc.*

Evans A.L. 1956: *The Story of Sker House* (Port Talbot; repr. 1957).

Evans A.L. 1958: *Margam Abbey* (Neath-Port Talbot; 2nd edn. 1996).

Evans A.O. 1928: 'Nicholas Robinson', *Y Cymm.* XXXIX.

Evans C.J.O. 1953: *Monmouthshire: Its History and Topography* (Cardiff).

Evans D.C. 1930: 'Rhydlan Deifi', *Trans. Cardiganshire Antiq. Soc.* VII.

Evans D.H. 1995: *Valle Crucis Abbey* (Cardiff; Cadw).

Evans G. 1915: 'Carmarthenshire Gleanings', *Y Cymm.* XXV.

Evans H.T. 1915: *Wales and the Wars of the Roses* (Cambridge).

Evans J. 1810: vol. 17 of: *The Beauties of England and Wales* (London).

Fenn R.W.D. and Sinclair J.B. 1989: 'Our Ubiquitous Friend', *Trans. Radn. Soc.*

Fenton R. 1917: *Tours in Wales (1804–1813)*, ed. J. Fisher (London, 1917).

Fowler R.C. 1908: 'Cistercian Scholars at Oxford', *English Hist. Rev.* XXIII.

Fulford M.G., Rippon S., Allen J.R.L. and Hillam J., 1992: 'The Medieval Quay at Woolaston Grange', *Trans. Bristol and Gloucs. Archaeol. Soc.* 110.

Gerulaitis L.V. 1967: 'The Canonization of Saint Thomas Aquinas', *Vivarium* V (No. 1).

Gillespie K. 1964: *Friends of Wales* (London; 2nd. edn.).

Gittins E.P. and Hancock T.W. 1883. 'Parochial History of Llanfair Caereinion', *Mont. Collns.* XVI.

Glynne S.R. 1897: 'Notes on the Older Churches ..', *Arch. Camb.*

Golding B.J. 1996: 'Gerald of Wales and the Cistercians', *Reading Medieval Studies* XXI.

Gray M. 1998: 'The politics of Cistercian grange foundation', *Medieval Settlement Research Group* (Annual Report 13).

Gray T. 1903, 1905: 'The Granges of Margam', *Jnl. Brit. Archaeol. Assocn.* N.S. (1) IX : 1903; (2). XI : 1905.

Gray T. 1903a: 'The Hermitage of Theodoric', *Arch. Camb.* (1903).

Greatrex J. 1994: 'Medieval Converts from Judaism in the Welsh Borders', *Monm. Antiq.* X.

Gresham C.A. 1939: 'The Aberconway Charter', *Arch. Camb.*

Gresham C.A. 1976: 'The Township of Neigwl', *Trans. Caernarvonshire Hist. Soc.* XXXVII.

Gresham C.A. 1983: 'The Aberconwy Charter: further consideration', *BBCS* XXX: 3–4.

Gresham C.A. 1984: 'The Cymer Abbey Charter', *BBCS* XXXI.

Griffiths R.A. 1972: *The Principality of Wales in the Later Middle Ages* I (Cardiff).

Guilloreau L. 1909: 'Les Fondations Anglaises de Savigny', *Revue Mabillon* V.

Gwynn A. 1970: Gwynn A. and Hadcock R.N. *Medieval Religious Houses: Ireland* (London).

Harri(e)s L. 1953: *Gwaith Huw Cae Llwyd ac Eraill* (Cardiff, 1953).

Harris S.M. 1951: 'Our Lady of Penrhys', *Ave* 21.

Harrison J. 1998: 'The troubled foundation of Grace Dieu Abbey', *Monm. Antiq.* XIV.

Harrison J. 2000: 'The Tintern Abbey Chronicles', *Monm. Antiq.* XVI.

Harrison S.A., Morris R.K. and Robinson D.M. 1998: 'A Fourteenth-Century *Pulpitum* Screen at Tintern Abbey', *Antiquaries Jnl.* 78.

Harrison S.A. Robinson D.M. *et al. The Cistercian Abbey of Strata Florida: Archaeology, Architecture, Art* (Cadw; forthcoming).

Hays R.W. 1963: *History of the Abbey of Aberconway* (Cardiff).

Hays R.W. 1971: 'The Welsh Monasteries and the Edwardian Conquest', *Studies in Medieval Cistercian History* (Cist. Studies Ser., 13; Shannon).

Heald G.O. 1976: 'Pentrefoelas Mill', *Trans. Denbighshire Hist. Soc.* 25.

Heath C. 1801, 1828: *Historical and Descriptive Accounts of Tintern Abbey* (Monmouth; 1828 = 10th edn.).

Hemp W.J. 1938: 'Two Burials in Tintern Abbey', *Arch. Camb.* (1938).

Hemp W.J. 1963: 'Theodoric's Grange, Note in *Arch. Camb.*

Heslop T.A. 1986: 'Cistercian Seals', in Norton C. and Park D., *Cistercian Art and Architecture in the British Isles* (Cambridge).

Hirsch-Davies J.E. de. 1916: *Catholicism in Medieval Wales* (London).

Hodges H. 1975: Notes in *British History Illustrated* I.

Hopkins T.J. 1967: 'David Jones of Wallington', *Glamorgan Historian* 4.

Hore P.H. 1901: *History of Wexford* (London).

Howel R: *The Story of the Monastery of Neath* (NLW, MS 4559C).

Huws D. 1980: *The Medieval Codex* (Aberystwyth).

Igliozi S. 1976: 'I Maggiori Dissidi fra Cîteaux e Clairvaux', *Notizie Cistercensi* IX.

Insley C. 1999: 'Fact and Fiction in Thirteenth-Century Gwynedd', *Studia Celtica* XXXIII.

Jacob E.F. 1961: *The Fifteenth Century* (Oxford).

Jack R.I. 1972: *Medieval Wales* (London).

James T. 1978: 'A Survey of Earthworks at the Site of Whitland Abbey', *Carms. Antiq.* XIV.

Jenkins D. and Owen M.E., 1982: 'Welsh Law in Carmarthenshire', *Carms. Antiq.* XVIII.

Jones A. 1933: 'Basingwerk Abbey', in Edwards, J.G. (and others), *Historical Essays in Honour of James Tait* (Manchester).

Jones A. 1937: 'The Estates of the Welsh Abbeys at the Dissolution', *Arch. Camb.* XCII.

Jones A.L. 1996: *Heraldry in Glamorgan* 7 (Cowbridge).

Jones D.R.L. 1981: 'Margam in the Post-Dissolution Era', *Trans. Port Talbot Hist. Soc.* III: No. 2.

Jones E.D. 1950: 'Ysgriflechi Cymraeg Ystrad Fflûr', *Llên Cymru* I.

Jones G. H(artwell) 1912: 'Celtic Britain and the Pilgrim Movement', *Y Cymm.* XXIII.

Jones H.L. 1846. 'Mona Medieva III', *Arch. Camb.* I.

Jones H.L. and Williams J. 1846: 'Basingwerk Abbey', *Arch. Camb.* I.

Jones J. 1997: *Monmouthshire Wills* (Cardiff).

Jones J.E.J. 1981: 'Old Fairs of Wales', *Jnl. Merioneth Hist. and Rec. Soc.* IX: Pt. 1.

Jones M.C. 1868: 'Feudal Barony of Powys', *Mont. Collns.* I.

Jones M.C. 1869: 'Some Account of Llanllugan Nunnery', *Mont. Collns.* II.

Jones M.C. 1871–73: 'The Abbey of Ystrad Marchell', *Mont. Collns.* IV–VI.

Jones M.C. 1873a: 'Shield of Arms in ... Buttington Church', *Mont. Collns.* VI.

Jones M.C. 1893: 'History of the Parish of Kerry', *Mont. Collns.* XXVII.

Jones Pierce T. 1949: 'Ancient Meirionydd', *Jnl. Merioneth Hist. and Rec. Soc.* I.

Jones Pierce T. 1950: 'Strata Florida Abbey', *Ceredigion* I.

Jones Pierce T. 1951: 'Medieval Settlement in Anglesey', *Trans. Anglesey Antiq. Soc. and Field Club.*

Jones Pierce T. 1959: 'The age of the Two Llywelyns', in Roderick A.J., *Wales through the Ages* (Llandybie).

Jones T. 1950: 'Place Names of Cardiff', *Publns. S. Wales and Monm. Record Soc.* II.

Kelly G.J. 1940: *The Monastery of Grace Dieu* (M.A. thesis; Fordham Univ. Graduate School).

Ker N.R. 1964: *Medieval Libraries of Great Britain* (2nd edn; Royal Hist. Soc. London).

Kerry C. 1893: 'History of Peak Forest', *Jnl. Derbyshire Arch. and Nat. Hist. Soc.* XV.

King A.A. 1954: *Cîteaux and her Elder Daughters* (London, 1954).

Knight J.K. 1972: 'Thomas Churchyard and the "Worthines of Wales"', *Severn and Wye Review* II: Pt. 2 (Winter, 1972).

Knight J.K. 1977: *Tintern and the Romantic Movement* (H.M.S.O.).

Knight L.S. 1920: 'The Welsh Monasteries and the Education of Later Medieval Wales', *Arch. Camb.*

Knowles M.D. 1979: *The Religious Orders in England* (Cambridge, 1948; repr. 1979).

Leach G.B. 1960: 'Excavations at Hen Blas', *Trans. Flintshire Hist. Soc.* XVIII.

Lekai L.J. 1977: *The Cistercians* (Kent State U.P.).

Leland J. 1715: Hearne T. (edit.), *Joannis Lelandi antiquarii de rebus Britannicis Collectanea* (Oxford).

Lewis E.T. 1975: *Efailwen to Whitland* I (Clunderwen).

Lewis F.R. 1938: 'History of Llanbadarn Fawr', *Trans. Cardiganshire Archaeol. Soc.* XIII.

Lewis J.M. 1973: (with Knight B.): 'Early Christian Burials', *Arch. Camb.*

Lewis J.M. 1976: *Welsh Medieval Paving Tiles* (Cardiff).

Lewis J.M. 1976a: (with Williams D.H.): *The White Monks in Wales* (Cardiff; 1976).

Lewis J.M. 1999: *Medieval Tiles of Wales* (Cardiff, 1999).

Lewis M. 1970: *Stained Glass in North Wales up to 1850* (Altrincham).

Lhuyd E. 1707: *Parochialia* (Suppl. to *Arch. Camb.* 1909–11).

Llewellyn R.W. 1898: 'The Borough of Kenfig', *Arch. Camb.* 1898.

Lloyd H.W: 1879: 'Ancient Welsh Poetry', *Mont. Collns.* XII.

Lloyd J.E. 1915: 'Edward I's Commission of Enquiry of 1280:1', *Y Cymm.* XXV.

Lloyd J.E. 1931: *Owen Glendower* (Oxford).

Lloyd J.E. 1939: *A History of Wales from the earliest times to the Edwardian Conquest* (London; 3rd edn.).

Lloyd J.Y.W. 1873: (Chevalier Lloyd). 'Lordship of Bromfield, Yale and Chirkland', *Arch. Camb.*

Lloyd J.Y.W. 1876: 'Lordship of Penllyn', *Mont. Collns.* IX.

Lloyd J.Y.W. 1885: *Powys Fadog* V (London).

Locock M. 1997: *Mynydd Maen and Mynydd Henllys* (Glamorgan-Gwent Archaeol. Trust, Report 97/005).

Lott G.K. and Barclay W.J. 1998. *The source of the stones used in the construction of Tintern Abbey* (British Geological Survey, Technical Report WH/98/13R).

Manley J.F. 1977: Note in *Arch. in Wales* XVII.

Matthew D. and A. 1929: 'The Survival of the Dissolved Monasteries in Wales', *Dublin Review* 184.

Mein A.G. and Lewis J.M. 1990: 'Floor Tiles from Llantarnam Abbey', *Medieval and Later Pottery in Wales* 12.

Midmer R. 1979: *English Mediaeval Monasteries: 1066–1540* (London).

M.N.J. 1926: *Byegone Days in the March Wall of Wales* (London).

Moore P.D. 1968: Notes in *Nature* 217.

Moore P.D. and Chater E.H. 1969: Notes in *Jnl. of Ecology* 57.

Morgan R. 1985: 'An early charter of Llanllugan Nunnery', *Mont. Collns.* LXXIII.

Morgan W.Ll. 1899: *Antiquarian survey of East Gower* (London).

Morris E.R. 1876, 1898: 'The Grange of Gelynog', *Mont. Collns* IX, XXX.

Morris E.R. 1889–90: 'History of the Parish of Kerry', *Mont. Collns*. XXIII–XXIV.

Morris E.R. 1892–93: *Ibid*. (cont'd). *Mont. Collns*. XXVI–XXVII.

Morris E.R. 1982: 'Monasteries, Religious Houses and their Properties', *Mont. Collns*. LXX

Morris E.R. 1983: *Ibid*. Loose revised map inserted in: *Mont. Collns*. LXXI.

Morris R.H. 1911: 'The Burial of Llywelyn', *Arch. Camb*.(1911).

Neaverson E. 1949: 'The Building Stones of Harlech Castle and Cymmer Abbey', *Arch. Camb*.

Newman J. 1995: *The Buildings of Wales: Glamorgan* (Penguin).

Nicholl L.D. 1936: *The Normans in Glamorgan, Gower and Kidweli* (Cardiff).

O'Dwyer B.W. 1975: 'Crisis in the Cistercian Monasteries in Ireland', *Analecta Cist*. (I) XXXI (1975: 2); (II) XXXII (1976: 1–2).

Ormerod G. 1861: *Strigulensia* (London).

Ormrod W.M. 1988: 'Edward II at Neath Abbey, 1326', *Neath Antiq. Soc,. Trans*.

O'Sullivan J.F. 1947: *Cistercian Settlements in Wales and Monmouthshire* (New York).

Owen E. 1896: 'The Bells of the Dissolved Welsh Monasteries', *Arch. Camb*. 1896.

Owen E. 1897: 'The Spoils of the Welsh Religious Houses', *Arch. Camb*. 1897.

Owen E. 1917: 'The Fate of the Structures of Conway Abbey, etc.', *Y Cymm*. XXVII.

Owen, E. 1919: 'Strata Marcella immediately before and after its Dissolution', *Y Cymm*. XXIX.

Owen E. 1920: 'The Monastery of Basingwerk', *Jnl. Flint Hist. Soc*. VII (1919–20).

Owen E. 1931: 'Vale Crucis Abbey', *Wrexham Guardian,* I (4 Nov. 1931), II (11 Nov. 1931).

Owen G.D. 1935: *Agricultural Conditions in West Wales* (Ph. D. thesis; Univ. of Wales).

Owen G.D. 1972: *Elizabethan Wales* (2nd edn., Cardiff).

Owen H. 1904: *Gerald the Welshman* (London).

Palmer A.N. 1886: *Town, fields and folk of Wrexham in the reign of James I* (Wrexham).

Palmer A.N. 1890: *History of Town of Wrexham* IV (Wrexham).

Palmer A.N. 1903: *The thirteen country townships of the old parish of Wrexham* (Wrexham).

Parkes L.N. and Webster P.V. 1974: 'Merthyrgeryn: A Grange of Tintern', *Arch. Camb*. CXXIII.

Parry T. 1952: *Gwaith Dafydd ap Gwilym* (Cardiff).

Parry T. 1962: *The Oxford Book of Welsh Verse* (Oxford).

Patterson R.B. 1992: 'The Author of the Margam Annals', *Anglo-Norman Studies* XIV (1991; publ. 1992).

Pegolotti F.B. 1936: *La Practica della Mercatura* (edit. A. Evans; Medieval Academy of America).

Pennant T. 1796: *The History of the Parishes of Whiteford and Holywell* (London).

Percival D. 1993: 'The Boundary of the Medieval Grange of Dolhelfa', *Trans. Radn. Soc*.

Phillimore E. 1920: 'Leprosy in Wales', *Arch. Camb*.

Phillips D.R. 1925: *History of the Vale of Neath* (Swansea).

Phillips N. and M. Hamilton. 2000. 'Geophysical Survey at Grace Dieu Abbey', *Monm. Antiq*. XVI.

Powel D. 1584: *Historie of Cambria* (London).

Powell A.D. 1964: 'Brilley Remembrance, 1590', *Trans. Radn. Soc*. XXXIV.

Powell S.M. 1931: 'Pilgrim routes to Strata Florida', *Trans. Cards. Antiq. Soc*. VIII.

Pratt D. 1997: *The Dissolution of Valle Crucis Abbey* (Bridge Books, Wrexham).

Price G.V. 1952: *Valle Crucis Abbey* (Liverpool).

Prichard J. 1881: 'Margam Abbey', *Cardiff Naturalists' Society: Transactions* XIII.

Pryce A.I. 1923: *The Diocese of Bangor in the Sixteenth Century* (Bangor).

Pugh R.H. 1934: *Glimpses of West Gwent* (Newport).

Pugh T.B. 1953: *The Marcher Lordships of South Wales* (Cardiff).

Radford C.A.R. 1974: *Strata Florida Abbey* (HMSO)

Radford C.A.R. 1982: 'The Cistercian Abbey of Cwmhir', *Arch. Camb.* CXXXI.

Randall H.J. 1955.: *Bridgend* (Newport, Mon.).

Randolph J.A. 1905: *Welsh Abbeys* (Carmarthen).

Redknap M. and Williams D.H. 1999: 'A Seal Matrix from Aberavon Beach', *Morgannwg* XLIII.

Rees D. 1984: 'Walterston', *Gower* 35.

Rees S.E. 1999: 'Abbey Cwmhir', pers. comm.

Rees W. 1957: ''Wreck de Mer', *Publns. S. Wales and Monm. Record Soc.* IV.

Rees W. 1972: *An Historical Atlas of Wales* (London).

Rees W.J. 1849: 'Account of Cwmhir Abbey', *Arch. Camb.* IV.

Remfry P.M. 1994: *A Political History of Abbey Cwmhir and its Patrons* (Worcester).

Rhys J. 1896: 'Epigraphic Notes', *Arch. Camb.* (1896), *Cf.* (1878).

Richards R. 1959: 'The Cistercians and Cymmer Abbey', *Jnl. Merioneth Hist. and Rec. Soc.* III.

Richardson W.C. 1961: *A History of the Court of Augmentations* (Baton Rouge).

Rigold S.E. 1977: 'Exhibitions at Ballots', *Antiq. Jnl.* LVII: Pt. 2.

Robinson D.M. 1990: *Tintern Abbey* (Cardiff; Cadw).

Robinson D.M. 1990a: *Cymer Abbey* (Cardiff; Cadw).

Robinson D.M. 1995: *Tintern Abbey* (Cardiff; Cadw).

Robinson D.M. 1996: *Basingwerk Abbey* (Cardiff; Cadw).

Robinson D.M. 1997: 'The Making of a Monument', *Monm. Antiq.* XIII.

Robinson D.M. and Platt C. 1998. *Strata Florida Abbey, Talley Abbey* (Cardiff; Cadw).

Robinson D.M. 1998a: (edit.), *The Cistercian Abbeys of Britain* (London).

Robinson W.R.B. 1967: 'The Litigation of Edward, Earl of Worcester, concerning Gower', *BBCS* XXII: Pt. 2 (May, 1967).

Rudder S. 1779: *A New History of Gloucestershire* (Cirencester).

Russell A.D. 1979: Note 82 in *Arch. in Wales* 19.

Salmon M. 1927: *Source Book of Welsh History* (Oxford).

Sayers J. 1964: 'English Cistercian Cases', *Analecta S.O. Cist.* (1964); *Cf.* 'Judicial Activities of the General Chapter', *Jnl. Eccles. Hist.* XV (1–2) 1964.

Schubert H.R. 1957: *History of British Iron and Steel Industry* (London).

Simpson Jones, T. 1889: 'History of the Parish of Guilsfield', *Mont. Collns.* XXXI.

Slater F. 1972: *Our Lady of Penrhys* (Treorchy).

Spurgeon C.J. and H.J. Thomas. 1975: note in *Arch. in Wales* 15.

Spurgeon C.J. and H.J. Thomas. 1980: note in *Arch. in Wales,* 20.

Spurgeon C.J. and H.J. Thomas. 1982: 'Monastic Granges', RCAHMW, *Glamorgan* III: Pt. 2.

Stalley R.A. 1987: *The Cistercian Monasteries of Ireland* (Yale U.P.).

Stedman Davies D. 1934. 'Abbey Cwmhir', *Trans. Radn. Society* IV.

Stephenson D. 1980: *Thirteenth Century Welsh Law Courts* (Aberystwyth).

Stevens B.J: *Tintern Abbey* (Forest of Dean Newspapers; n.d.).

St. John Hope W.H. and Brakspear H. 1904: 'The Cistercian Abbey of Beaulieu', *Archaeol. Jnl.* LXIII.

Sutton T.S. 1887: 'Neath Abbey', *Arch. Camb.* (1887).

Talbot C.H. 1939: *Cistercian Abbeys of Scotland* (London).

Talbot C.H. 1959: 'Cadogan of Bangor', *Cîteaux* IX.

Taylor A.J. 1947: 'The Greater Monastic Houses', in *A Hundred Years of Welsh Archaeology* (Cambrian Archaeol. Assoc. Centenary volume; Gloucester).

Taylor A.J. 1949: Report of field lecture, *Arch. Camb.*

Taylor A.J. 1971: *Basingwerk Abbey* (HMSO).

Taylor A.J. 1974: *The King's Works in Wales* (HMSO).

Taylor A.J. 1974a: 'A Fragment of a *Dona* Account', *BBCS* XXVII (Pt. 2).

Taylor A.J. 1976: 'Royal Alms and Oblations', in Emmison and Stephens, *Tribute to an Antiquary* (London).

Taylor A.J. 1977: 'Castle Building in Wales and Savoy', *Proc. British Academy* LXIII.

Taylor J. 1869: *Tintern Abbey and its Founders* (Bristol).

Thomas D. 1964: *The Parish of Holywell* (? Wrexham ; 1964).

Thomas D. 1998: *Cwmhir Abbey* (Clwyd-Powys Archaeological Trust, Report No. 278).

Thomas D.R. 1886: 'Merionethshire Six Hundred Years Ago', *Arch. Camb.* (1886).

Thomas D.R. 1913: *History of the Diocese of St. Asaph* I (Oswestry, I: 1908; III (1913)

Thomas H.J. 1992. 'The Mansion house of Magor', *Monm. Antiq.* VIII.

Thomas L. 1930: *The Reformation in the Old Diocese of Llandaff* (Cardiff).

Thomas R. G(wyn). 1976: 'Nineteenth-Century Tourists at Valle Crucis', *Denbighshire Hist. Soc. Trans.* XXV.

Thomas W.G(wyn). 1978: 'The Chancel of Llanbadarn Fawr Church', *Arch. Camb.* CXXVII

Thomas W.H. 1839: *Tinterne and its Vicinity* (2nd edn; London/Bristol).

Thomson D. 1982: 'Cistercians and Schools', *Cambridge Medieval Celtic Studies* 3 (Summer, 1982).

Toft L.A. 1983: 'Walterstone Grange', *Annual Report, Glamorgan-Gwent Archaeol. Trust* II (1983–84).

Toft L.A. 1988: 'A Study of a Coastal Village', *Morgannwg* 32.

Toft L.A. 1990: 'A Medieval Grange at Margam', *Trans. Port Talbot Hist. Soc.* I: Vol. 4.

Trott C.D.J. 1946: *Historical Geography of the Neath Region* (M.A. Wales, thesis).

Turner J. 1964: Notes in *New Phytologist* 63.

Usher G.A. 1974: 'The Black Prince's "Quo Warranto"', *Welsh History Review* VII: Pt. 1.

Wade-Evans A.W. 1910: 'Parochiale Wallicanum', *Y Cymm.*

Ward J. 1914: 'Our Lady of Penrhys', *Arch. Camb.* 1914.

Weeks R. 1998: 'Cillonydd grange landscape study', *Medieval Settlement Research Group Annual Report* 13.

Westwood J.O. 1863: 'Early Inscribed Stones of Wales', *Arch. Camb.*

Williams C.R. 1961: *The History of Flintshire* (Denbigh).

Williams D.H. 1964: 'Grace Dieu Abbey', *Monm. Antiq.* I: Pt. 4.

Williams D.H. 1965: 'Tintern Abbey: Its Economic History', *Monm. Antiq.* II: Pt. 1.

Williams D.H. 1966: 'Abbey Dore', *Monm. Antiq.* II: Pt. 2.

Williams D.H. 1967: 'Llantarnam Abbey', *Monm. Antiq.* II: Pt. 3.

Williams D.H. 1969: *The Welsh Cistercians* (Pontypool).

Williams D.H. 1970: 'Grace Dieu Abbey: An Exploratory Excavation', *Monm. Antiq.* III: Pt. 1.

Williams D.H. 1970a: 'Goldcliff Priory', *Monm. Antiq.* III: Pt. 1.

Williams D.H. 1975: 'Cistercian Nunneries in Medieval Wales', *Cîteaux* XXVI (1975: 3).

Williams D.H. 1976: *White Monks in Gwent and the Border* (Pontypool).

Williams D.H. 1976a: 'Cwmhir Abbey', *Cistercian Studies* XI: Pt. 2.

Williams D.H. 1976b: 'Strata Marcella Abbey', *Cistercian Studies* XI: Pt. 3

Williams D.H. 1980: 'The Welsh Cistercians and Ireland', *Cistercian Studies* XXXI.

Williams D.H. 1981a: 'Cymer Abbey', *Arch. Camb.* CXXX.

Williams D.H. 1981b: 'Basingwerk Abbey', *Cîteaux* XXXII.

Williams D.H. 1983: 'Corrodians and Residential Servants in Tudor Cistercian Monasteries', *Cîteaux* XXXIV: 1–2.

Williams D.H. 1984: *The Welsh Cistercians* (Caldey Island).

Williams D.H. 1987, 1988: 'Catalogue of Welsh Ecclesiastical Seals', *Arch. Camb.* CXXXVI–XXXVII.

Williams D.H. and C.J. Arnold 1992: 'An Appreciation of the Life and Work of Stephen William Williams', *Mont. Collns.* LXXX.

Williams D.H. 1995: 'Exploration and Excavation of Cistercian Sites', *Arch. Camb.* CXLIV.

Williams D.H. and Rippon S. 1996: 'Grangefield Moated Site, Redwick', *Monm. Antiq.* XII.

Williams D.H. 1998: *The Cistercians in the Early Middle Ages* (Leominster).

Williams D.H. 1998a: 'Cistercian Roads and Routeways', *Tarmac Papers* II..

Williams D.H. 1999a: 'Rogerstone Grange', *Monm. Antiq.* XV.

Williams D.H. 1999b: 'Cistercian Bridges', *Tarmac Papers* III.

Williams D.H. 1999c: 'Stephen William Williams', *Trans. Radn. Soc.* LXIX.

Williams D.H. 2000: 'The Cistercians and Quarrying', *Tarmac Papers* IV.

Williams D.H. 2000a: (edit.), *Trelech Grange* (in preparation).

Williams G. 1962: *The Welsh Church from Conquest to Reformation* (Cardiff; 2nd edn. 1976).

Williams G. 1967: *Welsh Reformation Essays* (Cardiff).

Williams G. 1974: 'Neath Abbey', in E. Jenkins, *Neath and District: A Symposium* (Neath).

Williams G. 1979: *Religion, Language and Nationality* (Cardiff).

Williams G. 1998: 'The Last Days of Margam Abbey', *Morgannwg* XLII.

Williams J. 1905: *General History of the County of Radnor* (Brecon; 2nd edn.).

Williams R. 1882: 'Cridia Abbey', *Mont. Collns.* XV.

Williams S W. 1889: *The Cistercian Abbey of Strata Florida* (London).

Williams S.W. 1890: 'The Cistercian Abbey of Cwmhir', *Mont. Collns.* XXIV.

Williams S.W. 1891: 'Excavations on the Site of Strata Marcella Abbey', *Mont. Collns.* XXV.

Williams-Jones K. 1976. *The Merioneth Lay Subsidy Roll, 1292–93* (Cardiff).

Willis-Bund J.W. 1900: 'Archbishop Peckham', *Trans. Cymm.* (Session 1900–01; publ. 1902).

Wood B.J. 1970: 'Llanderfil', *Pontypool and District Review* 5.

Wood J.G. 1936: 'Church and Parish of Lancaut', *Trans. Bristol and Gloucs. Archaeol. Soc.* LVIII.

Woodward C.W.O. 1966: *The Dissolution of the Monasteries* (London, 1966).

Wormald F. 1958: (with C.E. Wright) *The English Library before 1700* (London).

Wrenn D.P.H. 1975: *Shropshire History Makers* (Wakefield).

Wrottesley G. 1906: Notes in: *Collections for a History of Staffordshire* (William Salt Archaeol. Soc. N.S. IX).

Wyndham H.P. 1781: *A Tour through Monmouthshire and Wales* (London; 2nd edn.).

Youings J. 1971: *The Dissolution of the Monasteries* (London, 1971).

INDEX OF PRINCIPAL PERSONS

The names of medieval and modern poets and commentators are printed in *italic* type.

INDEX OF PRINCIPAL PLACES

INDEX OF PRINCIPAL SUBJECTS

The principal sections dealing with any topic are printed in **bold** type.